DON'T BRAND MY PUBLIC SPACE!

Contents

6
Introduction – Ruedi Baur and Sébastien Thiéry

9
Marketplace – Maria Roszkowska
Wherein the author, a graphic designer and graduate of EnsadLab, collects, compares, appropriates, parodies, and decodes the approaches to visual identity practiced by various European capitals. What are the differences between the studied imagery of public bodies, on the one hand, and advertising campaigns for mass-market products, on the other? What type of European citizenship is able to generate such emblems, designed along the lines of the most sophisticated marketing strategies?

65
The Conspicuous Absence of a Planetary Flag – Ruedi Baur
Wherein the author, a graphic designer, delves into the visual representations of various regions and nations of Europe. What is left of the future of flags, the piece of cloth bearing a national or regional mark that is supposed to express each and everyone's identity, proof of their existence? How does one go about locating, in the sleep or nightmare of signs, what nevertheless conveys future political representations and what may still serve as an expression of the public domain, starting with territorial signs?

131
Sugar Dictatorship – Great Nation
Wherein the authors, a collective of graphic designers, put together an edifying picture from the contemporary imagery of those who represent the law. Has the smile become the new attribute of government, and if so, what effect should we expect? Does the aesthetics of conviviality evince a new form of government, distinct from the classic forms of democracy, monarchy or oligarchy?

195
Everything Must Go! An Approach to Contemporary Ceremonial Writings – Sébastien Thiéry
Wherein the author, a political scientist, questions contemporary thought's lack of interest in the visual productions of public institutions. And yet, how can one take seriously the logomania of communities and the political impact of these anonymous productions? How can one clear a path to visual counter-productions that squarely face the poverty of the symbols affecting our public space?

205
The Logotomized City (or Patrick Le Lay's Victory) – Jean-Pierre Grunfeld
Wherein the author, a semiologist, offers a satirical review of the history and spaces of generalized commercialization. What can the genealogy of the logo as an act of faith and weapon of war teach us about its devastating power? What tragic correspondences can one make out between the logo-city and the logo-man, and how are we to understand the gradual dissolving of the subject in both cases?

237
There Are Cracks in the Walls... – Annick Lantenois
Wherein the author, an art historian, critically analyzes the visual essays featured in the present work. What do these layouts teach us about the contemporary poverty of symbols that isn't already known, what are they hiding that ought to be exposed? Beyond the devastating view of the demonstration, how can one blaze new trails of resistance that might take shape as graphic design?

257
"Branding," Faith, and Experience – Pierre-Damien Huyghe
Wherein the author, a philosopher, looks to describe what is indeed taking place before the signs of so-called supermodernity. Do the proliferating landscapes of logos produce a fatal effect of derealization and uniformization on places? Against the belief that on the horizon there is only desolation for branding strategies, how can we give back to the art of experience its active power and force for changing places and objects?

267
Against Disposable Territories: A Preliminary Critical Approach to Systems of Territorial Identification – Luc Gwiazdzinski
Wherein the author, a geographer, tackles the question of branding through an analysis of our contemporary connection with space and time. Do the contexts of mobility, "glocalization," and European integration allow us to take a fresh look at the issues affecting identification systems of territories? In what way do these visual productions capture the evolution of our social and political spaces, the risks associated with that evolution, and the possibilities that remain in spite of all the promise?

Introduction

Public collectivities are fictions addressed to everyone, magic beings. State, region, and commune prove themselves much more than the machines of government at whose controls one finds administrators and officials who impart a certain direction to them. These entities are not limited to the economic flows moving through them, nor the rationalized hierarchies defining them, if we confine ourselves to what administrative science tells us. These uppercase beings, which give life to the citizens we all are by delivering up duly stamped papers and guaranteeing the stability of our name, are indeed representations first and foremost. That is, behind the men and women who act every day on behalf of these institutions lie images without which no one could in fact act or feel the effect of so-called public action.

Here then, at the limits of politics, we ventured for several years to explore a place that is overlooked by researchers in both political science and art and design. Here, in the very thick of what we call the "ceremonial scriptures," we lingered in order to take seriously what is going on unnoticed in the eyes of supposedly serious sciences. Here, before the visual productions that serve as emblems for Europe's public collectivities, we asked ourselves a number of questions. We did so by working with these hypotheses: that these productions are not anecdotal, not the simple remains of folklore from a dark and distant time; and that these productions are crucial for the life, even the survival, of what we have in common. Drawing on these convictions—for the public good to exist requires taking the utmost care of not only the images that are the face it turns to the world, but also the quality of those images, and the depth of meaning that characterize them—we are convinced that the quality of life in common and the depth of meaning of what we still call "politics" depend on this. We then set about publishing the results of this research in the present book, demonstrating, we hope, that in abandoning the art of crafting these images to the precepts of branding and the sorcerer's apprentices of visual communications we render our public collectivities progressively inaudible and allow political action to break down to the point of becoming mere blind gesturing.

This book-manifesto is above all the result of research that was pursued under our direction by students of EnsadLab (Laboratoire de recherche de l'École nationale supérieure des arts décoratifs) of Paris, ZHdK (Zürcher Hochschule der Künste) of Zurich, and finally Head (Haute école d'art et de design) of Geneva. Their research was part of "Civic City," a program and transnational network that took shape in 2012. We would like to extend our warm thanks to those students, in particular Maria Roszkowska, who also served as the designer of the study's layout, and Irena Bockaj. In addition, this book is made up of texts whose authors were invited to write in light of what our research had made possible, that is, what we call "visual essays." We would also like to thank the design theoretician

Jean-Pierre Grunfeld, the geographer Luc Gwiazdzinski, the design theoretician Pierre-Damien Huyghe, and the design historian Annick Lantenois. The present work is thus the outcome of a collaborative effort conceived not only to diagnose the poverty of contemporary politics, but also to present a range of views on a rebellious creative approach to those future sponsors and future designers who will, we hope, lend a completely different look to what for us serves as public space.

Ruedi Baur and Sébastien Thiéry

UP

Marketplace

Maria Roszkowska

—

7 Up Brand

According to Professor Donald Sadoway, the name is derived from the atomic mass of Lithium, 7, which was originally one of the key ingredients of the drink (as lithium citrate). However, there are numerous myths explaining the name. One popular myth is that its creator named the soft drink after seeing a cattle brand with the number 7 and the letter U.

("7 Up Explained," everything.explained.at/7_Up/)

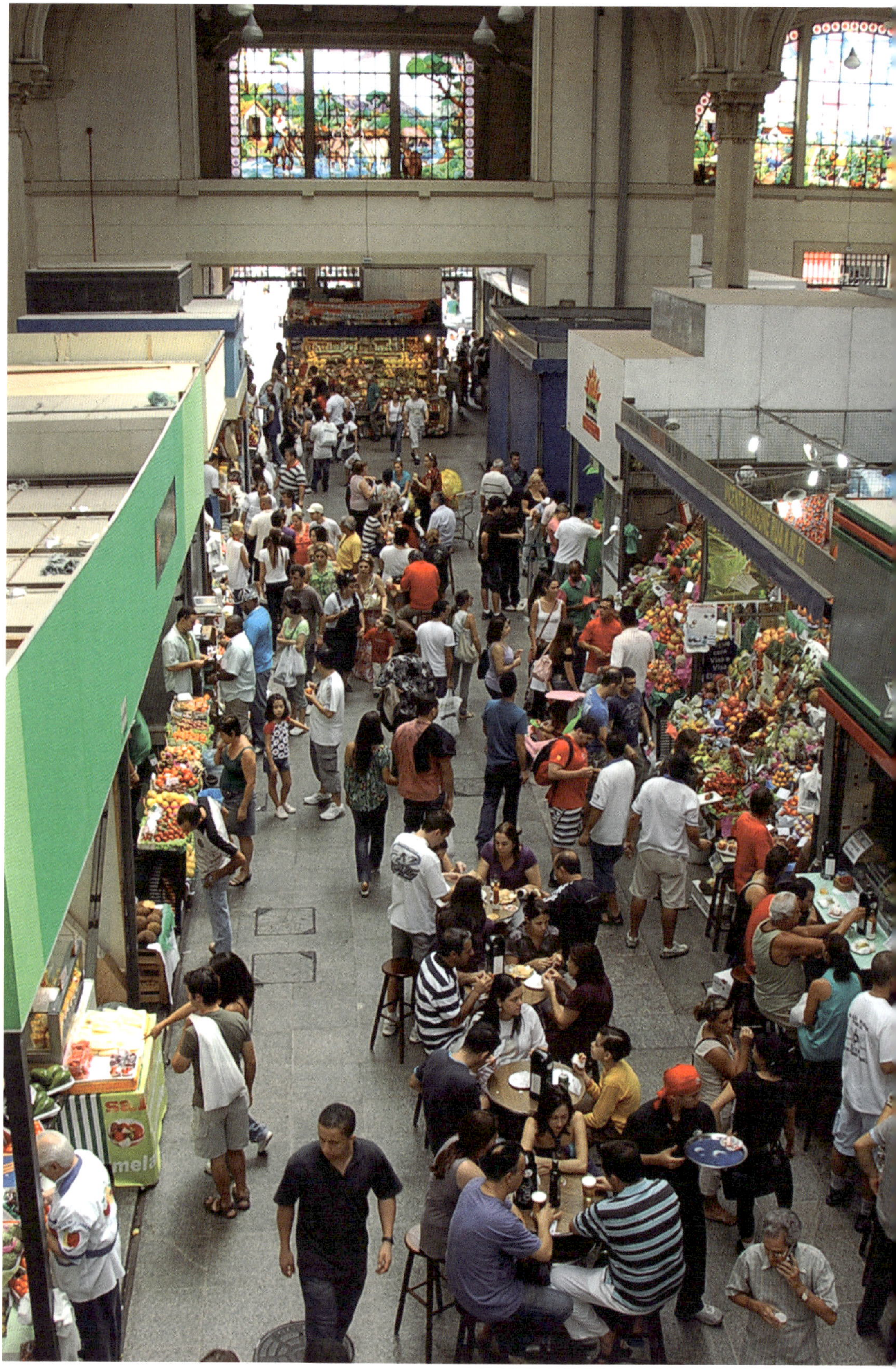

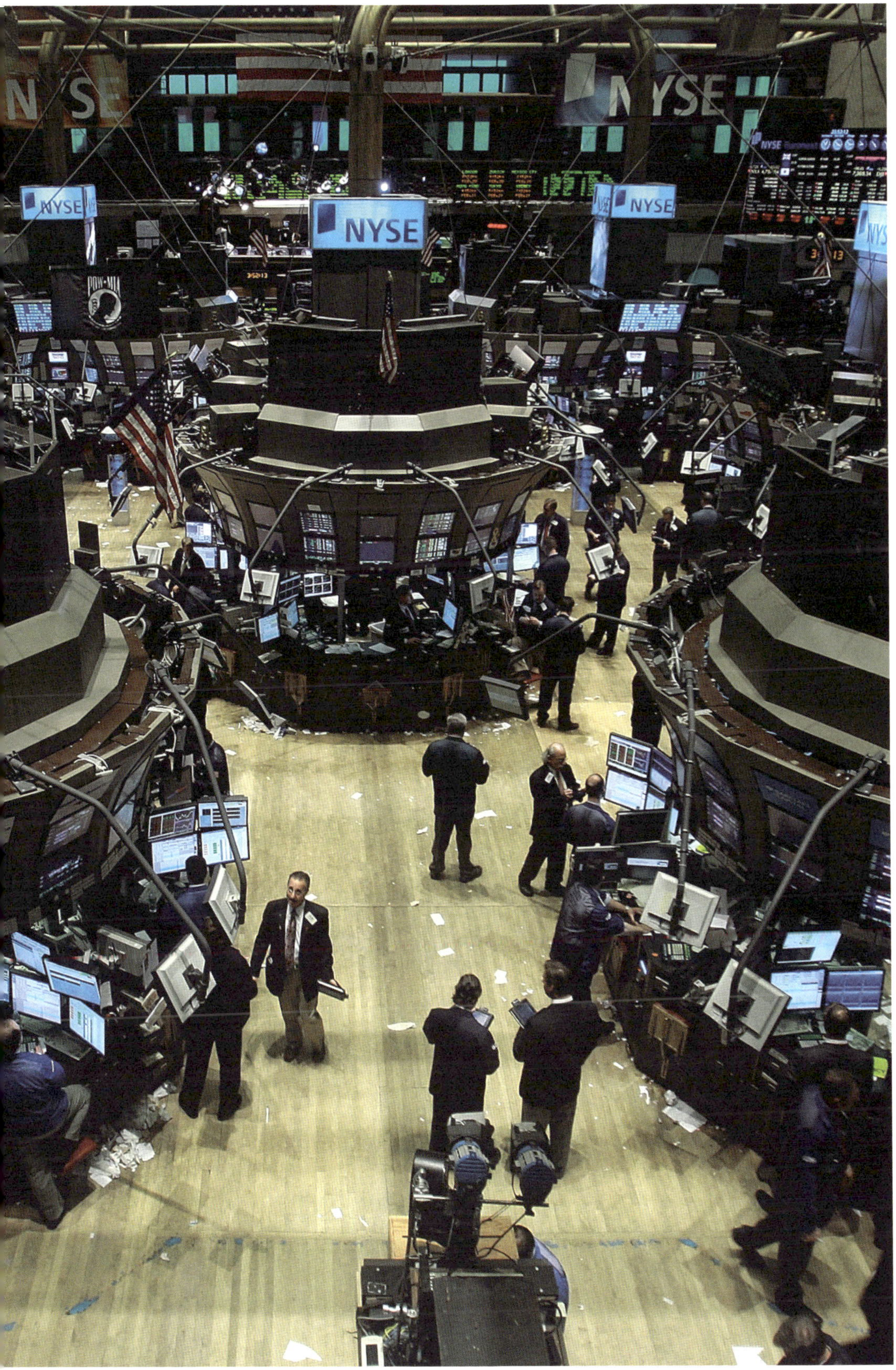
NYSE
NYSE
NYSE
NYSE
NYSE
POW-MIA

Chapter I
Cities and the Economy

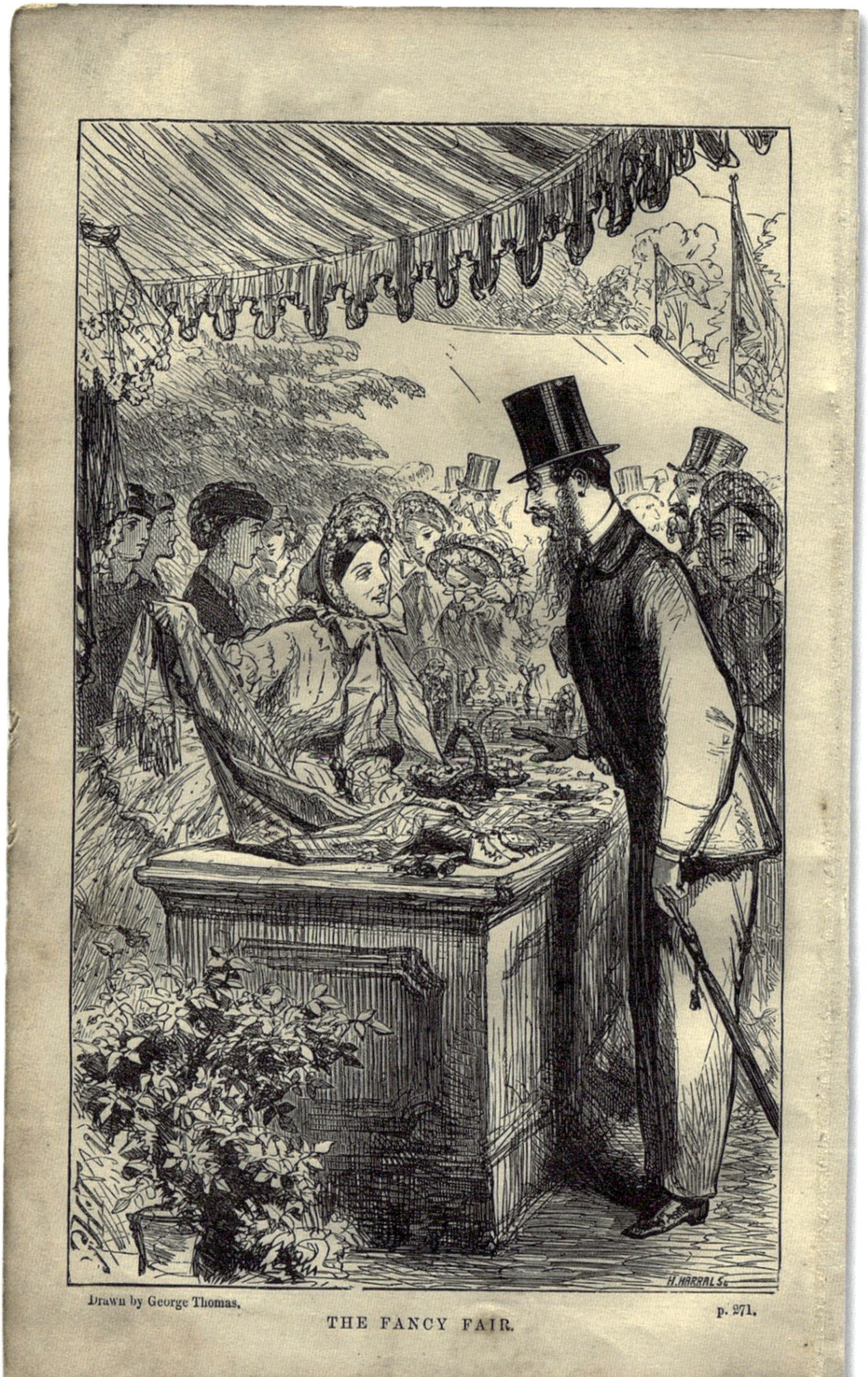

Above: G. H. Thomas, *The Fancy Fair*, 1862
Right page: Pieter Aertsen, *Market Scene*, ca. 1550

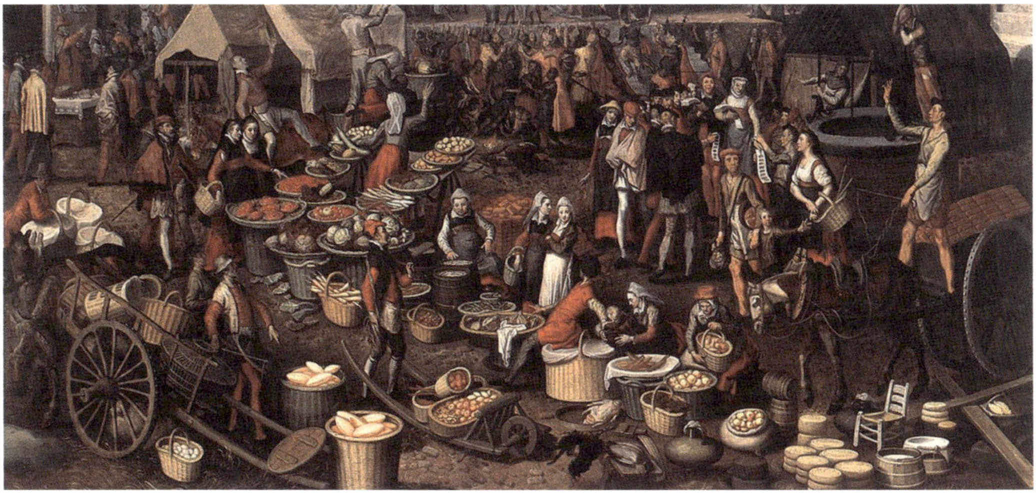

Why can it be so difficult to differentiate a city logo from a brand logo? Why resort to marketing techniques to represent a territory? "Marketplace" aims to analyze the recent tendency of Western cities to opt for a transition from coats of arms to logos. To this end, the present study looks back at the history of the relations between brands and cities in Europe. Their striking iconographic and historical proximity is symptomatic of a complex correlation that dates back to antiquity.

First of all, it is interesting to note that the very definition of the notion of city is intrinsically linked to economic and commercial development:
"The overland trade routes brought about the proliferation of cities from Turkestan to the Caspian Sea and then to the Persian Gulf and eastern Mediterranean. Their economic base in agriculture (supplemented by trade) and their political-religious institutions gave cities an unprecedented degree of occupational specialization and social stratification." (*Encyclopaedia Britannica Online*, s.v. "City")

Throughout the major historical periods, social transformations had a comparable impact upon commerce and economy (hence the brands) as they did upon the development of cities. During the Middle Ages, guild signs, workshop marks, and city coats of arms made their first appearance. At the time, the language of coats of arms, professional guilds, and workshop marks was so similar from a graphic point of view that they are easily confused with one another.

The Renaissance witnessed, alongside the development of large cities (Vienna, Turin, Naples, Amsterdam, Paris, London, etc.) and the flourishing of commerce, the appearance of the first brands in the modern sense of the term (e.g., Meissener Porzellan, 1723).

During the Industrial Revolution, cities and brands once again underwent transformations of a similar nature: the increase of mass production and the appearance of working-class towns and mass housing resulted in decreased quality, but also increased access to both commercial goods and housing. Brands and cities then expanded and entered the system of capitalism and international competition.

Beginning in the nineteenth century, the pace of change accelerated and instruments evolved. Brands adopted logos, subsequently a method of *branding*. Several cities also started adopting these methods of communication at the beginning of the Information Revolution, before this process became widespread through globalization.

Later on, the economic crises of 2007–10 revealed that cities managed like companies can also suffer from the consequences of the downturn, very much like a business would.

In short, their iconographic closeness seems to be a mere symptom of a complex correlation that has developed gradually ever since antiquity.

Cities and the Economy – Quotations

City marketing (related to city branding) is the promotion of a city, or a district within it, with the aim of encouraging certain activities to take place there. It is used to alter the external perceptions of a city in order to encourage tourism, attract inward migration of residents, or enable business relocation.... The development of cities as a marketable product has led to competition between them for inward investment and government funding.

—
Wikipedia contributors, "City marketing," *Wikipedia, The Free Encyclopedia*, en.wikipedia.org/wiki/City_marketing.

One of the specific aspects of local communication is that it applies not only to an institution, but also to a territory. To create true empathy among the inhabitants of a territory and its future, to give or restore the pride of belonging, to attract businesses and inhabitants—all of these are issues and aims embedded in the communication strategies.

—
Dominique Mégard and Bernard Deljarrie, *La communication des collectivités locales*, Paris 2003.

In our new economic context, enhancing the "product of territory" is necessary, but it is not enough! One must also work on marketing and inform the market!

—
Vincent Gollain, "Hambourg, le marketing territorial paie!," http://www.marketing-territorial.org/article-hambourg-le-marketing-territorial-paie--38431836.html.

Territorial marketing establishes a logic of competition between cities, and more generally between territories, which are called to compete in terms of "attractiveness" in order to win over their "clients." Local public action must satisfy the whims of the private sector: innovative taxation, exemptions via priority development areas: investments in first-rate infrastructure, roads, high-speed trains, urban transport, innovation and/or competition clusters. Cities must promote their "competitive advantages" for the greater benefit of businesses.

—

Julie Morange, "Les villes européennes et leurs audacieux managers," February 2010, ellynn.fr.dessousdebruxelles.spip.php?article104.

What is going on is a silent revolution—a silent revolution in terms of stronger economic governance by small steps. The member states have accepted—and I hope they understood it exactly—but they have accepted very important powers of the European institutions regarding surveillance, and a much stricter control of the public finances.

In the United States, the credit rating agency Moody's has recently—and for the first time—issued a warning against the risks represented by local communities.

—

José Manuel Barroso, President of the European Commission, Florence, June 18, 2010, http://euobserver.com/institutional/31993.

—

Isabelle Baraud-Serfaty, "La crise. Menace ou chance pour les villes?," *Esprit*, no. 359, 2009.

Chapter II

History of a Parallel Evolution

Ville le PUY en VELAY

Disneyland Resort

Vivre la Ville SAINT-AVOLD

ville de Périgueux

Baie-Saint-Paul
VILLE D'ART ET DE PATRIMOINE

hanse stadt wipperfürth

Stad Deinze
CENTRUM AAN DE LEIE

FÜSSEN
im Allgäu

STADT WÜRZBURG

Disneyland

MAIRIE DE BRIE-COMTE-ROBERT

Stadt Lichtenfels

Disneyland Resort Paris

Ville de Fresnay-sur-Sarthe

Ville de FRESNAY-SUR-SARTHE

Ville de L'Ancienne-Lorette

Nevers
cité européenne

Kalisz

Disneyland

BOISSY SAINT LEGER

Ville le PUY en VELAY

Disneyland Resort

Vivre la Ville SAINT-AVOLD

ville de Périgueux

Baie-Saint-Paul
VILLE D'ART ET DE PATRIMOINE

hanse stadt wipperfürth

Stad Deinze
CENTRUM AAN DE LEIE

FÜSSEN
im Allgäu

STADT WÜRZBURG

Disneyland

MAIRIE DE BRIE-COMTE-ROBERT

Stadt Lichtenfels

Disneyland Resort Paris

Ville de Fresnay-sur-Sarthe

Ville de FRESNAY-SUR-SARTHE

Ville de L'Ancienne-Lorette

Nevers
cité européenne

Kalisz

Definition – trademark, n.

TRADE-MARK, n.
Pronunciation: /ˈtreɪdmɑːk/
Etymology: < trade n. + mark n.
Definition:
a. A mark (secured by legal registration or, in some countries, established by use) used by a manufacturer or trader to distinguish his goods from similar wares of other firms; usually a distinctive device or figure, a fancy name or trade name, or the name of an individual or firm, marked or impressed on the article or upon the package, etc., in or with which it is sold.
[1571 *Letters Patent to R. Matthews* in Edmunds *Patent Law* (1897) 885 To make the said haftes called Turky haftes for knyves, and for his marke to haue vpon the blade and hafte of the same knyfes... a halfe Moone.]
1838 MYLNE & CRAIG *Rep. Cases III.* 338 The Court will grant a perpetual injunction against the use, by one tradesman, of the trade marks of another.
1862 *Act 25 & 26 Vict.* c. 88 §1 The Expression "Trade Mark" shall include any... Name, Signature, Word, Letter, Device [etc.] ...lawfully used by any Person to denote any Chattel, or (in Scotland) any Article of Trade [etc.] ...to be an Article or Thing of the Manufacture... of such Person, or to be an Article or Thing of any peculiar or particular Description made or sold by such Person.
1880 *Print. Trades Jrnl.* XXXI. 26 The owl is the trade-mark of the firm.
b. *fig.* A distinctive mark or token. Also attrib. as adj.
1869 M. TWAIN *Innocents Abroad* XXIII. 238 We see other monks looking tranquilly up to heaven, but having no trade-mark.
1873 R. BROWNING *Red Cotton Night-cap Country* i. 63 Trade-mark that stamps each word and deed.
1889 A. CONAN DOYLE *Micah Clarke* XXX. 311 The trade mark upon your forehead is especially hard to overlook.
1898 J. E. C. BODLEY *France* II. IV. VI. 406 Opportunists... utilised his name as the trade-mark of their parliamentary group.
1977 *South China Morning Post* (Hong Kong) 13 Apr. 7/2 Jimmy Shtoow'd, to phonetically adopt his trademark drawl, has an unnerving "look" for interviewers.
1983 *Daily Tel.* 18 Mar. 17/2 Fans need not worry: her trademark French rayon jersey made up at least half the collection.
c. *attrib.*, as **trade-mark name, trade-mark registration.**
1901 *Daily Chron.* 2 Dec. 7/1 A belated perambulator... with the trade-mark name of "The Prince of Wales."
1909 *Chem. & Druggist* 20 Feb. 315/2 Invented words should be protected by trade-mark registration; by themselves they cannot be copyrighted.

Derivatives:
TRADE-ˌMARK, v. (*trans.*) to affix or imprint a trade-mark upon.
TRADE-MARKED, adj.
1904 D. B. W. SLADEN *When we were Lovers in Japan* x, Bottled beer (made in Japan... and trade-marked with a big dragon).
1936 E. B. WHITE *Let.* 24 Dec. (1976) 146 Your public approval of a trademarked product and your influence can be bought at a price.
1983 P. DEVLIN *All of us There* XI. 133 The old [pub]... with its great copper-banded barrels and old trade-marked mirrors.
TRADE-MARKING, n.
1906 *Westm. Gaz.* 16 Mar. 5/2 The Bill... provided for the trade-marking of all imported beers.
(*Oxford English Dictionary Online*)

A TRADEMARK, TRADE MARK, OR TRADE-MARK is a recognizable sign, design or expression which identifies products or services of a particular source from those of others. The trademark owner can be an individual, business organization, or any legal entity. A trademark may be located on a package, a label, a voucher or on the product itself... A trademark may be designated by the following symbols:
™ (the "trademark symbol," which is the letters "TM," for an unregistered trademark, a mark used to promote or brand goods)
℠ (which is the letters "SM" in superscript, for an unregistered service mark, a mark used to promote or brand services)
® (the letter "R" surrounded by a circle, for a registered trademark)
(http://en.wikipedia.org/wiki/Trademark)

TRADEMARK, any visible sign or device used by a business enterprise to identify its goods and distinguish them from those made or carried by others. Trademarks may be words or groups of words, letters, numerals, devices, names, the shape or other presentation of products or their packages, color combinations with signs, combinations of colors, and combinations of any of the enumerated signs.... By indicating the origin of goods and services, trademarks serve two important purposes. They provide manufacturers and traders with protection from unfair competition (one person representing or passing for sale his goods as the goods of another), and they provide customers with protection from imitations (assuring them of a certain expected quality). In terms of the protection of the rights of trademark holders, the law in most countries extends beyond the rule of unfair competition, for a trademark is considered the property of the holder; and, as such, unauthorized use of the trademark constitutes not only misrepresentation and fraud but also a violation of the holder's private property rights...
(Encyclopaedia Britannica, s.v. "trademark" http://www.britannica.com/EBchecked/topic/601724/trademark)

A brand is a strong reference point on the market. (Georges Lewi, *Mythologie des marques, quand les marques font leur storytelling*, Paris 2009)

The difference between products and brands is fundamental. A product is something that is made in a factory; a brand is something that is bought by a consumer. (Peter Schweitzer, *People Buy Products Not Brands*)

CONSUMER, n
Pronunciation: (kənˈsjuːmə)
Definitions:
1. a person who acquires goods and services for his or her own personal needs
2. a person or thing that consumes
3. usually plural (ecology) an organism, esp. an animal, within a community that feeds upon plants or other animals
(*Collins Online English Dictionary*)

Definition – city, n.

CITY, n

Pronunciation: /ˈsɪtɪ/

Forms: ME–15 cyte, cite, (ME scite), ME cety, ME cytee, site, syte, ME–15 citee, cete, ME cetie, sete, ME–16 citie, 15 cittie, citte, cytte, setye, syttey, sittey; also Sc. ciete, cyete, scitie, 15–16 citty, (16 chitty), 15– city.

Etymology: Middle English cite, < Old French cité, earlier citet, corresponding to Provençal ciptat, Italian città, earlier cittade, Romanic *civ'tade < Latin cīvitāt-em. By another phonetic process the Romanic type gave Provençal ciutat, Catalan ciutat, Spanish ciudad, Portuguese cidade. Latin cīvitās, -tātem was n. of state or condition < cīvis citizen: its primary sense was therefore "citizenship"; thence concretely "the body of citizens, the community"; only in later times was the word taken as = urbs, the town or place occupied by the community. The historical relation between the Roman cīvitās and cīvis was thus the reverse of that between English city and citizen, which however is that of the Greek πόλις and πολίτη

1. *orig.* A town or other inhabited place. Not a native designation, but app. at first a somewhat grandiose title, used instead of the Old English burh, borough n. Frequently applied (after civitas of the Vulgate = πόλις of N.T. & LXX.) to places mentioned in the Bible which were really mere villages, e.g. Nazareth, Nain, Bethlehem...

2. *spec.* A title ranking above that of "town."

a. used vaguely, or of ancient or foreign places of note, as capitals, or the like.

b. In England... the title appears to be properly relative to "town," not to "borough." "Cities" and "towns," possessing a municipal corporation and local autonomy, are alike "boroughs," though those boroughs which are also cities may take precedence of those which are not.

c. In Scotland and Ireland (see the historical sketch above).

d. In U.S.: "A town or collective body of inhabitants incorporated and governed by a mayor and aldermen" (Webster); but applied, in the newer States, much more loosely (see quots.), and often given in anticipation. The legal characteristics of a city vary in different states ...

e. In the dominion of Canada: a municipality of the highest class ...

f. City of Refuge, in the Mosaic dispensation, a walled town set apart for the protection of those who had accidentally committed manslaughter. Holy City, Jerusalem, esp. in connection with pilgrims and crusaders. Eternal City, City of the Seven Hills, Rome: so with many similar epithets, for which see their alphabetical places.

(Oxford Online English Dictionary)

CITY, relatively permanent and highly organized center of population, of greater size or importance than a town or village. The name city is given to certain urban communities by virtue of some legal or conventional distinction that can vary between regions or nations. In most cases, however, the concept of city refers to a particular type of community, the urban community, and its culture, known as "urbanism."

(*Encyclopaedia Britannica Online*)

A CITY is a relatively large and permanent settlement. Although there is no agreement on how a city is distinguished from a town within general English language meanings, many cities have a particular administrative, legal, or historical status based on local law...

Cities generally have complex systems for sanitation, utilities, land usage, housing, and transportation. The concentration of development greatly facilitates interaction between people and businesses, benefiting both parties in the process.

(http://en.wikipedia.org/wiki/City)

TOWNS and urban agglomerations, also called urban units whereby delimitation is based solely on continuity of habitat, may comprise:

· two or more municipalities, that is, a town-center and its suburbs (exceptionally, several town-centers), on the territory of which an agglomerated zone contains more than 2,000 inhabitants; this sort of urban unit is called a multi-municipal agglomeration;

· just one municipality, the agglomerated population of which is at least 2,000; this sort of urban unit is called an isolated town or, more commonly, a town.

A first delimitation of towns and urban agglomerations was performed in the 1954 census. New urban units were constituted in the censuses of 1962, 1968, 1975, 1982, 1990, 1999, and 2010.

(French National Institute of Statistics and Economic Studies, INSEE)

CITIZEN, n.

Pronunciation: (ˈsɪtɪzən)

1. a native registered or naturalized member of a state, nation, or other political community. Compare alien

2. an inhabitant of a city or town

3. a native or inhabitant of any place

4. a civilian, as opposed to a soldier, public official, etc.

(*Collins Online English Dictionary*)

Antiquity – Trademark

1–

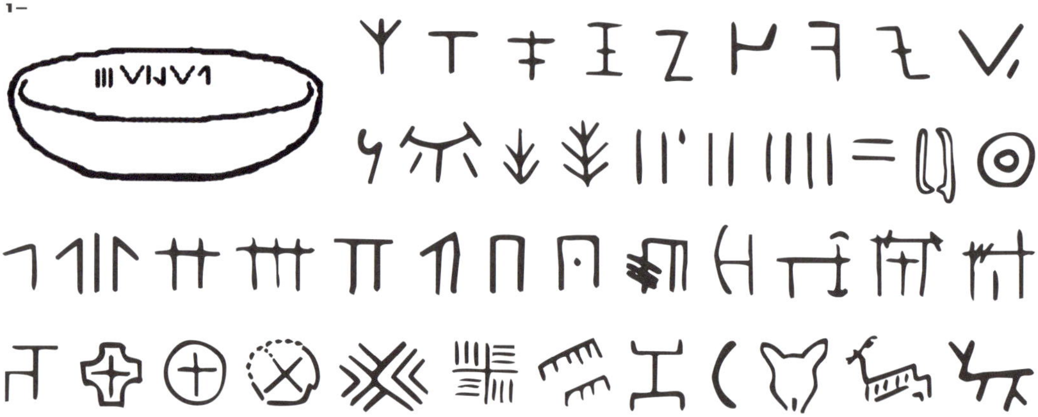

2–

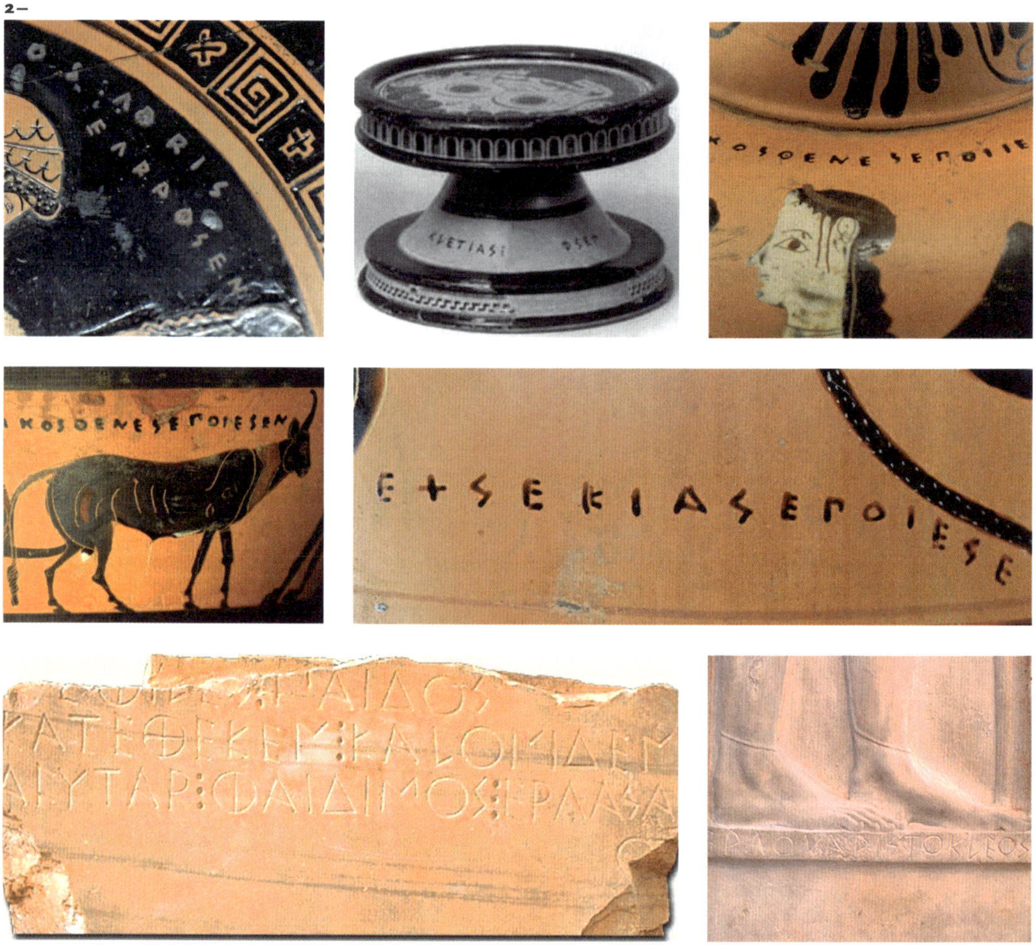

1–The first known branded objects (Vinča symbols on pottery) date back to 7,000 years ago. They are supposed to denote the place where they were manufactured.

2–In Greece, objects bore the signature of the artist; in China and Rome, the mark of the workshop. The mark functioned as a guarantee of quality (branding of pottery, ceramic, jewelry—gold, silver—craftsman's signature).

Antiquity – City

The overland trade routes brought about the proliferation of cities from Turkestan to the Caspian Sea and then to the Persian Gulf and eastern Mediterranean. Their economic base in agriculture (supplemented by trade) and their political-religious institutions gave cities an unprecedented degree of occupational specialization and social stratification. (*Encyclopaedia Britannica Online*)

3–

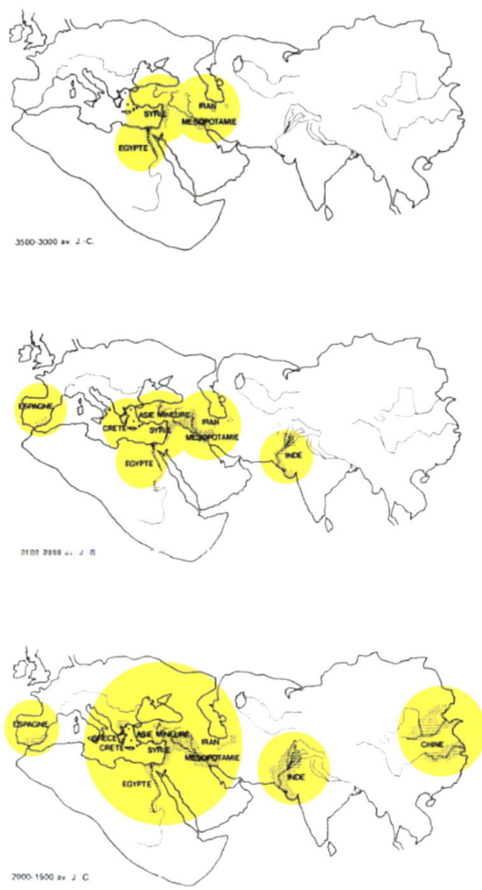

4–

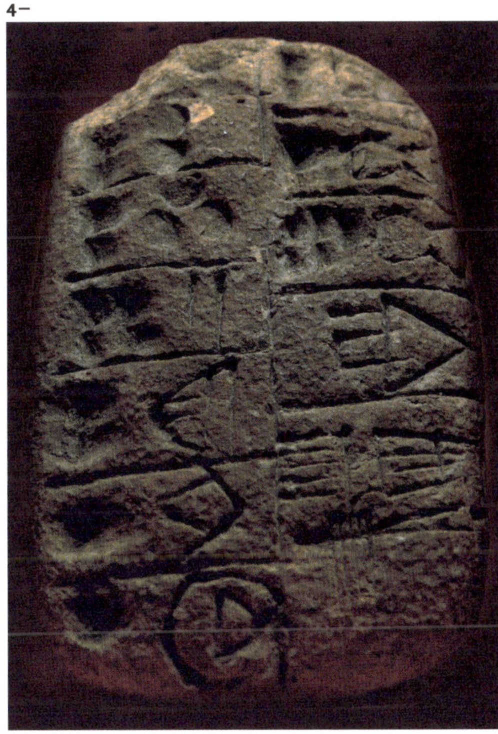

3–The *Encyclopaedia Britannica's* definition of city indicates that urban development in antiquity was already directly linked to economic and commercial development.

4–Uruk accounting tablet, Uruk III (ca. 3200–3000 BC), registering the delivery of cereal products for the feast of the goddess Inanna, Pergamonmuseum, Berlin.

The Middle Ages – Trademark

5–

6–

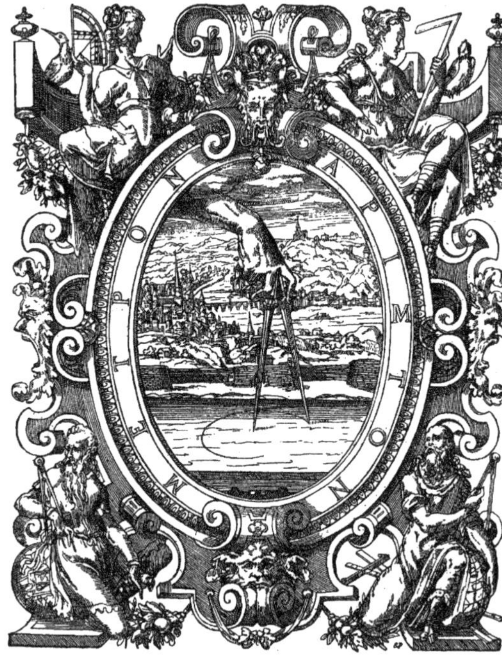

7–

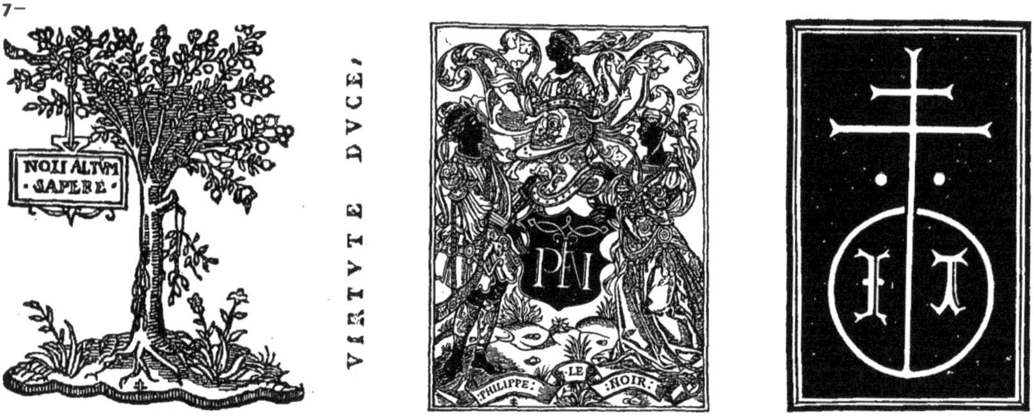

8–

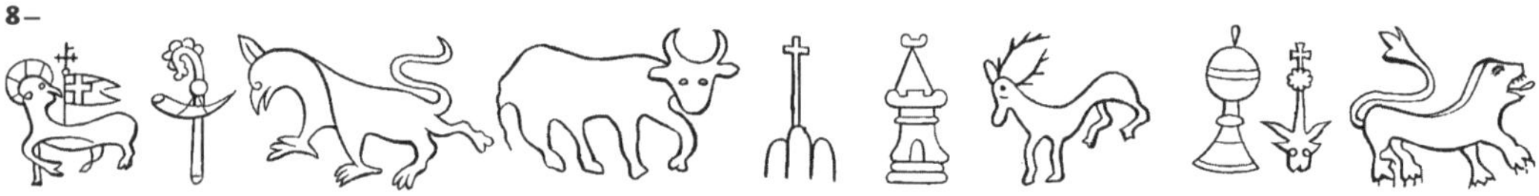

The end of the Middle Ages saw the appearance of guild signs, workshop marks, and city coats of arms. The languages of coats of arms, professional guilds, and workshop marks were already quite similar from a graphic viewpoint, to the point of being easily confused with one another.

5–Seal of the University of Oxford, featuring a book bound with coins and clasps. **6**–Mark used by Plantin, a printer from Antwerp, on the title pages of their scientific publications. The mark features the town of Tours, near which he was born. **7**–Marks by: Robert Estienne, printer from Paris (1536); Philippe le Noir, printer-bookseller from Paris (1536), established in rue Saint-Jacques, at the sign of the Crowned Rose; Trechsel, printer from Lyon (1489). **8**–Fourteenth- and fifteenth-century paper marks, France.

The Middle Ages – City

9–

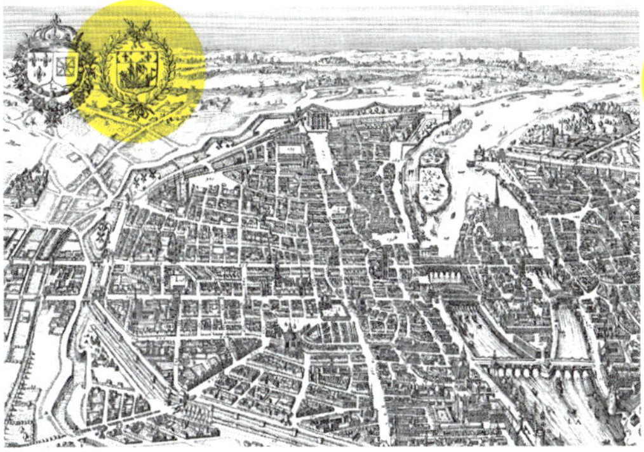

10–

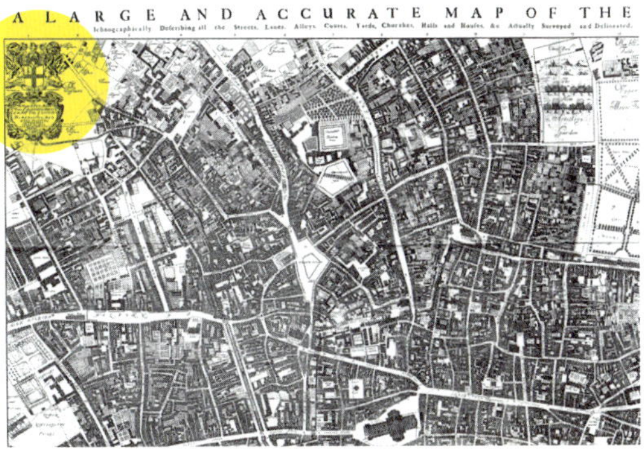

11–

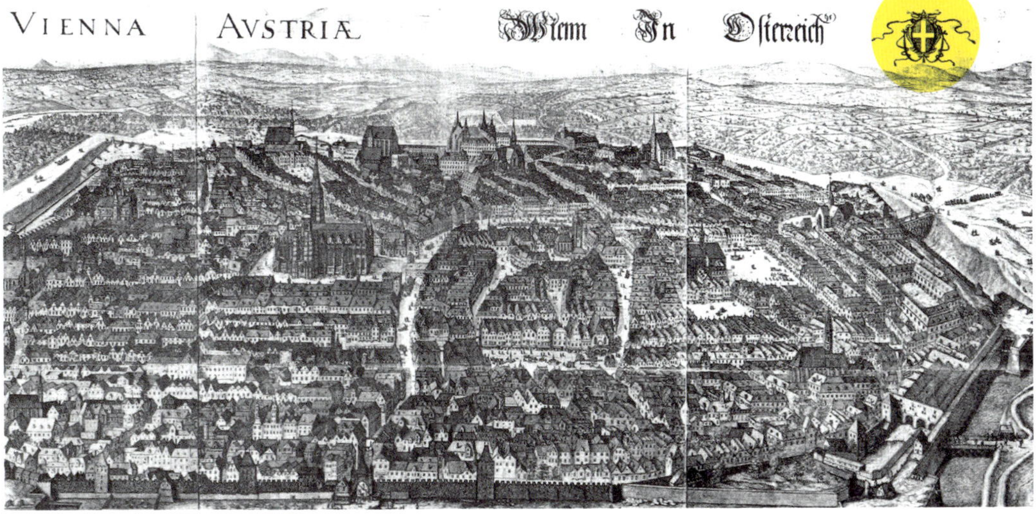

12–

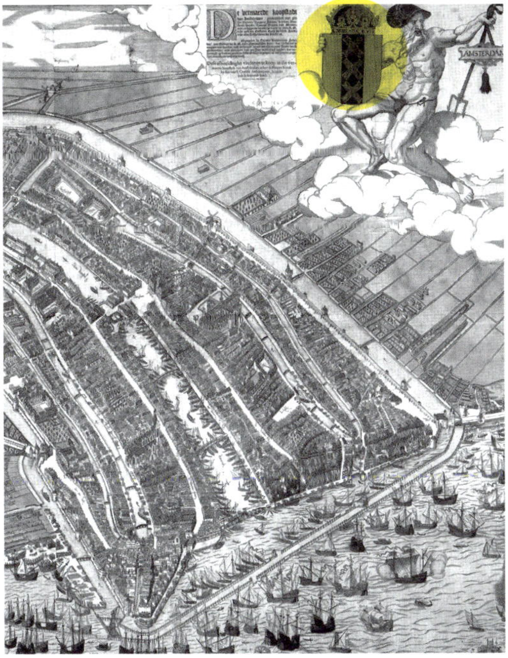

13–

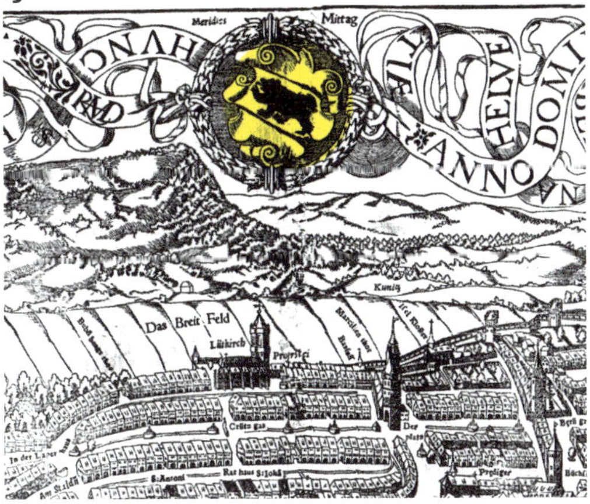

9–View of Paris in 1618 by Visscher. **10–**The City of London by Ogilby & Morgan (1673). **11–**Bird's-eye view of Vienna as seen from the north. Identical 1640 copy of the first 1609 print. **12–**Amsterdam, 1544. **13–**Map of Bern by Hans Rudolf Manuel, the oldest detailed topographic representation of Bern, 1549.

Times of Change – Trademark

14–

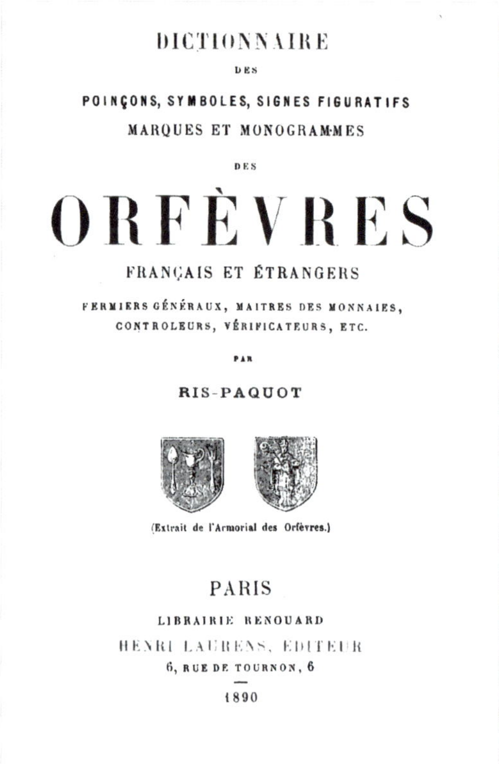

DICTIONNAIRE

DES

POINÇONS, SYMBOLES, SIGNES FIGURATIFS
MARQUES ET MONOGRAMMES

DES

ORFÈVRES

FRANÇAIS ET ÉTRANGERS

FERMIERS GÉNÉRAUX, MAITRES DES MONNAIES,
CONTROLEURS, VÉRIFICATEURS, ETC.

PAR

RIS-PAQUOT

(Extrait de l'Armorial des Orfèvres.)

PARIS

LIBRAIRIE RENOUARD

HENRI LAURENS, ÉDITEUR

6, RUE DE TOURNON, 6

—

1890

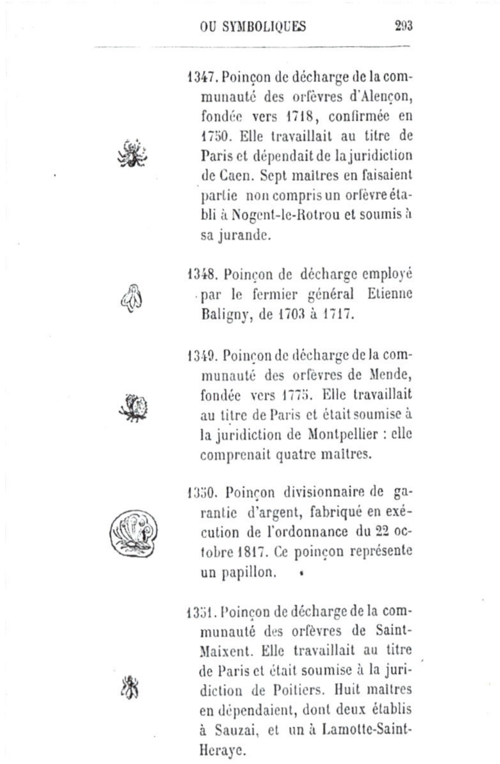

OU SYMBOLIQUES 293

1347. Poinçon de décharge de la communauté des orfèvres d'Alençon, fondée vers 1718, confirmée en 1750. Elle travaillait au titre de Paris et dépendait de la juridiction de Caen. Sept maîtres en faisaient partie non compris un orfèvre établi à Nogent-le-Rotrou et soumis à sa jurande.

1348. Poinçon de décharge employé par le fermier général Etienne Baligny, de 1703 à 1717.

1349. Poinçon de décharge de la communauté des orfèvres de Mende, fondée vers 1775. Elle travaillait au titre de Paris et était soumise à la juridiction de Montpellier : elle comprenait quatre maîtres.

1350. Poinçon divisionnaire de garantie d'argent, fabriqué en exécution de l'ordonnance du 22 octobre 1817. Ce poinçon représente un papillon.

1351. Poinçon de décharge de la communauté des orfèvres de Saint-Maixent. Elle travaillait au titre de Paris et était soumise à la juridiction de Poitiers. Huit maîtres en dépendaient, dont deux établis à Sauzai, et un à Lamotte-Saint-Heraye.

15–

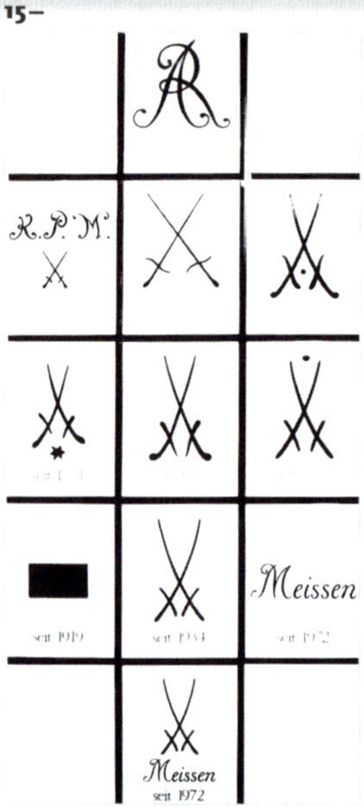

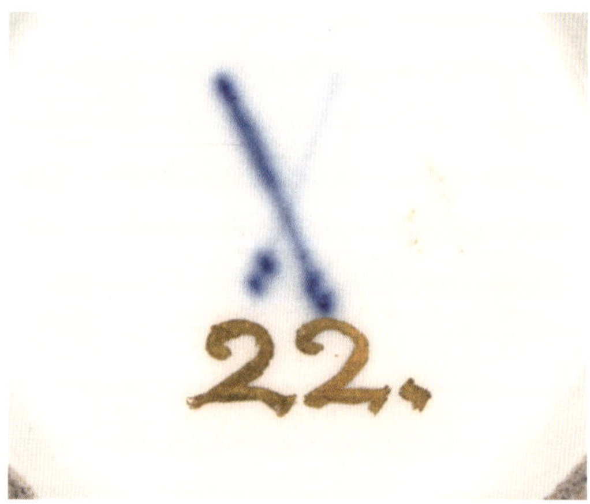

With the invention of printing, and especially from the Renaissance on, the growth of cities (Vienna, Turin, Naples...) and the flourishing of commerce are accompanied by the appearance of the first brands in the modern acceptance of the term (Meissener Porzellan, 1723).

14– Later on, commercial development leads to a multiplication of professional communities, guilds, and books of signs used by workshops and craftsmen (who were forbidden from using the same sign for a different client) as kinds of precursors of true trademarks for products such as gold, copper, soap, textiles, etc. **15–** Historically, the first European brand (1723) is attributed to the Saxon porcelain manufacturing company Meissener Porzellan (originally called Königliche Porzellan-Manufaktur Meissen).

274 MARQUES FIGURATIVES

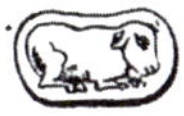

Ce poinçon est accompagné du double W, marque de John Wilkinson (1660) et d'un autre représentant une tour.

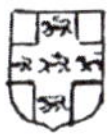

1247. Poinçon du bureau de la ville d'York, de 1710 à 1790. La forme extérieure a seule varié. En 1710 c'était une simple croix; en 1780 l'écu ci-contre et en 1790 une circonférence.

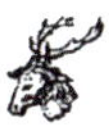

1248. Poinçon de décharge de la communauté des orfèvres de Compiègne, fondée en 1667; elle travaillait au titre de Paris et dépendait de la Cour des monnaies de Paris. elle était formée de six maitres dont un résidait à Villers-Cotterets.

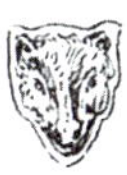

1249. Poinçon de décharge employé sous la régie de Jean-Baptiste Fouache, de 1774 à 1780, pour marquer les gros ouvrages d'argent. (Une tête d'ours.)

1250. Poinçon de décharge de la communauté des orfèvres de Lyon. Une déclaration en date du 9 mai titre de Paris et formait elle-même sa juridiction, dix maitres la composaient; les villes de Dax et de Saint-Jean-de-Luz en dépendaient.

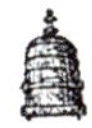

Cette communauté contremarquait les ouvrages qui étaient apportés à la maison commune avec deux poinçons différents, l'un était celui de la communauté dont l'empreinte est formée des deux lettres A B, adossées et surmontées de la couronne de France; l'autre est celui de la jurande, formé d'une seule lettre couronnée, lettre qui change à chaque mutation de garde.

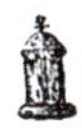

1320. Poinçon de décharge de la communauté des orfèvres de Loudun, fondée en 1646, elle travaillait au titre de Paris et dépendait de la juridiction de Tours. Elle se composait de six maitres.

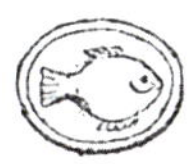

1321. Poinçon relevée sur des pièces d'argenterie provenant de la fabrication de Norwich, vers 1550.

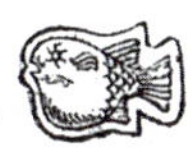

1322. Poinçon divisionnaire de la garantie d'argent, fabriqué en exécution de l'ordonnance du 22 octobre 1819. Ce poinçon représente une Lysse.

16–

328 MARQUES FIGURATIVES

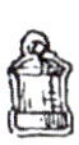

Baptiste), pour marquer les ouvrages d'or et menus ouvrages d'argent. (Ce poinçon représente un autel de l'amitié.)

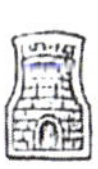

1503. Poinçon divisionnaire de recense, fabriqué en exécution de l'ordonnance du 22 octobre 1817. Sur ce poinçon est gravé le signe caractéristique, indiqué dans le tableau des bureaux de garantie (il représente un tour).

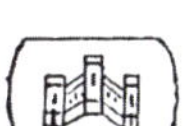

1504. Poinçon du bureau de la ville d'Exeter (Angleterre). Trois tours unies ou séparées, représentent les armes de la ville.

1505. Poinçon de décharge de la communauté des orfèvres de Châtillon-sur-Seine. Cette communauté travaillait au titre de Paris et dépendait de la juridiction de Dijon. Elle existait déjà dès le seizième siècle, elle était composée en 1785, de quatre maitres, non compris trois orfèvres établis, savoir : un

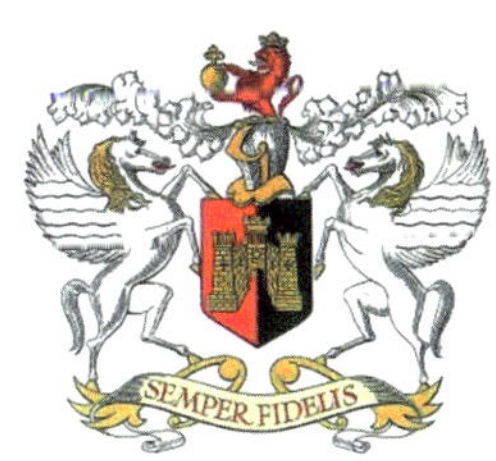

16– The hallmark and coat of arms of the city of Exeter. The symbols of the cities and craftsmen are on the same level.

Industrial Revolution – Trademark

17–

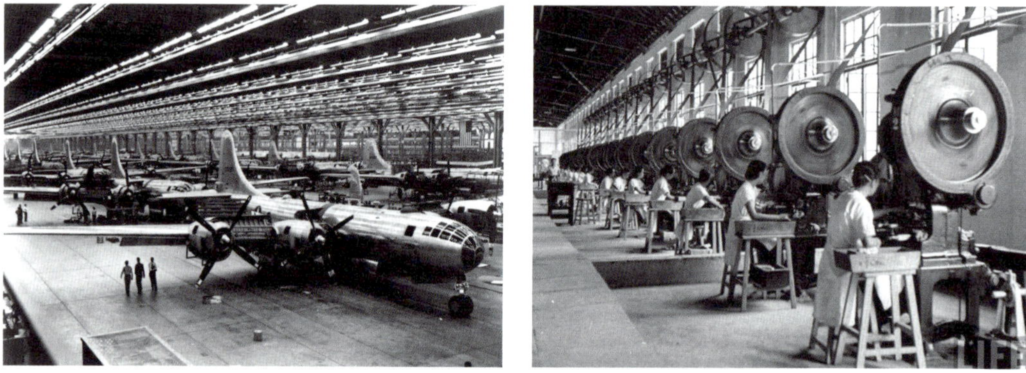

18–

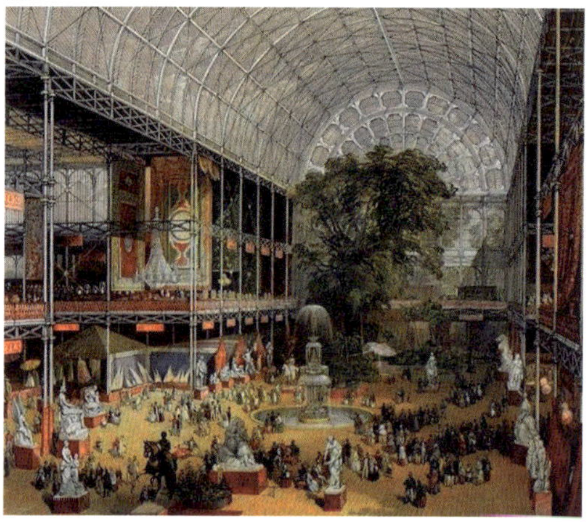

We are living at a period of most wonderful transition, which tends rapidly to accomplish that great end, to which, indeed, all history points—the realization of the unity of mankind.... The great principle of division of labor, which may be called the moving power of civilization, is being extended to all branches of science, industry, and art.... The products of all quarters of the globe are placed at our disposal, and we have only to choose which is the best and the cheapest for our purposes, and the powers of production are entrusted to the stimulus of competition and capital. (Albert Prince Consort's speech, given on March 21, 1850, in the course of preparations for London's Great Exhibition)

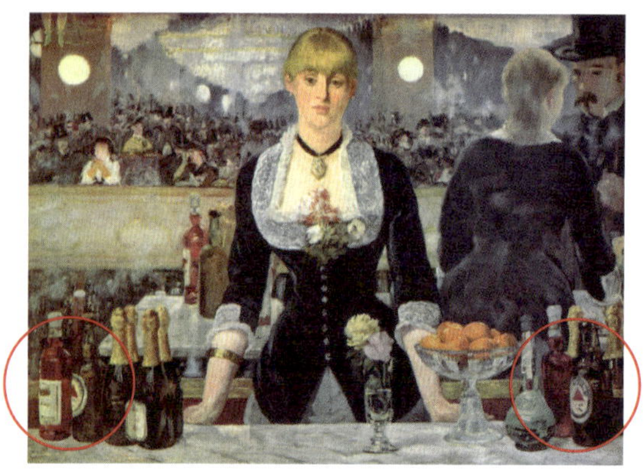

19–

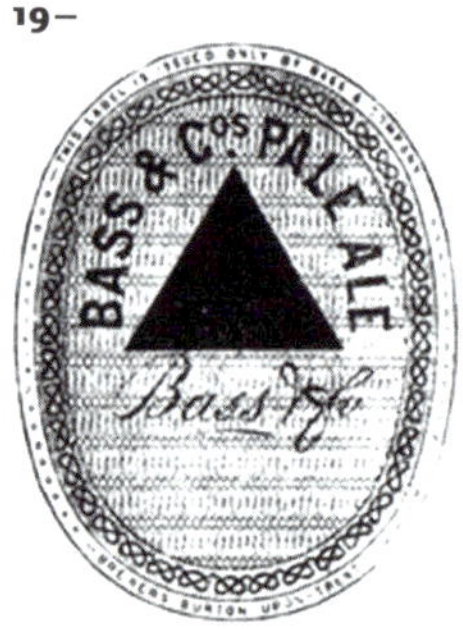

Increase in mass production and the emergence of working-class towns during the Industrial Revolution. Brands and cities expand as they enter the capitalist system and international competition.

17– Industrial Revolution, beginning of mechanized production. **18–** London's Great Exhibition of 1851. Declaration about the global market of goods. **19–** The first Trade Mark Registration Act was passed in England in 1875. The Bass Brewery's Red Triangle was the first trademark registered under this act.

Industrial Revolution – City

20–

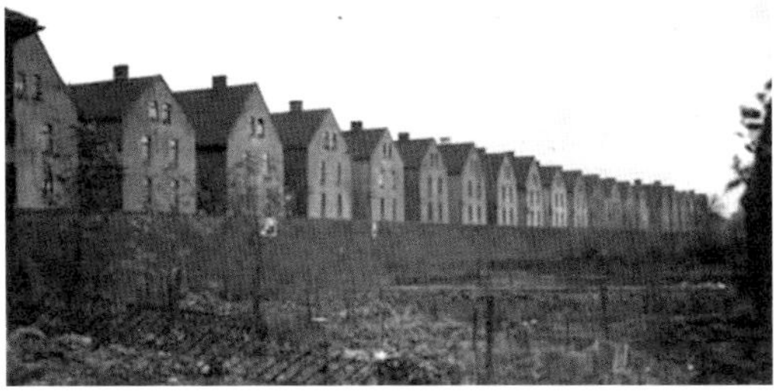

21–

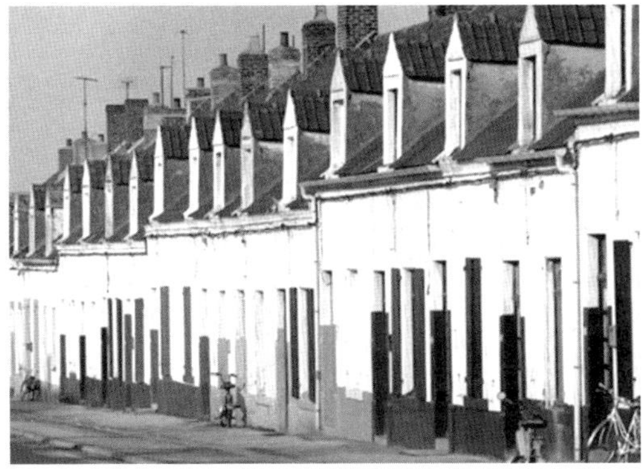

22–

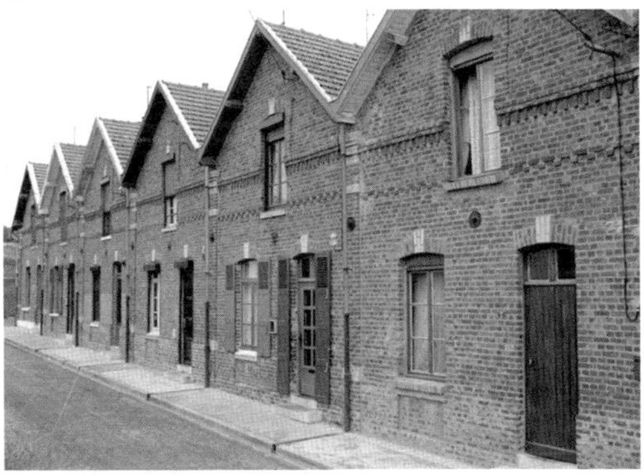

23–

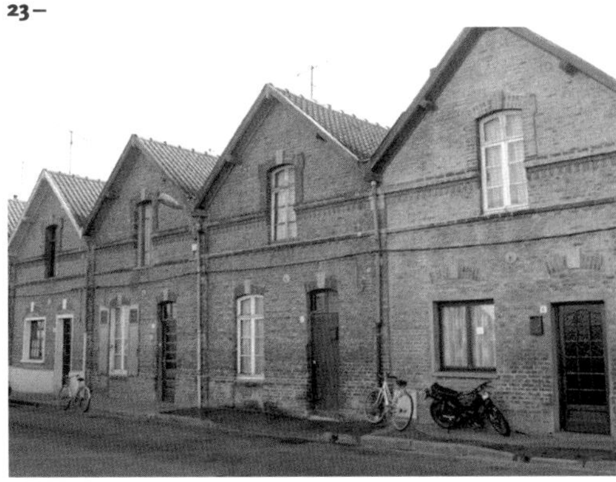

24–

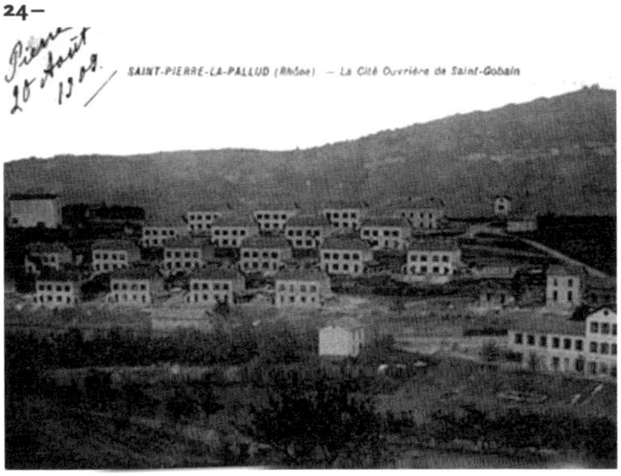

25–

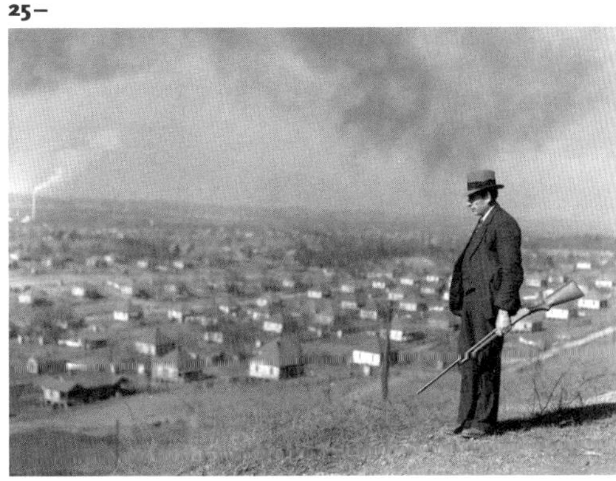

26–

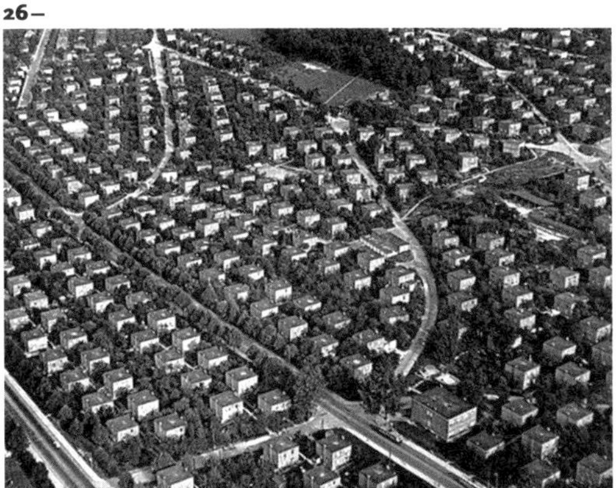

20–Working-class housing (steel factory), Duisburg, Germany. **21–**Working-class town, Le Coron, Nord-Pas-de-Calais, France. **22–**Working-class housing (Ancienne Briqueterie), Pont-Rémy, Picardy, France. **23–**Working-class housing (sugar beet factory; bottling factory), Martainneville, Picardy, France. **24–**Working-class town Saint-Gobain, Saint-Pierre-la-Palud, France. **25–**Working-class town watchman, Jefferson County, Alabama, US. **26–**Working-class housing (Bata factory), Zlín, Czech Republic.

Branding – Origins

27–

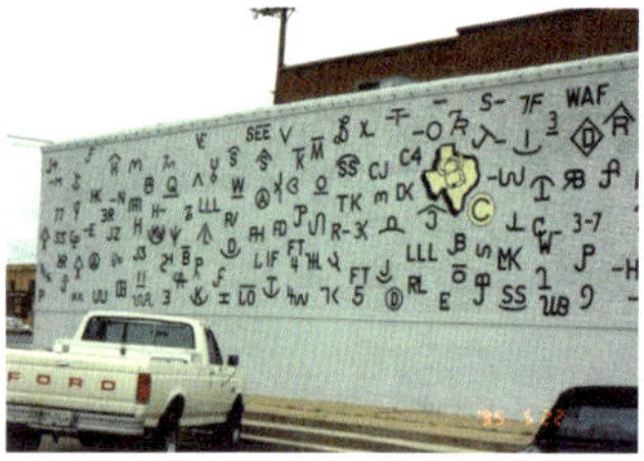

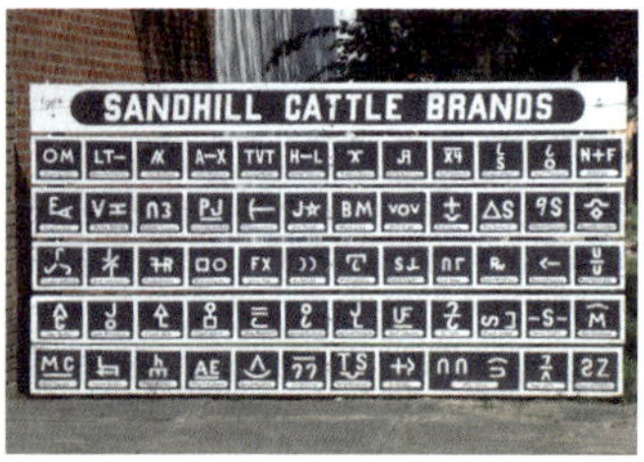

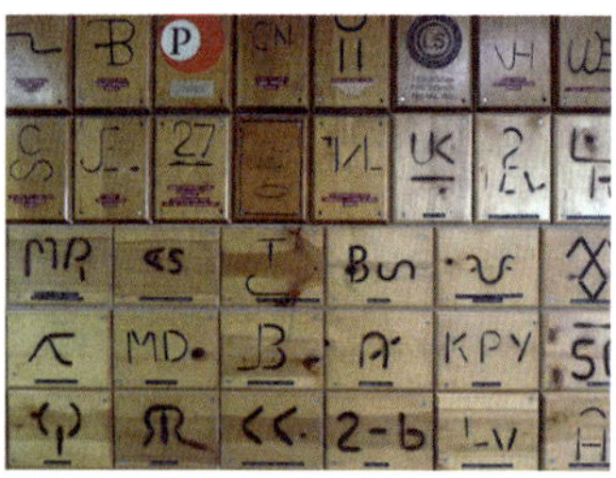

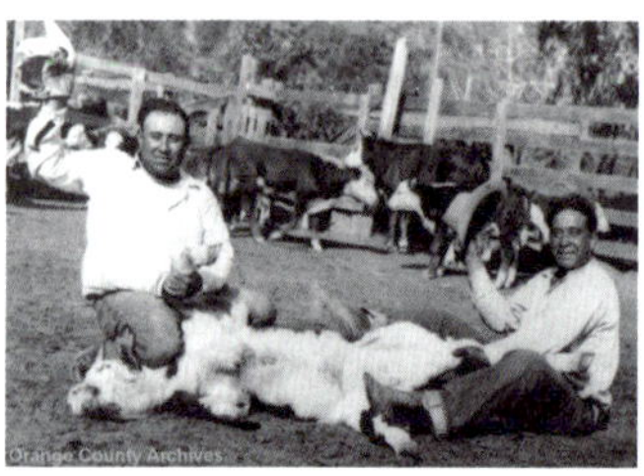

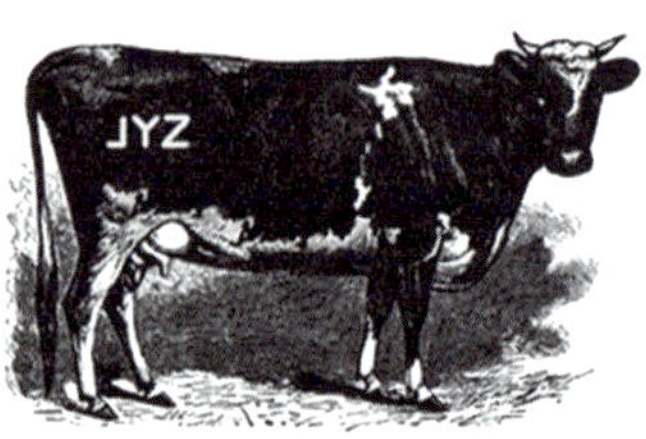

CATTLE BRAND.

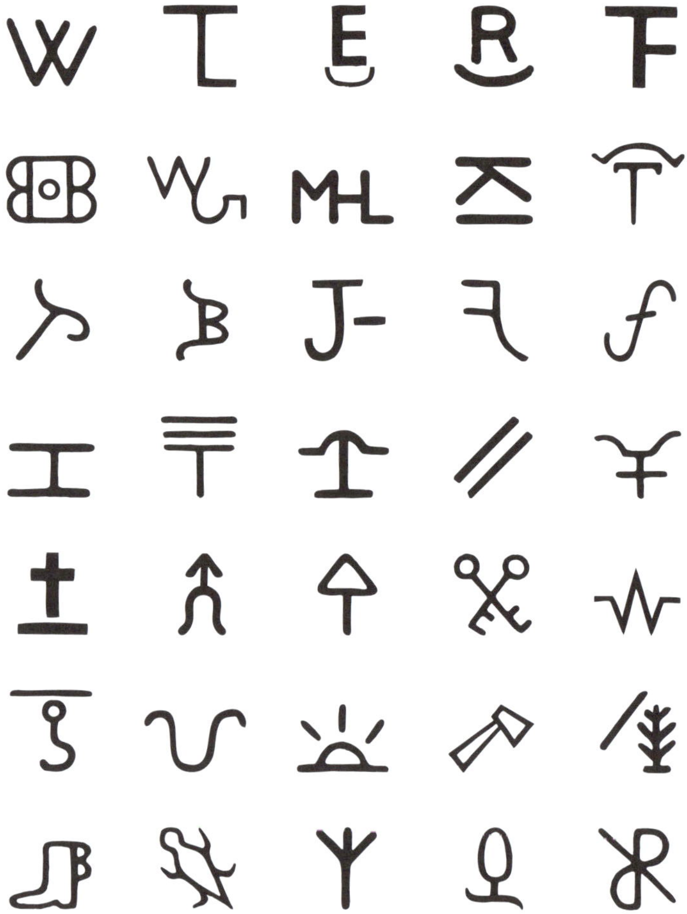

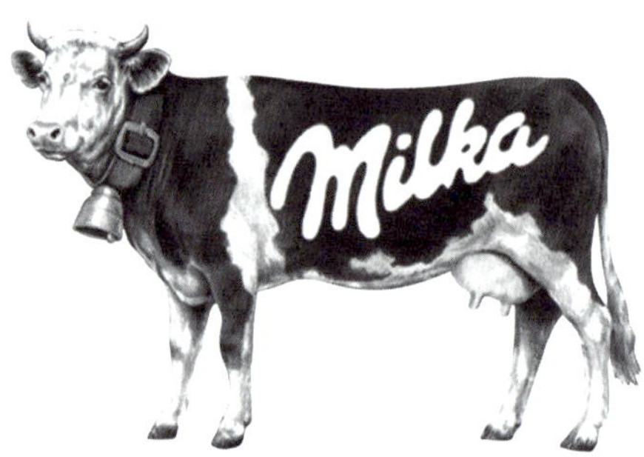

27– Livestock branding is a technique for marking livestock so as to identify the owner.

Originally, livestock branding only referred to a hot brand for large stock, though the term is now also used to refer to other alternative techniques such as freeze branding. Other forms of livestock identification include inner lip or ear tattoos, earmarking, ear tagging, and RFID tagging with a type of microchip. The semi-permanent paint markings used to identify sheep are called a paint or color brand. In the American West, branding evolved into a complex marking system still in use today. (http://en.wikipedia.org/wiki/Livestock_branding)

Branding – Management

A commodity appears, at first sight, a very trivial thing, and easily understood. Its analysis shows that it is, in reality, a very queer thing, abounding in metaphysical subtleties and theological niceties. So far as it is a value in use, there is nothing mysterious about it.... But, so soon as it steps forth as a commodity, it is changed into something transcendent. It not only stands with its feet on the ground, but, in relation to all other commodities, it stands on its head, and evolves out of its wooden brain grotesque ideas, far more wonderful than "table-turning" ever was. (Karl Marx, *Capital,* 1867)

28–

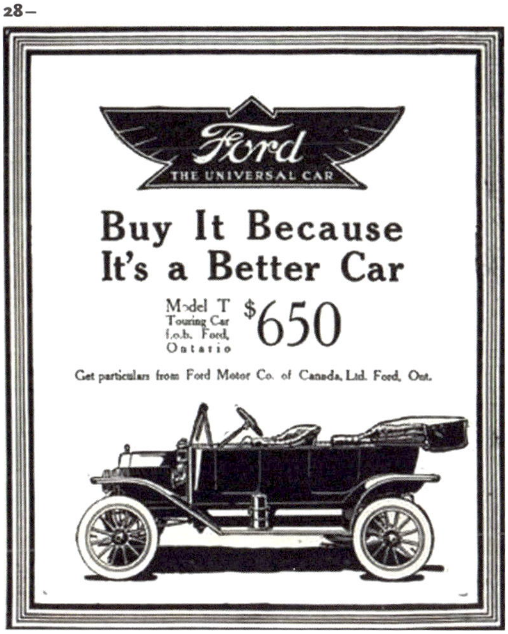

29–

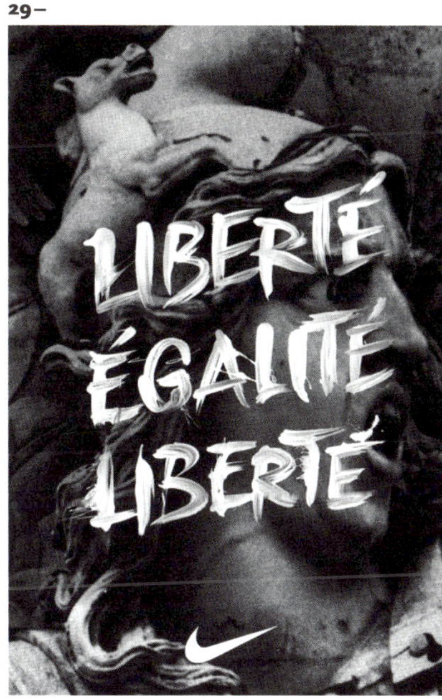

28– *Proto branding,* 1914. Henry Ford produces the black Model T on a large scale, lowers the price to 825 dollars, then to 500 dollars in 1914. By doubling the salary of his own workers, he turns them into his first customers. (Georges Lewi and Jérôme Lacœuilhe, *Branding management. La marque, de l'idée à l'action,* Paris, 2007)

29– *Branding management,* 1972
(Nike FFF campaign, Leg agency, Paris, 2011).
Phil Knight can be regarded as the man who perfected the mechanisms of marketing, and who developed, since the late 1990s, the phenomenon of branding on a planetary scale.... Nike does not have a production factory and plays on the concept of a "global village," both for its sales and for the manufacturing of its products in Asia. (Lewi and Lacœuilhe, *Branding management,* 2007)

Contamination – Brand → City

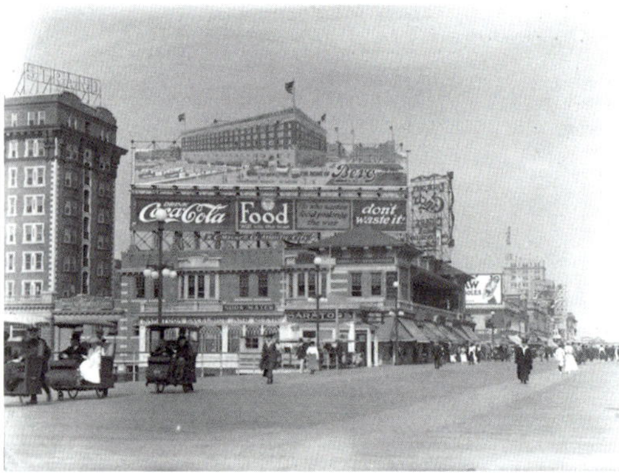

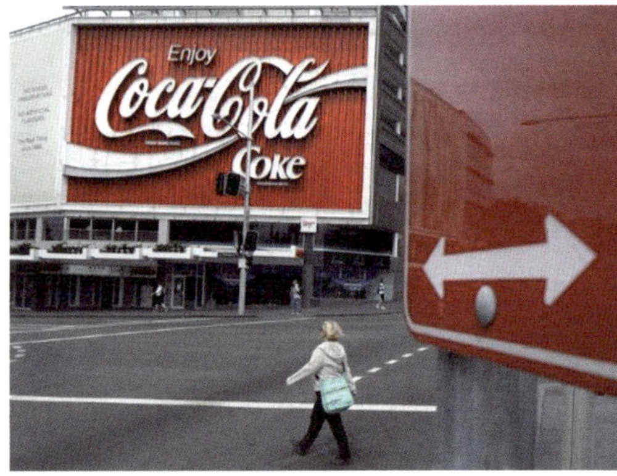

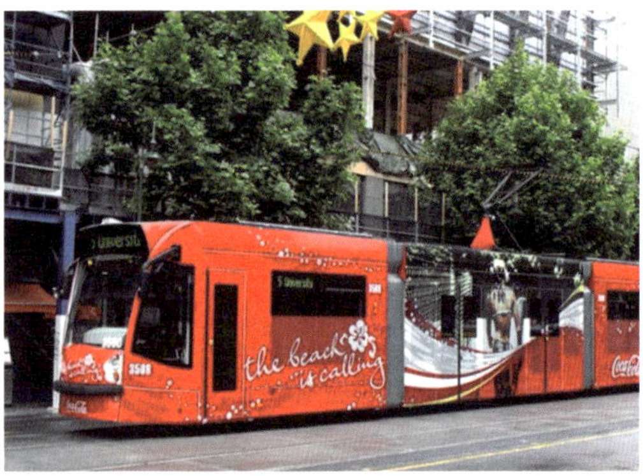

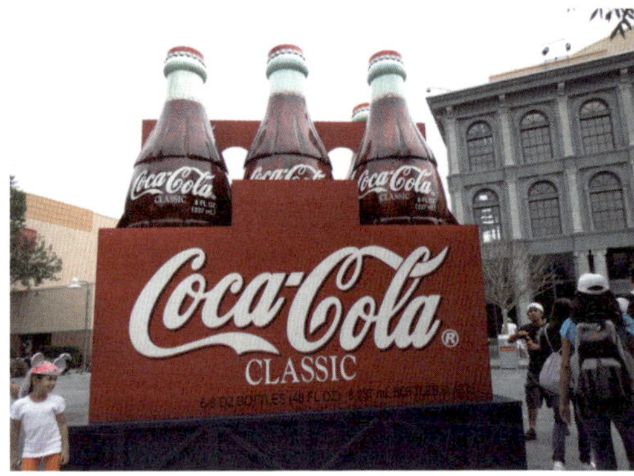

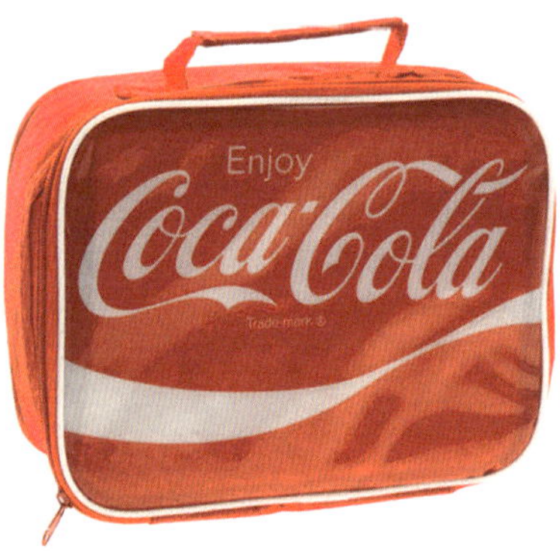

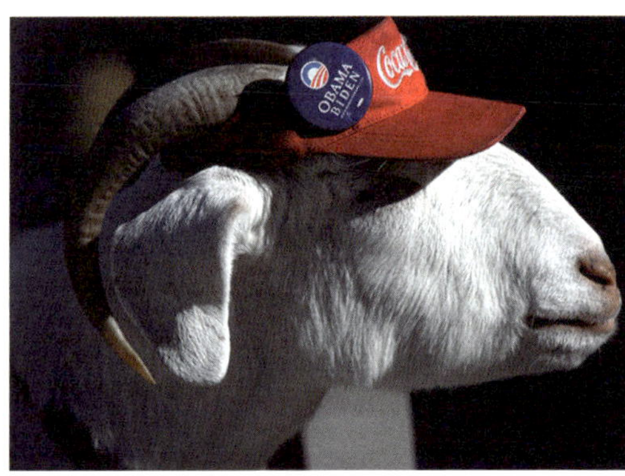

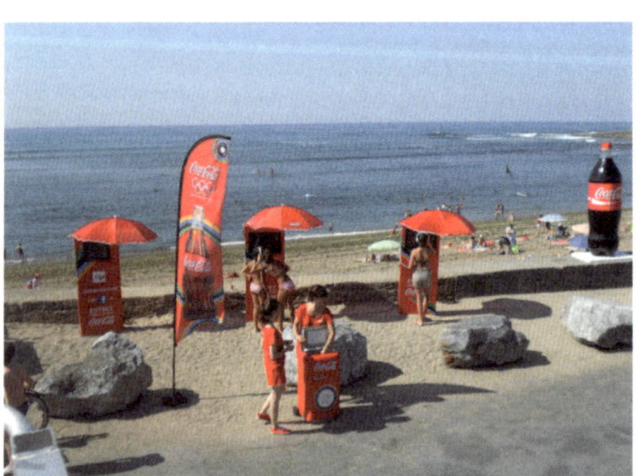

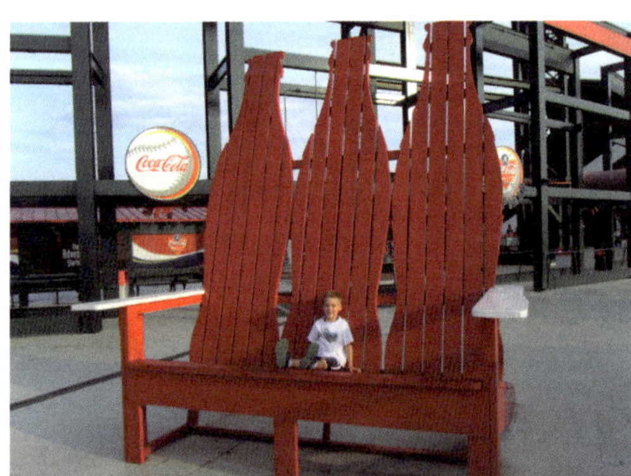

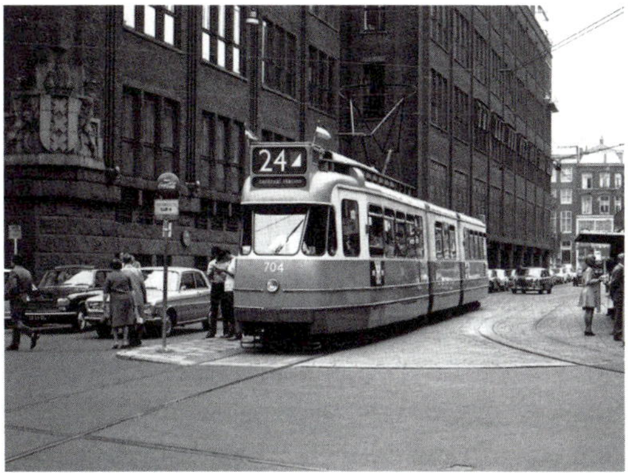
24

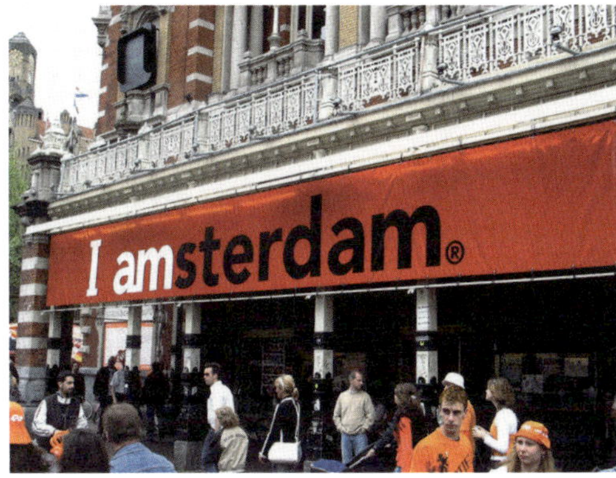
I amsterdam®

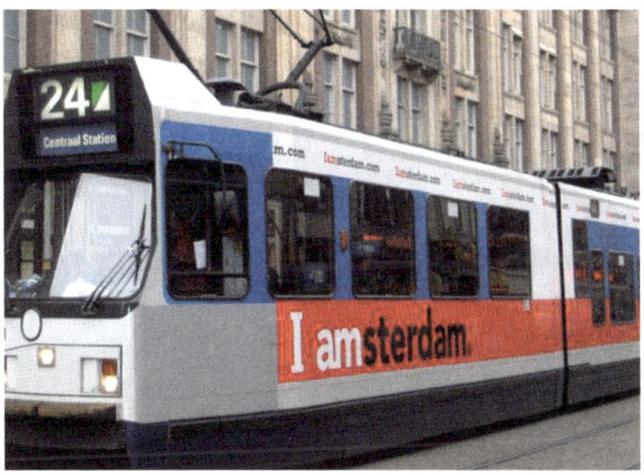
24
Centraal Station
I amsterdam.

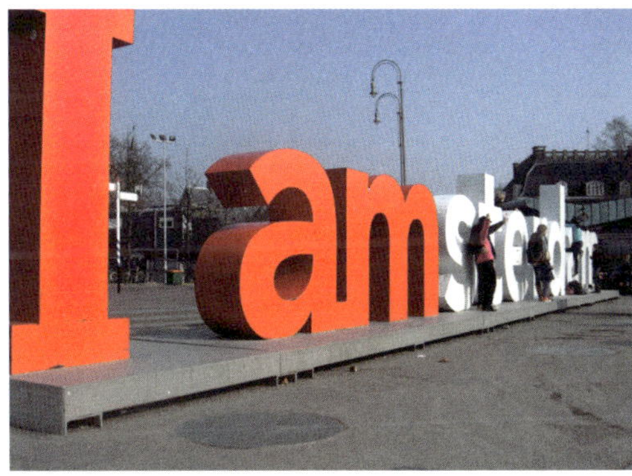

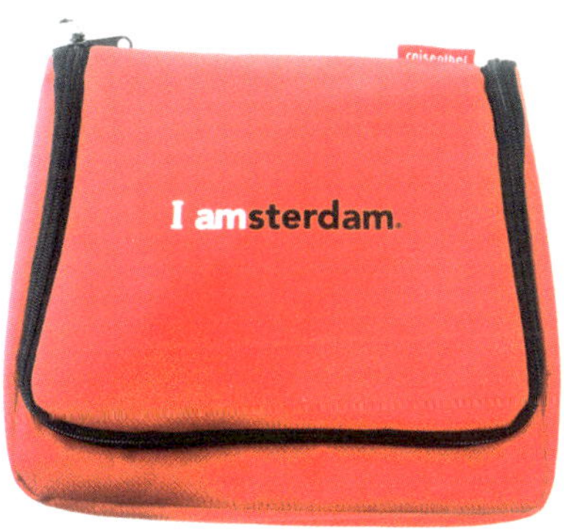
I amsterdam.

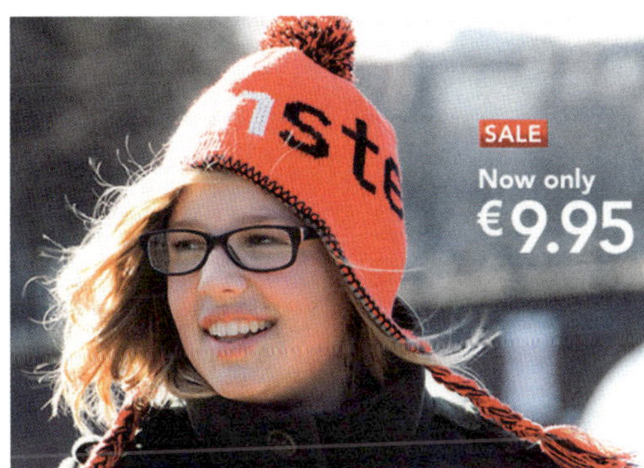
SALE
Now only
€9.95

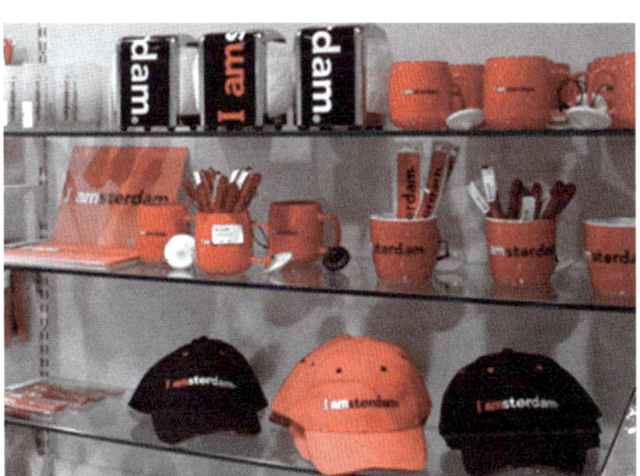

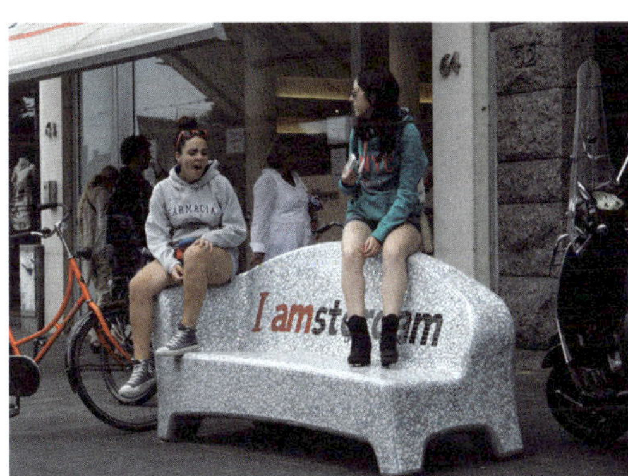

Chapter III

The Invasion of Branding

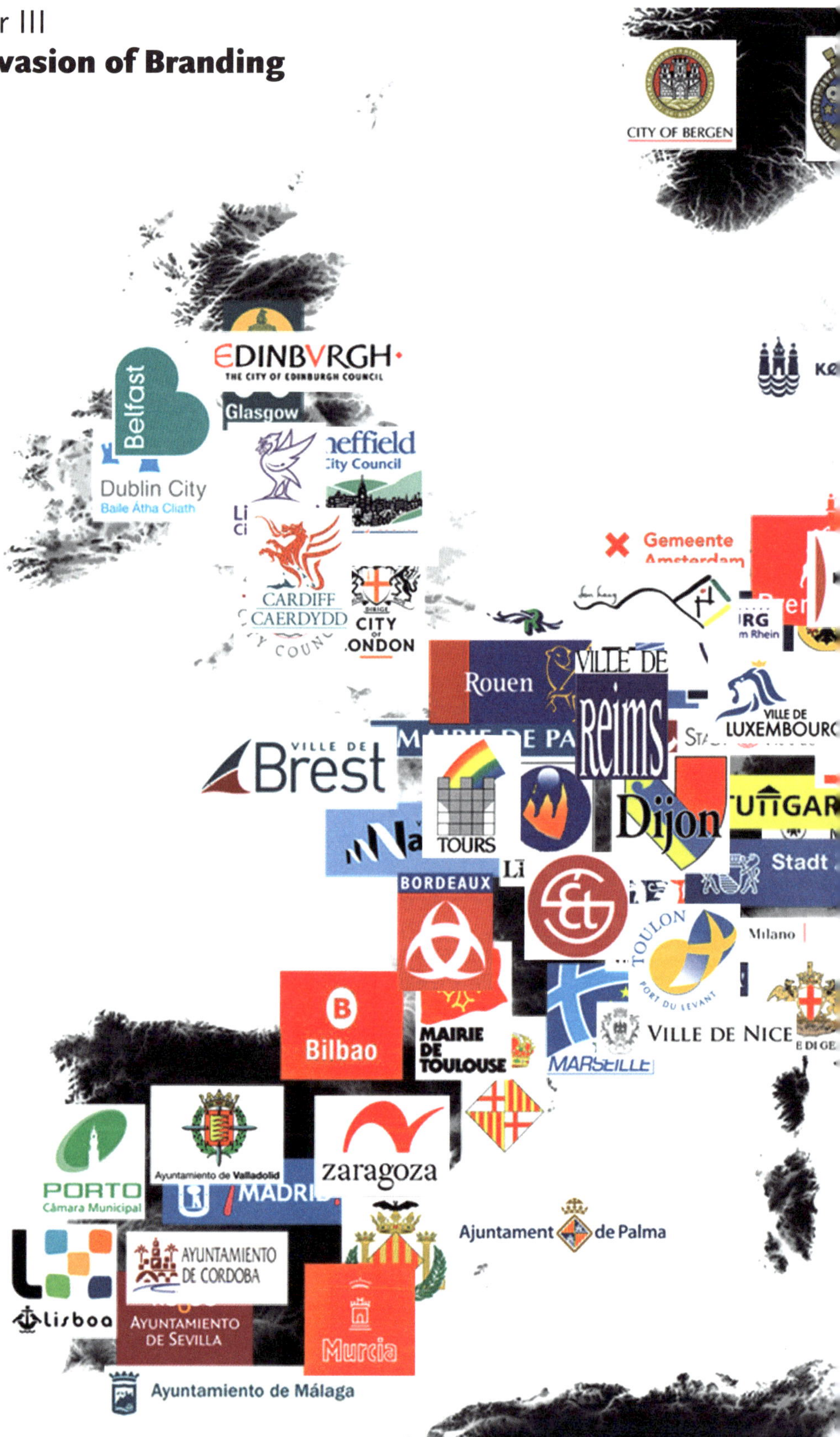

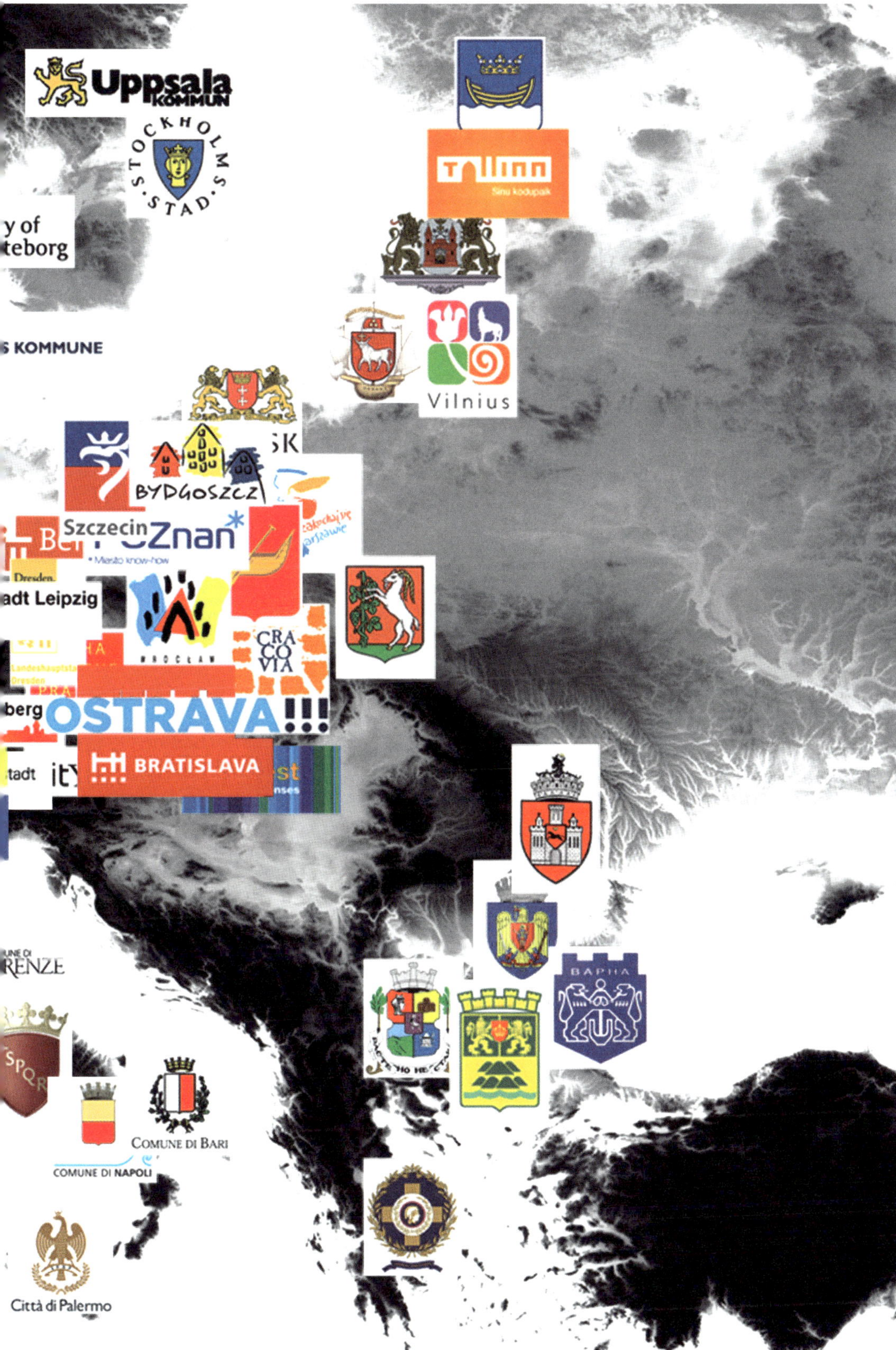

Uppsala
KOMMUN
STOCKHOLMS STAD
y of
teborg
Tallinn
S KOMMUNE
Vilnius
BYDGOSZCZ
Szczecin
Znan
Dresden.
adt Leipzig
CRA
CO
VIA
berg
OSTRAVA!!!
BRATISLAVA
tadt
RENZE
SPQR
COMUNE DI BARI
COMUNE DI NAPOLI
Città di Palermo
ВАРНА

The Invasion of Branding – France

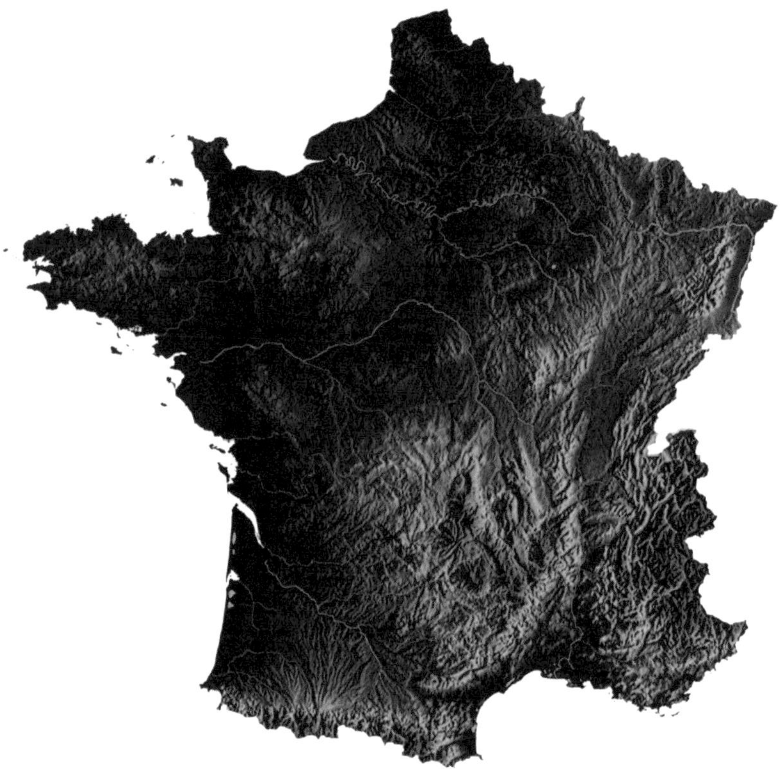

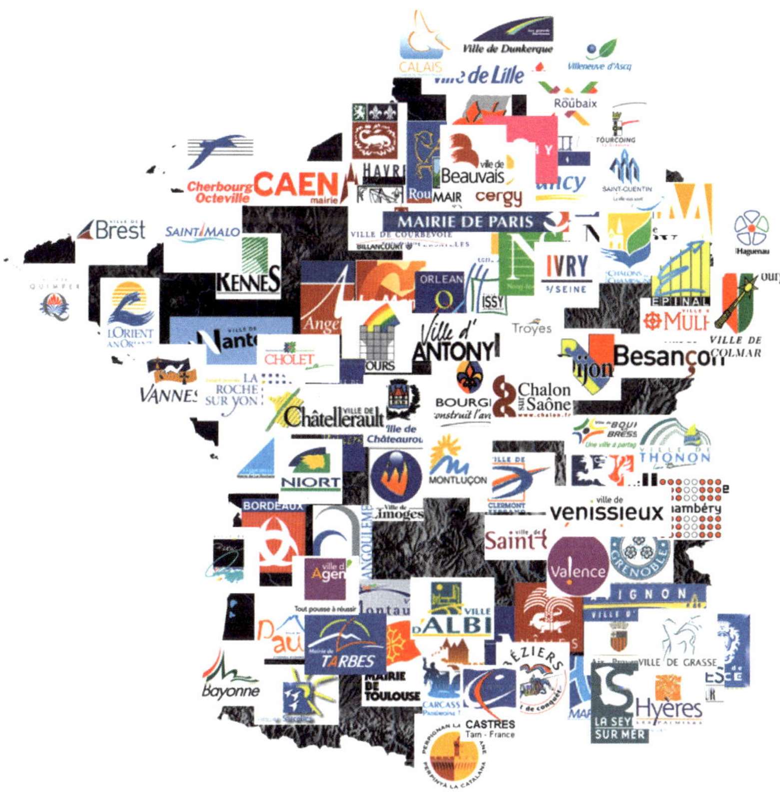
CALAIS
Ville de Dunkerque
Villeneuve d'Ascq
Ville de Lille
Roubaix
TOURCOING
SAINT-QUENTIN
Cherbourg Octeville
CAEN
Beauvais
cergy
MAIRIE DE PARIS
Brest
SAINT MALO
RENNES
QUIMPER
Haguenau
ORLEANS
IVRY S/SEINE
ISSY
Troyes
EPINAL
L'ORIENT
CHOLET
ANTONY
Besançon
VILLE DE COLMAR
VANNES
LA ROCHE SUR YON
Châtellerault
Ville de Châteauroux
BOURG
Chalon sur Saône
THONON
NIORT
MONTLUÇON
BORDEAUX
Limoges
ANGOULEME
venissieux
Valence
GRENOBLE
Agen
Tout pousse à réussir
ALBI
Pau
TARBES
MAIRIE DE TOULOUSE
Bayonne
CASTRES Tarn - France
VILLE DE GRASSE
Hyères
LA SEYNE SUR MER
PERPINYÀ LA CATALANA

The Invasion of Branding – Berlin

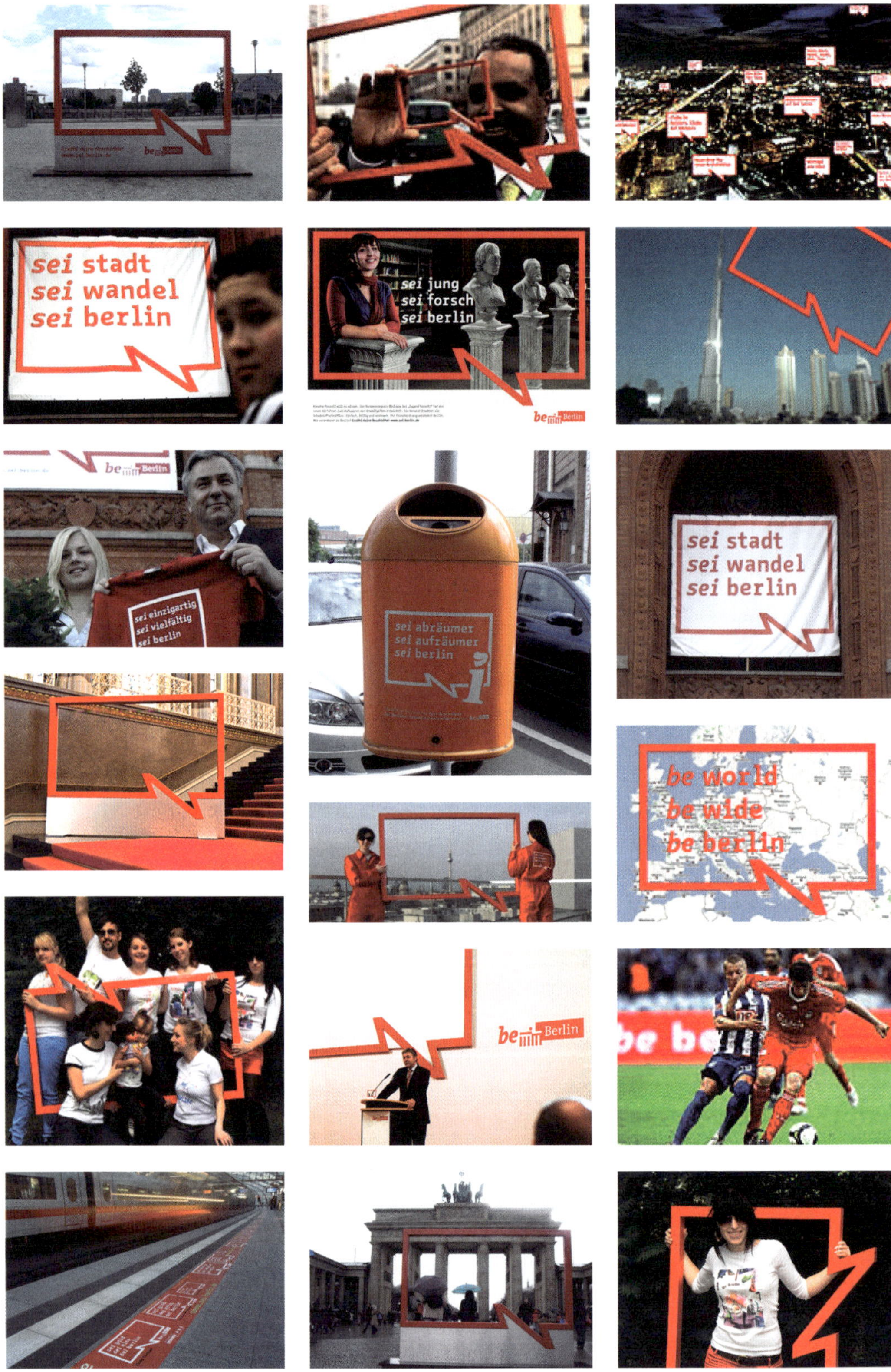

The Invasion of Branding – Bratislava

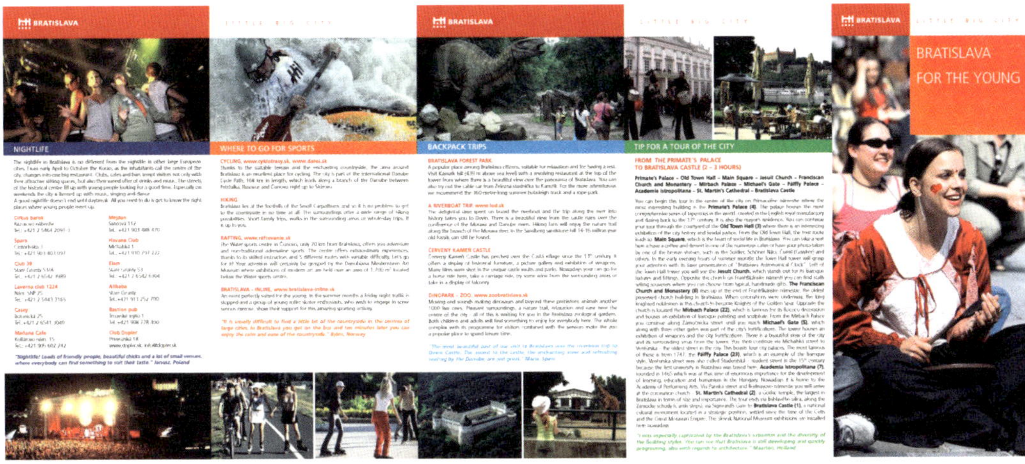

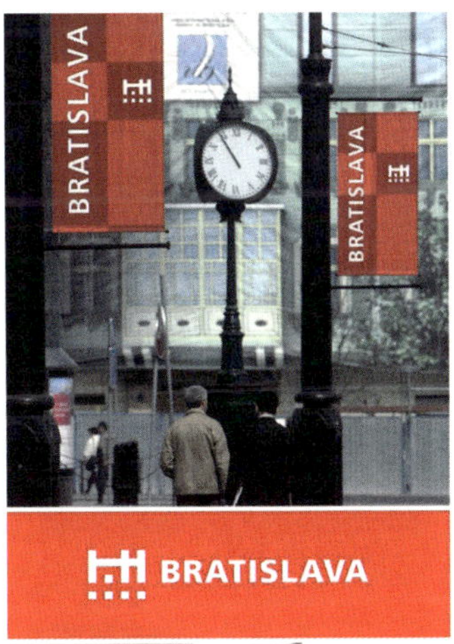

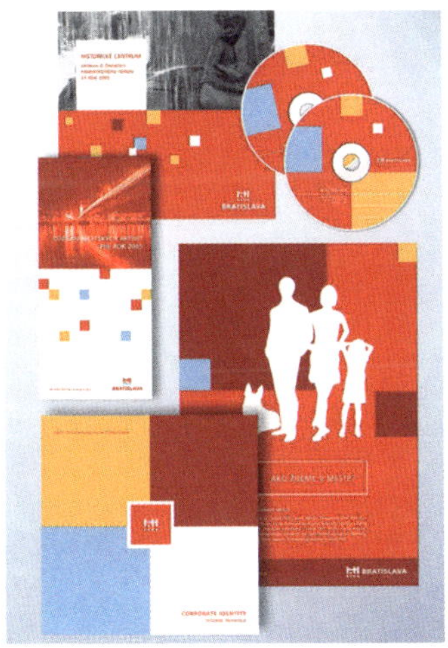

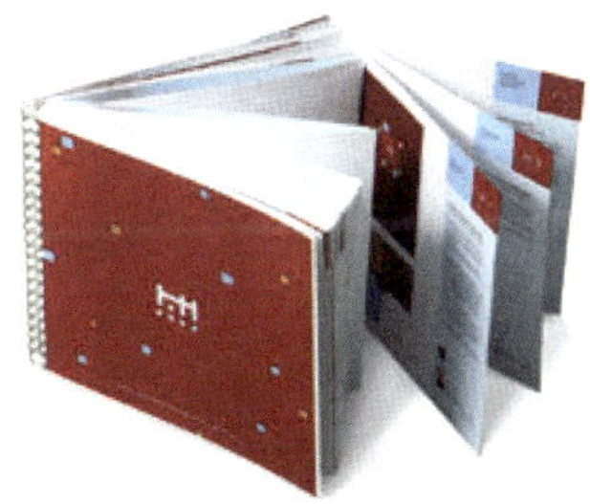

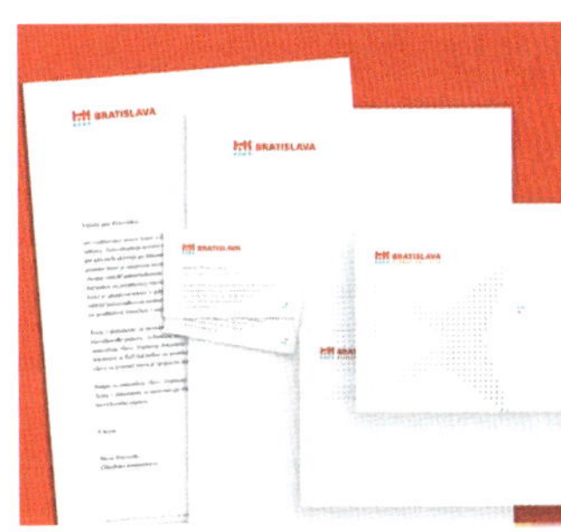

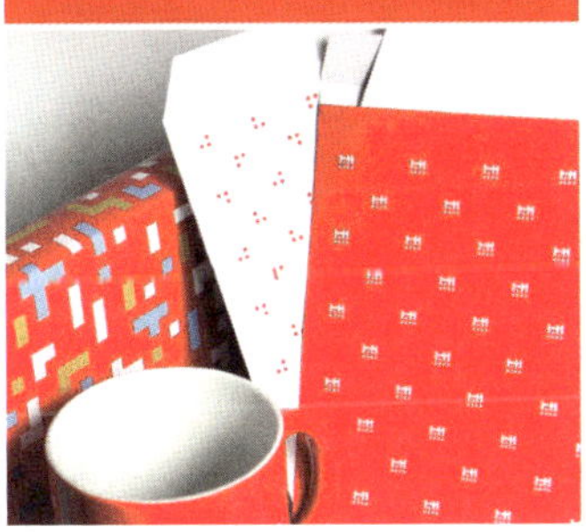

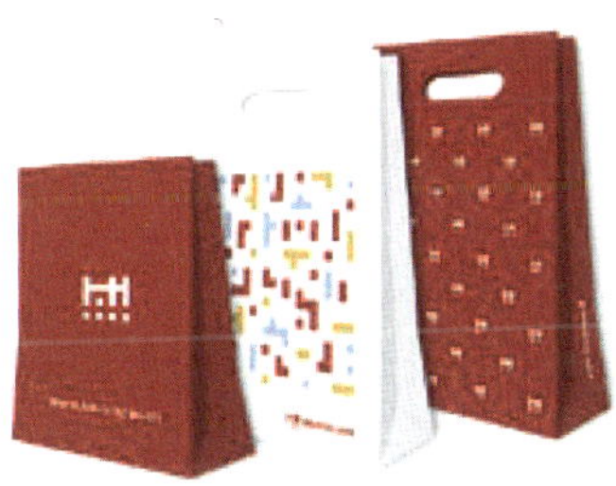

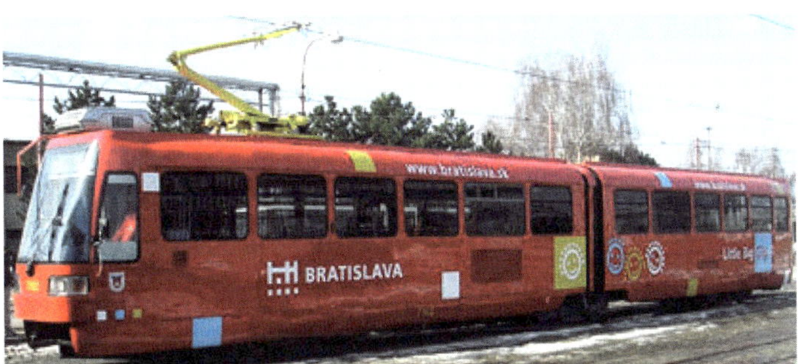

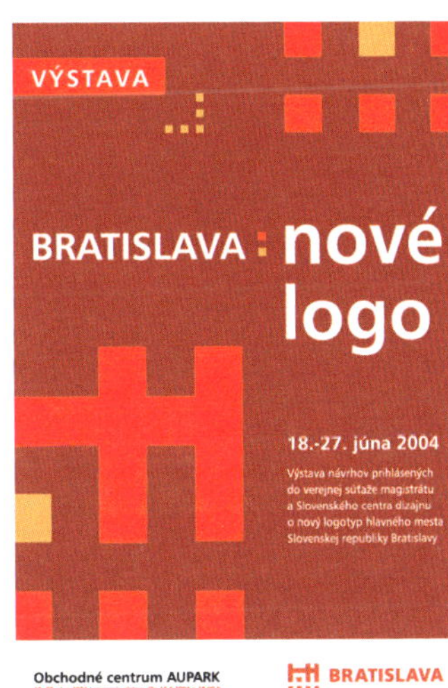

The Invasion of Branding – Prague

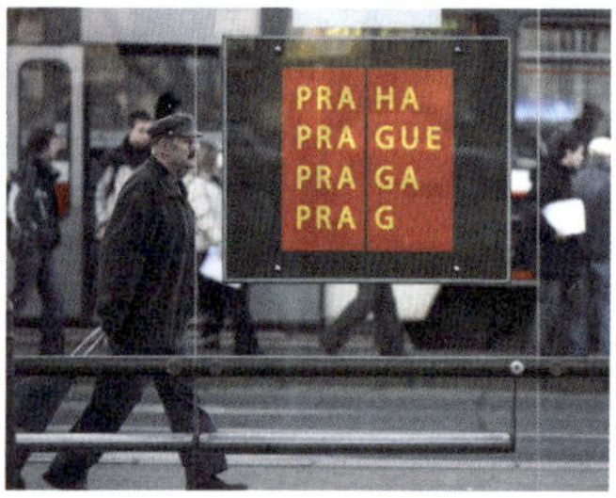

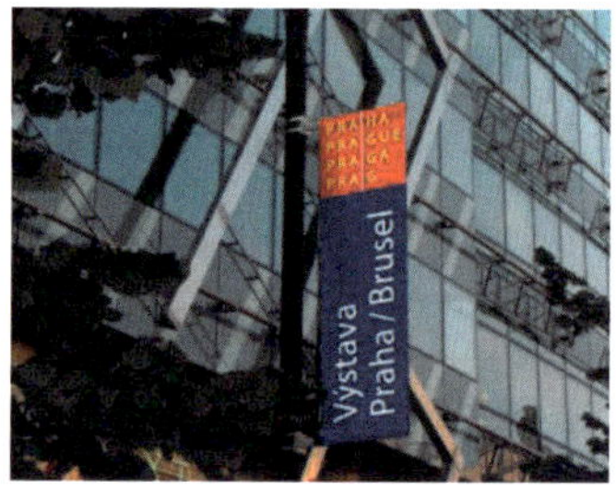

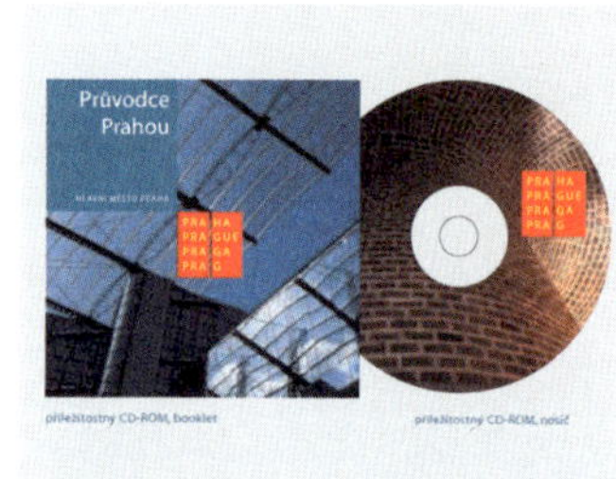

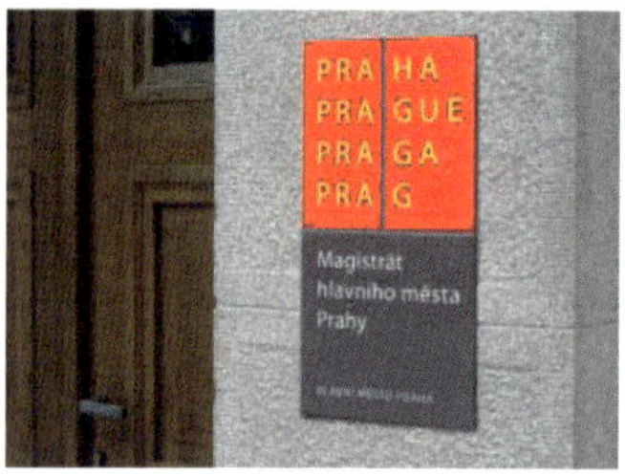

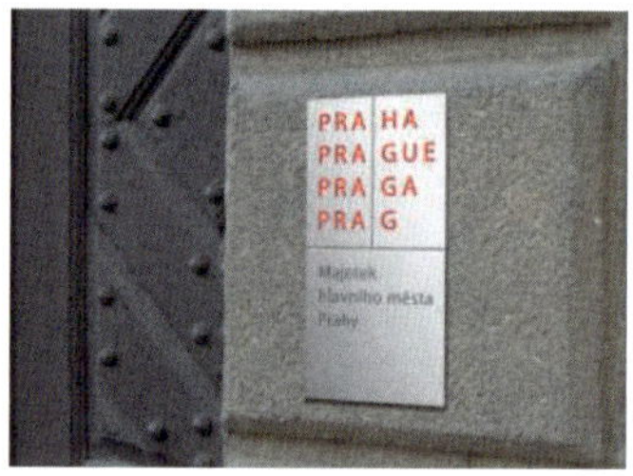

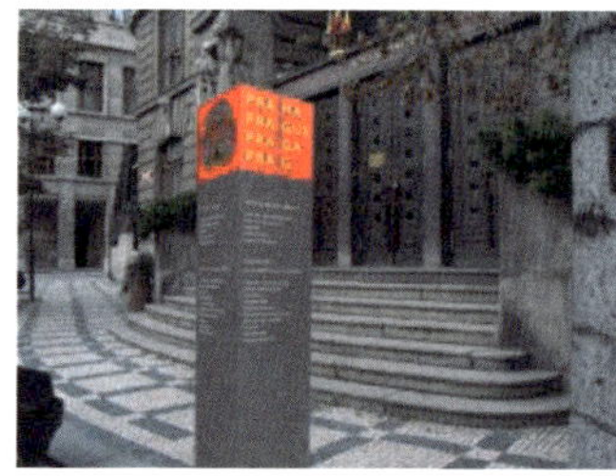

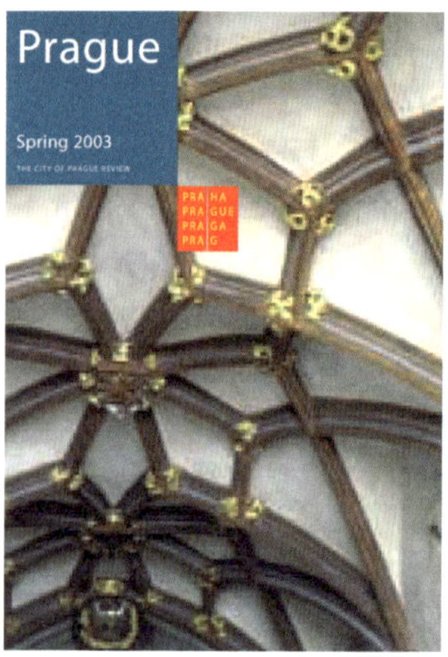

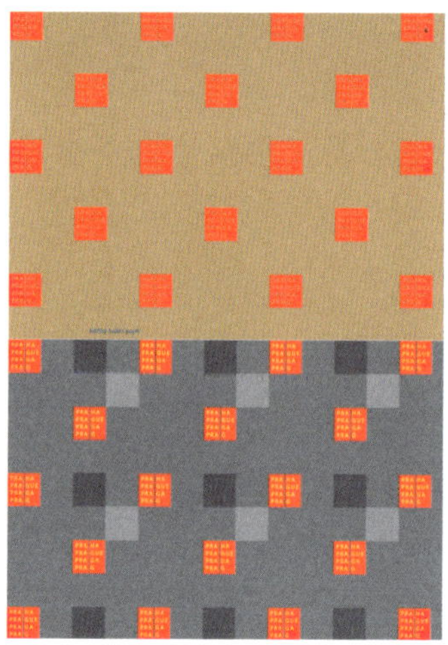

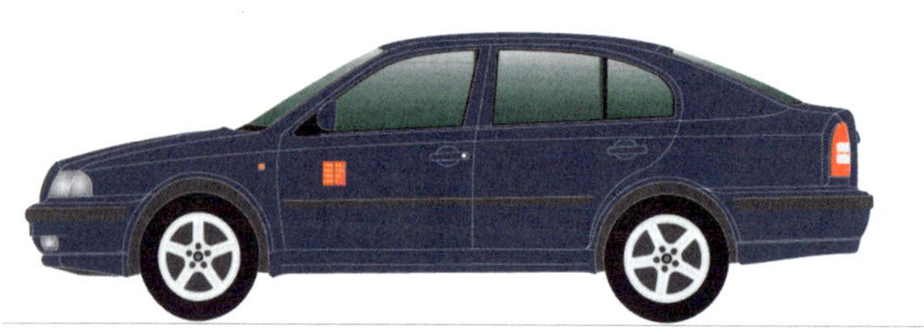

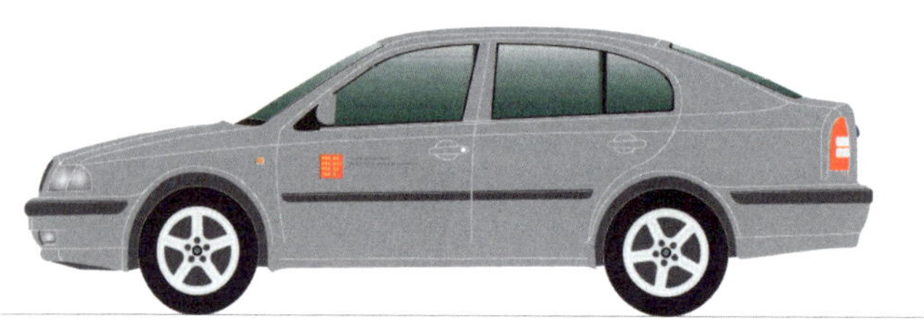

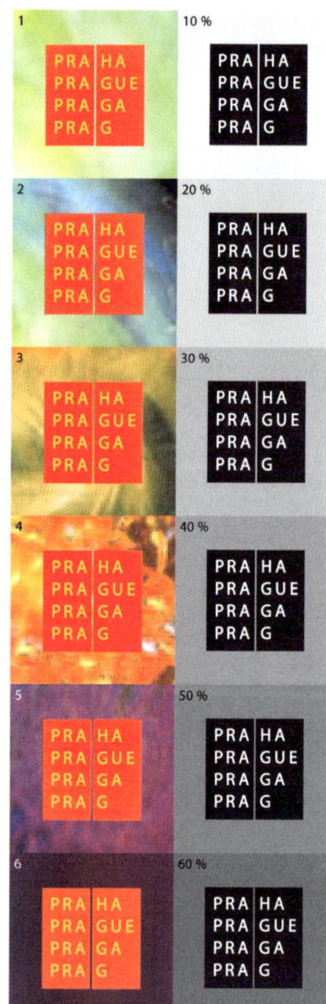

The Invasion of Branding – Stockholm

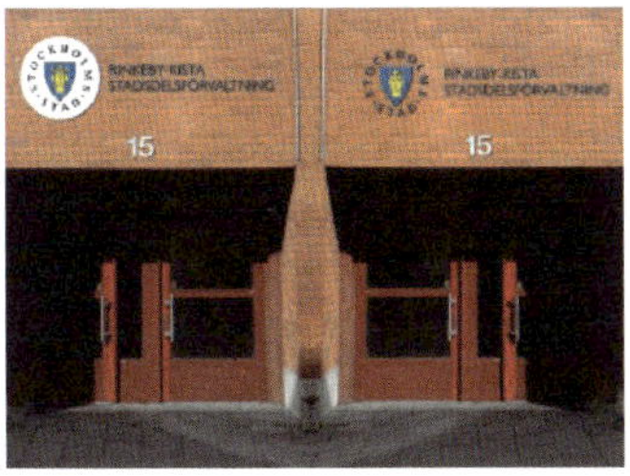

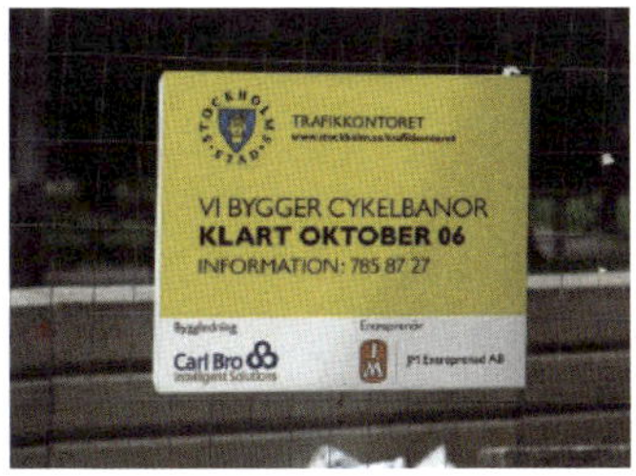

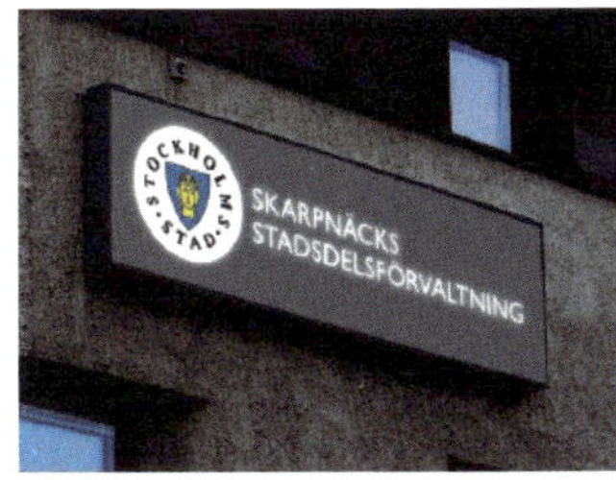

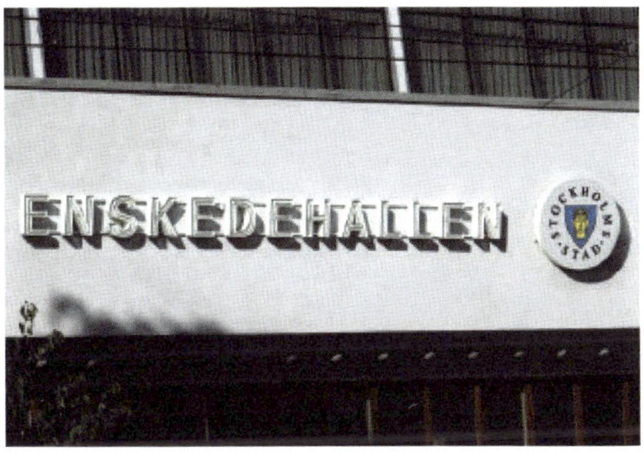

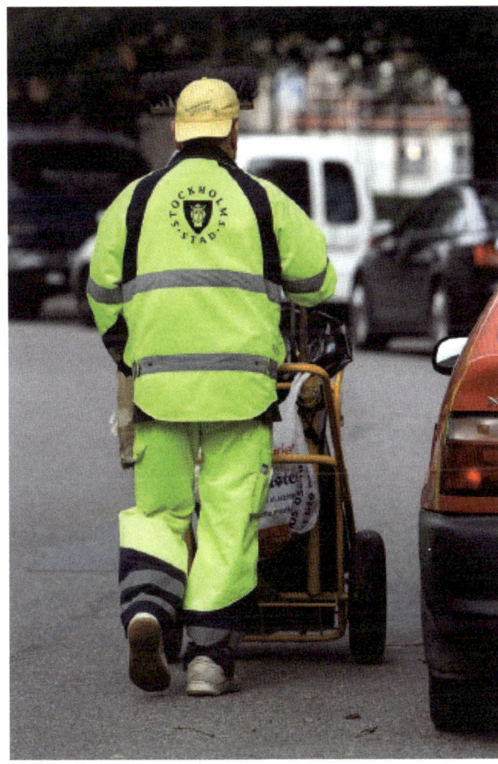

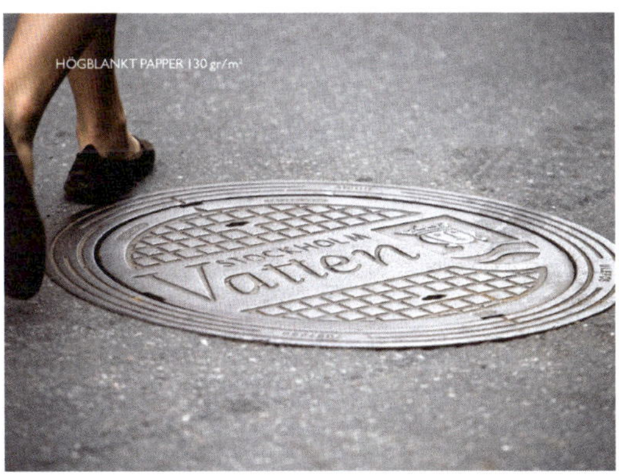

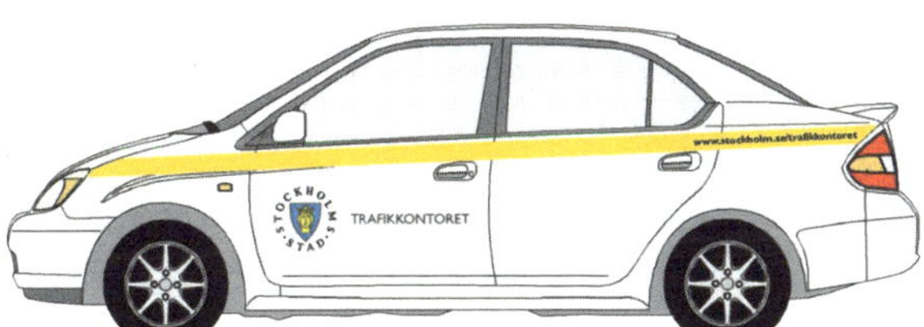

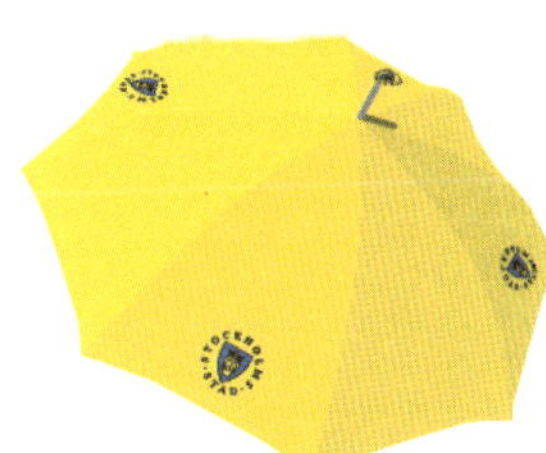

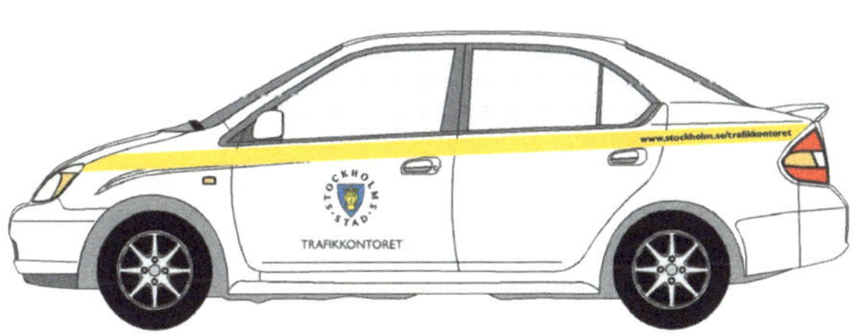

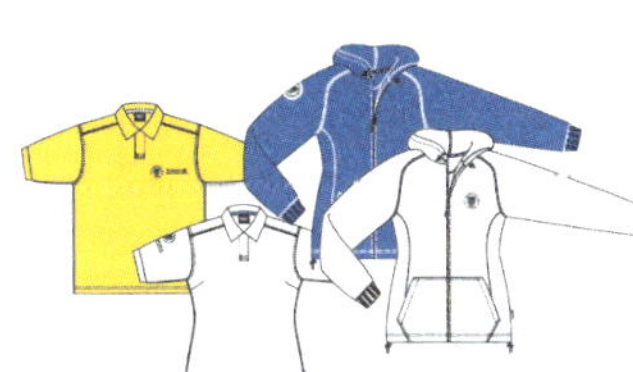

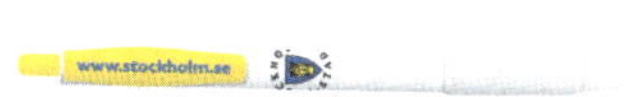

Chapter IV

Confusion and Interchangeability

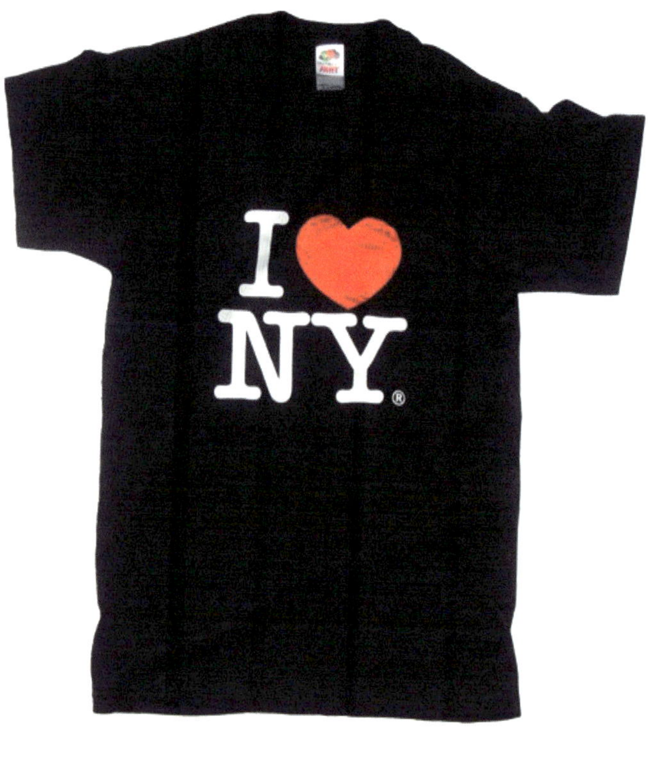

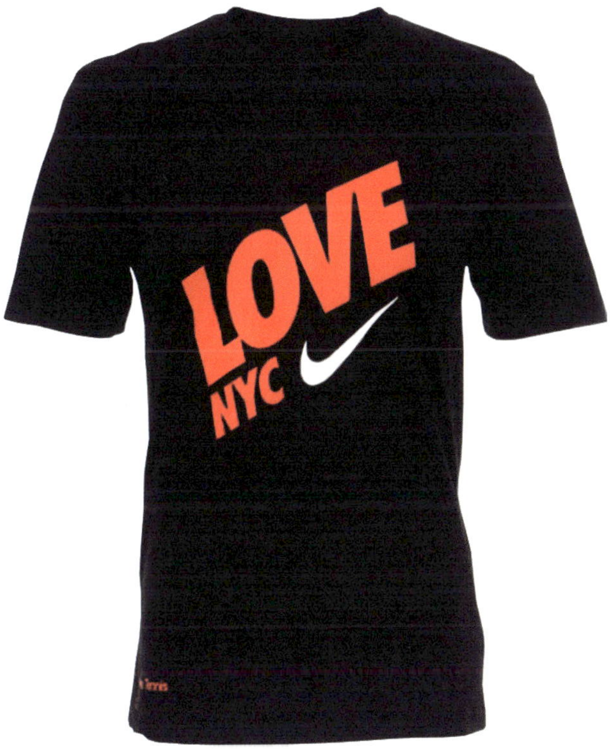
LOVE
NYC
Tennis

Shield and logo of Nike
Shield and logo of the City of Bratislava

Forgery: Nike / Hike
Forgery: I love NY / I love NancY

Food & Drink Devon / City of Belfast
Unilever / City of Tottenham

Adobe / City of Metz
Helly Hansen / City of Bratislava

VICHY
VILLE DE VICHY

PASTILLES
VICHY
SOURCE

VICHY
LABORATOIRES

VICHY
HIPPODROME

MAIRIE DE PARIS

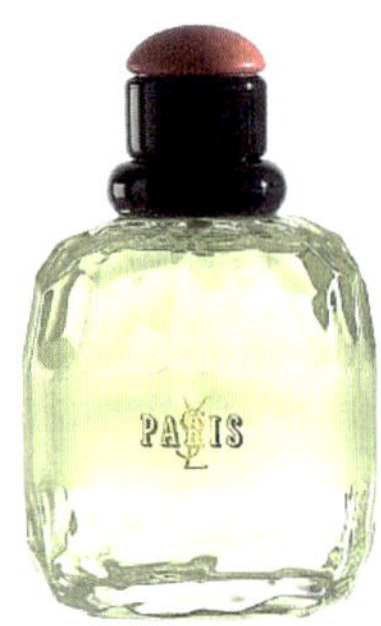

City of
Amsterdam

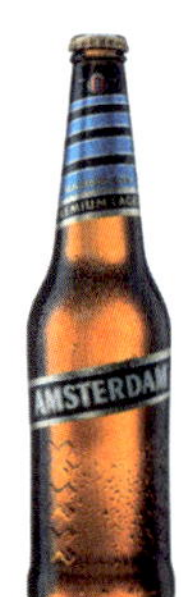

—

Town of Vichy / Vichy Source
Vichy Laboratoires / Vichy Hippodrome

—

City of Paris / Paris YSL
City of Amsterdam / Amsterdam

amsterdam partners 2007 ANNUAL REPORT

1858

1936

1955

1970

1998

PEUGEOT

—

The lion of Peugeot automobiles borrowed from the coat of arms of Franche-Comté

1880

1925

1960

1965

2002

2012

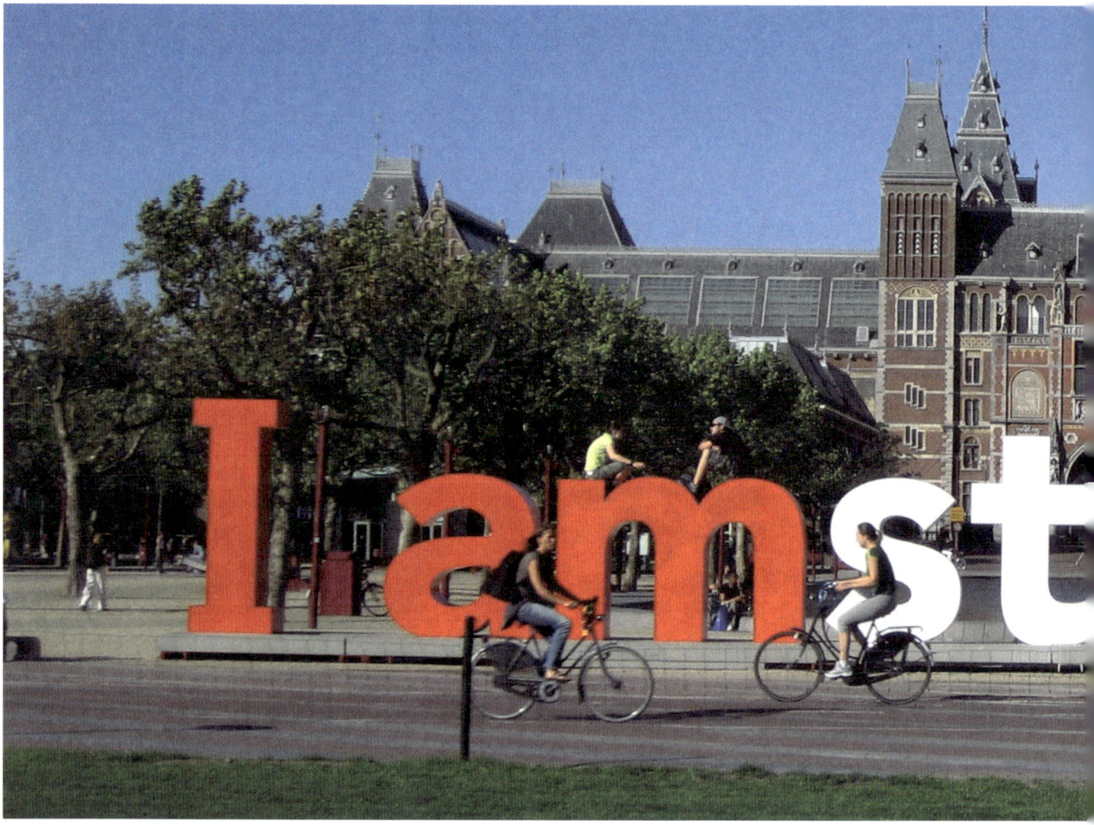

I am

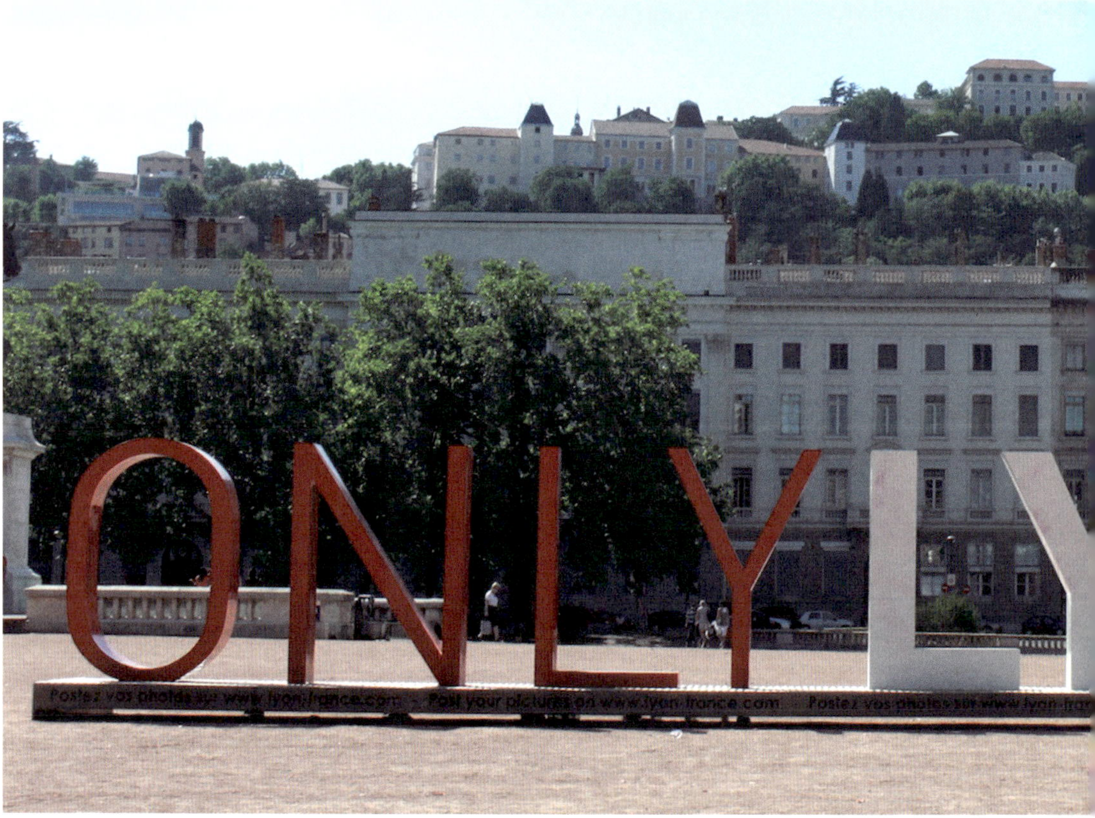

ONLY
Postez vos photos sur www.lyon-france.com – Post your pictures on www.lyon-france.com

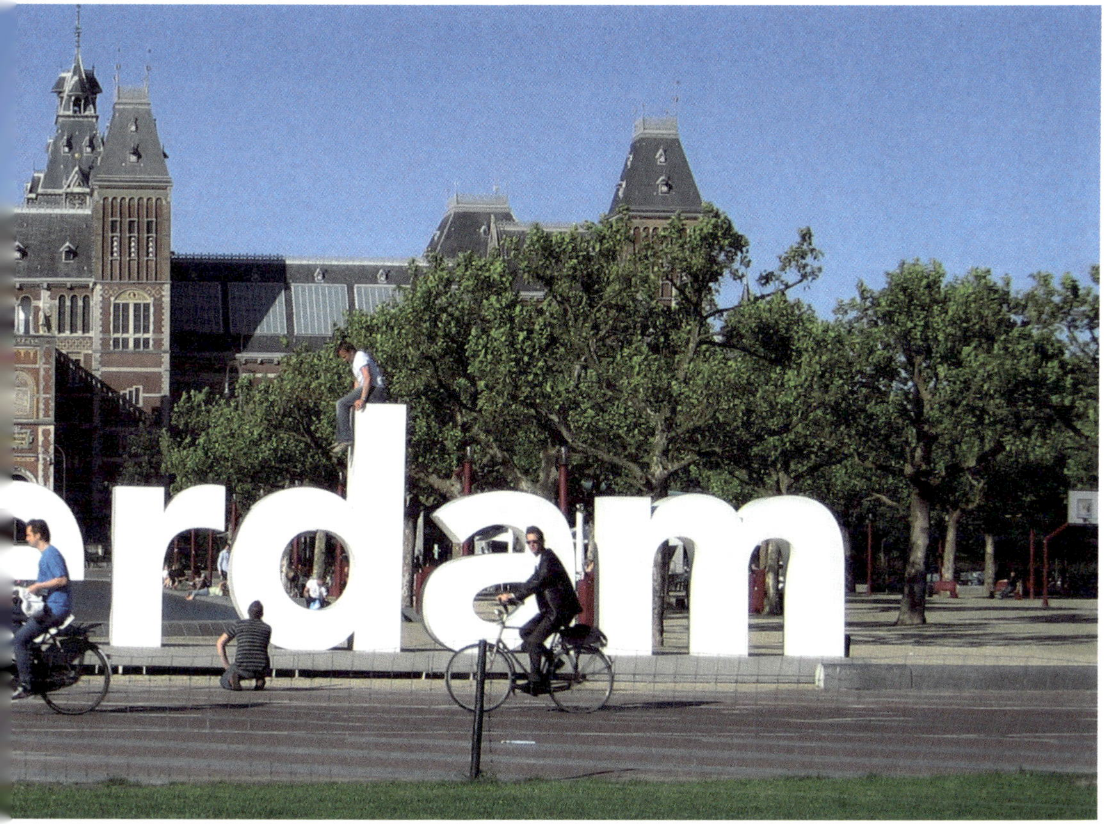
rdam

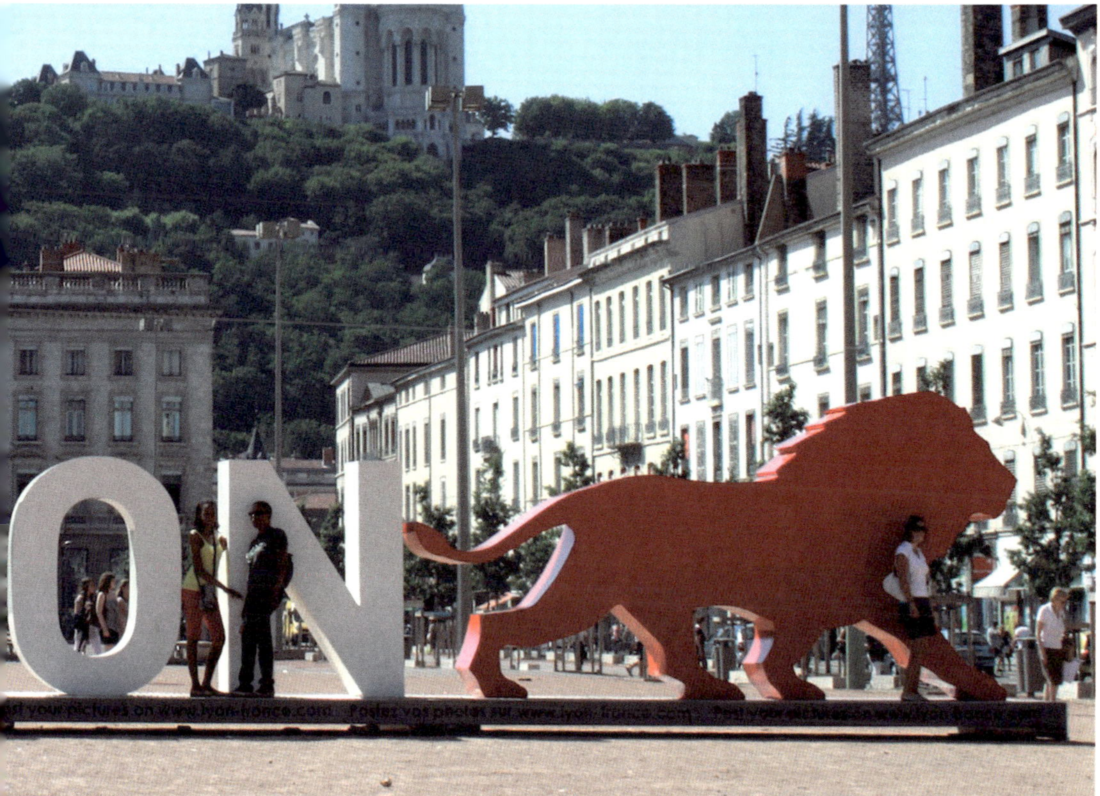
ON
st your pictures on www.lyon-france.com
Postez vos photos sur www.lyon-france.com

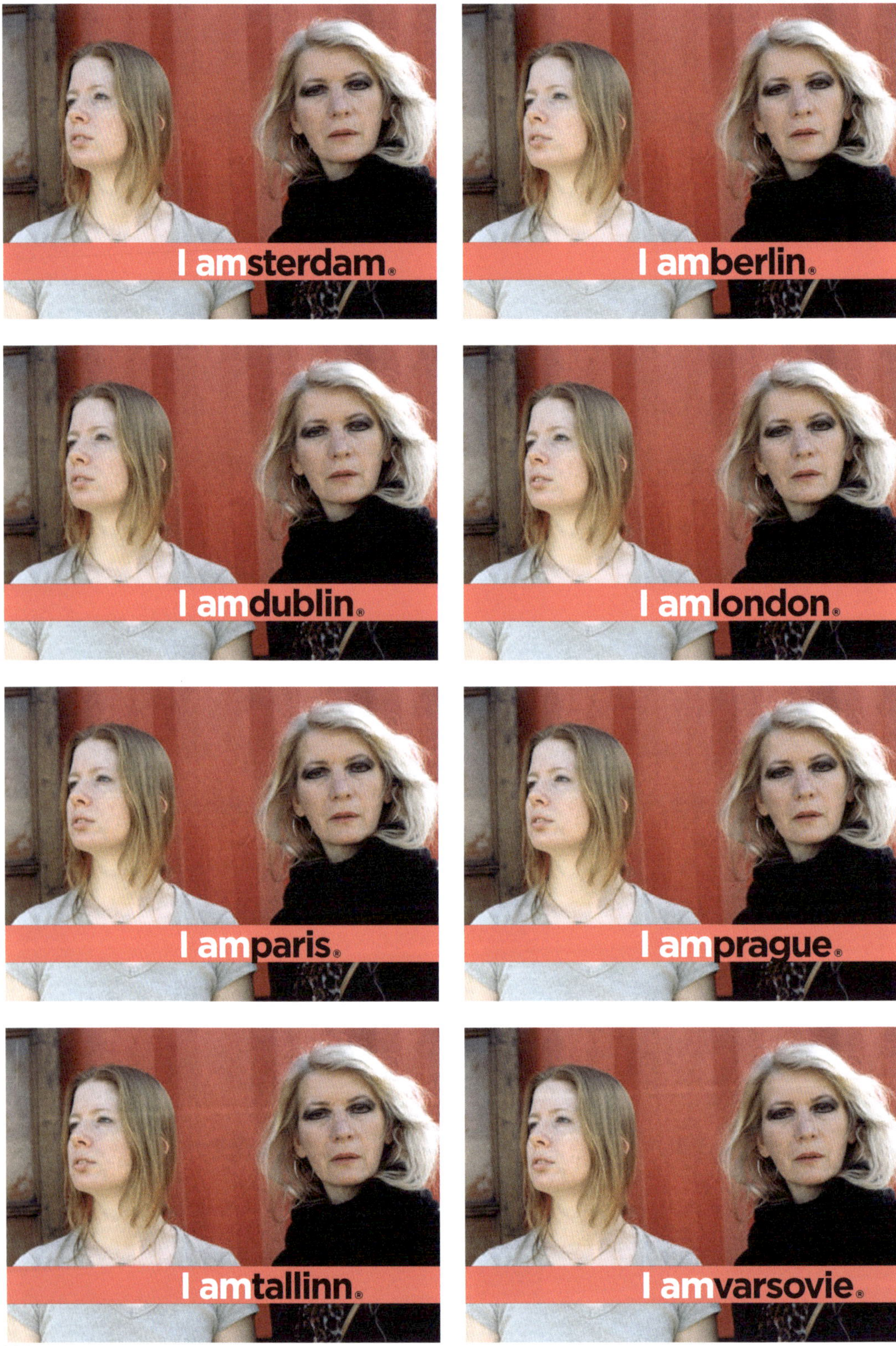

—

Appropriation of Amsterdam's advertising campaign ("I amsterdam" campaign).
Design: KesselsKramer, 2004, The Netherlands

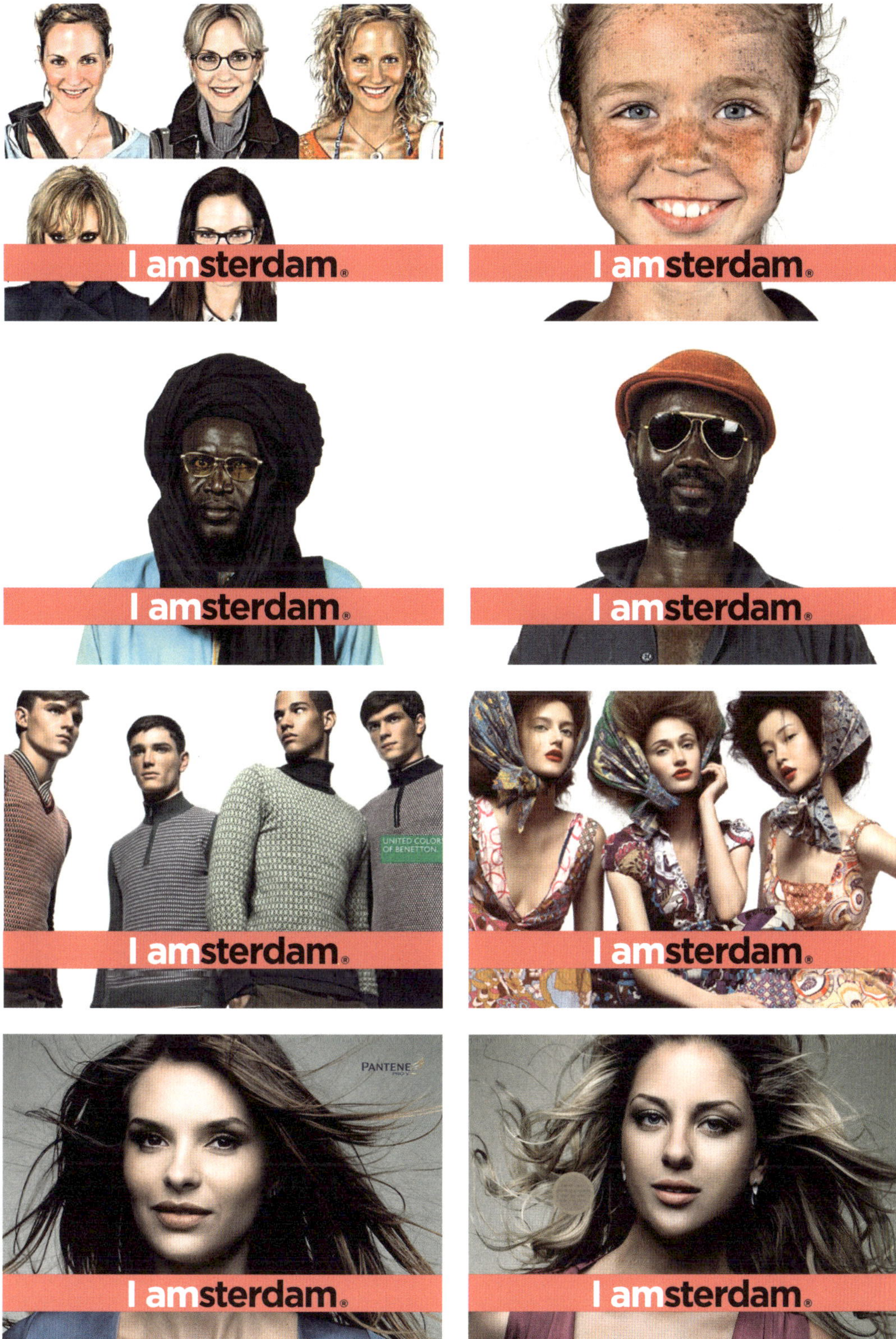

—

Background images: McDonald's, Benetton, Pantene

City of Vienna
Vienna is special.

City of Vienna
I am Vienna[1]

City of Vienna
Be Vienna[2]

City of Vienna
Think Vienna[3]

City of Vienna
Vienna, original, modern[4]

City of Vienna
Fall in love with Vienna[5]

City of Vienna
Visit Vienna[6]

City of Vienna
City of delights[7]

City of Vienna
Little big city[8]

City of Vienna
I ♥ Vienna[9]

City of Vienna
Get in on it[10]

City of Vienna
Mad about Vienna[11]

City of Vienna
Vienna, ma ville[12]

City of Vienna
Une ville d'impulsion[13]

City of Vienna
J'M Vienne[14]

City of Vienna
Fraîcheur de vivre[15]

City of Vienna
Always Vienna[16]

City of Vienna
United Colors of Vienna[17]

City of Vienna
like.no.other[18]

City of Vienna
Come as you are[19]

City of Vienna
Ask for Vienna.[20]

City of Vienna
Tous les bonheurs du monde[21]

City of Vienna
Vous le valez bien[22]

City of Vienna
La vie, la vraie. Vienna[23]

City of Vienna
Une histoire d'amour[24]

City of Vienna
Vienna j'adore![25]

City of Vienna
Vienna donne des ailes[26]

—

Appropriation of slogans for Vienna's logo
1. Amsterdam 2. Berlin 3. London 4. Manchester 5. Warsaw 6. London 7. Ljubljana 8. Bratislava 9. New York 10. Baltimore 11. Madrid 12. Fresnes 13. Nantes 14. Metz 15. Hollywood 16. Coca Cola 17. Benetton 18. Sony 19. McDonald's 20. Pepsi 21. Club Med 22. L'Oréal 23. Auchan 24. Kinder 25. Knorr 26. Red Bull

Berlin

Paris

Moscow

Dubai

Roma

Vienna

Tokyo

New York

Madrid

Dublin

Appropriation of Berlin's logo

Chapter V

Marketplaces

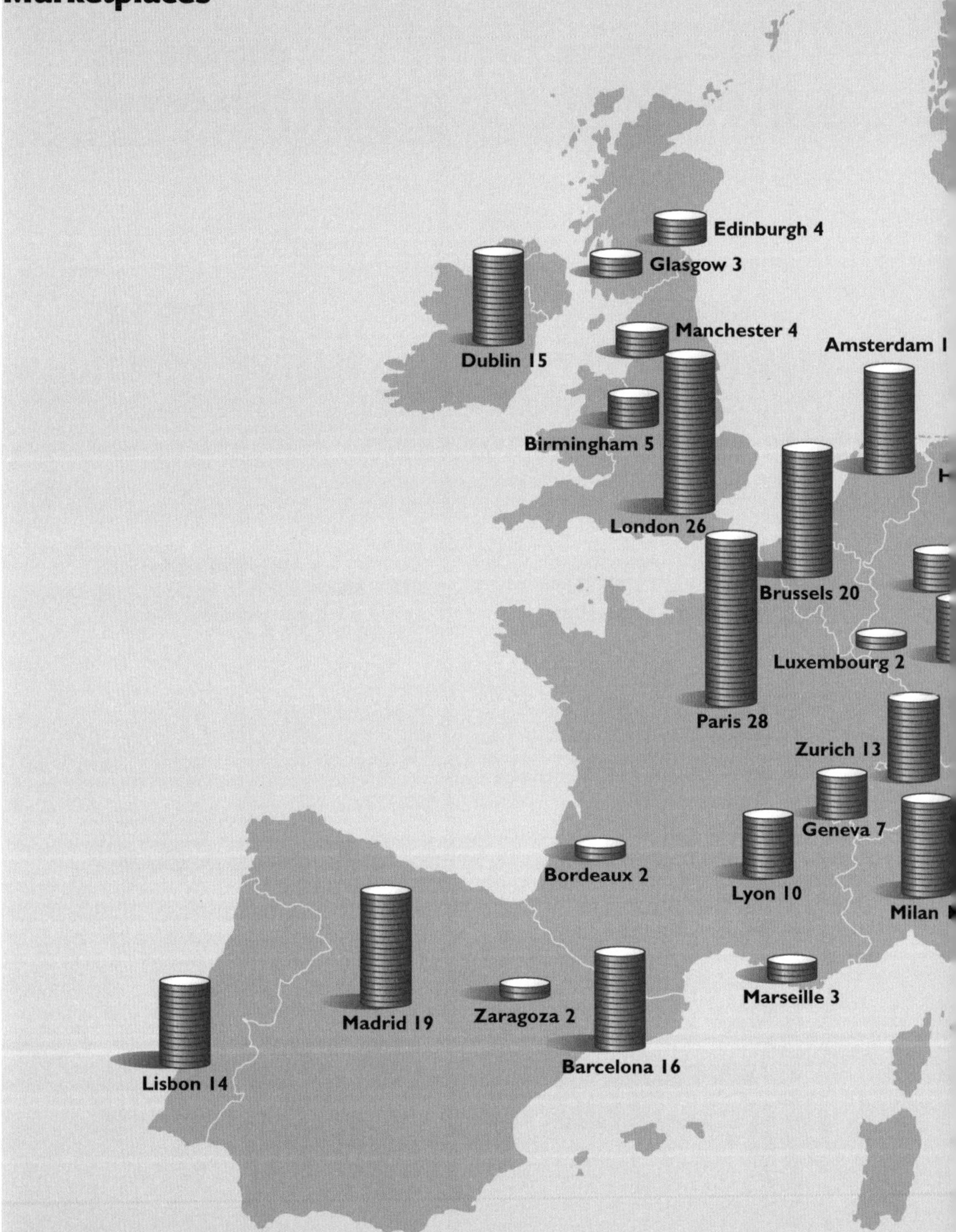

—

Cushman & Wakefield, *European Cities Monitor,* 2010
"Each year we ask companies about their future expansion plans across Europe. The map shows the number of companies expecting to locate in the cities shown within the next five years."

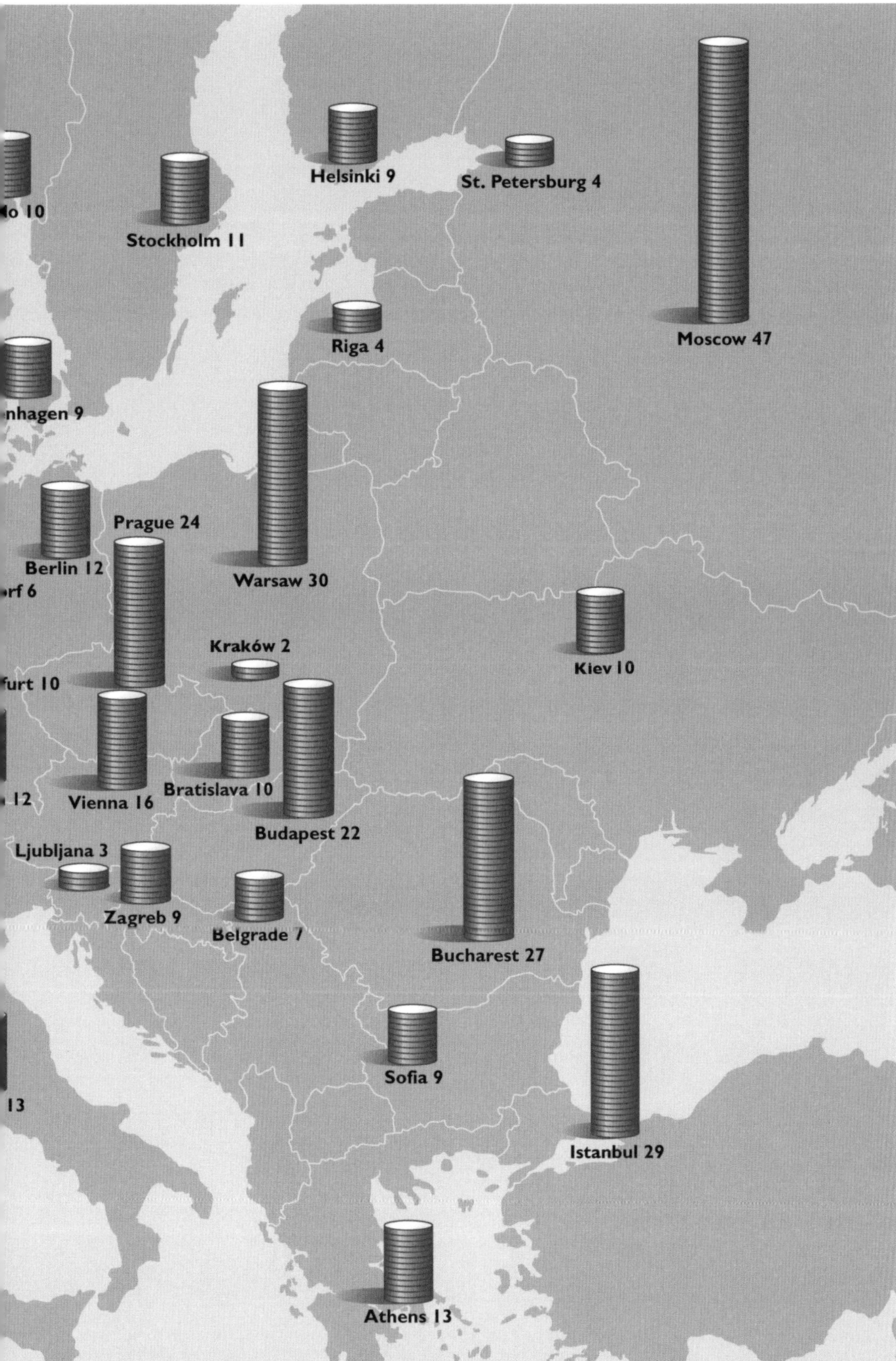
lo 10
Stockholm 11
Helsinki 9
St. Petersburg 4
Moscow 47
Riga 4
nhagen 9
Berlin 12
Prague 24
Warsaw 30
rf 6
Kraków 2
Kiev 10
furt 10
12
Vienna 16
Bratislava 10
Budapest 22
Ljubljana 3
Zagreb 9
Belgrade 7
Bucharest 27
Sofia 9
13
Istanbul 29
Athens 13

Identity by GDP

Sofia,
Bulgaria (PPS 45)

Bucharest,
Romania (PPS 49)

Riga,
Latvia (PPS 58)

Vilnius,
Lithuania (PPS 62)

Warsaw,
Poland (PPS 65)

Budapest,
Hungary (PPS 66)

Tallinn,
Estonia (PPS 67)

Bratislava,
Slovakia (PPS 73)

Lisbon,
Portugal (PPS 77)

Prague,
Czech Republic (PPS 80)

Athens,
Greece (PPS 82)

Valletta,
Malta (PPS 83)

Ljubljana,
Slovenia (PPS 84)

Nicosia,
Cyprus (PPS 92)

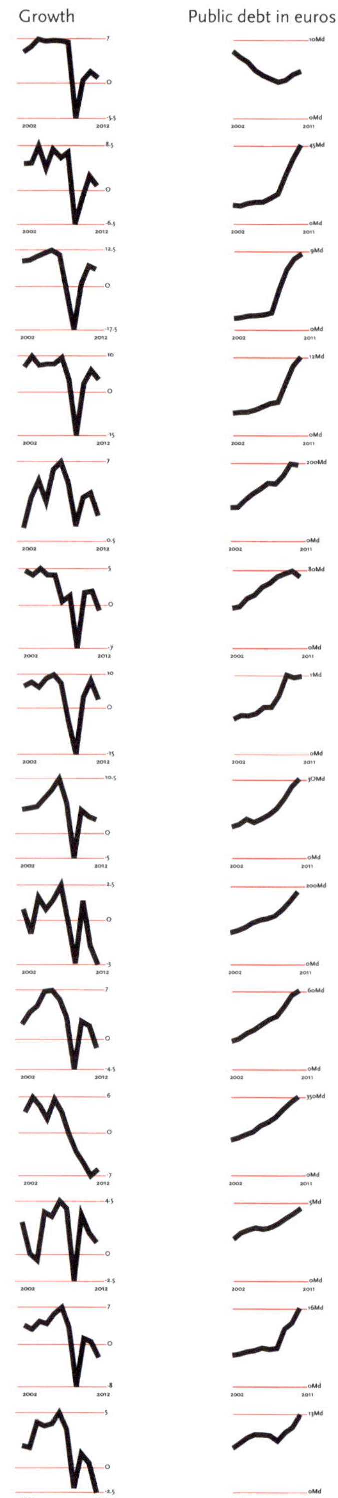

—

Coats of arms and logos of European capitals (+ Switzerland) classified by GDP per capita in PPS (Purchasing Power Standard)

Madrid,
Spain (PPS 99)

Rome,
Italy (PPS 101)

Paris,
France (PPS 107)

London,
UK (PPS 108)

Helsinki,
Finland (PPS 116)

Brussels,
Belgium (PPS 118)

Berlin,
Germany (PPS 120)

Copenhagen,
Denmark (PPS 125)

Stockholm,
Sweden (PPS 126)

Dublin,
Ireland (PPS 127)

Vienna,
Austria (PPS 129)

Amsterdam,
Netherlands (PPS 131)

Bern,
Switzerland (PPS 151)

Luxembourg,
Luxembourg (PPS 274)

Growth — Public debt in euros

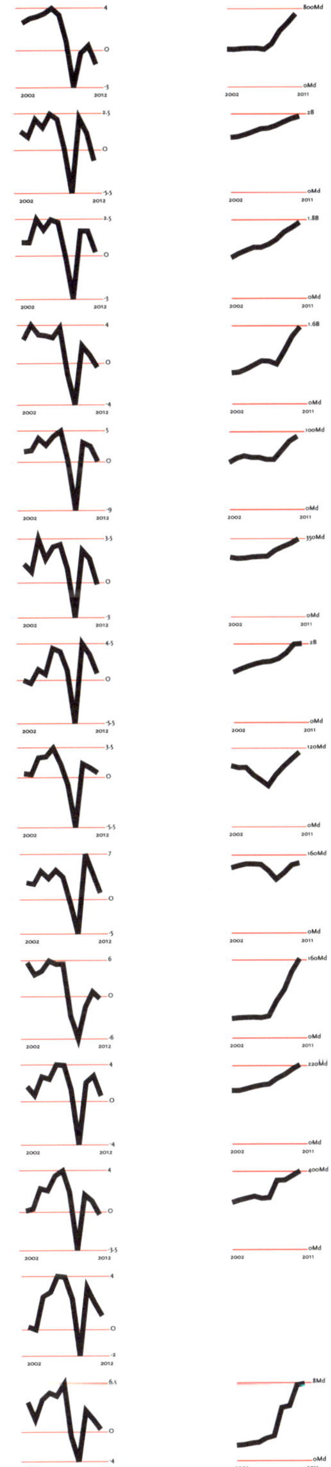

—

Index: EU27 = 100
Source of data: Eurostat – Year: 2011

The Best Cities to Do Business

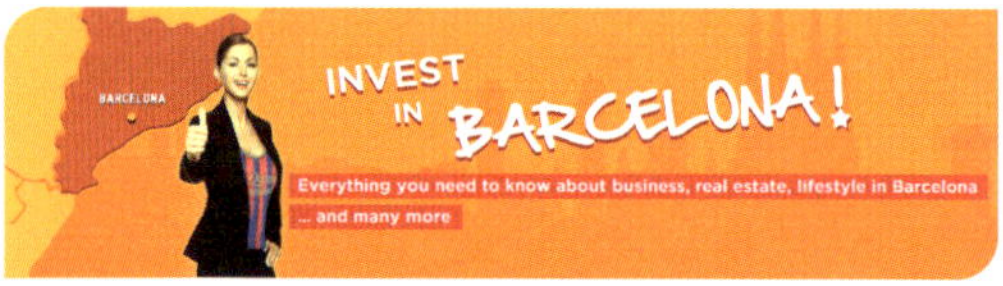

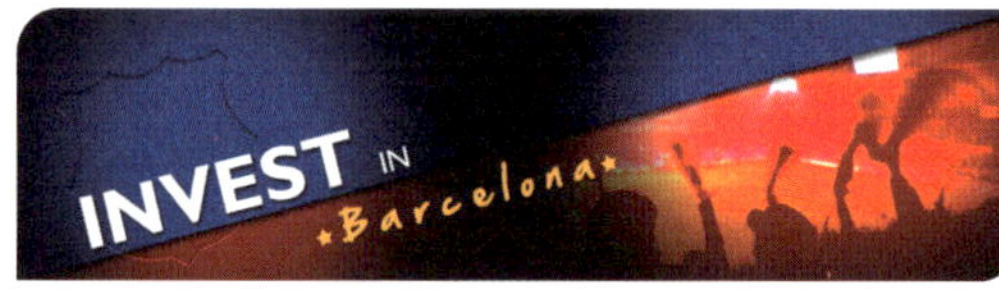

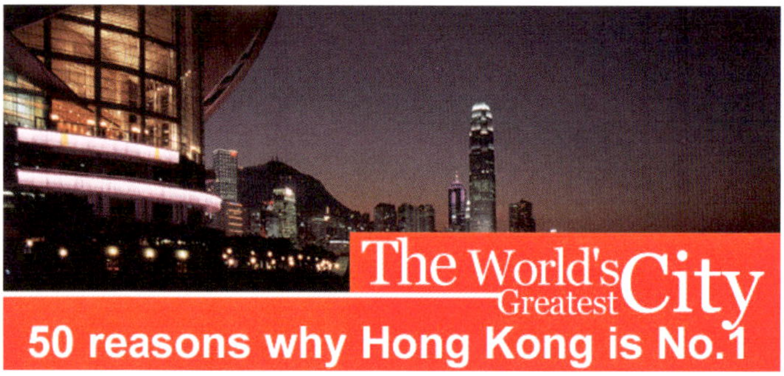

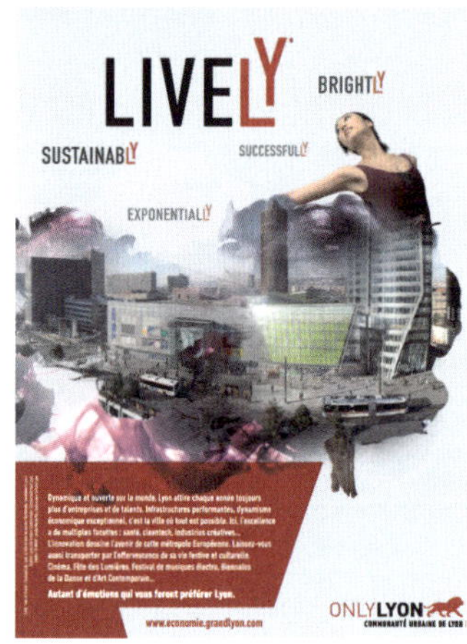

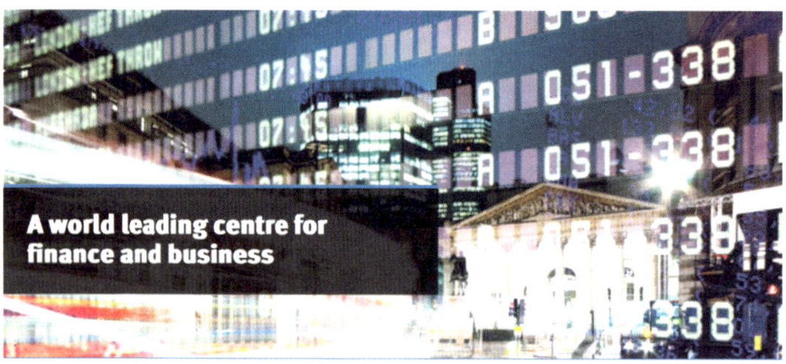

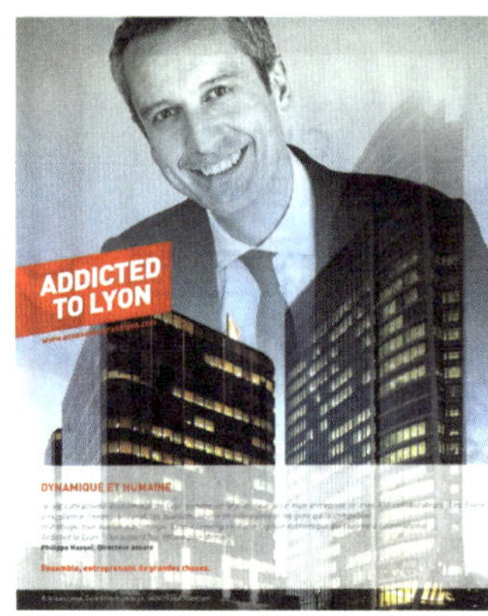

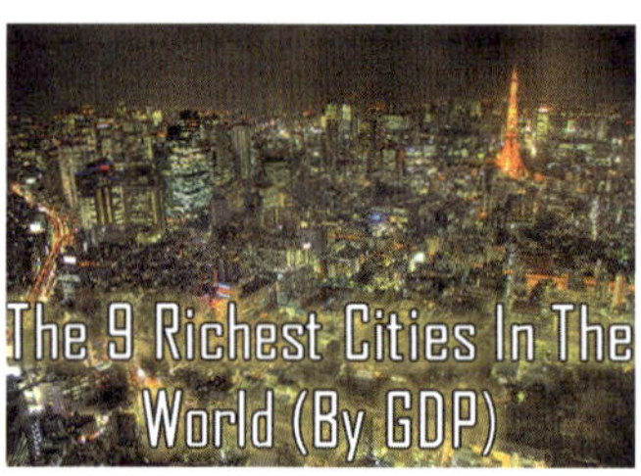

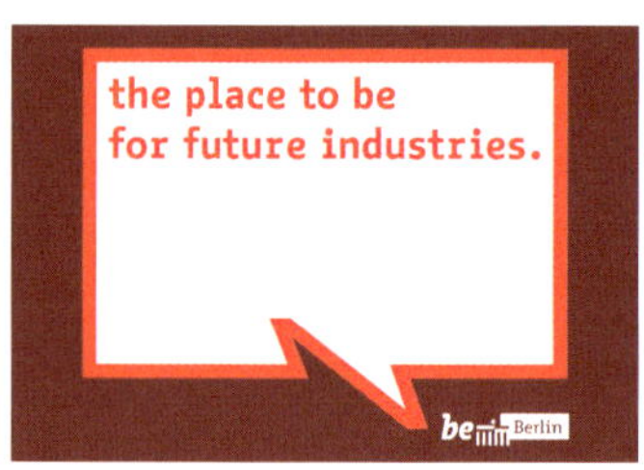

The main investment criteria

· Easy access to markets, customers, or clients
· Availability of qualified staff
· The quality of telecommunications
· Transport links with other cities and internationally
· Value for money of office space
· Cost of staff
· Availability of office space
· Languages spoken
· Ease of traveling around within the city
· The climate governments create for business through tax policies or financial incentives
· The quality of life for employees
· Freedom from pollution

—

Cushman & Wakefield, "European Expansion," in *European Cities Monitor*, 2011

The Best Cities to Live

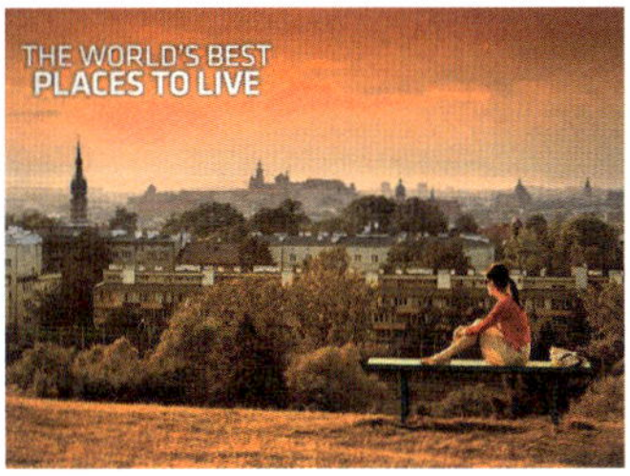

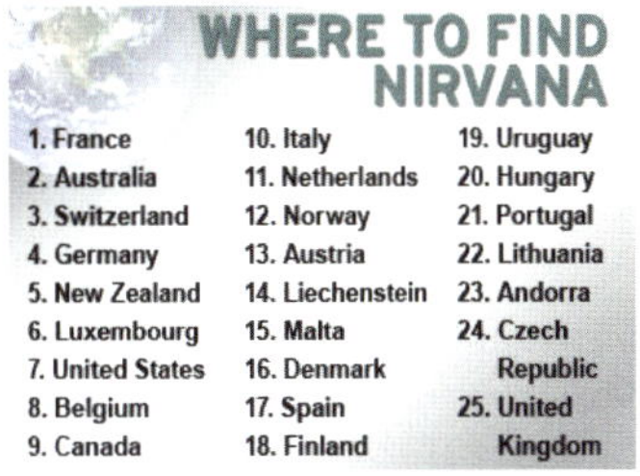

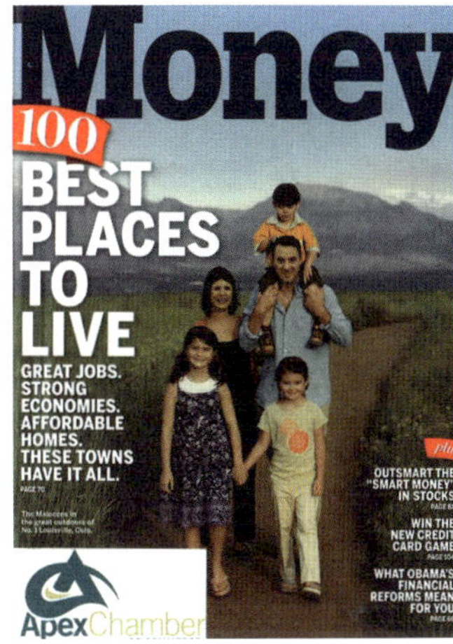

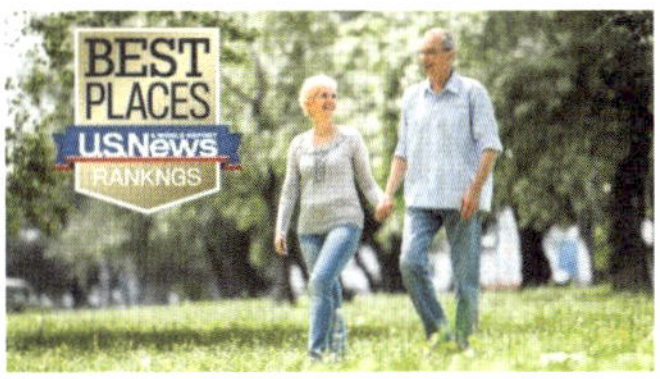

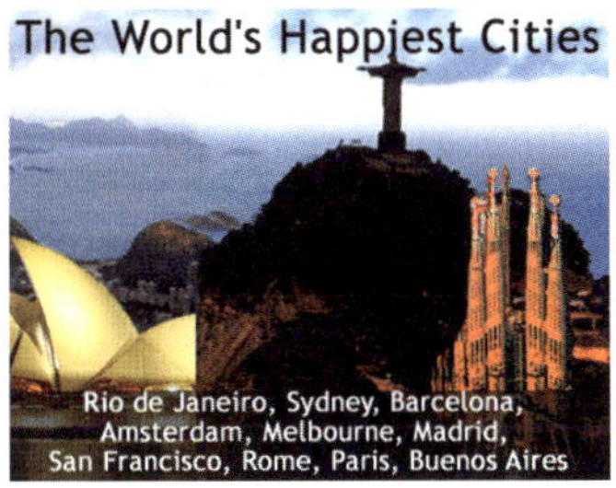

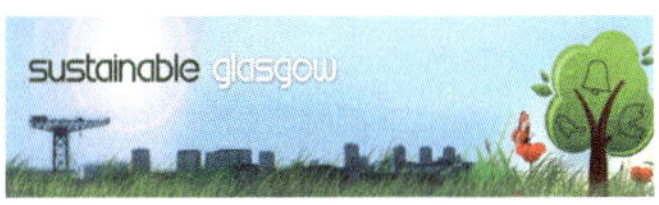

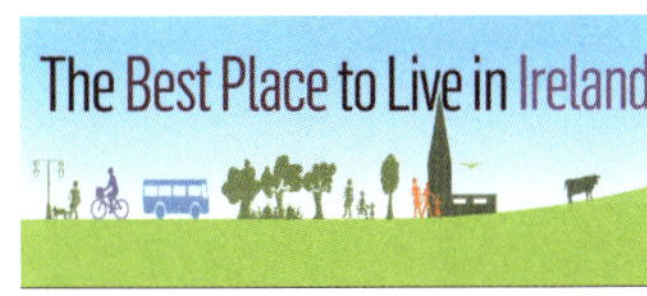

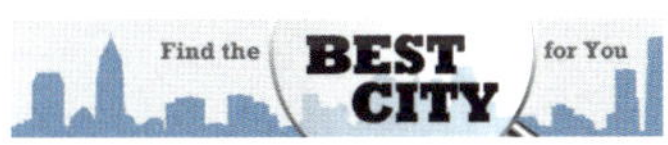

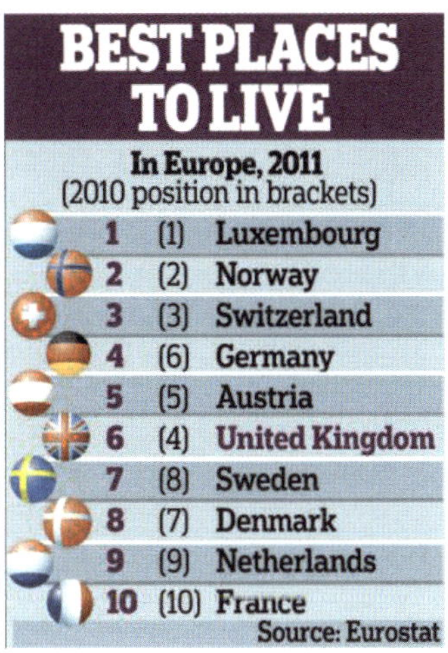

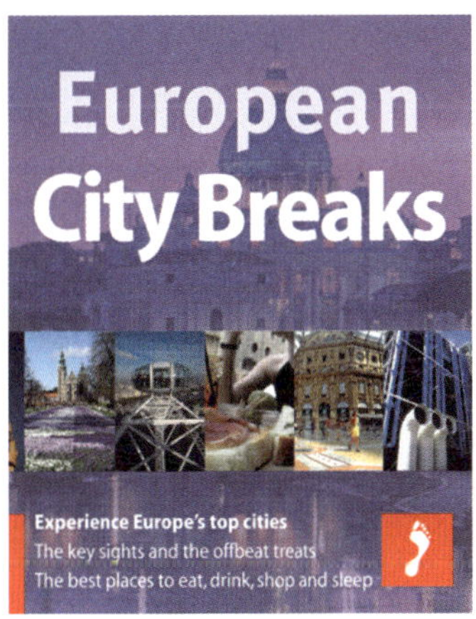

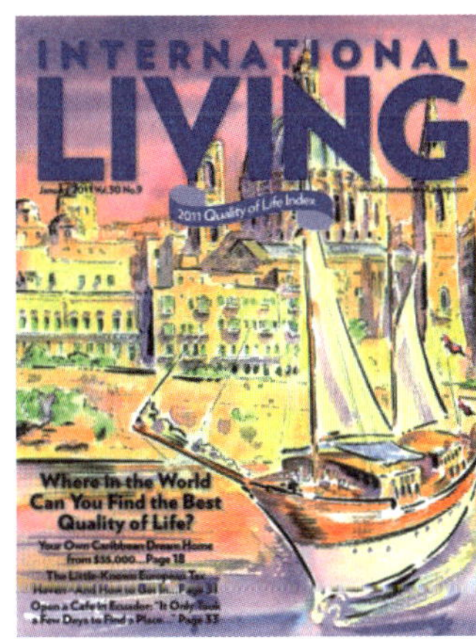

Quality of Living

- Political and social environment
- Economic environment
- Sociocultural environment
- Medical and health considerations
- Schools and education
- Public services and transportation
- Recreation
- Consumer goods
- Housing
- Natural environment

—

Mercer's 2012 International "Quality of Living" Survey. Comparative quality of living indexes between a base city and a host city are available, as are multiple-city comparisons. Mercer's global survey is based on an evaluation of thirty-nine criteria for each city, grouped in ten categories.

Epilogue – Territorial Marking: The Dawn of a New Era...

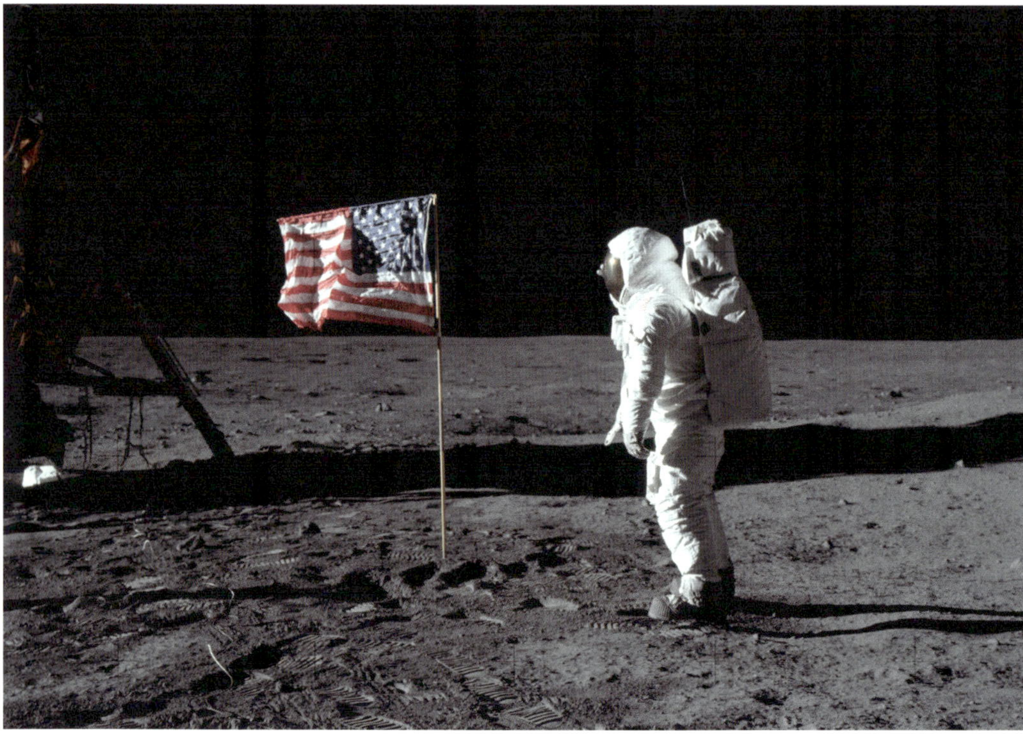

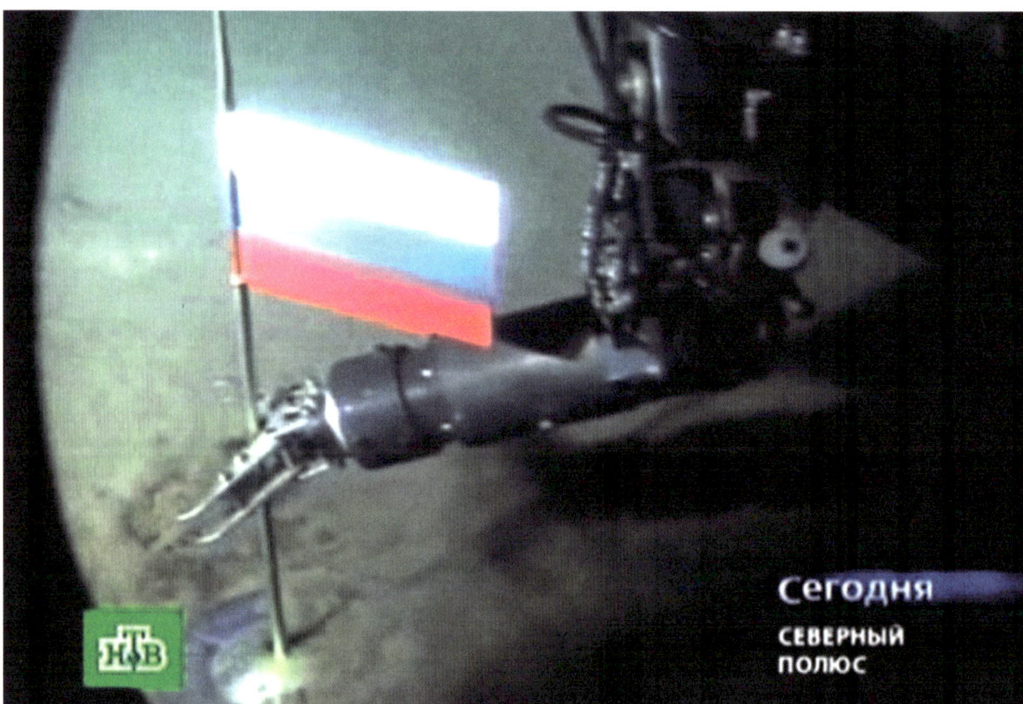

—
Buzz Aldrin/NASA, 1969

—
Russian flag at the bottom of the Arctic ocean, at more than 4,000 meters below the North Pole

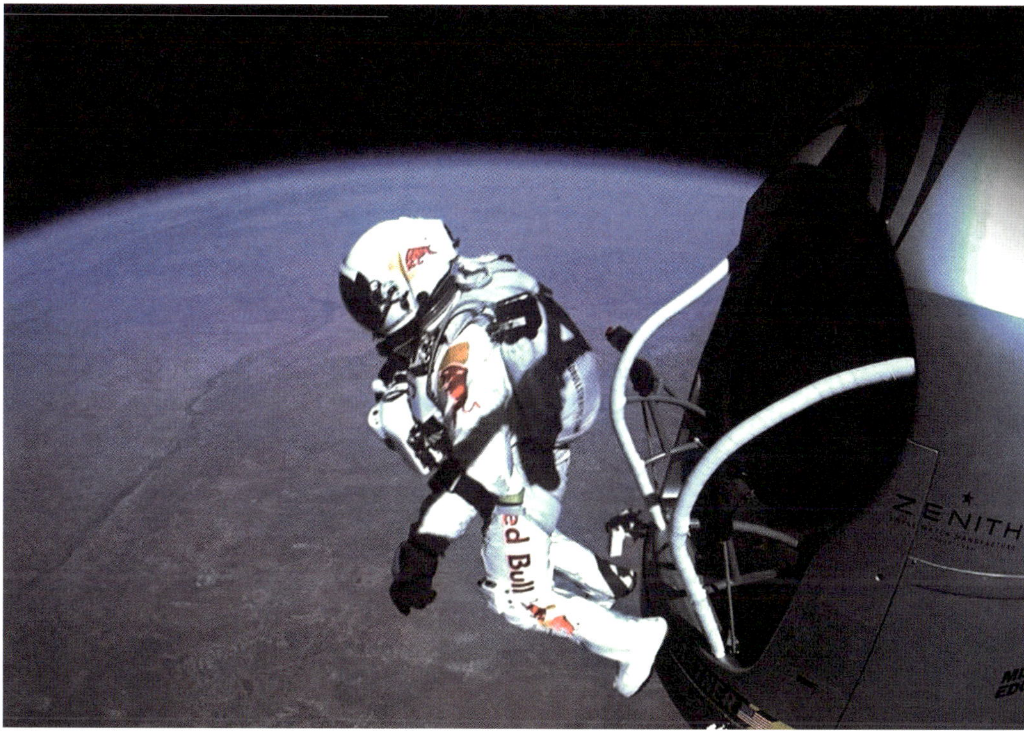

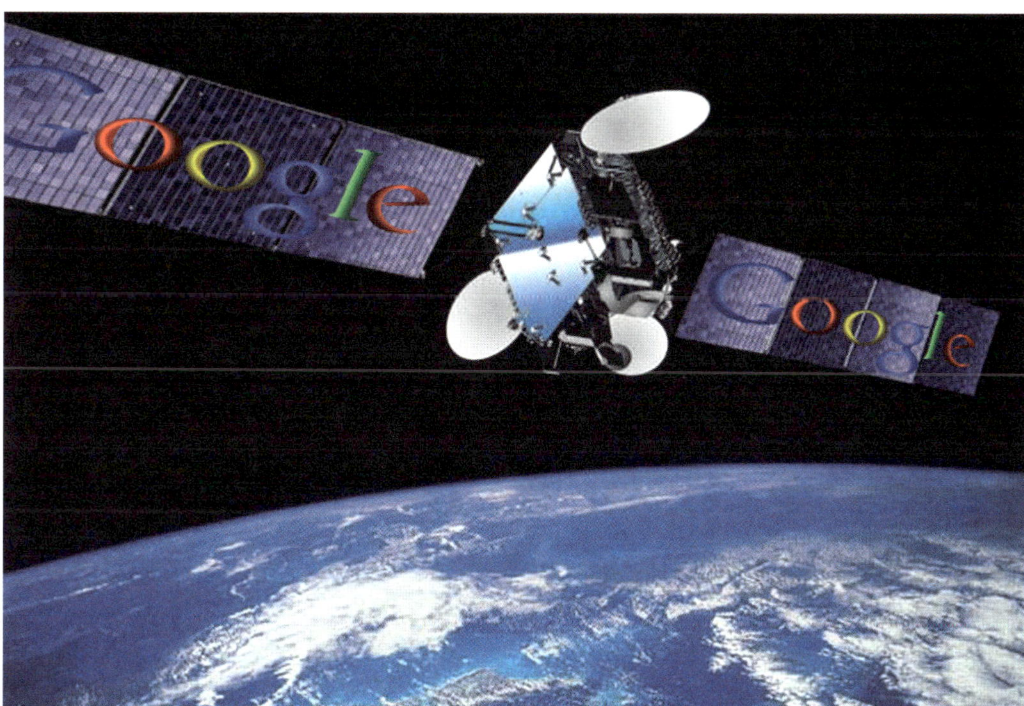

Felix Baumgartner/Red Bull, 2012

Google Satellite

The Conspicuous Absence of a Planetary Flag

Ruedi Baur

The Conspicuous Absence of a Planetary Flag

"If I knew something useful to me and harmful to my family, I should put it out of my mind. If I knew something useful to my family and not to my country, I should try to forget it. If I knew something useful to my country and harmful to Europe, or useful to Europe and harmful to the human race, I should consider it a crime."
MONTESQUIEU

No legislation requires a city, a region, a country, or even a territorial community to bedeck itself with coats of arms, flags, initials, logos, and other identification "systems" or "visual languages." Yet both the history of heraldry and, more recently, the history of "programs of visual identity," "branding," and territorial marketing strategies testify to the power of custom. As a rule, the successive forms of representation as well as the various strategies of visual promotion spread quite rapidly around the world. This took place through mimicry rather than by legal requirement—and, even more rarely, following a public discussion. If questions of recognition seem to be at the source of several of these systems of representation, this function is rapidly undermined in favor of the notions of the foil and "identity through difference" within a given mode of representation. Thus, the exceptional act of wishing to truly express a difference through the design of a particular mode of representation is rapidly transformed, by a mimetic effect, into a mere system of classification of virtually equivalent elements. Common rules are established without being actually dictated by any kind of superior instance. Only the originality of every individual sign has been protected, and this has been so since the late Middle Ages, when a number of famous trials for heraldic plagiarism took place. Proof, if any were needed, of the power of these signs.

Questions of credibility and competition are apparently the main reason for the reproduction of common models. It is as if the territories that failed to participate in this visual classification somehow ran the risk of sinking into a kind of invisibility or, even worse, tackiness. Competition among cities and political territories seems to need both originality and acceptance in its resort to modes of representation linked to an era and a dominant kind of strategy. As if the means of self-representation and the usage of these signs completely escaped not only the civic contract between citizens and rulers but also, and most importantly, the political question as such.

Signs of recognition, representation, identity, brands, rallying signs, and, often, signs of exclusion... their use transcends the mere question of informing citizens or identifying public affairs. The point is not merely to facilitate an accurate reading of the territory and the initiatives enacted by political institutions, but indeed, in many cases, to transform the perception of reality by creating an artificial identity in order to replace it. The "creation of floating identities" and their "artificial enhancement" are usually brought up with respect to this point. The aim is to read territories through "a major idea," to create an event in order to "focus and forget," not to mention more dangerous aims based on identitarian points of view that often entail fear, xenophobia, and reactionary ideas.

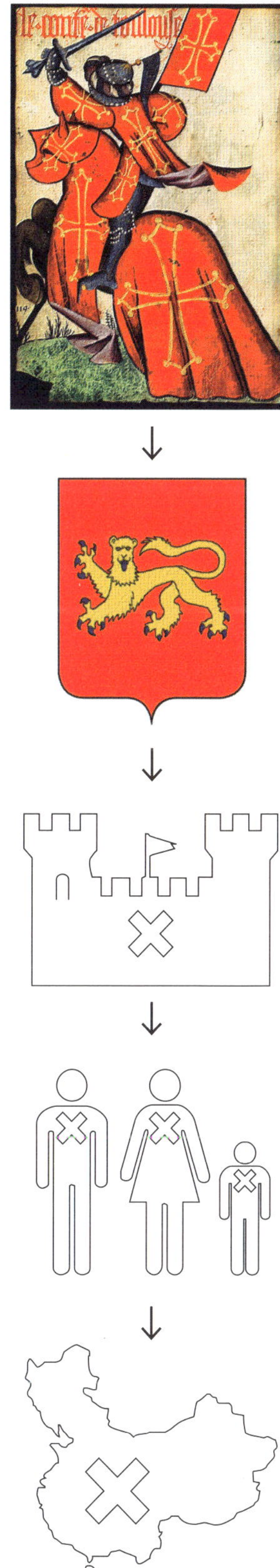

First there were the accoutrements of a knight, then the heraldic shield of the knight's family and its reproduction on various supports identifying their possessions and the territory they rule over, and eventually a town's coat of arms. Later, following the French Revolution, this sign was transferred to towns and cities to identify them as part of the Republic.

The present essay intends first to decode the operations at work on the basis of these various modes of identification. It proposes to question their respective civic values and offer, whenever possible, an alternative. To this end we must understand the issues at stake and their effects on the behavior of citizens. A comprehensive approach should allow us to free such actions from their dangerously apolitical status. It may help perhaps our understanding of these superimpositions, shifts, transfers, and mimetic acts. The intention is to force the political realm to assume its responsibilities, allow the citizen to better judge what is being done in that field, and raise a critical debate among professionals. But let us begin with the most traditional form of such veneers: the coat of arms.

The Knight, His Family, and His Kingdom

Research in the field of heraldry attributes the origin of the first emblems to the colored finery that made it possible, in the late Middle Ages, to recognize knights on the battlefield or during parades. Those human signs and their extensions in the form of pennants rapidly became coats of arms. These no longer served only to distinguish a knight, but were also signs of affiliation. Women, children, and more or less direct descendants proudly wore the sign representing the knight. All of the family property was gradually marked with the coat of arms. Thus, the sign came to symbolize a certain power, an area under a lord's rule, and the vassals' affiliation to these lands. Not to mention all the men who had

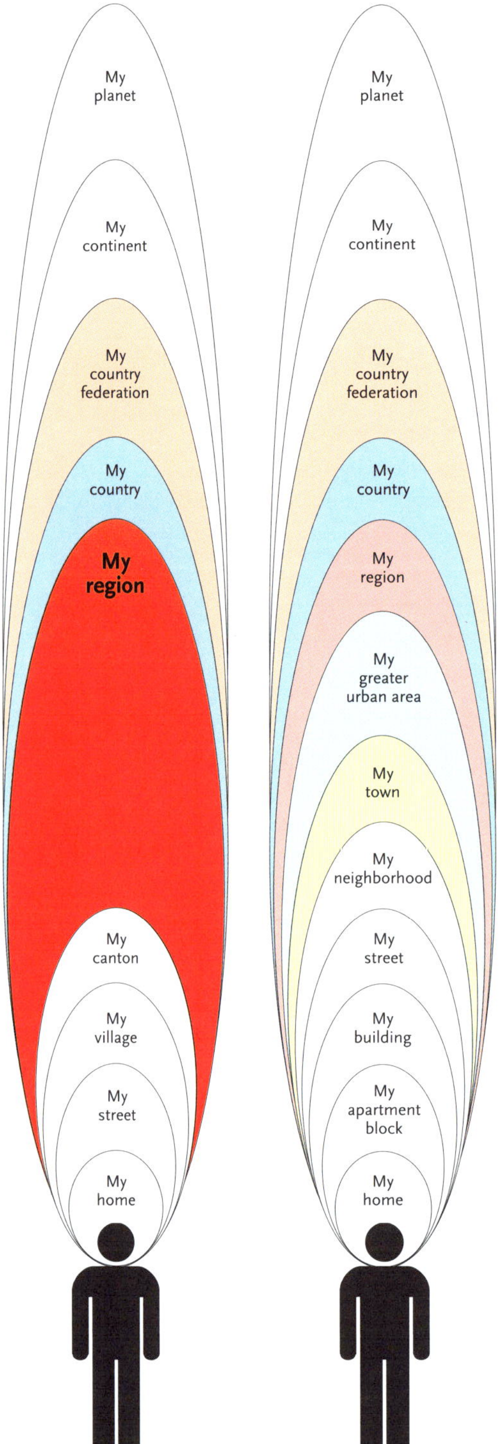

Nesting of the perception of different identities and, in certain cases, an overdetermination of one of them, leading to the disappearance of the others.

to wear these coats of arms and fight under them in the name of their lord. Thus, the same sign that allowed an individual to be recognized under his armor gradually became the symbol of the lineage and property of a feudal lord. A few centuries later, after the French Revolution, it came to symbolize a person's identification with a territory of the Republic. It was indeed this symbolic connection to feudal lands, moreover, that a number of French revolutionaries questioned. They criticized the system of territorial identification for its exceedingly direct relation to hereditary powers but without offering any valid alternative. This way of classifying different political territories became generalized throughout most European countries. Today, almost every commune, city, region, or country, even when endowed with logos and other identification systems, has its own emblem that often connects it to its history. Contrary to most other countries, republican France has no heraldic bearings, having abolished the royal coat of arms.

Root-Identity and Rhizome-Identity

The perception of these emblems has radically changed. First of all, their decoding is today the prerogative of a few experts, whereas during the Renaissance being able to read and identify them used to be part of mainstream culture. The main difference, however, resides in the relationship that the population once had with the coat of arms. Be it the emblem of a free city, a kingdom, or a seigneurial domain, the coat of arms generally was the one and only symbol of where one was born and lived. It represented the subjection to a unique power that could evolve only as a result of royal unions or invasions. Our contemporary perception of political territories is at once more stable and more complex. Like Russian dolls, the interlocking of territories goes from the more intimate dimension of one's staircase, building, neighborhood, to gradually extend to the nation—which still plays a major role—then to the continent or even the whole planet. Each level, except perhaps for the closest ones and for Earth—which still defines humanity as a whole—possesses different signs of identification. Beside the fact that, nowadays, we are often confronted in the course of our lives—through marriage, inheritance, or immigration—with several of these political combinations, their complexity somehow throws into perspective the excessive feeling of belonging to one of these political territories and the sign representing it.

Besides, is it not the case that focusing strongly on one of these interlocking entities, combined with the undermining of their true complexity, constitute the dangerous germ of attitudes of rejection of the other, whether xenophobic or racist? These attitudes are found at the level of a village, region, often a nation, or even a continent. They reappear like a plague in conjunction with social or societal problems, whenever a community feels—rightly or wrongly—that it is under attack. That is when signs of recognition, representation of power, and identification become one single sign of adoration and pride, a sign of identification and differentiation, but often also of exclusion of anyone unable to claim an "affiliation" to that symbol, whether by territorial "roots" or by blood. Numerous times throughout history, these identification signs suddenly overstepped their official role and proliferated in public space, becoming the symbol of a territorial cause for which it was necessary to fight, even die, and therefore kill. If today these signs mainly appear in connection with major football matches, make no mistake: the act of raising these flags often goes beyond the mere symbol of one's support for a team.

The last two centuries showed us the dangers of such exacerbated forms of nationalism or communitarianism. We thought that the horrors of the last century's fascist regimes would protect us, once and for all, from any such kind of backward-looking hatred. Unfortunately, European reality proved us wrong. Provincial and national egoism is re-emerging, flags are again flying, simplistic approaches are developing, borders are closing, and mentalities are becoming narrower. The "Tout-Monde" that we dreamed of beside Édouard Glissant and Patrick Chamoiseau, the world of "rhizome identities" and of the "poetics of relation," has apparently been postponed to a better time. Yet in our capacity as graphic designers did we manage to produce

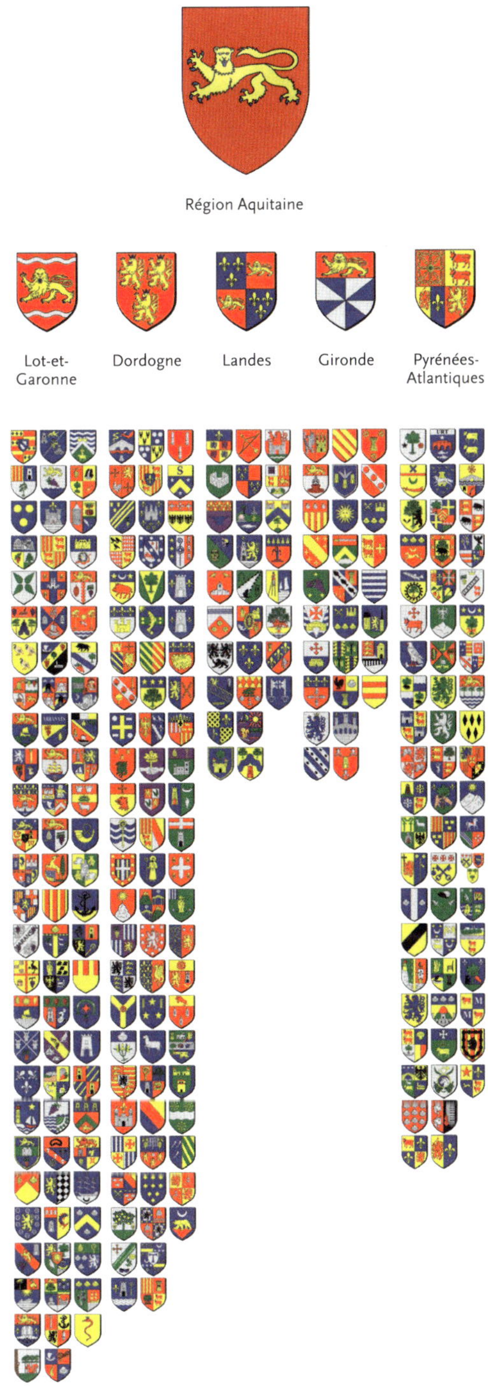

The coats of arms for the French region of Aquitaine, its five departments and the different communes making up each of those. Clearly the coat of arms does not by itself provide information on the kind of political territory referred to.

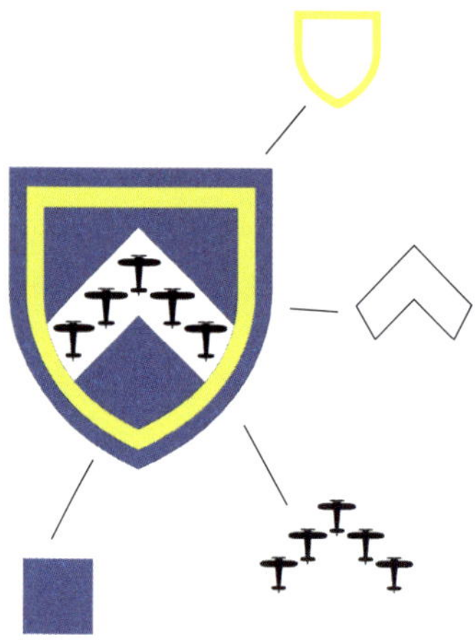

Breakdown of the coat of arms of the commune of Orly, which remains a kind of exception because of its use of contemporary motifs.

Saint-Denis

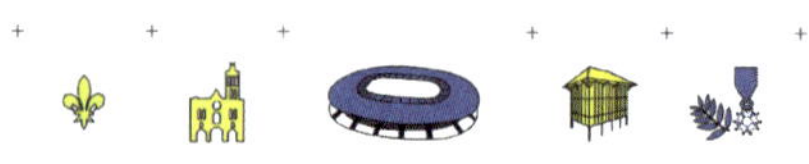

PARIS COSMOPOLITE

Vincennes

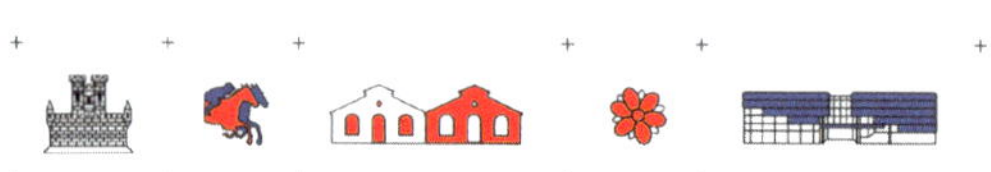

PARIS COSMOPOLITE

Bagnolet

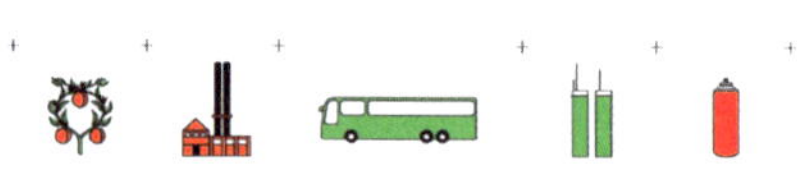

PARIS COSMOPOLITE

Proposal for rendering a number of communes in Greater Paris legible. This system is based on motifs drawn from various coats of arms to which more contemporary ones have been added.

accurate and fascinating interpretations of these concepts? How are we to represent the complexity of relations rather than the singularity of a root? How are we to talk about a cosmopolitan space, a special place open to every other place? As François Jullien has noted, "Today, the notion of otherness is being attacked on two fronts; on the one hand, it sees itself given over to a sacralization that absolutizes it, an ever-returning remainder of an act of divinization; on the other, it is abandoned to assimilation that standardizes, then sterilizes the world and makes it inert."

Classifying Singularities

Let us try to understand the reasons that prompted certain political entities to question the heraldic system, which was nonetheless quite coherent. Some arguments remained subjective, evoking the old-fashioned nature of coats of arms or reminding us of the reluctance shown towards them during the French Revolution. Today, we realize that coats of arms are being recycled in the advertising of trendy products and that these questions of fashion are indeed relative. Some emblems, as in the case the commune of Orly, also prove that the design of a coat of arms need not necessarily date back to the Middle Ages, and that it ought therefore to be possible to bring these signs up to date while respecting the rules of heraldry. Another advantage of these modes of identification certainly concerns the possibility of assembling different motifs without reducing a territory to its main monument. We can see that monuments are not systematically featured on coats of arms, and that a territory could just as well be defined by its agricultural production, river, or forest.

Incidentally, the relationship between these motifs and the context is quite a fascinating topic. Even if nowadays these signs have become more difficult to interpret, we can still use them to decode the peculiarities of the political territory they represent. Their contemporary usage, however, remains hindered by a number of factors of a more functional nature. A frequently evoked argument was that the coat of arms was difficult to read from a distance and could not be easily reproduced in different formats

The "arms of Aquitaine and Guyenne" are gules, leopard Or armed and langued azure. The choice of the leopard for the graphic representation remains relatively free. Integration of the typography makes it possible to associate the image more directly with the place it represents. These proposals were developed for a competition but were not chosen in the end.

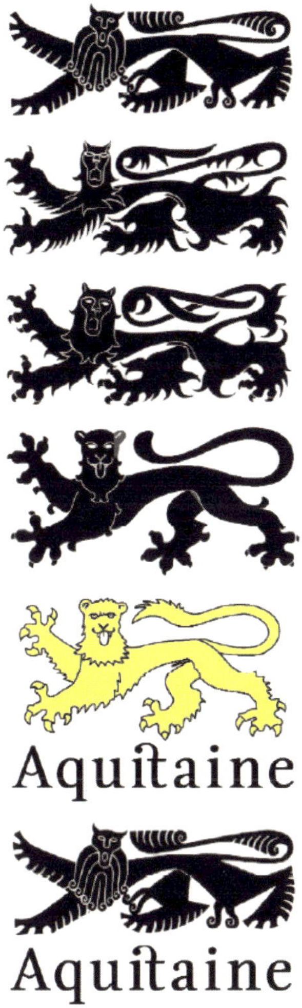

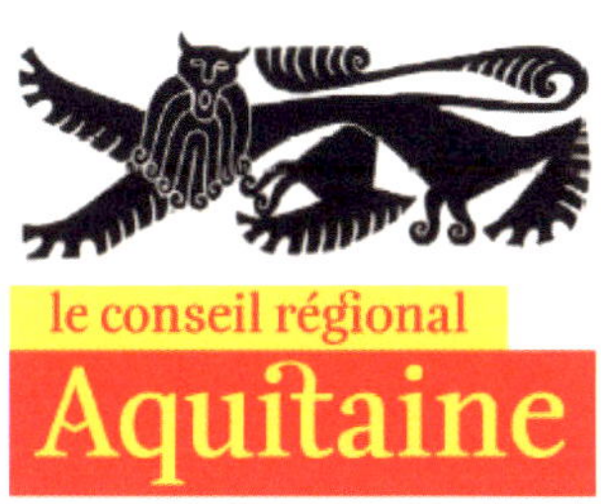

and on different media. However, redesigned coats of arms prove that this handicap can be overcome. A more challenging criticism concerns the fact that the rules of heraldry do not allow a distinction between different typologies of political territories. The same sign could represent a municipality, a canton, a department, a region, even a nation. Coats of arms therefore require a caption indicating both the political entity and the name of the territory.

Fascinated by the big companies whose signs of recognition were grounded in their name without any additional flourish, a few cities—later followed by other territories—started applying this approach to their own self-promotion. It is worth recalling that the first experiments were developed in a spirit of modernity and austerity. The aim was to reject outdated, exceedingly ornamental forms, and design a contemporary, democratic space. These first attempts took shape before World War II, in particular in some progressive cities. However, the major wave of logos and programs of visual identity only began to spread in the 1970s to the 1990s. The know-how of corporate identity and corporate design was directly applied to public domains, as if creating the identity of a transnational corporation could meet the needs for territorial identification and its smooth political functioning.

New Industrial Territories

Peter Behrens is generally regarded as the father of what would later be called corporate identity and corporate design. This architect and creator of the German Werkbund did not limit himself to transdisciplinary interventions on the products, advertisement, and design of factories and their furnishings; he also strove to provide a kind of visual cohesion to the whole production, a cohesion aimed at representing the AEG brand. Incidentally, unlike those who took over his approach, he did not proceed by merely repeating the logo, nor did he over-represent it as a unique recognizable permanent feature. During the time he was involved, the sign based on the letters *A, E,* and *G* took a variety of forms, but without weakening its cohesion in any way. Initially based on a decoration of

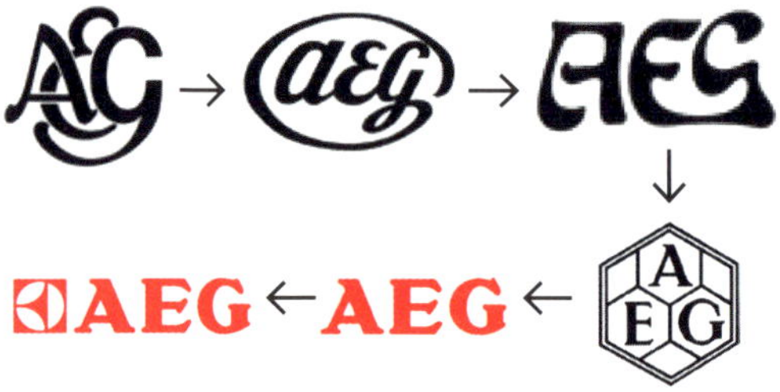

The evolution of the AEG logo in the 20th century. The initials of the Allgemeine Elektrizität Gesellschaft (General Electric Company) gradually become an acronym, then a neutral word/image vis-à-vis other languages.

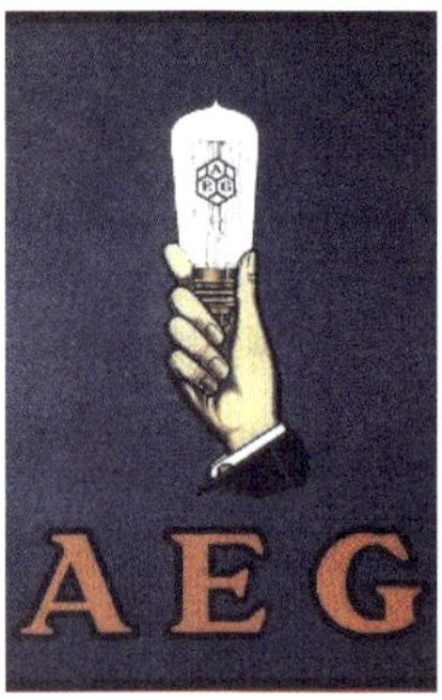

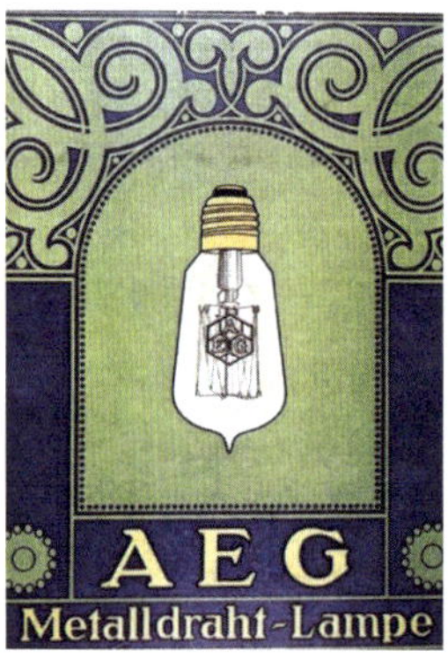

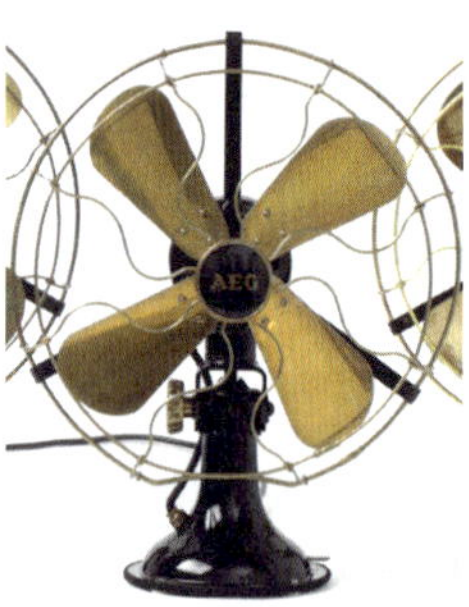

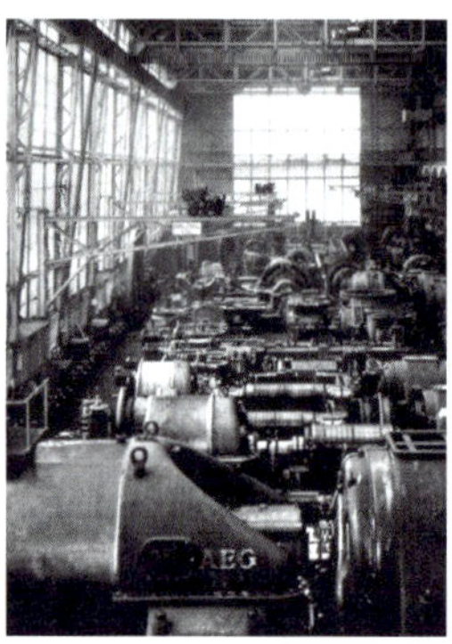

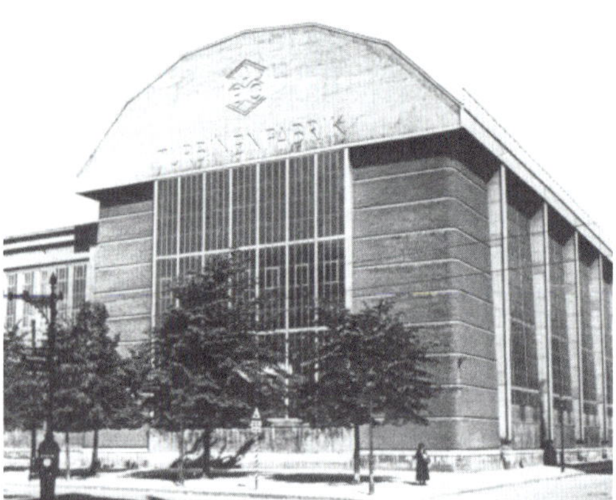

interlocking initials, the sign was gradually simplified to an extremely sober composition of lowercase letters. The sober, functional, and aesthetic value of this visual cohesion clearly transcended a simple matter of signature. It defined the company's entire visual approach, in the sense that it constituted a new financial and industrial feudalism.

This instance is interesting to us insofar as it shows that, as with several other major companies of the early twentieth century, the notion of territory was beginning to concern AEG and its designer. The aim was to design manufacturing spaces as if they were parts of a modern private city, but also to control the venues of promotion and sale worldwide. If the notions of export and planetary sales already defined these companies, their places of production were still strongly associated with a specific territory. There was thus a tension between the original place of manufacturing whence the company arose, and the need to develop outside of that territory as an international, decontextualized brand.

While several companies did not shy away from placing the representation of their brand squarely in the heritage of the coat of arms of their region, city, or nation, others tried to show a certain neutrality and extraterritoriality. This phenomenon was radicalized during the major operations of delocalization in the 1990s. The brand was made autonomous of the place of manufacture while keeping, in some cases, the label of the—usually wealthy—country of affiliation.

The beginning of this approach, however, was probably based on a certain notion of modernist authenticity. The idea was to establish a link between reality and representation by qualifying both, without forgetting the main objective of improving profits. This approach, variously called—depending on the language used—*progetazzione, Gestaltung,* "industrial creation," or "design," developed around an attitude of design in which the user occupied a central role. Unsurprisingly, this focus drew the attention of progressive politicians. However, in spite of their similarities, the two problems remain different in many respects.

We believe it is important to go back to the origins of this approach to better analyze these differences.

Identifying a Political Territory or a Company

Let's begin with the needs of citizens. In their capacity as residents, voters, and taxpayers, they are entitled to expect, in a democracy, clear legibility when it comes to the elements pertaining to the public management of territories. They must have easy access to all the services and information to which they are entitled, and must be able to easily recognize their ruling—or cofinancing—public entity. The citizens' well-being therefore also depends on the quality and legibility of the public space in which they live and act. By introducing the notions of civic-mindedness and shared space, what comes into play is a contract of mutual responsibility, based on respect between citizens and the elected officials in charge of managing the territory through the relevant administration. In our own system of interlocking territories, competences are distributed on different scales. The accurate reading of this complex whole becomes a crucial necessity. The citizen must be able to recognize who is responsible for what, and know how to interact at the various levels of the process. There is nothing worse than the feeling of powerlessness that one can experience when facing complex political mechanisms and their related administrations.

The question which concerns us is therefore whether the identification models based on initiatives of commercial competition can satisfy the need for legibility of our democratic spaces. It appears that an anonymous (corporate) society that wishes to mass-produce a given object and distribute it around the world needs an extremely high degree of visual cohesion and control, usually developed upon the endless repetition of the same logo imposed upon all the entities destined to disappear behind this visual sign and visual unity. If the question of recognizing the emitting entity is similar, perhaps that of the distinction between the subsets is, on the other hand, radically different.

Is it really necessary for a trash collection service to have an acronym and to be assimilated to the visual

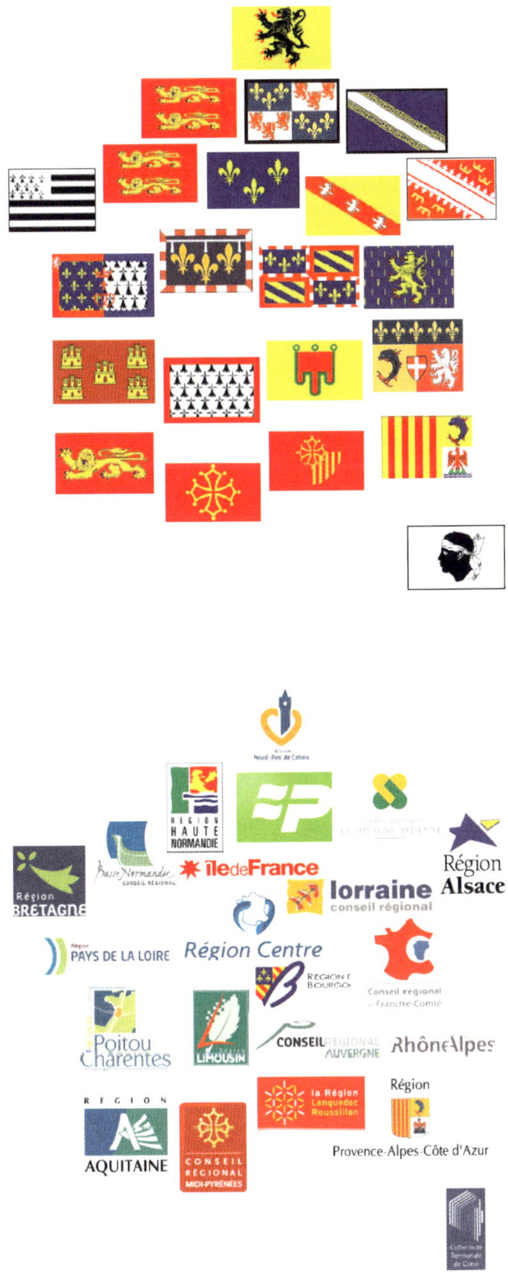

Comparison of a map of the coats of arms representing the regions of France and the map of the logos of the same territories shows the overall lack of coherence in the second approach. Each logo is fighting for itself in a way, laying down its own formal rules. The same holds for each country.

From the flag to the coat of arms to the logo: examples of representations of different regions in Europe.

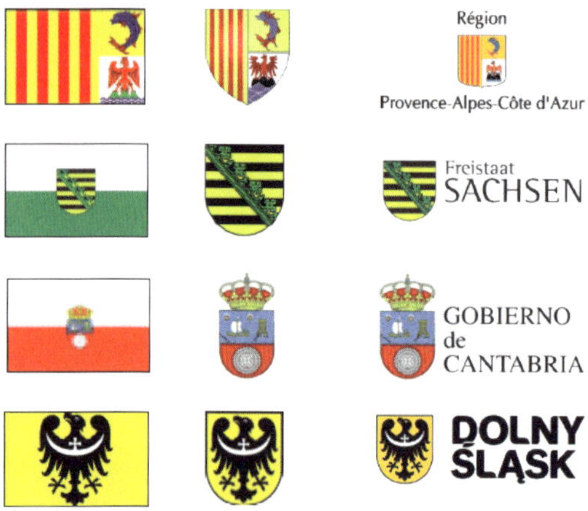

Type 1: the logo makes direct use of the coat of arms.

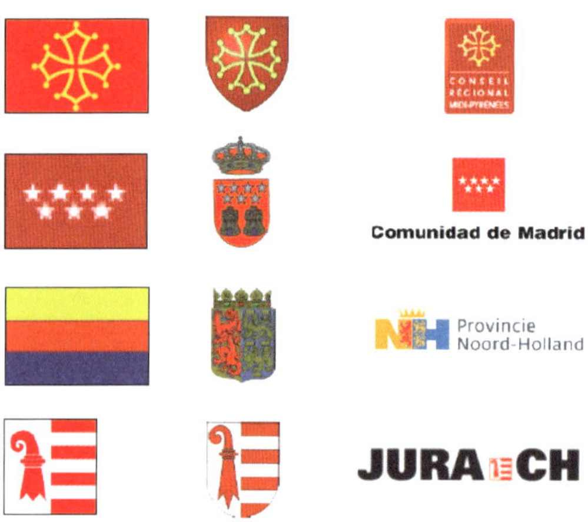

Type 2: the logo is inspired by the coat of arms.

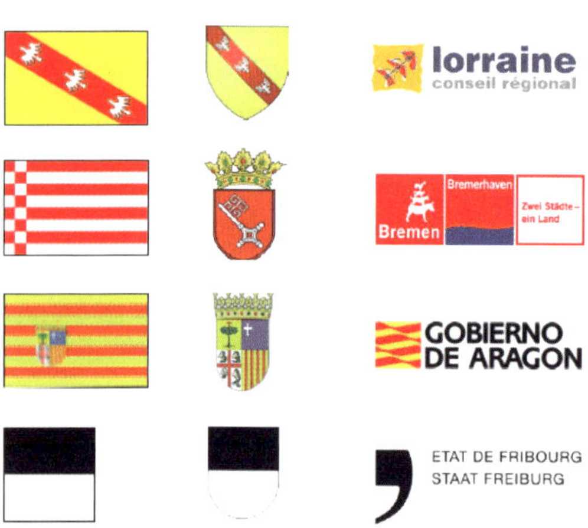

Type 3: the logo is in harmony with the coat of arms.

expression of the theater or social services? Should we not rather aim to set up a sound visual coordination that would allow entities with fundamentally different functions to express not only their particularities but also their role as a public service affiliated with a territory? One difficulty resides in the very meaning of a territorial sign. What does the sign signify—the territory as such, its government, its administration, or political action?

This lack of clarity can also be perceived when the creator of the sign is being briefed. For instance, the graphic designer may be asked to express through the logo the notions of "dynamism and modernity." Such notions are generally expressed by means of a simple line handwritten under the name. We could thus assemble a collection of such logos of municipalities and other small local divisions that very much want to be dynamic. What is the point of expressions such as these? To reelect a political leader, persuade investors, motivate administrative staff, or inform the citizenry?

The extreme confusion regarding the aim of these signs of recognition is plain to see, as well as the complete dismissal of the function—however important—of informing the citizens. If we take these needs seriously, it clearly appears that the question largely exceeds the expression of each individual entity, and that it becomes interlocked with the question of reading public institutions as a whole. This boils down to reading equivalences: all the municipalities of a region, say; but it also means reading the interlocking relations and responsibilities associated with different kinds of territorial institutions.

However, to complete the present analysis, we must understand a third model—a model which, today, has an increasing influence on the strategies of representation of political territories.

From Branding Cows to Territorial Marketing

To make the subject explicit and as simple as possible, let's begin with the identification marks applied by means of a red-hot iron to either the ear or hindquarters of cattle in the Far West. Indeed, is

Different types of logos representing regions of Europe with no connection to their coats of arms or flags.

Type 4: logo situating a place with respect to the nation.

Type 5: logo based on the region's initial.

Type 6: logo based on a monument.

Type 7: logo based on a singular geological feature.

Type 8: logo based on a singular historical feature.

Type 9: logo based on an atmosphere.

Type 10: logo with abstract motif.

Type 11: logotype without illustration.

it not the case that the trendy usage of the terms "brand" and "branding"—as applied to marketing strategies—originated in this means of identifying one's cattle?

In that case as well, the aim of the brand was to facilitate recognition. It testified to the fact that the cow belonged to that particular farmer, and, at the same time, it indirectly ensured recognition of the farmer's production. The cow's hindquarters, all branded with the same sign, proved that each and every one of them belonged to the farmer, and testified to the value of his production. The sign was the medium of a transfer from the quality of the cattle, to that of the meat and milk, to the farmer's reputation. In the absence of the farmer, the brand therefore functions as a guarantee. Some would claim that the brand attributes an identity to the cow. This is completely false. All we know about the cow is that mark of ownership. The cow therefore loses its identity in favor of a sign indicating that it belongs to the farmer. All its life, the cow will be associated to that farmer by virtue of the brand. One could talk of symbolic capital being transferred from the farmer to the cow through the sign. The latter undermines the cow's actual identity while transforming it into a product, as when we say, for instance, "That farmer's cows are nothing if not excellent." Or the opposite, "I wouldn't trust that cow; it belongs to that owner." These examples illustrate a simple and direct connection between the sign and its symbolic value.

Let's push the cow story a bit further by introducing the notions of "corporation" and "global market." Let us suppose that the mark branded on the cow no longer refers to a specific farm, but to a company established in an obscure tax haven. It belongs to unidentified investors who probably come from all over the world and own a number of farms and meat factories in different countries. As a result of such depersonalization, delocalization, and, most important, the secrecy surrounding the actual ownership, the notion that "this cow must be good because it carries that identifying sign" becomes considerably more complex. Why must I believe that this branded cow is indeed of good quality? Does the qualification depend on the frequency with which we find ourselves facing the sign? Is it because the brand is internationally recognized, or because its qualities are promoted by advertisements? Or is it because I enhance my own value by consuming that symbolic article? In any case, the brand refers neither to the cow, nor to the farmer who takes care of the cow, and not even to the anonymous investors who cash in on the profits. It refers to itself.

As it circulates, independently from any referent, the brand acquires an entirely autonomous symbolic value. It will need to be protected, and its importance will increase commensurately with the anonymity of the producer and the distance from the consumer. In spite of the progress in the symbolic capital of the sign and of what it stands for, the cow will remain what it is—a cow destined to become meat. The brand on its hindquarters will also remain unchanged. Only the overall perception will be transformed. The branded cow will become a branded product. It must conform to our idea of that product. To become a brand, it will be subjected to norms and will lose its personality once and for all.

We can therefore assert that branding and marketing strategies rely on indirect trust or fascination. But how can such a trust be artificially produced, and what is it exactly that we trust? Certainly not those anonymous investors, who, as we all know, think only of the profits they can derive from a commercial operation. This capital of trust must therefore be built upon an artificial reality that does not merely conceal negative realities, but must also divert the attention from the actual item in order to create a dream. Indirectly, the point is also to discredit other symbolic values susceptible to overshadow the brand because they look more authentic. The first targets of these undermining operations will be precisely those anarchic cows that are not subjected to any particular brand, then the farmers who want to remain independent, and finally the small local businesses with still identifiable owners. Little by little, through a succession of exclusions, bankruptcies, and buybacks,

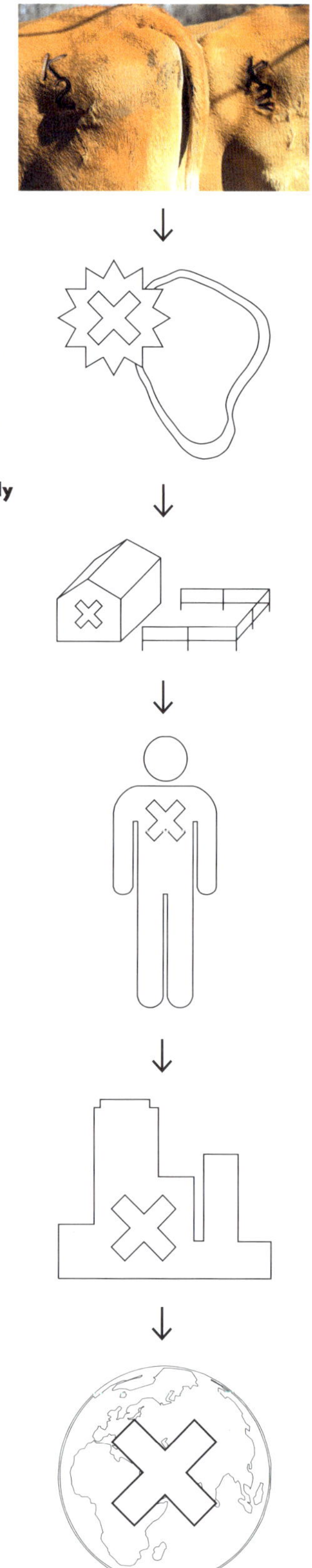

As with the knight, the brand went from a sign for recognizing a cow that is liable to wander away, to a value, i.e., the quality of the kind of meat bearing that brand, to the farm, to the farmer guaranteeing the brand and the area where the animal was raised, to finally the brand itself.

one eventually reaches a situation where all that remains are the major global companies among themselves.

The market seems under control. It is shared among entities of the same kind. Anonymity becomes the rule, and everyone strives to homogenize these products. The actual difference between cows or farms gradually disappears. Everything becomes standardized. The consumer is supposedly "free to choose!" between brand X and brand Y, both of which correspond to similar strategies. Meanwhile, and with increasing intensity, global brands continue their endless drumbeat around these ever-repeated signs. Thanks to their increasingly colossal budgets, they can develop more and more sophisticated communication strategies. Their aim is to constantly enhance their visual domination on a global level, in the context of a global visual war in which only the strongest powers can express themselves.

This close-up centered on the branding of cows allowed us to appreciate the gradual shift from questions related to the recognition of real elements to those pertaining to an entirely different speculative logic. We observe that the same sign, identically repeated, ends up at the core of two radically different logics. In the first case, the sign has an identifying purpose; in the second, it functions as an enhancer and an instrument of domination, and gradually frees itself from the reality it is supposed to represent. As we have seen, in order to win over consumers and make the dream being built around the sign work, they will not hesitate to embellish or conceal reality, be it in part or even in its entirety.

The Territorial Brand

As they compete on the global markets and strive to attract tourists, businesses, and investors, cities, nations, and other political territories try to become more visible, attractive, and interesting to an international public. They no longer shy from applying branding strategies that are directly inspired by the private sector. The notions of "city-branding," "nation-branding," or, more broadly speaking,

The brand makes it possible to delocalize a company. It no longer represents a particular production quality in a certain place but rather a visual coherence, a kind of dream that is independent of the actual making of the product. The Armani empire naturally expresses to perfection this global power of a brand that is both anonymous and personalized through the construction of an identity unconnected with any reality.

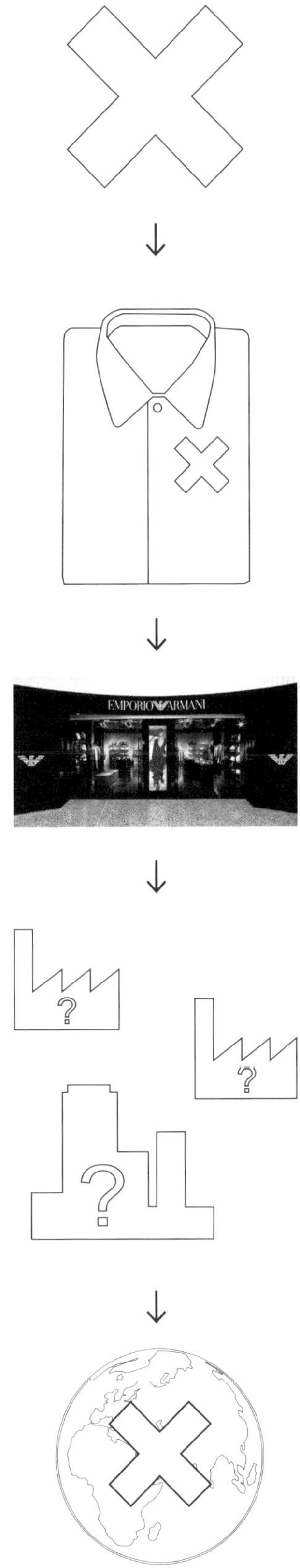

From the logo to the brand: examples of different tourism-oriented representations of European regions. Except for the last one, the connection between the two signs is nonexistent.

territorial marketing seem to be gradually taking hold in public discourse. Directly transposed from consumer sectors, these approaches are imposing profound changes, both symbolic and concrete, on the democratic space. What comes into play is no longer a question of private brands invading the public space, a blurring of boundaries between public and private sectors, but also the transformation of these spaces into symbolic values of a speculative nature. What is affected is not only how these territories are identified and represented and how they communicate, but also the manner in which they present their connection with first the world and then citizens and other people residing there. Beyond the communicative dimension, these presentational strategies radically call into question the way in which we approach, conceive, and transform a political territory and, in particular, a shared space.

According to experts, the reinforcement of a territorial brand requires homogenization, or even a kind of visual hygiene that consists of reinforcing the main positive characteristics while undermining the rest. The emphasis is usually on existing or prospective monuments that are good candidates for mediatization. The politics of seduction and staging, the relentless search for competitive originality, the reduction to the least common denominator seem to gradually and simultaneously dominate the instruments of recognition and institutional communication, but also temporary programs, or even what is already built and definitive.

This branding policy is expressed not only through graphic style, but also through design, architecture, urban planning, and, more generally, through the staging of those forms of entertainment that are gradually replacing culture. The entire ceremonial writing of "citizen spaces" is thus affected by the strategies of these brands. On the one hand, it becomes aseptic by virtue of an allegedly original global aesthetics; on the other, it automatically places the citizen in the position of a consumer deprived of any responsibility. We can indeed observe that, in spite of important investments in the field of design and creation, the expressions of these operations remain extremely similar. Even though the original intent is one of distinction, the result often conveys an impression of interchangeability and above all non-integration in the territorial context. Approached in the same manner regardless of the place of implantation, ceremonial writing partakes in the new global aesthetics derived from commercial strategies: a new modernity under the direct influence of global marketing. Like any other fashion, it imposes itself by discrediting whatever is excluded from its system of reference. Indeed, these questions of credibility seem to be taking the place of questions about actual distinctiveness or capacity for identification connected to the context and its specific needs.

While this attitude indeed brings profound changes to the whole visual approach then, and to what we may call the ceremonial writing of global hyperliberalism, it is based on a notion of brand that needs to be analyzed if we want to understand its effects on democracy and civic spirit.

Same Signs, Different Uses

As we shall see, the notions of brand and brand image are not new. After being reconsidered in the framework of the delocalization characterizing these past few decades of globalization, today they have replaced in our minds the models of corporate identity or corporate design, also derived from the private sector. If these new territorial signs continue to be expressed on occasion through centuries-old logos and emblems, their usage is nevertheless radically transformed. The tool of identification no longer reflects an actual or desired reality, but finds itself at the core of the construction of a floating symbolic value well beyond mere questions of communication. This recent transformation is therefore expressed not through the specific form adopted by signs of representations, but though their use.

In our analysis, we must therefore separate the evolution of identification modes from the use these signs are put to. A historical overview would allow us to analyze the connection between the forms of visual representation and governmental trends. We will try to show the extent to which these trends can radically conflict with the foundation of the civic contract—if not from the viewpoint of democracy, at least from that of the republic. Even now, we can observe that such an invasion of the logic of marketing takes place, at least in Europe, in the context of the return of discourses and behaviors that are identitarian, protectionist, even racist and nationalist. As if the only choice left to the citizen were between a globalizing neoliberalism, based on artificial constructions of identity, and an equally identitarian policy of withdrawal. We shall see that these dialectics combine several populist behaviors which will have to be questioned.

Sometimes won over by these actions, or even proud of certain exceptional feats, citizens also feel entirely powerless when facing operations that represent them as well as fall outside of the democratic system. Confined to a status of mere consumers, they realize they no longer have any influence on that evolution which, they feel, is addressed to others rather than to themselves or their fellow citizens. As a consequence, they almost automatically find themselves in the position of reacting negatively to novelty, whereas they could easily be won over by it, were they given the opportunity to participate in the process.

Refusal and lack of civic spirit then become the sole possible modes of expression outside acceptance. The republican exchange between rulers and their constituents therefore appears to be deeply disturbed in its relation to both place and representation. Could it be that the current disaffection toward politics and public affairs is also the result of a deep crisis in the instruments of public recognition and representation? Unable to distinguish between the representation of a civic space and that of consumerism, today's neoliberal democracies run the risk of endangering the moral contract between their citizens, the institutions of the republic, and the need for collective control which they imply. The hypothesis that civic-mindedness is being destroyed by marketing strategies applied to a territory and focused in particular on notions of brand must be taken very seriously.

But before proceeding, shouldn't we try to understand the effects of the transformation of a political territory into a brand? I shall begin with an analysis of extreme cases—geological icons—then move on to the link between cartographic representation and the notion of land. This will help us understand the possible connections between the promotion of a territory and outbreaks of xenophobia.

Geological Icons

Although the simple images of Mont Saint-Michel, the Matterhorn, or Mount Fuji are enough to symbolize their three respective territories, these are very exceptional cases. Only a few locations lend themselves to being directly transposed into an easily identifiable graphic sign. Their outline and geological appearance are in themselves a recognizable symbol. The passage from photography to graphic reproduction is a direct one. However, this does not apply to each and every viewpoint on these three icons, or to each of their outlines. In this respect, we are far from the "Eiffel Tower" phenomenon, in which the object is recognizable from virtually any perspective. In the case of our three mountains, the recognition is limited to the reproduction of one or a handful of specific viewpoints. Graphic variations are far less important than the presence of codes that allow them to be identified. One just has to climb up the Matterhorn, walk on top of Mount Fuji, or go near Mont Saint-Michel and stroll along its narrow streets to lose the iconic vision that corresponds to most representations of these locations. Only those who have walked many times along their paths can recognize the excerpts from the whole and the other, less singular viewpoints. There is therefore a choice of representation, a kind of visual convention that facilitates the passage from these endless potential interpretations to what will constitute a symbolic viewpoint upon the territory. The latter will be confirmed by tens of thousands of photographers and observers who favor that same viewpoint. Thus, the coastal view of Mont Saint-Michel is unquestionably the dominant representation. Sometimes, however, an artist or a graphic designer manages to impose their own particular viewpoint on the location. Reality will then be approached through that new interpretation, which can be more or less realist. Whatever its correlation to reality, the sign of recognition will correspond only to a fraction of it. Such a representation is generally reduced to an ideal shape. It limits the range of representation of and perspectives on the territory.

The considerable variation in the names of the famous Swiss mountain—called Matterhorn in German, Cervin in French, and Cervino in Italian—would suggest a similar variation in the symbolic representation of the mountain, depending on the side from which it is observed. However, if one compares the images featured on Google under these different denominations, it appears that the different viewpoints are dominated by a single emblematic image, namely, the mountain seen from Zermatt. This is the perspective that has been chosen and graphically reworked in order to symbolize not only that mountain with two names, but also, through that image, the Alps, the canton of Valais, the neighboring resorts, local tourism and, more broadly, Switzerland, or even mountains in general. Disneyland did not hesitate to reproduce it in 3D in Disney's first amusement park. That same image has been used for publicity purposes, as a patriotic symbol or as an item of nationalist propaganda. The same happened to Mount Fuji. Hundreds of companies integrated its graphic representation to signify their ancestral connection to Japan's timeless traditions. Nor did the sign escape the country's nationalist movements. On the other hand, despite its symbolic force, and probably because of the construction's religious legacy, the image of Mont Saint-Michel remains confined to the realm of tourism.

Graphic treatments of other equally famous mountains have not succeeded in becoming iconic. For instance, in spite of being the highest mountain in Europe, Mont Blanc is considerably less fascinating from a visual standpoint. The Great St. Bernard Pass even had to resort to an external symbol—the dog of the same name—in order to better represent itself. But before addressing these "ersatz" identifiers, we should go back to symbolic

Initial Google images after typing in the name of these geological icons or territorial brands.
A kind of ideal image can be extracted from these many reproductions. It is the image found in these prints possessing a broad range of designs.

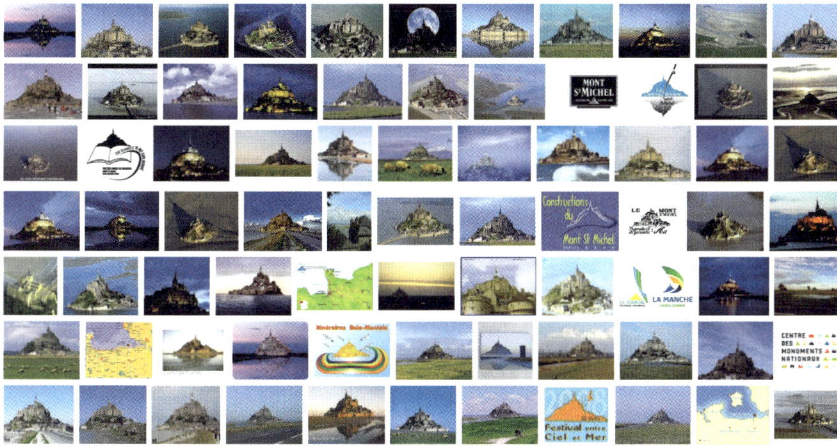

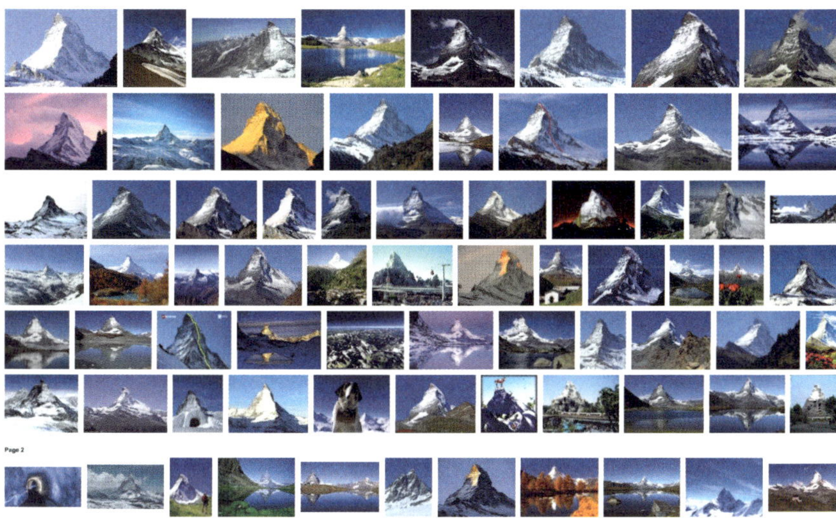

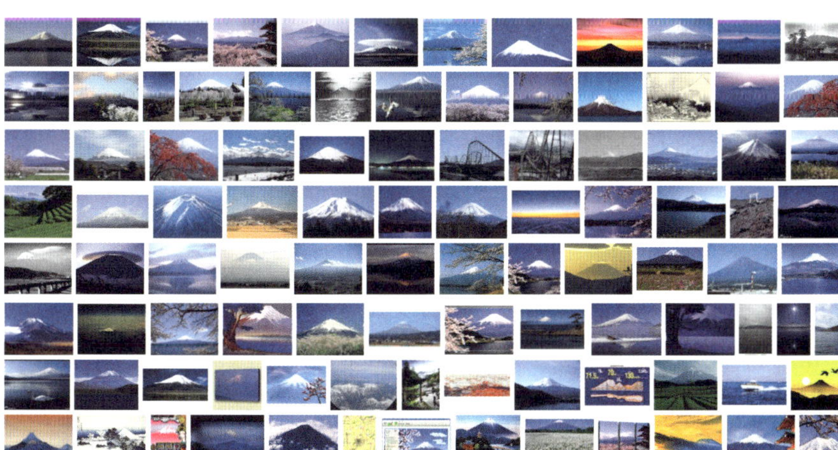

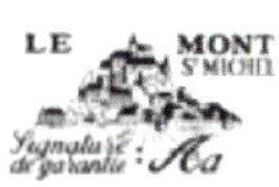

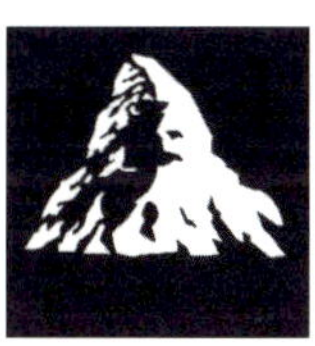

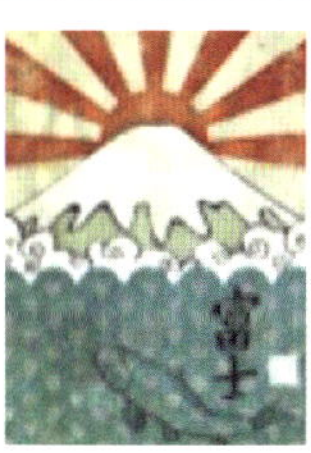

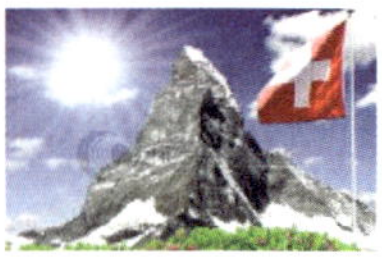

Year round, the Matterhorn (Mont Cervin, Monte Cervino)

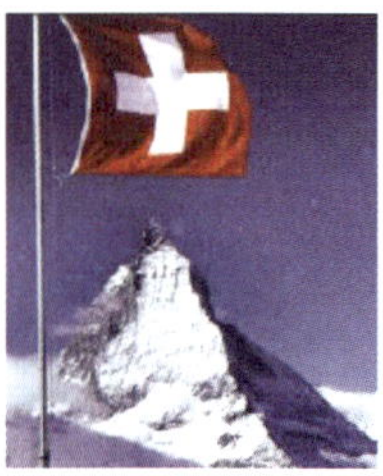

is associated with the Swiss flag. The latter sometimes even overshadows it. Or such as it was often represented in the heyday of Switzerland's federal iconography

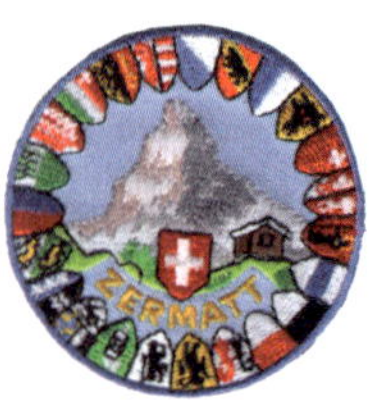

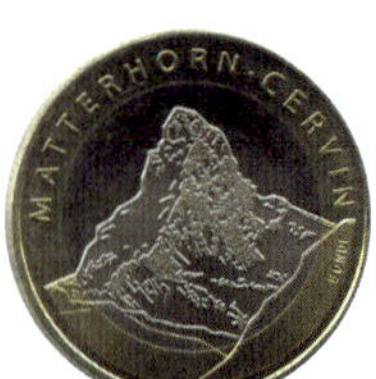

with the flags of the cantons, on national coins,

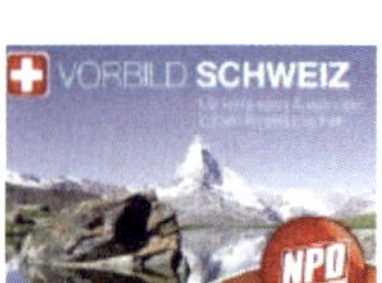

or as propaganda of nationalist parties, or as a commemorative military image.

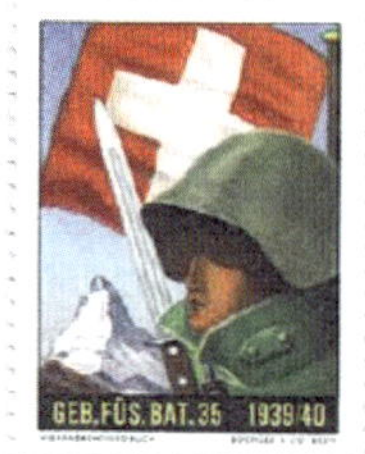

Also as a promotional image for tourism in the country.

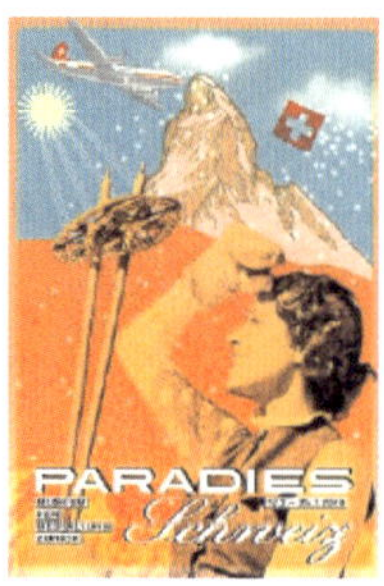

As a brand for the canton of Valais, the Matterhorn, or the ski resort of Zermatt.

Wallis

MATTERHORN REGION

ZERMATT MATTERHORN

ZERMATT MATTERHORN TREK

To promote activities in the region.

Matterhorn Valley Hotels
ursprünglich vielfältig · Grächen

To reinforce the brand of a local festival,

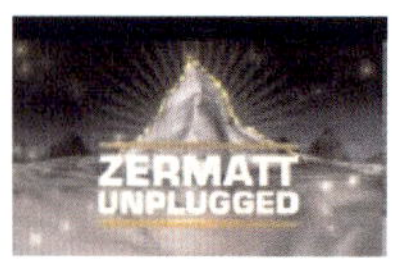

ZERMATT UNPLUGGED

or to express in an ironic way the excellence of research done in "paradise" (Switzerland).

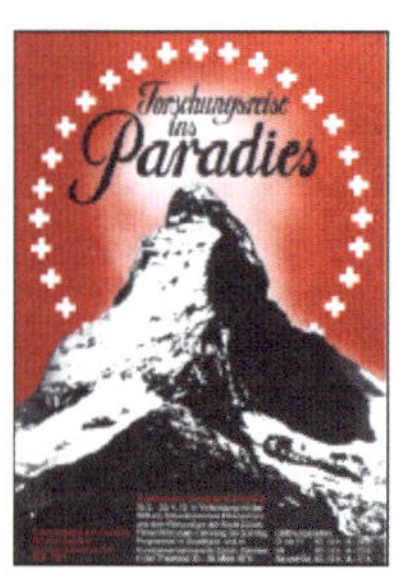

More generally, to promote a Swiss product.

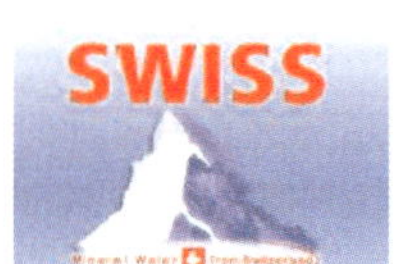

TOBLERONE

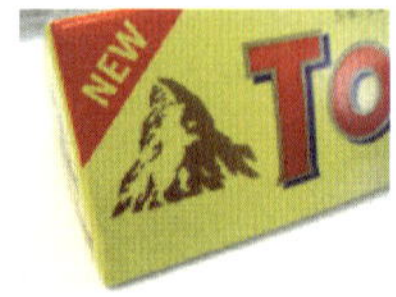

A brand that clearly states its Swiss roots, its "Swissness."

HRI.ch

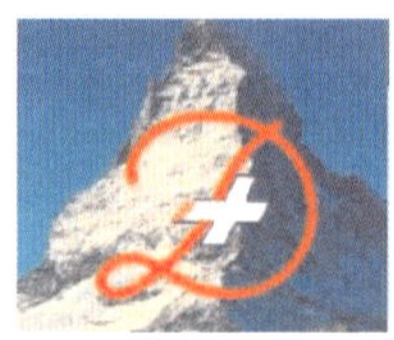

And many others addressed to the Swiss or to people abroad. In a word,

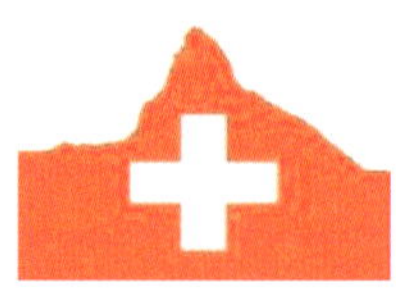

a real subject for advertising.

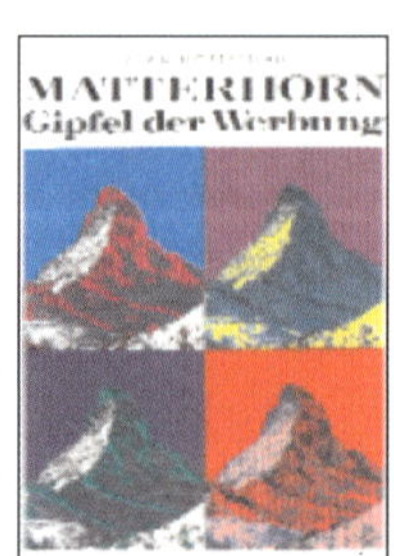

See Yvan Hostettler, *Cervin Matterhorn. Top model des Alpes*, Geneva, 2006.

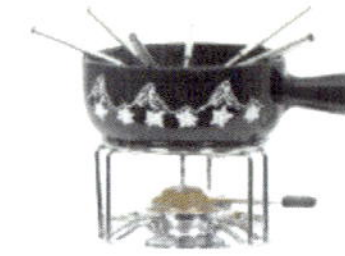

As a decoration on products symbolizing Swiss customs

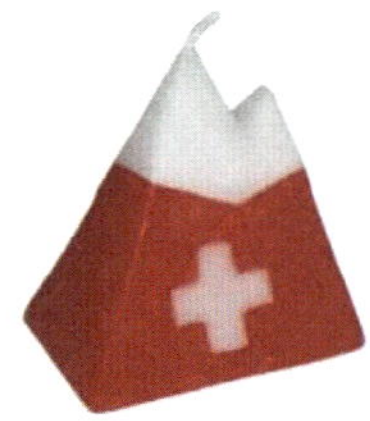

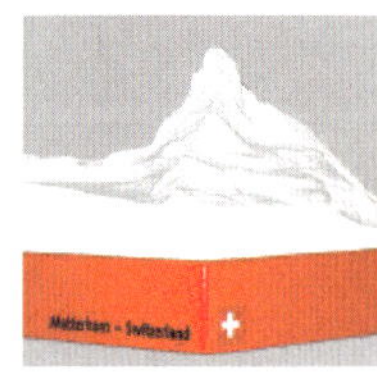

or on objects promoting Switzerland.

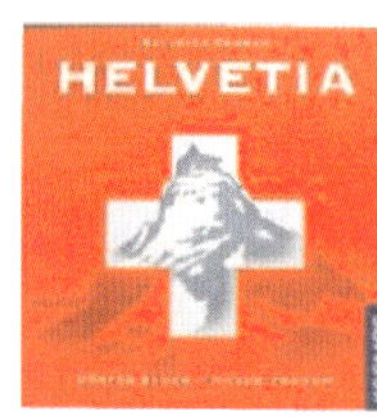

As a reinforcement of national symbolism,

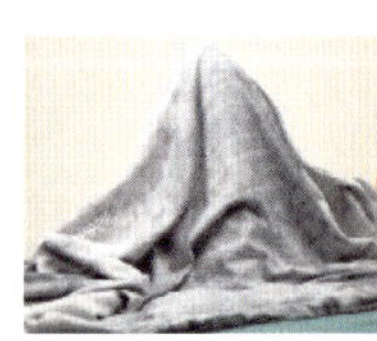

or as self-mockery in works of art, illustrations, or comic books.

reproductions of territories with clearly identifiable geological structures. The example of the Italian "boot" shows that a given reality need not be actually seen in order to be transformed into a symbol. The ancient maps of the Mediterranean and later the world established this boot shape—based entirely on calculations—as a strong symbol, a characteristic of that territory. As abstract as it may be, the analogy between a shape and an object that anyone can identify and name consolidates the level of memorization of and adhesion to the symbol. The symbol represents not only the territory, but also the actual or constructed values associated with it. Long before photographic documentation, the simple reproduction of a calculated image was therefore considered not only a sign of recognition, but also the actual symbolic value of that long-divided territory. Long after the formation of the Italian nation in the late nineteenth century, and once the symbol was already considerably widespread, the first twentieth-century aerial views confirmed the particular outline of that country. Although such views from above have now been made commonplace by Google Maps, the interpretation remains an indirect one. Who can claim to have seen with their own eyes the sight indirectly brought to us via satellite? Who has actually seen the boot? However, that shape is present in almost every pizzeria as an expression of Italy's culinary culture and lifestyle. These photographic or even merely cartographic documents, admittedly by virtue of endless repetition, are therefore sufficient to create consensus around an icon. They constitute a common platform that allows us to recognize countless graphic interpretations with various agendas and symbolic values.

Whereas a large part of Italy is outlined by this visible limit between land and sea, and that outline's surprising resemblance to a boot lends itself to reproduction, this is not the case of many other nations. Firstly, the shape outlined by their borders evokes no association whatsoever. It remains abstract and therefore less memorable. Secondly, that external outline often corresponds to no visible geological reality. It needs to be artificially added to maps, and remains indistinguishable in aerial

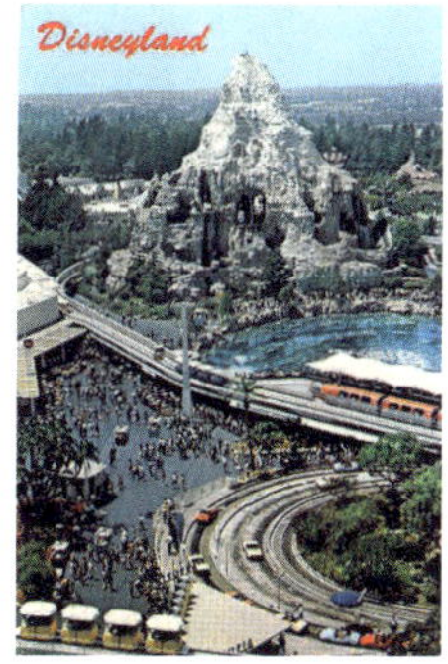

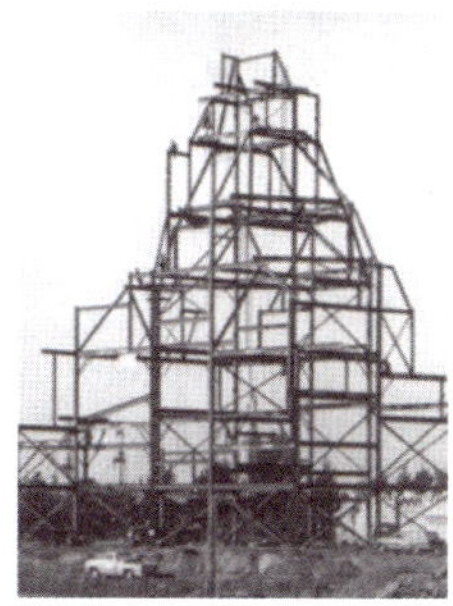

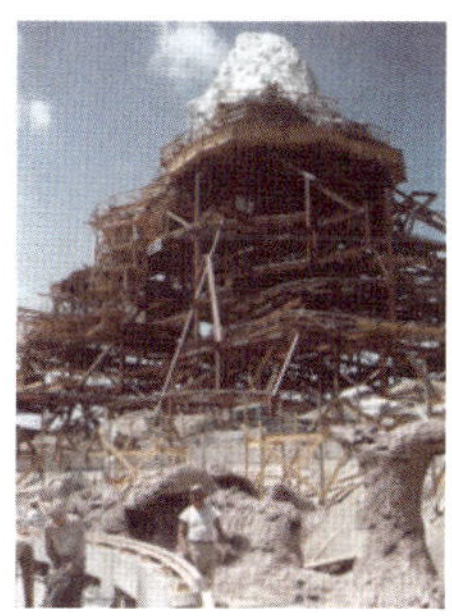

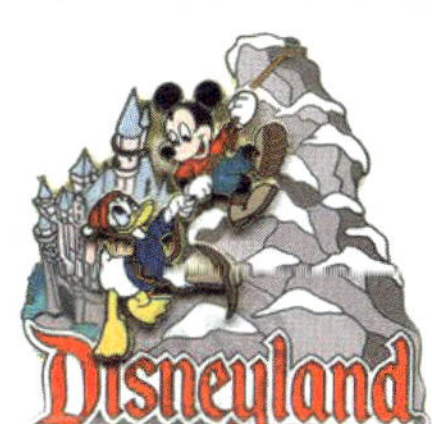

The icon in this case goes beyond the framework of the nation since the first Disneyland amusement park recreated the mountain and introduced it into its magic world.
The question then of who owns such icons is raised. Who indeed owns which brand?

Here, thanks to the progress that occurred in mapmaking, the form of the boot gradually grew more accurate. It only became a national symbol, however, in the nineteenth century. It is no less true for most maps representing nations. Their history is in fact more recent than they suggest.

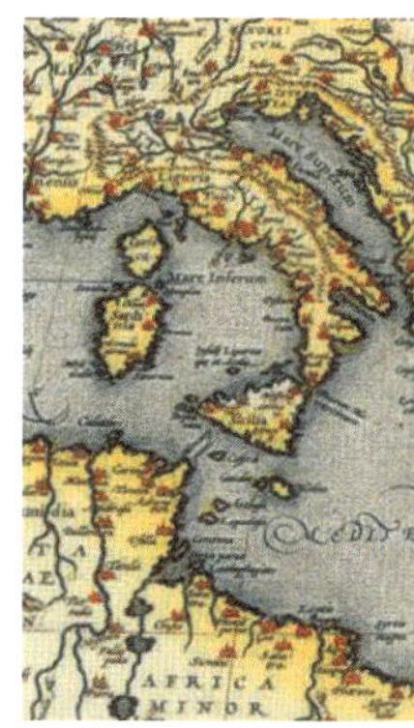

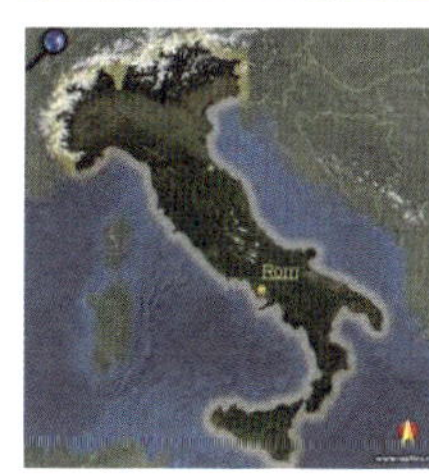

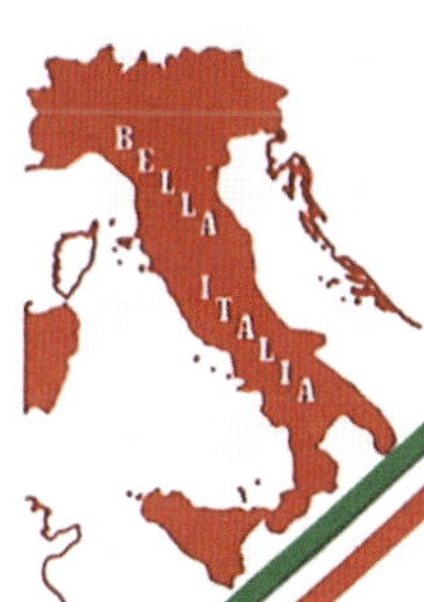

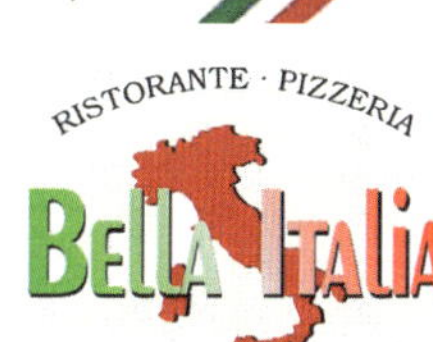

A country's map with an overlay of the national flag...

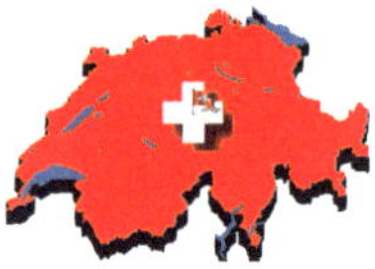

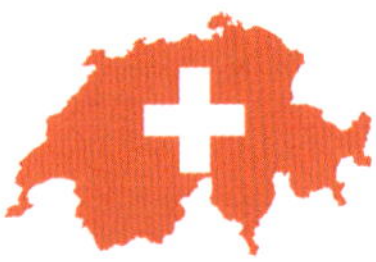

or the position of its various cantons...

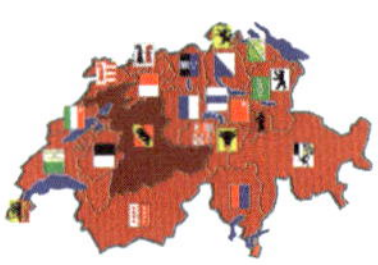

the map becomes a symbol...

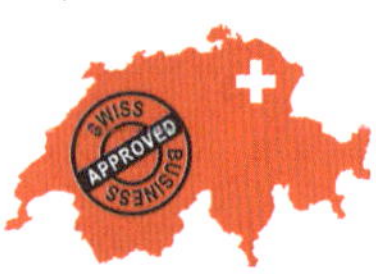

grows bigger...

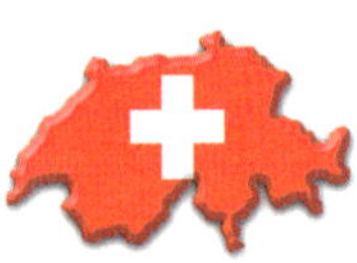

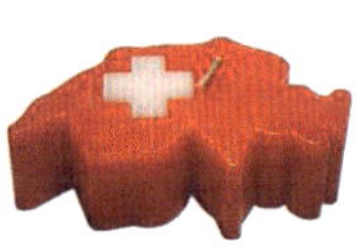

the flag bulks up...

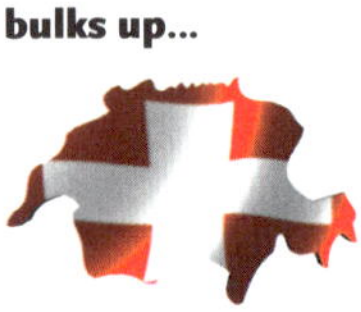

becomes the homeland.

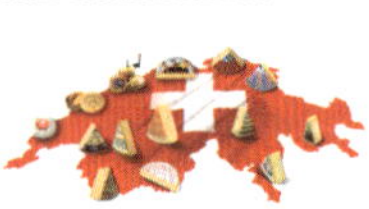

What does putting the map in perspective mean?

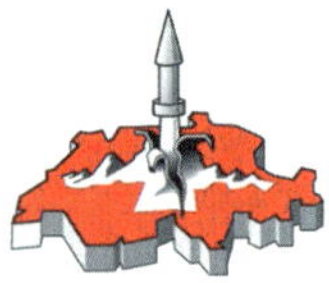

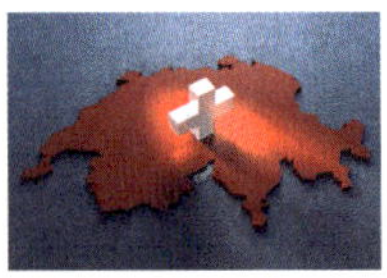

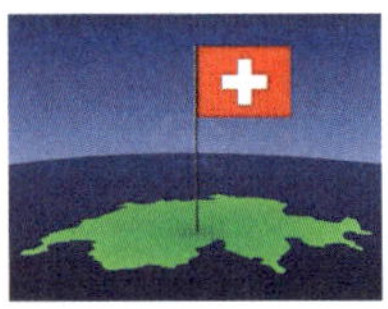

A land that a flag rules over.

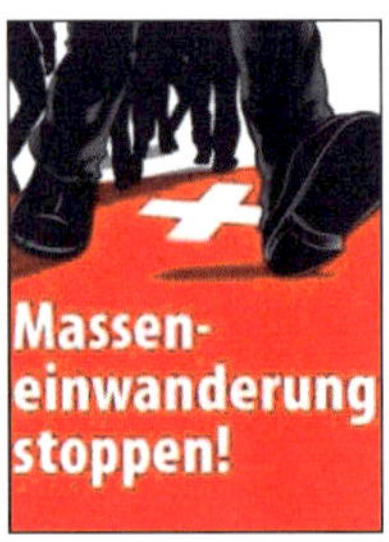

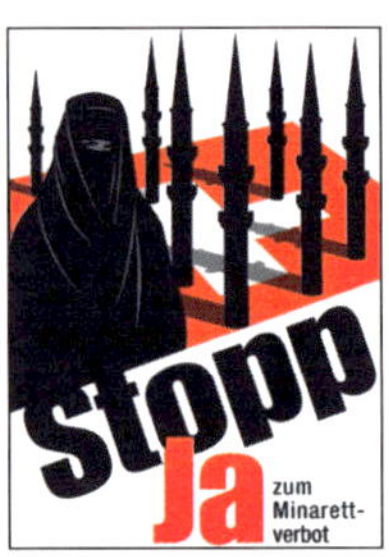

A similar perspective used to symbolize a country that is said to be threatened by immigration. Gradual shift towards a fascist iconography...

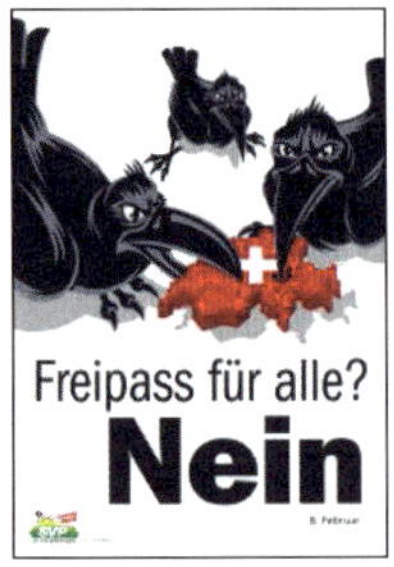

Where does the border lie, where do xenophobia, racism, visual nationalism begin?

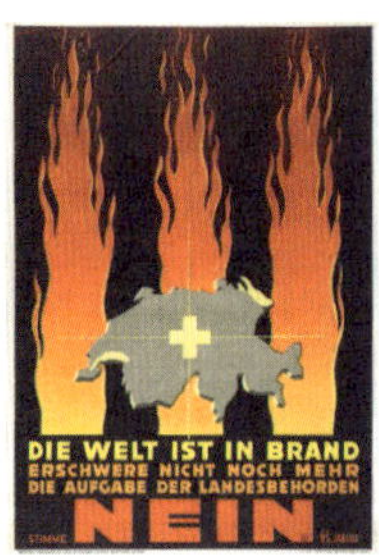

The same signs were already used in the 1930s.

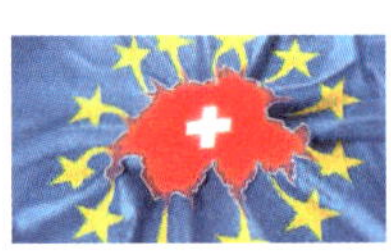

And again the construction of a national symbol, as a first step, which is then easily shown to be endangered.

The choice of Switzerland to raise this question of brand and branding is based on the fact that over the past few decades the country has fundamentally transformed its mode of representation, completely erasing its federal dimension, which is what sets it apart. This country, which has always been based on the culture of its differences, its linguistic differences, for example, has opted for a policy of representation that tends towards an erasure of all that.

It seems, for example, that people prefer the message given in English over multiplicity and contrast. Thus, the country seems to increasingly use the name "Swiss" rather than Suisse, Schweiz, or Svizerra.

The equilateral cross is now at the center of this visual bombardment.

It is interesting to recall here that this sign was only made official as a national emblem by the constitution of 1848.

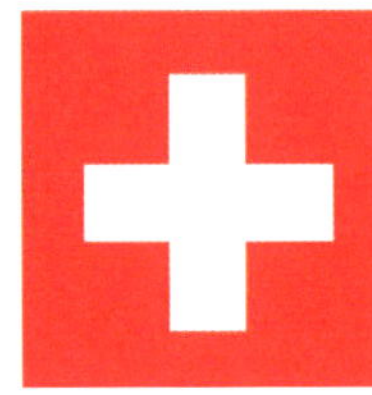

Nor is it the first Swiss flag because an initial national flag with horizontal stripes floated over the land when the republic was proclaimed in 1798.

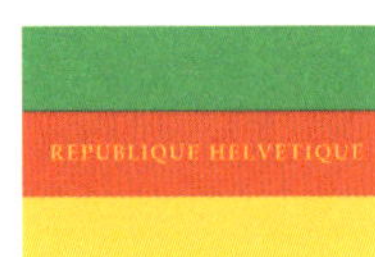

It disappeared as an official emblem in 1803.

The *Corporate Identity Manual Switzerland* dates from 2008. It defines the usage rules of official representations of the Swiss Confederation.

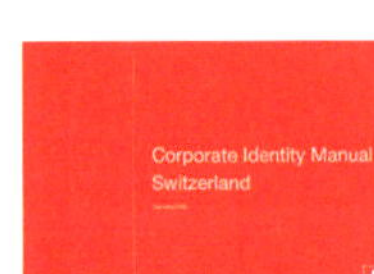

pictures. Finally, even though borders have remained relatively stable over the past decades, they have frequently changed in the course of various historical episodes. Yet these nondescript shapes constitute, for numerous nations, an important symbol alongside their national flag, a kind of conquered trophy, the proof of their existence, the expression of their exclusive dwelling, of territorial pride distinct from a non-represented "elsewhere." Easier to decode, the sign will mostly concern internal communication. It rallies everyone who identifies with it, and excludes those who cannot claim to belong to that territory. We are dealing here with the more or less direct legacy of nineteenth-century nationalisms, which bring us closer to the dubious notions of land and motherland.

Without generalizing the nationalist and often regionalist character of territorial representations, the point still remains to distinguish the reproductions of geological realities from the act of enhancing the visibility of political borders. While an analysis of the official logos of countries and regions worldwide shows that islands are the territories which most often resort to that kind of official representation, this is no longer the case when we incorporate in our analysis other accompanying signs of national identity such as stamps, coins, and the logos of national organizations. Switzerland, for instance, an isolated island in the center of Europe, striving with some difficulty to go beyond its national concept, makes extensive use of that territorial symbol. Its surface area is thus reproduced at every opportunity, no longer—as used to be the case—in order to map its dimension as a confederacy, its cantons, or its wealth of languages, but indeed to express the territory's national unity. In addition, the racist posters produced by nationalist and populist parties rely precisely on the representation of a red-colored territory from which white sheep are kicking out the black ones.

The Flag as Brand

The signs analyzed above, even if they are part of the symbolic environment of a territory, do not have the official character of the emblem or the flag. They do not directly represent an elected political body, although they do have an influence on its representation. Through the similarity of their visual approaches, an important confusion is established between what falls within the domain of the state and hence the political, and what would be the nation, that is, the land with its borders, interior and exterior.

To continue with our analysis of the example of Switzerland, it is clear that territorial symbols are many. They are put to completely different ends by a range of actors. They can be seen promoting the country, notably abroad, both politically and economically. The different actors in the tourism sector make particular use of these symbols to promote a uniform territorial ideal in a way, which for Switzerland is quite a stretch. At the same time, political movements, and notably those extolling a nationalist agenda, use these same signs as propaganda and informational tools. Referendums and other questions put to Swiss voters thus produce a plethora of expressions based on these symbols whose aim is to convince citizens of the risk of one decision or another for the nation, even to rally them around the latter. For some citizens, the connection with these signs is even more direct. They use them to symbolize their home, their country, or values they are proud of. They are not shy about bringing out the flag, including abroad. Thus, the white equilateral cross on a red background floats over campgrounds around the world, for example. Inside the country, these patriotic signs serve as a tool for hierarchization, even exclusion—expressing the fact that one comes from this territory, and thinking one has therefore a greater right than those who cannot claim the same status.

Use of these patriotic symbols is not limited to individuals, parties, or political entities, since they are borrowed as a label or brand for companies wanting to express their value as a product of Switzerland, but also for those wanting to symbolize their national field of activity, their domain of responsibility, or their connection with the state. All of them use these same symbols to excess. The most visible example remains naturally the airline that took over from Swissair, whose bankruptcy was felt to be a national tragedy. The decision to draw even closer to Swiss symbolism by using the name Swiss and dressing it up with a Swiss cross was undermined a bit by the fact that the airline was bought out by the German company Lufthansa. The branding strategy based on Swiss symbols was shamelessly continued. Reality is overlooked. This is proof, if ever there was, of the capacity to construct a national delusion based on corporations. Moreover, who knows who owns Lufthansa's capital? All of this mixes and merges, creating complete illegibility or perhaps a visual unity that in the end differs little from what was once decried as propaganda.

Historical analysis of the use of this country's symbols shows an increasing disappearance of the expression of the Swiss confederacy in favor of this national visual unity. The image of this joining of cantons able to express their differences while forming a coherent whole becomes illegible. Beyond the political reason for this visual uniformization taking shape around national symbols only, another question is raised: What is the contemporary capacity of the representation of a coherent diversity or even of a cosmopolitanism that is quite real all the same?

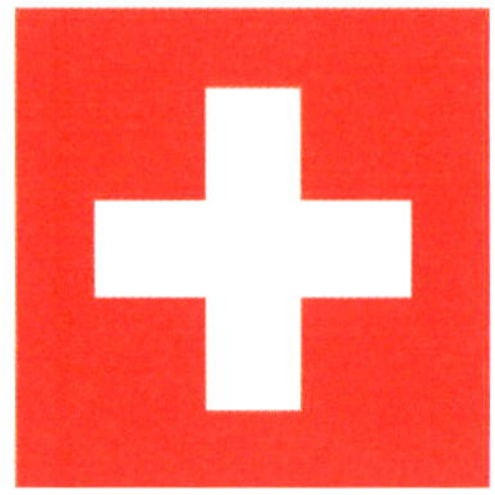

The flag is probably the most official emblem of the Swiss Confederation. At the same time, it is also the one that is used the most by the greatest range of designers.

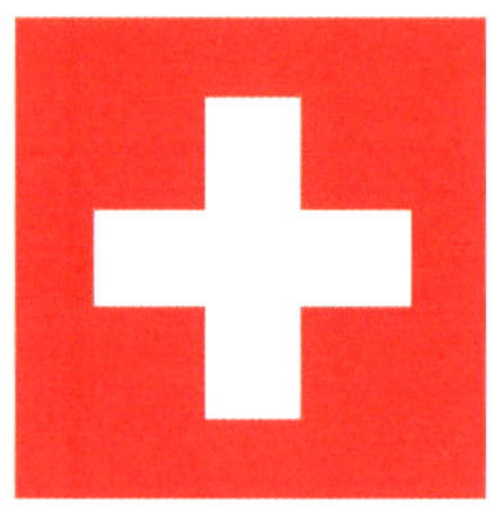

Switzerland.

The official brand taken from the visual identity manual is none other than the Swiss national emblem with the subtitle "Switzerland" followed by a full stop, written out in Helvetica and translated into the language of the target country.

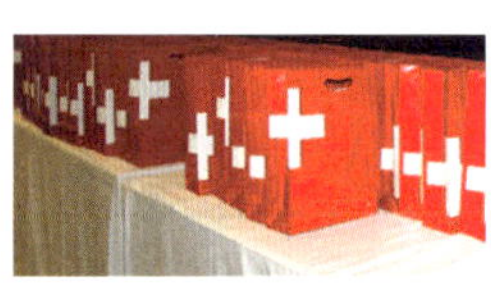

The organization Presence Switzerland is in charge of the Swiss image abroad.

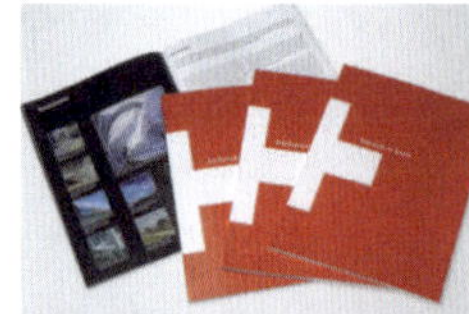

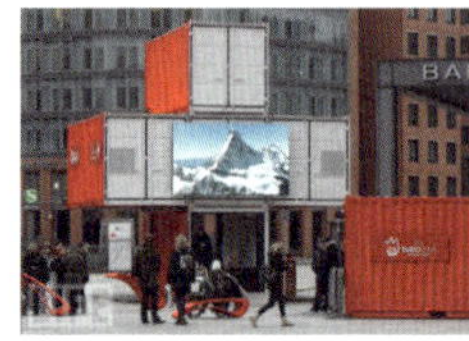

On the other hand, the state is presented quite plainly and employs the heraldic shield generally accompanied by "Swiss Confederation" written out in the country's four official languages.

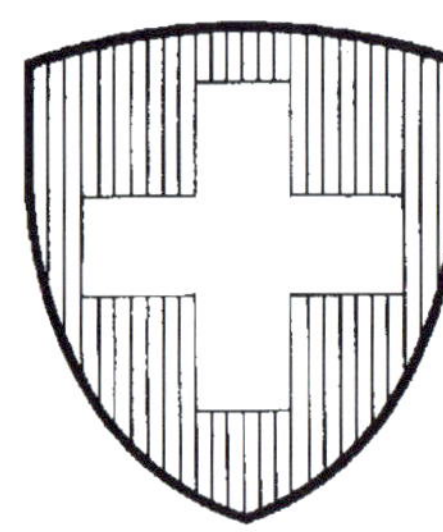

Schweizerische Eidgenossenschaft
Confédération suisse
Confederazione Svizzera
Confederaziun svizra

Another manual defines the way in which each state body must be presented. The whole is very dry and serious, with no visual difference setting off the various public services. Only culture escapes this absolute uniformity so often difficult to decode.

Citizens are equipped with passports and identity cards;

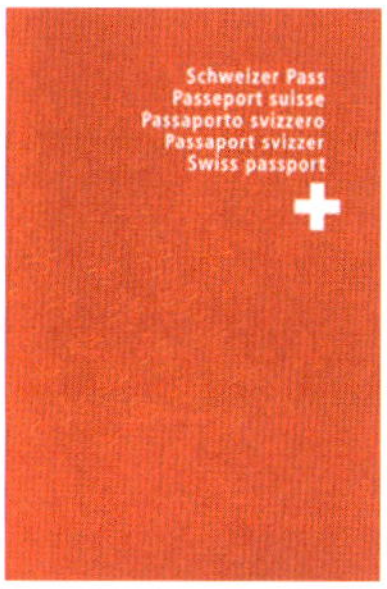

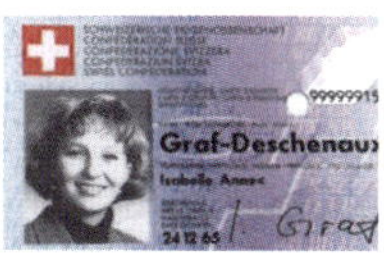

they handle the national currency that bears both Helvetia, an effigy of nineteenth-century national construction, and Swiss figures from the world of culture such as Le Corbusier and Giacometti.

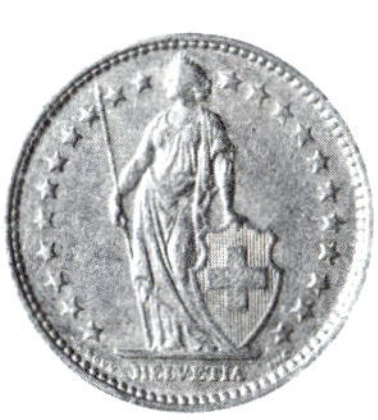

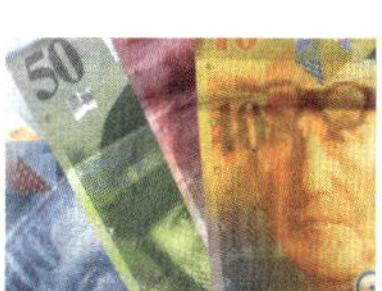

These banknotes miraculously avoid the visual bombardment of a message.

A series of acronyms identify the major public institutions.

A specific brand promotes Swiss tourism,

while a range of other signs act to protect Swiss products.

Public services, even more or less privatized ones, are in the same vein.

This visual atmosphere isn't just a state matter. Many trade associations and the like have adopted similar emblems.

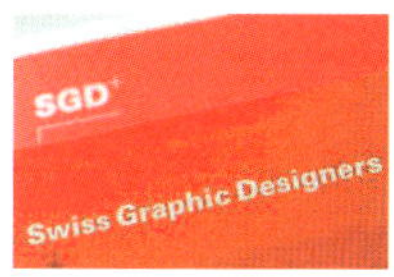

The colors red and white equipped with a cross likewise dominate lots of sports federations.

With advertising budgets that dwarf governmental ones, large companies that are more or less Swiss couch their visual identity in the same visual principles.

A few examples among many.

It should be clear that the term Swiss dominates.

Nor is the church remiss here. More surprising is the sign's reappropriation by opposition movements.

Some companies tie their image to the state's in an even more direct manner.

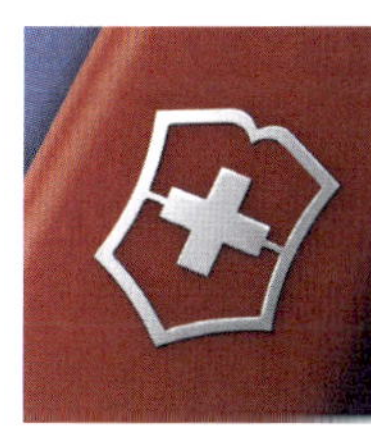

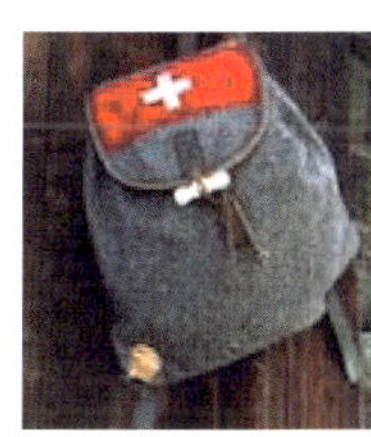

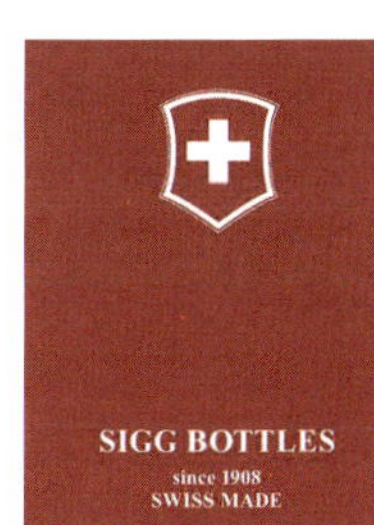

The term *branding*, however, perfectly designates those examples that consist of applying to any object or event a mark, a brand, that makes us view the former through the latter.

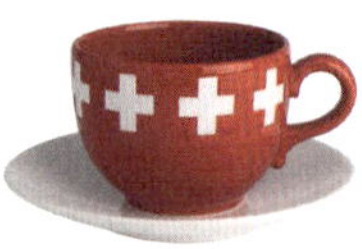

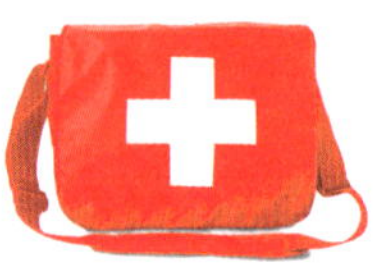

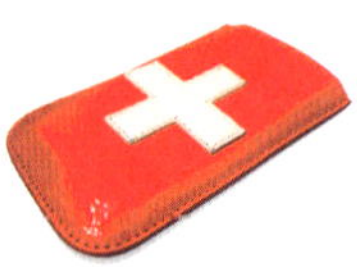

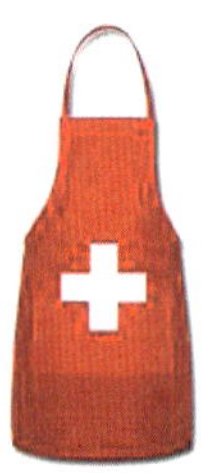

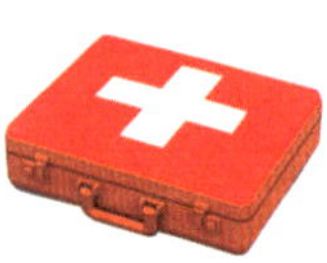

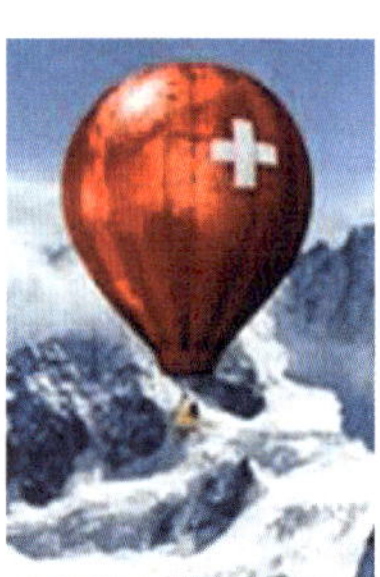

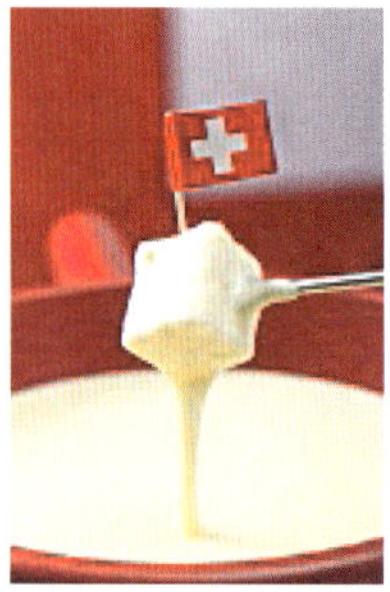

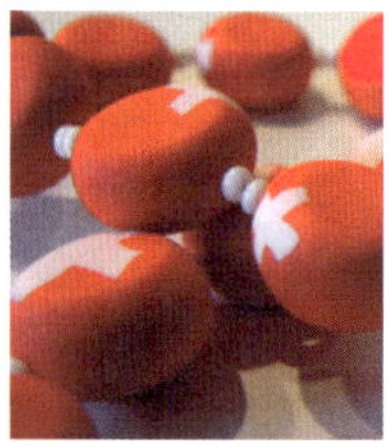

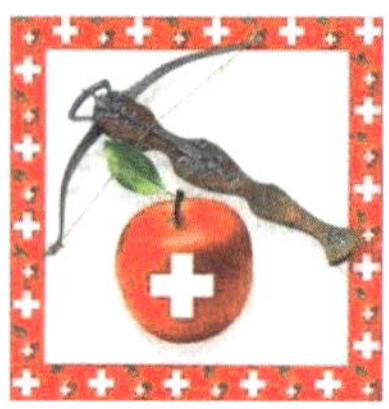

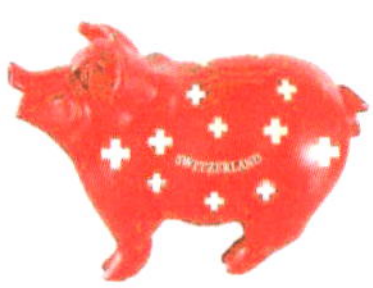

Terrible simplification, reduction of differences, disappearance of minorities. What was once the symbol of a dual regional and cantonal identity is the mere splitting of the same thing.

Swiss products seem only able to hang on by clinging

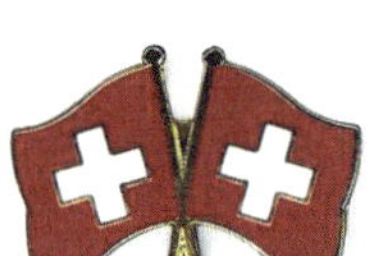

to their brand, proof positive of their Swissness if ever there was. Does one eat a certain type of

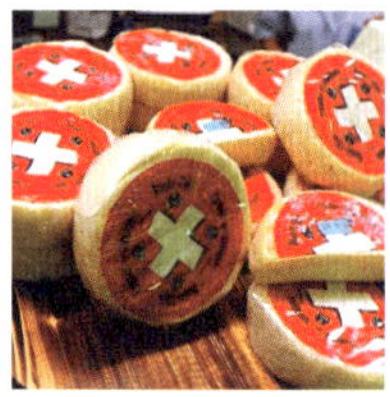

cheese for its taste, or for the place where it was made? Can the latter guarantee by itself the quality of the cheese?

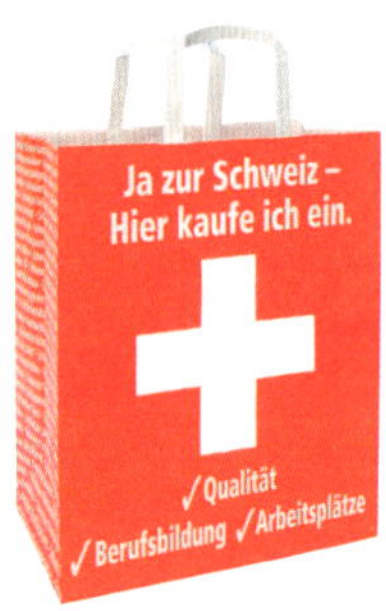

Ihr Schweizer Gewerbe
in-der-Schweiz-gekauft.ch

Clearly a new form of protectionism is taking shape through the image.

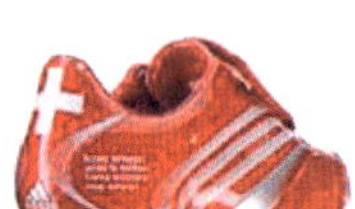

The cross lends value to the product, even when produced far from the country it symbolizes. I shall come back to this.

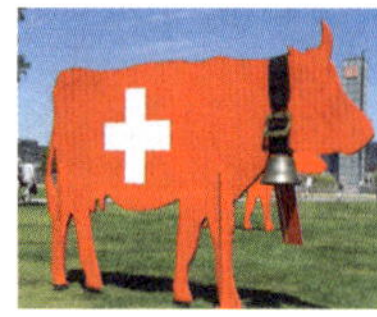

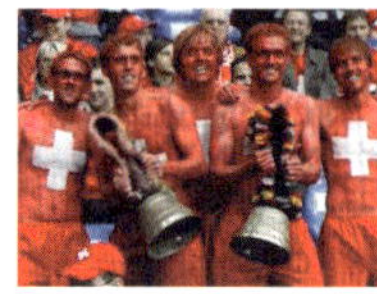

Of course traditions keep bursting in on every side, but beware, the expression will be all the more formidable when it has a contemporary stamp.

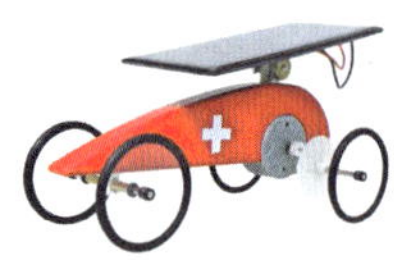

And once again there is that shift without borders towards the populist simplifications…

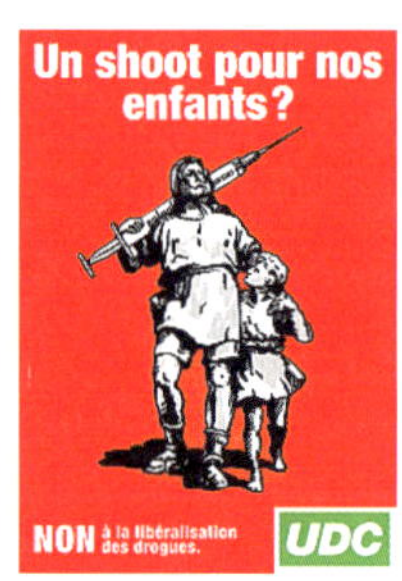

Branding: more than air bubbles.

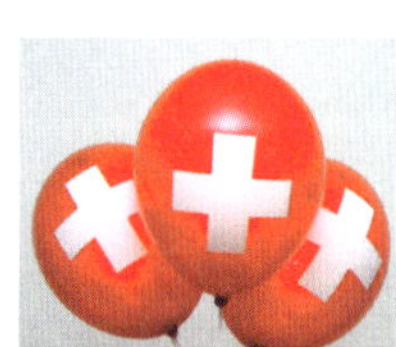

Whether improvised or well organized, fan demonstrations perfectly echo all of this.

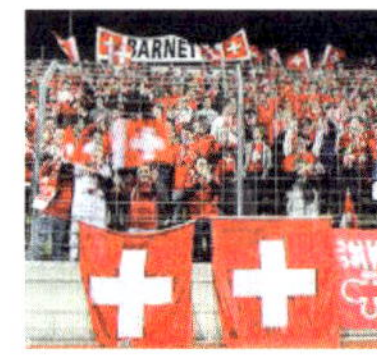

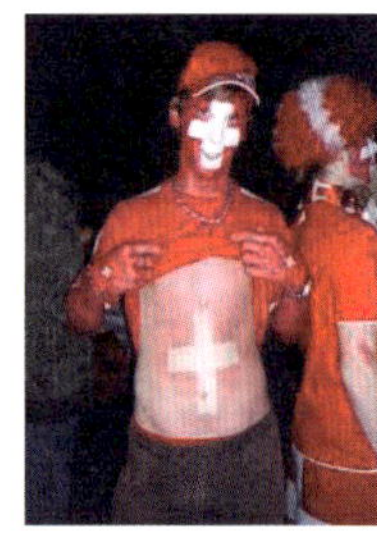

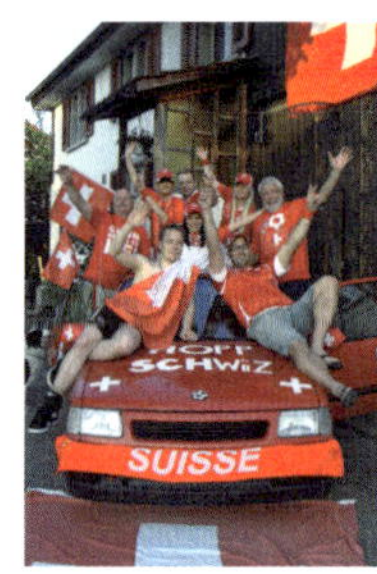

The whole phenomenon is harmless, some will say, while others will assert that it is a typically Swiss exception, the most perfect of democracies, what a success, the citizens are backing it…

These opinions remain hard to refute, and are part of a coherent whole: a successful brand?

The Manual of the Territorial Brand

It is called the *Corporate Identity Manual Switzerland,* as if Switzerland were a corporation. Use of the copy-paste function is obvious. Yet already in the introduction we find the objective clearly spelled out. The aim is to establish "nation Switzerland" as a strong international brand. "The uniform appearance is the base to increase the impact of our activities by a higher degree of recognition [*sic*]." One of the first chapters deals with the connection between the corporate design of the Swiss Confederation, which is "the visual identity of the federal administration," and "Corporate Identity Switzerland," which "is an instrument of Nation Branding." Identity Switzerland defines Switzerland's values and messages... It is a matter of imposing the image one wants to project of oneself on the image that others on their own will construct for themselves—transmitting a positive image of the country. If this is not propaganda, it certainly looks a lot like it. To define that image, one has to choose the average points of intersection between expectations abroad and the image the Swiss have of their own country. Thus we see, for example, that the question of diversity is excluded from the zone where reality, personal image, and exterior image intersect. That the red and white and the Swiss cross are depicted there. That direct democracy and international organizations are absent while financial centers are very well placed. These values later appear broken down so as to define in one part the appearances in which all the clichés are found (mountain, Swiss cross, red and white, bank and bank secrecy, pocket knife, wristwatch, chocolate, and cheese). All of this is simplified around mountain inhabitants, the Swiss cross, the colors red and white, and the people. You have got to have human smiles in creating advertising. We are plunged here in that form of extreme simplification that fortunately renders in the end each of these branding operations both similar and unbelievable. The question that concerns us is: Can Swiss citizens, in their significant diversity, see themselves in this? That is, whether the image being disseminated here truly corresponds with what they are, experience, and wish for. Whether another world isn't being imposed on them.

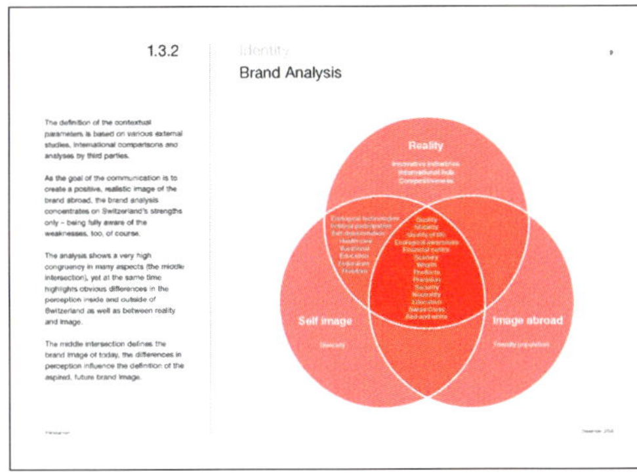

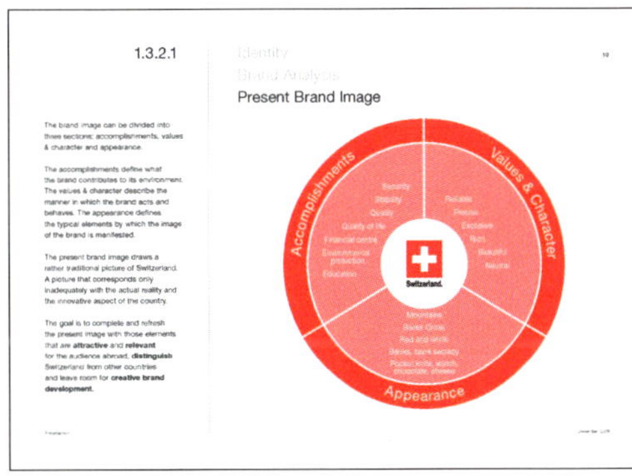

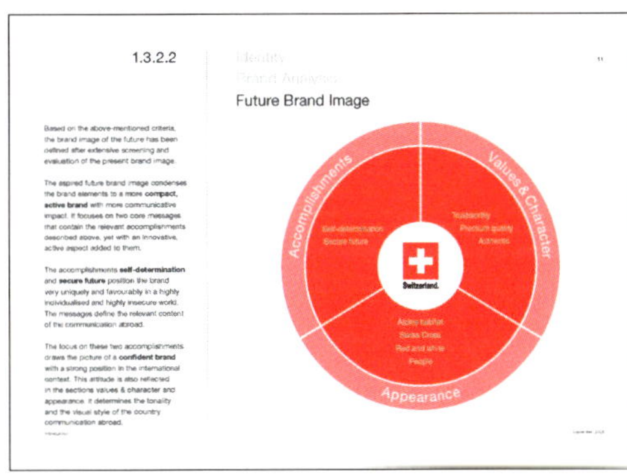

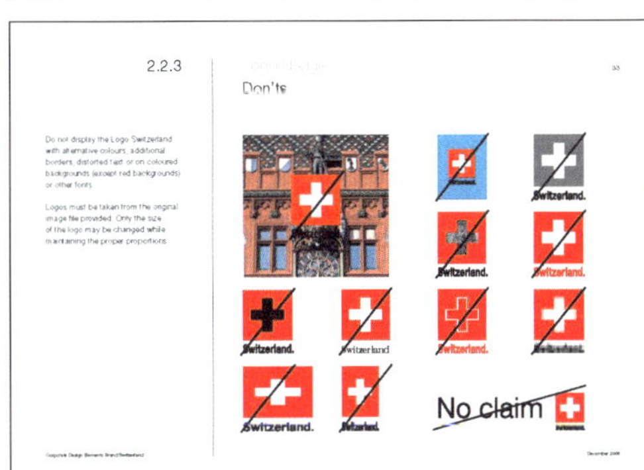

Following these introductory pages on the values that ought to be transmitted, the manual deals with geographical questions by attempting to master visual appearance on the broadest range of supports.

The semiotic environment of a Swiss citizen in the 2010s

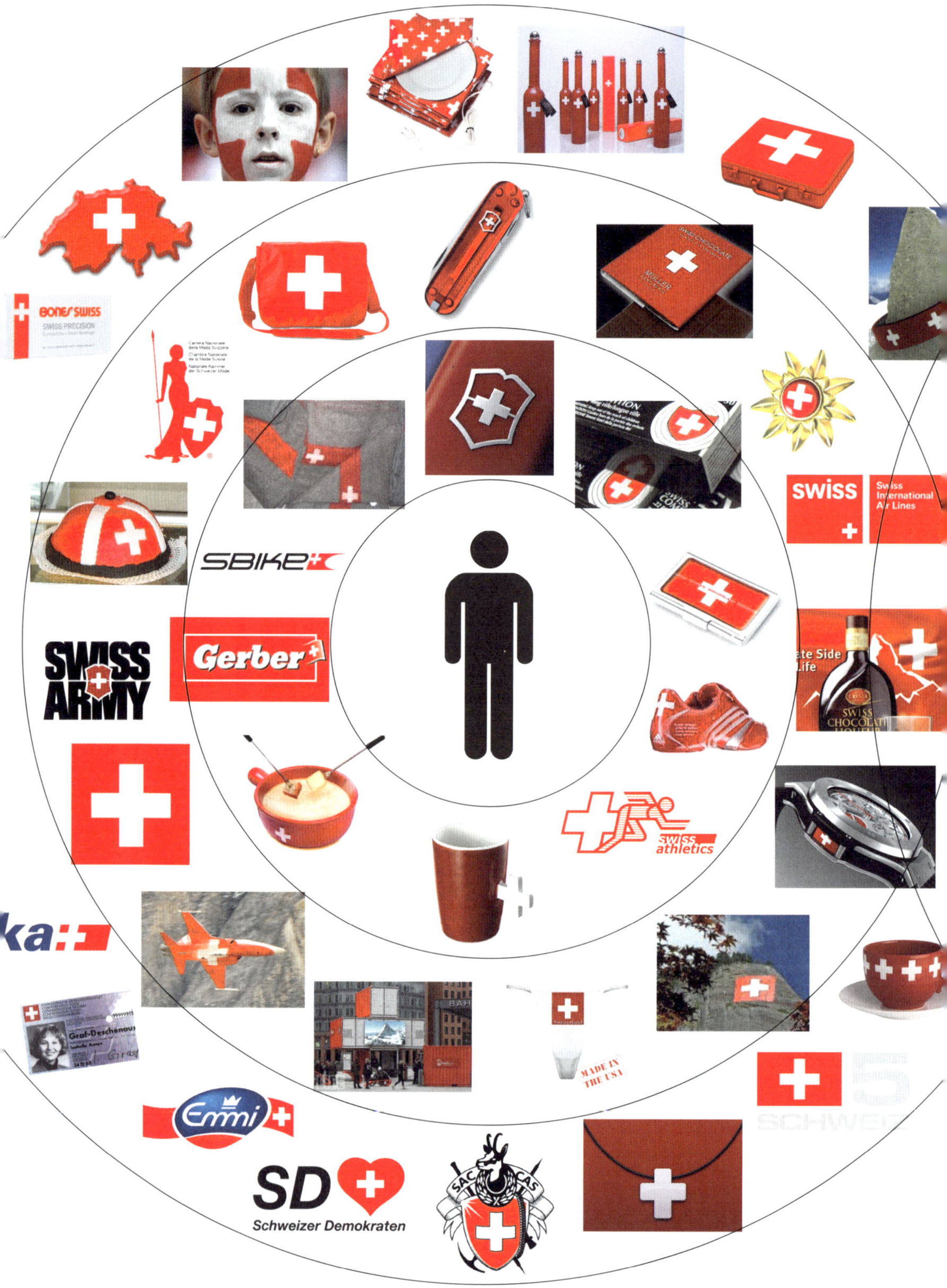

The semiotic environment of a Chinese citizen in the 1970s through 1990s

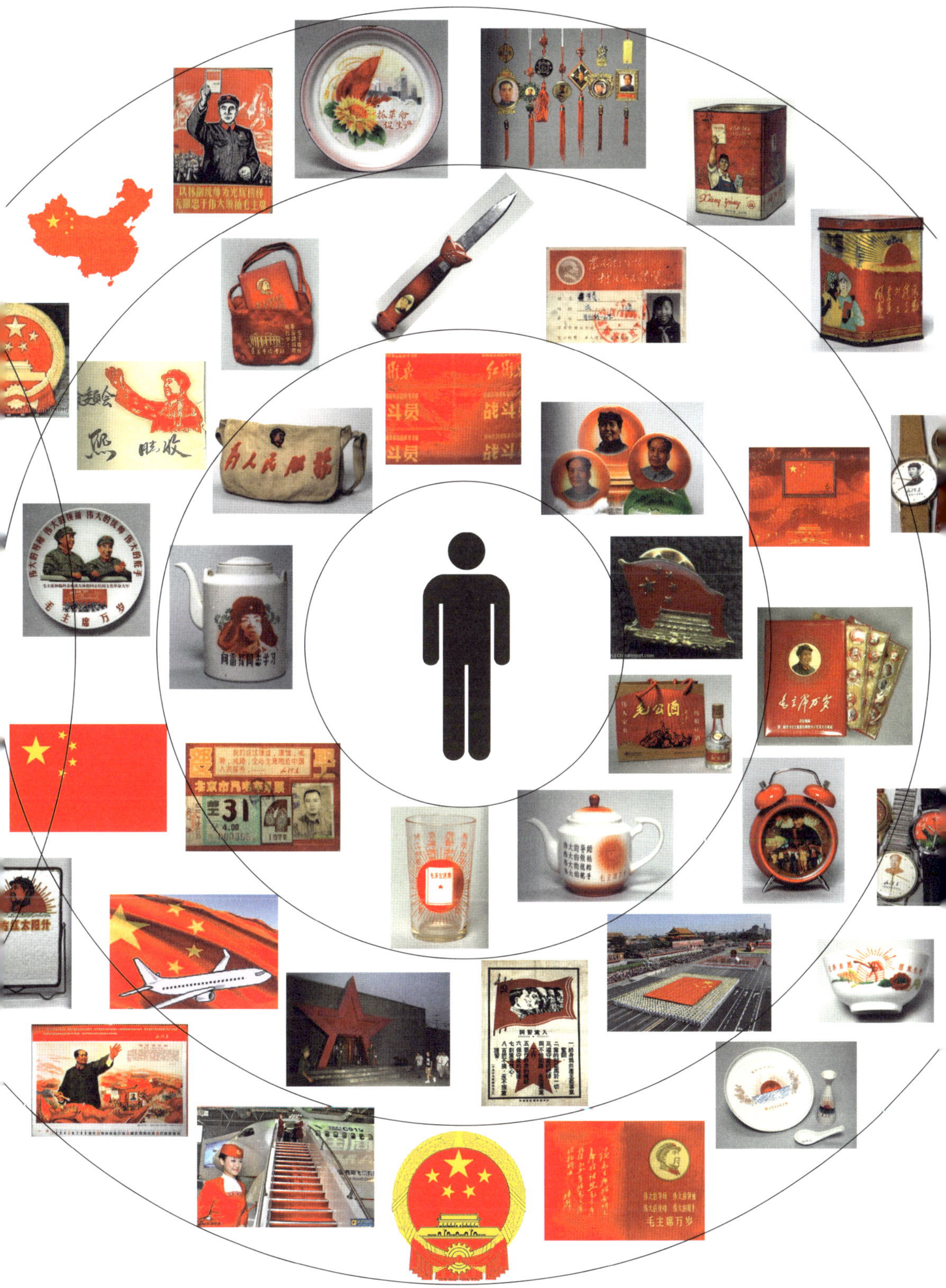

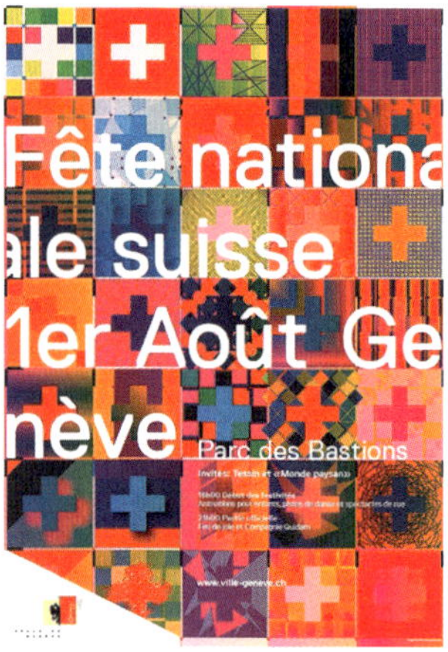

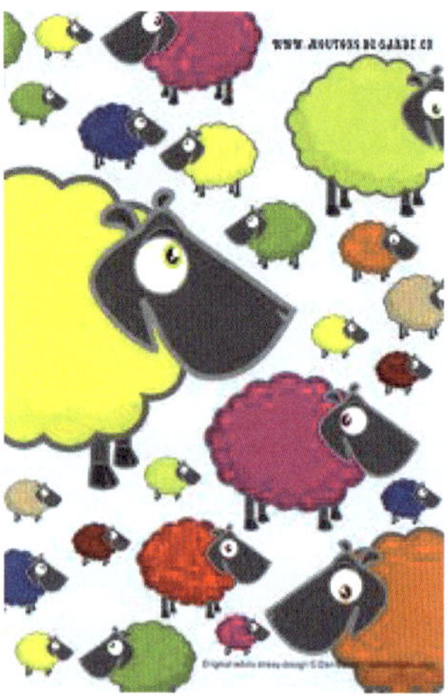

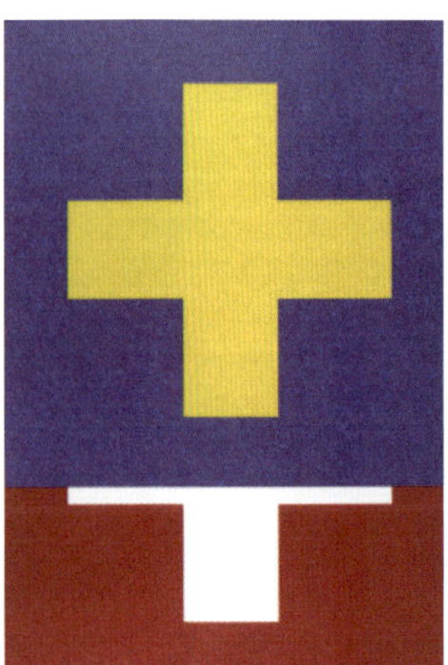

Three ways of representing Switzerland differently, three reactions to visual uniformity and the policy of branding. Many other examples could be included on this page, of course.

This case study would not be complete, however, if we did not present those areas of resistance which, unlike under a dictatorship, aren't censured and are even occasionally commissioned by state entities. We shall not linger long over this counterproduction since it is not the subject of this study. More interesting is the analysis of several other examples drawn from different contexts. They will allow us to leave this particular case and return to the principles that concern us here. First, however, we shall remain with the case of national territories before turning to other entities in a second part.

The Brand of a Developing Country

Having analyzed the brand of one of the richest countries in the world, it might be interesting to make the comparison with several developing countries. We observe two types of brands, those which correspond to the local visual culture, and those, on the contrary, which try to correspond to the visual culture of rich countries. Peru's new brand, for example, also red and white by the way, was designed by a major company in London and very clearly displays a number of graphic qualities. The sign, however, offers us an altogether predictable image of a Peru that resembles those luxury hotels that cultivate a minimum of exoticism in structures that are absolutely identical to the ones found everywhere around the world. Do we have here a new international code dictating that this country be marked by a cross while that other one must sport a spiral, a bit like the coats of arms in the late Middle Ages; or are we in a neoliberal competitive framework where even individual territories struggle among themselves, at the risk of simply reproducing models that work? Both seem true.

First of all, graphic designers, branding agencies, and the people who hire them are all in a system so self-referential that very quickly a model that works is reproduced along with that necessary little adaptation. In a word, we are not in a stable system like heraldry. For some fifty years, signs and identification systems have existed in permanent visual change. They follow trends that hardly last more than those of advertising campaigns, then fall out of favor and become tiresome.

Like logos, these national brands could be typified. It is clear, however, that there is a heightened tendency toward the seductive image of advertising. One often sees slogans and visualizations that are akin to ads.

Below: Three brands of Italy since the 1980s.

This raises the question of the more important durability of certain signs with respect to others. While we might suppose that the brand devised for Singapore, which is based on a graphic effect that is now very much in vogue, will prove hard to justify in a few years, we see that the Spanish Miró, though quite convincing, is beginning to show its age. Whereas it continues to function as a recognizable element, it symbolizes, I think, an age that no longer really exists.

All this wouldn't be half so serious if it weren't in fact the state that was defining those points of view, that vision, that staged presentation to which citizens can only submit. For it is indeed they who find themselves symbolized through the chosen values. All Spaniards thus find themselves represented through the artistic sign of Spain. No Swiss citizen can escape the absolutism of the cross, and what will the Serbs think of the representation of their country?

Yet, as we have seen, our identity is fortunately not defined only through a single territorial scale, i.e., the nation, and many of us would feel quite hemmed in if we had to identify with one nation alone. This is not to say we wouldn't accept civic contracts and political rules from the different political authorities we have to face.

Made in...

The 2012 parliamentary debates on the regulations affecting the "Made in Switzerland" designation symbolize fairly clearly the contradictions that arise in these national quality-assurance labels within the context of globalization. The Swiss government proposed heightening the value of the label by controlling its use and limiting it to goods in which 60 percent of the finished product could be attributed to Swiss factories or companies. The enormous fuss that was kicked up, notably by small and medium-sized companies, showed that this measure affects the very heart and soul of how they work. They believe that these measures are likely to put them at a disadvantage, either by forcing them to produce at a higher cost inside the country, or by excluding them from the symbolism of the

The brand can be had by any company now producing in France.

A minimum of 50 percent of the cost price per unit must be French and the product must have in large part French characteristics. In the name of the free circulation of goods and services, European member states do not have the right to provide direct support for national labeling efforts.

Despite these laws, the labels exist. They try to voice their official character. Contrary to appearances, each sign only guarantees a slight percentage of what is expressed.

The labels are not only related to national territories. They touch on regions, even mountain ranges in the Alps, for instance.

nation. Many of them referred to Germany, which is happy with a production of 45 percent on the national territory in order for the "Made in Germany" label to apply. France stands about midway with its 50 percent. Neither the lie perpetrated against the consumer, nor the subject of workers who are more deeply exploited abroad, is brought up in these nationalist debates. However, at the same time, the traceability of products is indeed being demanded. "Product standardization and anonymity are contrary to efforts in favor of traceability, transparency, and proximity within a context of overwhelming globalization," Yves Jégo declared at the presentation of the logo "Origine France Garantie." Products might be deprived of a label that sets them apart, putting them in competition with products subjected to environmental, social, or quality regulations that are less stringent.

This tiny sign which indicates the origin of a product, and whose use is regulated by the public domain, is thus at the center of the contradictions affecting capitalism in its current form. Because of delocalization, products have lost their connection with their production site. As Naomi Klein shows in *No Logo*, the manufacturing of brand products is generally carried out by anonymous subcontractors according to production costs. Since the cost of transportation is often lower than the profit from an overexploited workforce in a distant country, there is little question of delocalizing production wholly or in part. In order to sell in rich countries and set oneself apart from a down-market product, such a product must, on the contrary, make clear that it belongs to the trustworthy countries.

Whether it is by the "made in" label or more directly through the name and identity of the brand, the connection with a nation is expressed in a more or less obvious way. What used to involve import taxes is nowadays replaced by an expression of territorial identity in products and companies that creates a border just as formidable while not really corresponding to reality. This phenomenon affects both medium-sized and large companies. For the latter, the phenomenon is further heightened by the anonymity of capital that no longer corresponds with the country claimed by the brand, as we have seen, for example, with the airline company called Swiss.

In this context then, the "made in" label looks to protect those enterprises which, more than many others, are still trying perhaps to produce locally for social or ecological reasons, or reasons having to do with protecting the local area. At the same time, negotiations around the percentages of what is really developed in the country make plain the limits of the operation. The consumer, both in the country and abroad, little aware of these negotiations about percentages, does not know that a guarantee of product origin rests on a figure of only 60 percent, even 45 percent of the product. The sign, which is nonetheless certified by officials at the national level, thus does not correspond with the truth. It raises the question of the need—in terms of correct information—to impose real product traceability that would make it possible to inform consumers about the place where the product was designed and manufactured, attendant social and environmental conditions, the materials and advertising budgets that were mobilized, even the capital involved. This kind of product legibility would be more honest than the fake national labels.

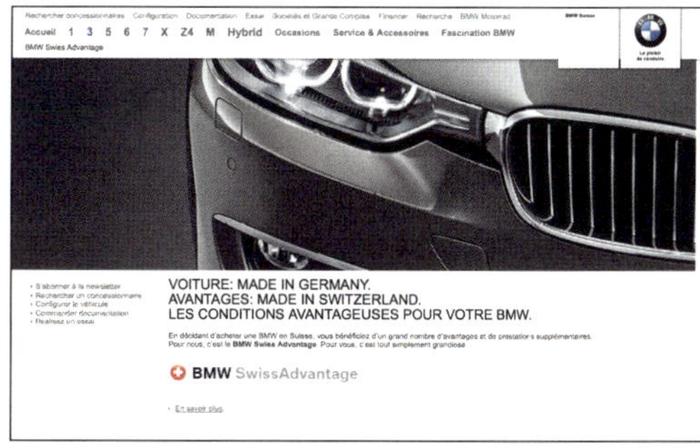

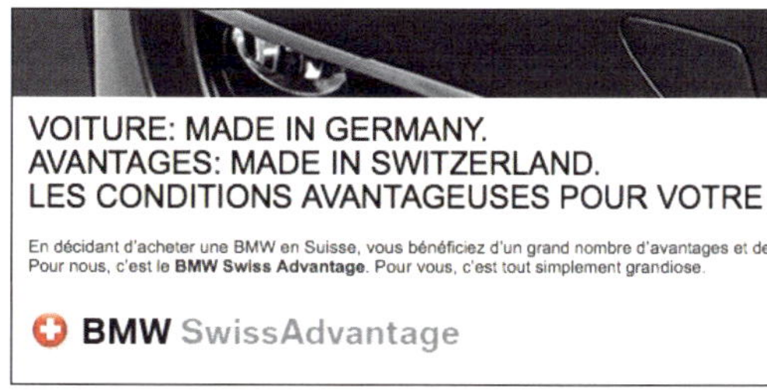

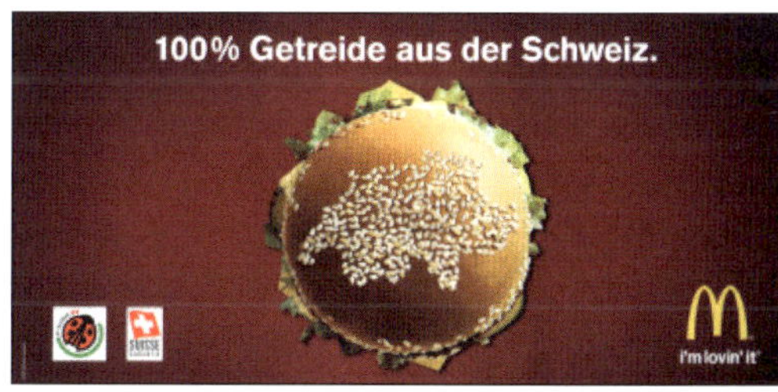

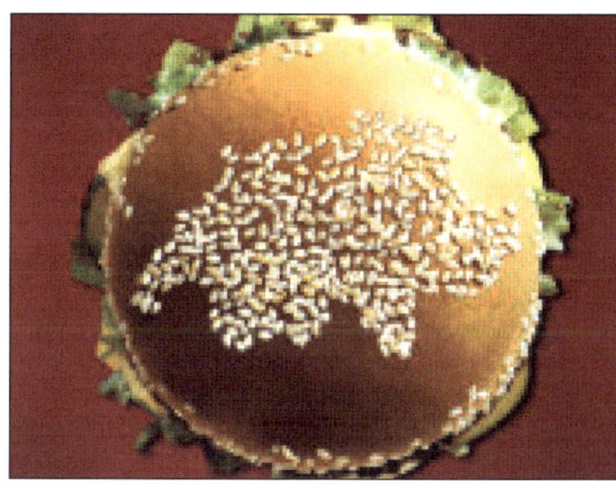

Your ID!

Some customs resist transformation. The custom of defining a human being starting with a family's country of origin doesn't seem to be really affected by the evolution going on in our lifestyles, a radical evolution nonetheless. Beyond the immigrations and multigenerational mixing of ethnicities, our reality as consumers of products, impressions, and information rejects in a deep way the notions of national borders. The perfecting of interactions at a distance is completing a long process of "simultaneization" of the planet, which began with the invention of the printing press and the dissemination of millions of Bibles, then picked up steam once the planet had been utterly conquered by the revolution in our means of communication and the great European migrations to America. It has continued with the internationalization and subsequent globalization of markets, real-time access to the same information, and especially the digitalization and

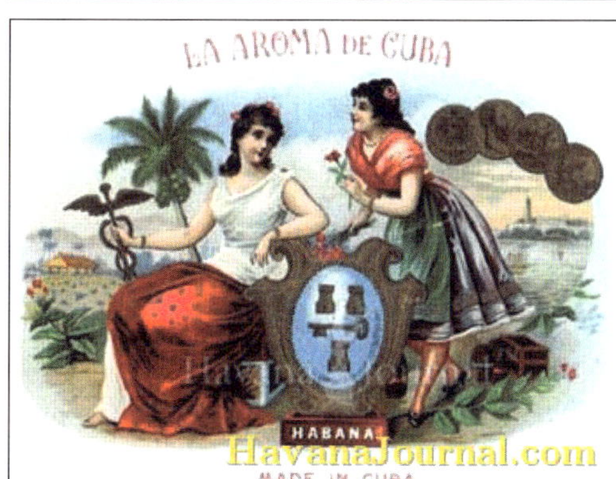

Sad French invention: the nationalist government of Vichy forced everyone within its borders to obtain an identity card. Jews and other communities that were suspect to this racist political organization were identified by an additional stamp. The identity card was not rescinded after the Occupation, however. The principle has even been picked up by a significant number of countries around the world. Nowadays computer technology extensively reinforces this principle of keeping tabs on citizens, even in their own land.

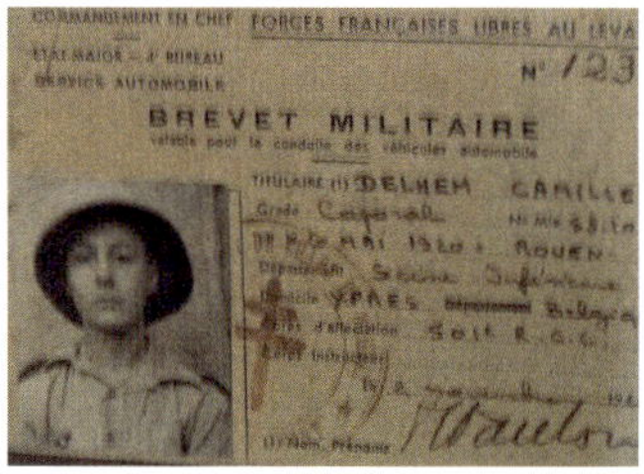

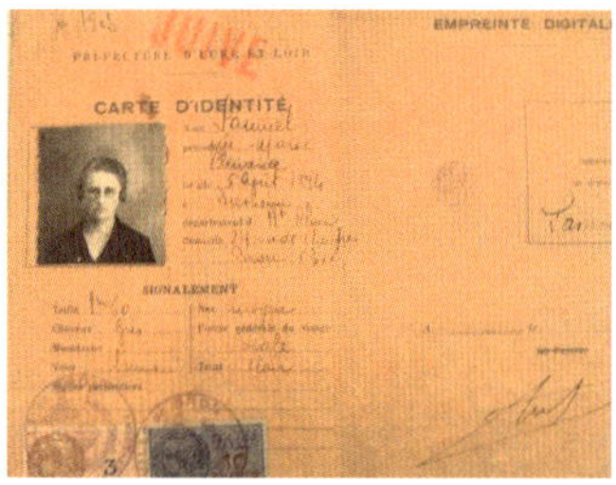

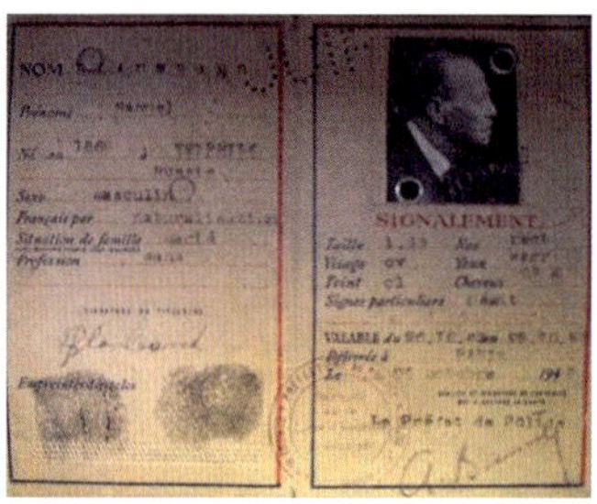

online posting of a tremendous amount of knowledge along with industrial and even cultural output. If not the peoples of the different countries, at least the inhabitants of the large cities find themselves today on the same network of references, which is more interurban than international, moreover. It is based on a certain planetary cosmopolitanism. However one judges this evolution, it seems absolutely irreversible. Even if preserving cultural diversity forms an indispensable objective, it cannot involve either isolating peoples or hindering access to this planetary reality. It is impossible to imagine today a country that is not in a situation of interdependency with the rest of the world. The absurd example of North Korea is ample proof of that.

Yet it is in the course of building this world based on exchange and mixture that borders crystalized, governments and legal systems were reinforced, and these systems of national representation and myths took shape. The entire planet seems almost just as definitively divided up into so-called sovereign territories with airtight borders and more or less independent governments, although containing a specific population. To be stateless in this systematic division of the planet's surface suggests the impossible or Kafkaesque horror. Doesn't the concept of citizen of the world or even citizen of Europe correspond to a status that today would liberate one from the status related to the nation? Every newborn continues to systematically inherit a nationality. In other words, a territory to which one belongs, the territory of at least one of one's parents and at best the place of one's birth. But whatever the choice and situation of one's kin, one is immediately tied—for better or worse and in a lasting way—to that territory. Identity papers quickly make this tie of dependency official, placing some among the privileged, and others, often definitively, among the wretched of the earth. It is a legal, cultural, and symbolic connection that profoundly defines each existence and takes shape as a kind of confinement for some and an elite status for others. Rare are those who, at the risk of their lives at times, manage after long and hard-fought battles with red tape to change the territory to which they are attached. They will remain suspect,

Above: Ludwig van Beethoven's genealogical tree indicating the trades and places of birth of his ancestors.

Below: Map representing migration and refugee flows. We see that Europe has been relatively spared these population movements by comparison with other points around the globe.

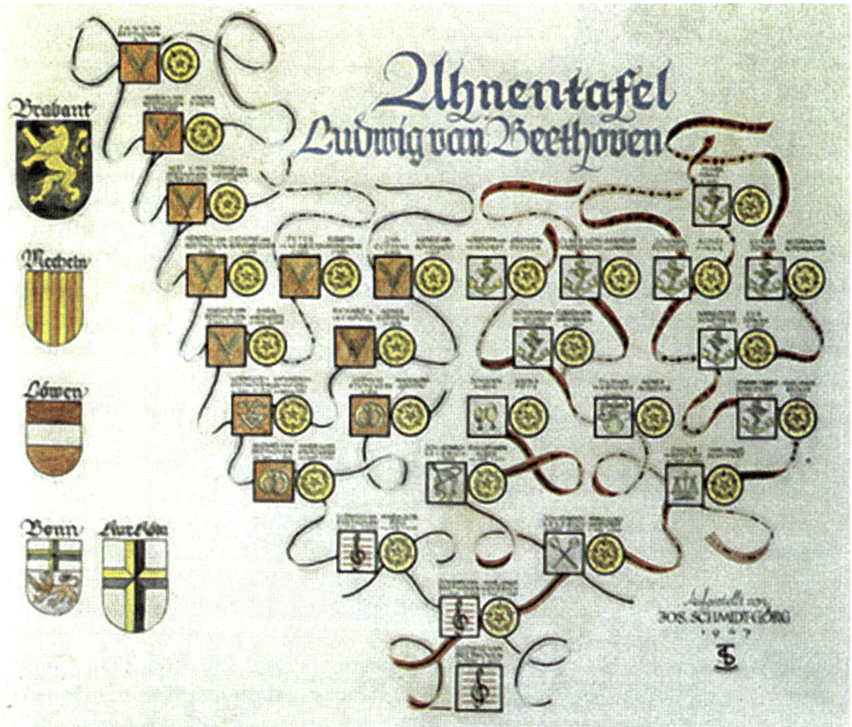

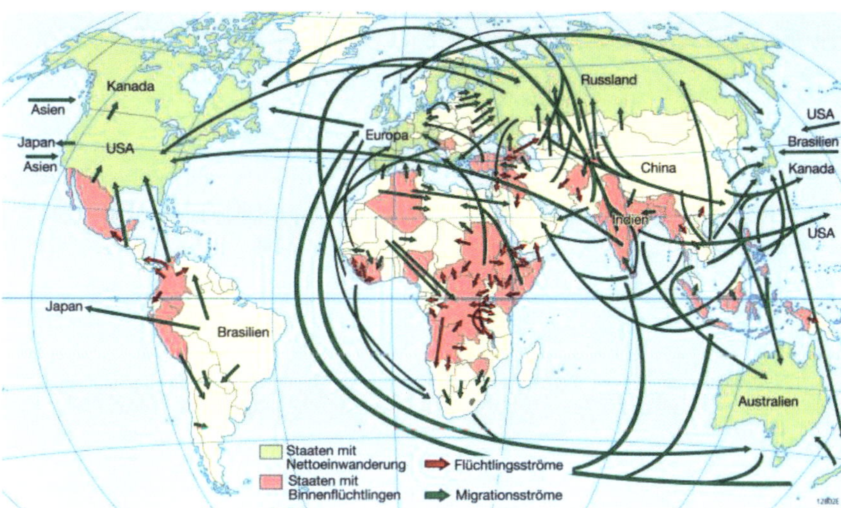

Flags of several regions fighting for their indepen-dence or minorities without a homeland such as the Rom community, today the most important of Europe in terms of numbers.

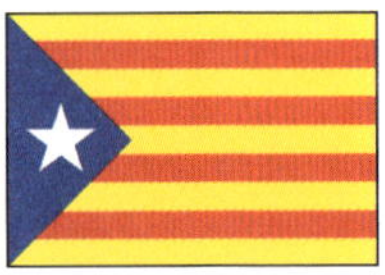

Estelada: the flag symbolizing the fight for the independence of Catalonia.

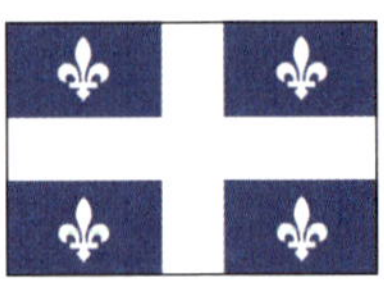

Fleurdelisé: national flag of Quebec used by separatist movements.

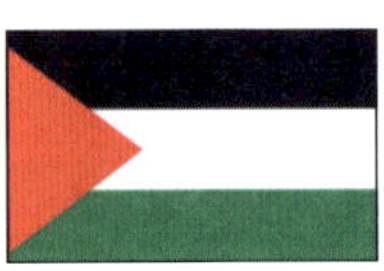

Flag of the Palestinian authority or flag of Palestine.

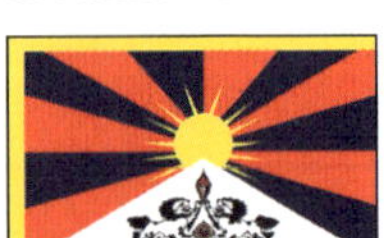

Snow lion flag of the Tibetan government in exile, banned since 1959 in the People's Republic of China.

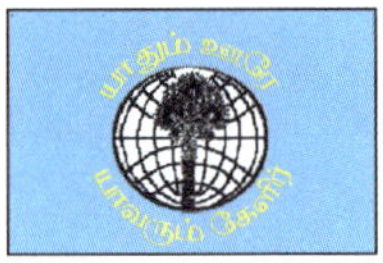

Tamil flag repre-senting the Tamil people everywhere in the world.

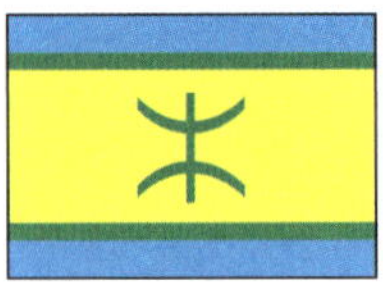

Flag of the Berber people of North Africa.

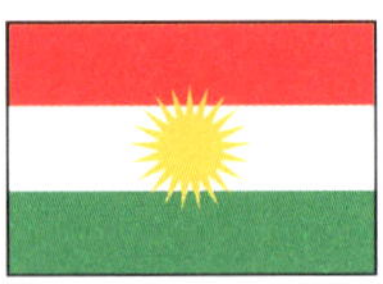

Flag of Kurdistan.

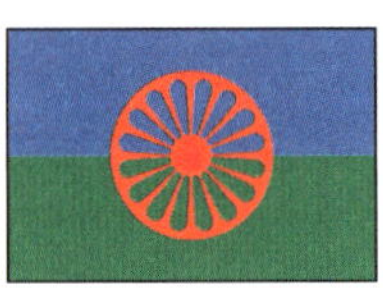

Flag of part of the Rom community.

Several flags borrowed from the table of seventy-two flags of the fifty-two countries of the world. A number of them had both a commercial and a battle flag.

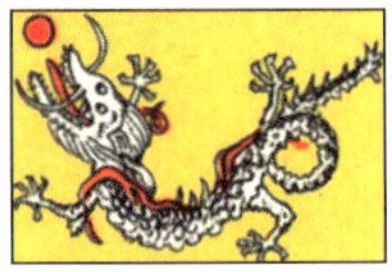

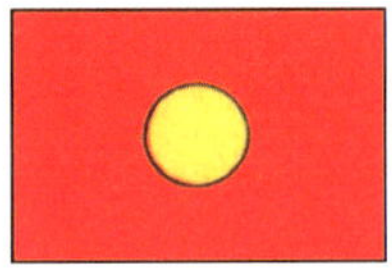

The commercial and battle flags of China. Japanese battle flag.

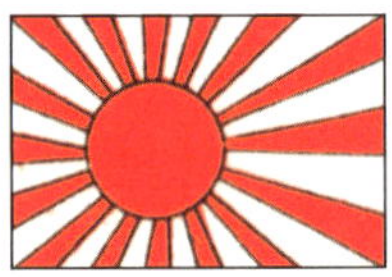

The Japanese commercial flag is the equivalent of the country's current flag.

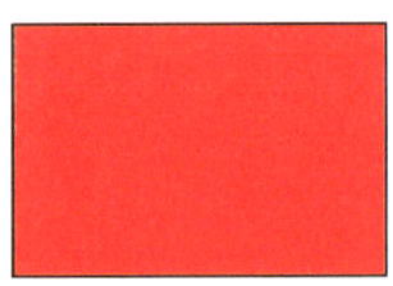

Red flag of both Zanzibar and Morocco.

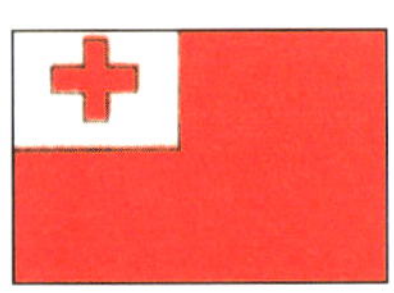

Flag of Tonga.

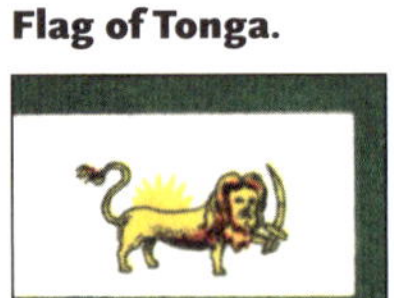

Flag of Persia.

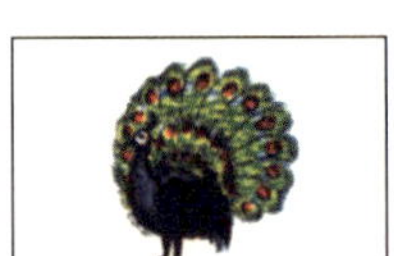

Flag of Burma.

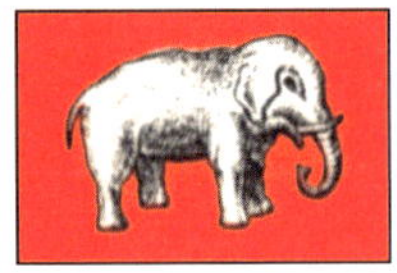

Flag of Siam.

Finally a few flags of fictional countries.

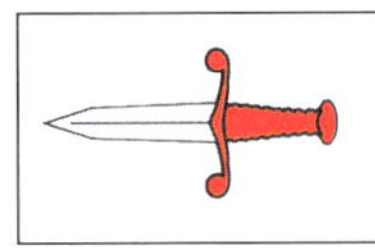

Flag of Brutopia in Eastern Europe, which is born of the world of Donald Duck (Disney).

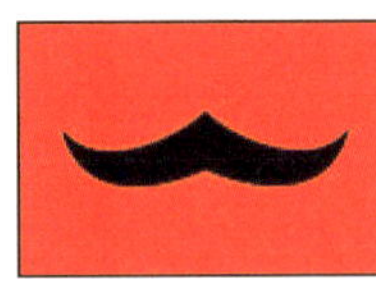

And that of Borduria, totalita-rian dictatorship of Eastern Europe in the world of Tintin.

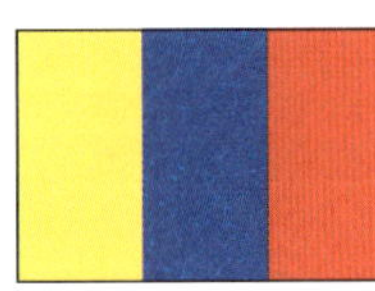

Flag of Palombia, between Venezuela and Colombia, from *Spirou and Fantasio*.

Flag of Groland dreamt up by Jules-Édouard Moustic.

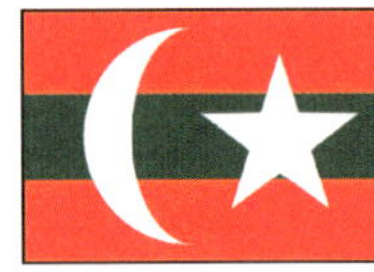

That of Khemed, on the Arabian Peninsula, from the world of Tintin.

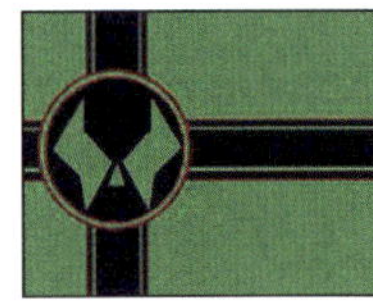

Flag of Marvel Comics' Latveria in the Balkans.

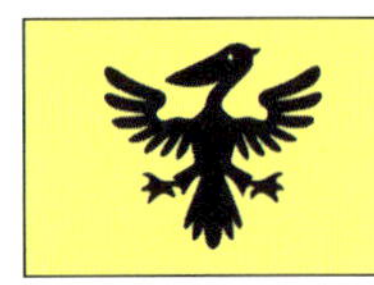

Flag of Tintin's Syldavia, an Eastern European monarchy.

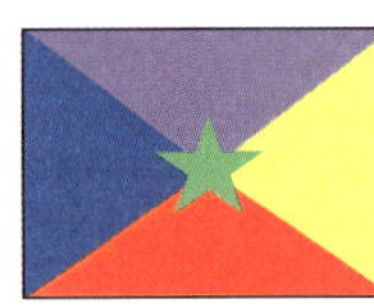

Flag of Oz, the country found in *The Wizard of Oz*.

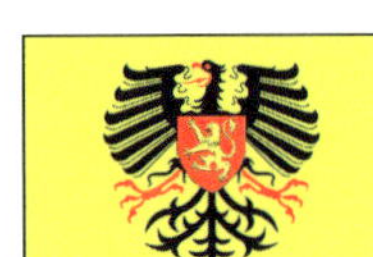

Flag of Swedenborg, an independent country in Norway, invented by Serge Dalens.

however, in the eyes of the so-called native-born, and sometimes for generations.

The history of an important part of contemporary families, however, shows that life choices, the reality of moving, immigration, be it temporary or permanent, chosen or forced, transnational marriages—that this mixing, sometimes spanning several generations, is a great deal more complex than what is conceded by official papers and categorizing individuals in terms of nationhood. One can feel close to a city, region, or culture, but not really a nation. One can, for example, consider oneself simultaneously Parisian, Swiss but from the Romansh minority of the Engadin, culturally French, married to a German woman of half-Polish descent, radically European and above all a citizen of the world, while possessing two passports, one referring to one's place of birth and the first eighteen years of one's life, and the other which mentions a city-canton, distant origin of one's family on one's father's side. It is a place for which you have no feelings of belonging. This situation is not exceptional. And for all that, it does not imply denigration or disloyalty, but rather, on the contrary, a certain clear-sightedness that is an effect of comparison. A distancing that bothers those who stand to gain from national nearsightedness and egotism. Those who want bodies as much as minds to remain attached to the nation from which their family originally hails, a territory that one has to love, which one is willing to fight for, and soon, why not, even die for once again. But all of the above especially suggests that era, fortunately past now, when parents imposed their choice in arranged marriages for their children and divorce remained practically impossible. In the case of one's connection with a territory, custom hasn't really evolved. An open marriage for life or just for a time with one or more countries one feels close to is still the exception. Each human being must fit back into the box of their country of origin.

This connection goes beyond, at least legally and politically, those we have with our neighborhood, city, urban area, canton, region, or continent, even quite simply our fragile planet made up of those human beings who are so alike yet so wonderfully different. Can one feel as though one belongs to a culture, a political structure, a city, the republic, without belonging to this national patriotism? The formidable legacies of the nineteenth century, with the building and overvaluation of national myths, seem to have destroyed the concept of the original republic, the one that brought together worthy and responsible citizens around a civic contract. Only those who accepted the rules, regardless of their origin, could take part in it. In the end, doesn't that spirit correspond with our contemporary reality, the reality of those immense megacities where transnationally an important part of the world's population—nowadays predominantly urban—is congregating?

The Flags of Nations

The history of national flags, which began in a way with the French Revolution in the eighteenth century, makes plain that this form of communication took over a century to be truly deployed as a coherent system. While the proportion of the background rectangle still varies, very few countries really stand apart from the graphic system, even though Nepal remains an exception. Fortunately this form seems to be accepted as is without giving rise to legions of imitators. As with heraldry—which remains a source of information—the world has achieved a kind of common rule that is universally accepted. The United Nations with its majestic entry of flags defines the obligations, implicitly in a way, while the rest is defined on the basis of existing models and the needs of local expression. The people fighting to be able to form a nation, moreover, already possess a flag in general. The whole is coherent without putting either of these at a disadvantage. I don't make this observation in order to champion either nations or flags, far from it. Rather, I do so in order to consider that there is indeed an advantage, in terms of institutional communication, to stepping outside the logic inspired by the sectors having something to do with the consumer economy in order to implement identification systems based on common conventions. Much more highly complex agreements are then able to take shape. Why wouldn't it be possible in this way to tackle

Classification of national flags according to their type of design. Surface with circular motif:

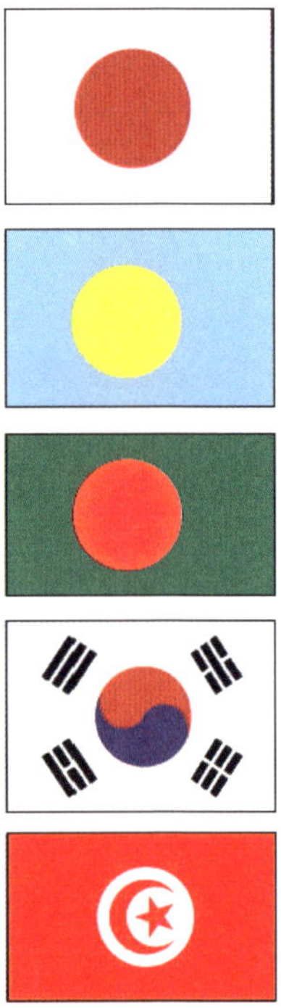

Japan, Palau, Bangladesh, South Korea, Tunisia...

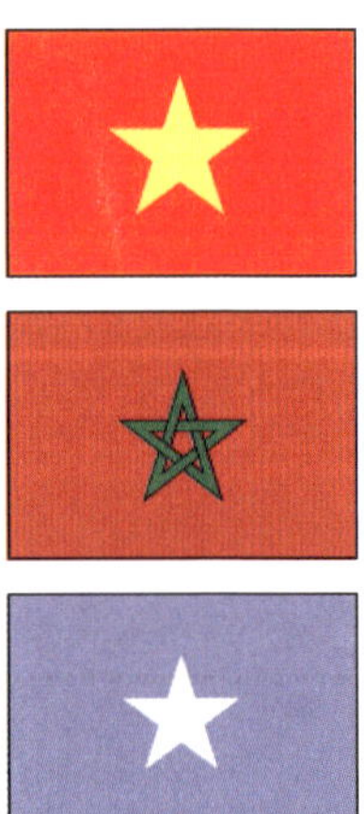

With a star: Vietnam, Morocco, Somalia...

Surface with centered motif:

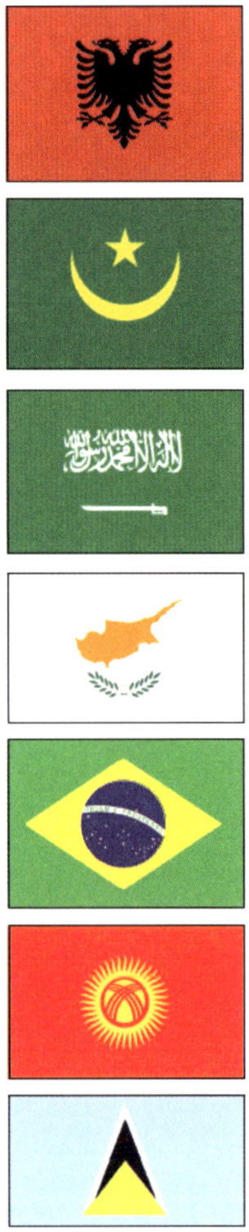

Albania, Mauritania, Saudi Arabia, Cyprus, Brazil, Kyrgyzstan, Saint Lucia...

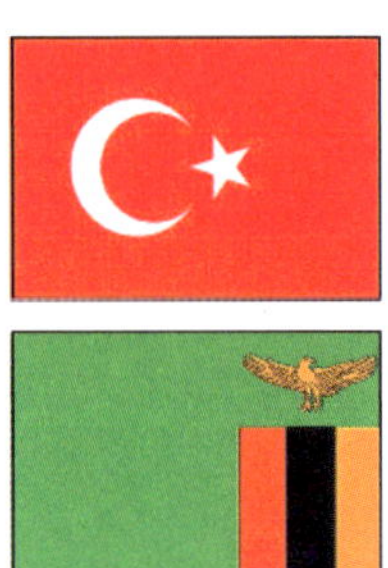

Surface with off-center motif: Turkey, Zambia.

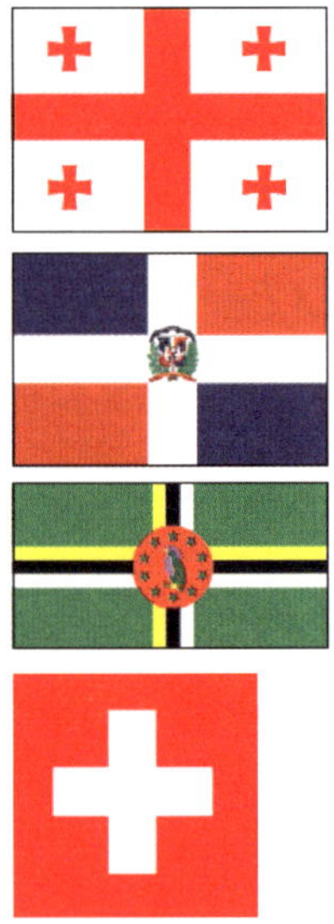

Centered crosses: Georgia, Dominican Republic, Dominica, the Swiss Confederation.

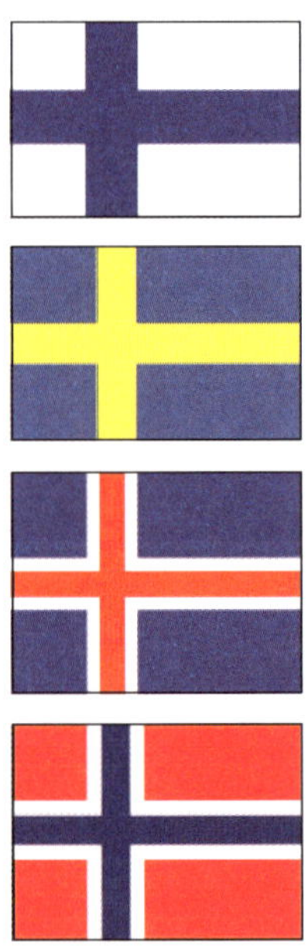

Off-center crosses: Finland, Sweden, Iceland, Norway...

Horizontal surface divided in two:

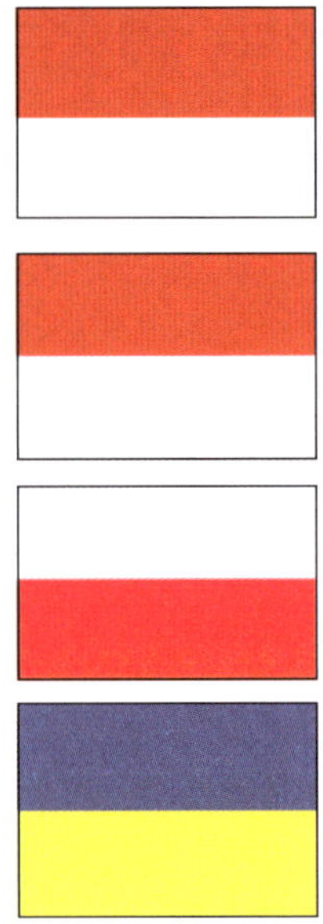

Monaco, Indonesia, Poland, Ukraine... Same with motifs: Singapore, Burkina Faso, Angola, Haiti, Liechtenstein...

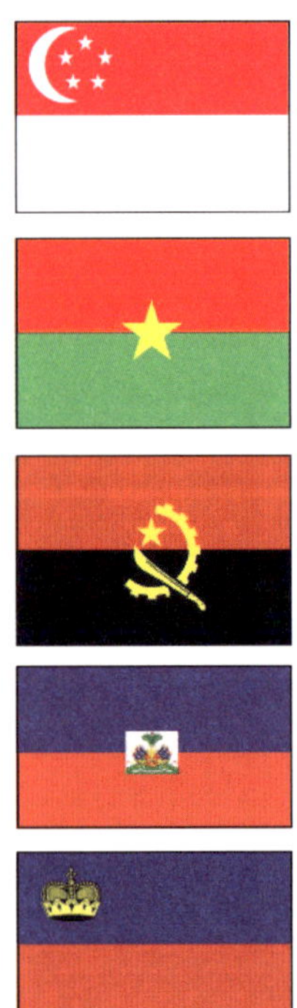

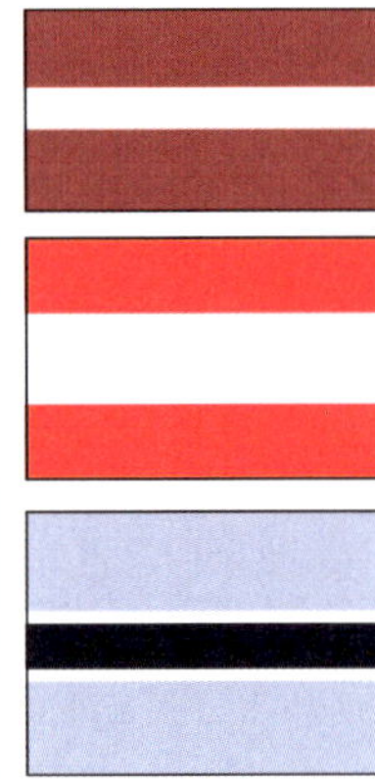

Surface crossed by one or more horizontal stripes: Latvia, Austria, Botswana...

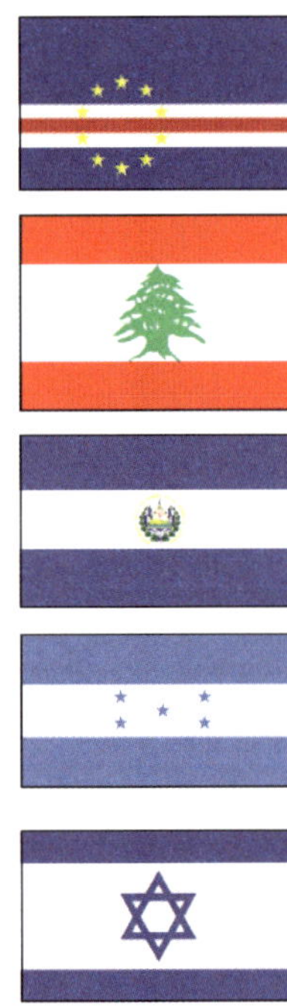

With motifs: Cape Verde, Lebanon, Salvador, Honduras, Israel...

Then comes the great series of three-color flags.

First, horizontally:

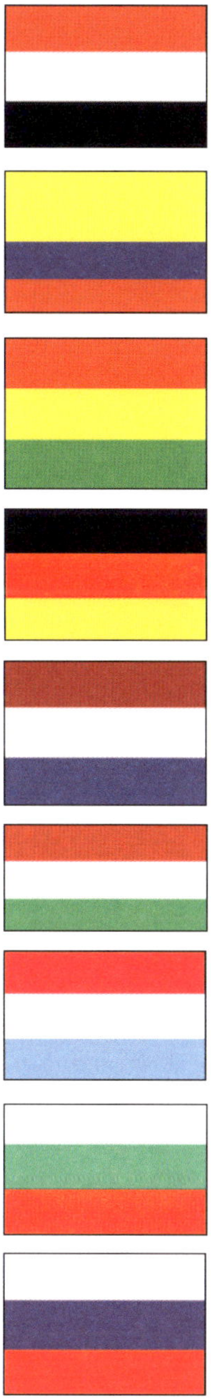

Yemen, Colombia, Bolivia, Germany, the Netherlands, Hungary, Luxembourg, Bulgaria, Russia...

Then with motifs:

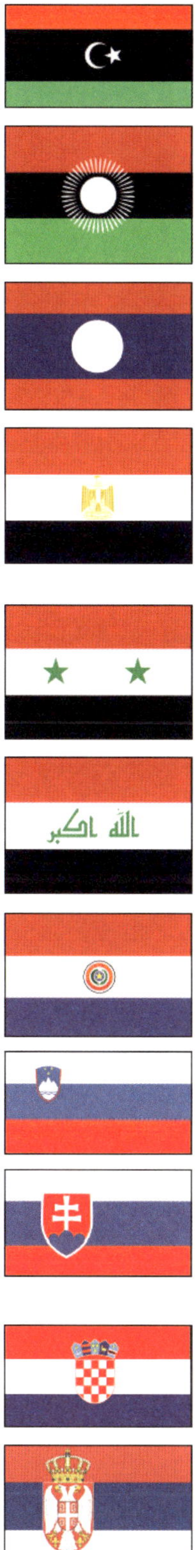

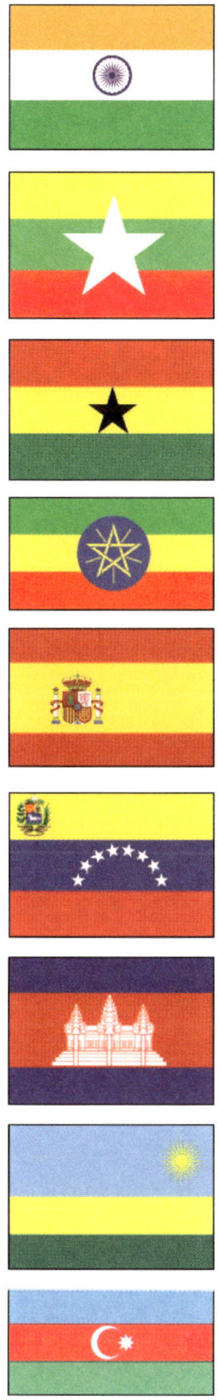

Libya, Malawi, Laos, Egypt, Syria, Iraq, Paraguay, Slovenia, Slovakia, Croatia, Serbia, India, Myanmar, Ghana, Ethiopia, Spain, Venezuela, Cambodia, Rwanda, Azerbaijan...

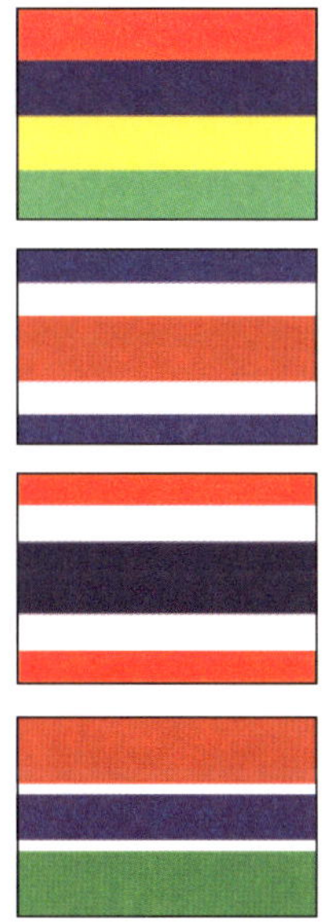

Flag with more than three horizontal stripes: Mauritius, Costa Rica, Thailand, the Gambia...

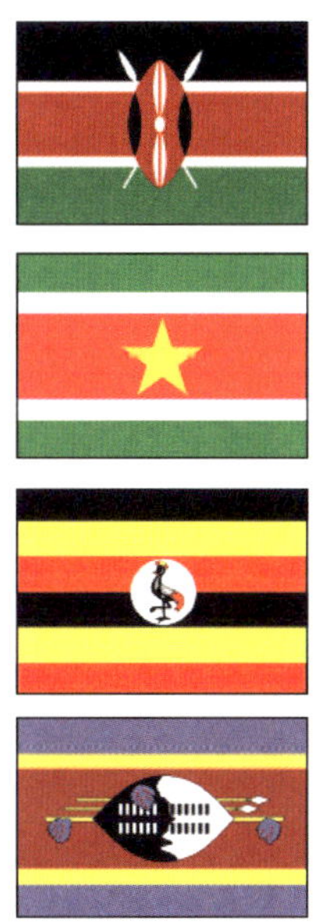

Kenya, Suriname, Uganda, Swaziland

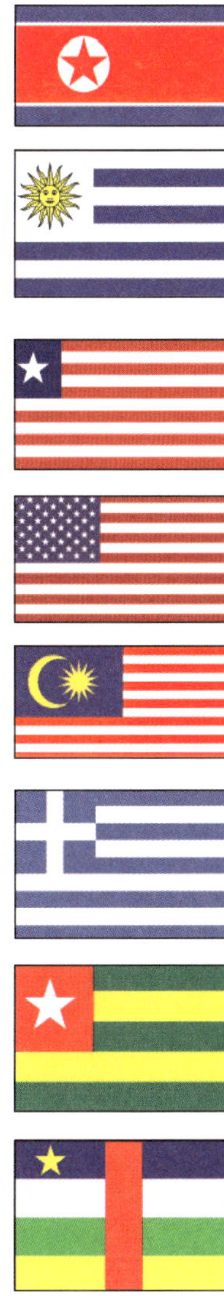

North Korea, Uruguay, Liberia, the United States, Malaysia, Greece, Togo, Central African Republic...

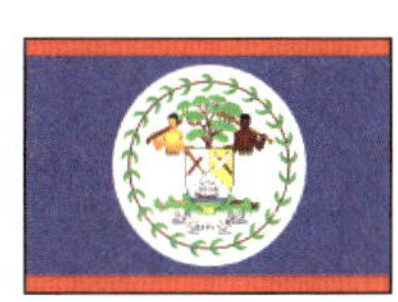

With a horizontal frame: Belize. Few flags are framed.

Surface divided in two vertically:

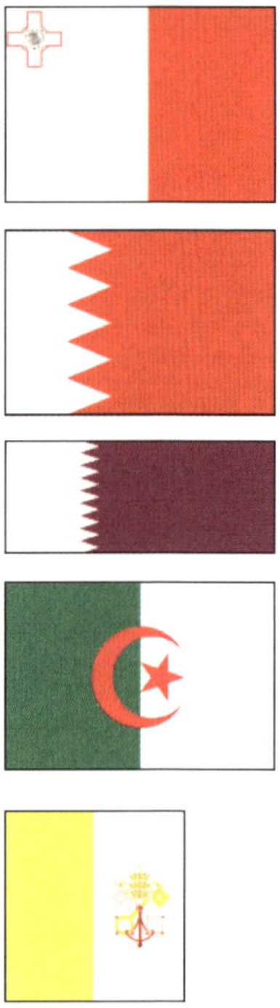

Malta, Bahrain, Qatar, Algeria, the Vatican.

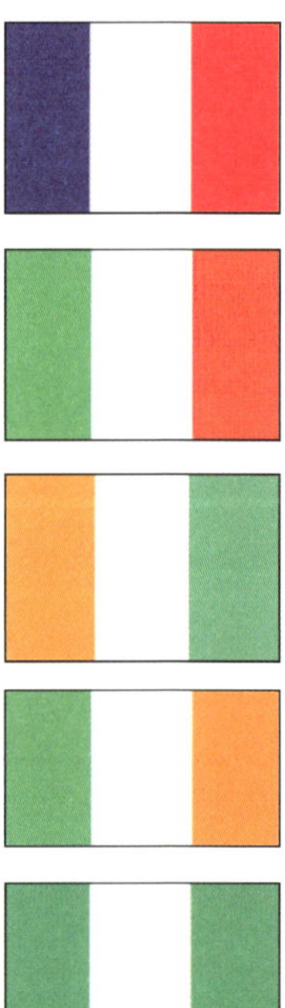

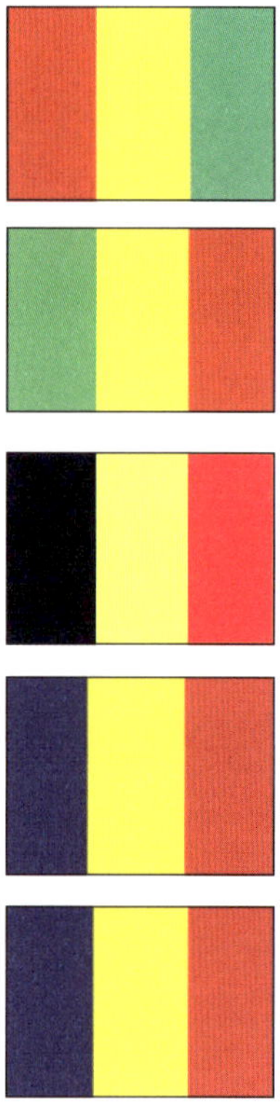

Vertical three-color flags: France, Italy, Côte d'Ivoire, Ireland, Nigeria, Mali, Guinea, Belgium, Chad, Romania,

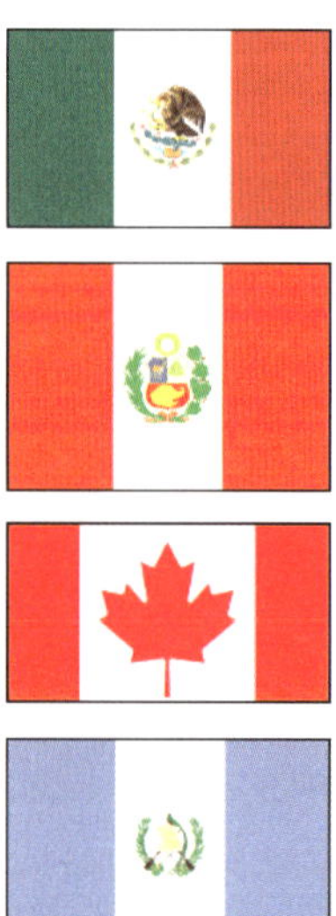

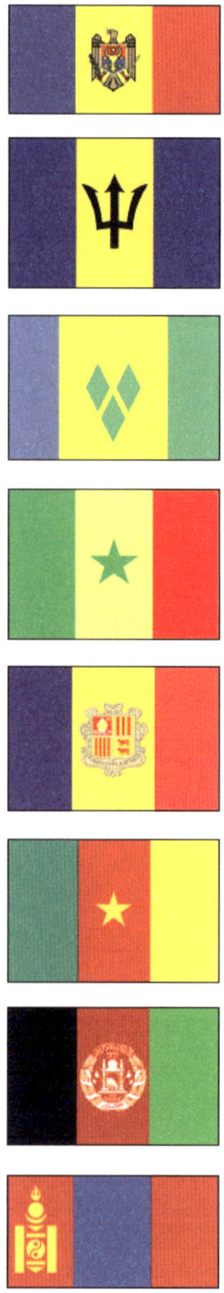

Mexico, Peru, Canada, Guatemala, Moldavia, Barbados, Saint Vincent and the Grenadines, Senegal, Andorra, Cameroon, Afghanistan, Mongolia...

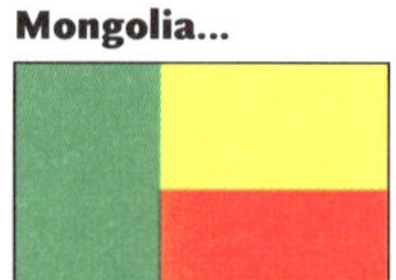

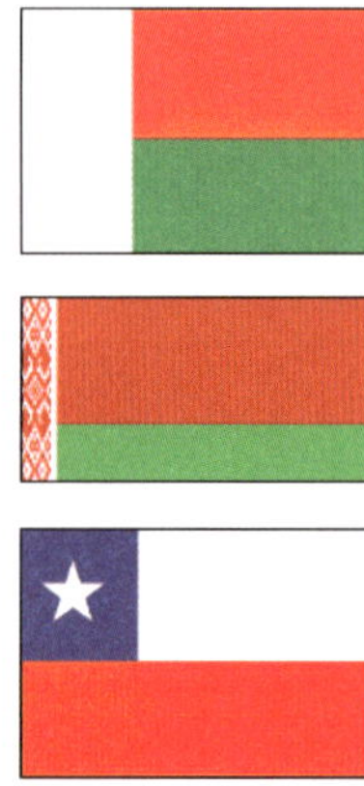

Few flags with both vertical and horizontal stripes: Benin, Belarus, Madagascar, Chili...

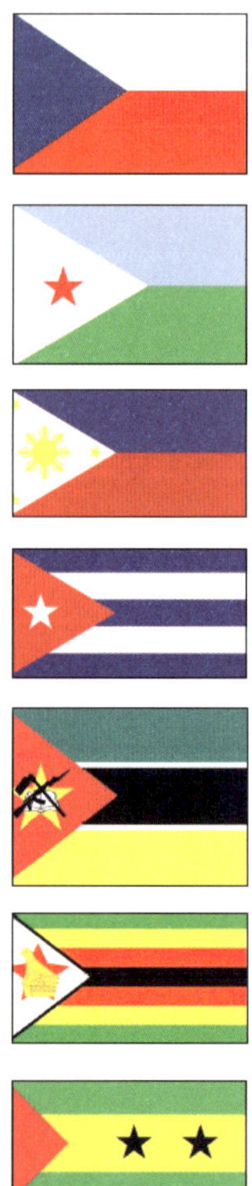

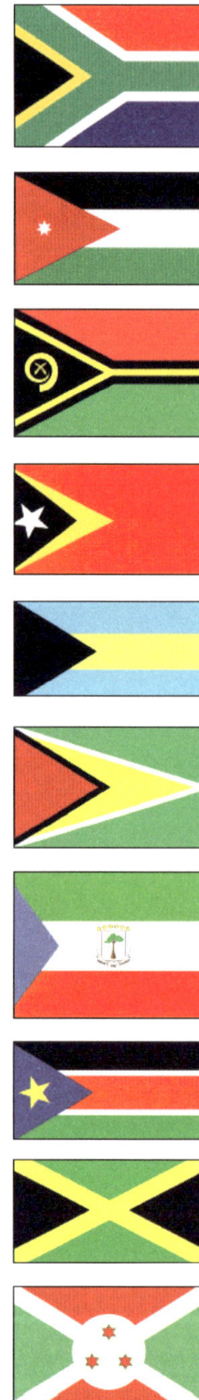

A significant number of flags designed with a triangle placed on the left: the Czech Republic, Djibouti, Philippines,

Cuba, Mozambique, Zimbabwe, São Tomé and Príncipe, South Africa, Jordan, Vanuatu, East Timor, Bahamas, Guyana, Equatorial Guinea, South Sudan, Jamaica, Burundi…

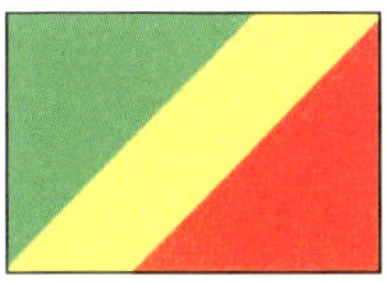
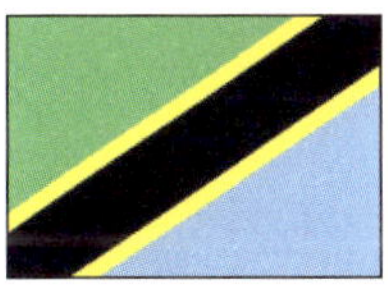
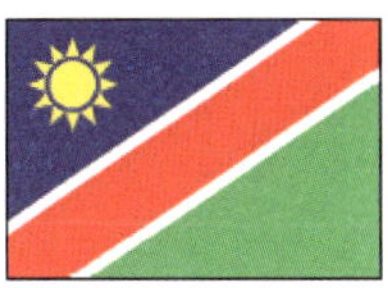
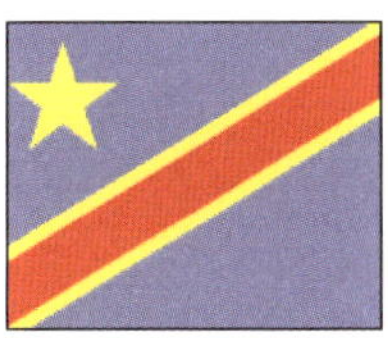
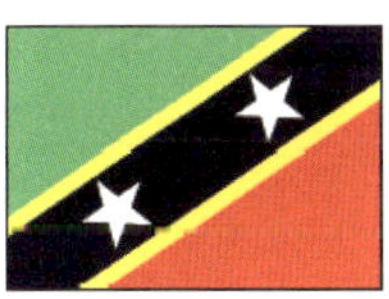
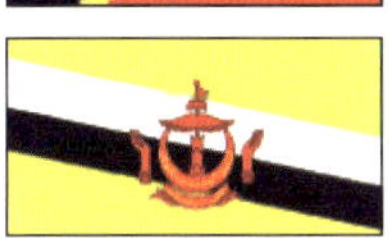
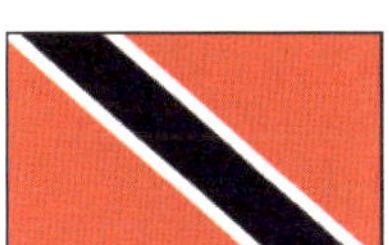

Diagonally striped flag: Republic of the Congo, Tanzania, Namibia, Democratic Republic of the Congo, Saint Kitts and Nevis, Brunei, Trinidad and Tobago…

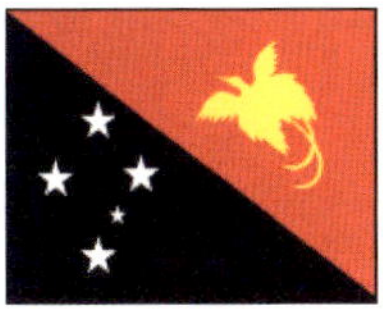
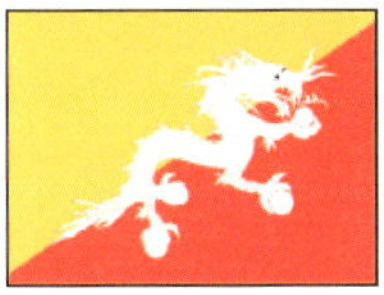
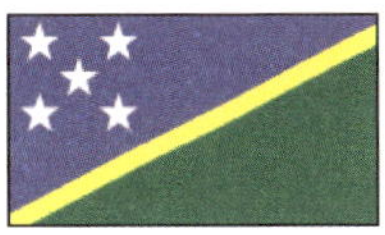

Diagonally divided in two: Papua New Guinea, Bhutan, Solomon Islands…

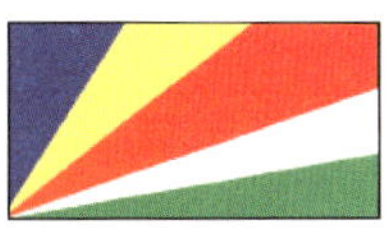
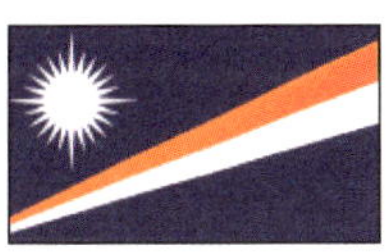

Divided by radiating stripes: Seychelles, Marshall Islands…

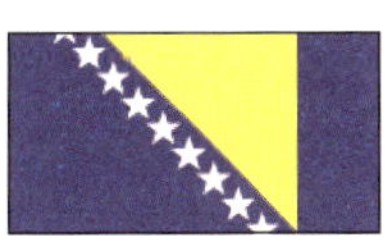

Borrowing a European star, a flag in the visual cultural of a logo: Bosnia and Herzegovina

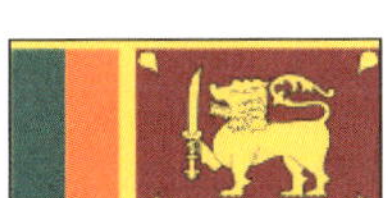

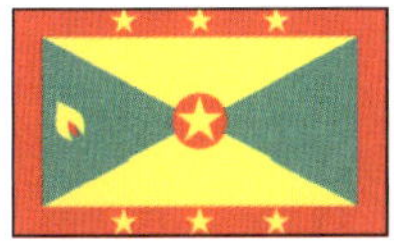
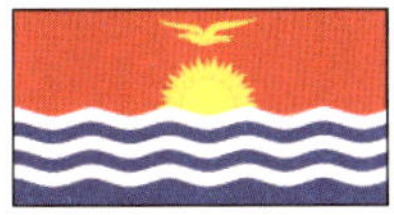
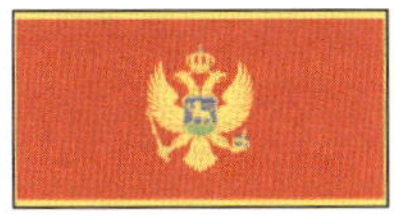
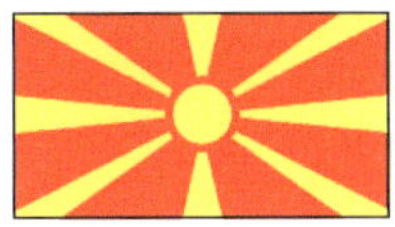

Several flags that are harder to classify, although integrated in a visual system: Grenada, Kiribati, Montenegro, Macedonia…

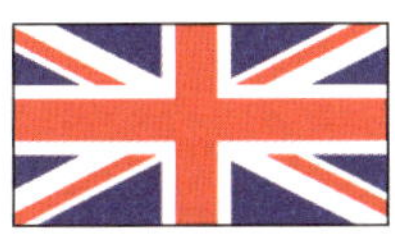
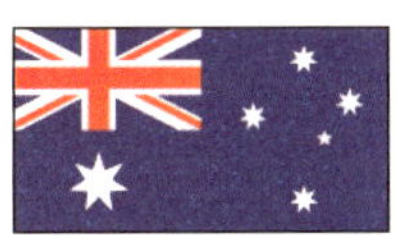
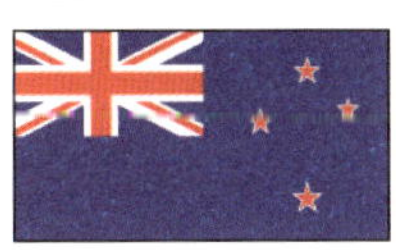
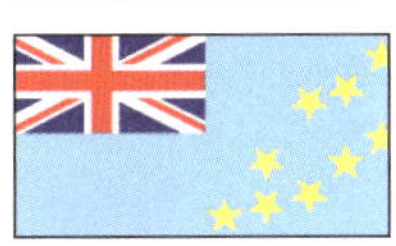
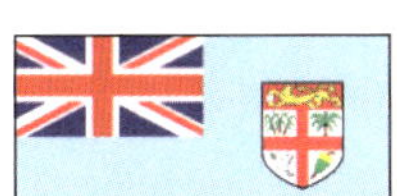

A subgroup that aims for coherence: the United Kingdom, Australia, New Zealand, Tuvalu, Fiji.

And finally a granted exception that is justified by the local flag culture and makes the coherence of the rest of the system legible: Nepal.

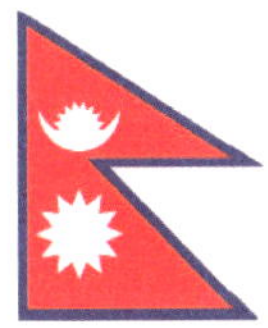

Not all of the flags of the world's nations are reproduced here. Those that are missing, however, do correspond to one of the types described above. Denmark, for example, completes the series of crosses of Scandinavian countries. The list of countries, moreover, isn't set in stone; despite the permanence of some nations, others are still dividing and reforming around new entities. While in 1900 there were fifty-two nations, today we have some two hundred if we refer simply to the number of members of the United Nations.

questions of identification and political territories? To remove them from the field of marketing would make it possible to lend democracy credibility once again.

Render More Legible

Contemporary citizens are profoundly disillusioned. They feel they are being manipulated constantly. The overall view escapes them and they sense they have no grip on it. Leaders have flashed before their eyes their here and now without taking into account connections with the complexity of the whole. Yet each person knows the importance of both vertical and horizontal interconnections in our contemporary world. The brand and the politics of branding, to my mind, play a role in disinformation and especially the impression of being that we are constantly fed. Citizens are quite capable of decoding the strategies imposed on them by public services. They rightly feel they are infringements on the civil contract linking them to government entities. Be it in their immediate vicinity or, on the contrary, in terms of the organizations in charge of dealing with problems on a planetary scale, illegibility is a well-known fact. Its solution lies not in the leaflets that are distributed for temporary use, but rather in the way each of these territorial powers represents itself.

The example of states clearly shows us the complexity involved. Around two hundred nations share the surface of the earth. Each of these, as we have seen, boasts a flag. That flag represents simultaneously the territory, the population living there, and the state making up that territory. In the case of Switzerland, this sign is used to promote the country. In the case of Peru, it is a complementary sign that officiates. A bit like the dual flags of war and trade in the nineteenth century, the state might equip itself with a formal flag and a promotional trademark. The two are representational signs but in different ways. Yet neither refers to the state, the people's elected representatives, the government, its activity, and the activity of the departments related to it. This "legibilitization" of the nation's operations ought to be repeated at every territorial level.

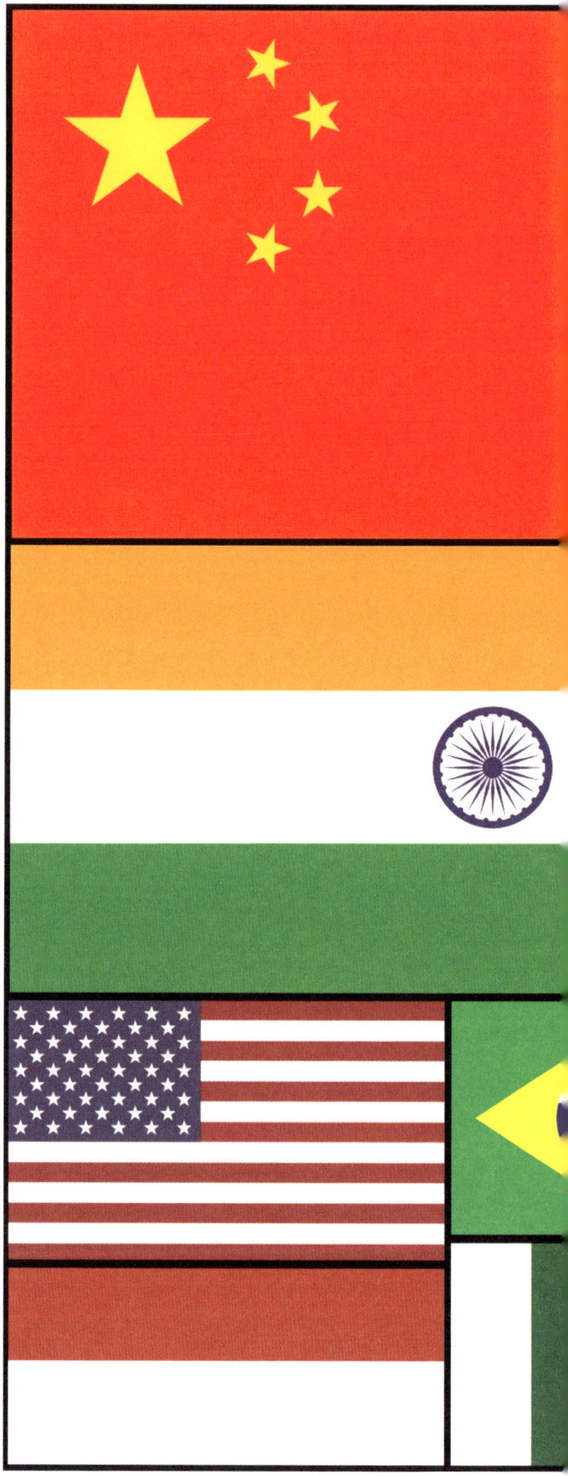

Global population distribution with respect to the different national territories. While each nation is represented in the

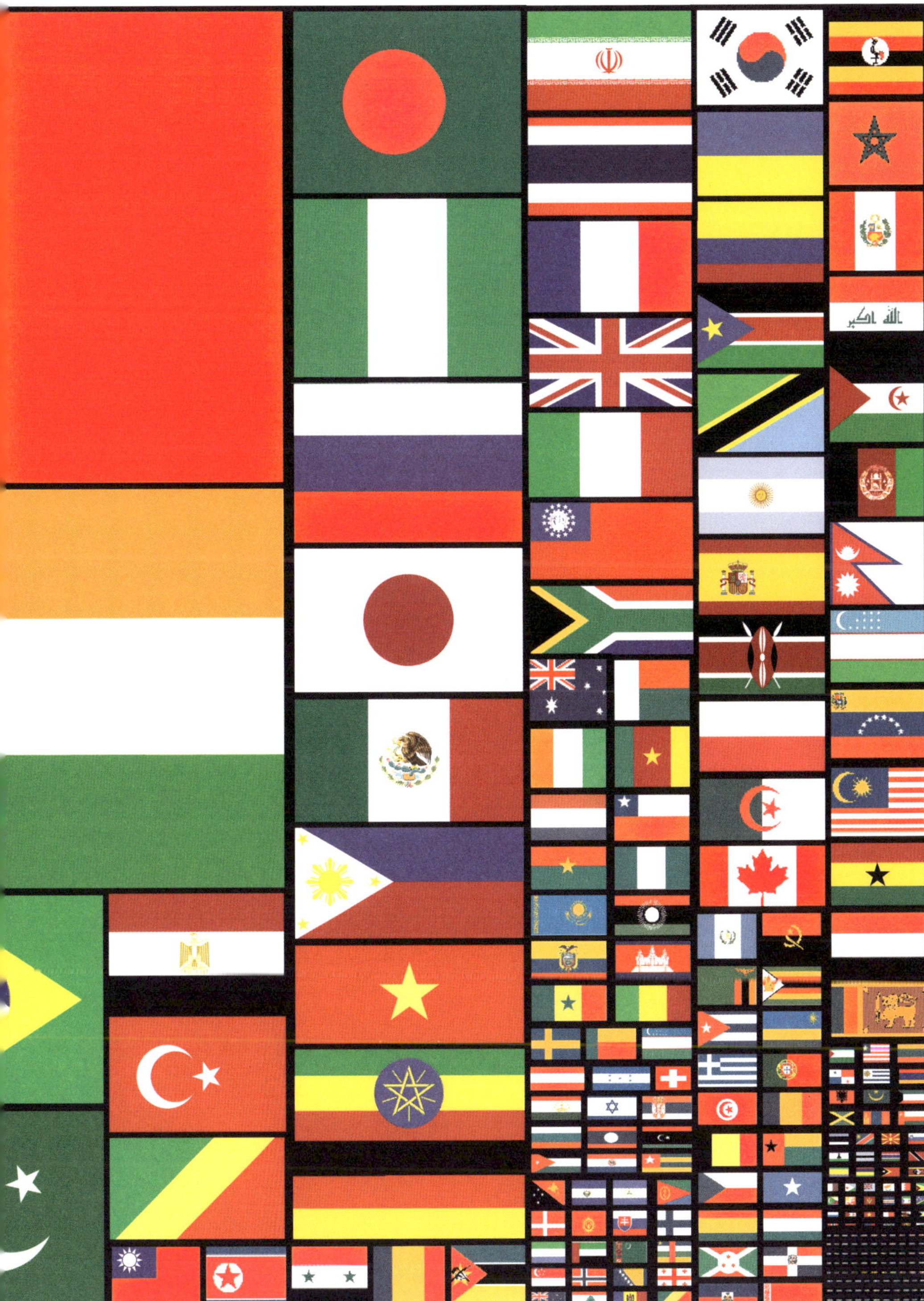

international organizations, democratic principles of proportional representation are hardly applied universally at this level.

How then do we render this complex whole, the links between the different institutions, the scope of their powers, and hence, more broadly, the workings of democracy legible? Let's examine these modes of representation at the level of nation-states and draw the necessary lessons from them in the hope of gaining a more transversal legibility.

Representation of the Nation and the State

Limiting still my analysis of visual representation to the question of the flag or the signature, one notes the discretion that reigns in most emblems and logos of the state's political entities. The connection between the flag and the signatures of these political institutions is best established through color. Parliament and senate generally fall within codes that often date from their creation. It is worth noting that little pressure is exerted at this level. Rather fascinating is the example of Canada, which manages to connect flag, the logo of the government and different departments, and brands, a graphic design that goes back to the 1980s. One ought to verify whether it suffers from the same effect as Switzerland and its confusion between the state and private signs, but without having done any extensive analysis, I would probably say that the distinction is a more significant one. This may be due as well to the work done by a clear widespread signage that makes it possible to reinforce recognition through recognition of the supports. In Quebec, for instance, the distinction between signs having to do with the state and those related to the province is very clear. The whole expresses the institutional, even civic dimension, and the long term seems to predominate over the immediate reaction.

France, on the other hand, offers a negative demonstration of the independence of each institution. Each sign is the result of its own invention, which doesn't seem to take into account the presence of other signs, except to affirm its difference. The only rule in common seems to be the traditional three colors of the French flag. Is this really enough? I wonder. An advertising-like aspect introduces a doubt with regard to the seriousness of these state institutions. I shall delve into this

Here we compare flags, brands, and representational signs of governments, parliaments, and senates.

A lack of coherence but an expression of seriousness.

The kangaroo as a connecting thread!

Somewhat codified, visualization borrows from oral expression.

Color coherence for Pakistan.

Great restrain for India.

Here again we find great rigor.

The signs are built around the coat of arms.

The coherent identity of the government is not carried over to Parliament.

A great soberness, almost modesty, despite the coat of arms of the eagle.

Certainly an expression of seriousness and coherence.

Despite the similarity with Germany, coherence isn't part of the picture.

The blue, white, and red alone lend consistency. Is that enough?

Ultimately in the local style.

case more deeply by attempting to represent an institutional column starting with the very local institution, the French commune, and going as far as the whole of Europe.

The Nesting of Territorial Identities

If it were still necessary to do so, the demonstration indeed confirms expectations. Living in the community of X, we find ourselves before a series of signs all of which refer to this place as part of a number of nesting territories, territories that fit into increasingly larger entities, as we have seen. While the greatest proximity remains relatively silent and even the European Community doesn't overwhelm us with its signs, which are too distant perhaps, that is not the case for intermediary territories. By themselves they express the incoherence of public representational systems. At the same time, we need to be wary of the immediate reflex, i.e., wanting to unify everything because of the obvious chaos. This is the attitude of the corporate designer, a kind of visual hygienist. Likewise, a certain clarity in the headings and a common typography could provide the legibility that is lacking. And a shared constraint, it is worth noting, does not abolish the differences for all that. It simply allows the difference to be cultivated within a defined framework. Heraldry and the visual language of flags are grounded in such rules.

In this regard, it is interesting to analyze the evolution of French regional logos, for example, once they were allowed to be reproduced on license plates. It amounts to an extremely generous presence that is a bit like Swiss license plates with their coats of arms of both the Confederation and the cantons. The blue support is a powerful constraint that may gradually transform these signs.

Ceremonial Writing

The term is borrowed from the field of ethnology. It involves analyzing the signs produced by a society following various rituals instituted by the society. To observe this production of signs or this visual environment seems to me to be something that is necessary today. What is this so-called developed and democratic, though politically weakened,

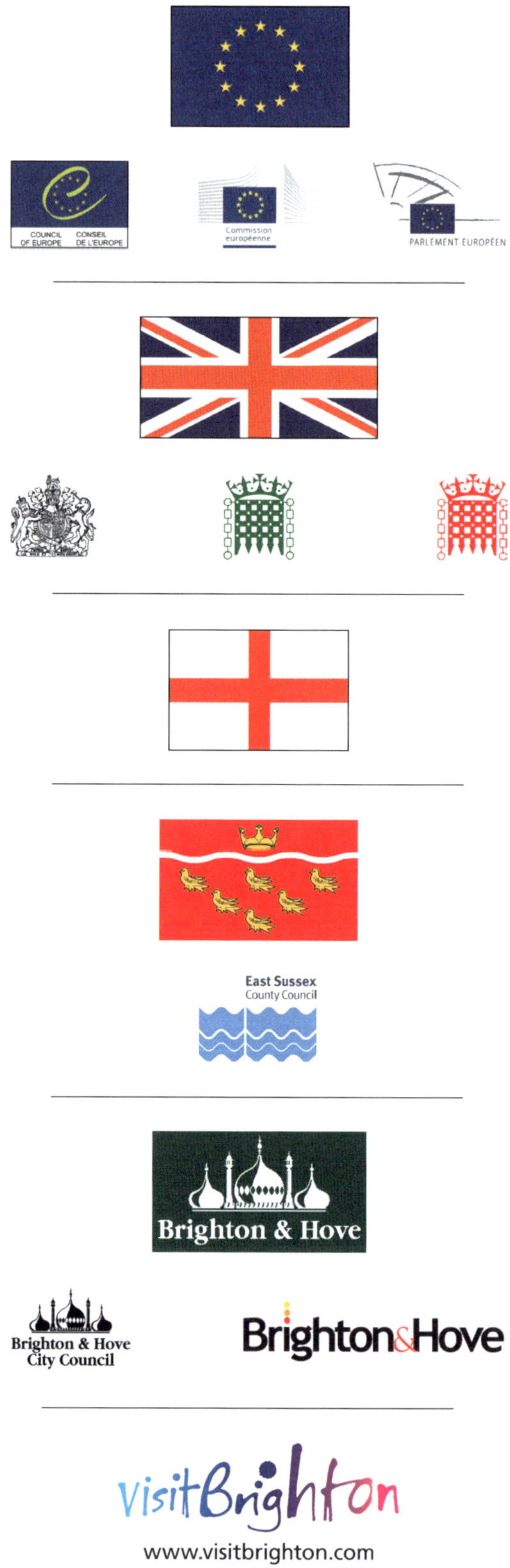

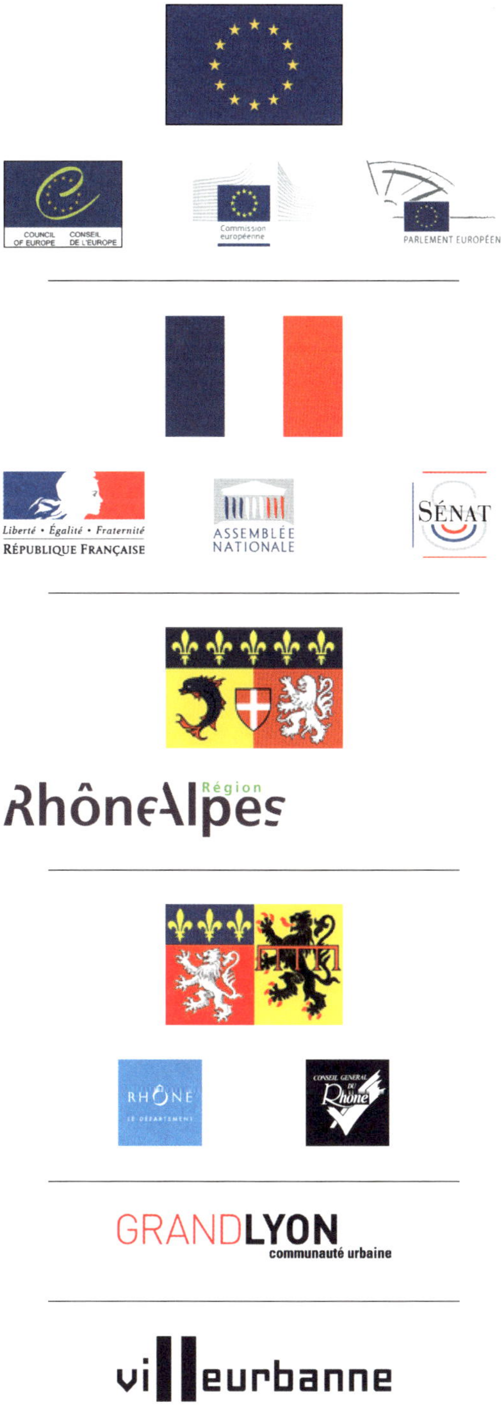

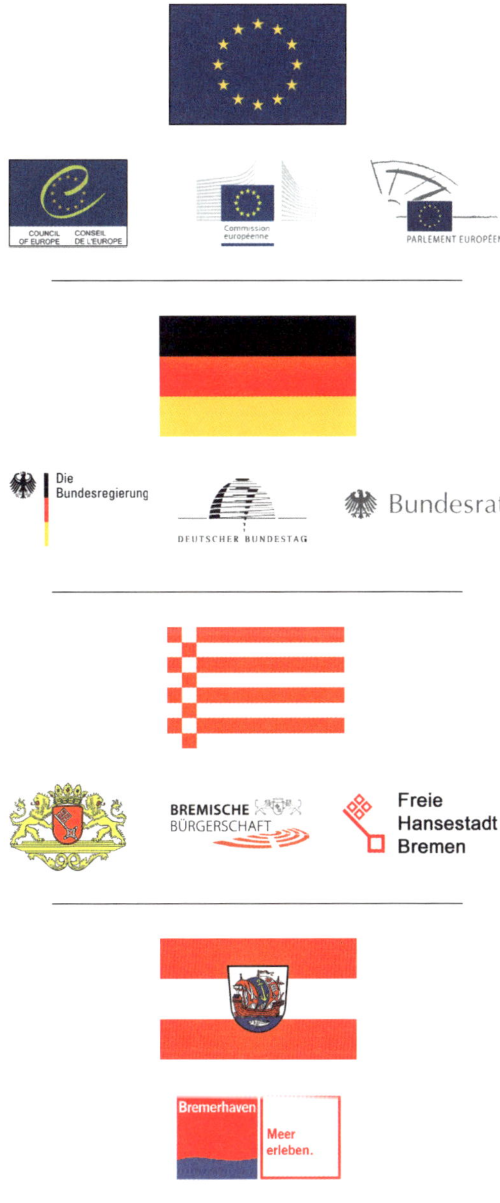

Nesting of territorial identities on the basis of three European cities (Brighton, Villeurbanne, and Bremerhaven), trying to show at each level the image of the territory and its governance. If none of these gradations seem truly coherent, some do work out additional steps and signs. How can citizens feel the notion of public interest, for example, if the territories representing them are symbolized in this way?

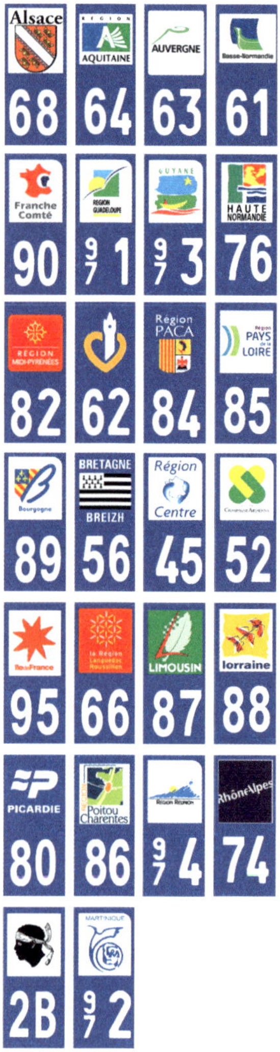

French license plates (since April 2009): the region's logo appears in a white rectangle above the department's number. By law one must indicate a department (freely chosen by the owner of the vehicle); the region is then the one in which that department is located. For example, 60 (Oise) is associated with the logo of the Picardy region. While only a very few logos work in this context, most reveal their ineffectiveness, mediocre aesthetic, even their amateurism. The omnipresence of these signs, however, ought to force the authorities to professionalize their graphic design.

society that represents itself in such an incoherent, often vulgar manner? What is this so-called public entity giving itself over to the world of advertising in order to represent itself? Which finds it no longer has the ability to invent a writing that is its very own and corresponds, not to the needs of politicians, but rather to those of its citizens? A public entity whose different components are in constant visual competition, like some seller of detergent. If the representation crisis in democracies is indeed widespread, clearly it is much more pronounced in certain countries that nonetheless assert their republican tradition, civic-mindedness, even humanism. Criticism not only takes aim at those small territories that find themselves short of means, it addresses just as much a European Community that still cannot manage to win the hearts of its peoples. A European Community that appears so very distant and bureaucratic to everyone. Yet, shouldn't it be from this point in common with all of Europe, or nearly all, that a reform of territorial representation ought to be mounted? Of course, but in the meantime it can emanate from a national or even regional or peri-urban territorial reform.

Let's imagine nevertheless a reform taking place at a Europe-wide level. Obviously it is not about erasing local diversities but rather integrating them in a common system. It is up to the lawyers and legal experts to craft laws that will encourage a visual cohesion that respects cultural differences. I shall limit myself to a modest proposal that might make an improvement of overall legibility possible.

A certain number of types of territories and political entities haven't yet been the subject of the necessary in-depth study. Let's begin with the one that brings together nearly everyone on the Continent yet still struggles to win hearts. One part of this disenchantment might well involve the mode of representation.

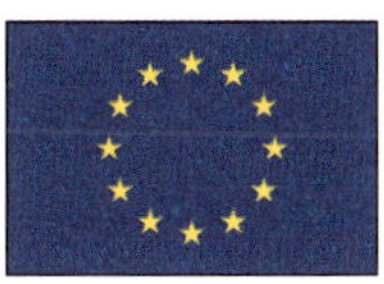

Blue background at the center of which is a circle made up of twelve stars. A cool color then that displays, unlike all other flags with a single color background, not a strong sign but a sort of empty center. The intention, i.e., to symbolize the coming together of European states after so many conflicts, is easily read there. It borrows the symbolism of the United States but without the power and warmth of the red and white stripes of the American flag. This cool and balanced expression, the equivalence between each of the stars, looks more like a kind of bureaucratic constraint aiming to eliminate differences than the expression of a real European desire.

This impression of extreme distance is reinforced by the logos of the different governing institutions. Conspicuous lack of character, even force. Yet one need only take part in one of these parliamentary reunions to realize a wonderful number of combinations exist in this multiplicity. Isn't it that variety and wealth of combinations then that needs to be cultivated rather than the flat, uninteresting least common denominator? Once again, the representation of the interconnections deserves better than what is indeed devoted to identity.

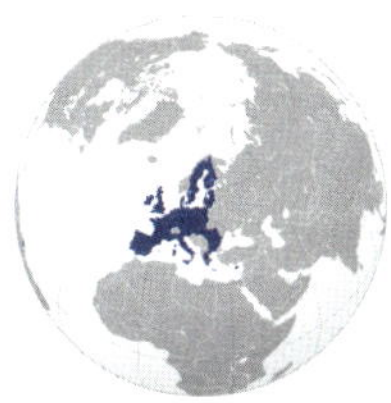

In 2001, the president of the European Commission, Romano Prodi, and the president of the Council of the European Union, Guy Verhofstadt, sought out Rem Koolhaas and asked the Dutch architect and urban designer to think about the visual symbols of the European Union. The proposed flag is a compilation of all the flags of the member states. This visual marker remained merely a proposal. A different, livelier, more complex Europe would have thus been symbolized.

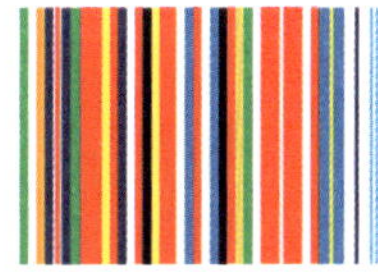

But Europe seems to be more a matter of the internal competition of the member states. The logos of European presidencies say as much in any case.

Does any one of these logos manage to express what is at stake? Don't hold your breath. It looks like a tourist brochure.

But before going any further, let's examine the situation of individual European citizens by analyzing what binds them symbolically to this territory. Today the euro constitutes the principal symbol. Here again Europe has not really shown true excellence in this regard, inviting, for instance, the very best designers of the Continent to compete with respect to the representations. No, we find ourselves facing the bland result of a call for tenders and a thousand compromises.

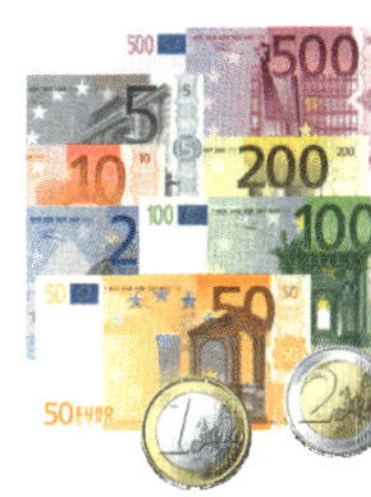

The demonstration could go on for a long time. The situation dashes the hopes of even the most dyed-in-the-wool Europeans. What is this ceremonial writing that is so mediocre? That of a political power in the hands of as many states as there are member countries.

Let's begin this search for legibility by focusing on a region, Aquitaine, its departments and department capitals. Our initial analysis will then be applied to other levels and other regions.
At first then, the principle is to limit the transformation of current signs.

REGION
AQUITAINE

Let's start with the logo of France's Aquitaine region.

Région
Aquitaine

We shall retain the visual and append a highly legible typeface that can be used for all territories, "Fedra-Sans," for example.

Région
Aquitaine

Now we shall invert the hierarchy by placing the information outside the sign, which we reduce in size.

La région
Aquitaine

We now reconnect this territory and locate it with respect to the national entity.

La région
Aquitaine
en France

With words or the symbol that corresponds to it.

Aquitaine

Région de

This principle, which bears on the name of the territory and not its government, might be extended to the European level.

Région
Aquitaine

The whole can assume an informative dimension or,

Région
Aquitaine

on the contrary, a more graphic one.

Région
Aquitaine

And what applies to a region of France could likewise function for any other region of Europe.

Freistaat
Bayern

Región de
Aragón

Provincie
Noord-
Holland

Clearly the concept can be applied to countries that favor flags and emblems, as well as to certain logos that fit into a rectangle.

Région
wallonne

The presence or absence of national or European flags would indicate a clear position.

Vlaams
Gewest

This would risk, however, confusing people since this mode of expression ought to correspond to nations.

France

España

Česká republika

But perhaps it would be more apt to talk about the Czech Republic...

Since it is indeed a question of making more readable the difference between the nation, France, and its state, the French Republic, with its government and its constituent assemblies. The equivalent would be available for regions and other types of territories.

To conclude this part, let's come back to Aquitaine and try to render our nesting of territorial identities from Europe on down legible.

Union européenne

République française

Région Aquitaine

département de la Gironde

commune de Bordeaux

Of course, not all logos can be included in such a system or in such a limiting way as we have seen for French license plates. One might hope that the constraints would force a gradual evolution.

la région Aquitaine

et ses cinq départements:

la Dordogne

la Gironde

les Landes

le Lot-et-Garonne

et les Pyrénées-Atlantiques

Unfortunately it is not enough to place a bad logo in a rectangle to make it more interesting. Sometimes the question arises of why one doesn't simply go back to the emblems or flags.

la région Aquitaine

et ses cinq départements:

la Dordogne

la Gironde

les Landes

le Lot-et-Garonne

et les Pyrénées-Atlantiques

Strange evolution, the same region is expressed through those historical flags in red and through its logos in green. Visually, representation through heraldry is much more convincing. The hope remains, however, that this type of legibilitization will introduce a new culture of the territorial sign.

These few examples are given to demonstrate that diversity, effectiveness, and contemporaneousness would be possible in this framework.

Yet for all that, the problems of legibility on the whole are not solved. We need to tackle the question of the connection between the representation of the political territory and the territory of its governance, or even of the sign that represents the least political dimension of the territory.

Région
Aquitaine

Aquitaine
le Conseil
régional

l'Aquitaine

The first question then is whether to use the same sign or, on the contrary, different signs for these three uses. It seems quite fitting to employ similar signs to indicate the political territory and its governance. The distinction can be made through a clear inscription of titles. Continuing with the rule of not transforming existing signs, let's try to distinguish the identification of the regional council from its action or financial support, for instance. We shall choose, however, the emblem for this expression. The writing that is

Conseil
régional
Aquitaine

Avec le
soutien
du Conseil
régional
Aquitaine

involved here leads us away from commercial logos. It ought to be generalized throughout the whole of the public message. Careful, though, this is not about a slogan but about information. Examples:

Financé
grâce
soutien
du Conseil
régional
des Landes

Sous la
tutelle
du Conseil
de l'Europe

Cofinancé
par le Conseil
de l'Europe
le
Gouvernement
français
le Conseil
régional
Aquitaine
et le Conseil
général
des Landes

Expression of this kind of collaboration may correspond with the different supervisory bodies for one and the same territory, or with the joint activities between similar institutions.

Eine Partner-
schaft
zwischen
Freie und
Hanselstadt
Hamburg
Communidad
de Madrid
Gemeente
Amsterdam

Another need involves legibility within the departments of these various governmental entities. While certain functions are the responsibility of the people's elected representatives, they must be clearly distinguished from those that fall under any administrative department.

Département
de la petite
enfance
du Conseil
régional de
la Lorraine

M. Dedatre
élu à la
culture
Conseil
régional de
la Lorraine

It is well known that for citizens, the need to distinguish and to recognize lies at this level of proximity. They are often at a complete loss when faced with a public service that fulfills a number of functions. For them it is not so much the competition between the different territories that matters, but rather the clear identification of the service they need. Here as well the question of exact designation is of consequence, but beyond that, signs of recognition are useful.

These pictograms (pp. 116–17) could be put at the disposal of public services in such a way as to be recognizable from one department to the next. While the spirit and the rectangular frame are respected, the color and style of the motifs could certainly evolve.

Département de la petite enfance

du Conseil régional de la Lorraine

It is worth noting that unlike organizational charts and the traditions that companies follow, it is proximity that is found at the top of the page. The nesting develops downward towards the bottom of the page. It is indeed the identification of the service that interests citizens. Its place in the organization is an internal question rather than a matter for the user.

École élémentaire publique Voltaire

Établissement scolaire de la mairie de Montreuil

dépend pour l'éducation de l'académie de Créteil

Ministère de l'Éducation nationale

Liberté • Égalité • Fraternité
République Française

In this informational process, several levels of visual identification disappear. As does the level of the Ministry of National Education, which we designed a few years ago and which partly borrows this principle.

académie Créteil
éducation nationale enseignement supérieur recherche
Liberté • Égalité • Fraternité
République Française

Clearly things get complicated at that level. Yet it is indeed the legibility of this administrative dimension that is every citizen's due. It seems absolutely normal to know that the school attended by one's children is indeed a municipal responsibility, and that the teaching that goes on there falls within the Ministry of National Education's purview. Yet both communicate and both are rarely found on the same informational support. This is also due to the lack of visual coordination that affects identifying signs. For each political entity, the identification system needs to be brought under control.

This is not limited, of course, to the question of signatures alone. Clearly, at this level, addressing the question of signatures brings us back to that of signage, on the one hand, and Internet sites, on the other. It is a matter of enabling all citizens to get their bearings within the labyrinthine halls of officialdom. We certainly will not have solved everything with this proposal, which, it should be remembered, does not have a graphic value. It is limited to trying to point up a possible visual wisdom that seems quite simply logical to me. Despite the difficulties of the operation, applying such a common visual system at the European Community level would make it possible to create a clear link between local politics and politics on the level of Europe. To show that these ideas are more in line with a kind of urbanity of signs, we propose here a few graphic applications that remain in the realm of possibility, of course. They do have the advantage of integrating logos in the same way flags or even coats of arms do, and therefore leave it up to each place to devise its mode of representation. What would be regulated would depend solely on the link and information.

europe
conseil de l'europe
france
assemblée nationale
rhône-alpes
RhôneAlpes conseil régional
rhône
conseil général
GRANDLYON grand lyon
villeurbanne villeurbanne

villeurbanne villeurbanne
GRANDLYON grand lyon
conseil général
rhône
RhôneAlpes conseil régional
rhône-alpes
assemblée nationale
france
conseil de l'europe
europe

villeurbanne villeurbanne
GRANDLYON grand lyon
conseil général
rhône
RhôneAlpes conseil régional
rhône-alpes
assemblée nationale
france
conseil de l'europe
europe

meer erleben
bremerhaven
Freie Hansestadt Bremen freie hansestadt
breme
bundesrat
deutschland
rat von europa
europa

conseil général
rhône
RhôneAlpes conseil régional
rhône-alpes
assemblée nationale
france
conseil de l'europe
europe

VisitBrighton brighton
Brighton&Hove brighton & hove
Brighton & Hove brighton & hove
East Sussex County Council county council
east sussex
england
U.K. commons
united kingdom
europe council
europe

europe conseil de l'europe
france assemblée nationale
rhône-alpes RhôneAlpes conseil régional
rhône conseil général
GRANDLYON grand lyon villeurbanne villeurbanne

europe conseil de l'europe
france assemblée nationale
rhône-alpes RhôneAlpes conseil régional
rhône conseil général
GRANDLYON grand lyon villeurbanne villeurbanne

europe
allemagne autriche belgique
bulgarie chypre danemark
espagne estonie finlande france
grèce hongrie irlande italie
lettonie luxembourg lituanie
malte pays-bas pologne suède
république-tchèque roumanie portugal
slovaquie slovénie royaume-uni

france
alsace aquitaine auvergne
bourgogne bretagne centre corse
champagne-ardenne franche-comté
guadeloupe guyane île-de-france
languedoc-roussillon limousin lorraine
martinique mayotte midi-pyrénées
nord-pas-de-calais basse-normandie
haute-normandie pays de la loire picardi
poitou-charentes provence-alpes-côte d'azur
la réunion rhône-alpes

While waiting for the sweet dream of Europe to materialize, wouldn't it be interesting to experience this type of approach at a less complex level? I am thinking here of the new territories that are forming around the consolidations taking place among communes. The state of representation ought to prove that the current approach that consists in finding its expression without worrying about its equivalents while trying to keep one's distance leads nowhere. During a competition for the visual identity of Greater Lyon that was won by the Catalan graphic designer Peret in 2003, we tried to represent that territory in connection with the communes making it up.

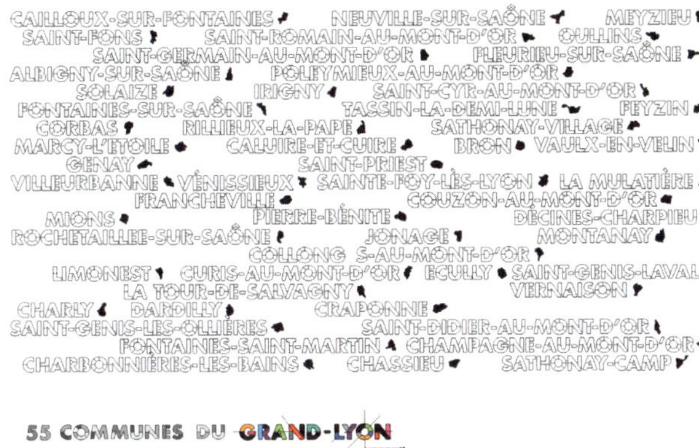

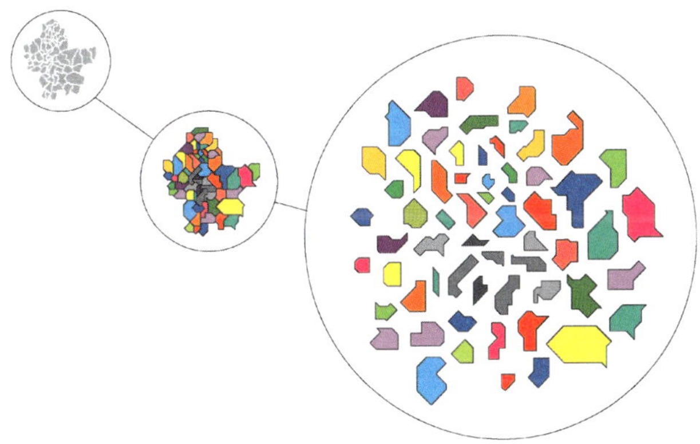

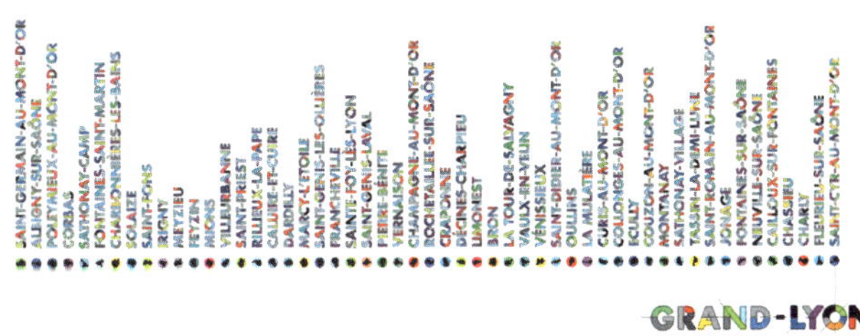

The winning proposal, above, featured a convincing soberness. Our proposal, below, attempted to respond to the needs of legibility of the subgroups.

Various signature modes should be conceivable. The forms or names of the communes were integrated as early as possible.

The proposed system also goes so far as to identify the various public services of the urban community. A more in-depth analysis of the needs of these communities in terms of legibility would make it possible to define representational modes that are appropriate to this urban scale and these indirect representations, often fairly obscure for citizens.

International Organizations

The postrevolutionary world order established in the nineteenth century, in the days when the world was divided into colonial empires, remains fundamentally the one still in force at present. It is still the nation, which represents tens of thousands of citizens or hundreds of millions of people, that remains the central link of the global organization. The United Nations Organization, the principal planetary government organ, designed after the last world war, says as much in its name. Its mode of representation seems to be definitely in retreat, as if faded or subdued in that baby blue it has adopted. Deeper analysis, however, shows a codified coherence around the olive branches. Different world organizations that depend on the UN have in their own way borrowed this sign. The diminutives used for their names form codes that are hard to decipher. For these different reasons, culture (Unesco) and economic organizations (WTO, IMF, World Bank, and BIC) avoid this visual uniformization. The signs as a whole are closer to those symbolizing governments rather than territories. Not easy for people to unite around these bureaucratic signs. It seems every effort is made so that "citizens of the world," all those who put the interests of the planet before those of nations, have no territorial representation. Here once again we run into the territorial abstraction of urban communities, on the one hand, and perhaps the European community, on the other. It corresponds to a conscious or unconscious desire to not create a link between the citizen and these entities.

The consequence of such an approach is their weakening through a want of citizen support, a weakening that affects the democratic system as a whole. Citizens can no longer bring themselves to believe that their votes and the election of their representatives have a genuine impact on these global, megacity organizations. Questions touching on visual representations of governmental entities, of the accurate perception of their authority and style of governance, must not be underestimated. They are part and parcel of the ceremonial writing.

While the flag of planet earth is indeed missing, there is no shortage of signs of its multinational governing institutions.

As with the signs of Europe, blue is the dominant color.

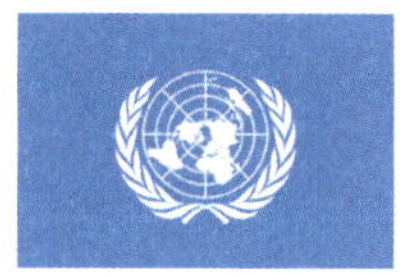

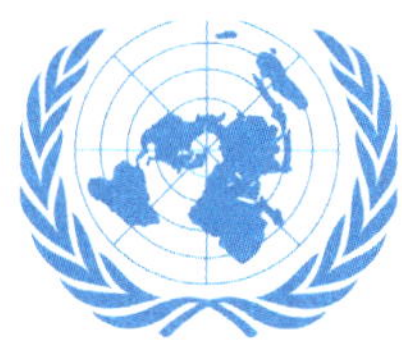

The flag and the logo of the UN and its many variations for affiliated organizations.

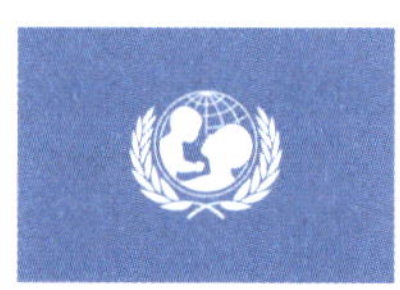

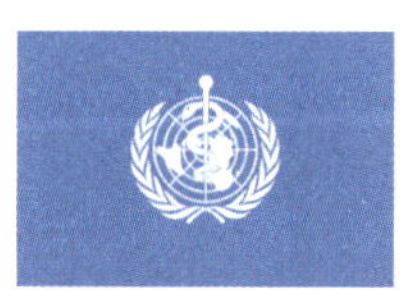

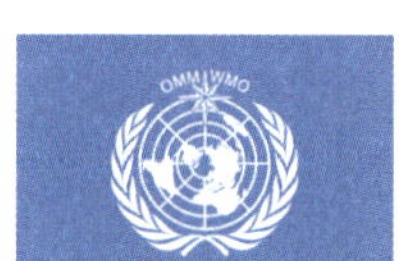

The United Nations International Emergency Children's Fund (Unicef), the World Health Organization (WHO), the World Meteorological Organization (WMO),

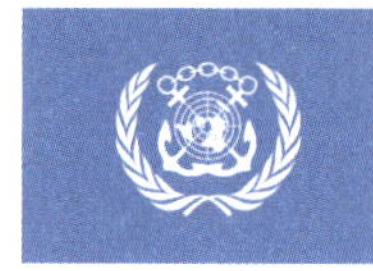

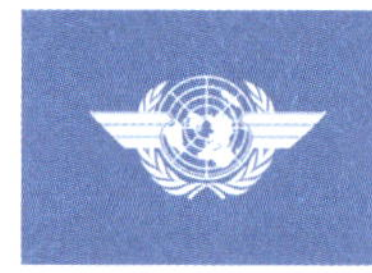

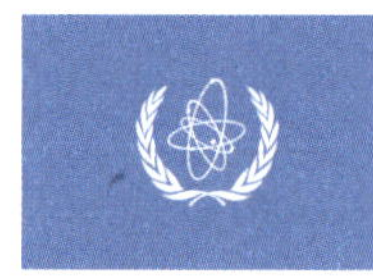

the International Maritime Organization (IMO), the International Civil Aviation Organization (ICAO), the International Atomic Energy Agency (IAEA)...

And less successfully inspired.

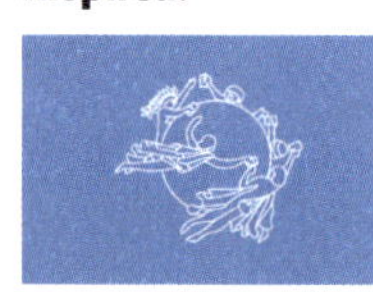

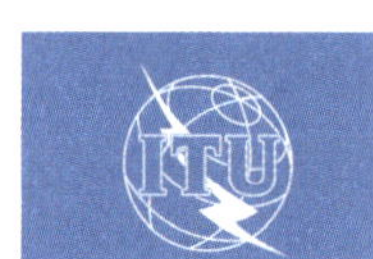

The Universal Postal Union (UPU), the International Telecommunication Union (ITU).

The olive branches symbolizing peace seem to attest to a direct link with the UN.

The logos show less mastery than the flags, although the whole remains coherent.

Certain agencies or organizations refer more directly to the UN, while others make clear their difference.

The World Trade Organization, for instance, though close to the UN, clearly states its independence.

The International Criminal Court is integrated in the UN's visual concept.

Likewise for the International Criminal Tribunal. On the other hand, the International Court of Justice (ICJ), which answers directly to the UN, has its own visual expression.

The same goes for the World Intellectual Property Organization (WIPO), although it is also connected with the UN.

An older institution, the Inter-Parliamentary Union (IPU) displays the olive branches, though without being a part of the UN, with which it works all the same.

The list could easily go on of course. It allows us to compare these signs with more obscure organizations that wield immense power:

the World Economic Forum of Davos, the International Monetary Fund, or the World Bank, the latter being connected with the UN, although it lacks the olive branches. Admittedly its goal is not really to work for peace. Continuing with the same aesthetic of shades of blue, the international organizations that are limited to a certain set of countries make use of their members' flags.

We find this same representation of the flags of participating countries for the G7, G8, and G20 summits.

To summarize, these global organizations seem to cultivate a kind of distancing and froideur that is heightened by a culture largely developed from the diminutive or from code. This bland blue represents perhaps that art of the least common denominator.

Something quite different is going on with nongovernmental organizations and other alternative groups and associations. They, too, express themselves through a great number of logos which are interesting to analyze. Some make clear their alternative position or the popular dimension of their actions, while others aren't shy about borrowing the codes of governmental organizations, undoubtedly in a bid to display their seriousness.

Still others are so familiar to us that they are part of our visual environment. And a great many others deserve a spot on this list but, at this point, we are falling into that logomania where each organization indeed manages to set itself off, yet the whole appears neither coherent nor credible. Non-logos or typograms such as "Emergency Architects" appear to fare the best.

Beyond NGOs, we must also analyze the identification signs of the major movements dealing with global questions.
I shall take three examples from among the legion of possibilities, i.e., the world social forums, the protest movements against speculators and the consequences of the stock market crash due to the policies of economic liberalism, and finally the movements against the summits held by the presidents of the rich countries, be they G7, G8, G9, or G20 in number.

It is perhaps the link between the site of the action and the global cause, or, on the contrary, going as far as to embrace total anonymity, that characterizes these signs of current struggles. This here and now linked with the global even designates activities by the names of the public squares where they play out.

It is only fitting that we should end this analysis on the signs that have something to do with that shared territory that is our planet, indeed with the one sign that the "citizens of planet earth" have offered themselves. Fortunately this does not involve some pictogram from Otl Aicher, nor one of those soppy illustrations of kindhearted humans holding hands, but rather a sign that has a prehistoric connotation, from a time that preceded the concept of nation and maybe even that of private property. But if we conjure up those citizens whose lands become an entity which is more referential than the nation, we need to connect that with the opposite movement that springs from the search for greater civic proximity to the neighborhood, village, etc. The two movements are not opposites, since there are visual similarities between them. For them the logos are far more narrative than posters.

It is that exchange or participation of the citizen, not neighborhoods as political entities, that is represented through these signs. While more than one of these signs involves that form of dumbed-down communication, others try to represent the desired interaction. More than a few convey the plural, which makes plain they indicate a kind of coming together in a city or commune rather than a particular neighborhood. We cannot really conjure up the initiative of citizens since generally this involves the attempt by a municipality or another organization to connect with its population.

The Tunisian citizens' initiative, for example, as its name indicates, is indeed that initiative that spurs both action and debate.

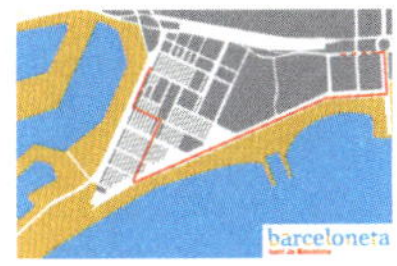

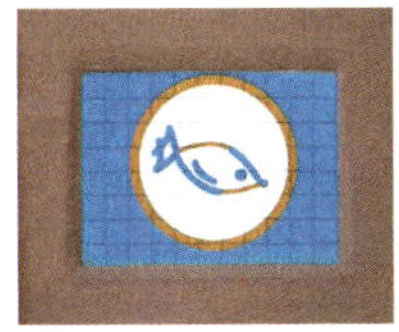

We have also developed, with the students of the ELISAVA design school, an identification proposal for Barcelona's different barrios, the aim being to render the city's neighborhoods more legible. To give them the ability to express themselves as they are. Three-quarters of them are reproduced here, along with others, with the development of a visual language for each that is meant to reflect the particularities of the barrio while taking into account the fact that it, and all the others, are a part of the city of Barcelona. This was not a question of adding logos to other logos but rather of finding codes for diversifying the modes of expression and representation of these adjacent locations. These languages ought to provide a representation of the real atmosphere and particularities of each neighborhood. Rather than a competition, this entails a visibilitization of the differences. But it is difficult to talk, however, about these kinds of projects for neighborhoods without bringing up the fruitful experience of the Quartier des spectacles, the nightlife district of Montreal. A non-administrative territory decreed by the heads of various cultural institutions, this neighborhood only gradually became known thanks to the presence of its visual language. Communications doesn't act independently, it takes its place in synergy with the transformation of the on-site reality. The visual language was constructed around the notion of light. Thus, the logo played only a secondary role. For us it was much more important to find a common thread allowing each action to be specified, without losing the advantage of the synergy for all that. The extensive work of composing public space has gradually become the subject of communications. Many designers took part in this process, which made it possible to characterize the neighborhood.

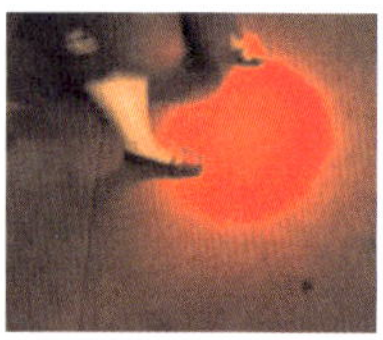

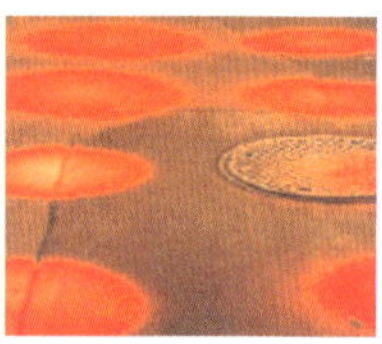

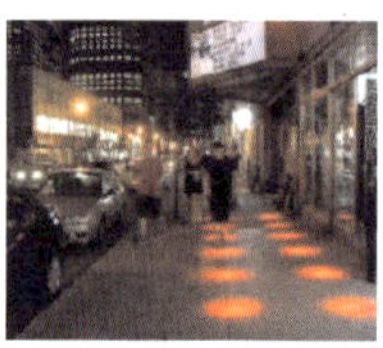

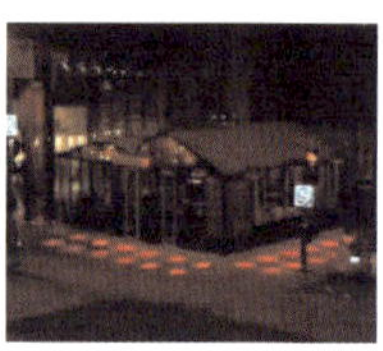

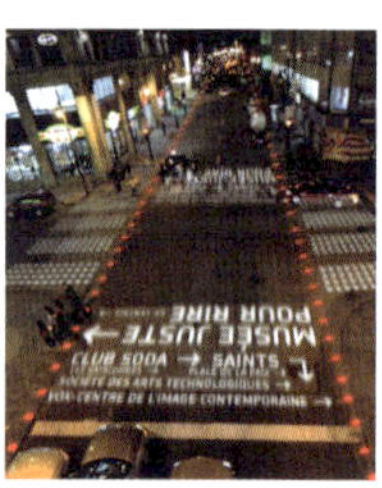

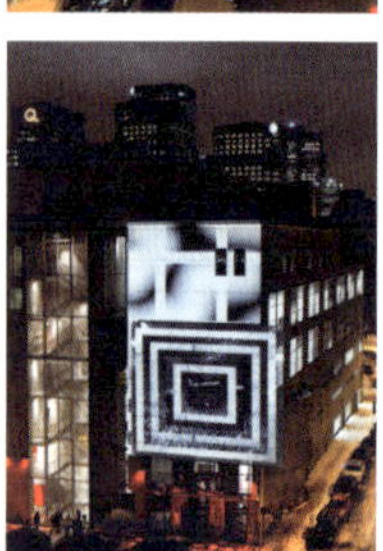

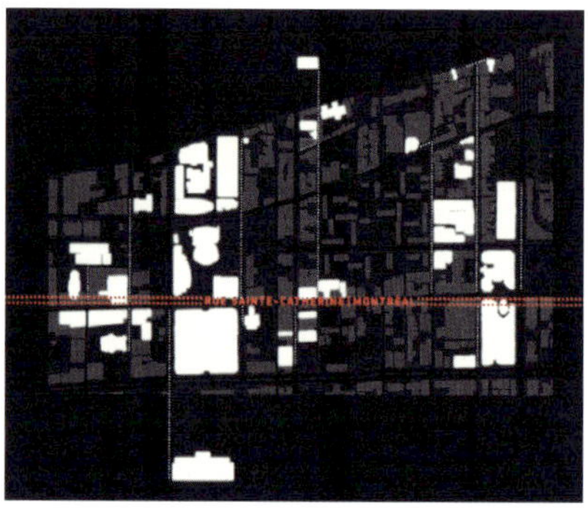

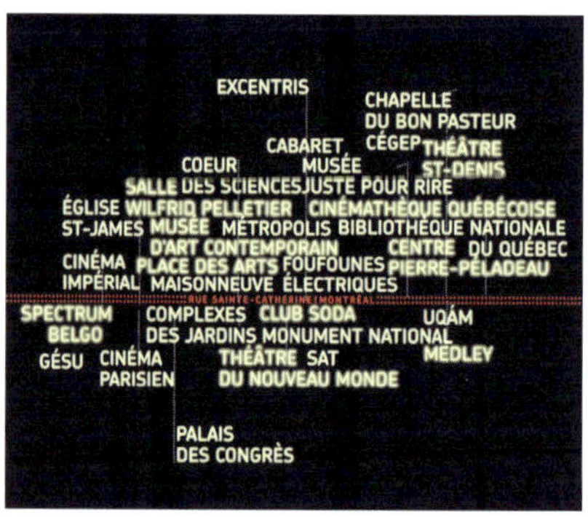

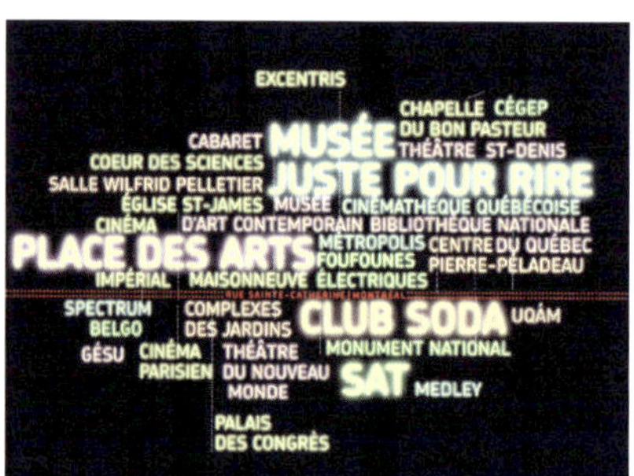

QUARTIER DES SPECTACLES MONTRÉAL

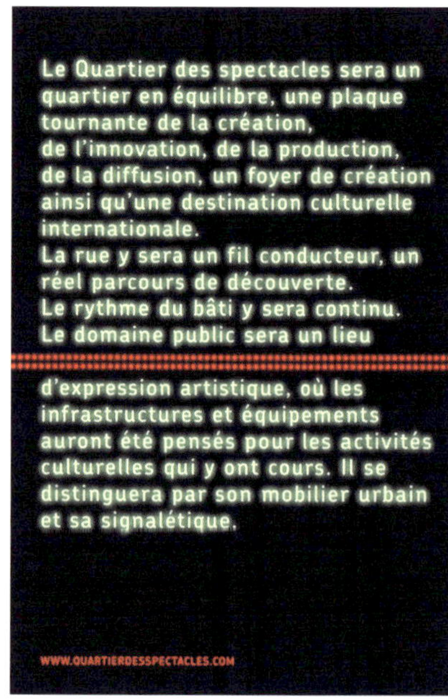

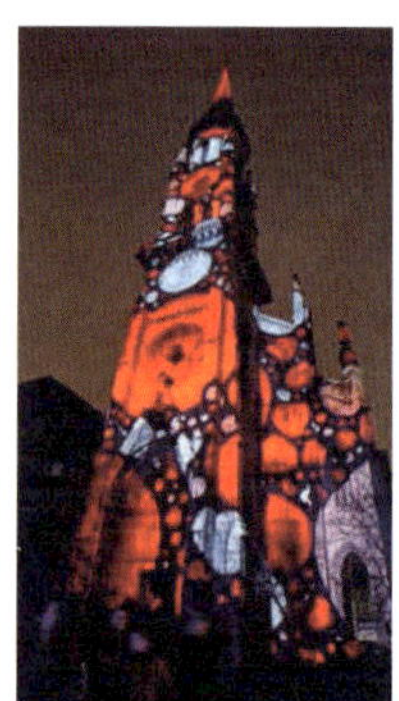

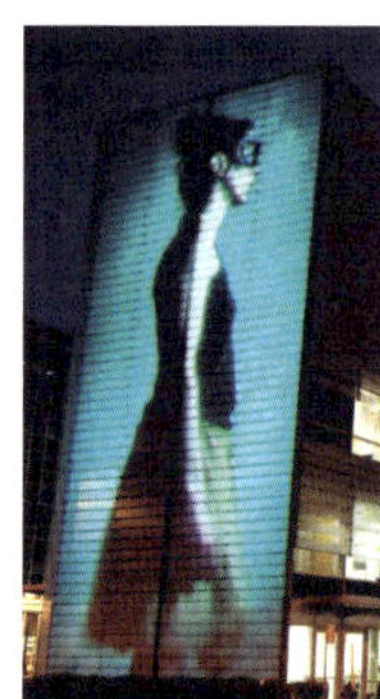

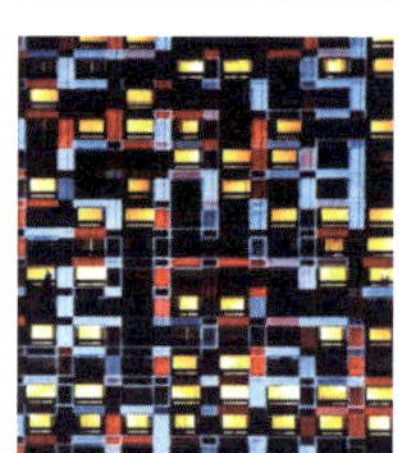

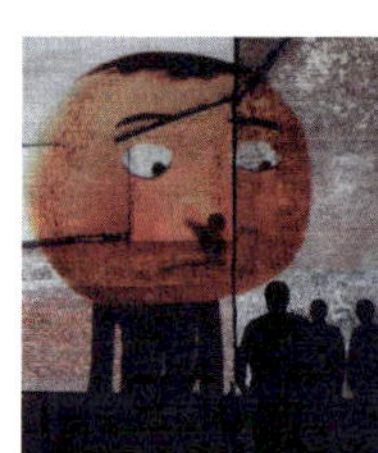

The Citizen of the World and Hyperproximity

Whether one wants it or not, there exists an increasingly strong link between the here and now, the local, the neighborhood, that public space that is crossed daily, what Bruno Latour calls the choices of the photocopier space, in a word hyperproximity, on the one hand, and the planet, on the other. Citizens are aware that the quality of their personal lives is often dependent on events that are hyperlocal and bound up with forces that are beyond the scope of political authorities. This realization, moreover, does not call into question the role of politics but does open up a complementary space in which citizens take direct charge of operations, sometimes against the opinion of their elected representatives. It is interesting to note the visual link between the representations of these local initiatives and visual expressions of nongovernmental organizations and other international movements fighting for various planetary causes. It is a connection that goes beyond the question of logos and above all the question of the administrative territory, with its borders that are famous or simply inscribed in a more or less long history.

In the space of this here and now, closely connected with the rest of the earth, projects that make sense are able to take shape today, it seems. To do so, however, one will need to break free from the burden of that sort of permanent planetary observatory that encourages us to favor events that are likely to interest the rest of the world. A good number of branding strategies work in this register, representing and constructing in a way a territory for someone who will not experience it, for the person who one tries to both convince and captivate. A healthier and certainly more civic approach would involve accepting what one is and clearly formulating what one wants, building around that focused intention, and then informing others. This link between serenely doing and then expressing it has to be reinvented. It works, in my opinion, in that place of resistance represented by spaces of proximity that manage to surpass the notions of territories defined by pre-established borders and governmental authorities. If these often prove conservative or caught up in the social egotism that consists of strongly supporting only one's own circle of family and friends, and the organizations beneficial to them, it manages at times to move beyond this pettiness and place itself locally at the service of shared interests, while cultivating its specificity. The question of representation in these cases is repositioned with respect to doing and not the location of its immutable territorial status.

Evolutive Identity and Visual Language

While evolutive systems of representation have been the subject of numerous experiments in the past few years, we can subdivide those that are purely decorative variations and those that allow one to render processes that are undergoing development and whose evolution cannot be anticipated. Unlike a closed system, a language can evolve. It is recognizable regardless of the message that is given expression, the person using it, and the chosen style. Learning a language is of course more complex than recognizing the same sign repeated over and over, but it makes it possible to express oneself, evolve, adapt, inform and bear witness, chart differences and repetitions. Mustn't we try to imagine public spaces in terms of this shared grammar and vocabulary that leaves room for a range of expressions?

To design a logo for a space is to represent in a way its constancy, roots, opposition to change; to offer it a visual language is already to enable it to be expressed. To imagine visual language for political fields as complex as those tackled in the present study is to imagine systems that can be read as a whole, but which allow each subgroup to be defined within them. These common languages could, when coordinated, define shared space in contrast to space that is private for us. Another kind of analytical ability that is a far cry from the logic of business might thus create the serene space that is necessary to the smooth functioning of information for citizens in shared space.

From Markings to Writing

With these questions of signature being laid to rest so to speak, we now have to study their functional presence in public space. While it is good that citizens can know an institution's or a specific action's connection with a political entity, this should not be a pretext for a mass dissemination of the logo, as if it were a place to be occupied visually, as if some commercial success depended on it. It is quite difficult to get communications people, who are trained to win market share, to grasp this point. Yet civil peace is also at stake. If the presence of advertising in public space is today almost universally considered a factor of disturbance that ought to be regulated, institutional logomania seems to escape this constraint. Yet, when one gets beyond functional information, it is possible to consider this repetition of the same identifying sign as stemming from the same visual pollution. Must we mark with one and the same signature each informational support, each object financed by the political authorities, each action that is linked to them? If it is indeed right to extend to citizens the possibility of recognizing what they are financing with their taxes, this identification need not necessarily involve this identification stamp, this mark repeated forever.

Rather than marking public space, isn't it rather a question of writing it? Writing it with words, but also with forms, colors, uses, ways of saying things that react to needs and contexts. Writing so that each intervention is part of an identifiable whole, a kind of visual language that is recognizable from its structure. A style that can evolve over time, adapt to various situations as it does to the different authors of this study.

The analogy with language appears justified since it is indeed a question of determining a grammar, a vocabulary that everyone can use in their way to express themselves. Thus, alongside the signature system that is common to all political territories, there might develop a real difference in terms of the way of writing this shared space qualitatively and respectfully.

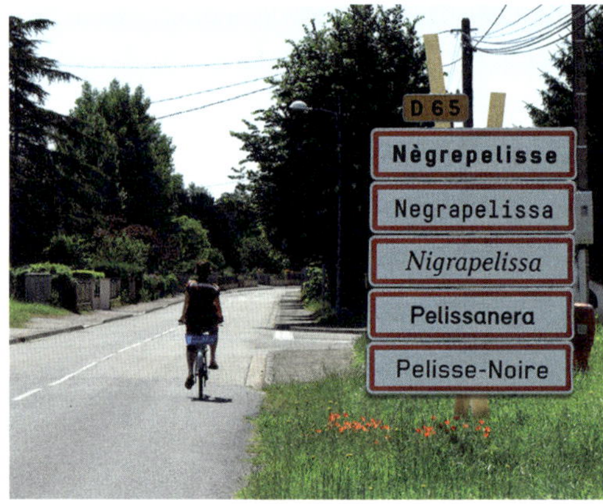

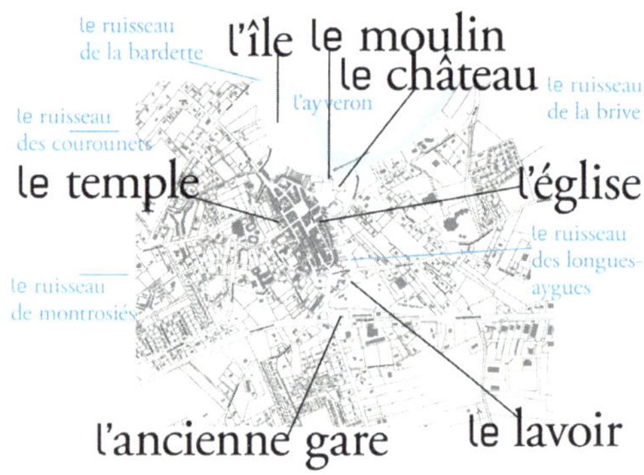

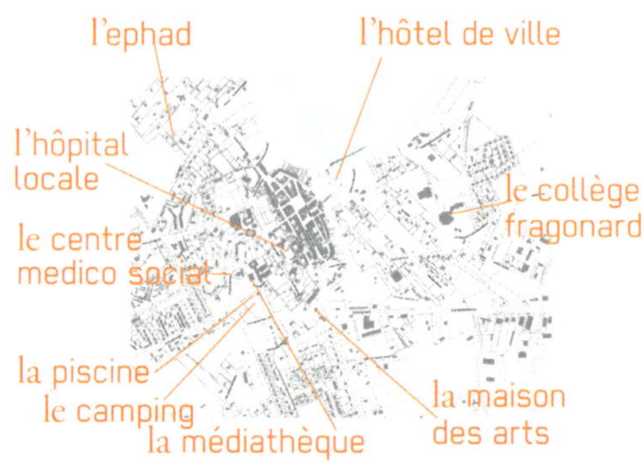

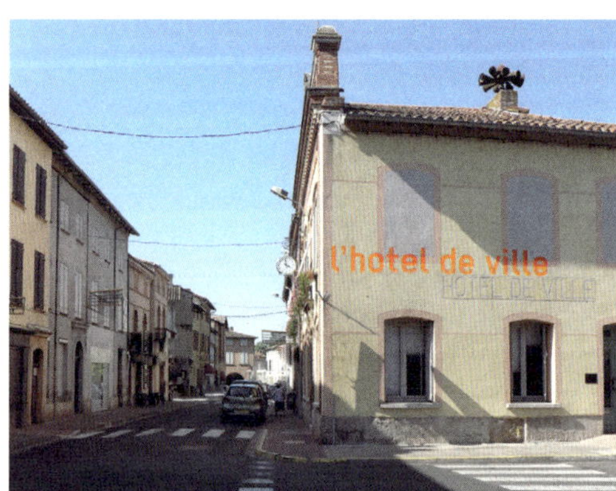

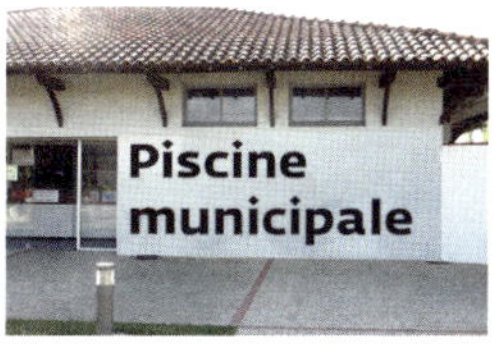

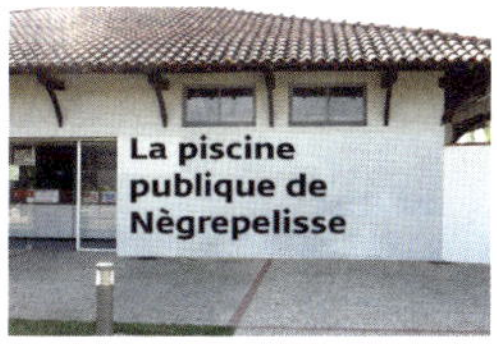

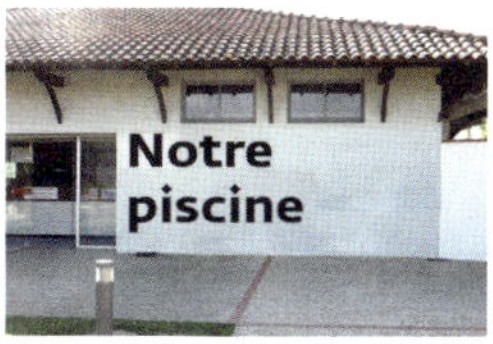

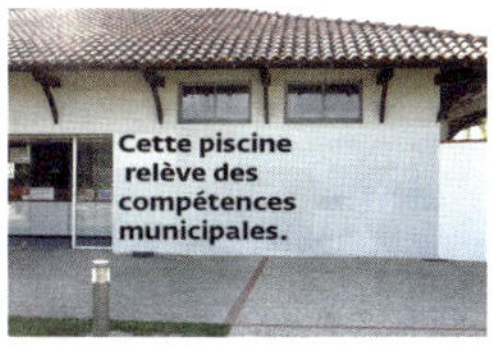

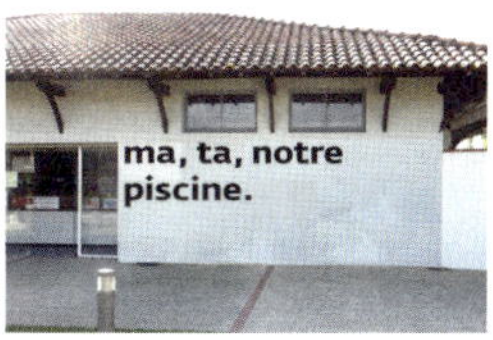

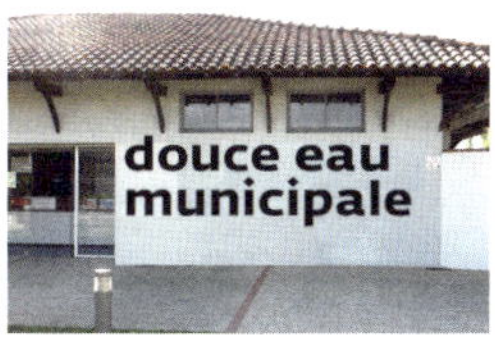

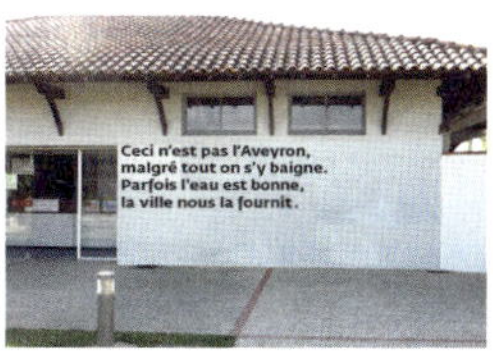

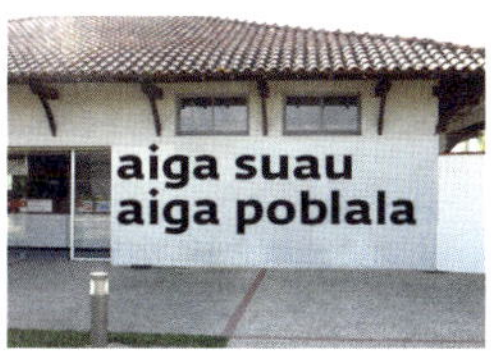

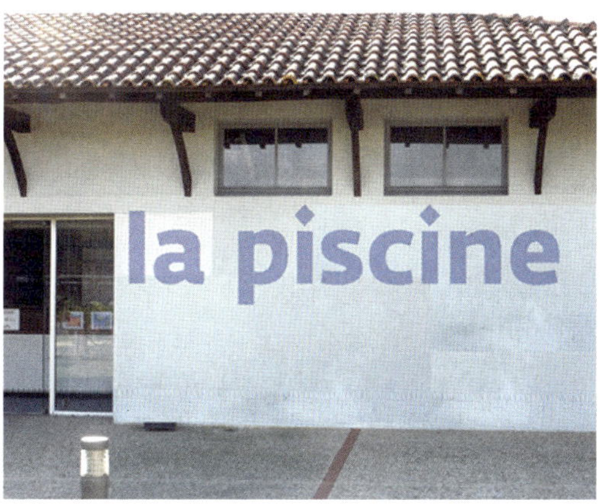

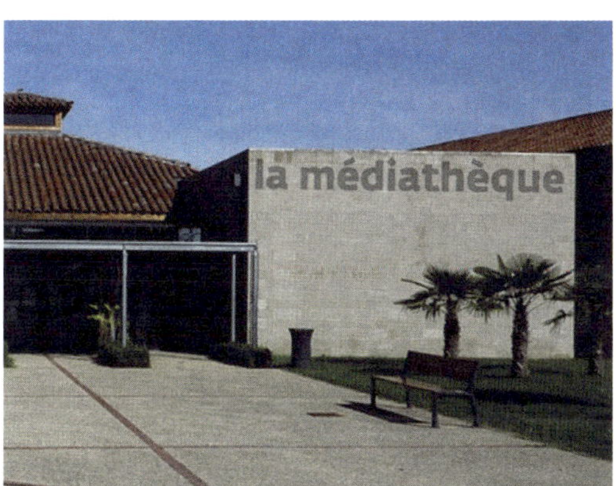

With the Civic City Institute and Head Geneva, we were invited to reconsider the public graphic signage of the small town of Négrepelisse near Toulouse. After carrying out a detailed study of the existing system, we focused on the identification used for the municipal swimming pool. How should one greet citizens without subjecting them to the succession of signs banning one thing or another that is posted solely for legal coverage or to be able to impose fines? If it were really a matter of informing the public, other means would be necessary. But beyond this broader question of the way public space is addressed to citizens lies the question of identification, which concerns us more directly. Thus, is it really necessary to write "municipal" in big letters in this context? The letters' form agrees with the formulation in this sense. The comparative proposals show the extent to which these modes of identification influence our perception of one and the same service. The removal of the term "municipal" and the addition of the definite article was the obvious choice. "The Pool" clearly means that it is the only one and is open to all. The systematic application of this approach selected for all of the buildings linked with city hall would make reading this public space easier. We would thus leave the logic of advertising behind and content ourselves with informing people and rendering the city more legible. While these words and phrases meant for the city's inhabitants can be pared down to a simple name, signage on the city's historical legacy, on the other hand, would involve descriptions enabling the curious to understand the site.

From Marking to Information

The present essay on the brand images of political territories has gradually developed into a plea for a kind of peace with respect to the signs of identification in the public domain. This is an appeal to officials asking them to accept a visual civility in the interest of their citizens, by giving priority to questions of recognition and information over those of captivating viewers and territorial marketing; by rendering political authorities and the ties with other public entities more legible; by accepting to follow rules in common enabling us all to find a clear perception of the competent political and administrative structure in our living and working spaces; by cultivating the representation of proximity and differences rather than that of the least common denominator; by considering information as an integral part of the design of public space; and by dedicating to it artistic requirements as much as regional planning, and by considering it as such.

Questions of artistic form and creativity have not been raised in these pages. The worst and the best are juxtaposed here, as they are in our daily environment. A quality sign—corresponding to the functional constraints of reading, making sense with respect to the context it represents, appropriate and simultaneously contemporary, formally interesting—contributes like a good architectural design to a gesture that is quite simply civic. Representing oneself correctly is nothing less than dressing in a dignified manner, neither in too showy a way nor vulgarly. At the same time, such qualities become almost illegible in a visual environment where shameless strategies transform these representational spaces into a vulgar free-for-all. Thus, it is not enough today to individually design quality signs; rather we must define together modes of representation that express this space where citizens are asked to behave in a responsible and dignified manner. This important building site could be the subject of a prototyping at the urban community level, for example. Ideally—but this is utopian—these questions will be worked on in the interest of the citizens of the earth by international institutions that have been sensitized to the problem.

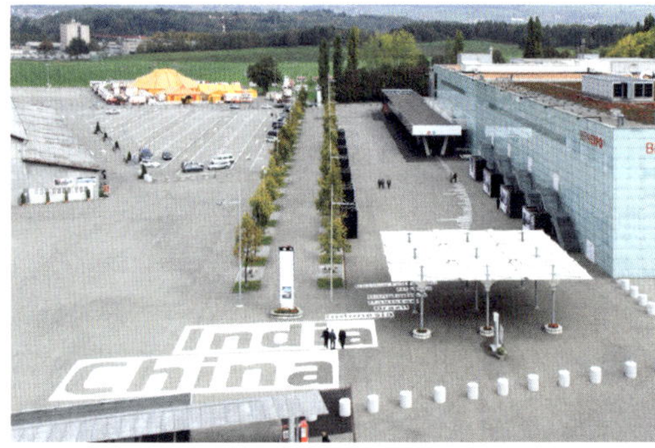

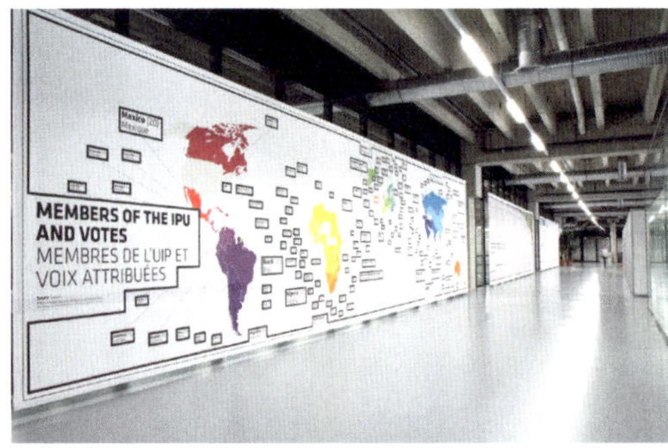

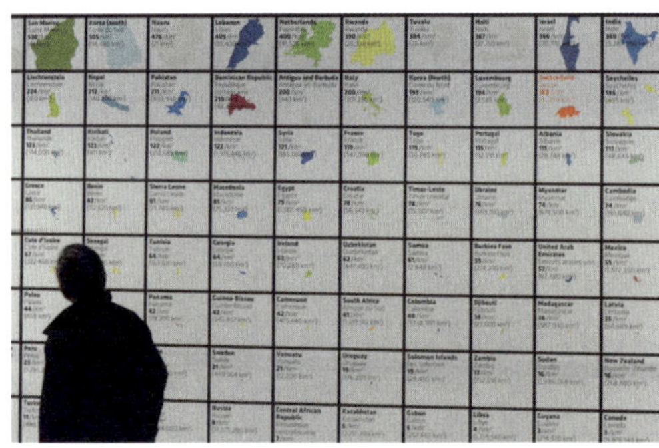

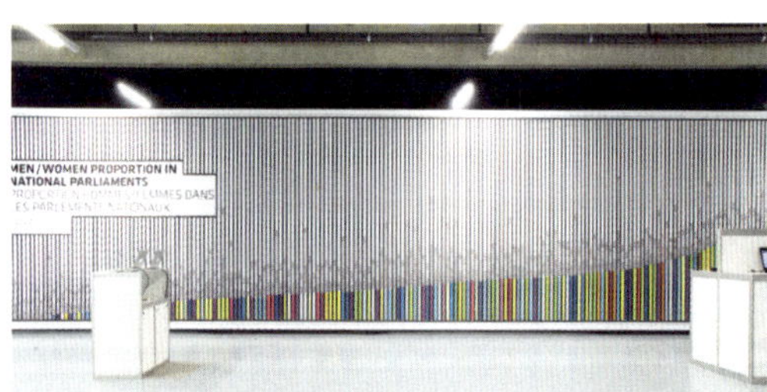

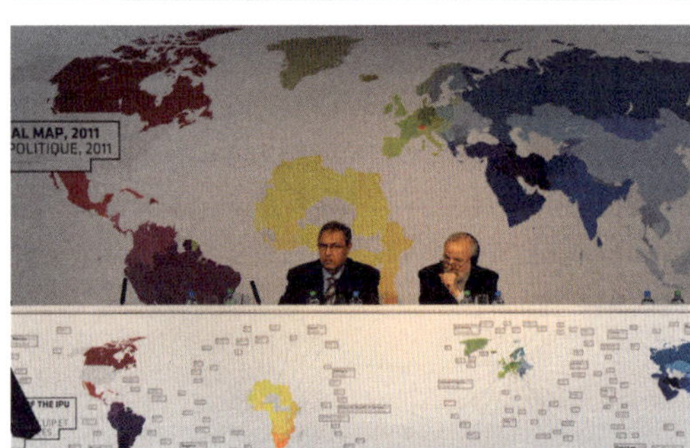

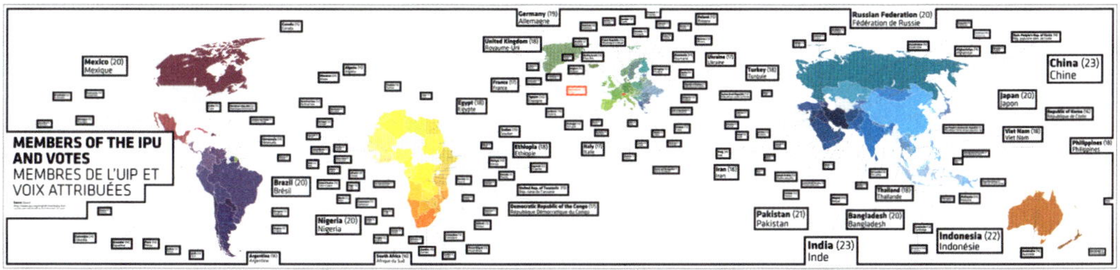

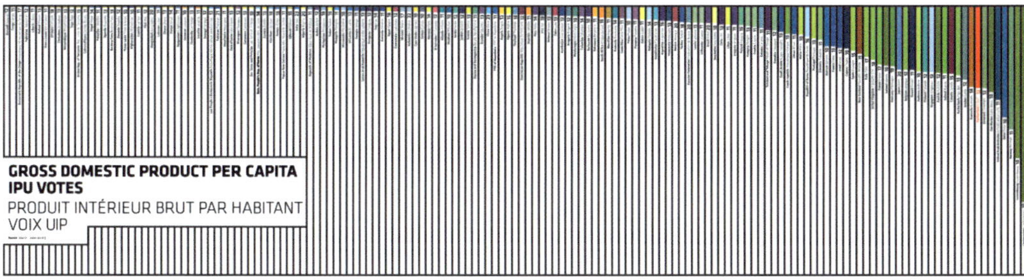

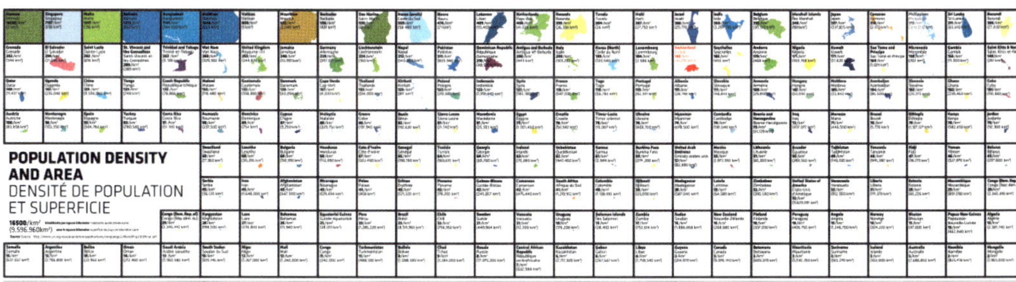

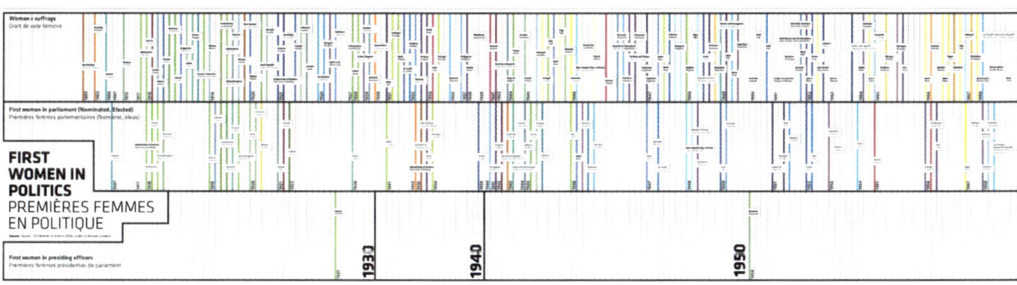

The International Parliamentary Union was holding a congress in Bern. Rather than mark this temporary territory with the organization's logos and decorate the site as is done for any other congress, we thought it would be fitting to immerse the delegates in statistics concerning the state of the world. An initial outside installation (a painting on the ground) indicated the number of inhabitants for each country. Thus China and India greeted visitors, who then followed the names of the other countries listed in descending order right up to the building's entrance (the population of the host country, Switzerland, placed it far down the list from the first examples). Once they entered the building, delegates then found themselves immersed in statistics on the state of democracy throughout the world. The subject of the congress became its visual framework while the organization's regular logo remained in the background. These color visuals lent the subject both atmosphere and a serious aspect. This was only a temporary intervention, which nevertheless shows how to shift, at this level as well, from the brand to visual language.

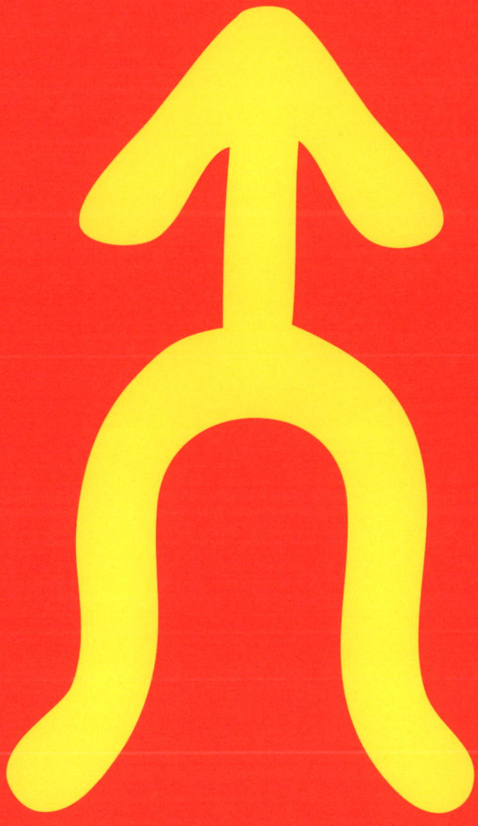

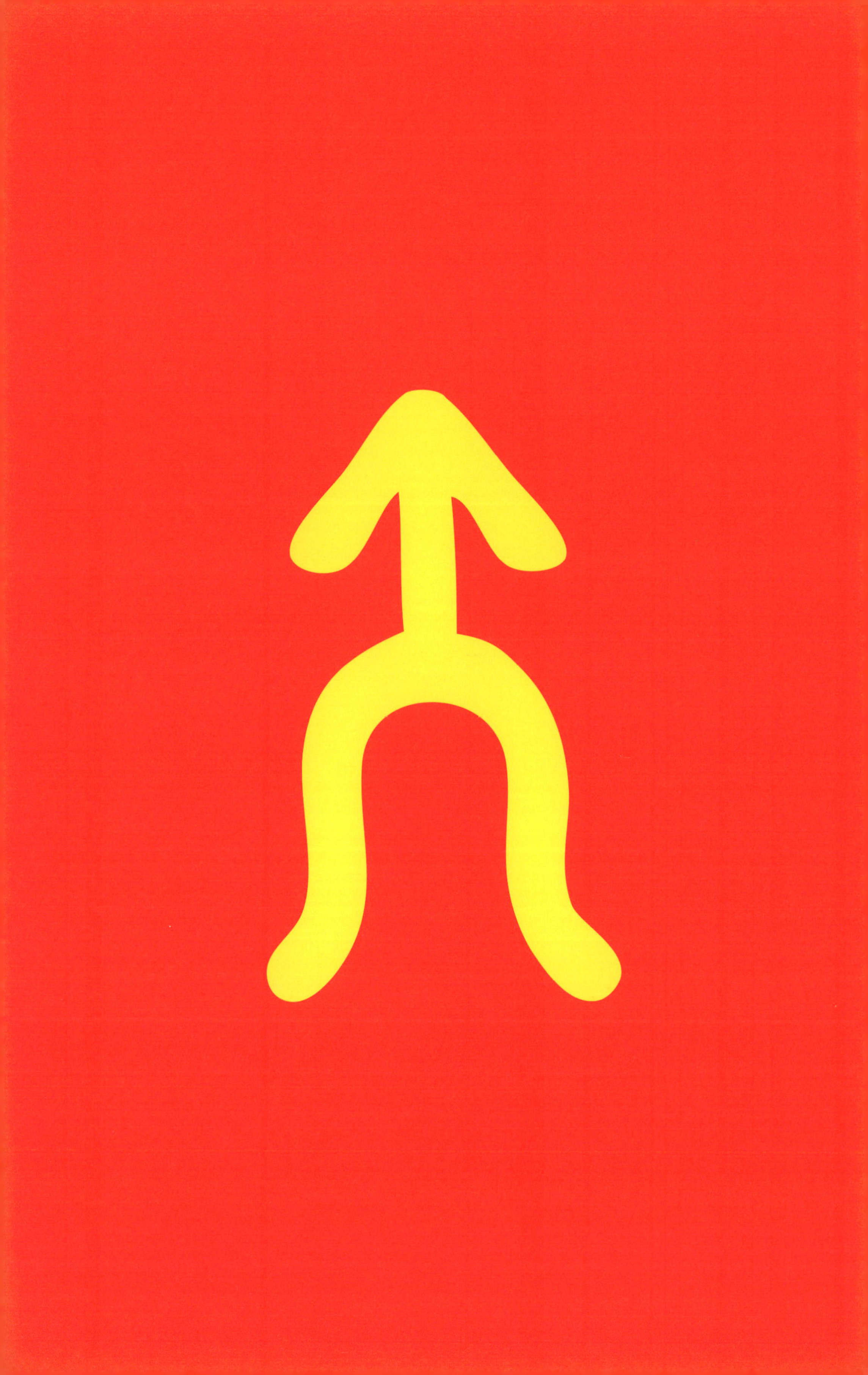

Sugar Dictatorship
Great Nation

Abstract

"Sugar Dictatorship" examines the connection between the principles of branding and political imagery through a selection of heads of state. Based on four recent examples (Angela Merkel, Vladimir Putin, Silvio Berlusconi, and Barack Obama), the study attempts to work out the modern principles behind the branding of political figures, the individual manifestations of the phenomenon, and the means chosen to implement it.

This visual investigation, moreover, features additional chiefs of state, presidential candidates, former presidents, and significant historical figures. They serve as benchmarks and reference points to help us understand the sociopolitical phenomenon of presenting and shaping political actors in visual terms, certainly not a recent development but one that has gained both importance and relevance worldwide.[1]

The expression "sugar dictatorship," our coinage, serves here as an open framework for a creative study. The association of the two terms functions as an anchor for the subject under discussion, an anchor that is striking and above all untainted by any professional point of view.

The resulting visual analysis of the two poles of tension, i.e., branding and "the political," is based on freely chosen examples of photorealist images and graphics. And behind these featured examples lies a textual organization by which the individual principles of branding are examined both individually and together as a whole.

The present chapter claims neither to treat the subject exhaustively nor to propose a qualitative evaluation of the individual personalities and their milieu, be it their culture or political system.

Rather, the thematic sections studied here display graphically the depoliticizing of various state entities as well as the emotionalizing and instrumentalizing of representatives and heads of state in light of branding's mechanisms and the use of well-known marketing strategies.

This visual analysis focuses on each political actor within his or her branding system while holding all of them up for scrutiny.

The notion of branding should be seen in a relative way throughout the following study. Rather than understanding the discipline in a classical sense, we ought to grasp it in terms of a mise en scène of political actors and therefore a far-reaching sociological problem with a range of characteristics.

—

1 See Jay G. Blumler and Dennis Kavanagh, "The Third Age of Political Communication: Influences and Features," *Political Communication* 16, no. 3 (1999), pp. 209–30.

It is especially interesting in this regard to consider what it means for a modern understanding of politics and democracy.

The visual presentation of political figures is today becoming increasingly significant in the political process, although seen historically this has been the case for some time. Over the years, however, only the prevailing conditions, i.e., the possibilities of communication, have generally evolved far more than the principles that visual presentation obeys. Nearly each of history's major leaders—from Caesar to Napoleon to Hitler to Obama—is closely bound up with a concrete image in which a claim to leadership is both given voice and made good on. Both the image and the claim stem from the national or transnational situation of the respective country.

The parallels in the visual mise en scène of political figures are to be found superficially in the connection between the ruler (the heads of state) and the ruled (the people),[2] as well as in their historical and sociocultural context. Considering Max Weber's theory from the contemporary point of view raises the question of whether we are in fact seeing, in modern political representation, a more or less rapid shift toward high modernity's "charismatic authority" (after the traditional and rational-legal types of authority of Weber's analysis). Within this phenomenon, the legitimacy of leadership plays out in both the emotional and visual communalization of the political. In addition, the ruler's deft charismatic or communicative abilities determine the persuasiveness and lasting quality of the image.

Contemporary actors in leadership roles are increasingly subjected to pluralization, fragmentation, and economization.[3] And in a related phenomenon, these leaders themselves, like the political demands of their countries, are turning with increasing frequency to societal trends and mass products to get their message out. Of major relevance in this regard, in addition to the ruler-ruled relationship mentioned above, we now are seeing the attraction and recognition—symbolic and popularized by the mass media—as well as the division of interests of leaders among themselves.[4]

—

2 Max Weber, "The Three Pure Types of Authority," in *Economy and Society*, Berkeley et al., 1978, pp. 215–16; originally published in German in 1922 as "Die drei reinen Typen der legitimen Herrschaft."

3 Claudia Ritzi and Gary S. Schaal, "Politische Führung in der Postdemokratie," *Aus Politik und Zeitgeschichte* 60, nos. 2–3 (2010).

4 See Jonathan McClory, *The New Persuaders II: A 2011 Global Ranking of Soft Power*, London, 2010.

"Sugar Dictatorship" constructs a visual bridge between the carrot and the stick, propagandist constructions and neo-populist manifestations. The two notions face off symbolically as two opposite poles of tension. The degrees of adaptation of current political systems make this clear, in terms of an increasingly professionalized and "seductive" aestheticization on the one hand, and the visually contrived manipulation and incapacitation of the citizen on the other.
The stage is set.

Definitions

Sugar
is a generic term that covers all sweet-flavored saccharides (mono- and disaccharides), as well as the commercial term for disaccharide sucrose. It is considered both a staple foodstuff and a luxury. It is part of those foods that have no use-by date. Numerous studies have looked into the correlation between sugar consumption and addiction. However, science continues to debate whether the results of these lab studies, usually carried out on rats, also apply to humans.

Dictatorship
(ultimately from the Latin *dictator* and *dictatura*) is a form of government in which absolute political power is wielded by either one person, the dictator (leader), or by a group (e.g., a party, military junta, or family). According to the particular form, nowadays we distinguish between authoritarian and totalitarian dictatorships.

Research Policy

The concept of our research work is based on making a subjective selection of the hits that Google Images provides in response to a series of search terms targeting the chosen protagonists.

The key words used in these searches are the outcome of reflection as well as our own experience with the representation of heads of state in the framework of their national brand.

The results of our occasionally over-the-top research put us variously in touch with news portals—from the serious to the questionable—and social media tools, as well as nightlife and celebrity-gossip portals, even private collections (blogs like tumblr, for example). Of course the official media outlets of government representatives played an important role, too. Government sites and social media tools like Facebook and Twitter accounts proved a rich source of material for analyzing the visual language and tone of different government media.

The subject of Google Images in connection with a creative outcome is hardly new to us given we had often turned to this method for our graduate thesis "Good People, Great Nation" and so had learned in the meantime to wield it practically and above all precisely. One can quickly get lost in this kind of research since almost no limits are imposed on either the particular "stalker" facet of the project or the variety of the results.

In the run-up to the visual research and its application in our chapter entitled "Sugar Dictatorship," we took advantage of many classic reference sources and contemporary contributions to political science, along with well-known writings in sociology (for example, Max Weber's "The Three Pure Types of Authority"). Moreover, there are books on design whose approach suggests a real kinship, and whose ostensibly populist visual aspect of political representations sheds additional light (*Iron Fists: Branding the 20th Century Totalitarian State* by Steven Heller). The same goes for the foundational texts and definitions in the sociopolitical field. This sound textual portion of our study, i.e., the conceptual work, proved very useful during the stage of empirical visual research, and again as a basis for understanding in our own analysis. And it proved useful, too, in developing a personal—and very vivid and striking—narrative for our subject.

Christian Rau and Lukas Weber

Branding Through Merchandise

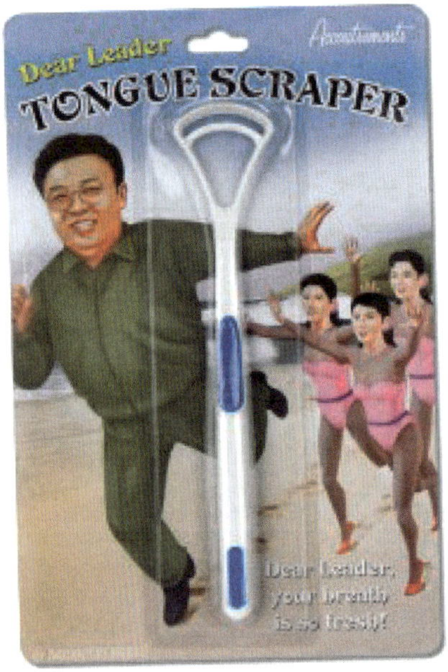

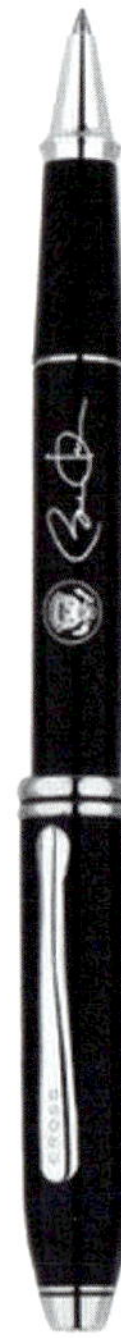

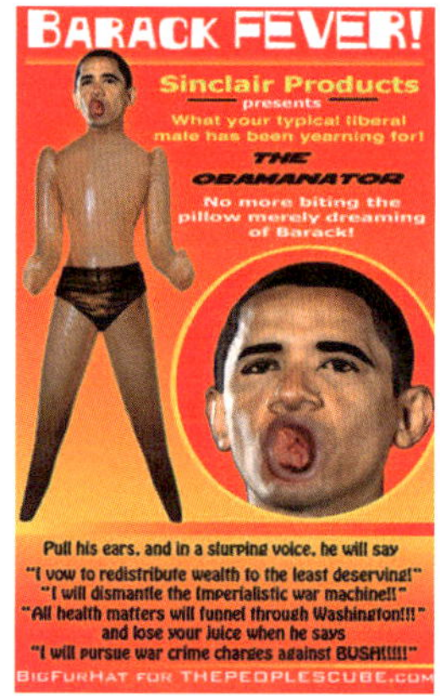

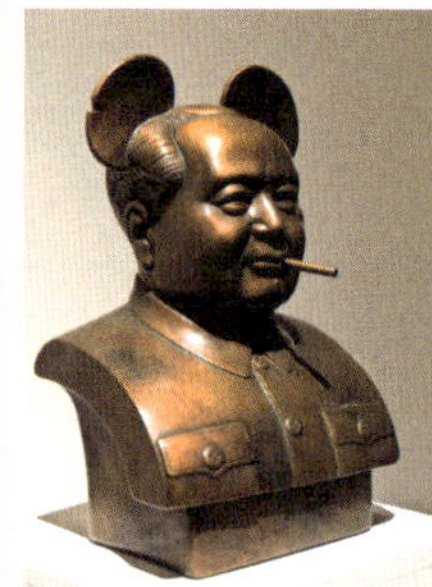

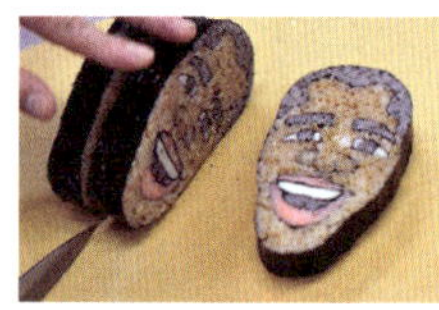

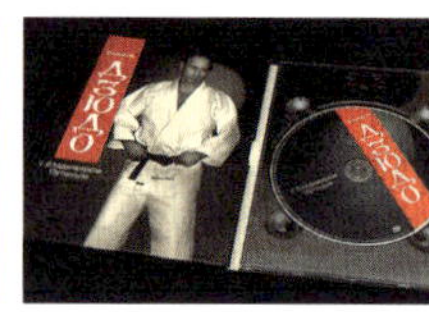

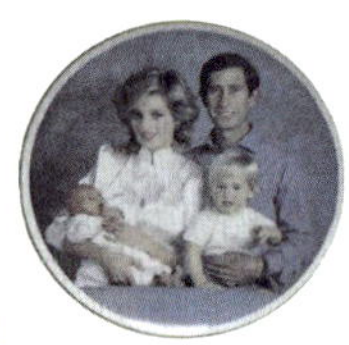

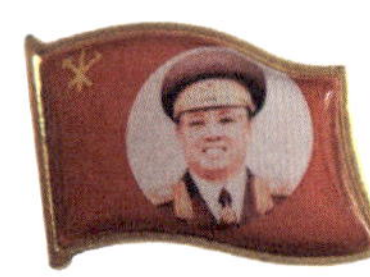

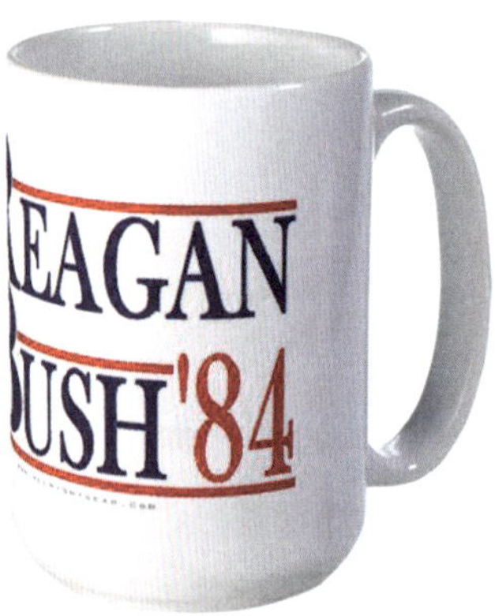

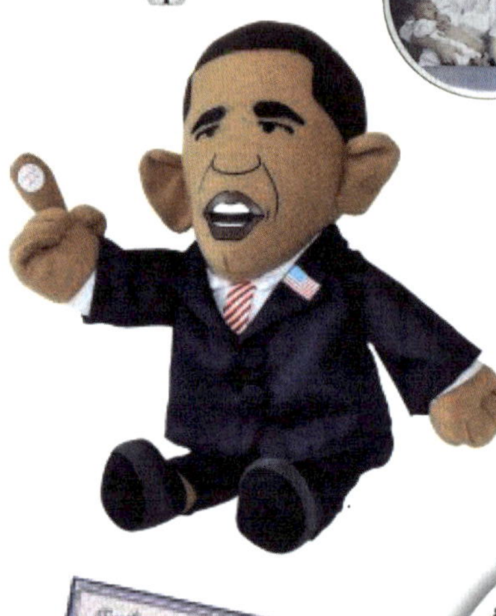

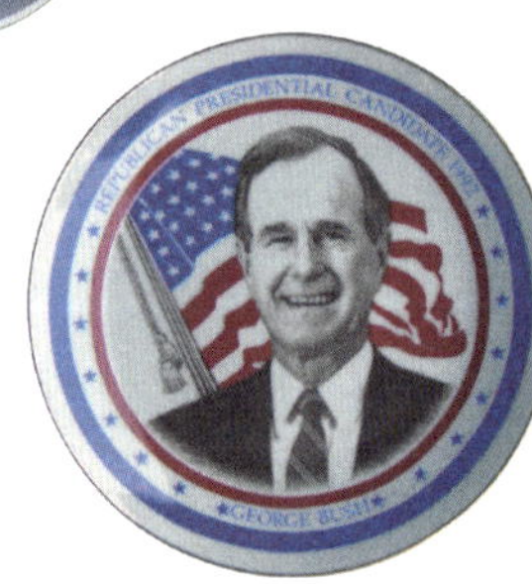

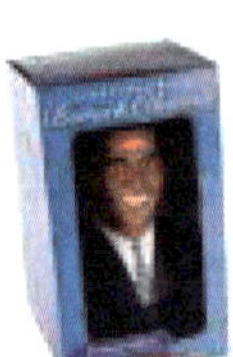

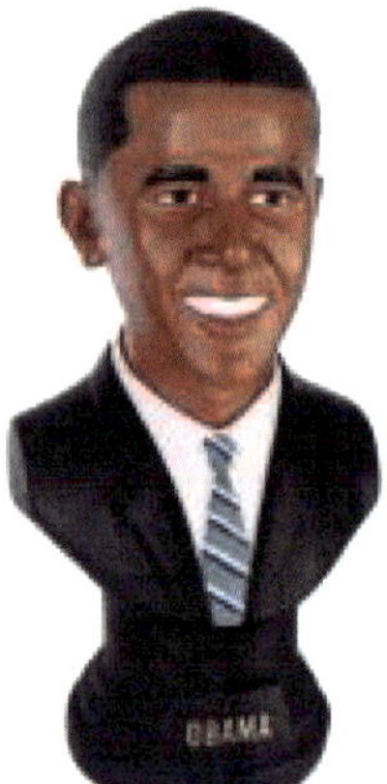

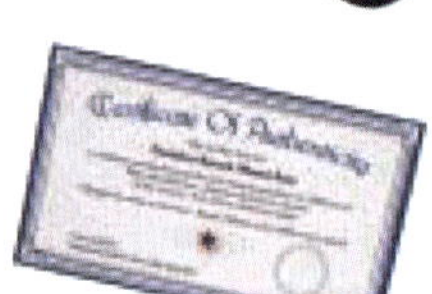

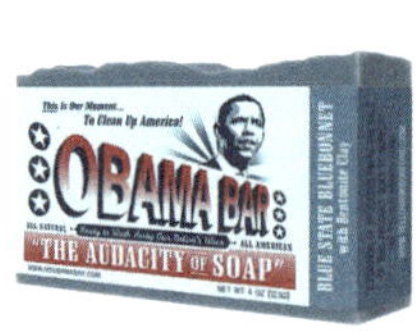

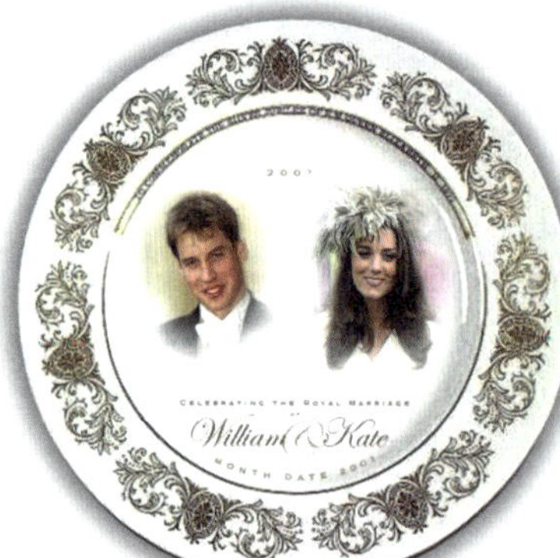

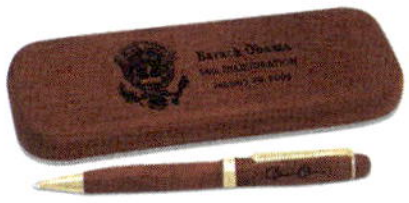

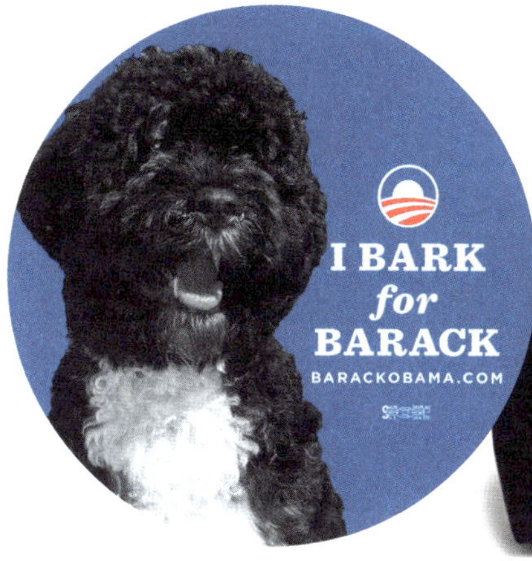
I BARK
for
BARACK
BARACKOBAMA.COM

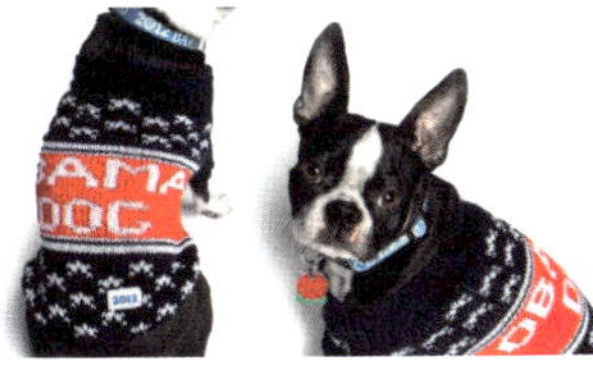

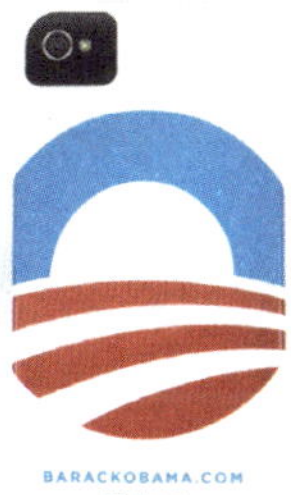
BARACKOBAMA.COM

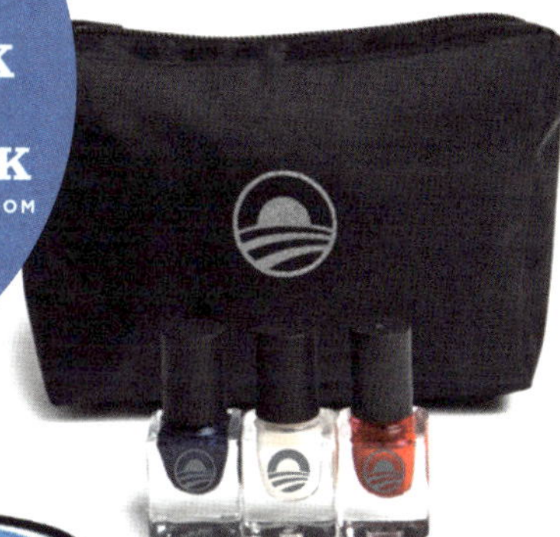

OBAMA

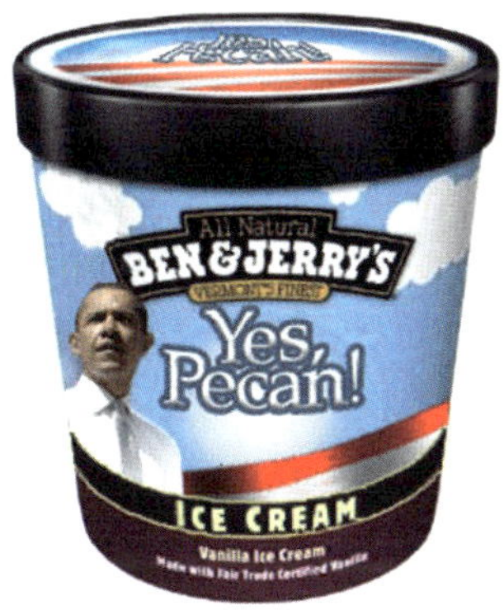
All Natural
BEN&JERRY'S
VERMONT'S FINEST
Yes, Pecan!
ICE CREAM
Vanilla Ice Cream
Made with Fair Trade Certified Vanilla

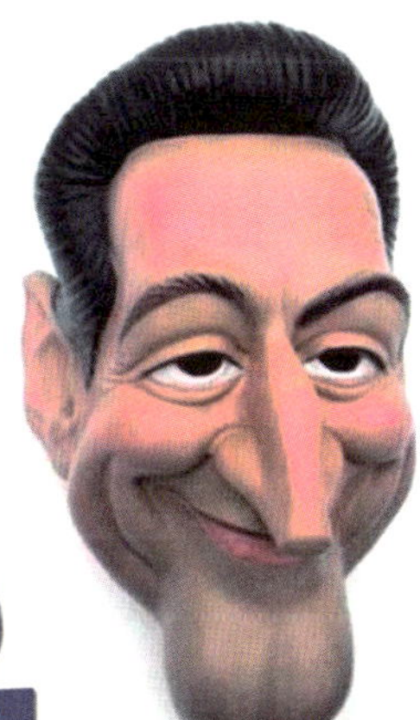

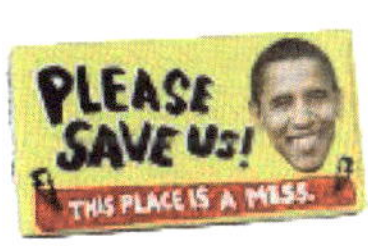
PLEASE SAVE US!
THIS PLACE IS A MESS.

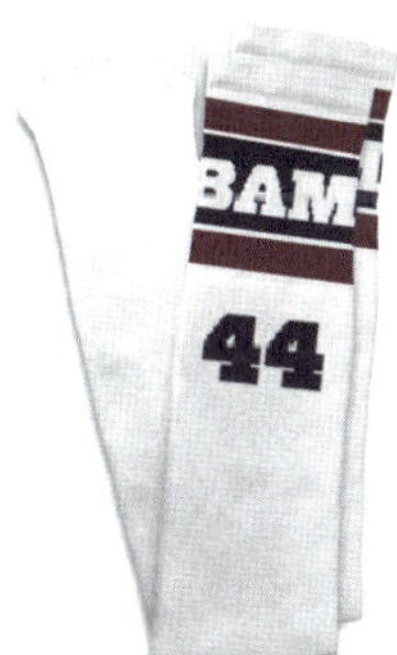
BAM
44

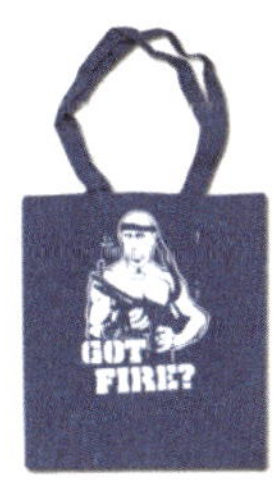
GOT FIRE?

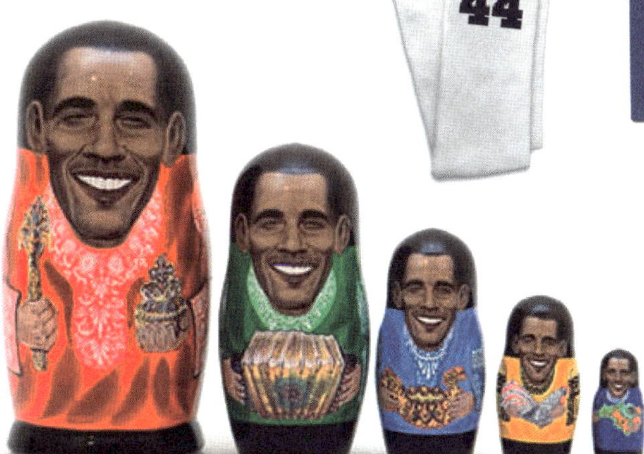

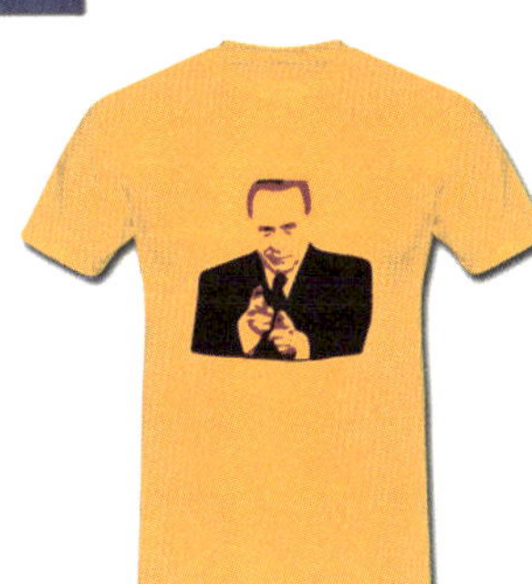

Branding Through Merchandise

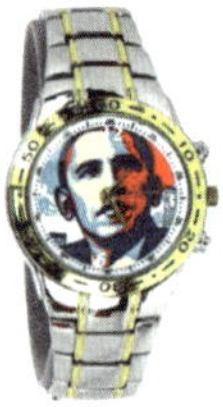

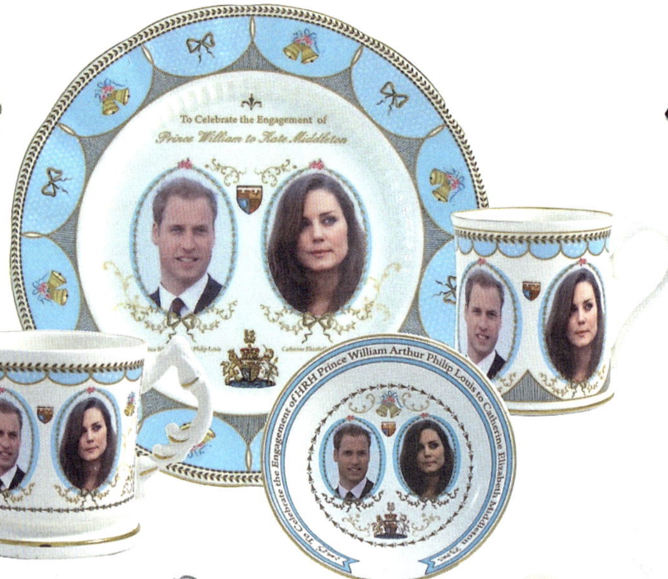

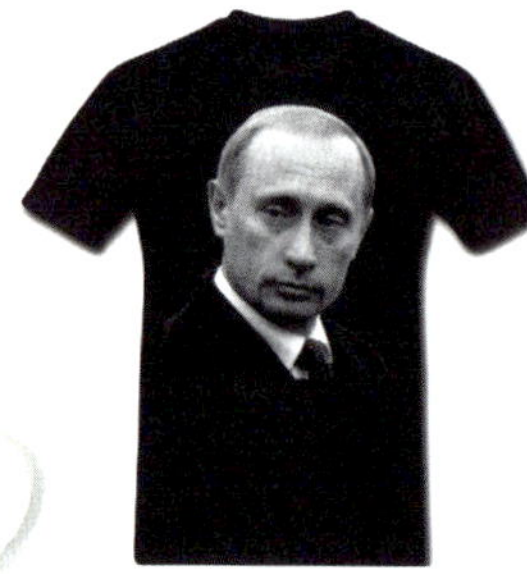

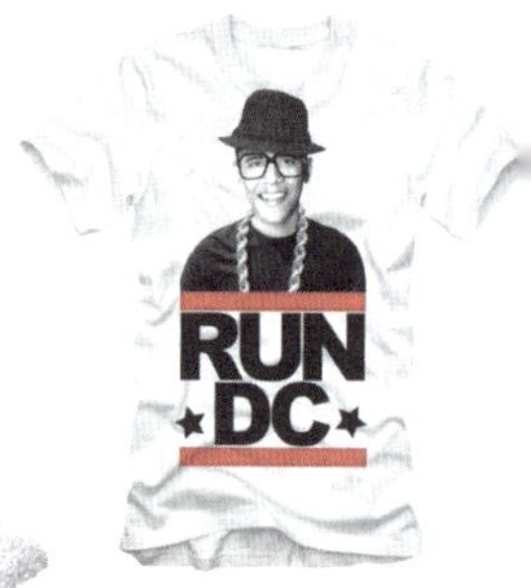

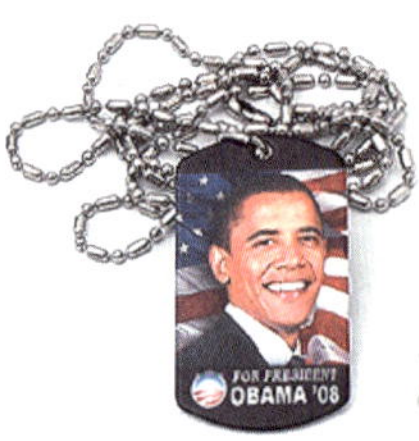

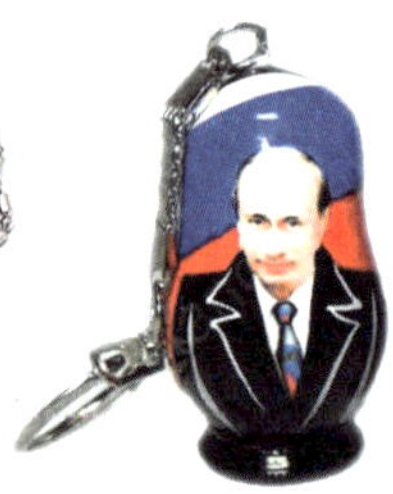

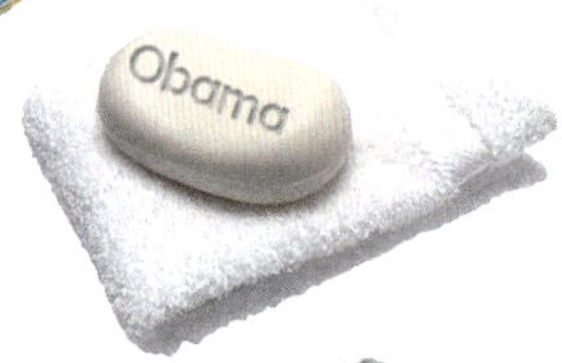

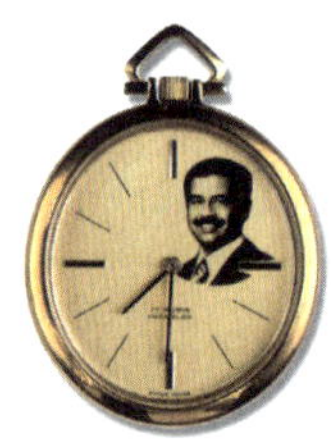

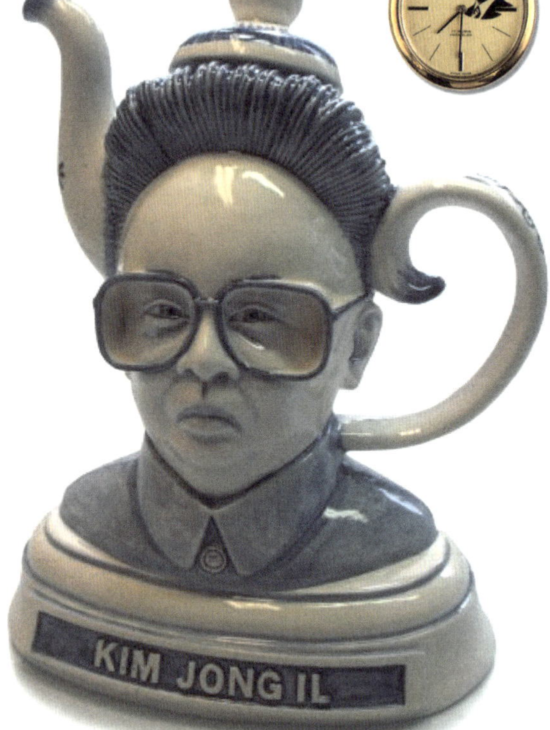

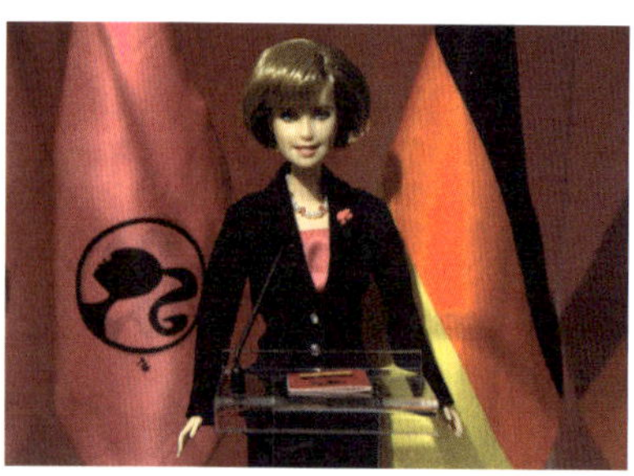

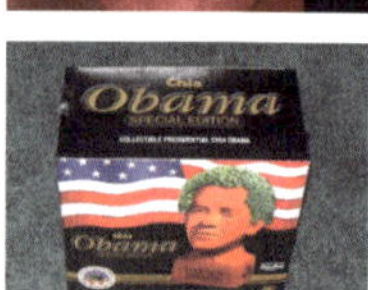

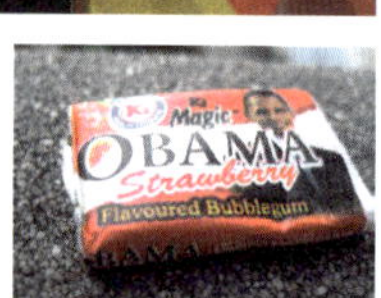

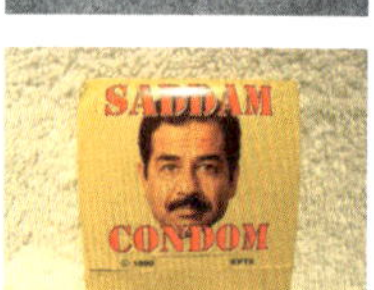

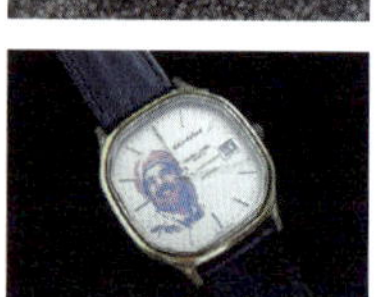

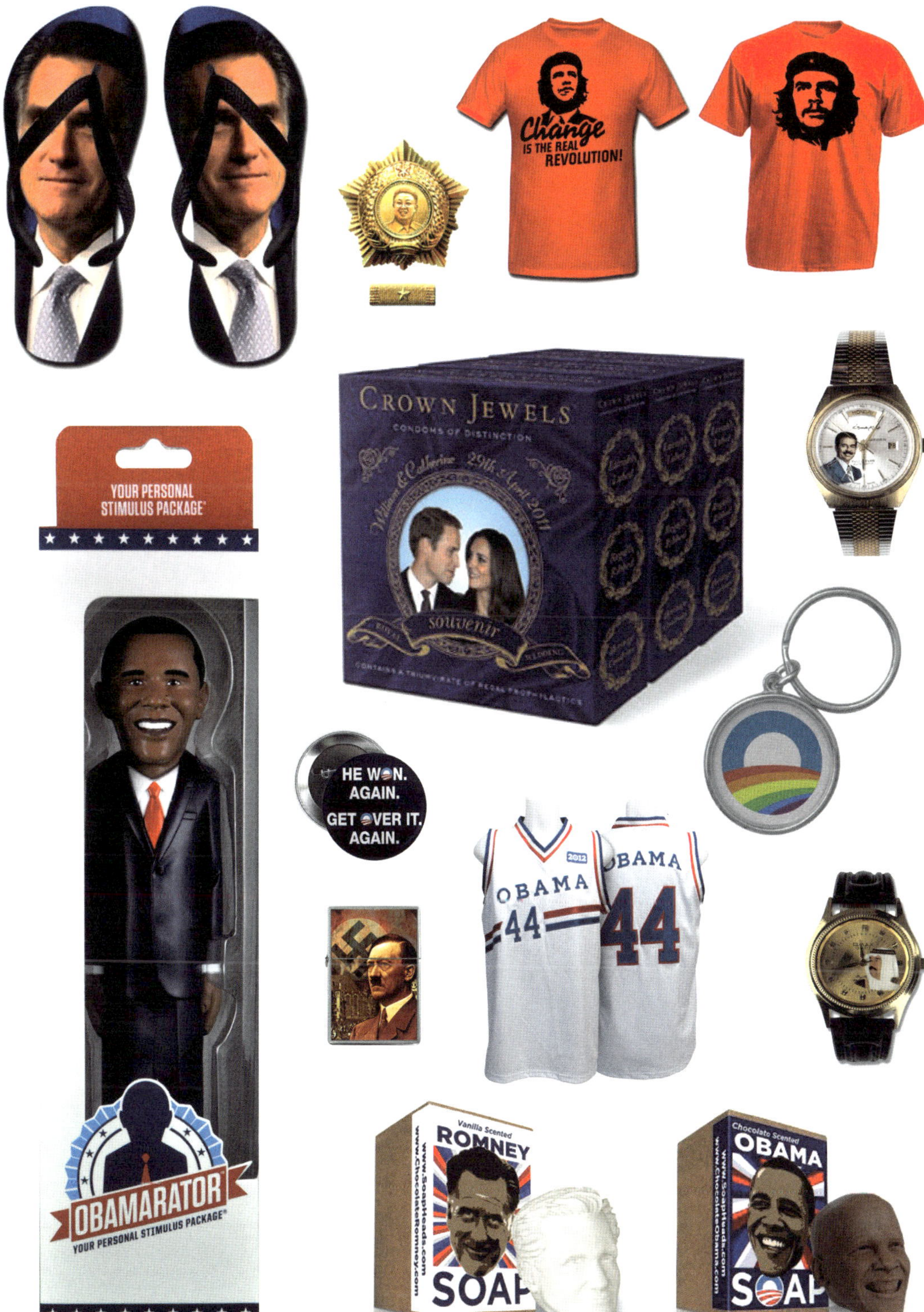
Change
IS THE REAL
REVOLUTION!
CROWN JEWELS
CONDOMS OF DISTINCTION
William & Catherine 29th April 2011
souvenir
CONTAINS A TRIUMVIRATE OF REGAL PROPHYLACTICS
YOUR PERSONAL
STIMULUS PACKAGE
HE WON.
AGAIN.
GET OVER IT.
AGAIN.
2012
OBAMA
44
OBAMA
44
OBAMARATOR
YOUR PERSONAL STIMULUS PACKAGE
Vanilla Scented
ROMNEY
SOAP
www.SoapHeads.com
www.ChocolateRomney.com
Chocolate Scented
OBAMA
SOAP
www.SoapHeads.com
www.ChocolateObama.com

Branding Through Merchandise

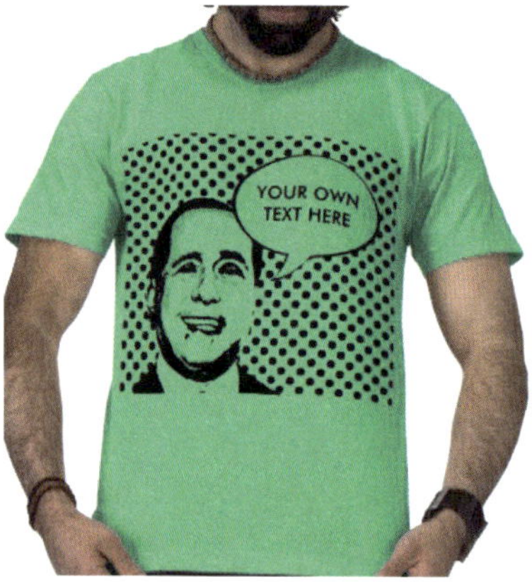

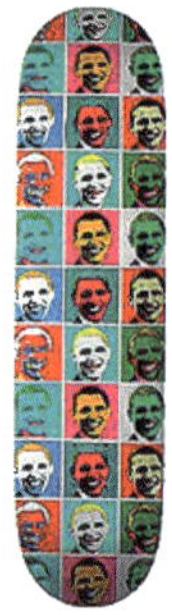

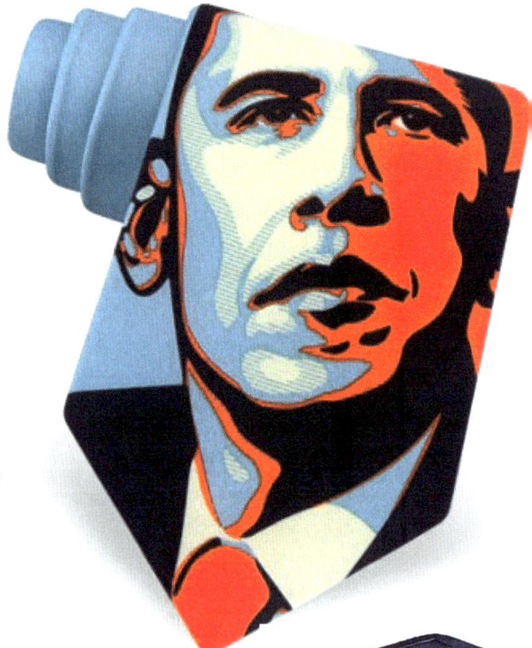

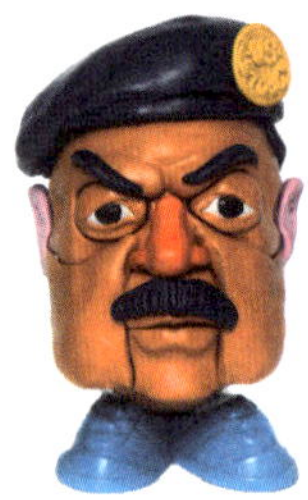

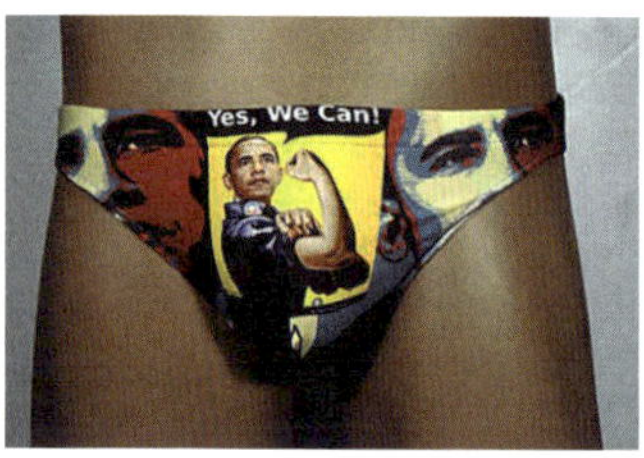

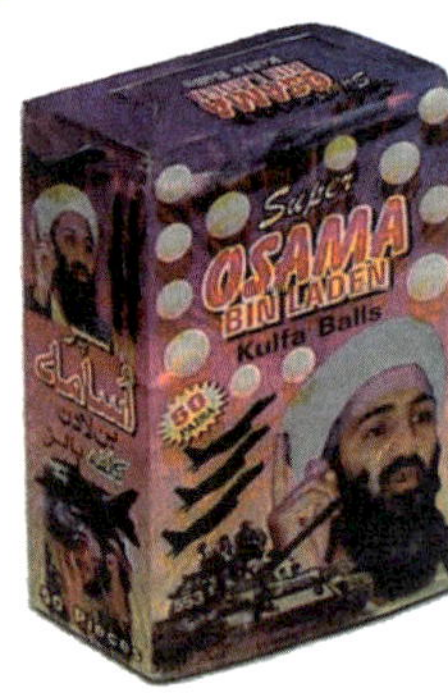

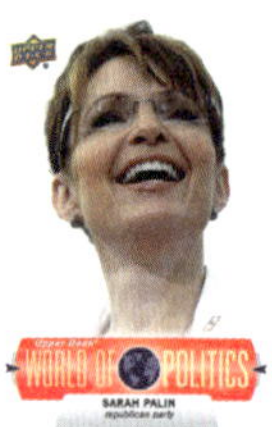

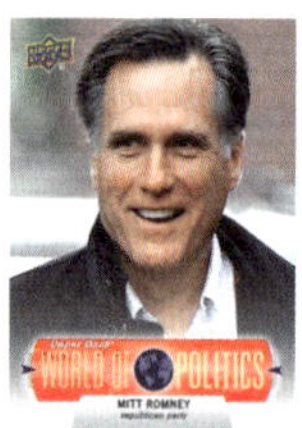

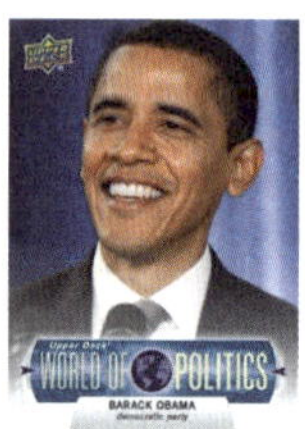

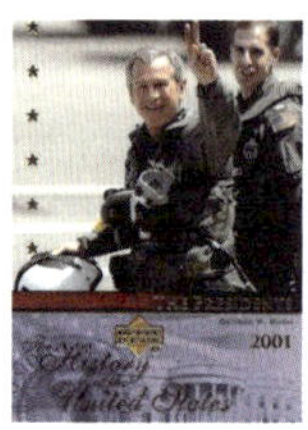

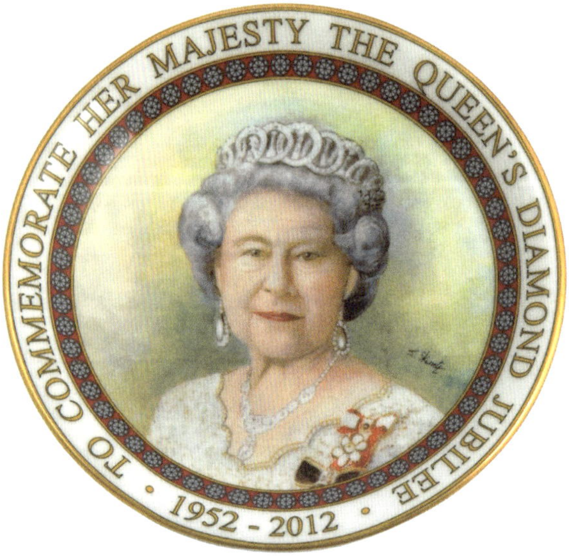

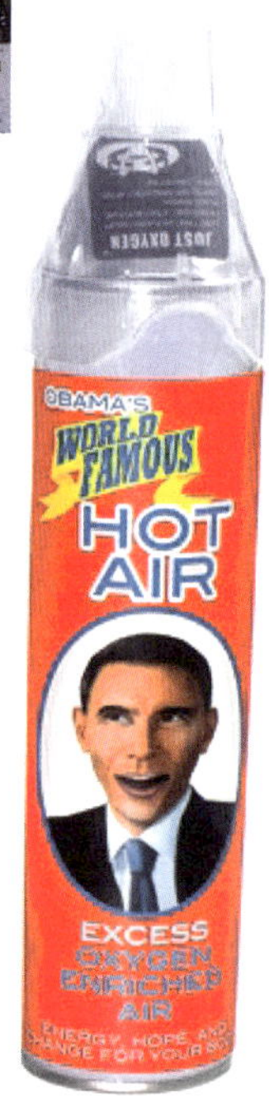

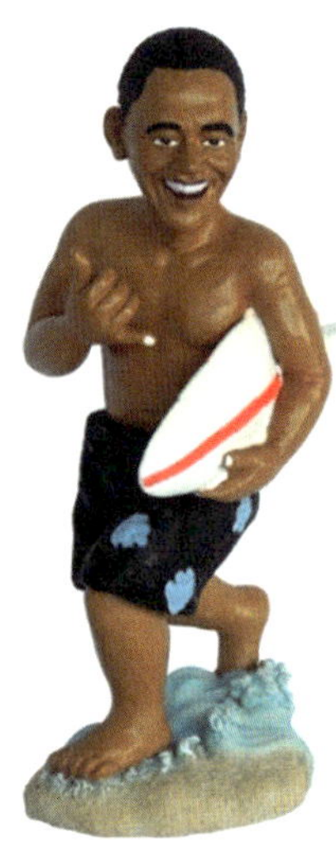

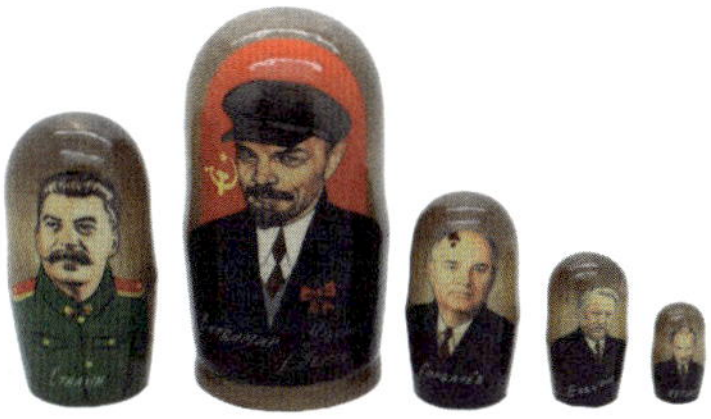

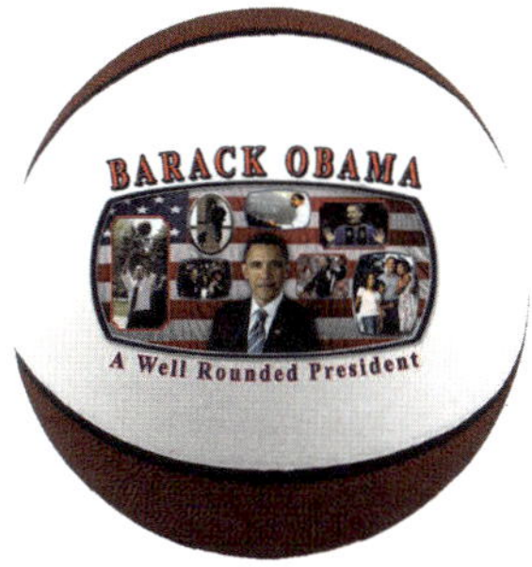
BARACK OBAMA
A Well Rounded President

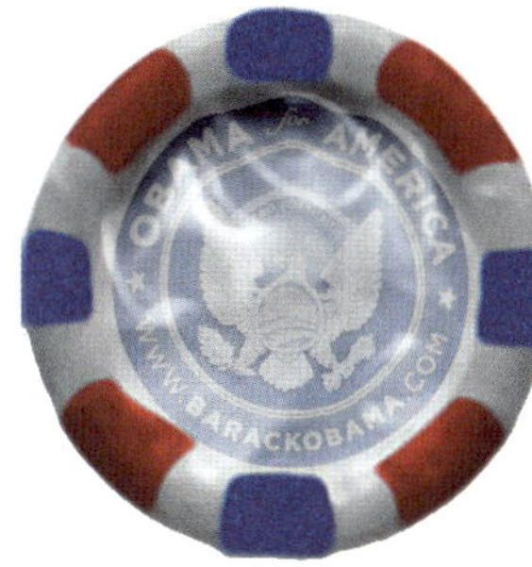
OBAMA AMERICA
WWW.BARACKOBAMA.COM

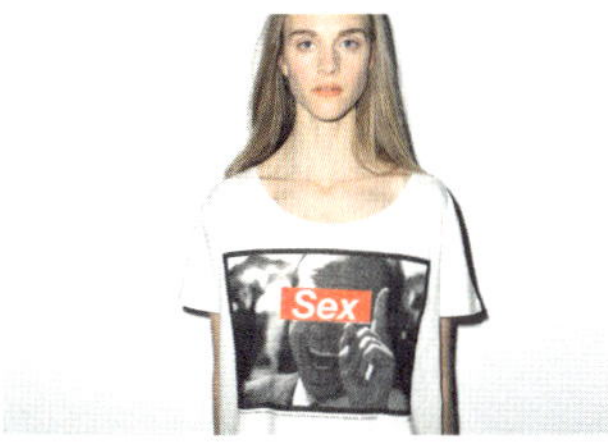
Sex

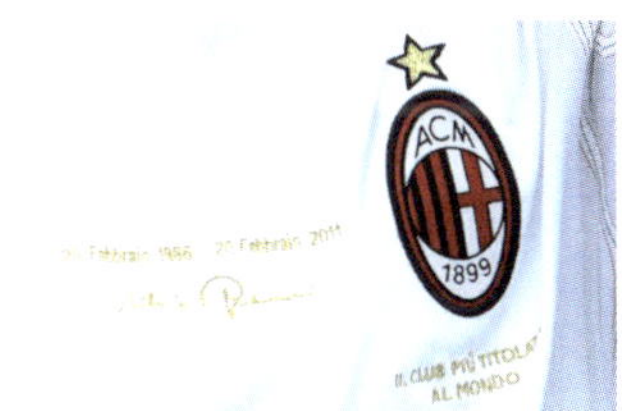
ACM
1899
IL CLUB PIÙ TITOLATO AL MONDO

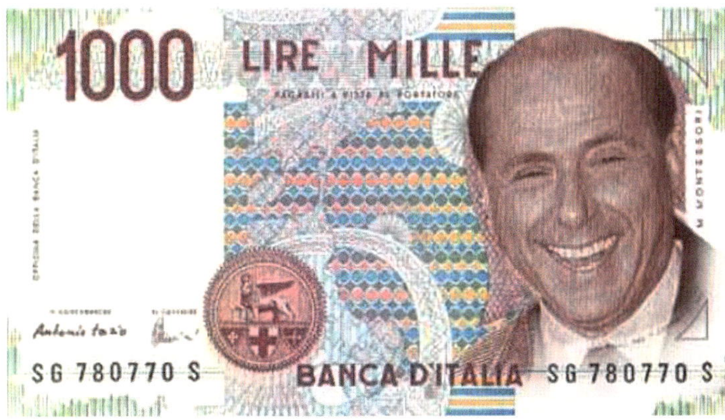
1000
LIRE MILLE
SG 780770 S
BANCA D'ITALIA
SG 780770 S

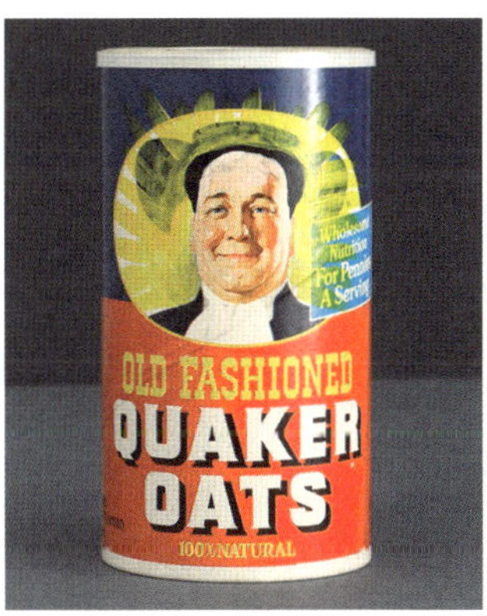
OLD FASHIONED
QUAKER
OATS
100% NATURAL

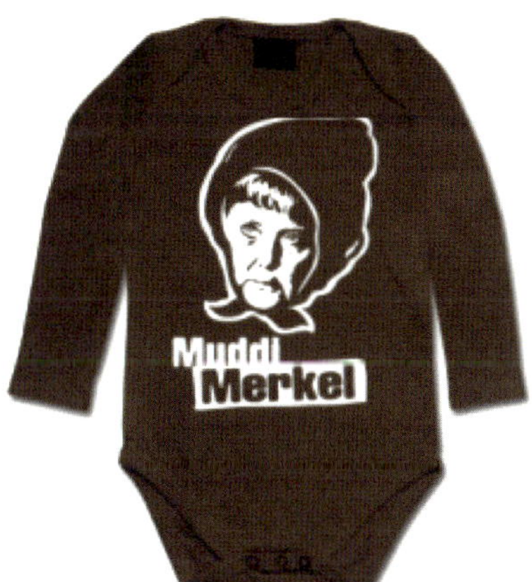
Muddi
Merkel

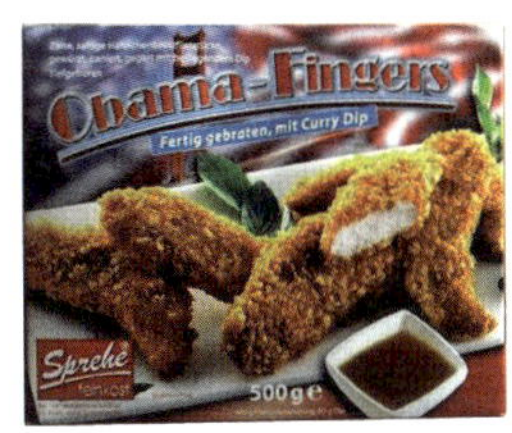
Obama-Fingers
Fertig gebraten, mit Curry Dip
500 g

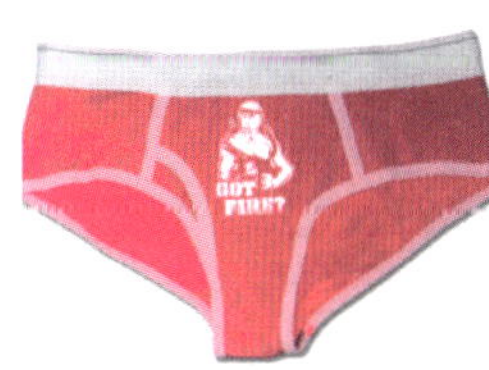

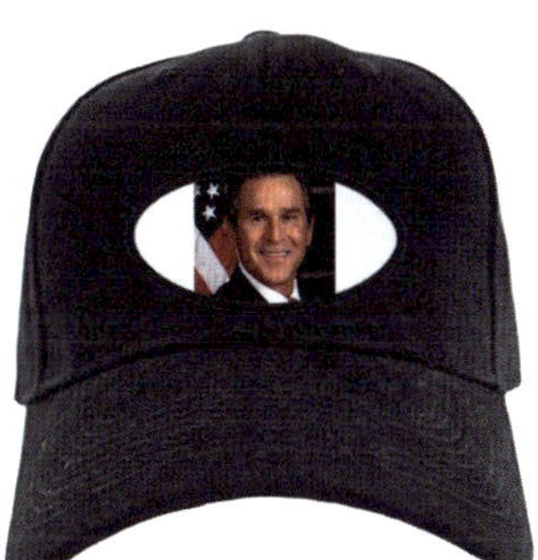

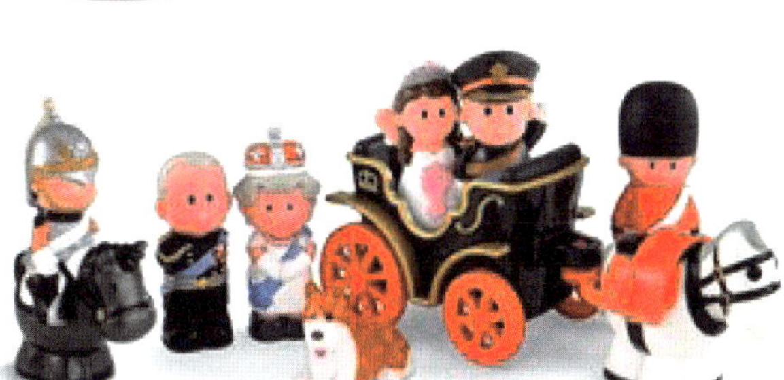

Branding Through Merchandise

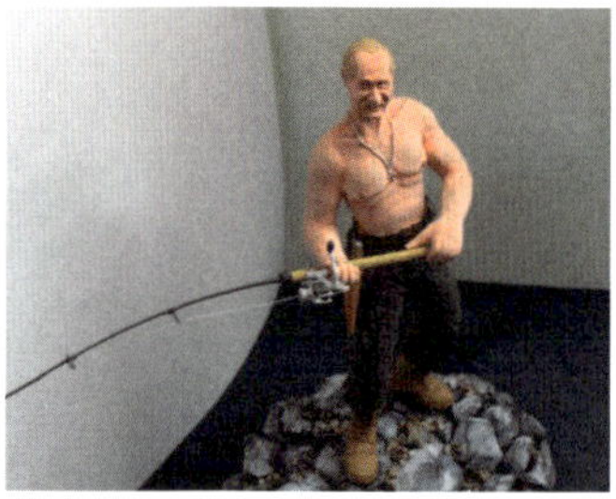

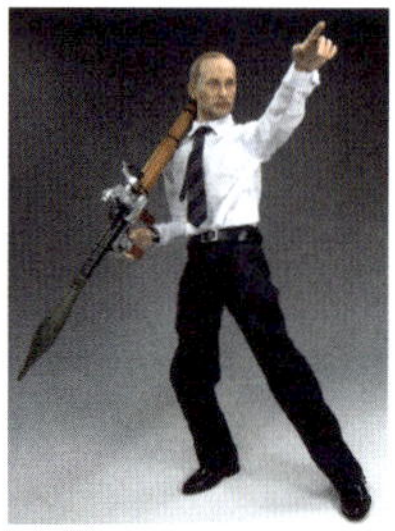

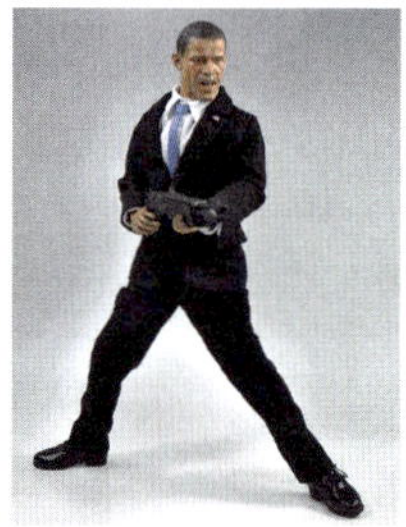

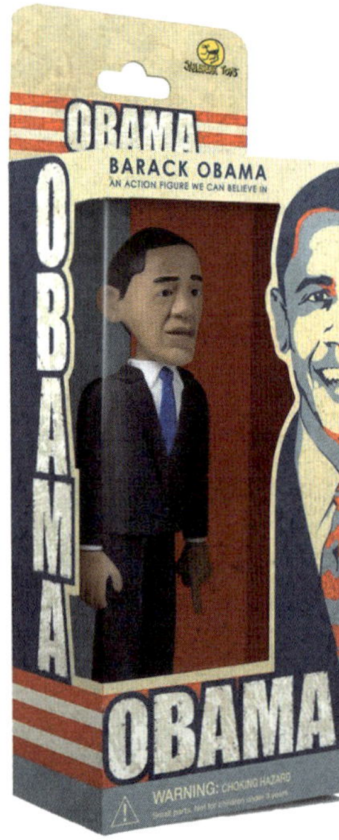

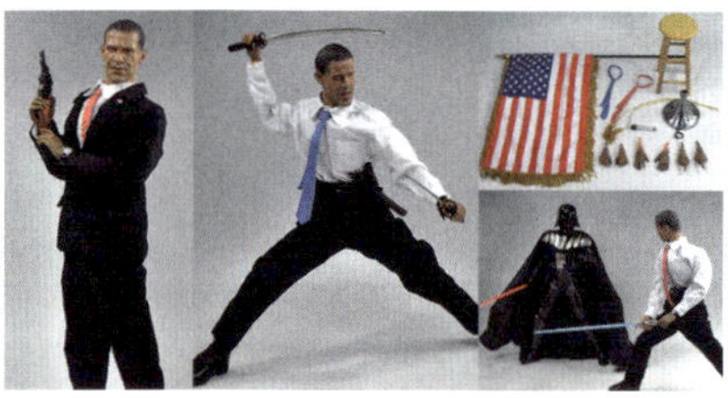

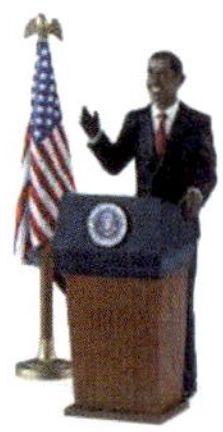

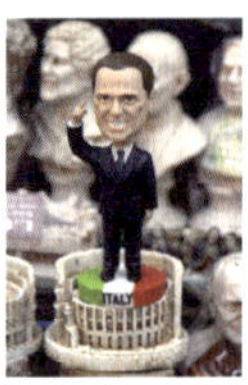

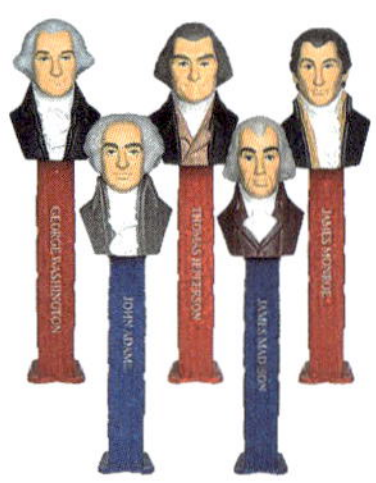

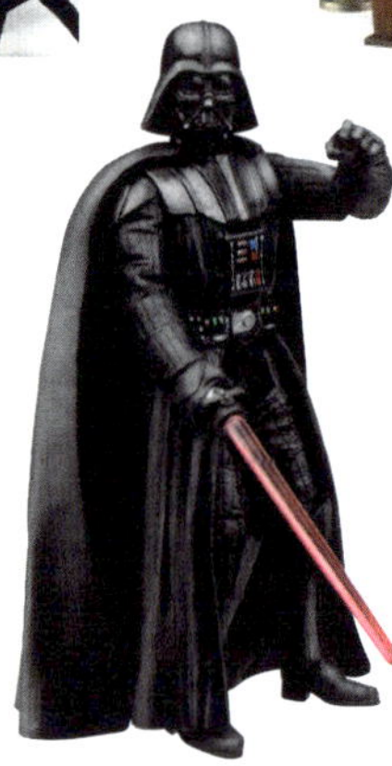

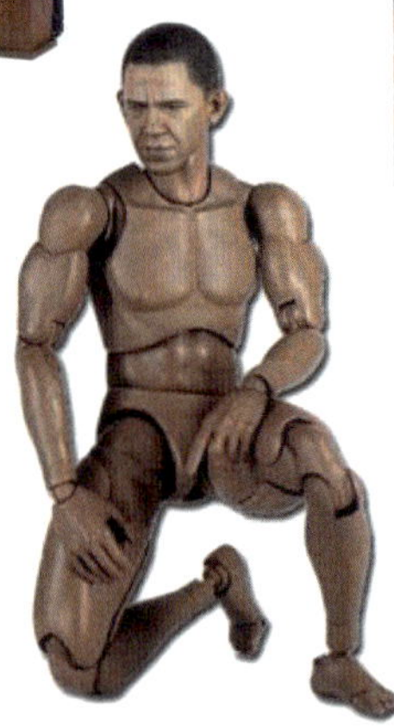

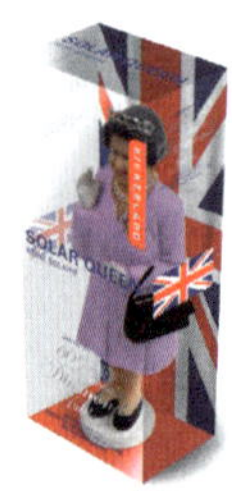

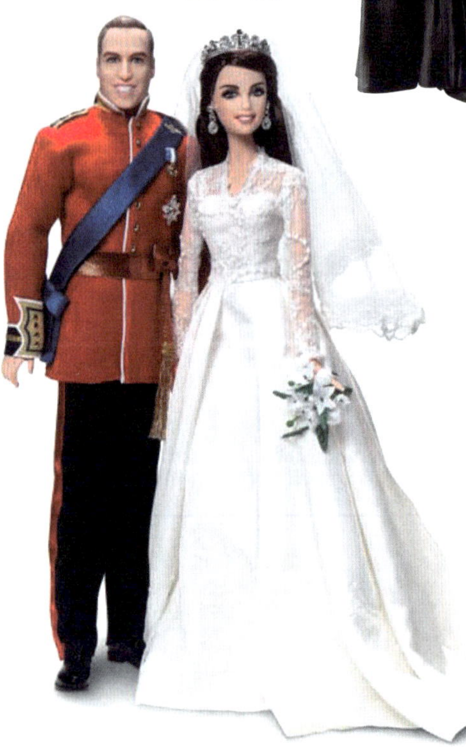

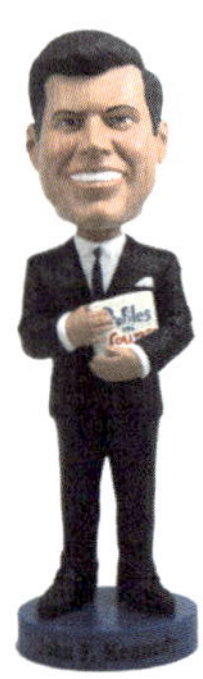

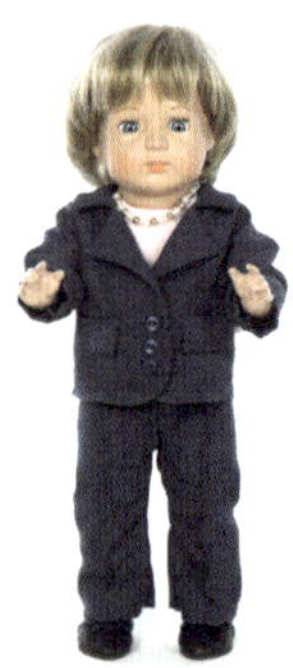

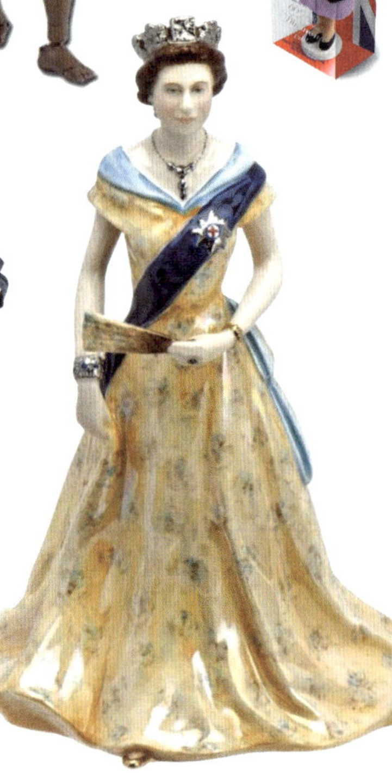

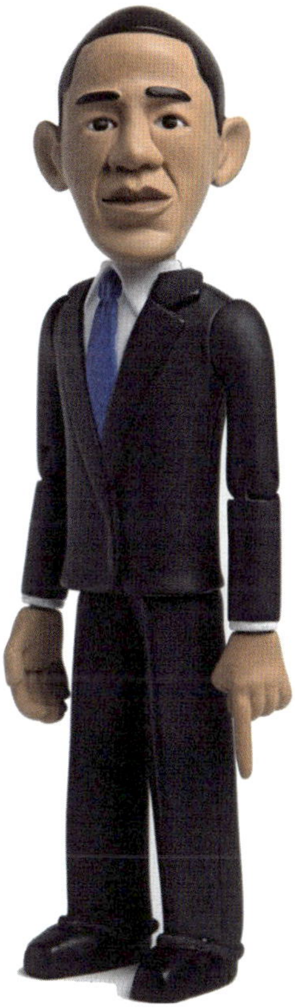

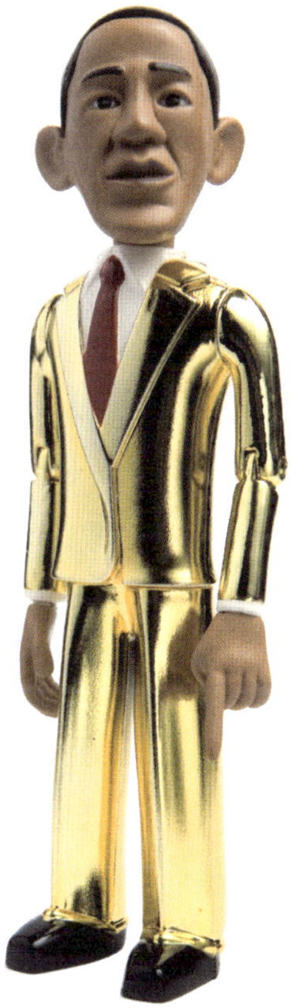

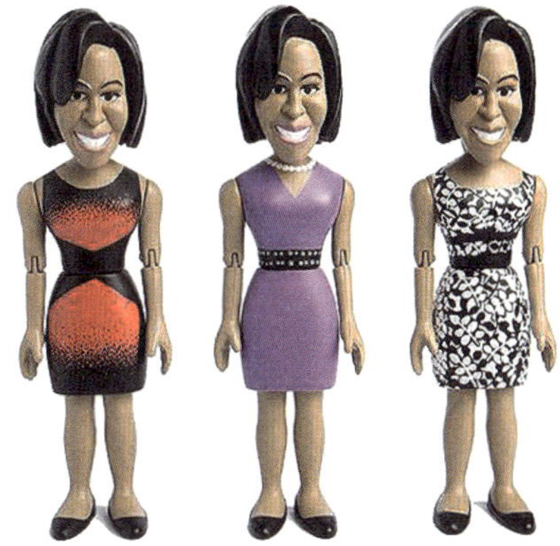

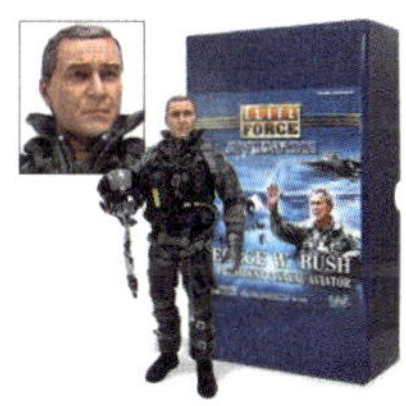

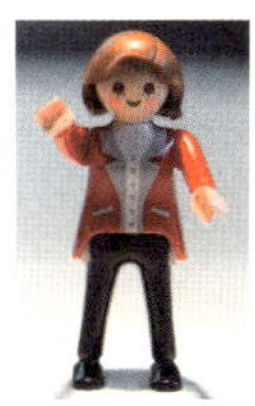

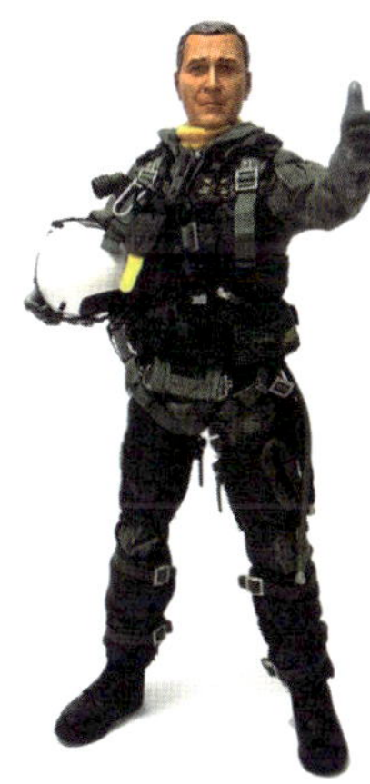

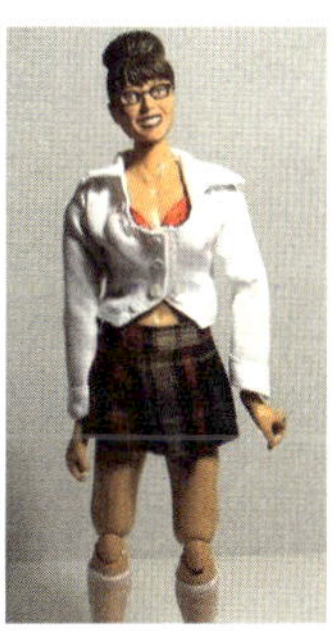

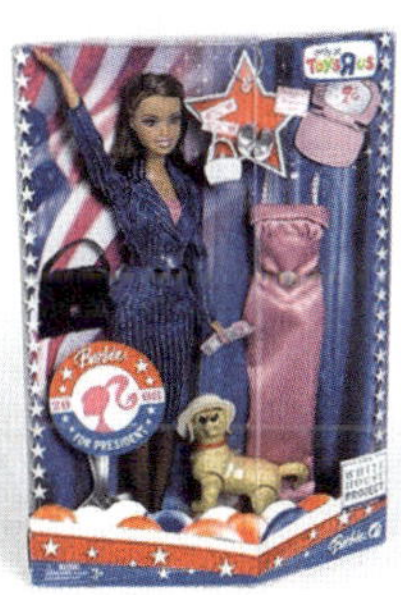

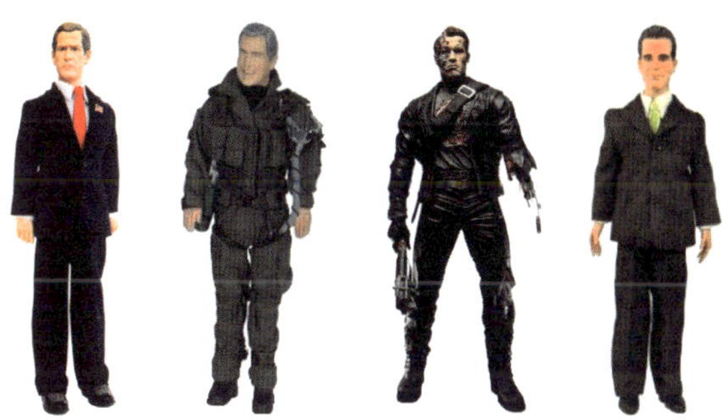

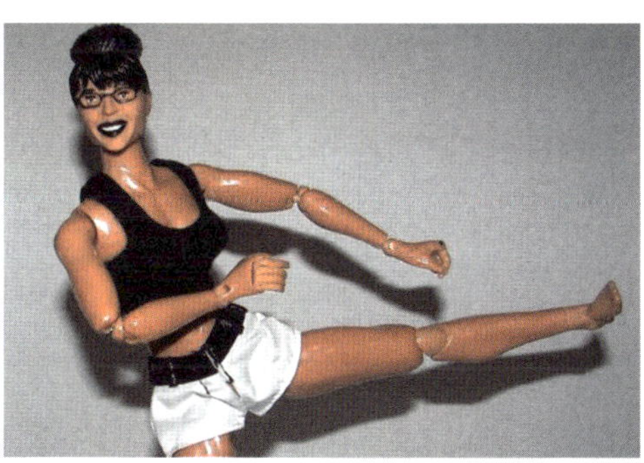

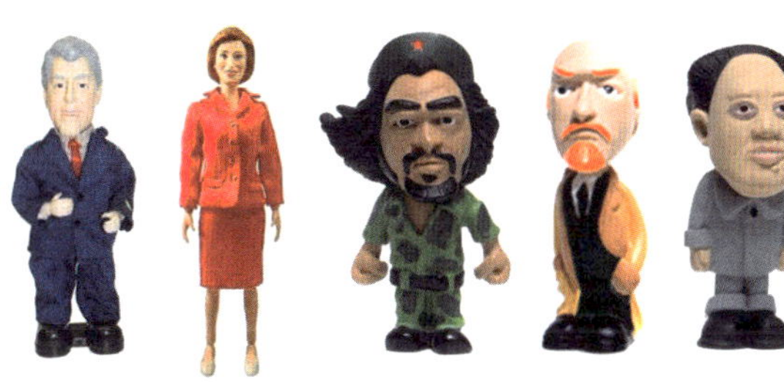

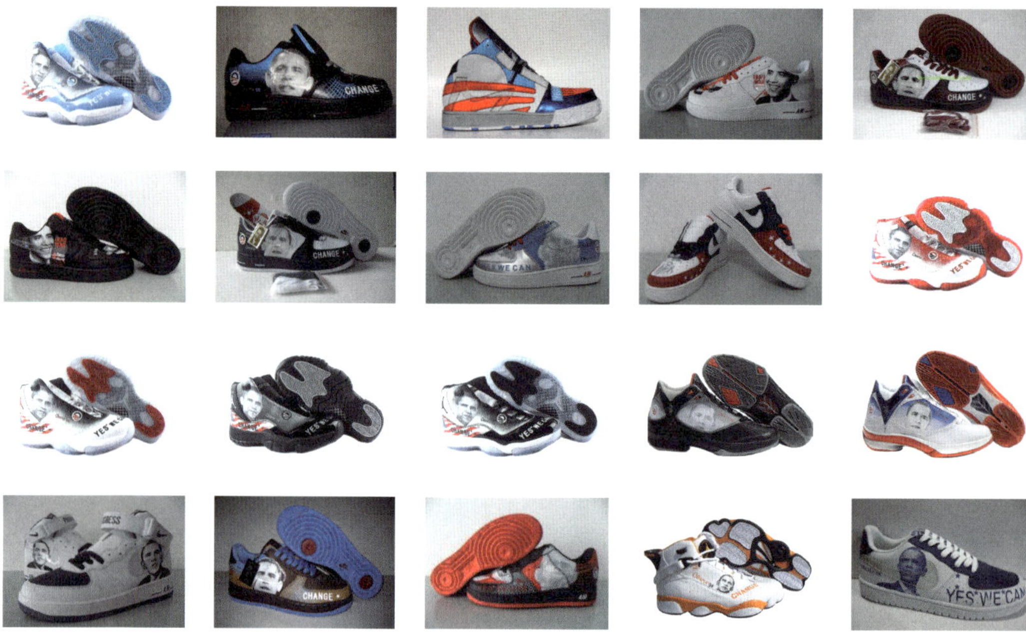

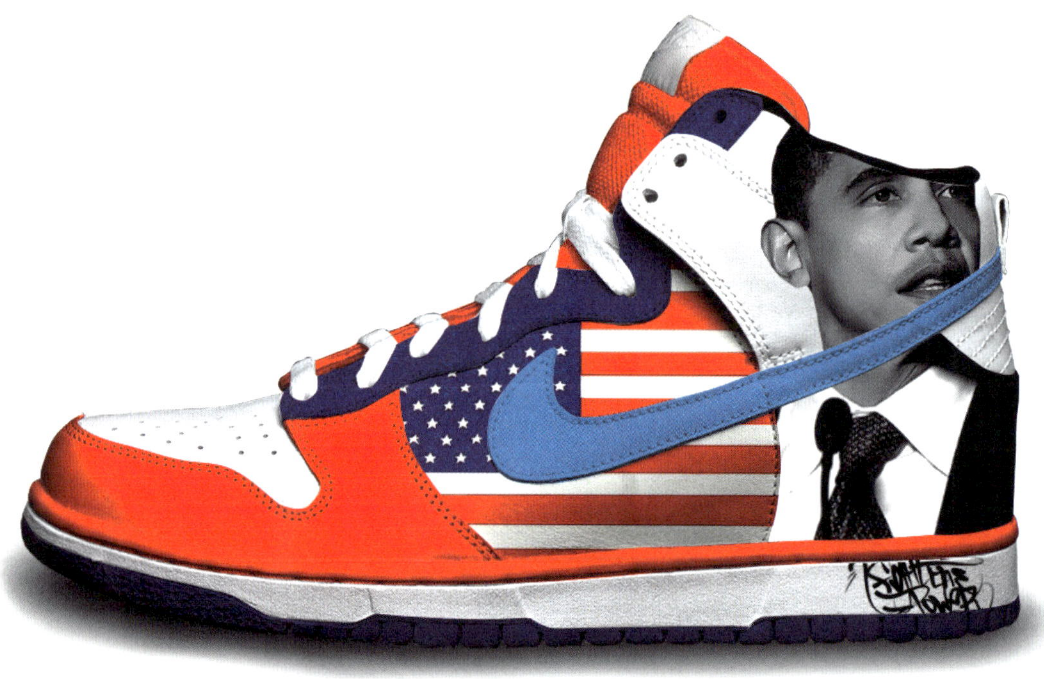

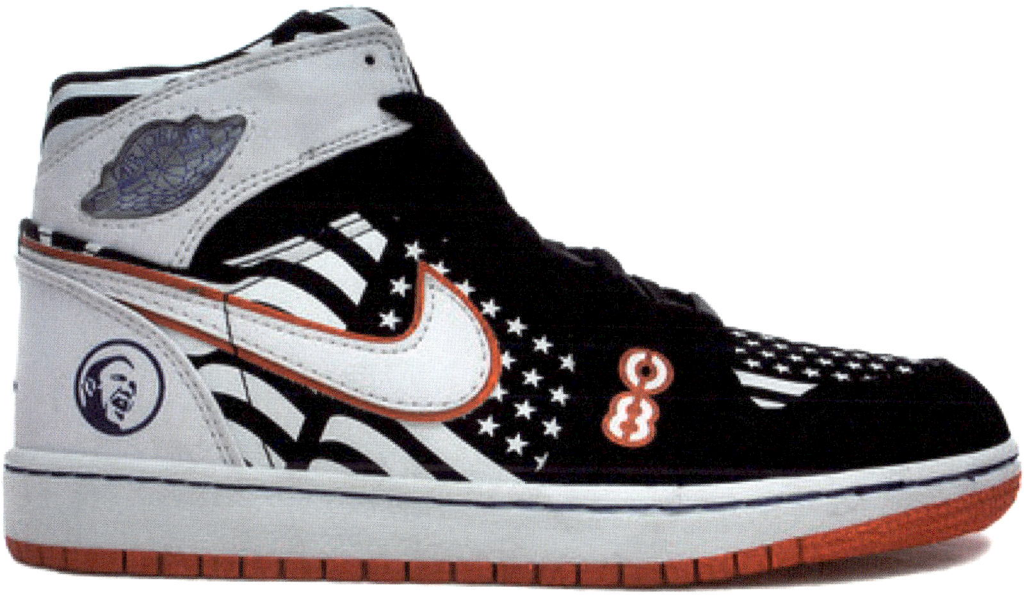

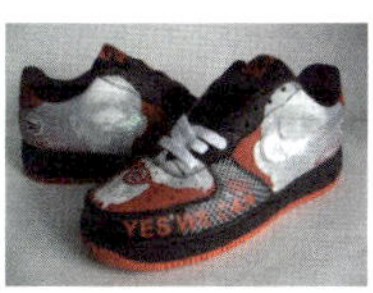

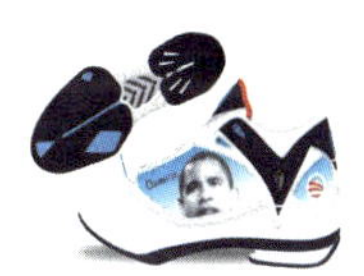

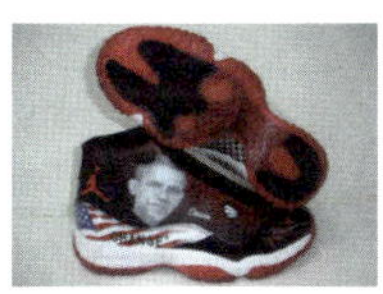

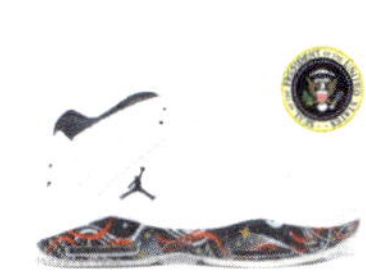

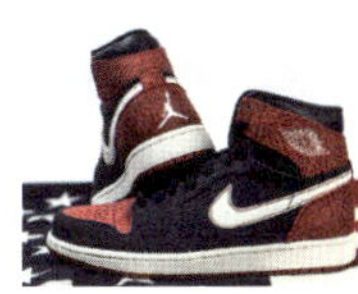

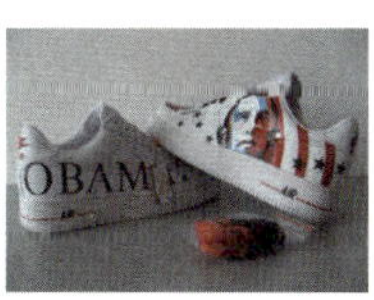

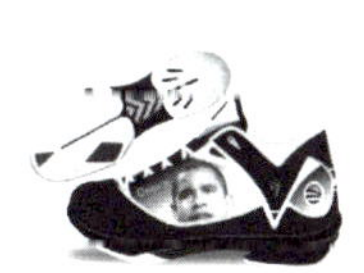

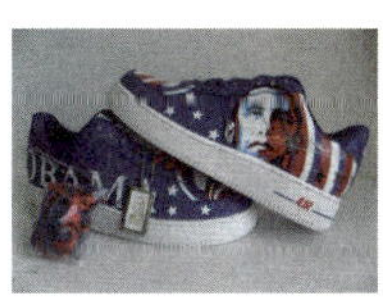

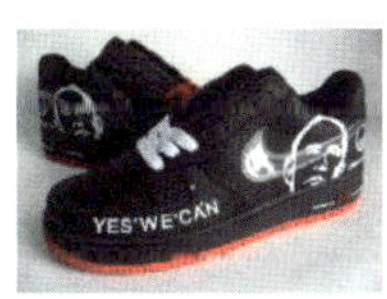
YES'WE'CAN

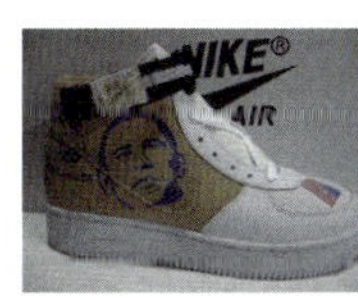

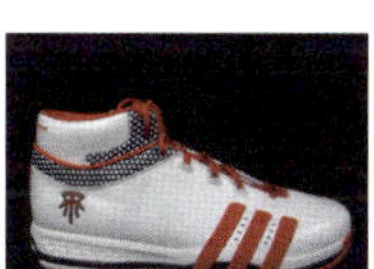

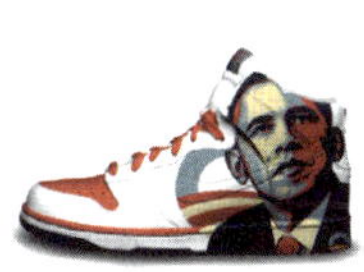

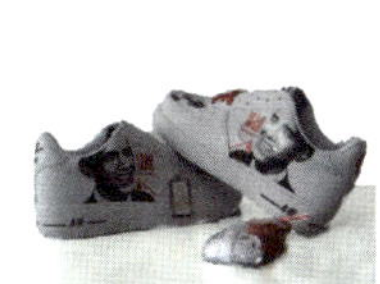

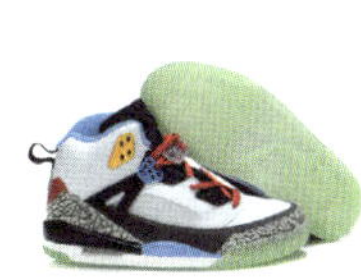

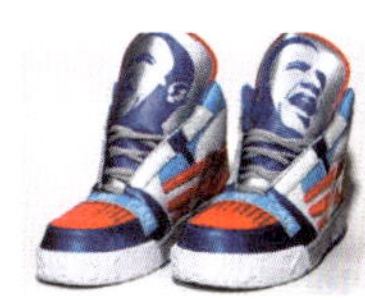

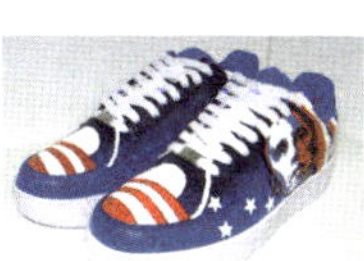

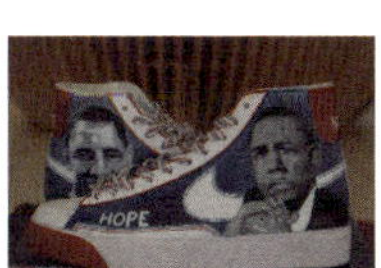
HOPE

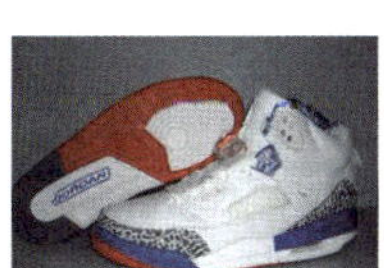

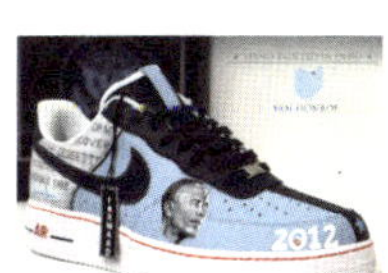
2012

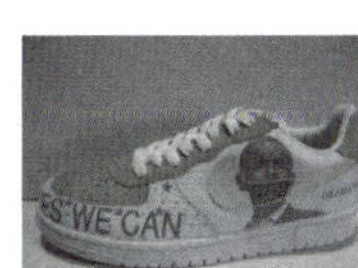

Branding Through Iconography

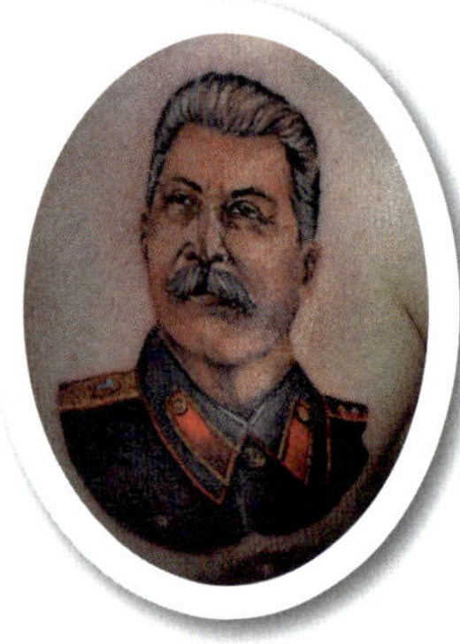

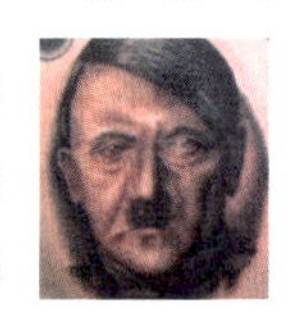

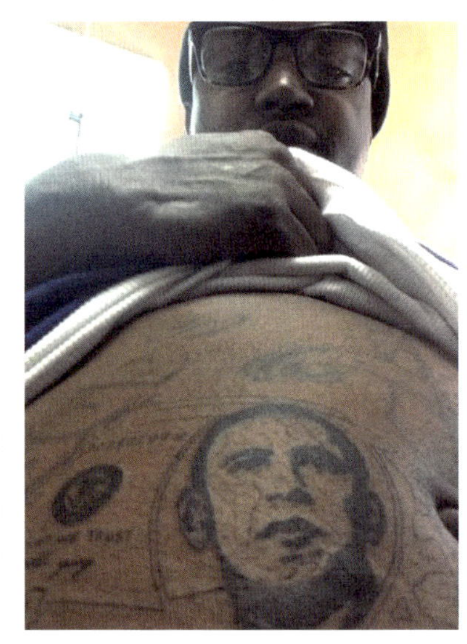

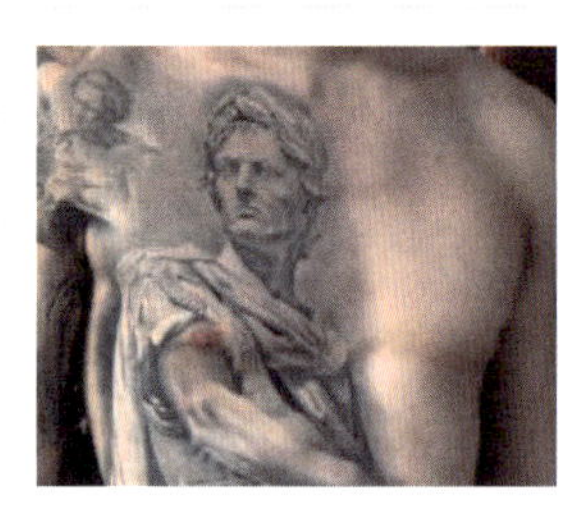

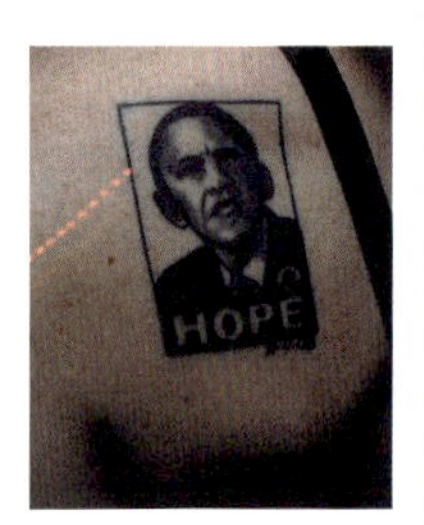

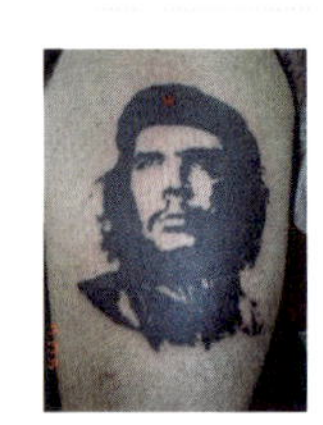

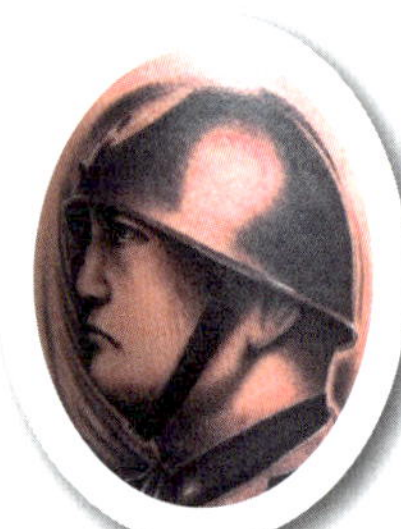

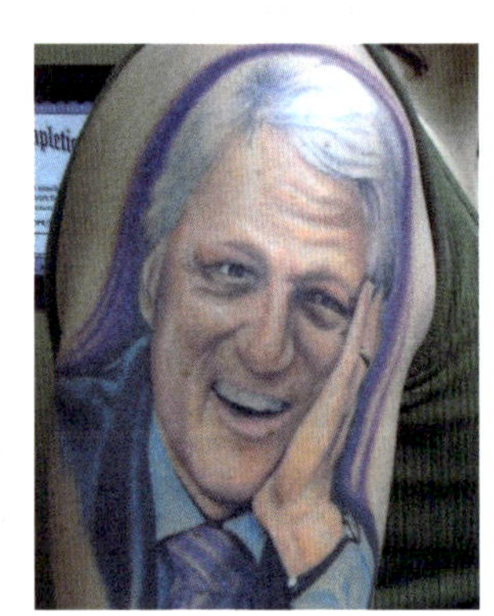

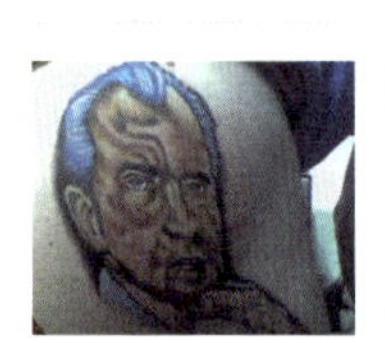

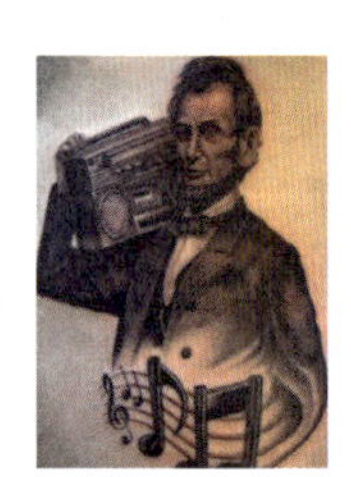

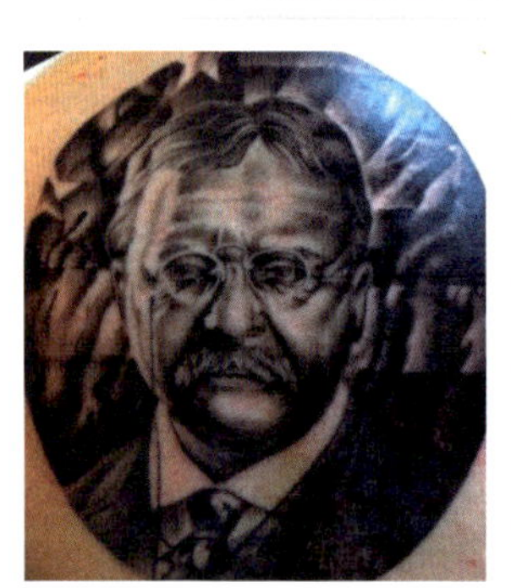

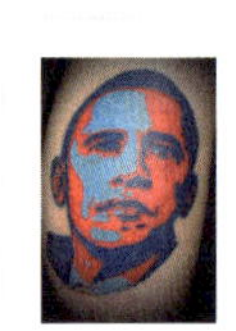

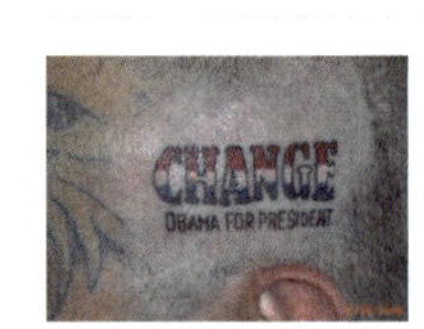

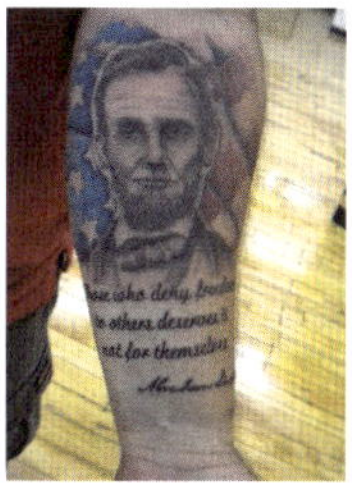
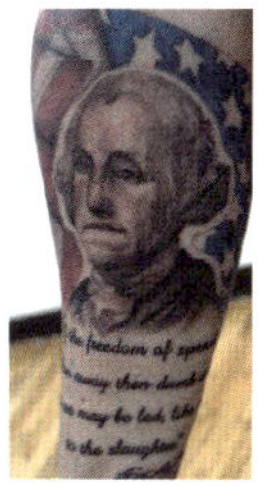
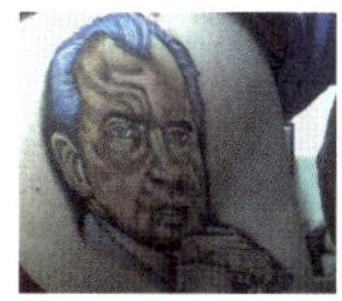
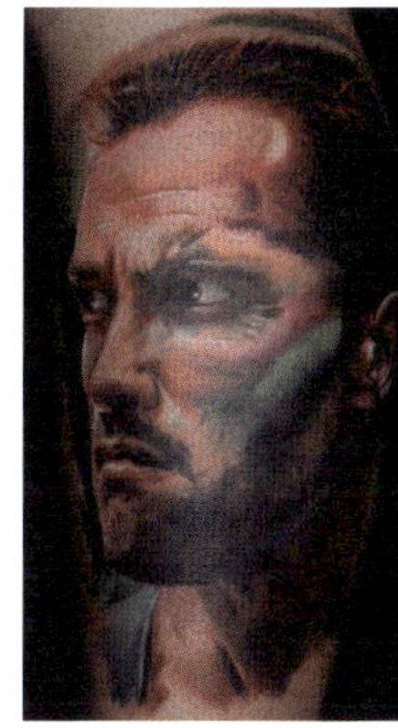
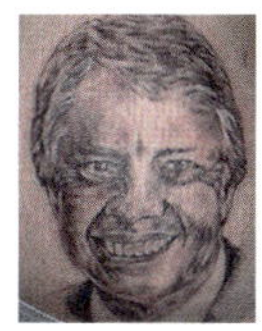
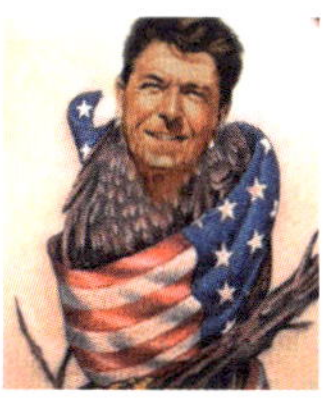
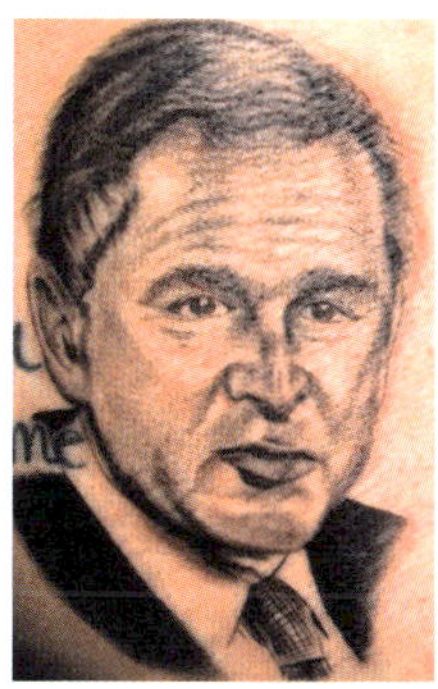
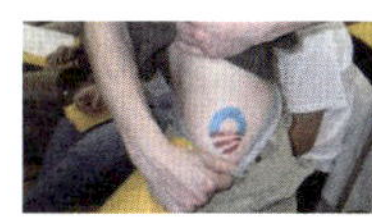
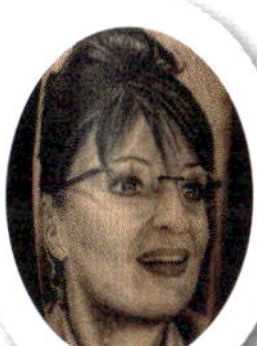
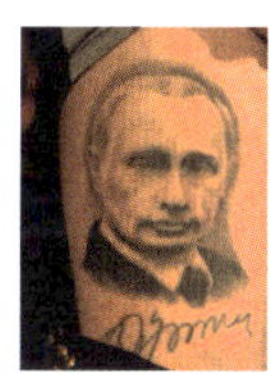
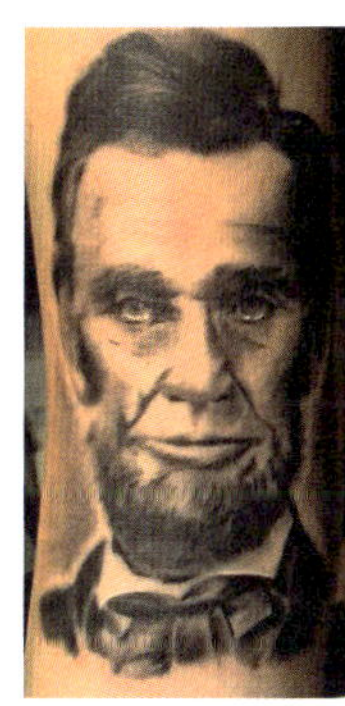
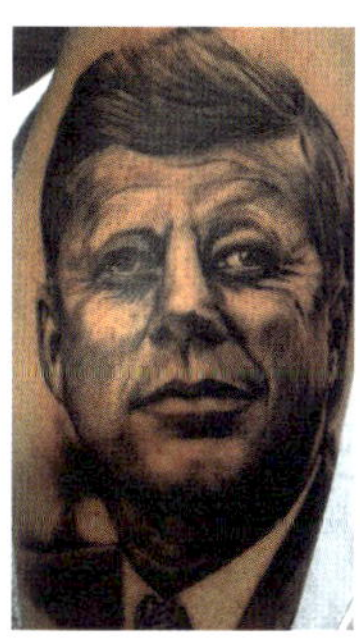
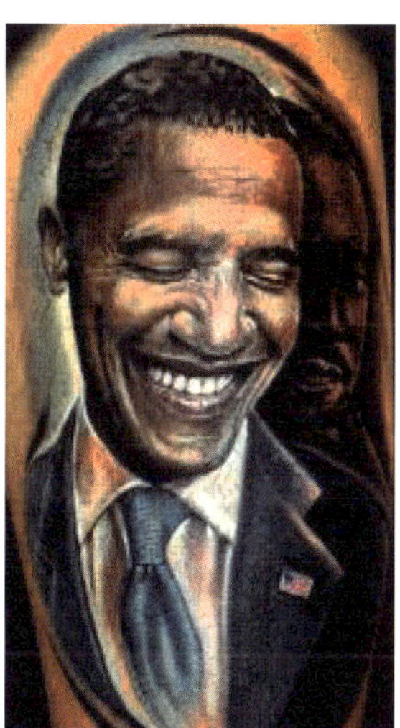
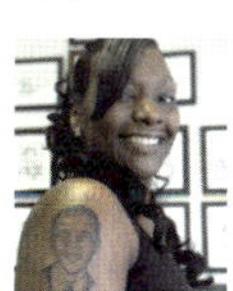
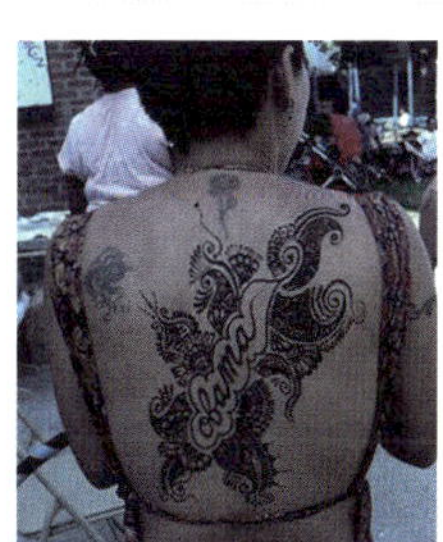
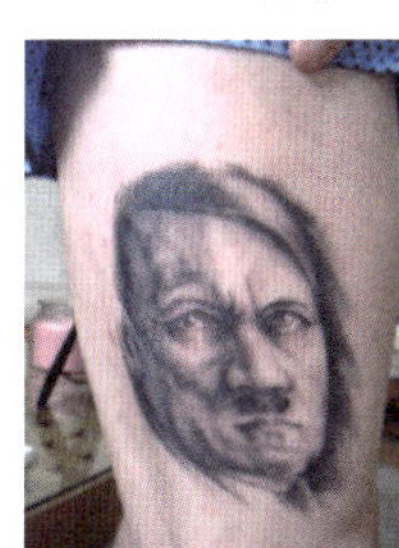

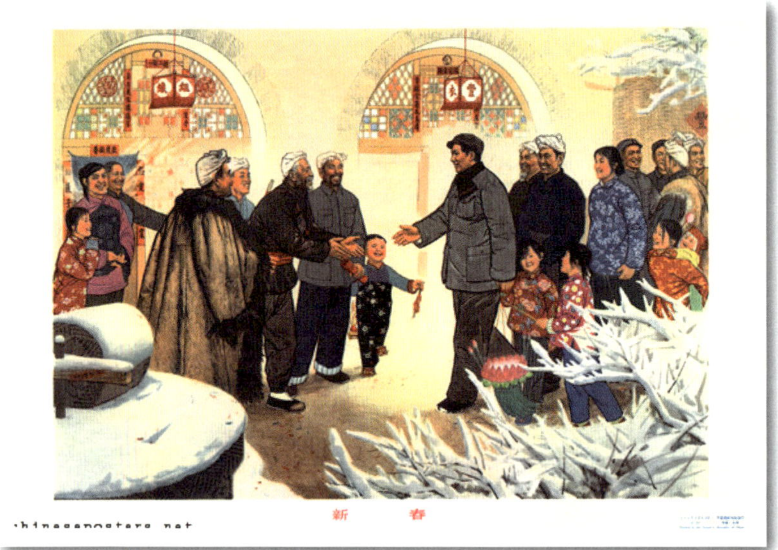
新　春

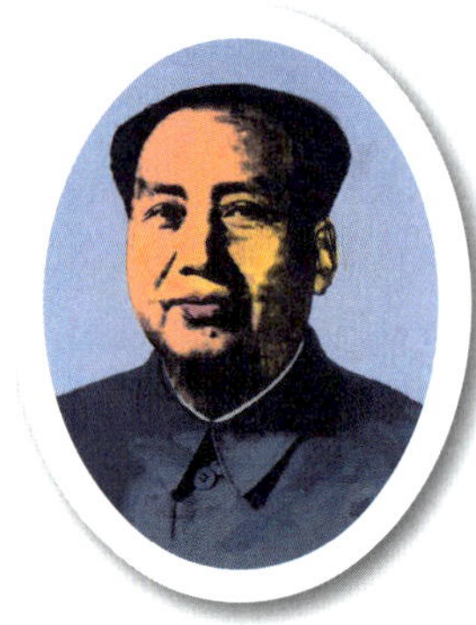

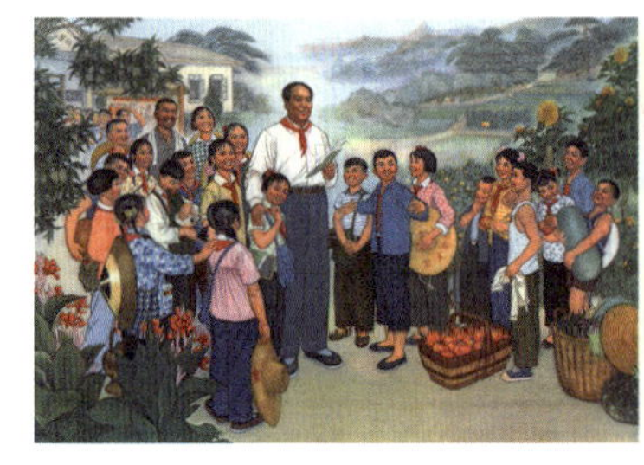

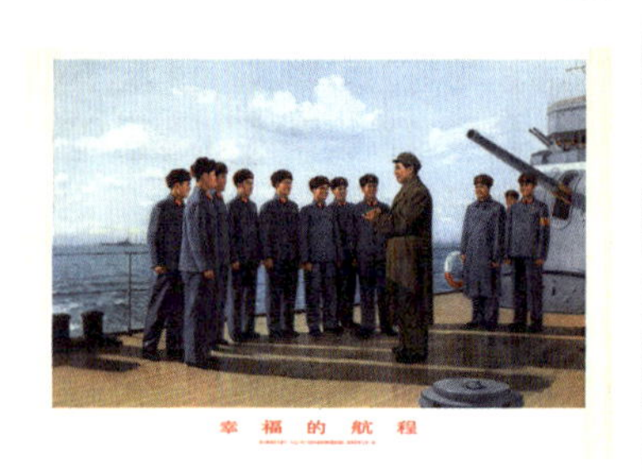
幸 福 的 航 程

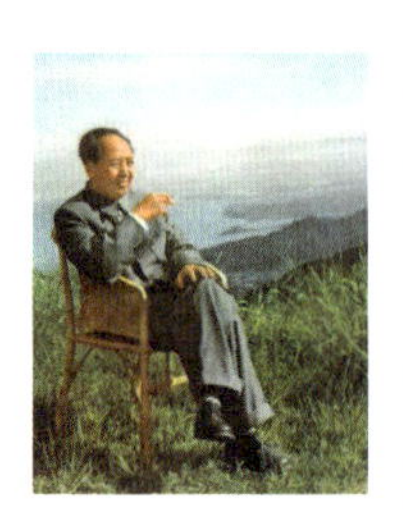

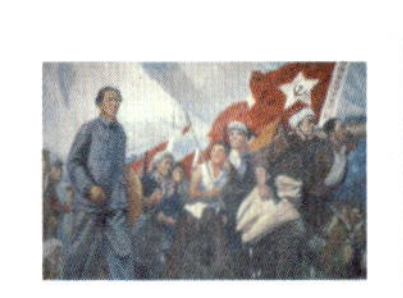

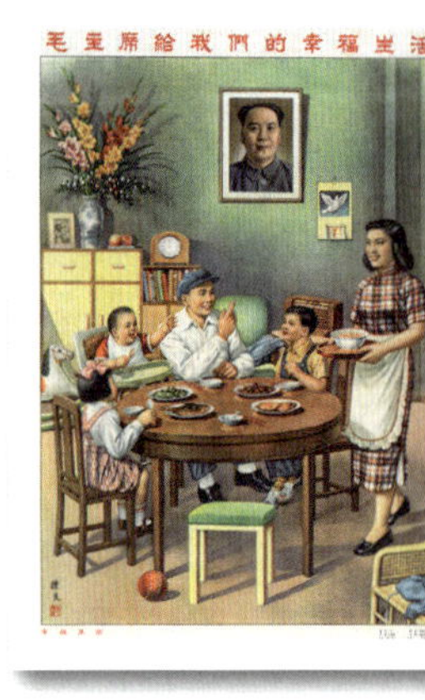
毛主席給我們的幸福生活

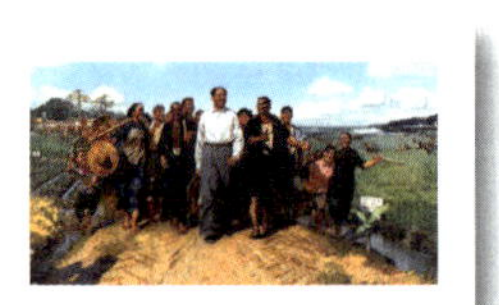

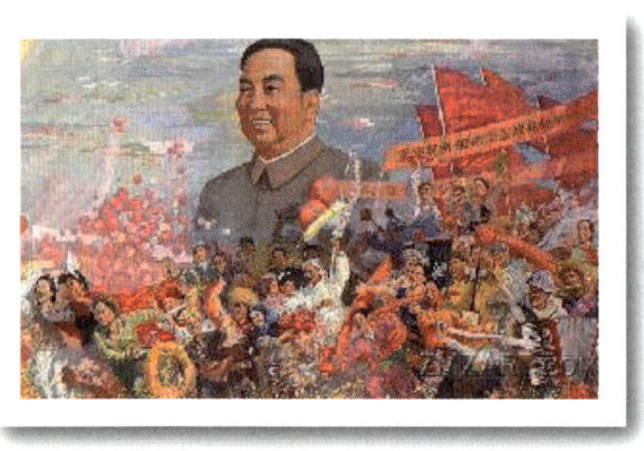

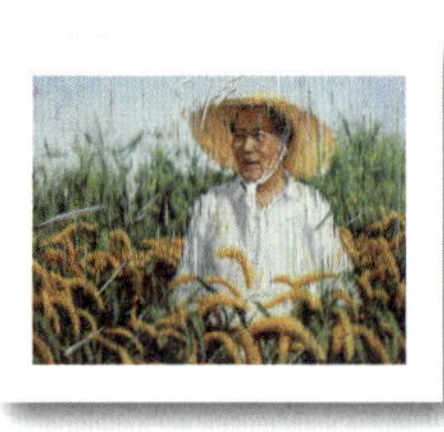

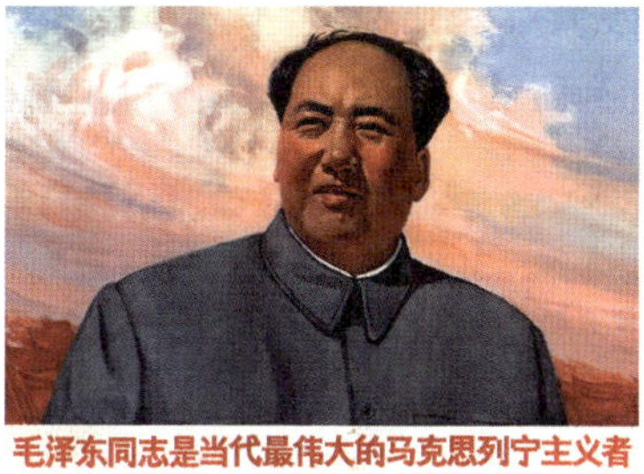
毛泽东同志是当代最伟大的马克思列宁主义者

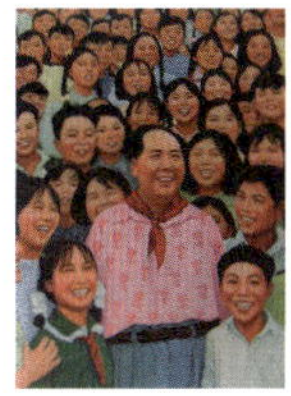

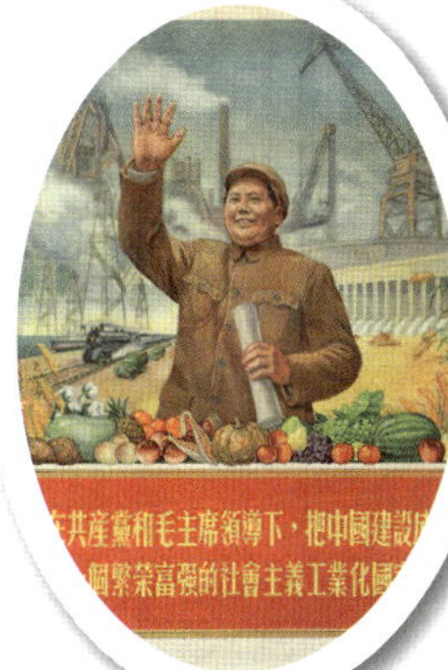
共産黨和毛主席領導下，把中國建設
個繁榮富强的社會主義工業化

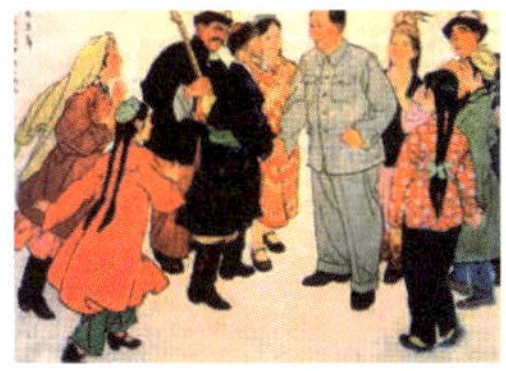

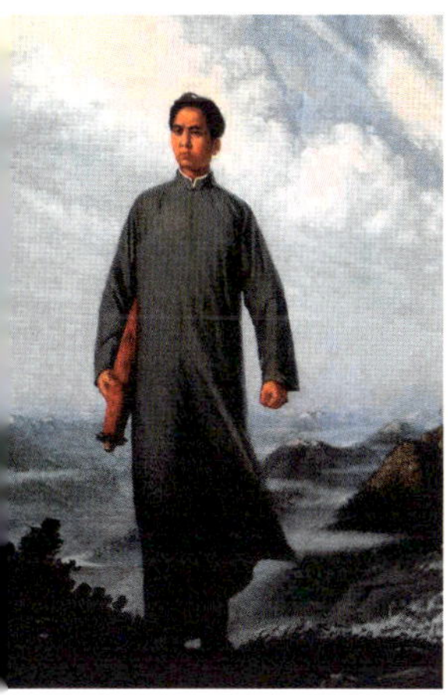

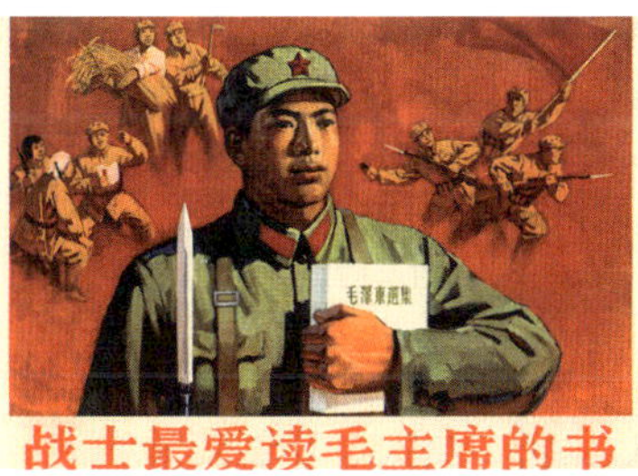
战士最爱读毛主席的书

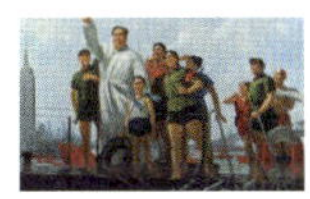

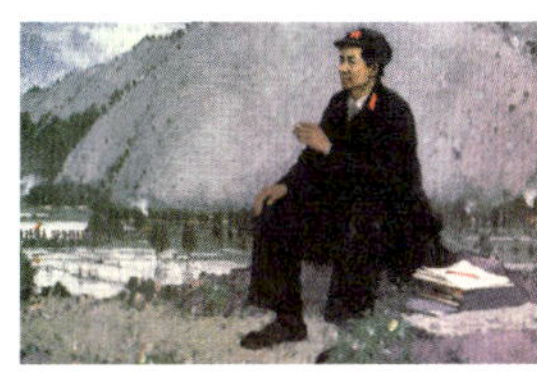

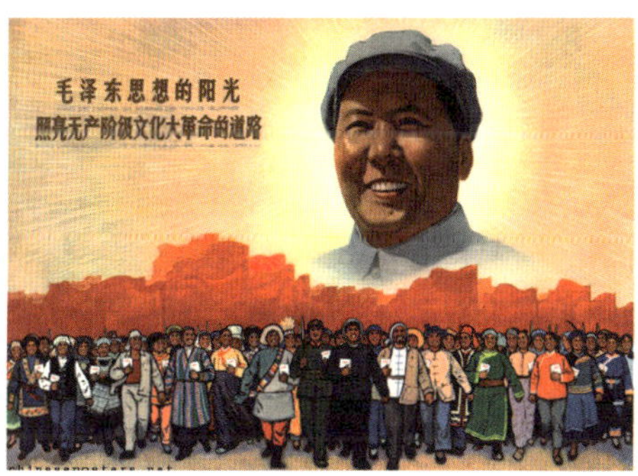
毛泽东思想的阳光
照亮无产阶级文化大革命的道路

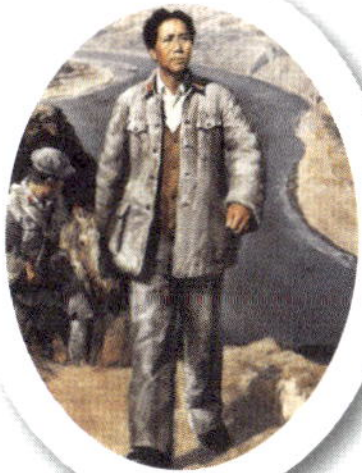

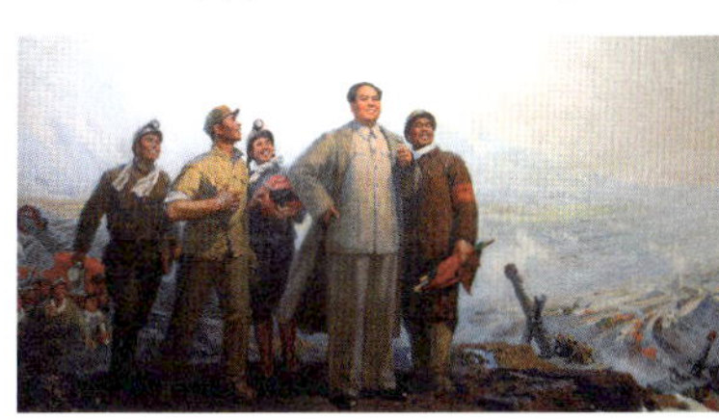

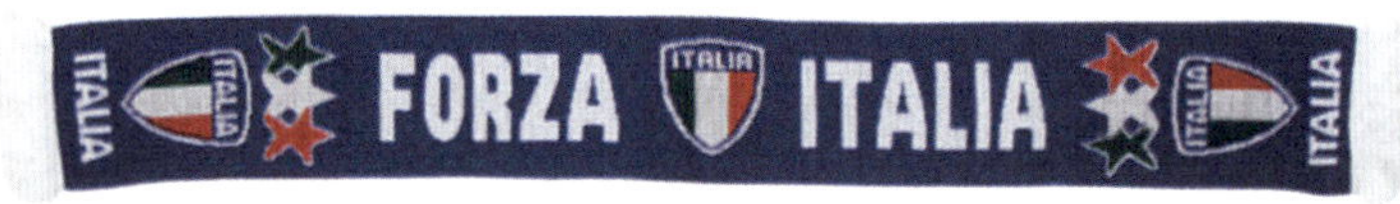
ITALIA
FORZA
ITALIA
ITALIA
ITALIA
ITALIA

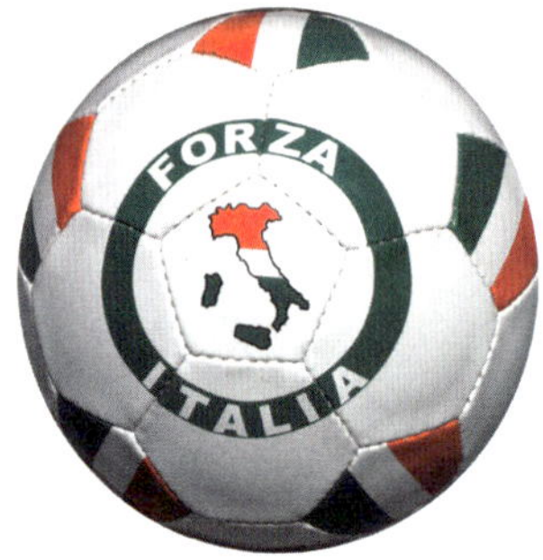
FORZA
ITALIA

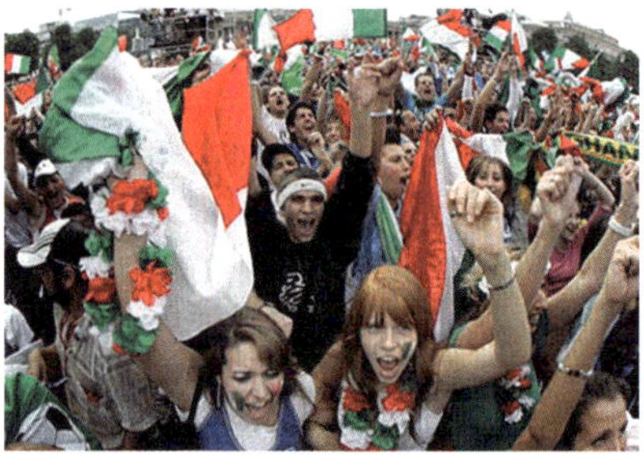

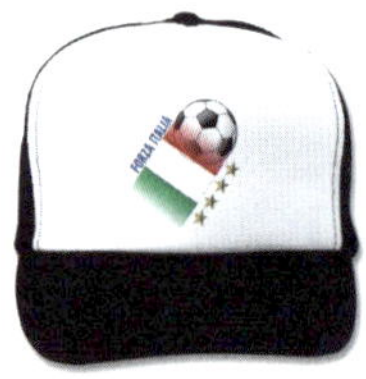

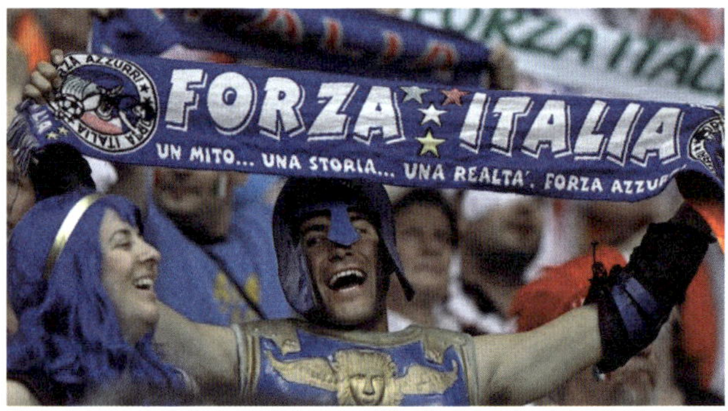
FORZA ITALIA
UN MITO... UNA STORIA... UNA REALTA'. FORZA

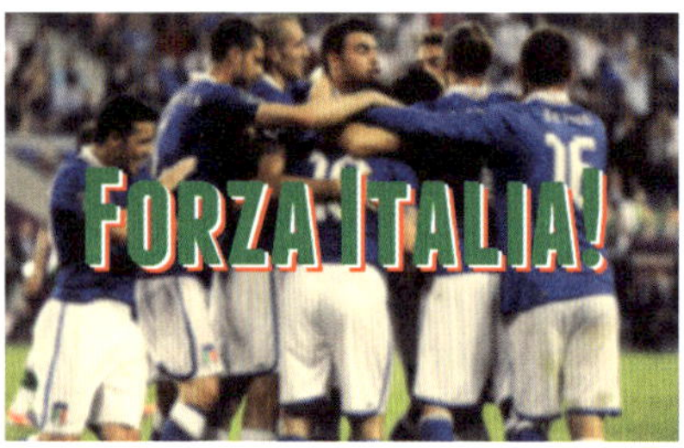
FORZA ITALIA!

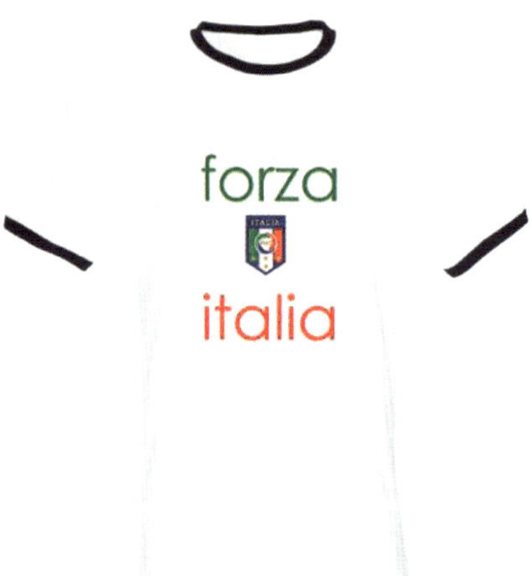
forza
italia

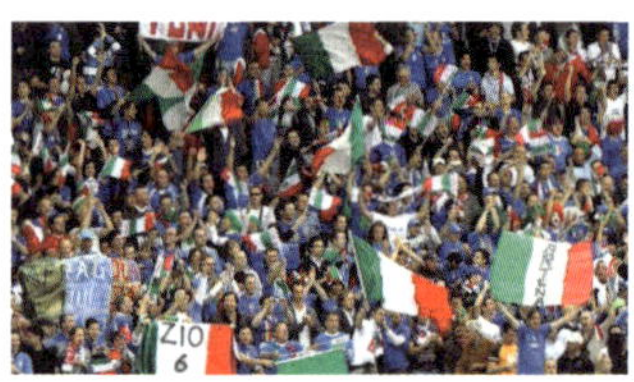

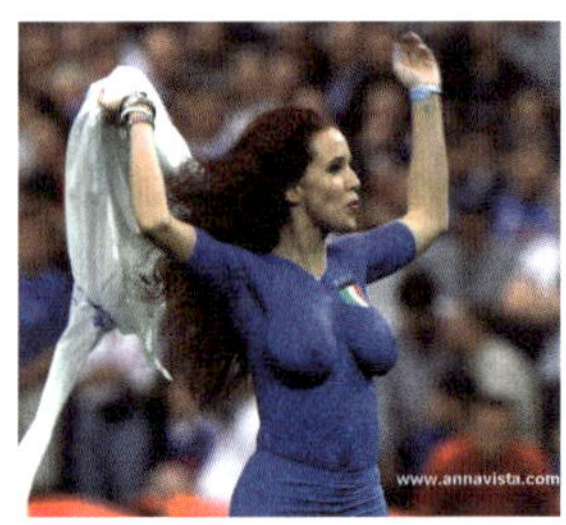
www.annavista.com

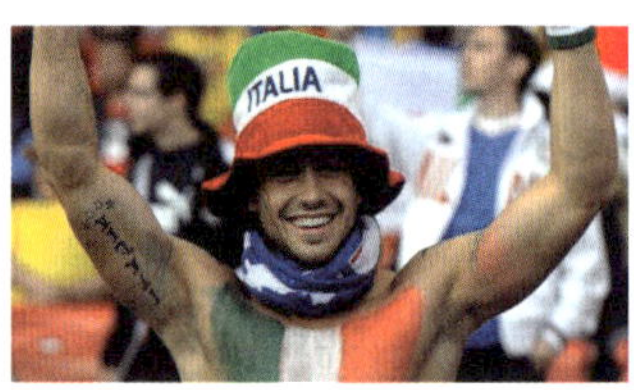
ITALIA

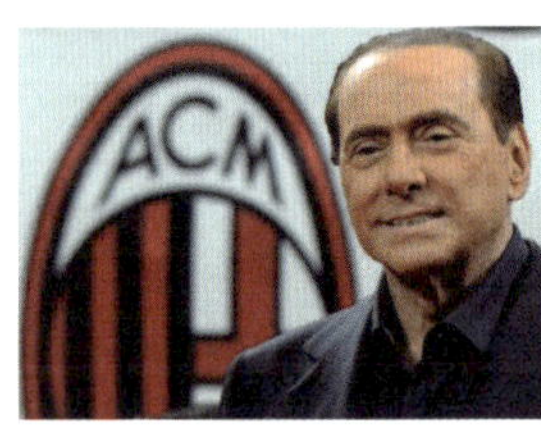
ACM

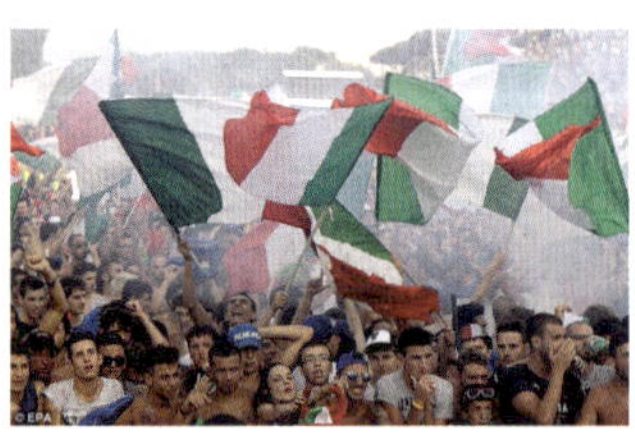

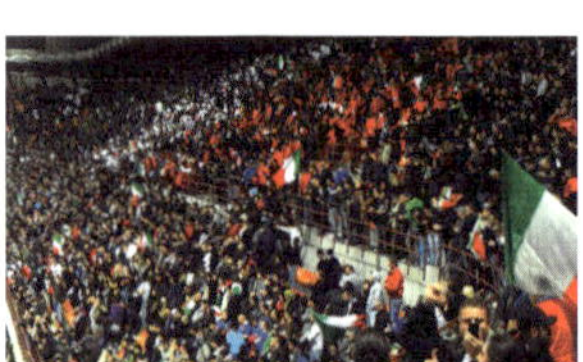

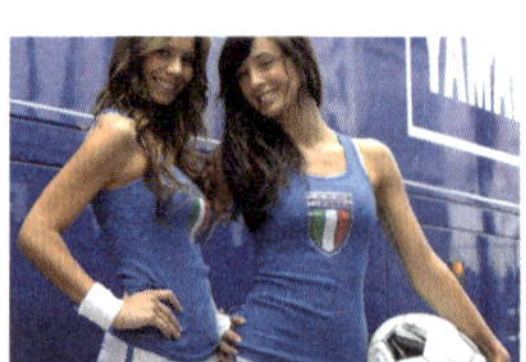

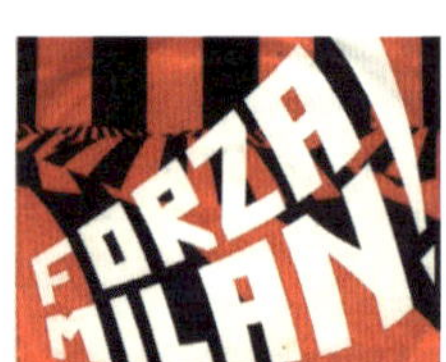
FORZA MILAN!

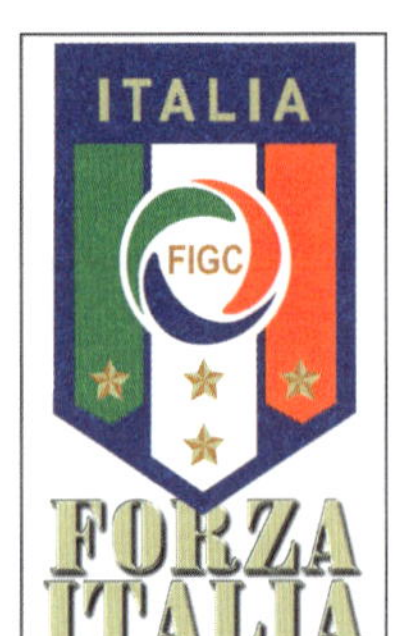
ITALIA
FIGC
FORZA ITALIA

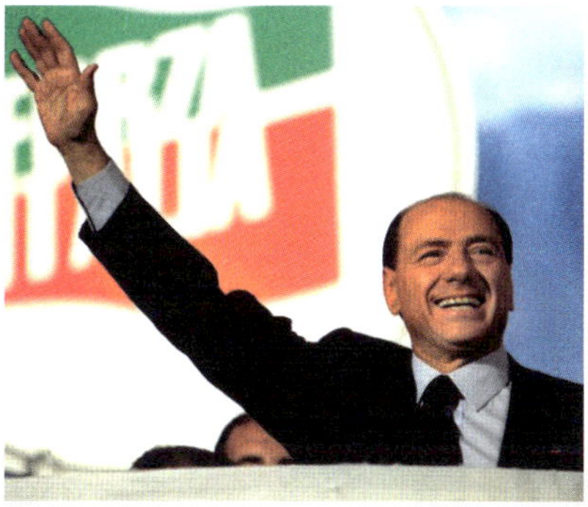

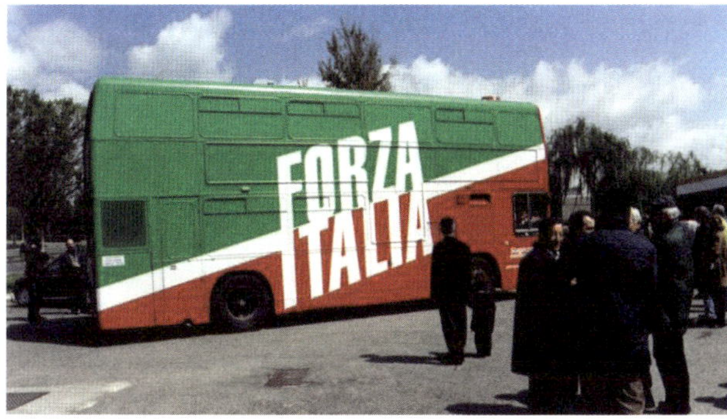

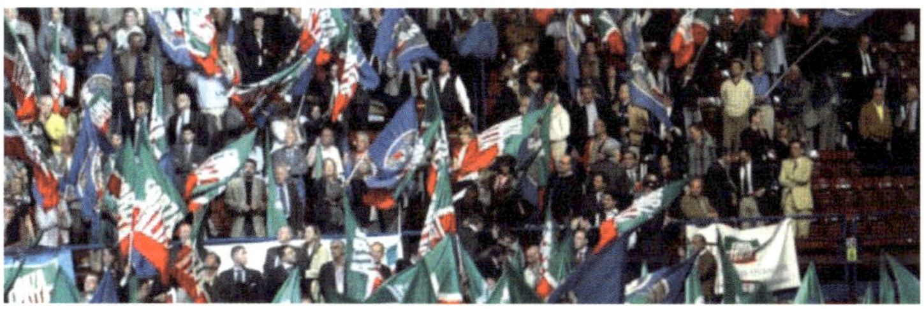

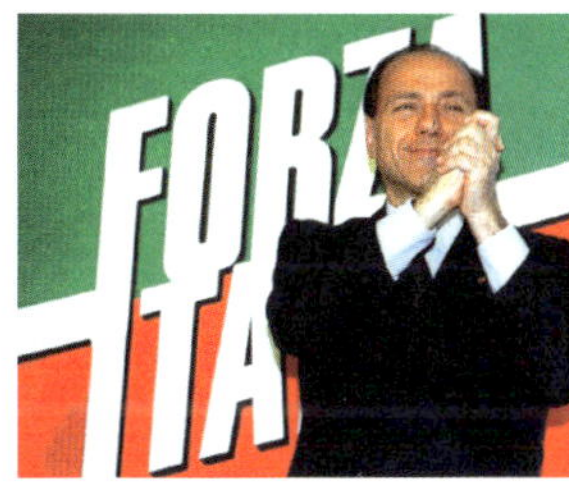

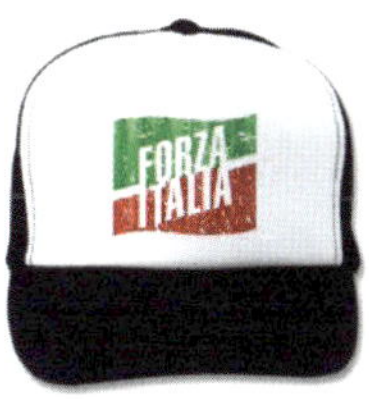

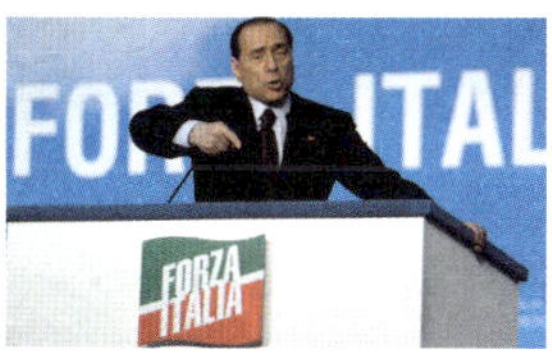

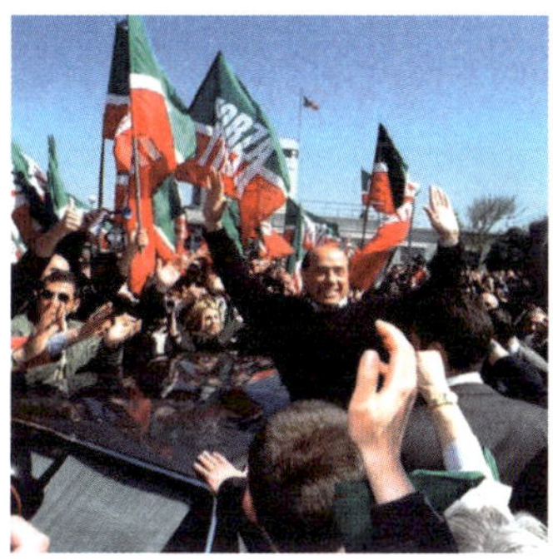

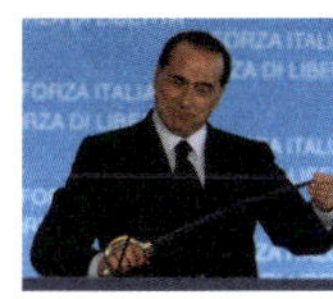

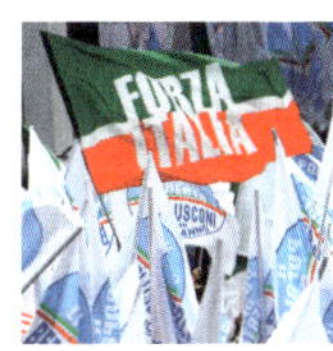

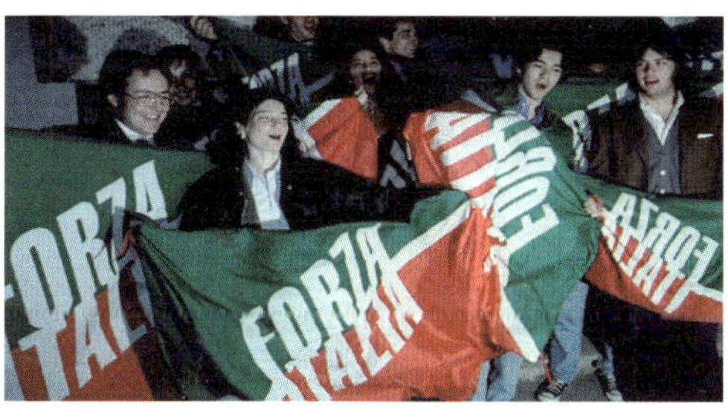

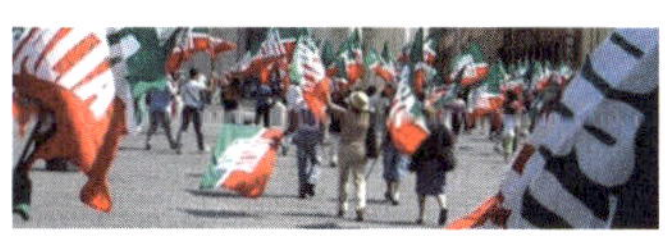

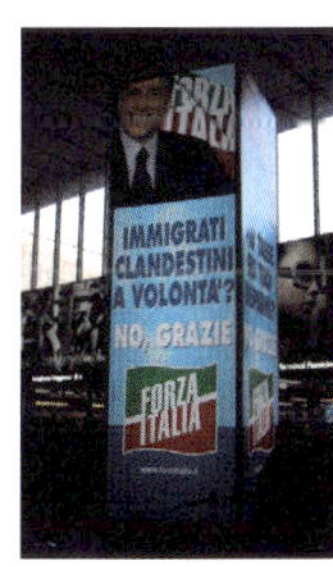

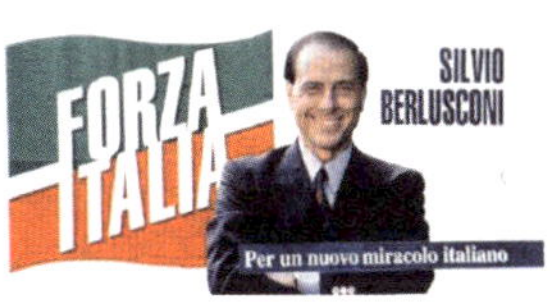

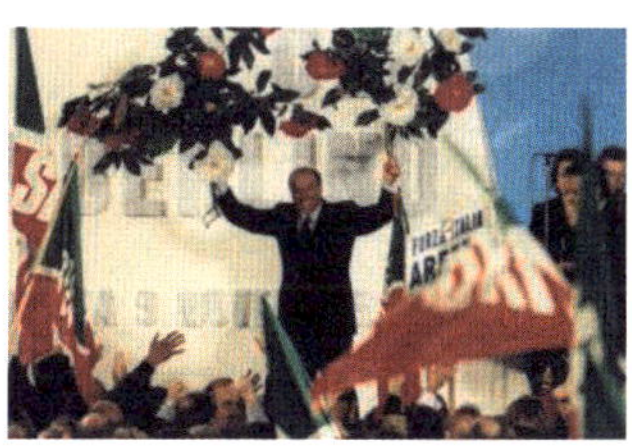

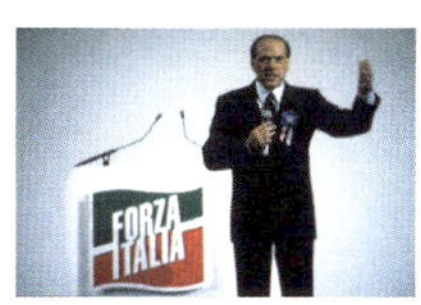

FORZA ITALIA BERLUSCONI PRESIDENTE

FORZA ITALIA UdC - CCD - PLD

LA CASA DELLE LIBERTÀ BERLUSCONI PRESIDENTE

IL POPOLO DELLA LIBERTÀ

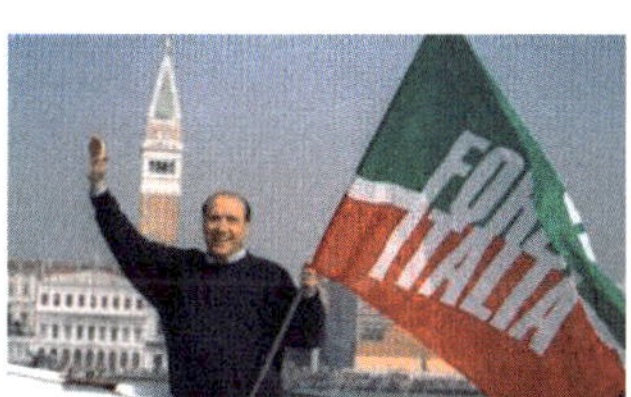

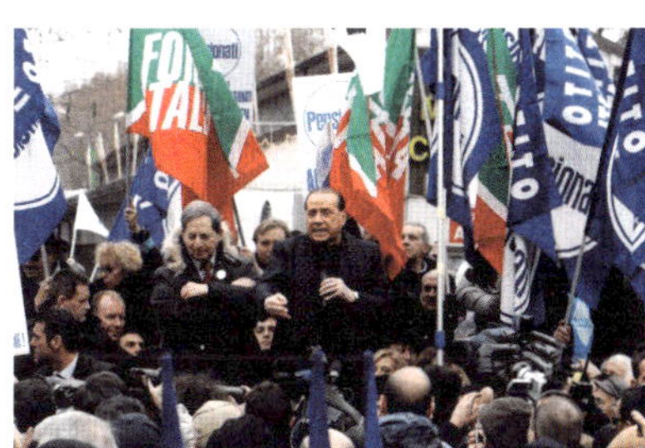

Branding Through Image

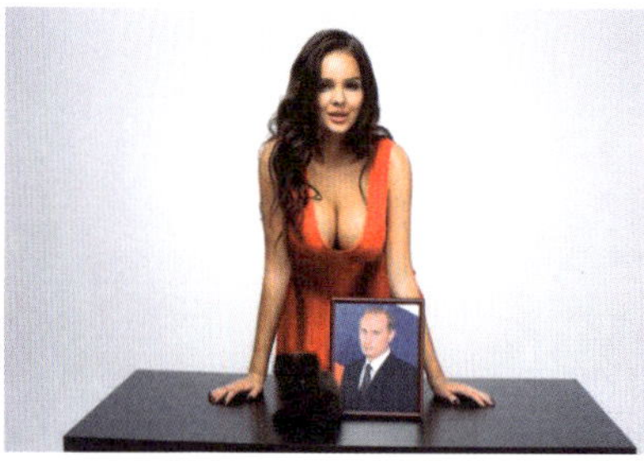

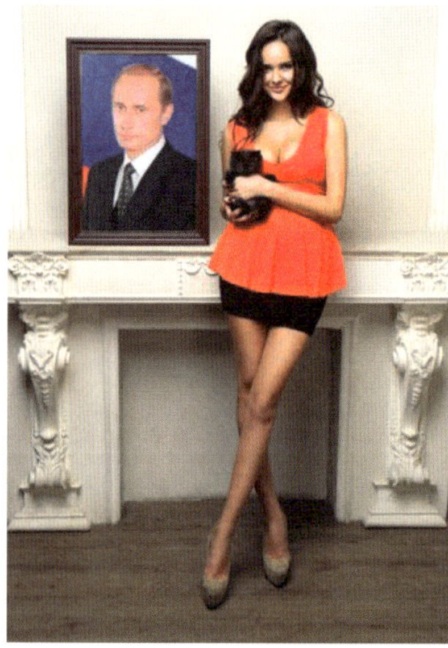

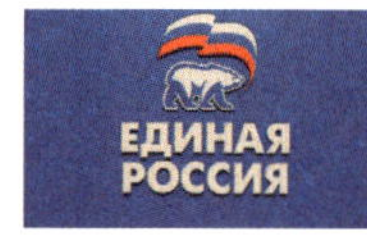

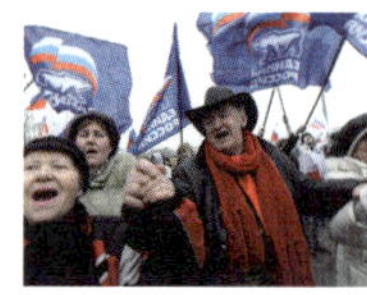

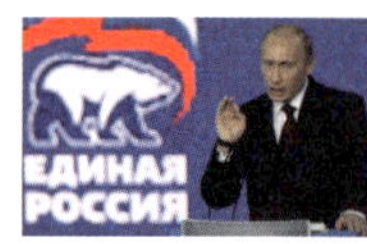

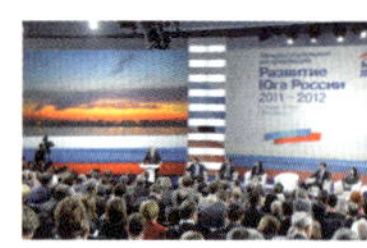

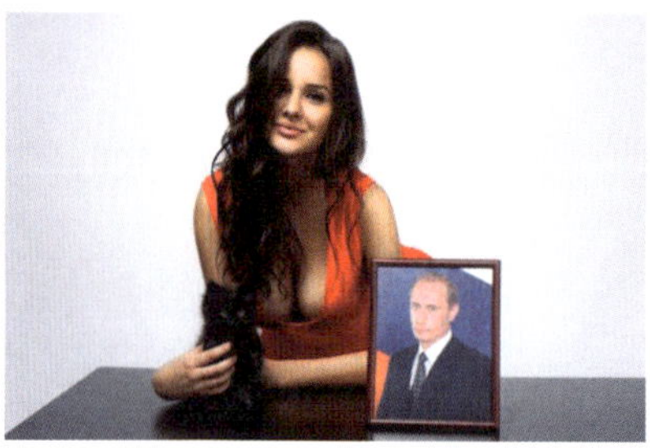

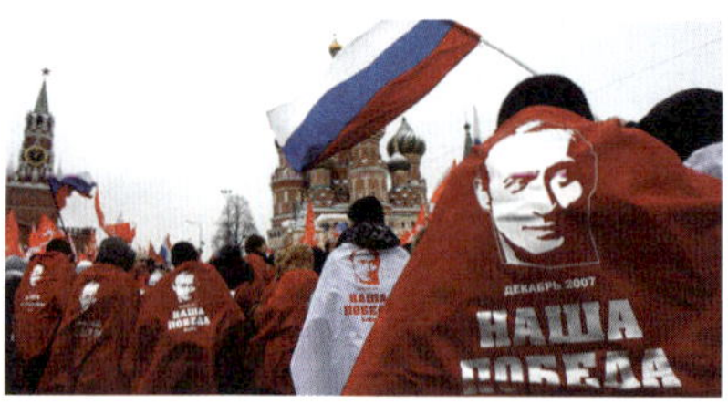

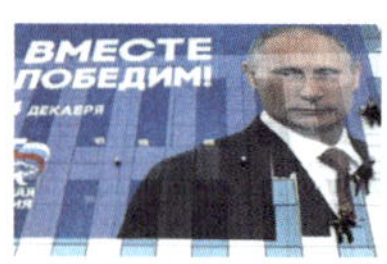

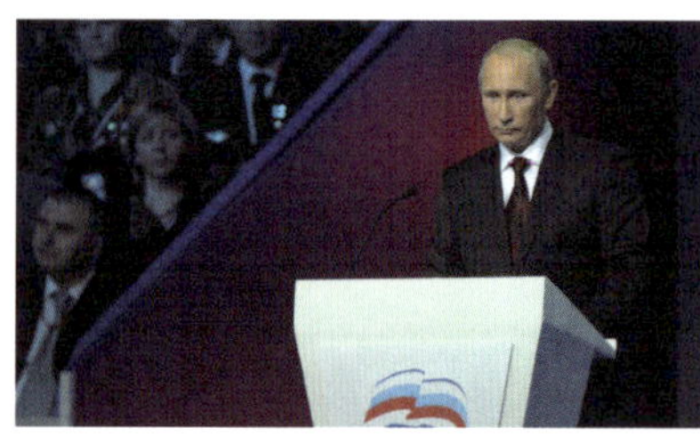

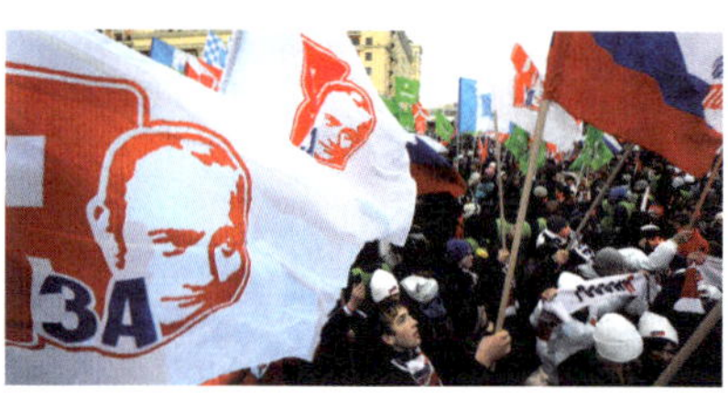

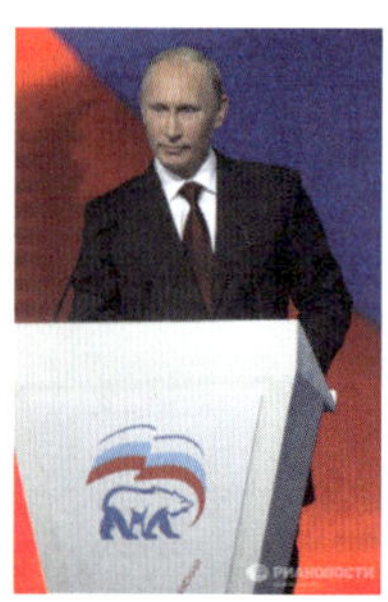

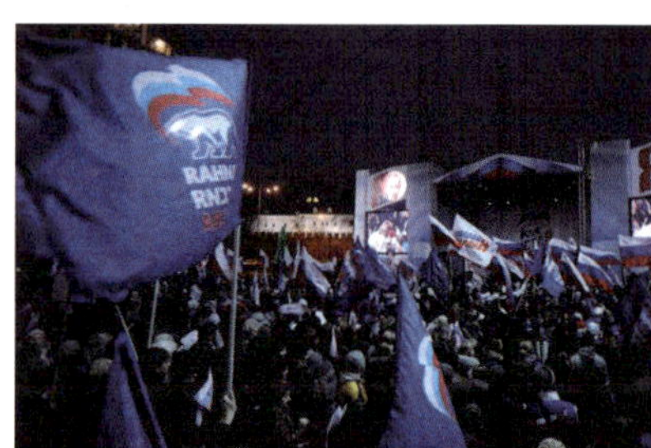

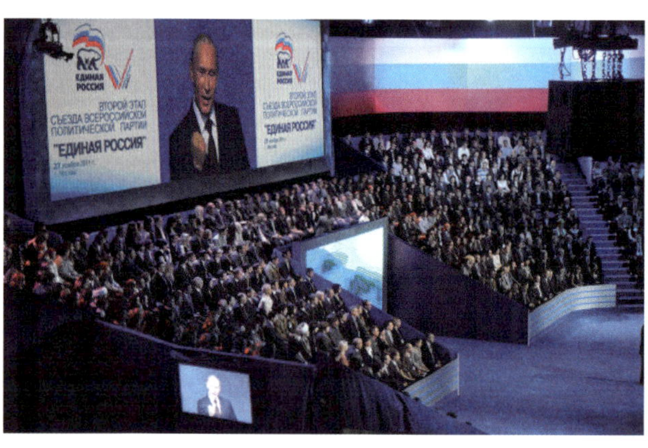

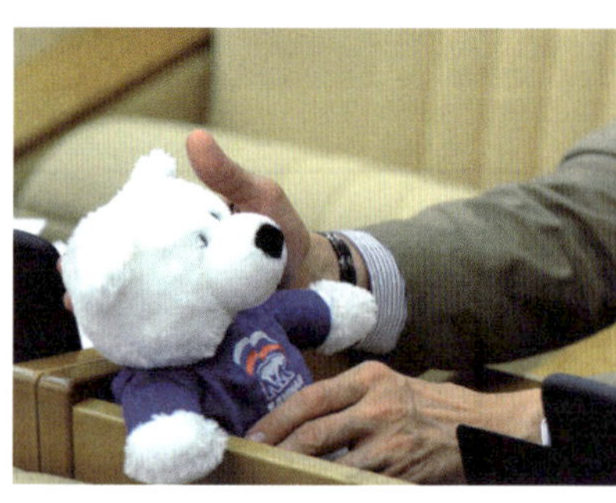

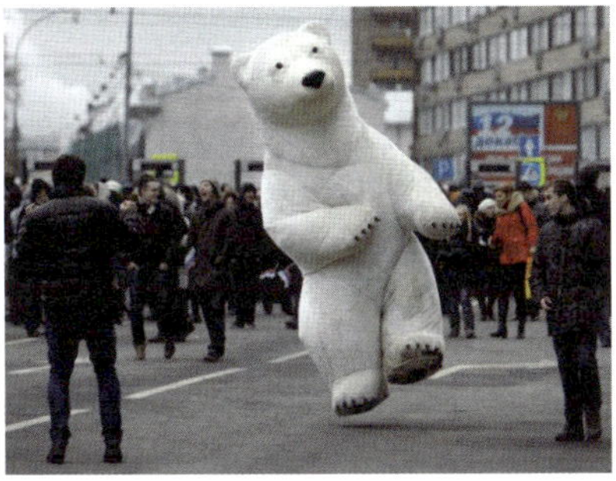

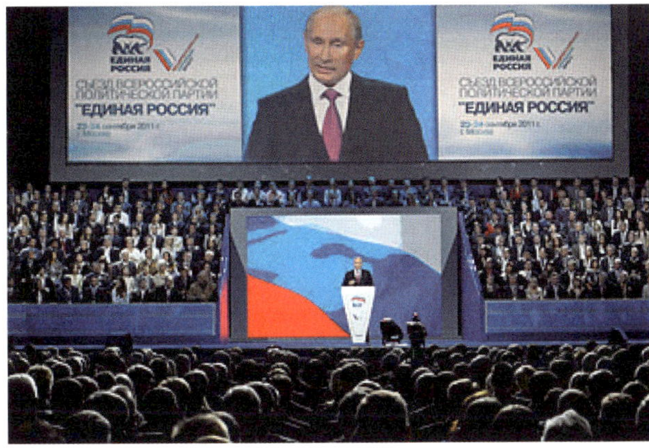
СЪЕЗД ВСЕРОССИЙСКОЙ
ПОЛИТИЧЕСКОЙ ПАРТИИ
"ЕДИНАЯ РОССИЯ"
СЪЕЗД ВСЕРОССИЙСКОЙ
ПОЛИТИЧЕСКОЙ ПАРТИИ
"ЕДИНАЯ РОССИЯ"

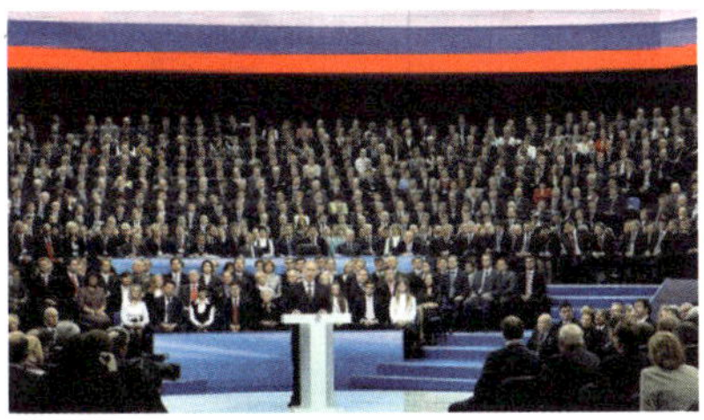

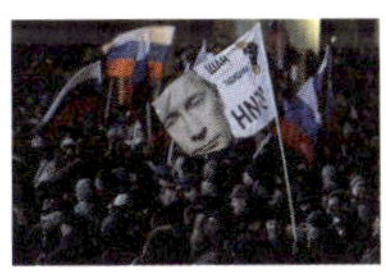

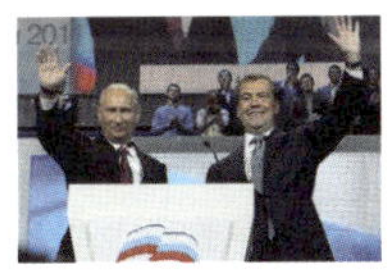

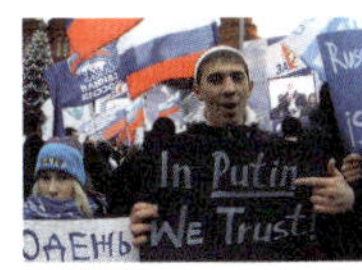
In Putin
We Trust!

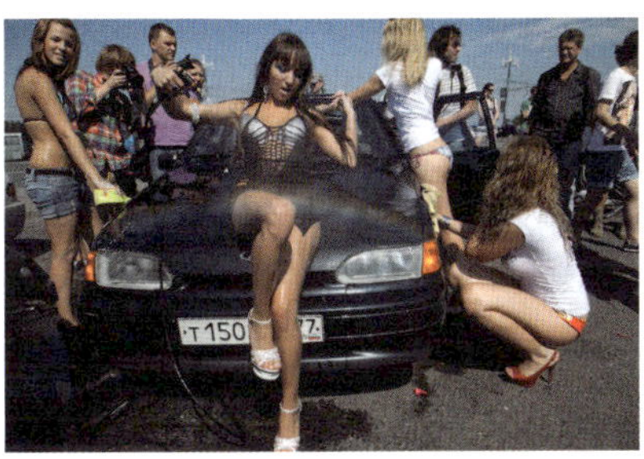

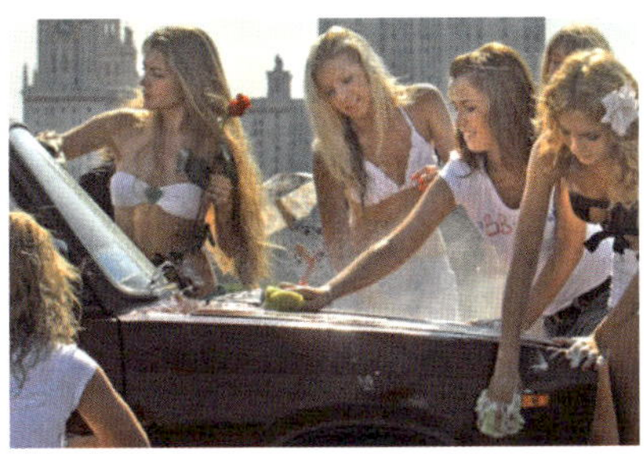

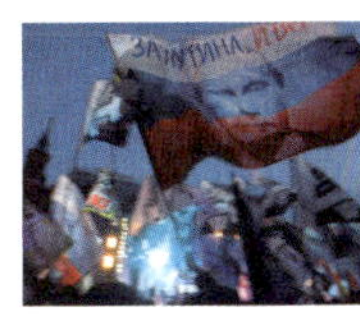

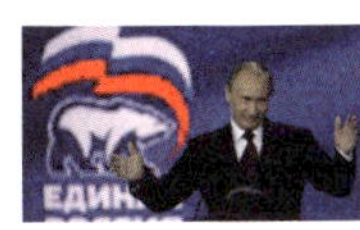

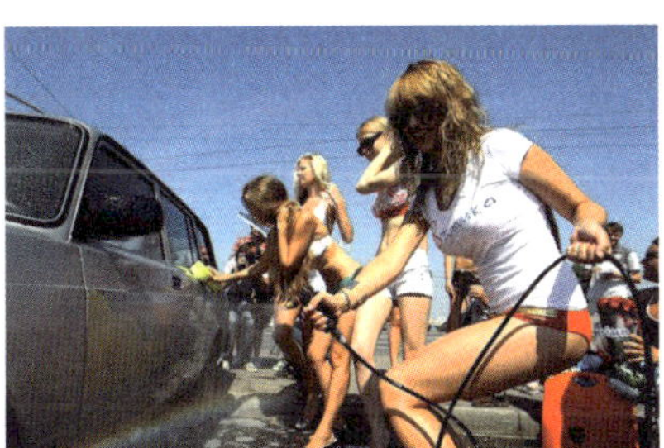

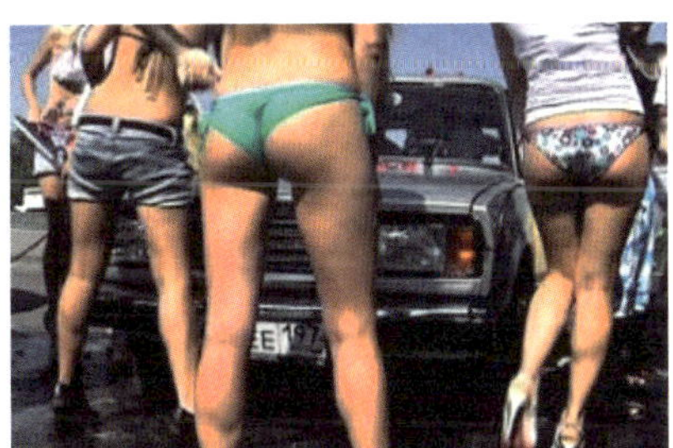

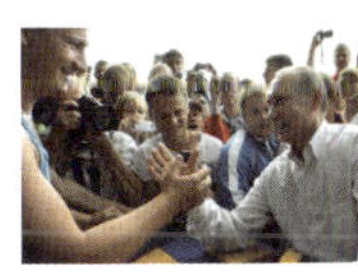

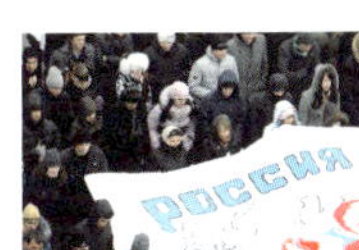
РОССИЯ

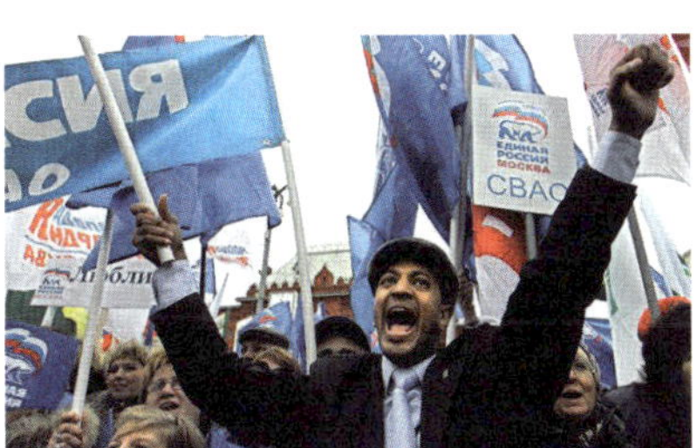

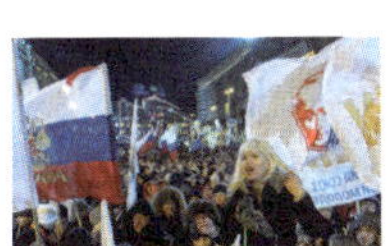

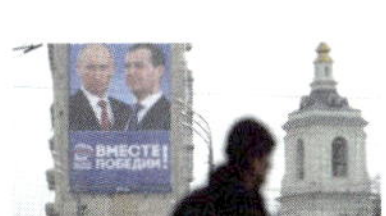

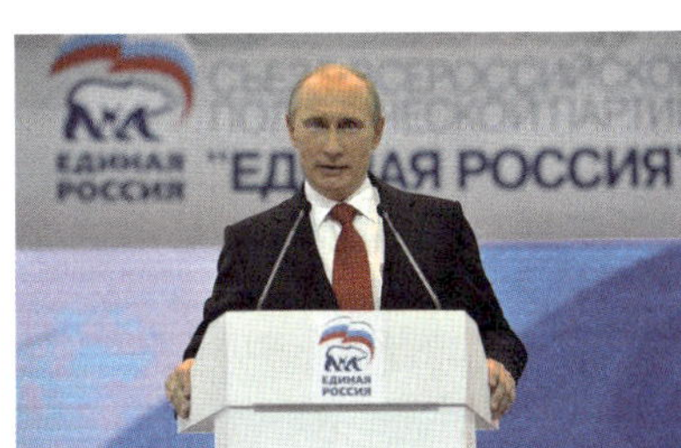
ЕДИНАЯ
РОССИЯ

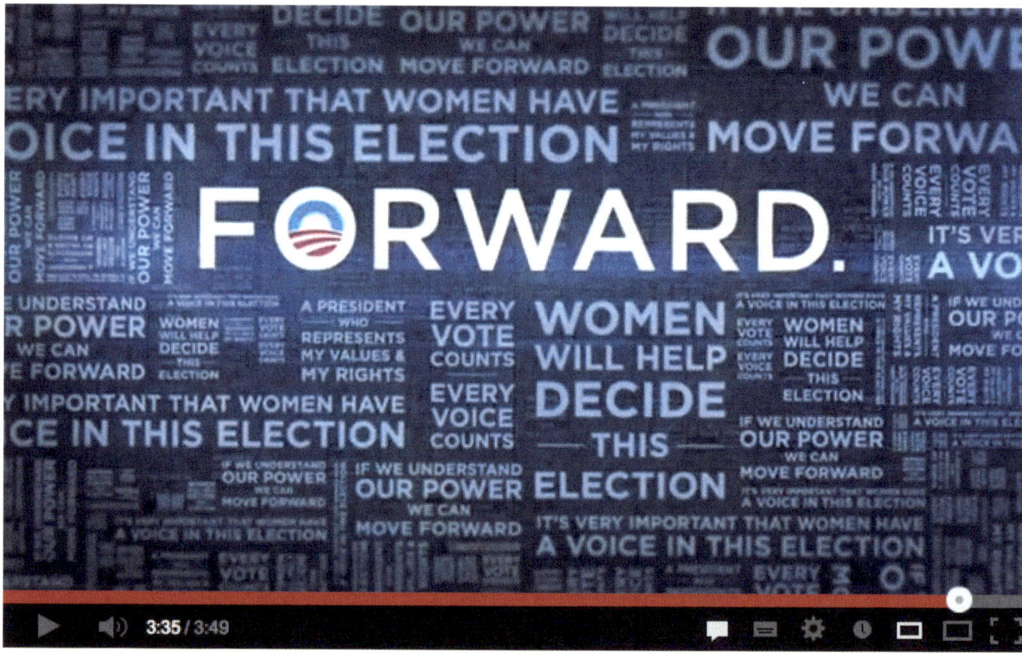
DECIDE
OUR POWER
WE CAN
MOVE FORWARD
ELECTION
OUR POWE
WE CAN
MOVE FORWA
ERY IMPORTANT THAT WOMEN HAVE
OICE IN THIS ELECTION
FORWARD.
IT'S VER
A VO
UNDERSTAND
R POWER
WE CAN
E FORWARD
A PRESIDENT
WHO
REPRESENTS
MY VALUES &
MY RIGHTS
EVERY
VOTE
COUNTS
EVERY
VOICE
COUNTS
WOMEN
WILL HELP
DECIDE
THIS
ELECTION
WOMEN
WILL HELP
DECIDE
THIS
ELECTION
Y IMPORTANT THAT WOMEN HAVE
CE IN THIS ELECTION
IF WE UNDERSTAND
OUR POWER
WE CAN
MOVE FORWARD
IF WE UNDERSTAND
OUR POWER
WE CAN
MOVE FORWARD
IT'S VERY IMPORTANT THAT WOMEN HAVE
A VOICE IN THIS ELECTION
3:35 / 3:49

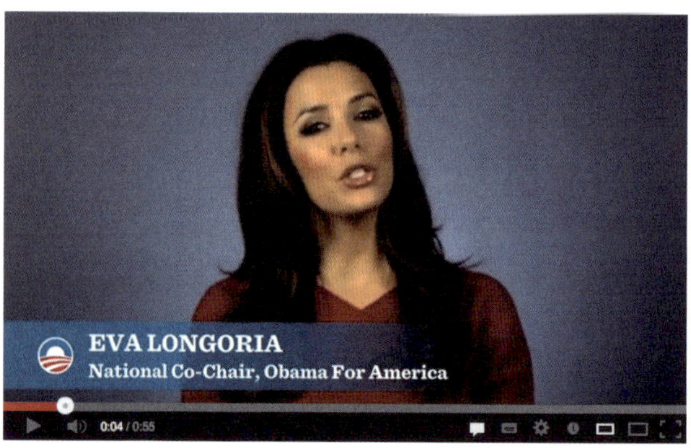
EVA LONGORIA
National Co-Chair, Obama For America
0:04 / 0:55

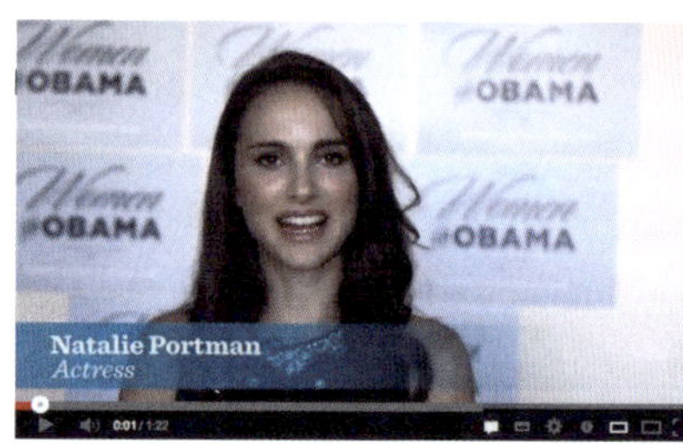
OBAMA
OBAMA
OBAMA
OBAMA
Natalie Portman
Actress

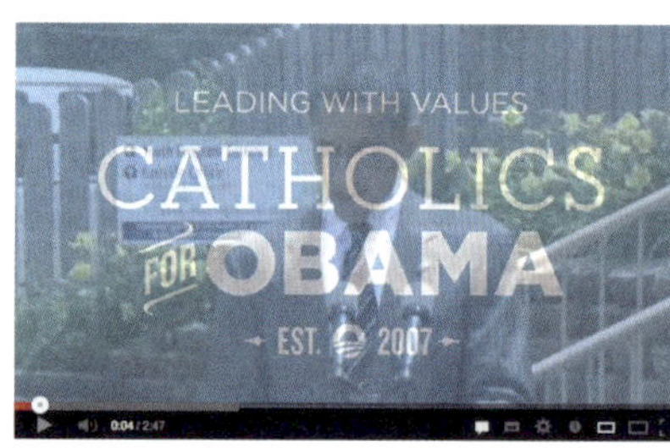
LEADING WITH VALUES
CATHOLICS
FOR OBAMA
EST. 2007

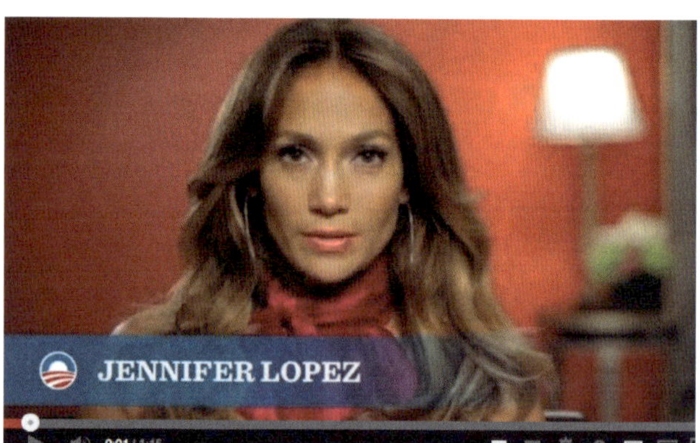
JENNIFER LOPEZ
0:01 / 1:15

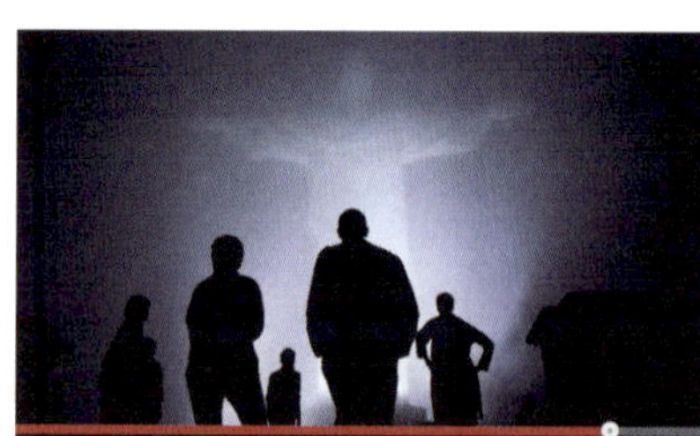

ESTAMOS UNIDOS
LATINOS
FOR OBAMA
EST. 2007

SPORTSMEN
FOR OBAMA
EST. 2007

ARTISTS
FOR OBAMA

AFRICAN
AMERICANS
FOR OBAMA
EST. 2007

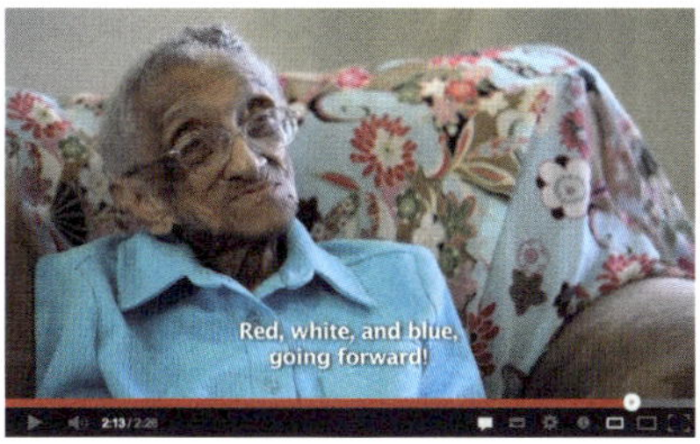

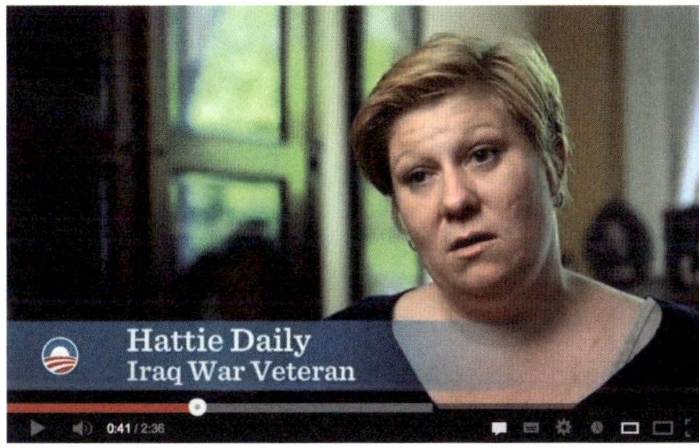

VETERANS
& MILITARY FAMILIES
FOR OBAMA
EST. 2007

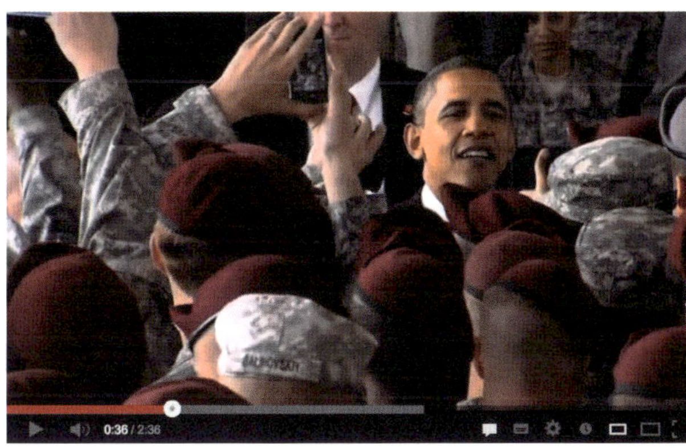

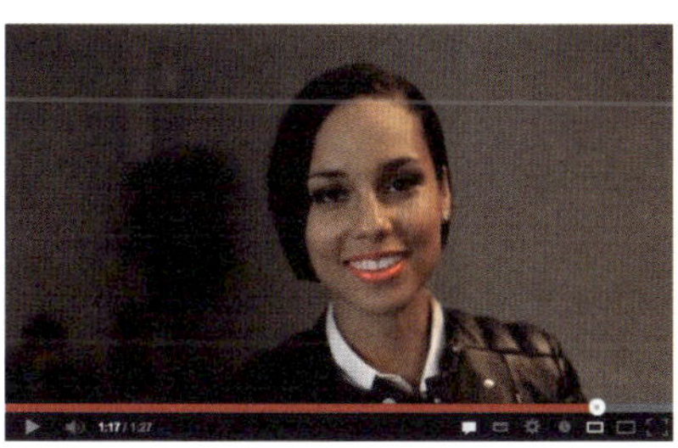

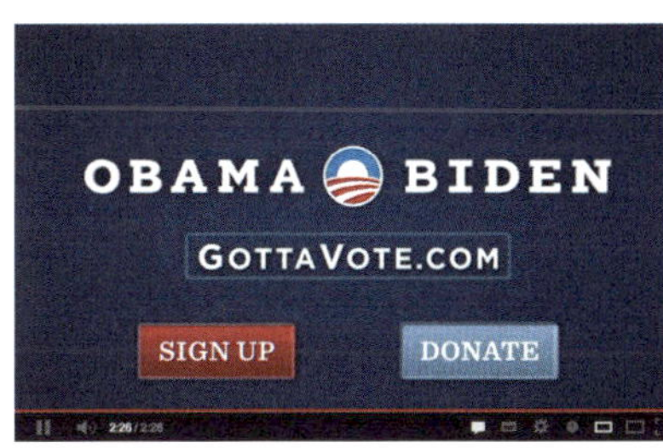

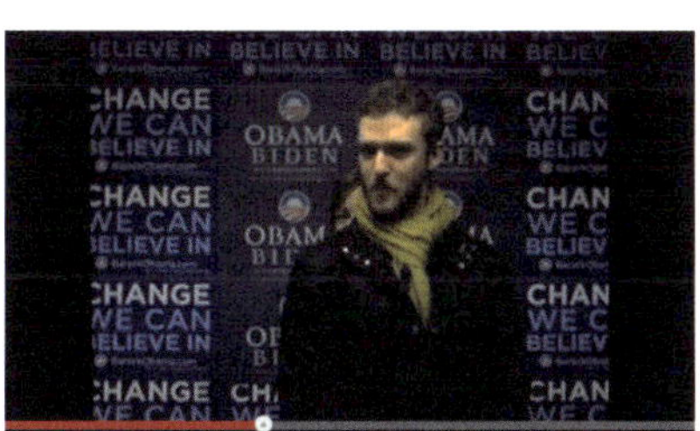

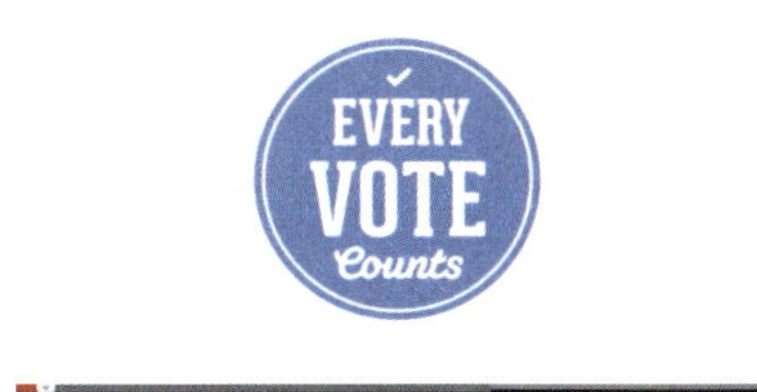

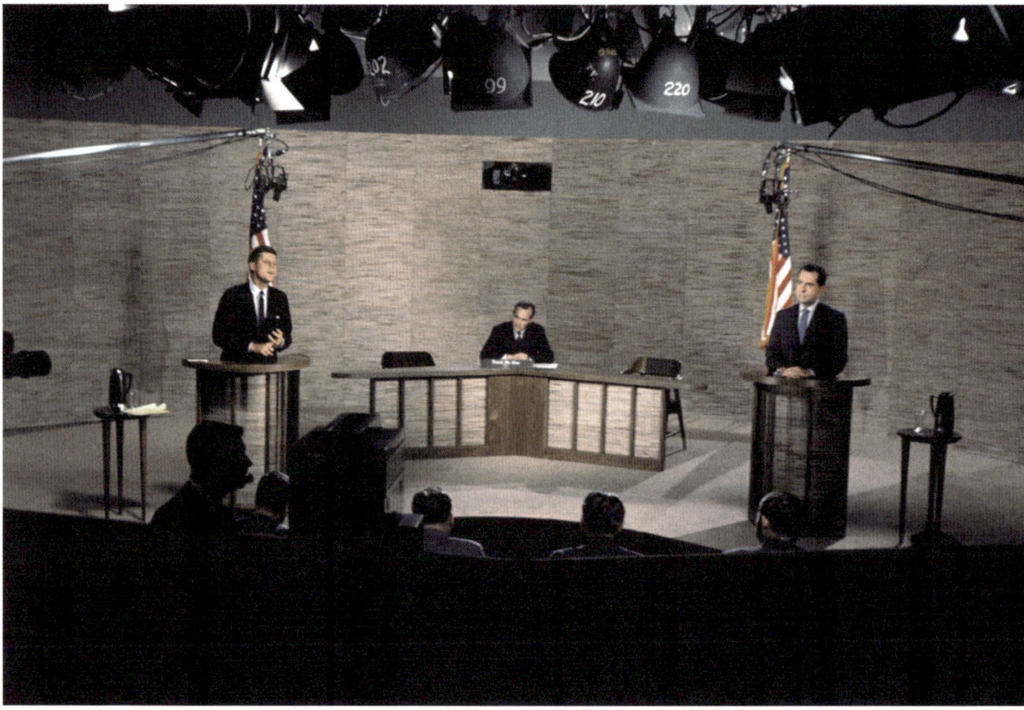
99
210
220

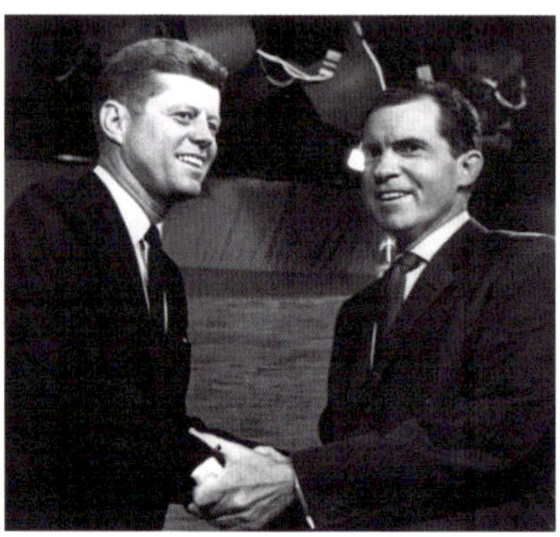

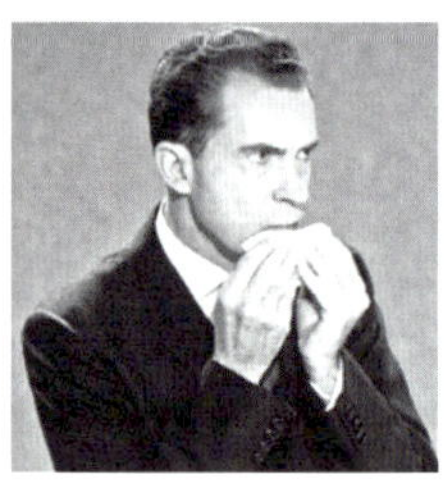

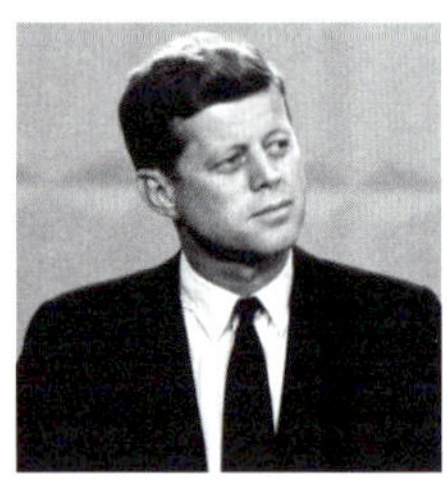

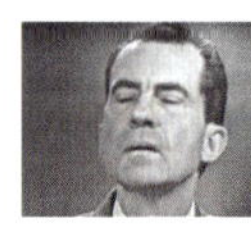

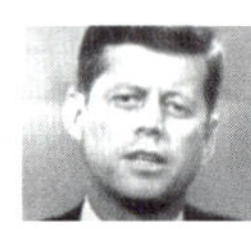

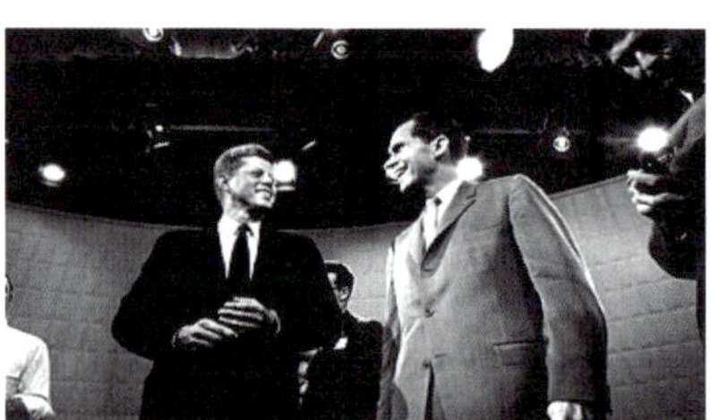

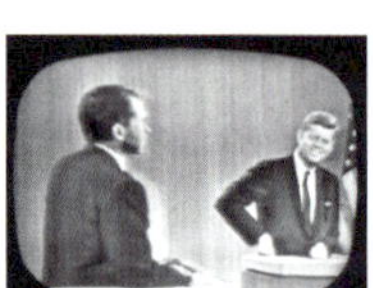

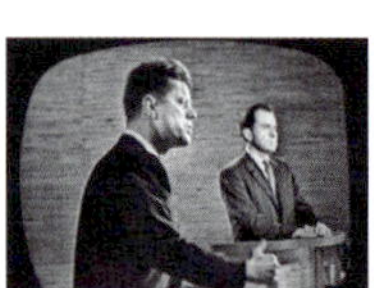

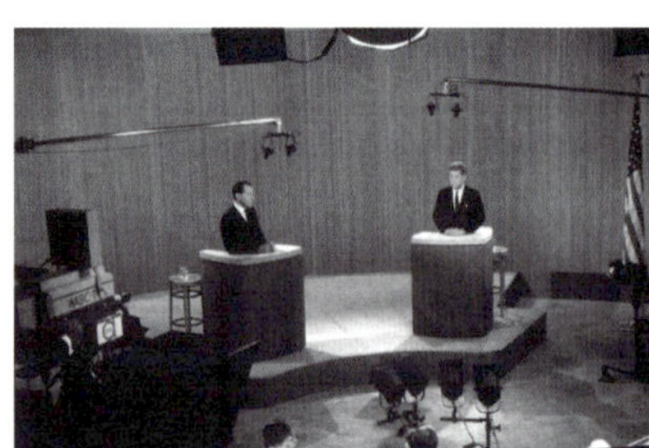

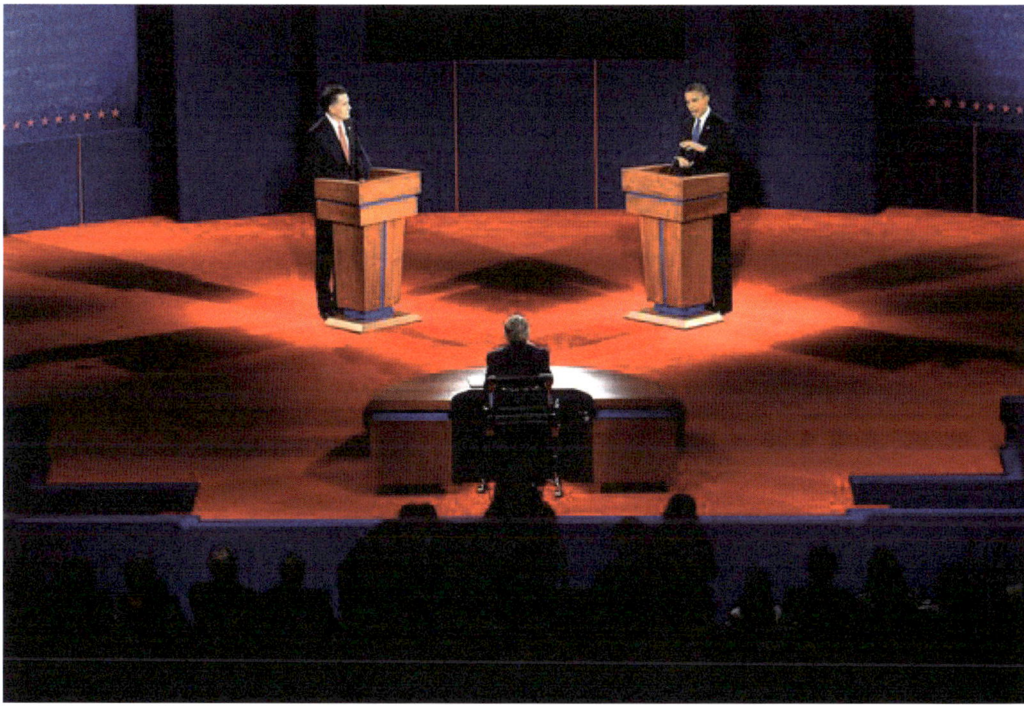

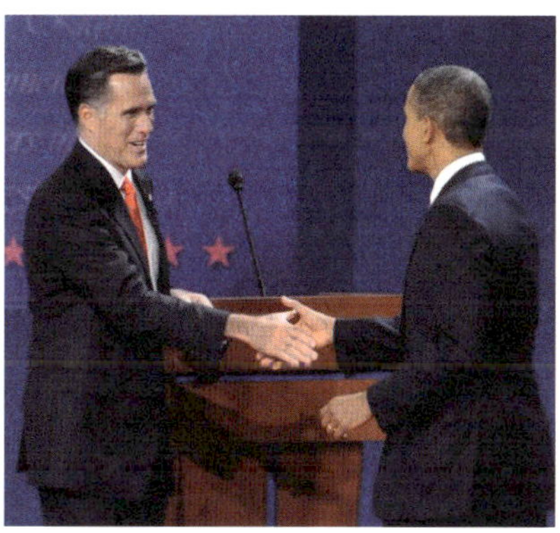

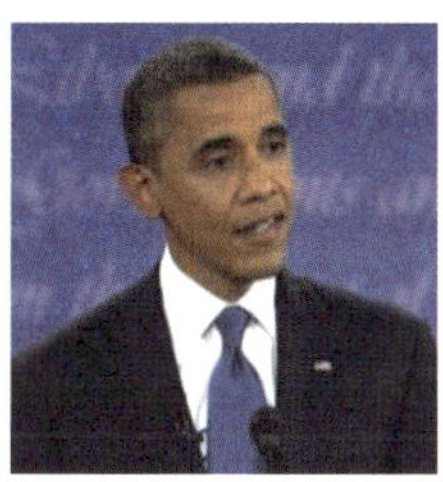

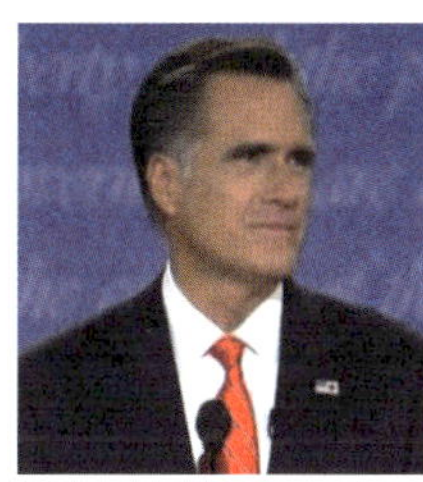

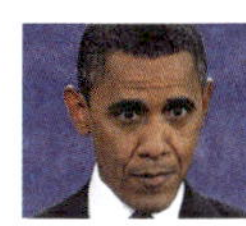

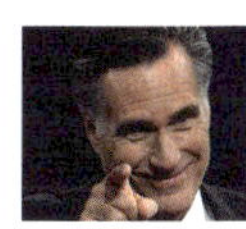

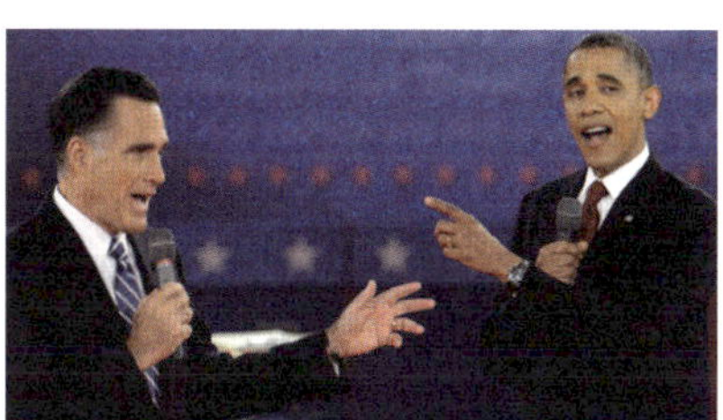

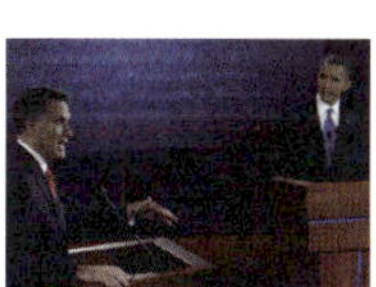

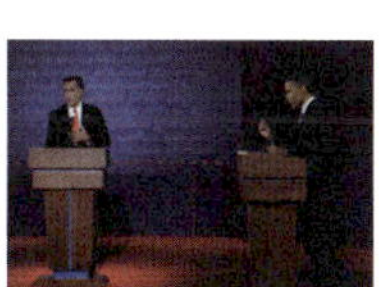

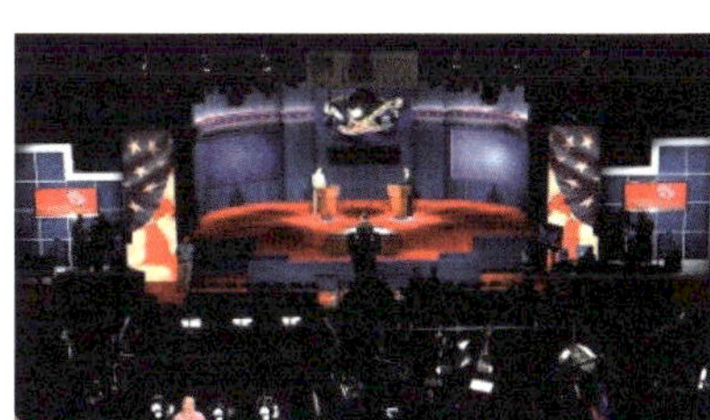

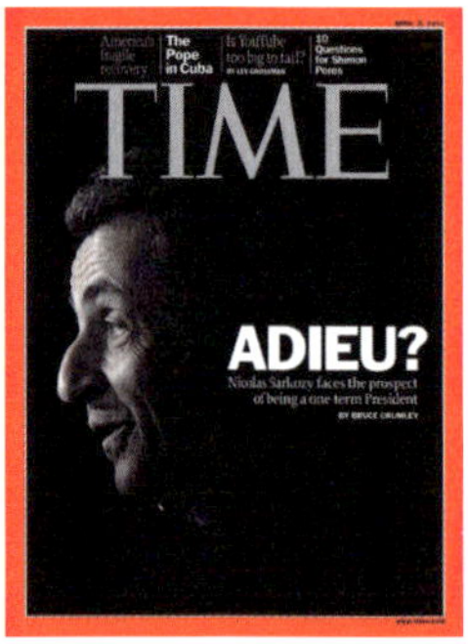
TIME
ADIEU?
Nicolas Sarkozy faces the prospect of being a one-term President

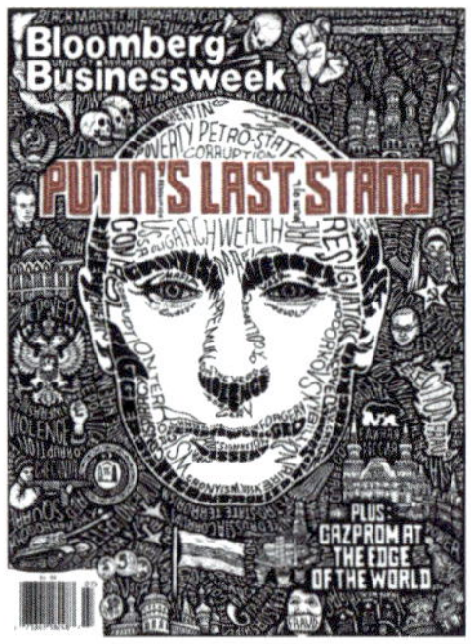
Bloomberg Businessweek
PUTIN'S LAST STAND
PLUS: GAZPROM AT THE EDGE OF THE WORLD

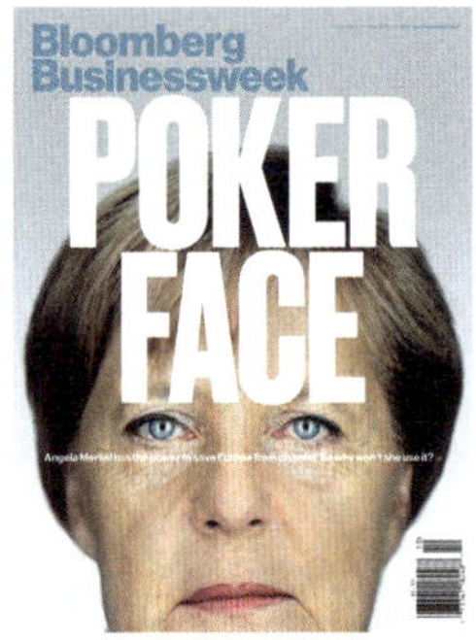
Bloomberg Businessweek
POKER FACE

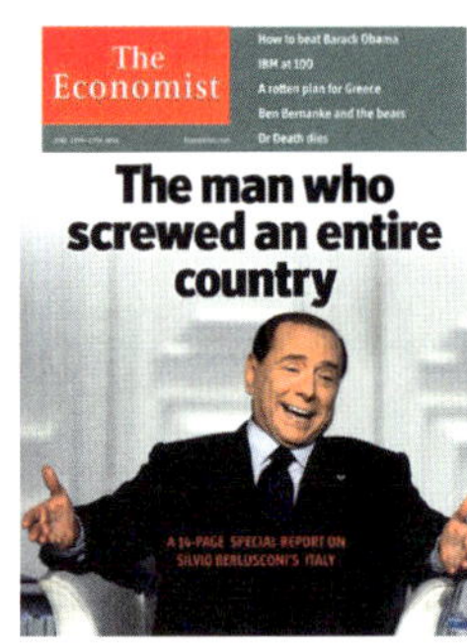
The Economist
The man who screwed an entire country

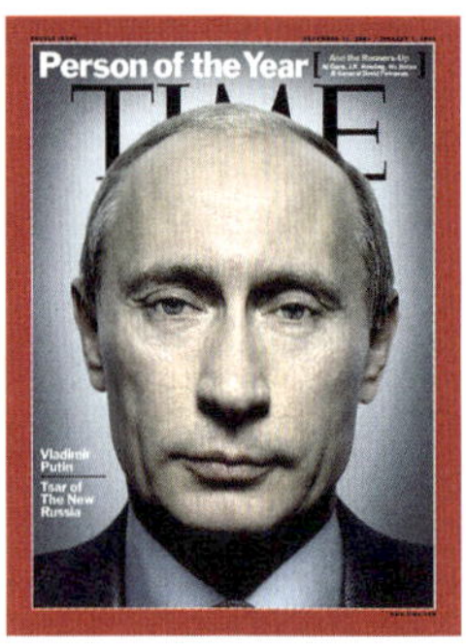
Person of the Year
TIME
Vladimir Putin
Tsar of The New Russia

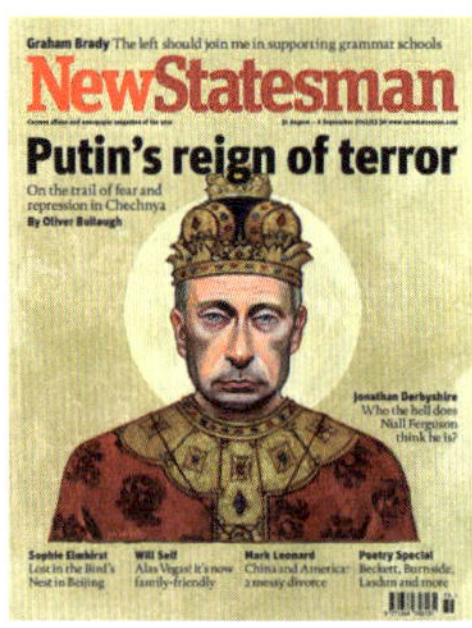
NewStatesman
Putin's reign of terror
On the trail of fear and repression in Chechnya

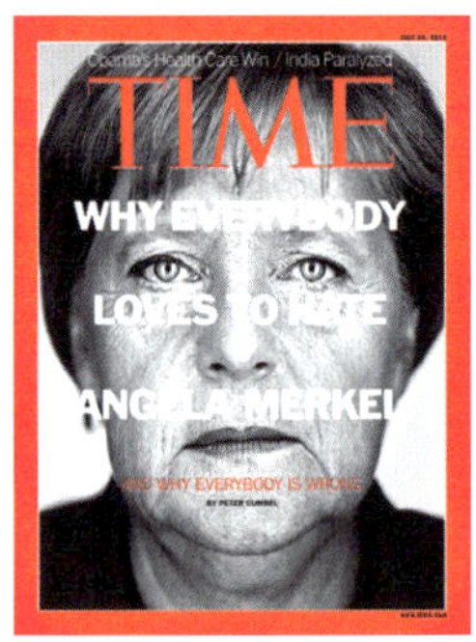
TIME
WHY EVERYBODY LOVES TO HATE ANGELA MERKEL

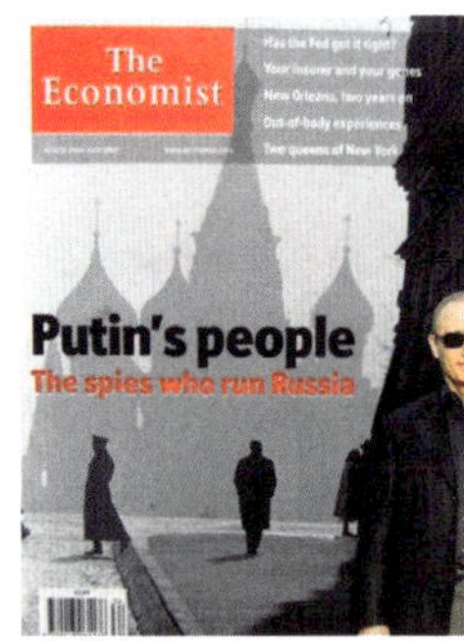
The Economist
Putin's people
The spies who run Russia

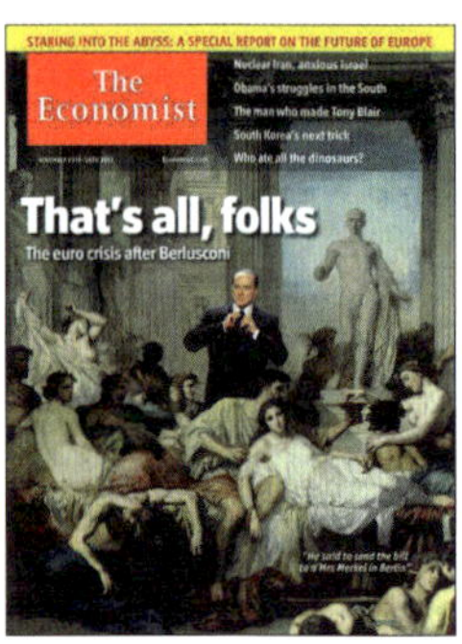
The Economist
That's all, folks
The euro crisis after Berlusconi

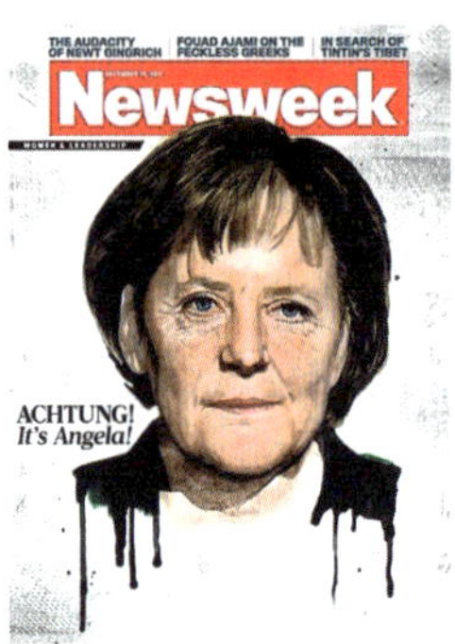
Newsweek
ACHTUNG! It's Angela!

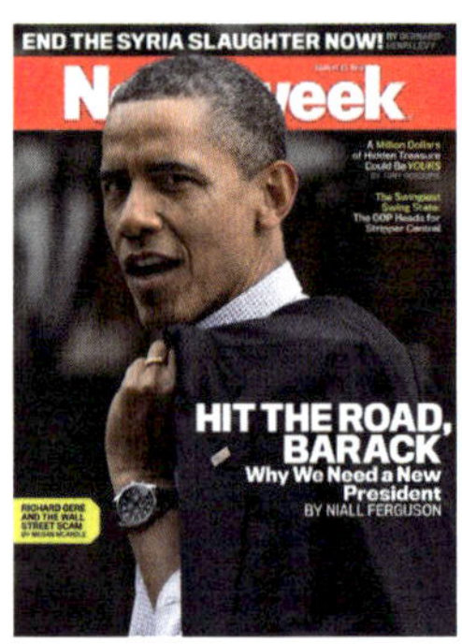
END THE SYRIA SLAUGHTER NOW!
HIT THE ROAD, BARACK
Why We Need a New President
BY NIALL FERGUSON

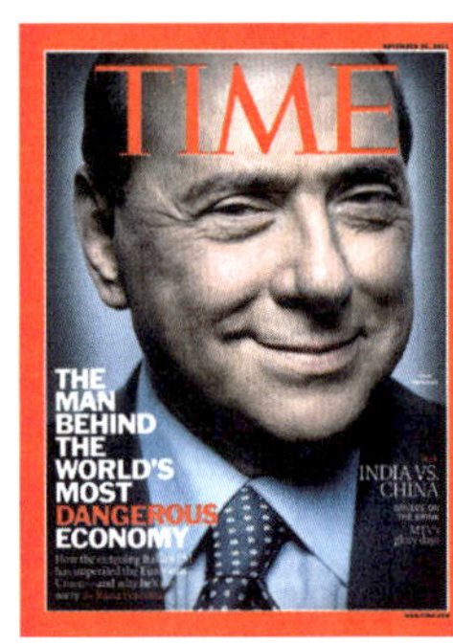
TIME
THE MAN BEHIND THE WORLD'S MOST DANGEROUS ECONOMY

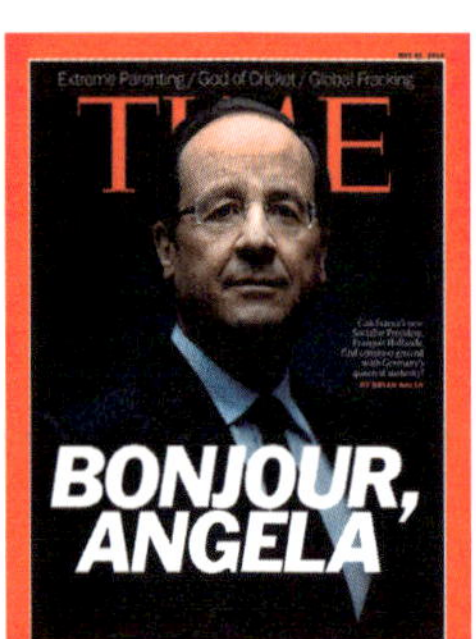
TIME
BONJOUR, ANGELA

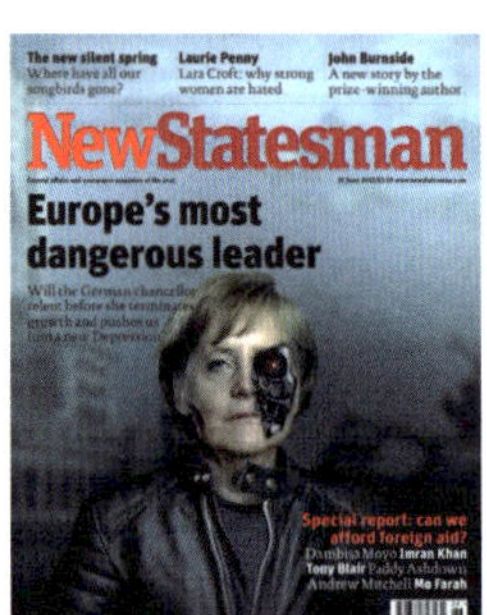
NewStatesman
Europe's most dangerous leader

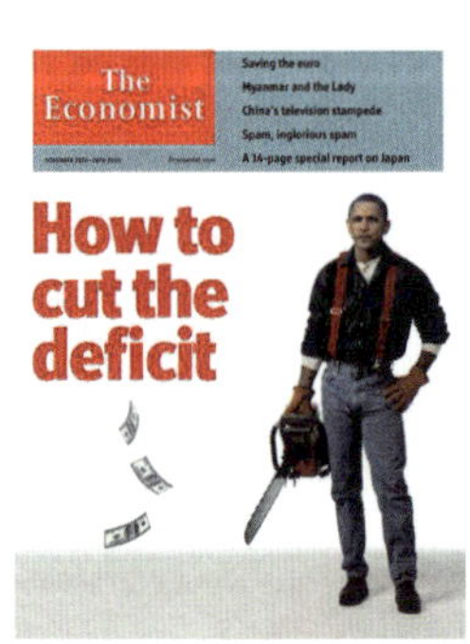
The Economist
How to cut the deficit

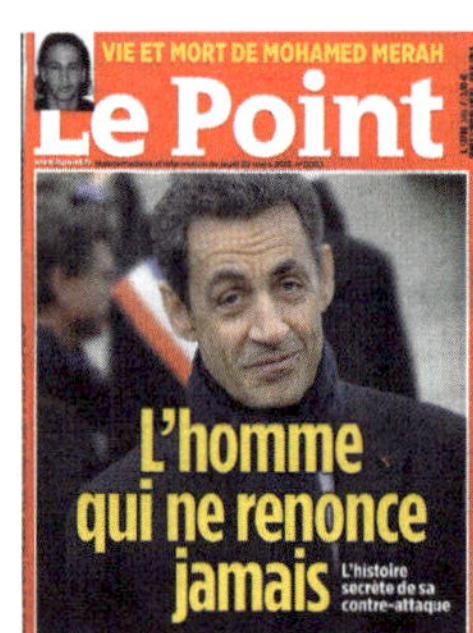
VIE ET MORT DE MOHAMED MERAH
Le Point
L'homme qui ne renonce jamais
L'histoire secrète de sa contre-attaque

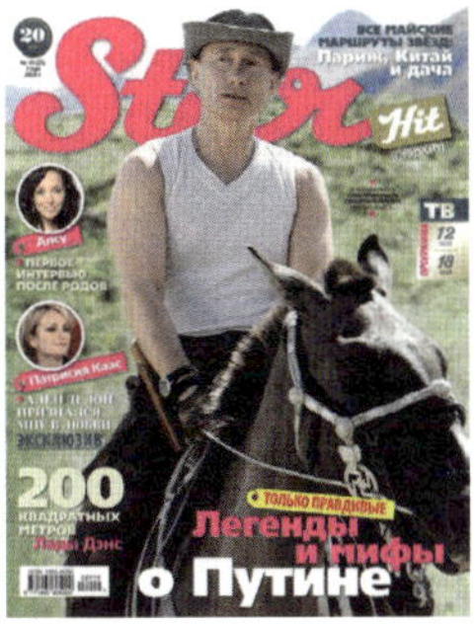
Star
Hit
200
Легенды и мифы о Путине

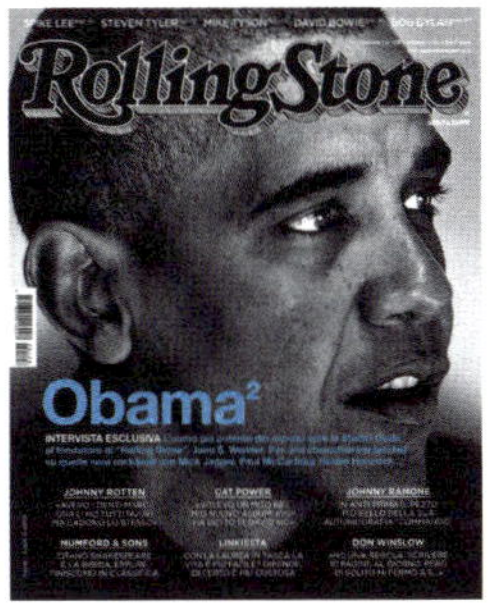
Rolling Stone
Obama²

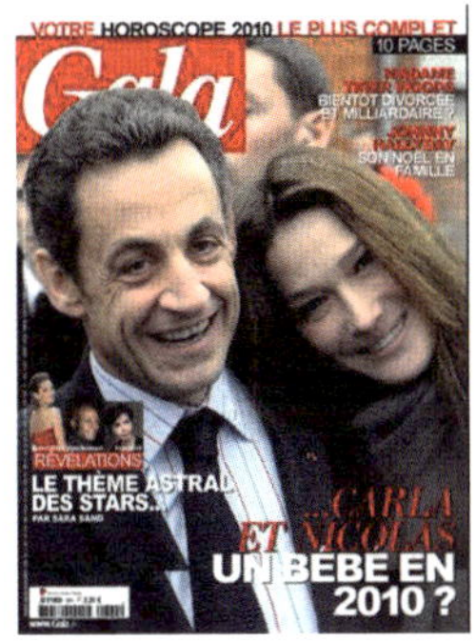
VOTRE HOROSCOPE 2010 LE PLUS COMPLET
Gala
10 PAGES
RÉVÉLATIONS
LE THÈME ASTRAL DES STARS
CARLA ET NICOLAS
UN BÉBÉ EN 2010 ?

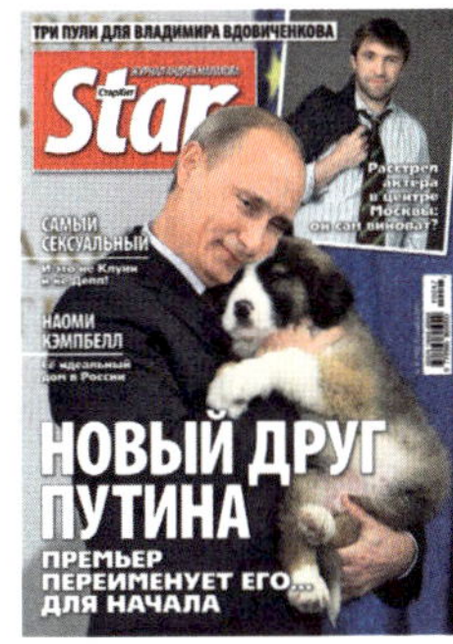
Star
НОВЫЙ ДРУГ ПУТИНА
ПРЕМЬЕР ПЕРЕИМЕНУЕТ ЕГО... ДЛЯ НАЧАЛА

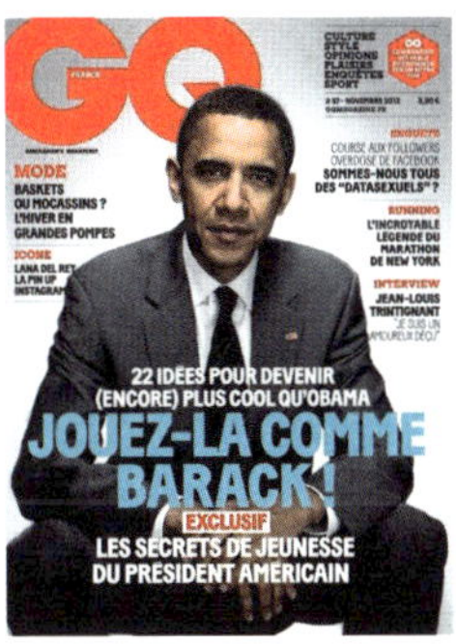
GQ
22 IDÉES POUR DEVENIR (ENCORE) PLUS COOL QU'OBAMA
JOUEZ-LA COMME BARACK !
EXCLUSIF
LES SECRETS DE JEUNESSE DU PRÉSIDENT AMÉRICAIN

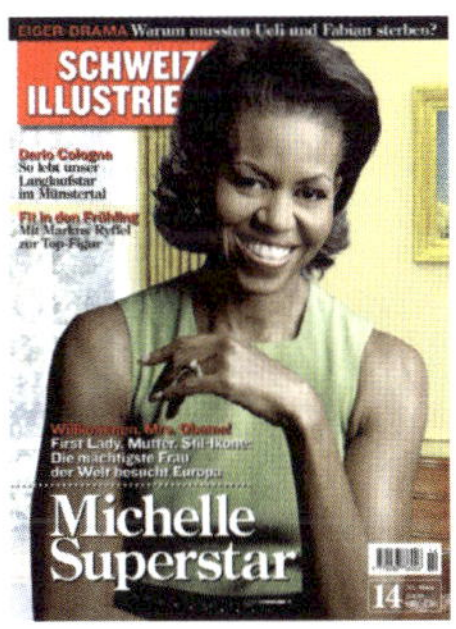
SCHWEIZER ILLUSTRIERTE
Michelle Superstar

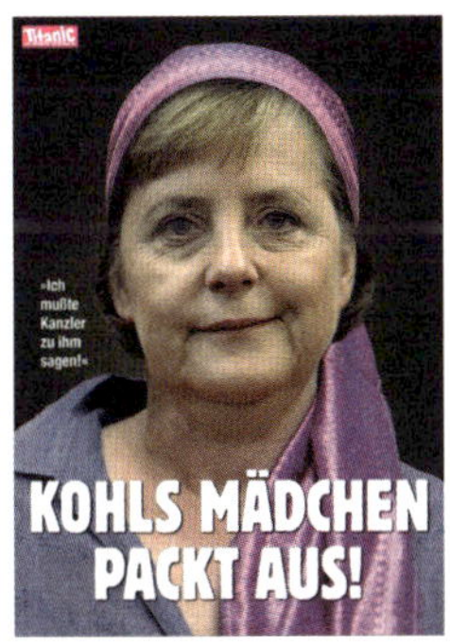
Titanic
»Ich mußte Kanzler zu ihm sagen!«
KOHLS MÄDCHEN PACKT AUS!

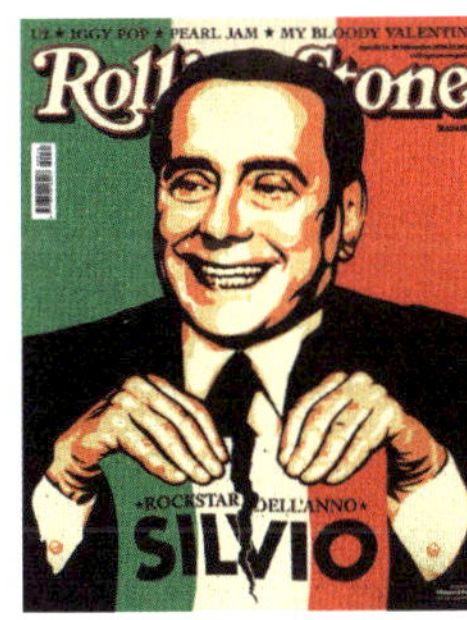
Rolling Stone
SILVIO

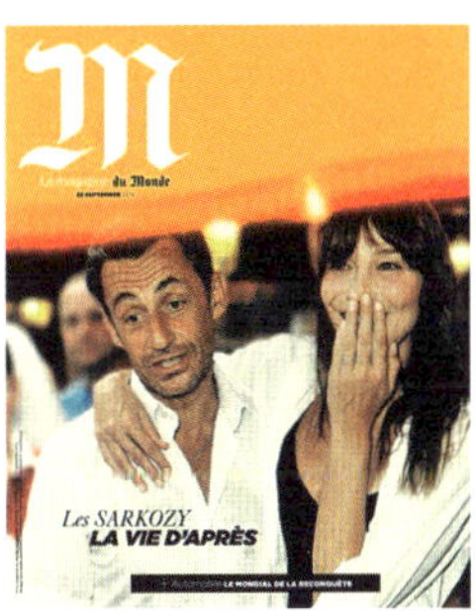
M
Les SARKOZY
LA VIE D'APRÈS

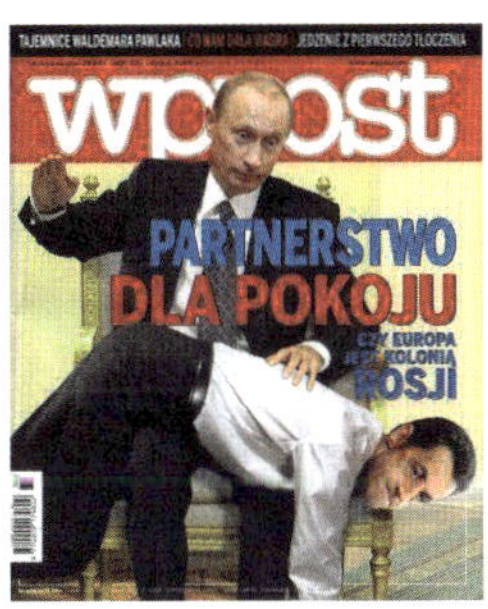
wprost
PARTNERSTWO DLA POKOJU
ROSJI

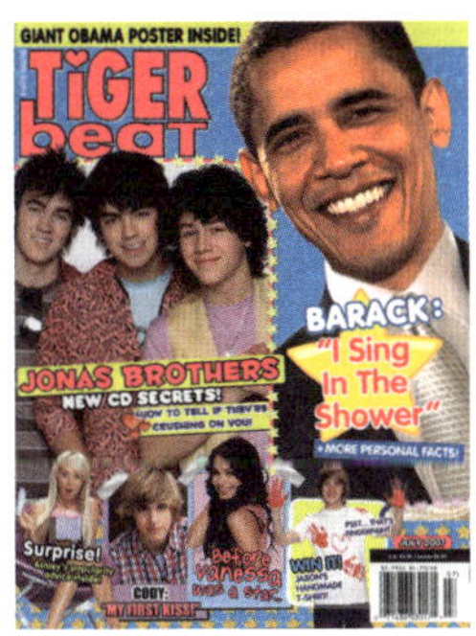
GIANT OBAMA POSTER INSIDE!
Tiger beat
BARACK: "I Sing In The Shower"
JONAS BROTHERS
NEW CD SECRETS!

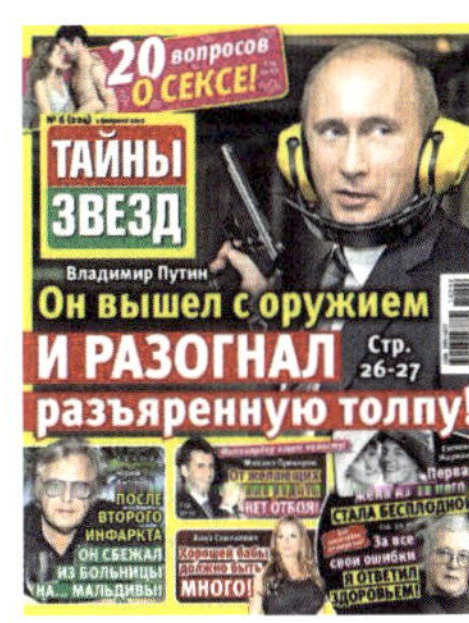
20 вопросов о сексе!
ТАЙНЫ ЗВЕЗД
Владимир Путин
Он вышел с оружием и РАЗОГНАЛ разъяренную толпу!
Стр. 26-27

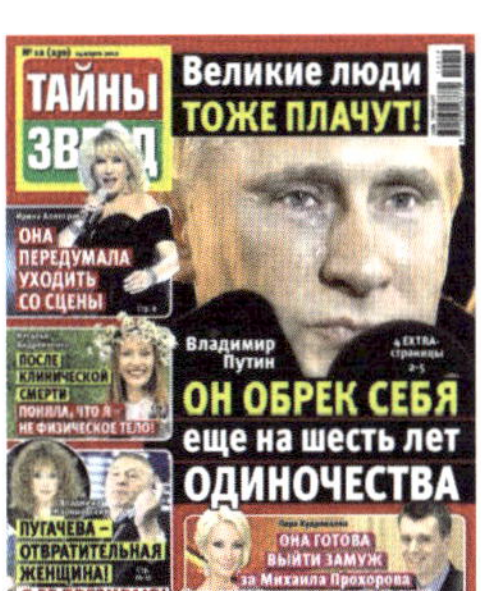
ТАЙНЫ ЗВЕЗД
Великие люди ТОЖЕ ПЛАЧУТ!
Владимир Путин
ОН ОБРЕК СЕБЯ еще на шесть лет ОДИНОЧЕСТВА

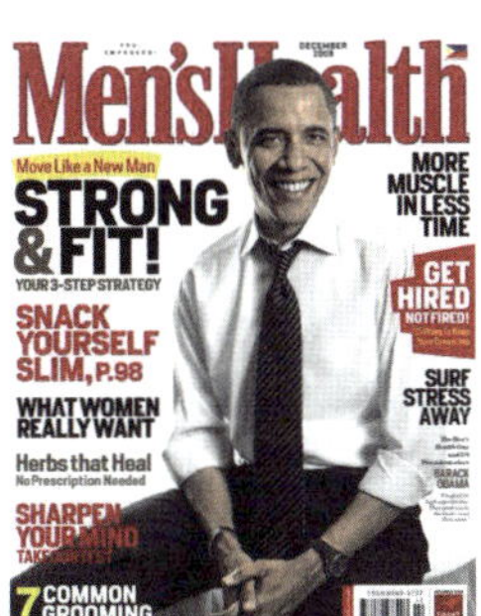
Men'sHealth
MORE MUSCLE IN LESS TIME
STRONG & FIT!
GET HIRED
SNACK YOURSELF SLIM, P.98
WHAT WOMEN REALLY WANT
SURF STRESS AWAY
7 COMMON GROOMING ISSUES—SOLVED

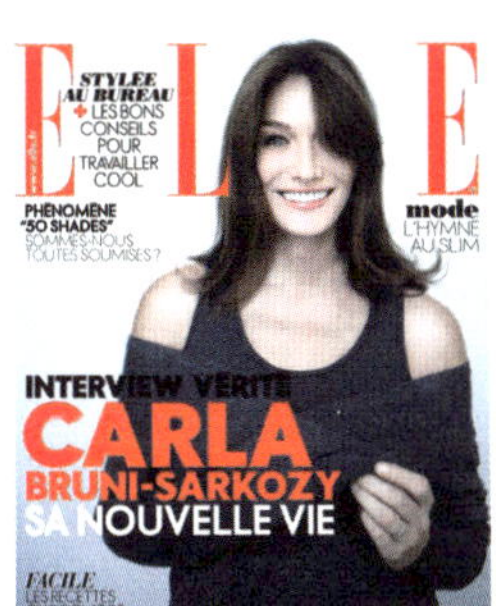
ELLE
INTERVIEW VÉRITÉ
CARLA BRUNI-SARKOZY
SA NOUVELLE VIE

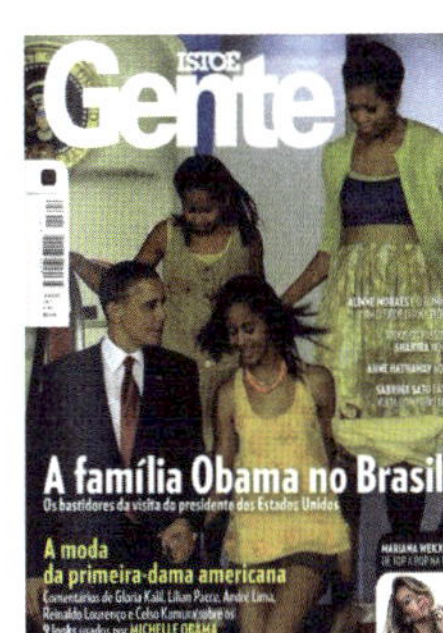
Gente
A família Obama no Brasil
A moda da primeira-dama americana

Branding Through the Media

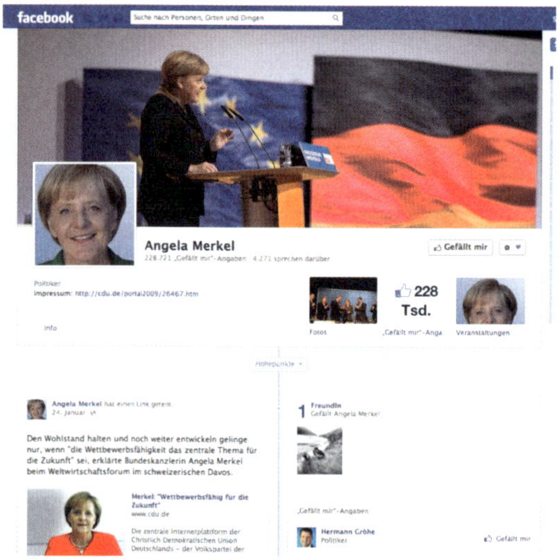

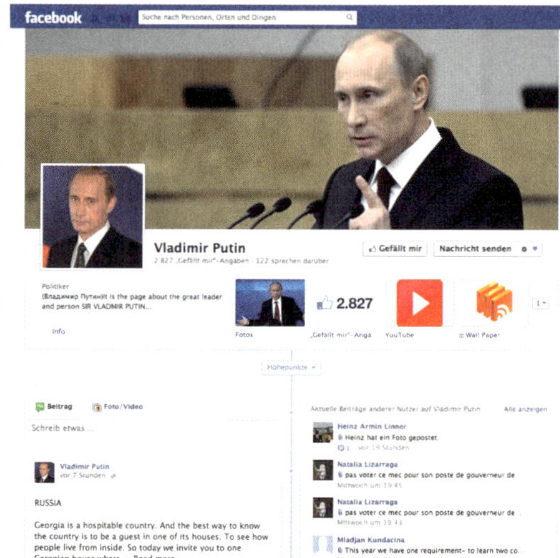

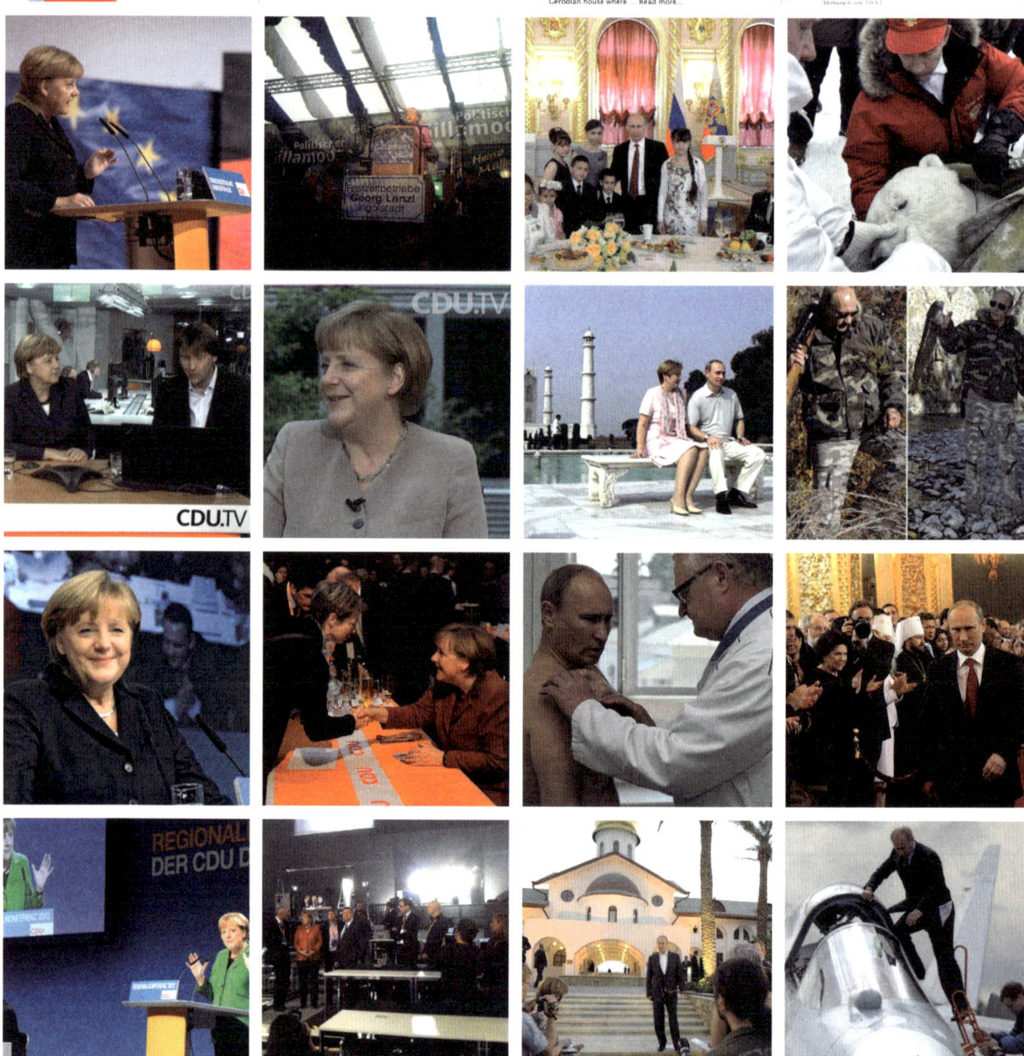

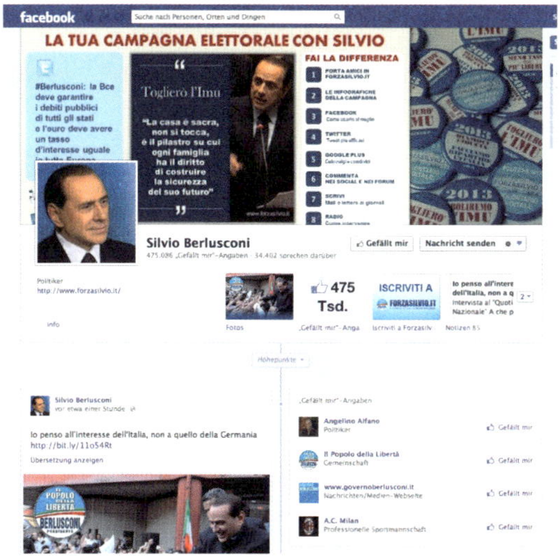
facebook
LA TUA CAMPAGNA ELETTORALE CON SILVIO
FAI LA DIFFERENZA
Toglierò l'Imu
"La casa è sacra, non si tocca, è il pilastro su cui ogni famiglia ha il diritto di costruire la sicurezza del suo futuro"
Silvio Berlusconi
Gefällt mir
Nachricht senden
475 Tsd.
ISCRIVITI A
Io penso all'interesse dell'Italia, non a quello della Germania

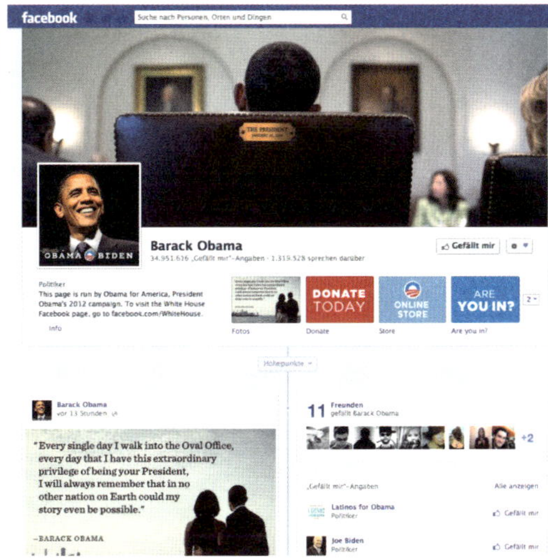
facebook
Barack Obama
Gefällt mir
DONATE TODAY
ONLINE STORE
ARE YOU IN?
11 Freunden
"Every single day I walk into the Oval Office, every day that I have this extraordinary privilege of being your President, I will always remember that in no other nation on Earth could my story even be possible."
–BARACK OBAMA

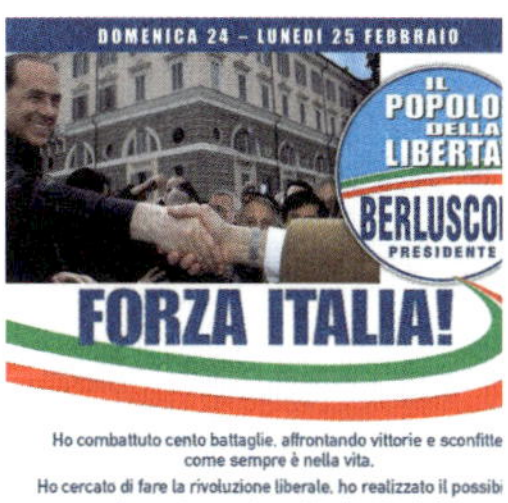
DOMENICA 24 – LUNEDÌ 25 FEBBRAIO
IL POPOLO DELLA LIBERTÀ
BERLUSCONI PRESIDENTE
FORZA ITALIA!
Ho combattuto cento battaglie, affrontando vittorie e sconfitte come sempre è nella vita.
Per questo me ne hanno fatte di tutti i colori.

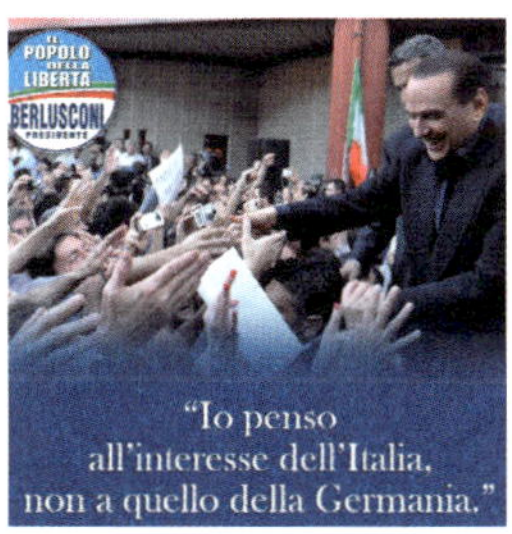
"Io penso all'interesse dell'Italia, non a quello della Germania."

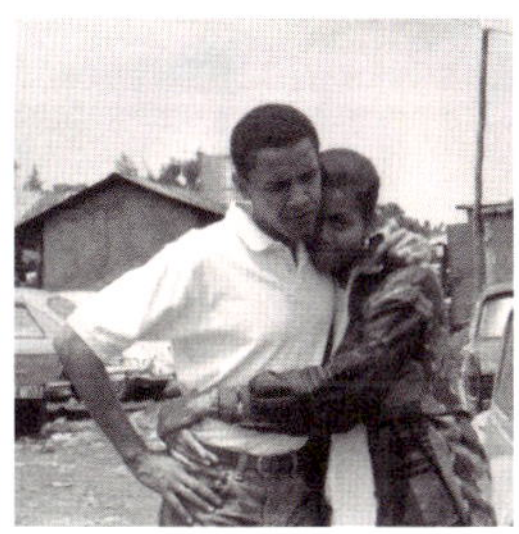

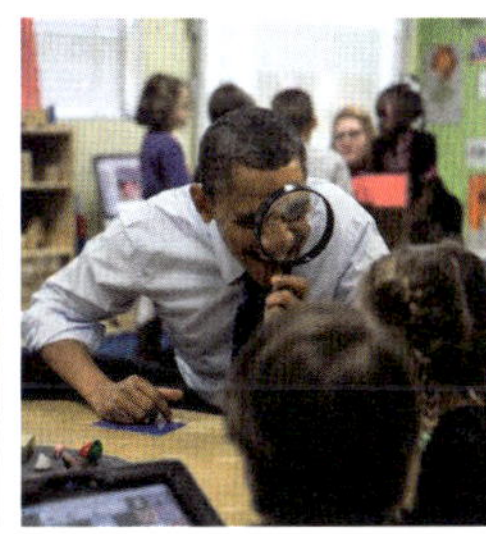

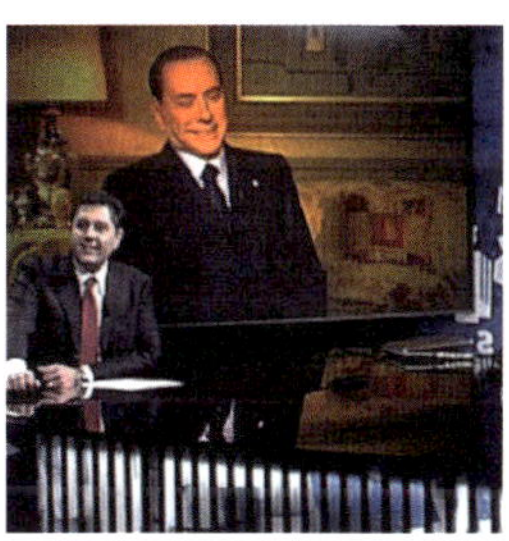

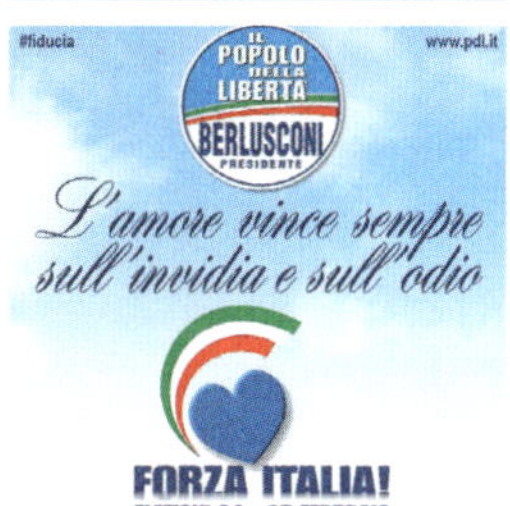
#fiducia
www.pdl.it
IL POPOLO DELLA LIBERTÀ
BERLUSCONI PRESIDENTE
L'amore vince sempre sull'invidia e sull'odio
FORZA ITALIA!
ELEZIONI 24 - 25 FEBBRAIO

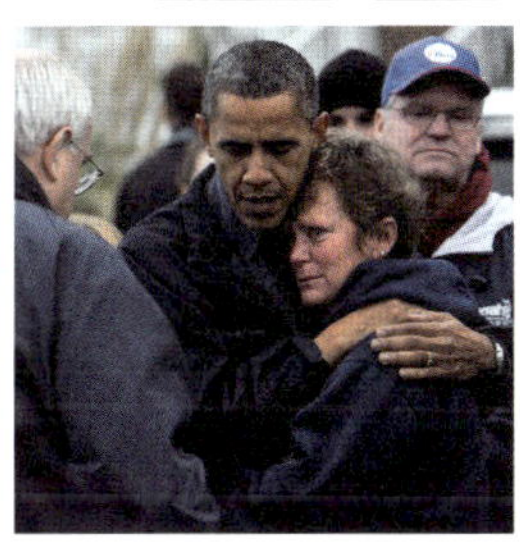

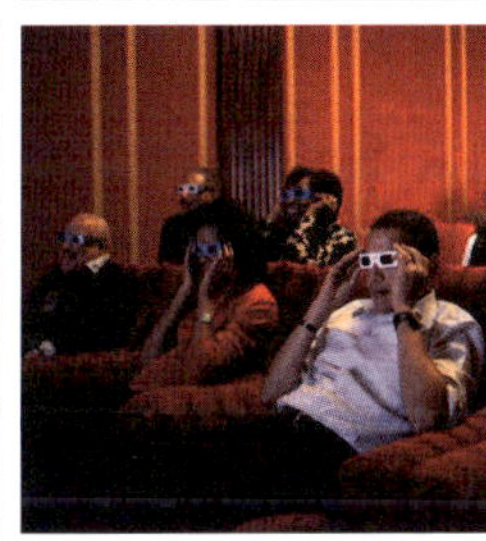

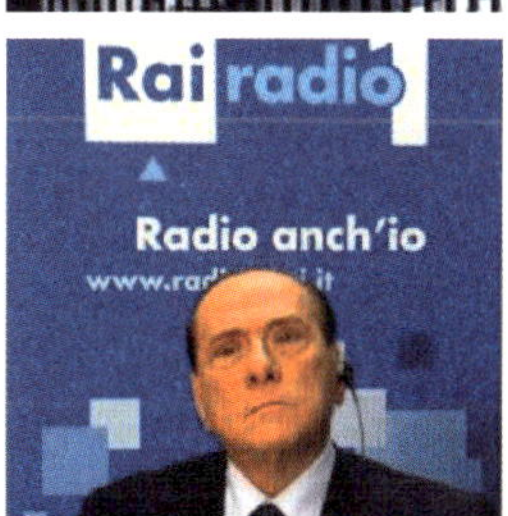
Rai radio 1
Radio anch'io

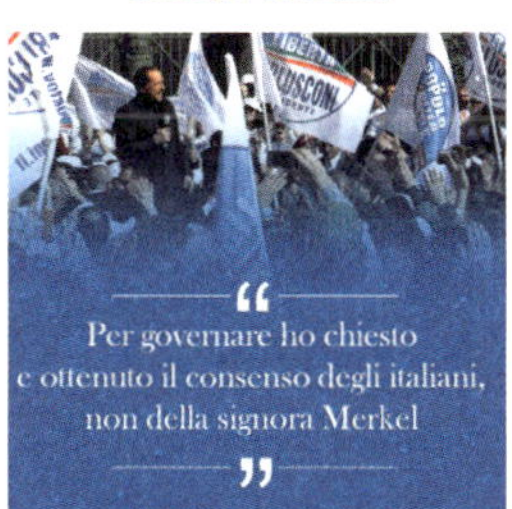
"Per governare ho chiesto e ottenuto il consenso degli italiani, non della signora Merkel"
SILVIO BERLUSCONI

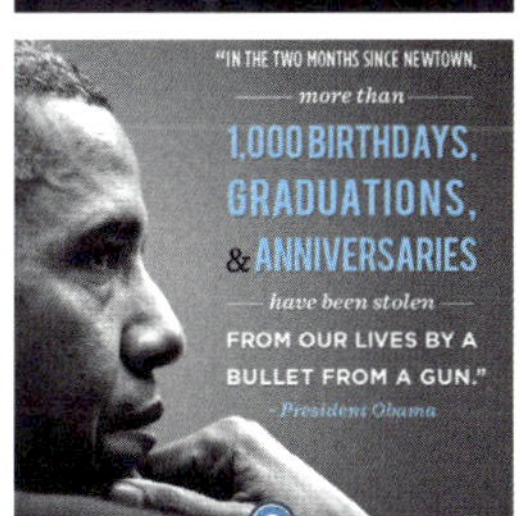
"IN THE TWO MONTHS SINCE NEWTOWN,
more than
1,000 BIRTHDAYS,
GRADUATIONS,
& ANNIVERSARIES
have been stolen
FROM OUR LIVES BY A BULLET FROM A GUN."
– President Obama

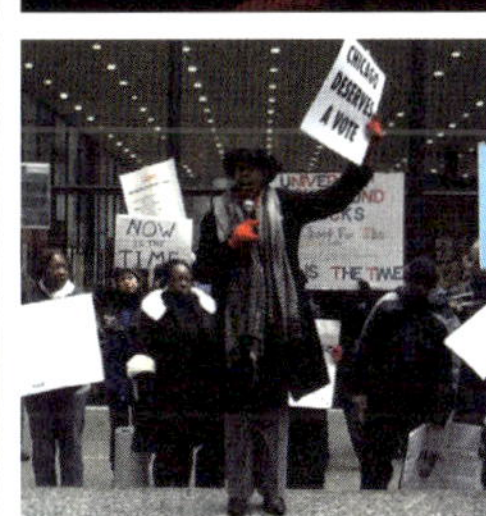

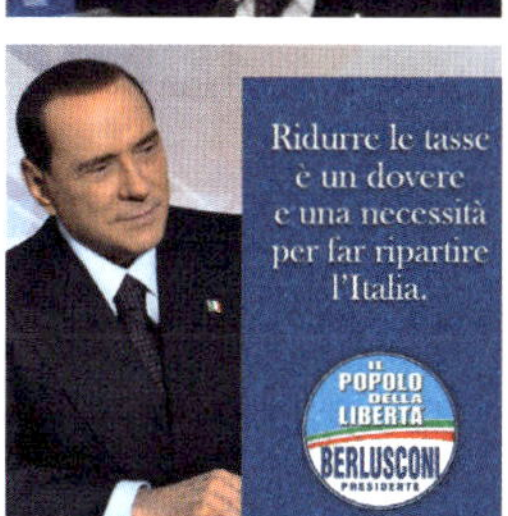
Ridurre le tasse è un dovere e una necessità per far ripartire l'Italia.
IL POPOLO DELLA LIBERTÀ
BERLUSCONI PRESIDENTE
www.forzasilvio.it

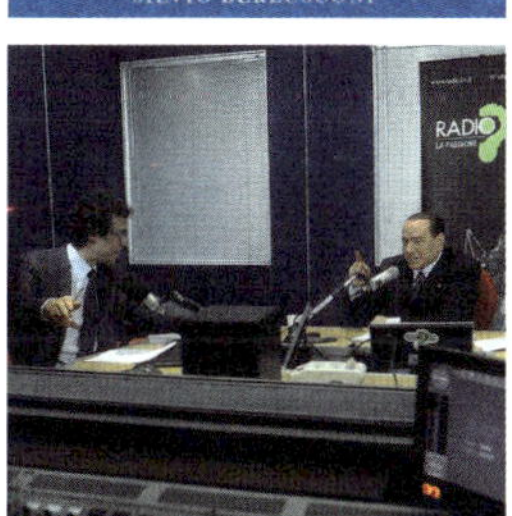

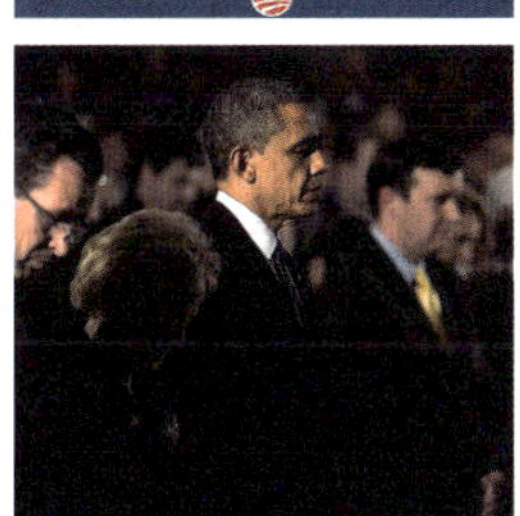

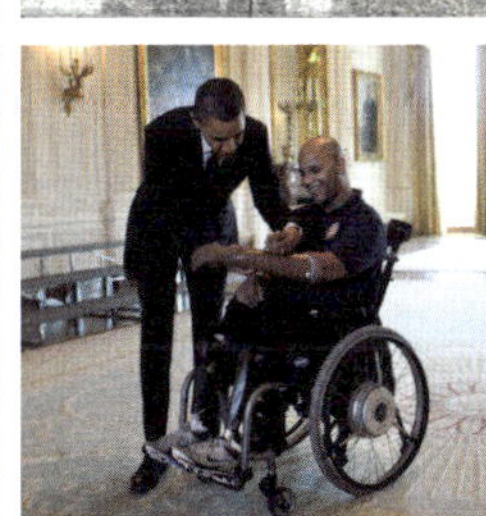

Branding Through Personality

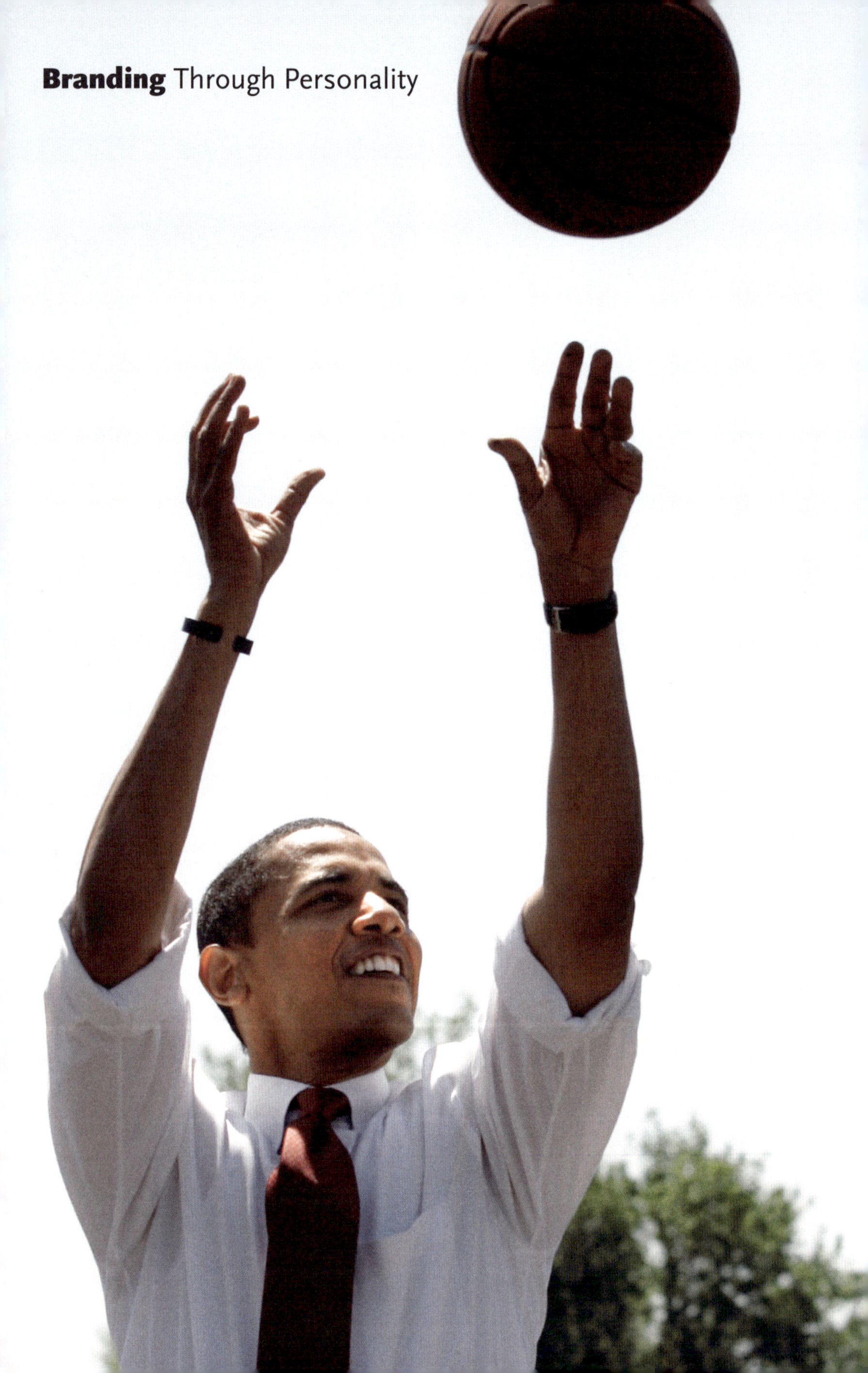

Family/partner

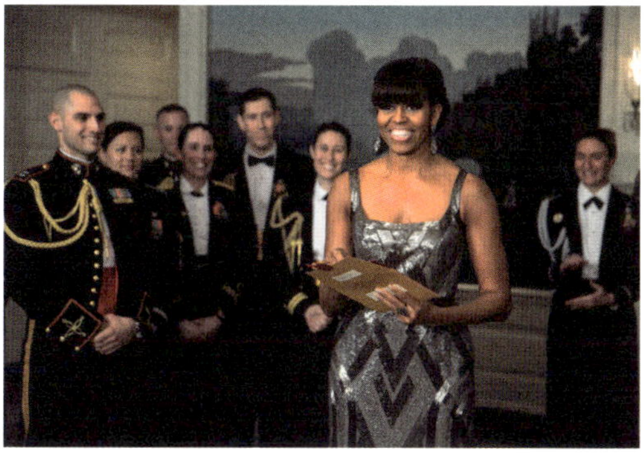

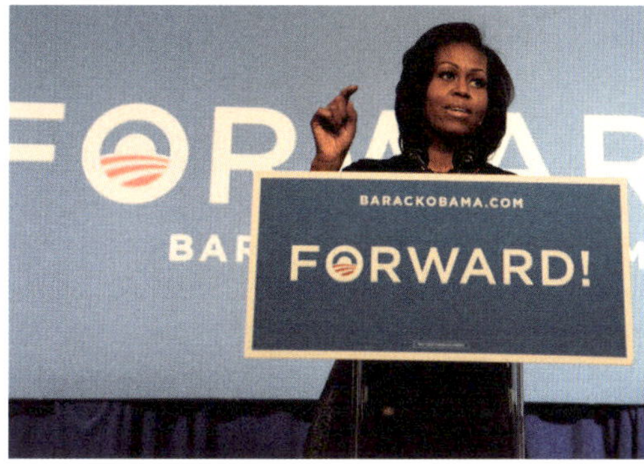

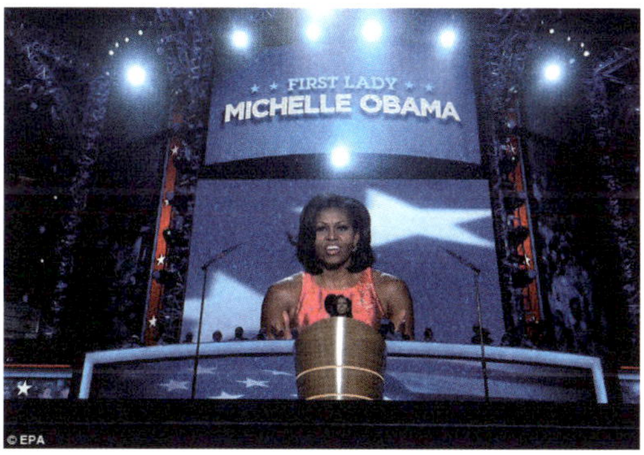

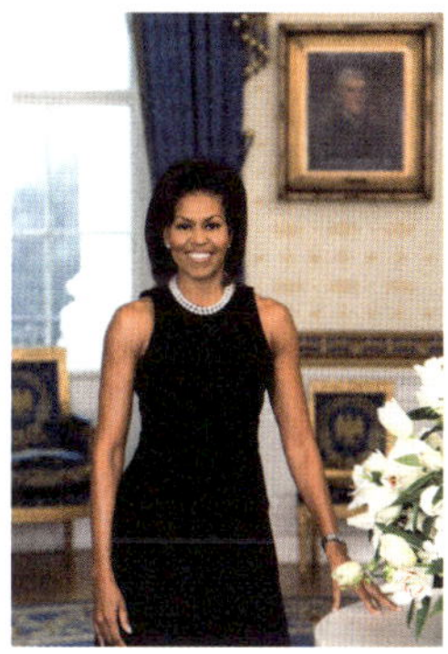

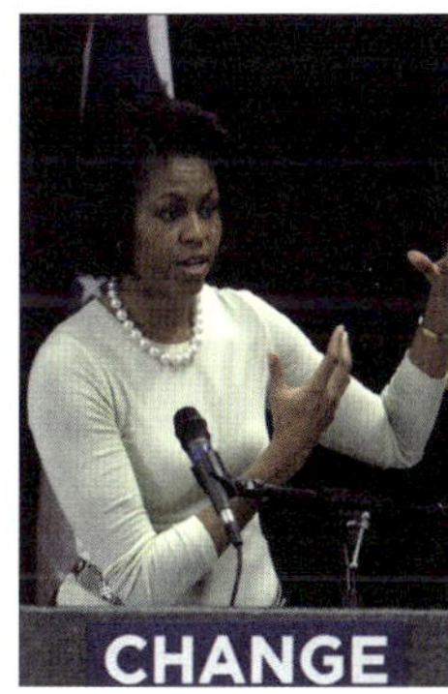

Children

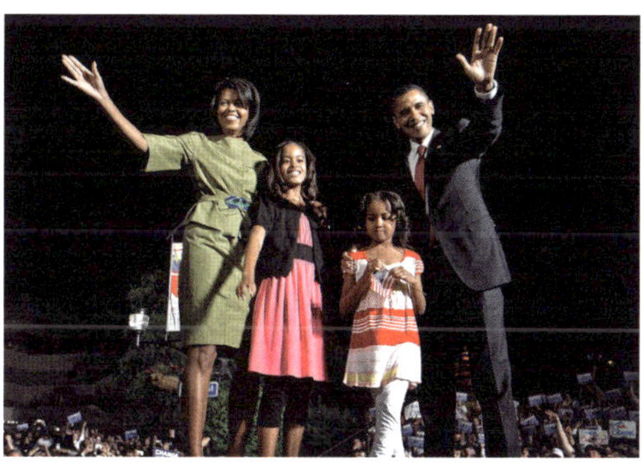

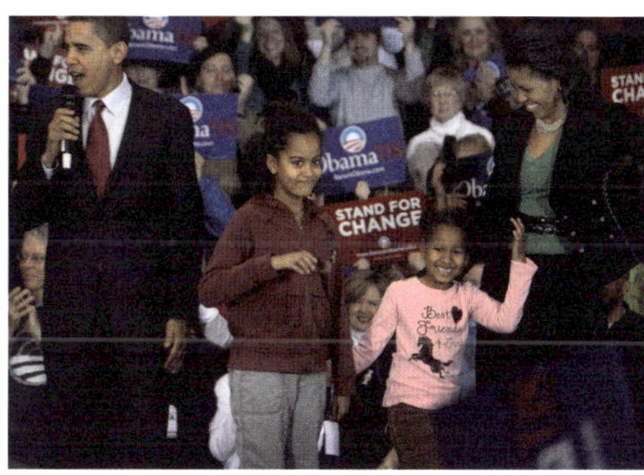

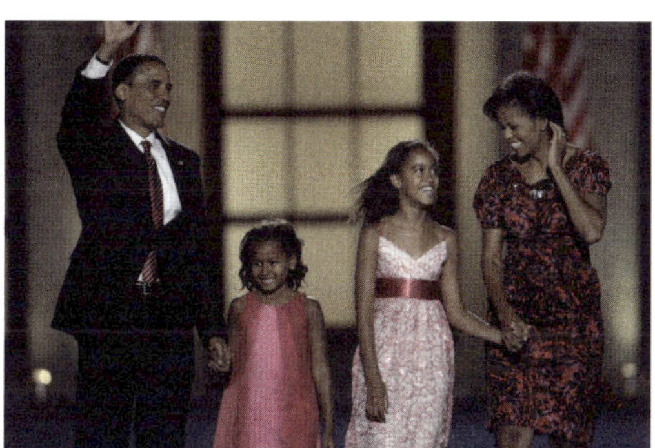

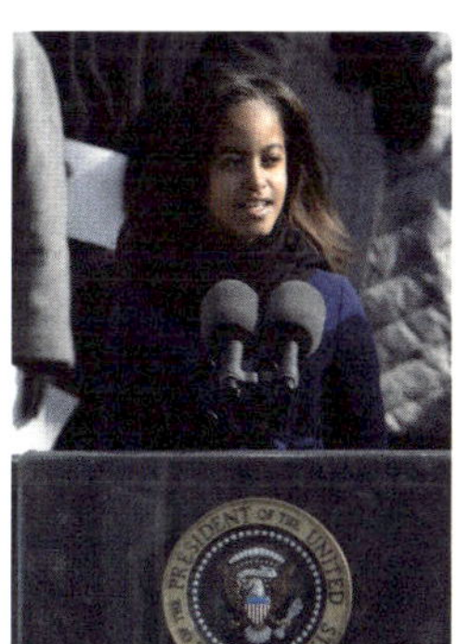

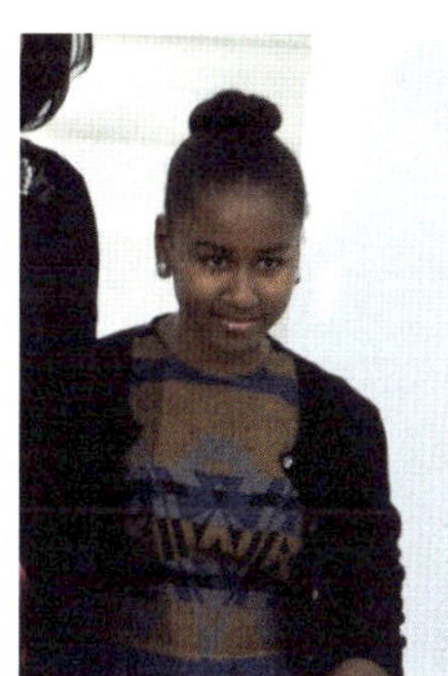

Branding Through Personality

Pets

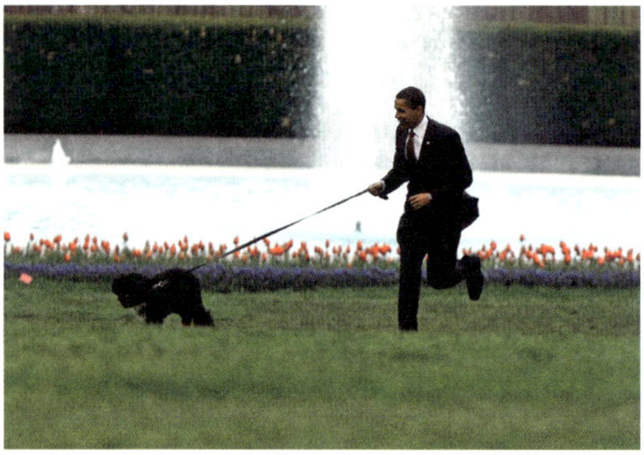

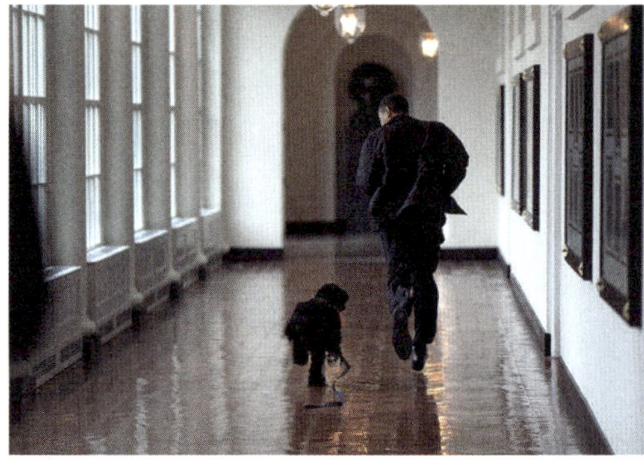

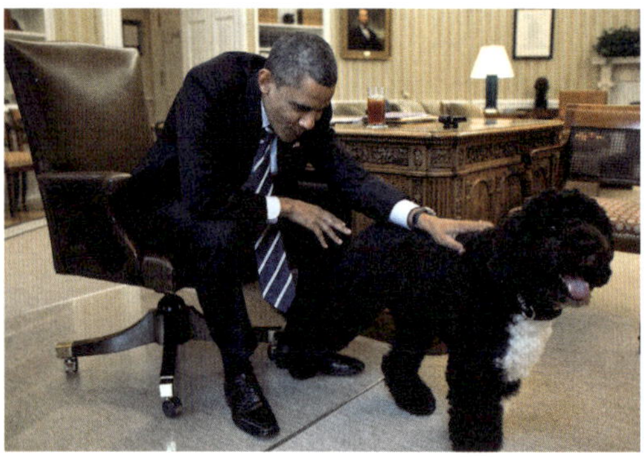

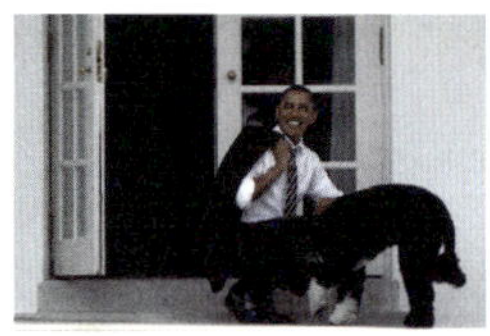

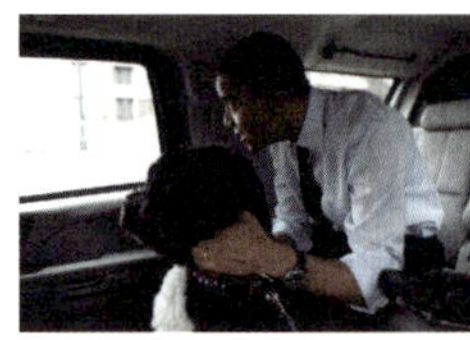

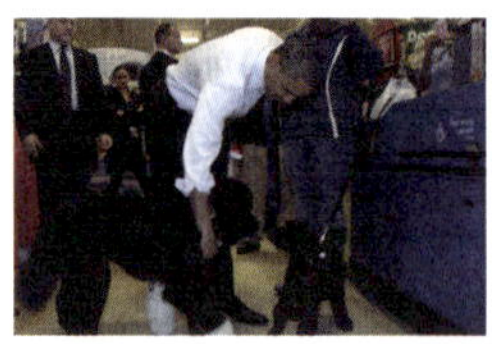

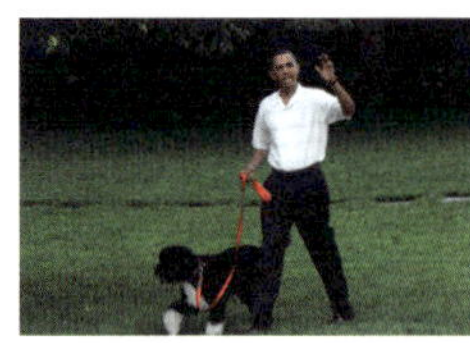

Friends

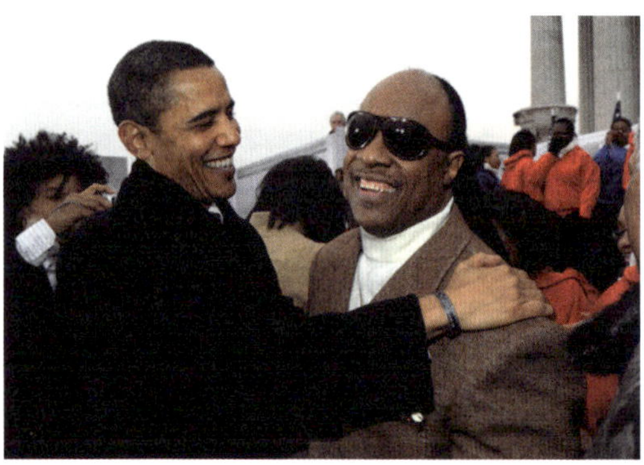

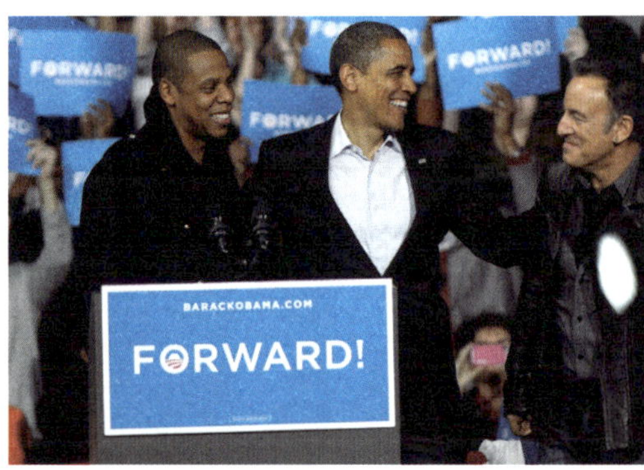

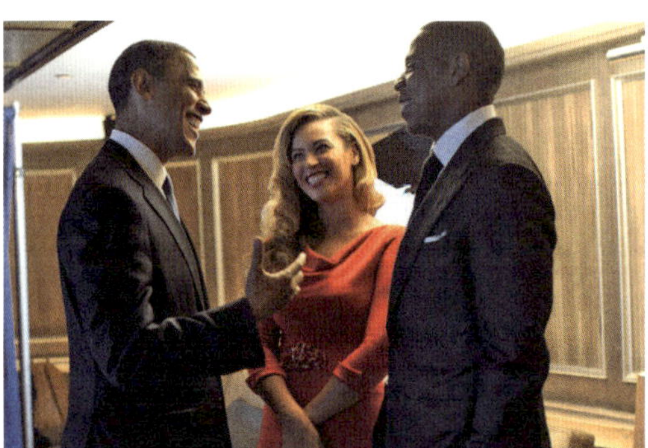

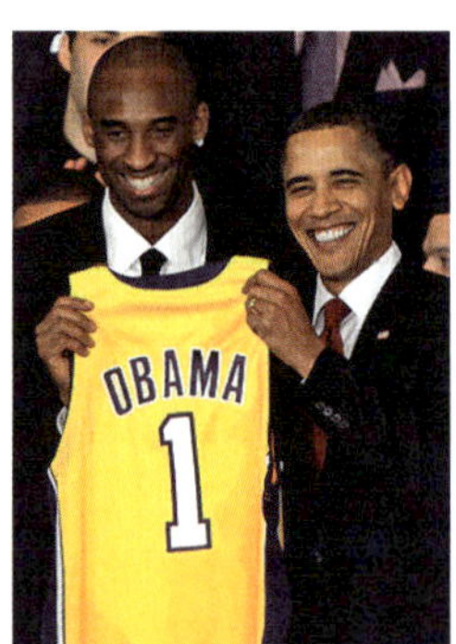

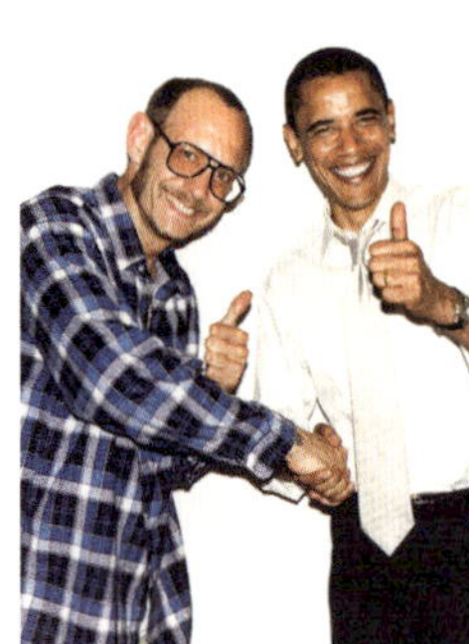

Hobbies

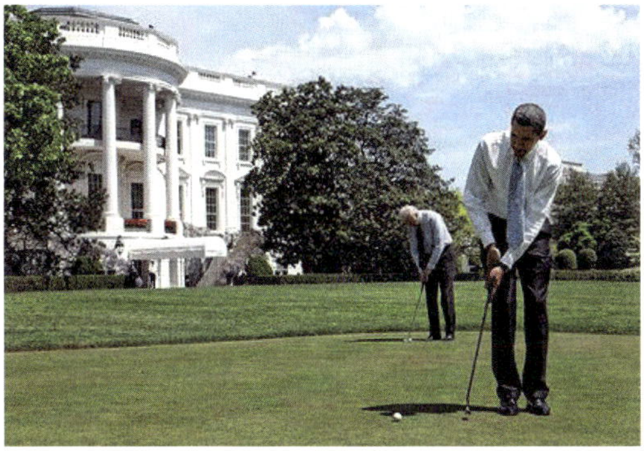

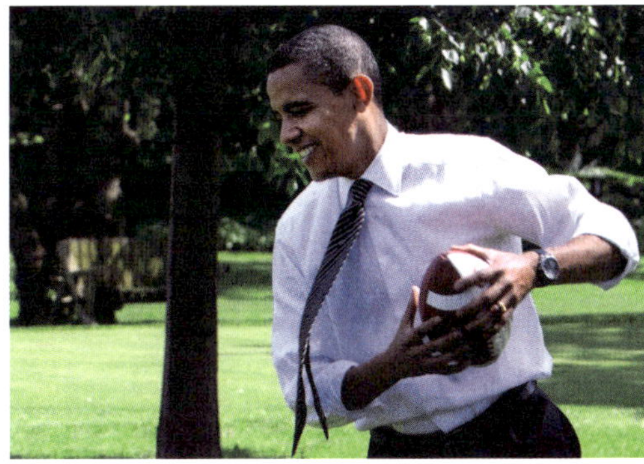

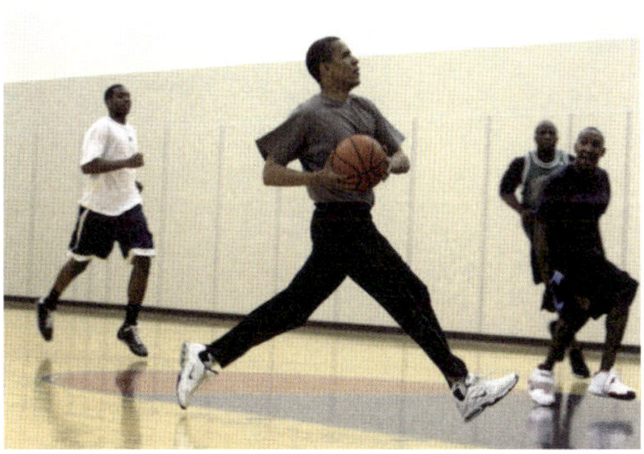

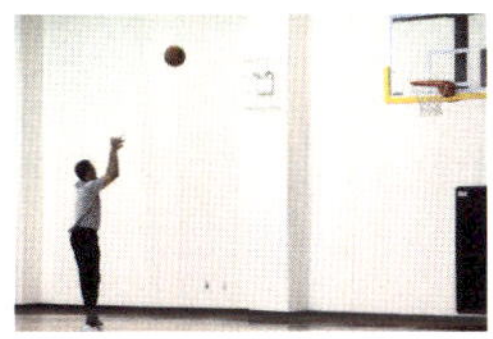

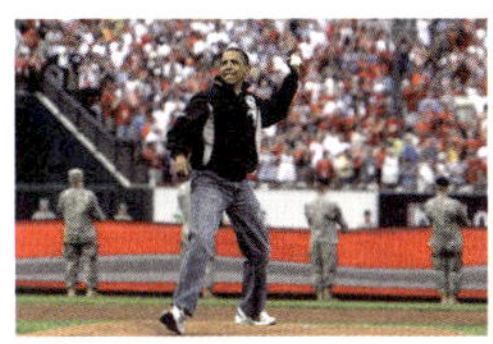

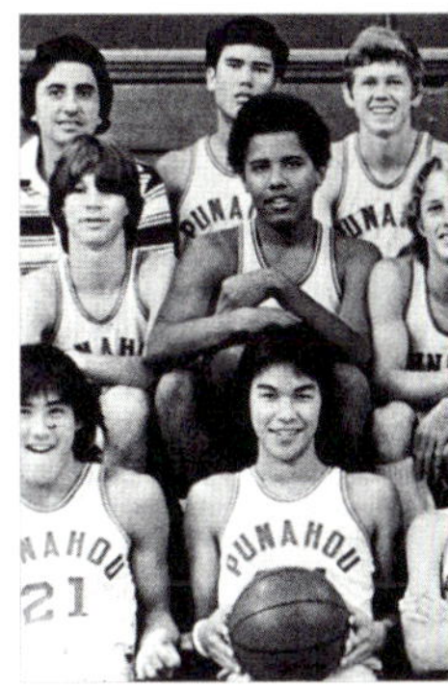

Character traits and gestures

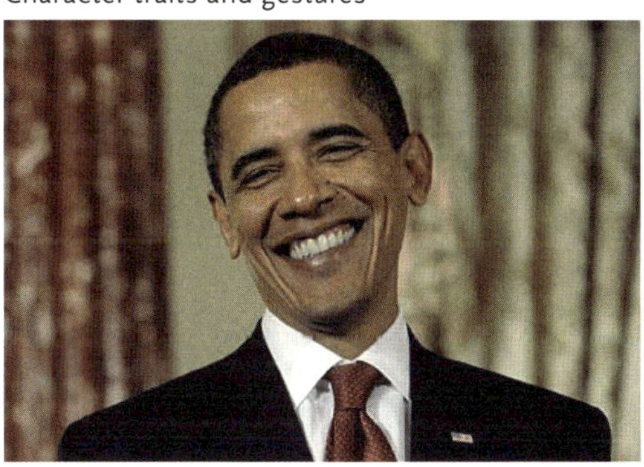

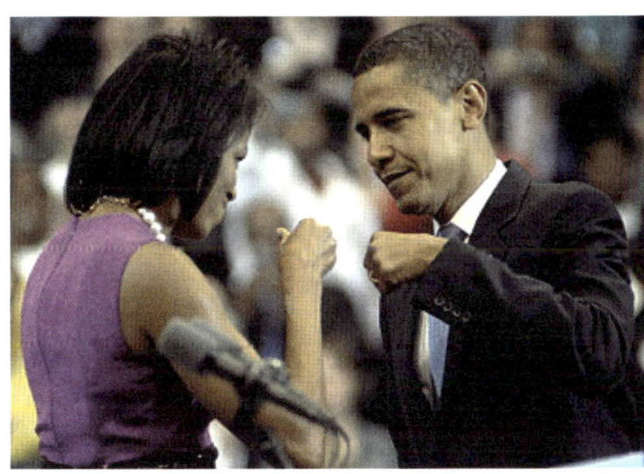

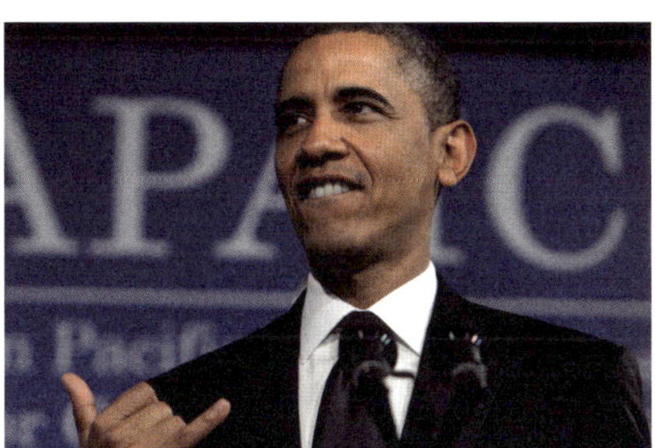

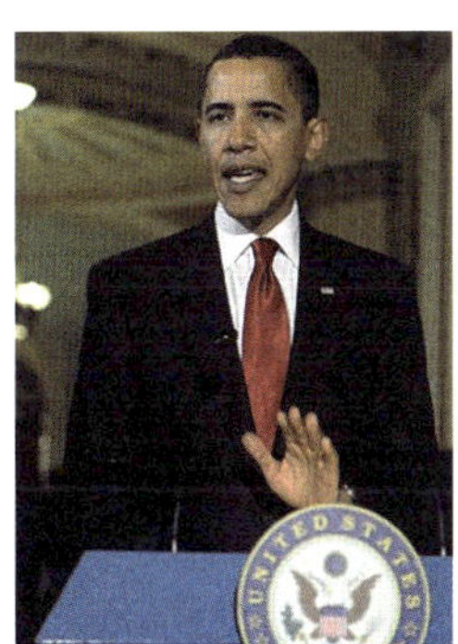

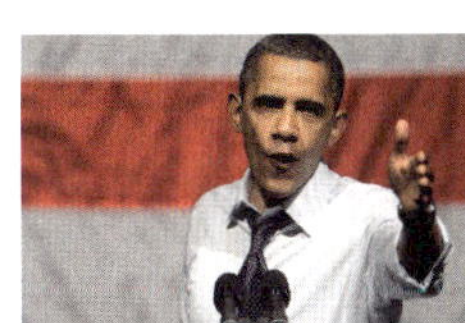

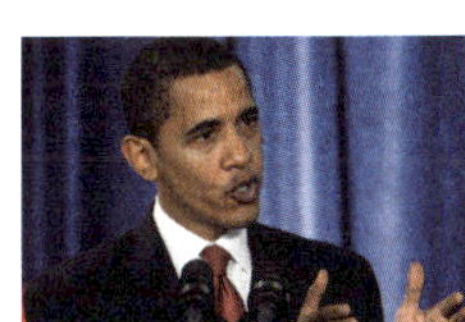

Branding Through Personality

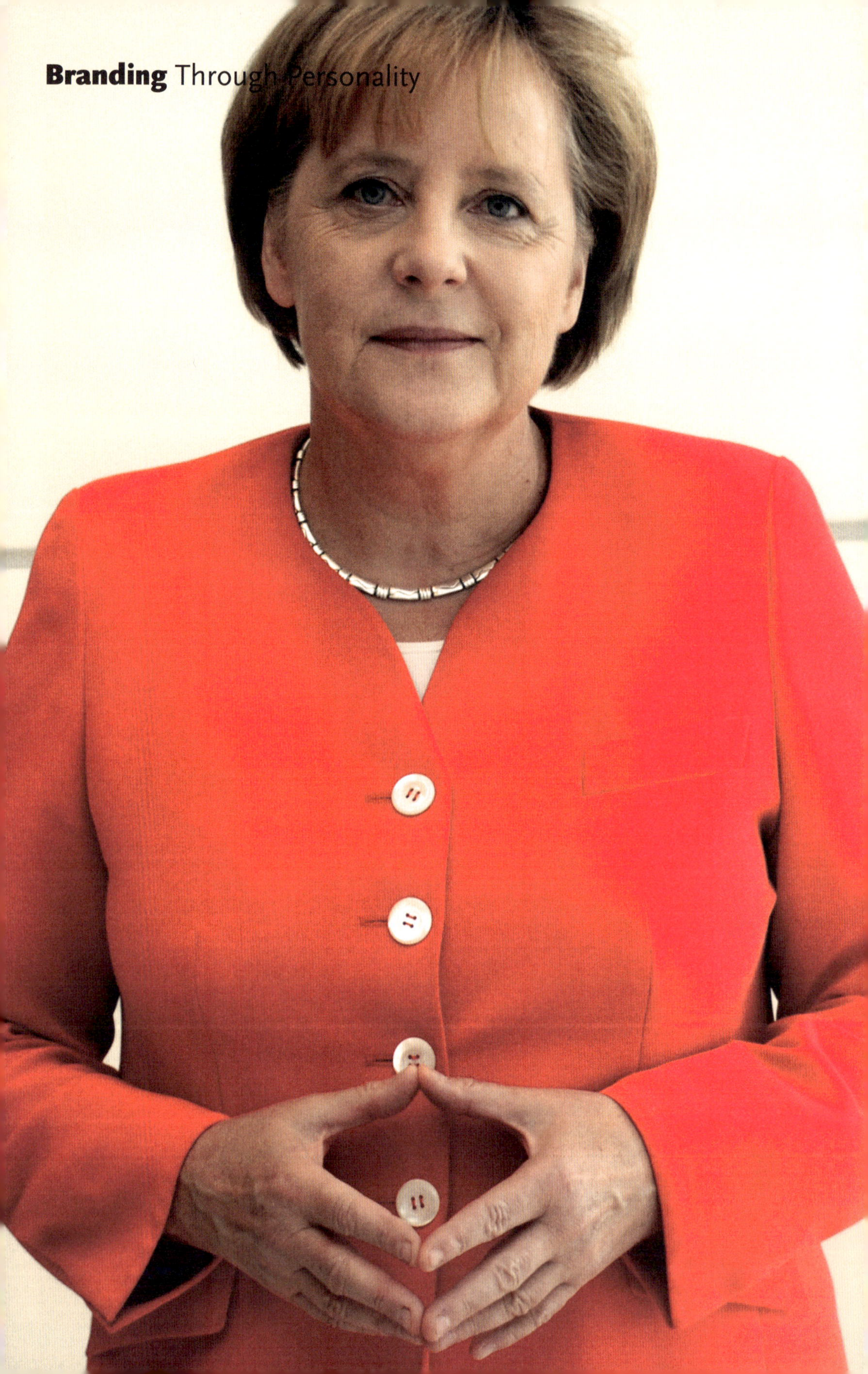

Family/partner

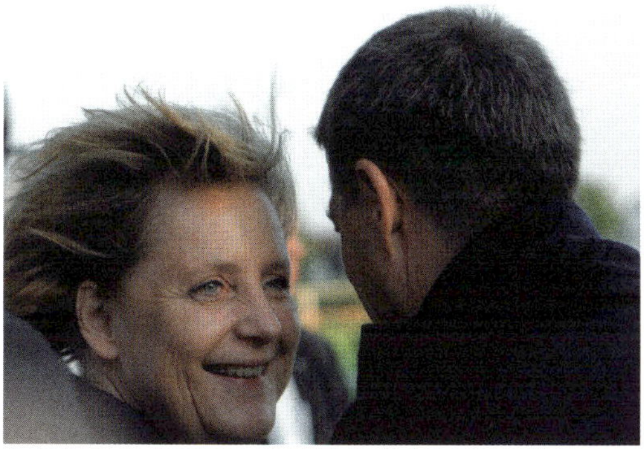

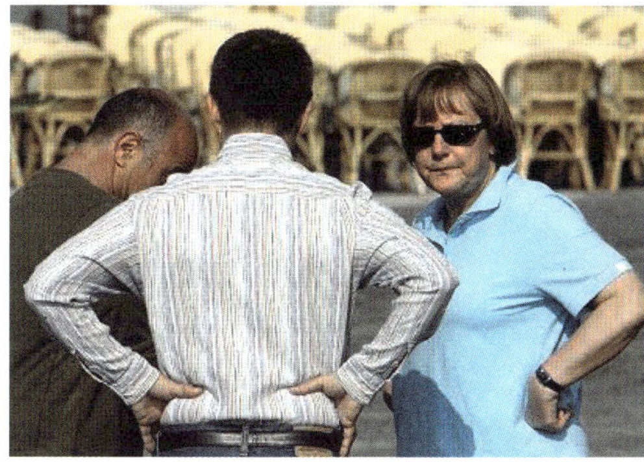

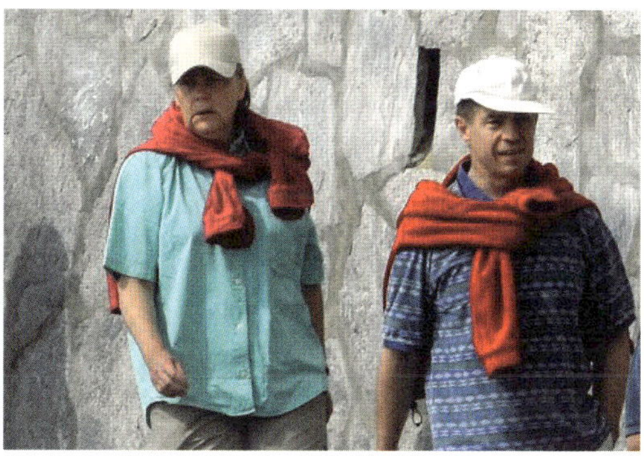

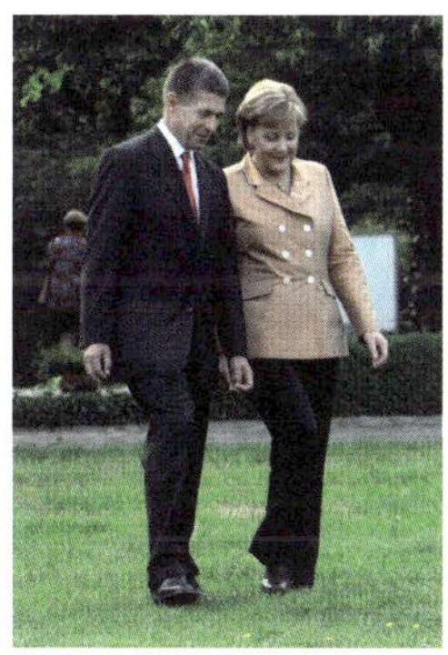

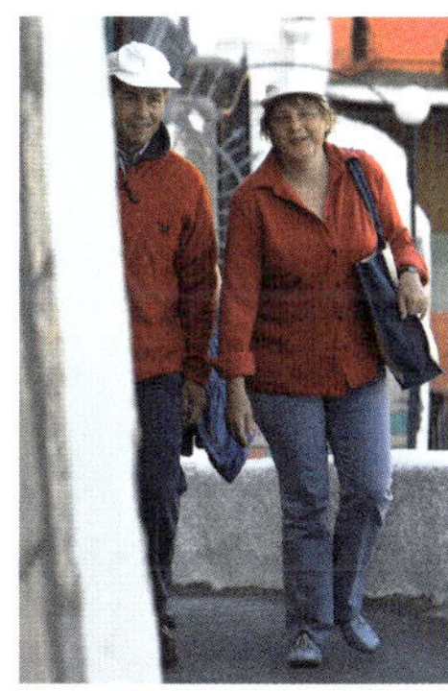

Children

Branding Through Personality

Pets

Friends

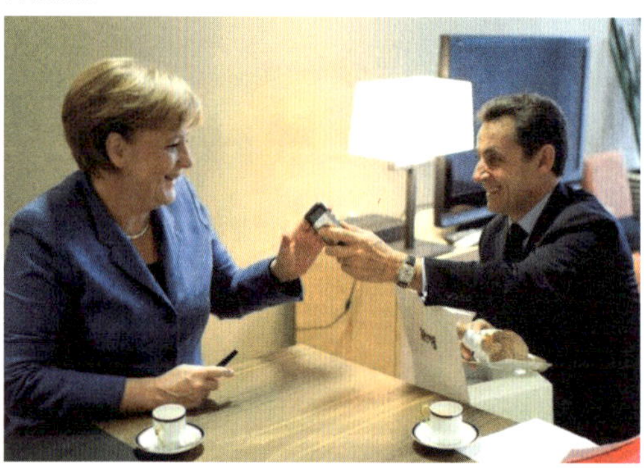

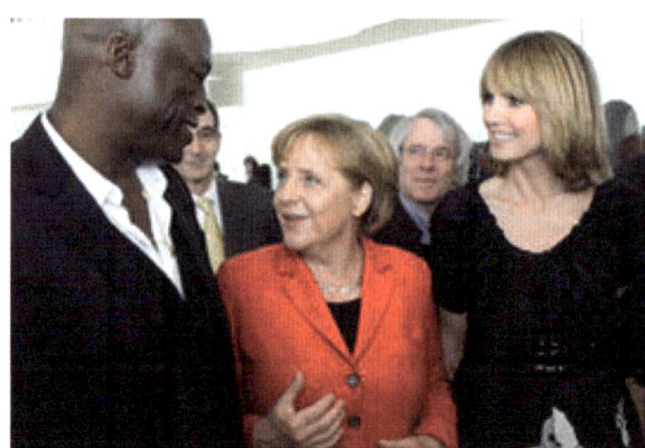

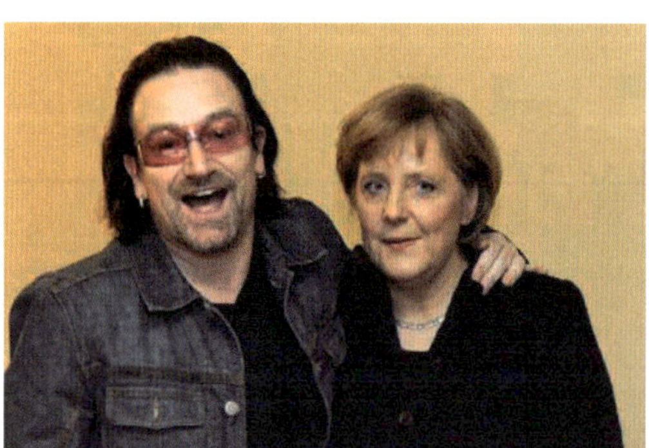

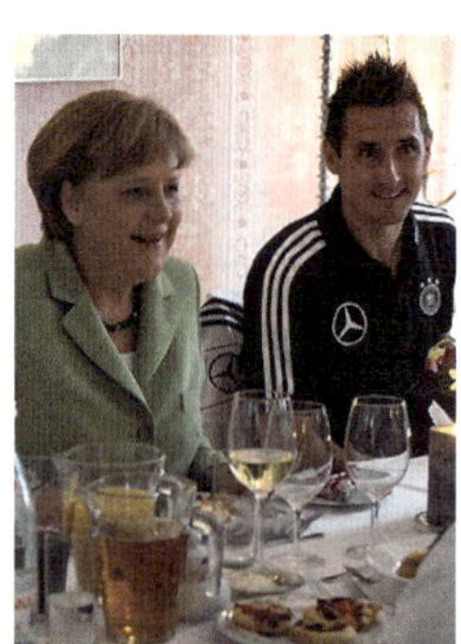

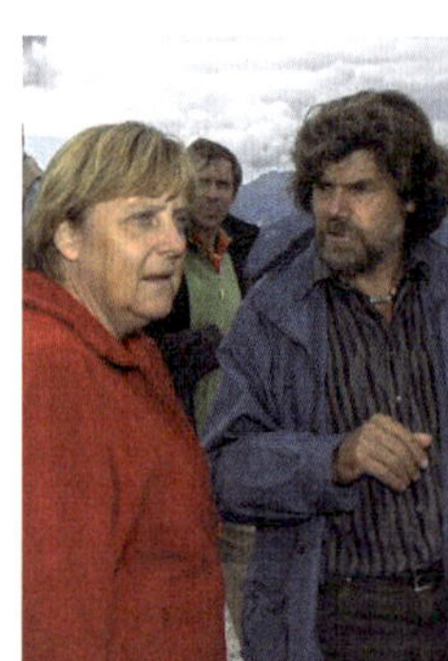

Hobbies

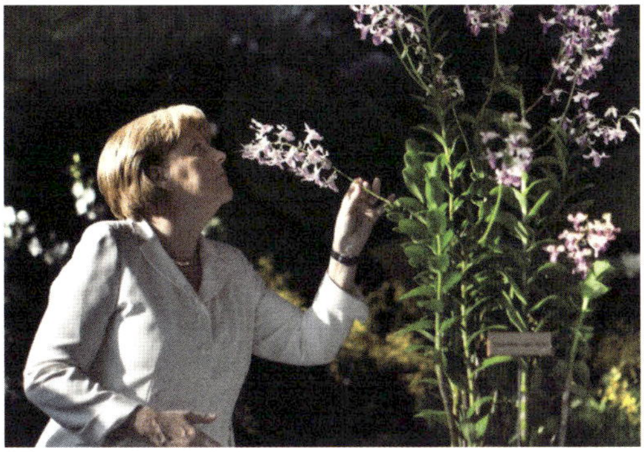

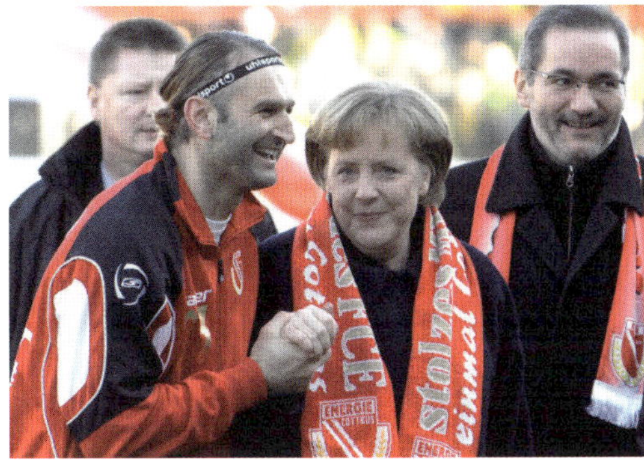

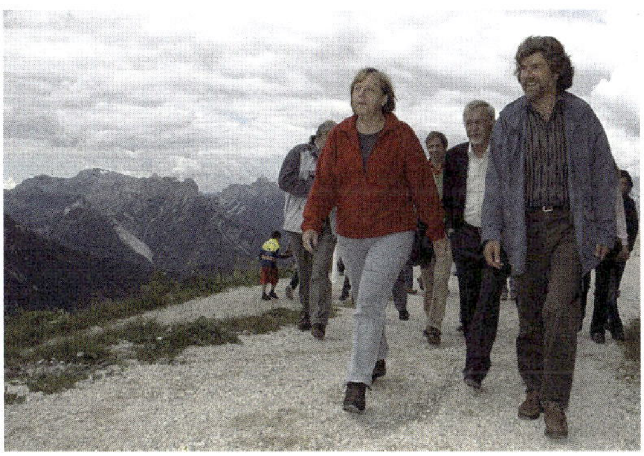

Character traits and gestures

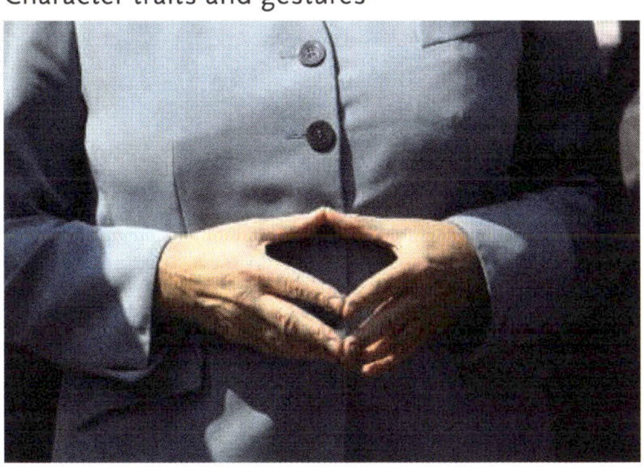

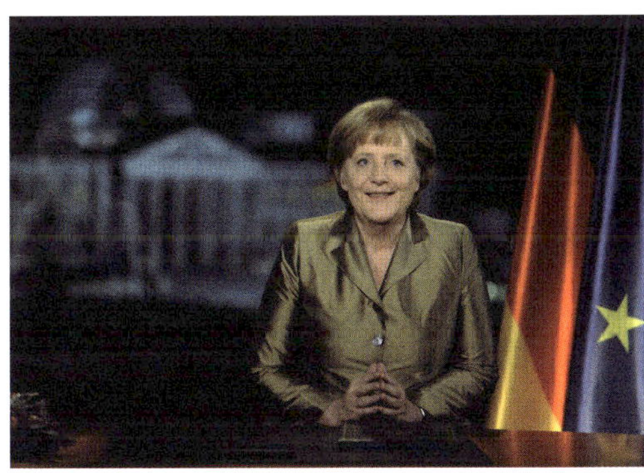

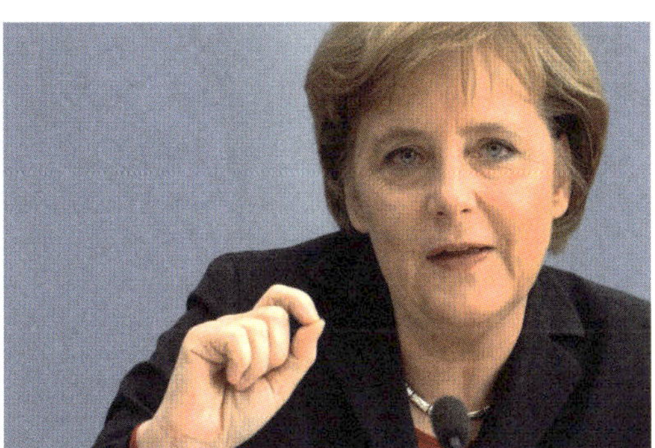

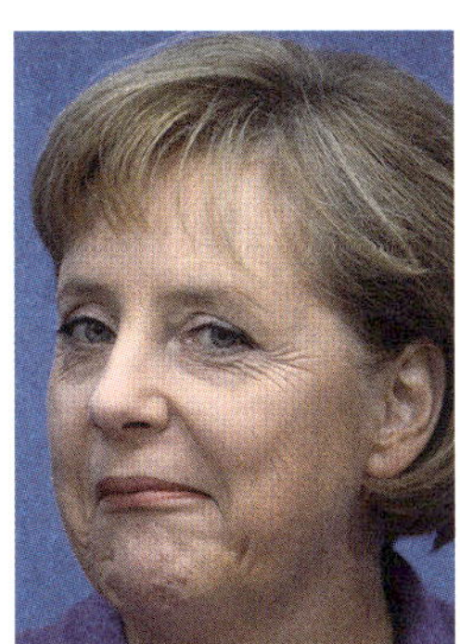

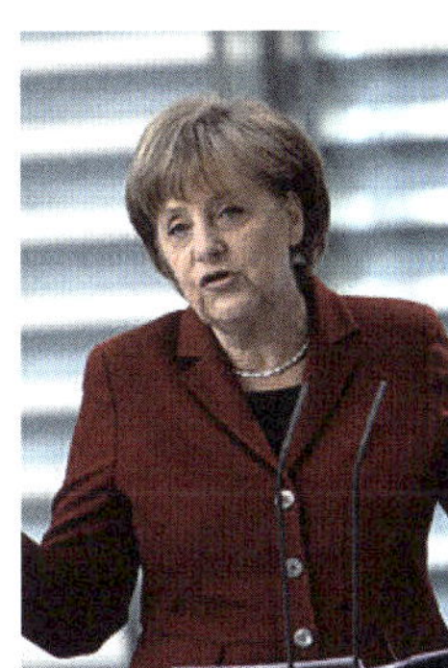

Branding Through Personality

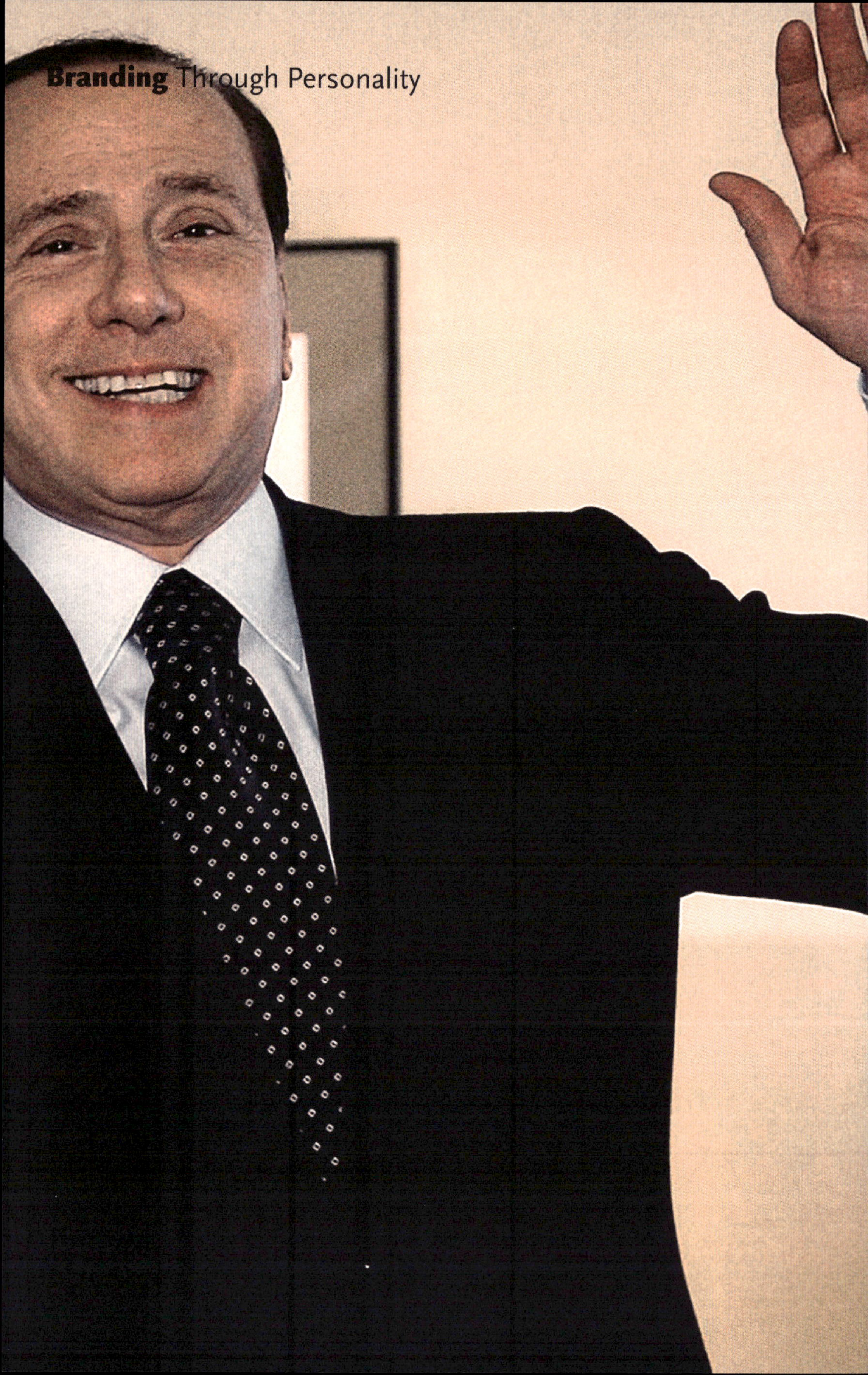

Family/partner

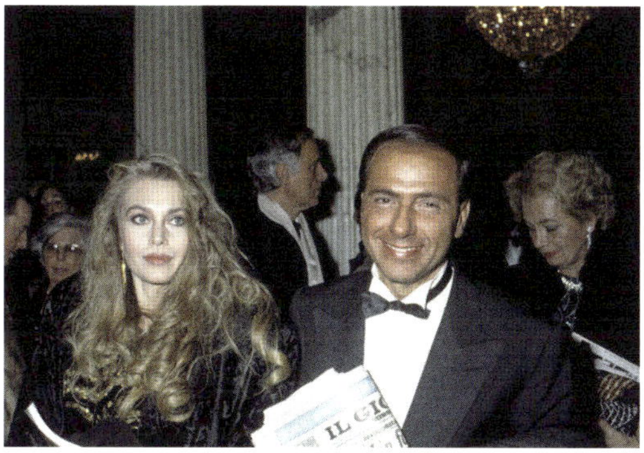
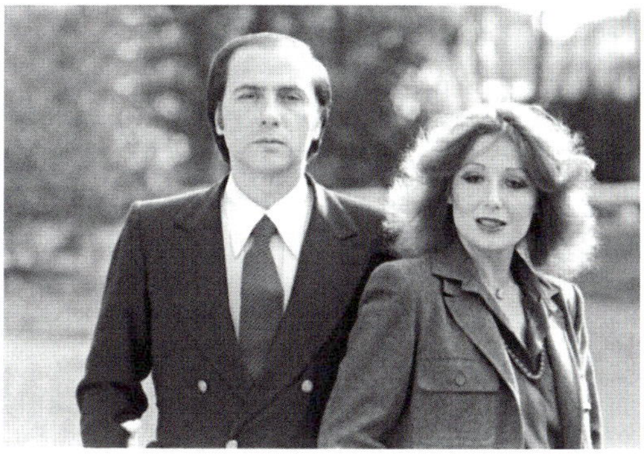
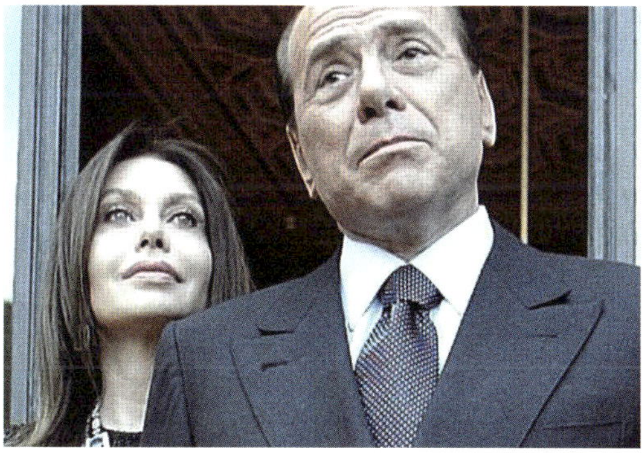
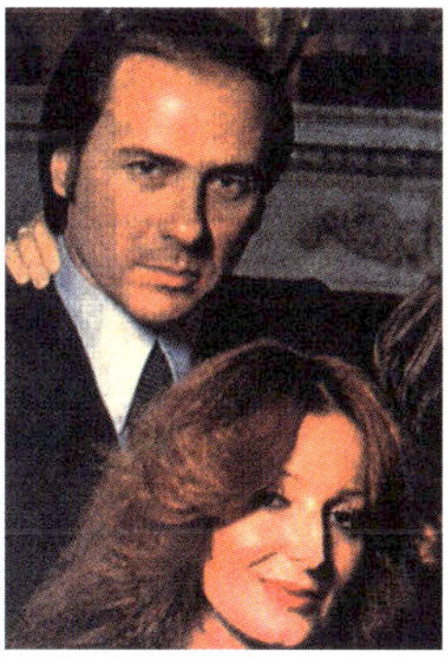
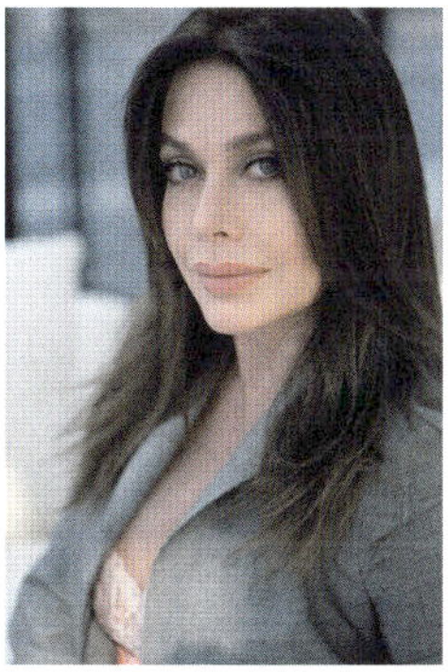

Children

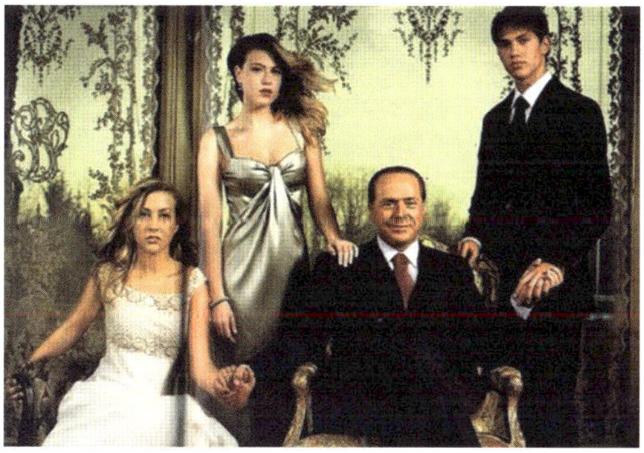
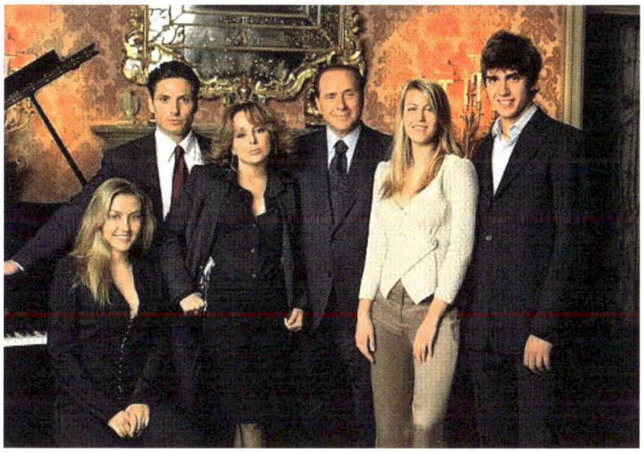
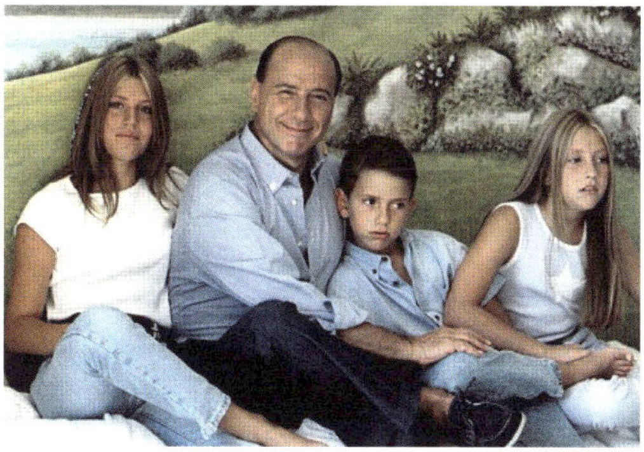
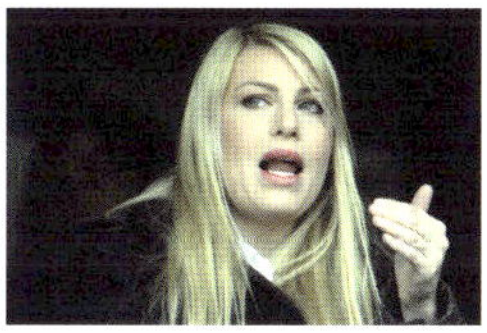
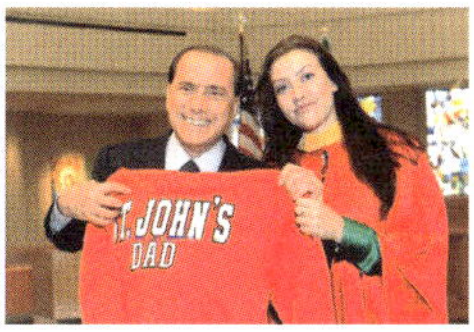

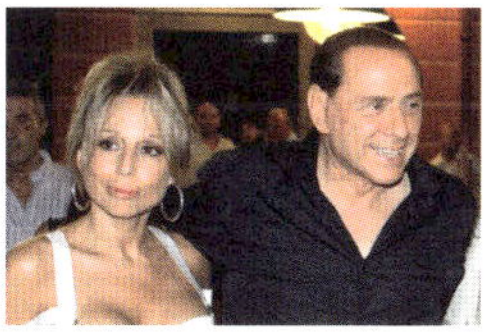
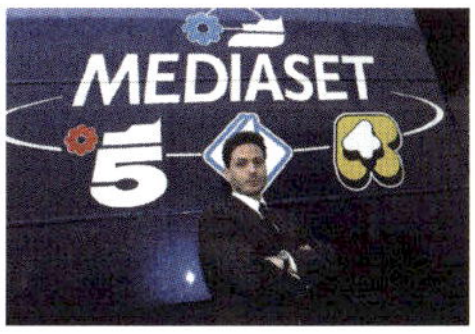

Branding Through Personality

Pets

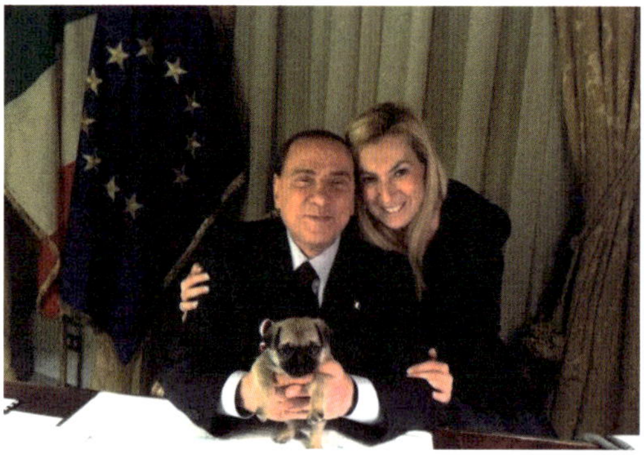
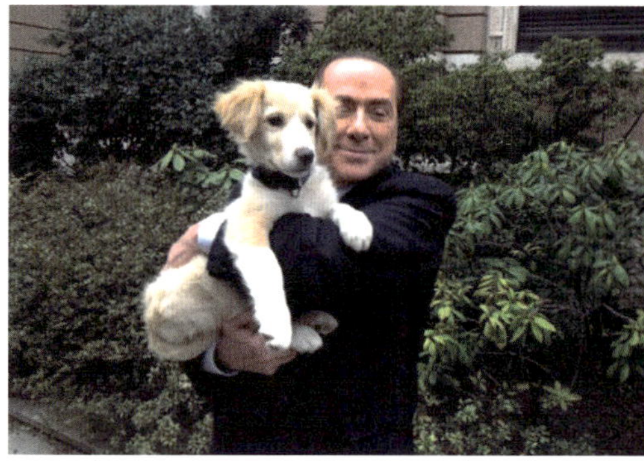
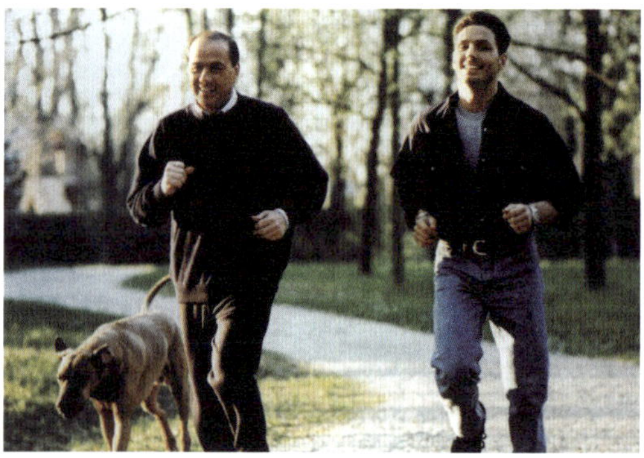

Friends

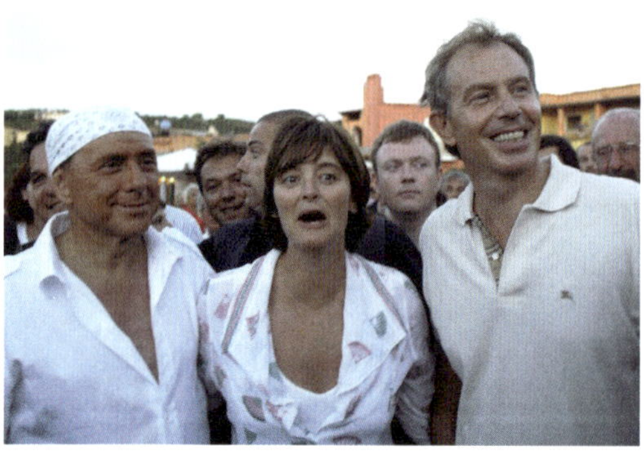
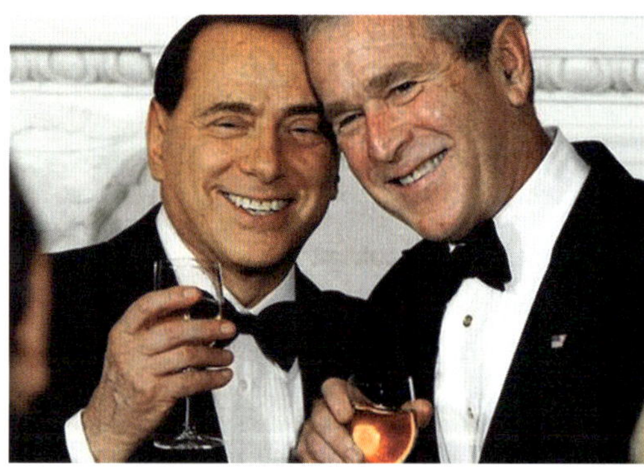
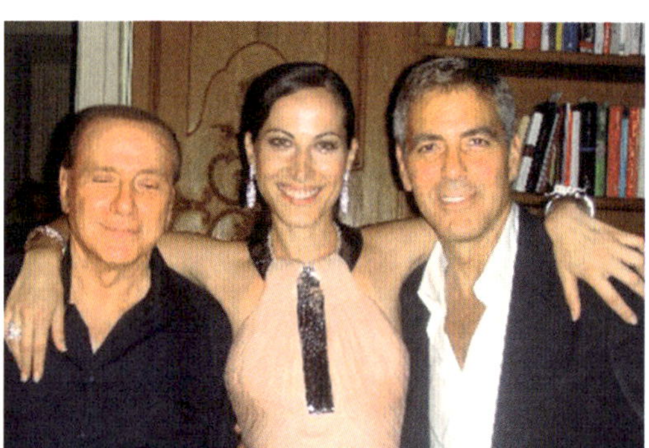
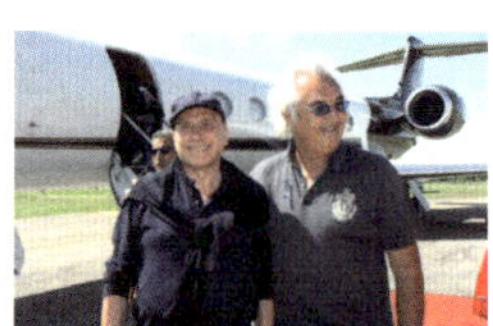
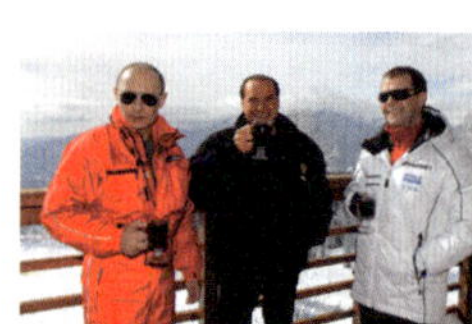
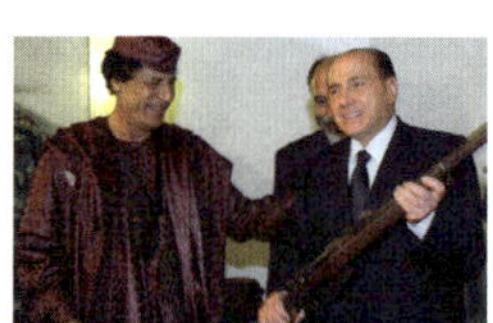
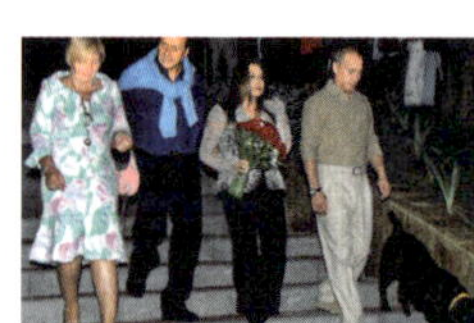

Hobbies

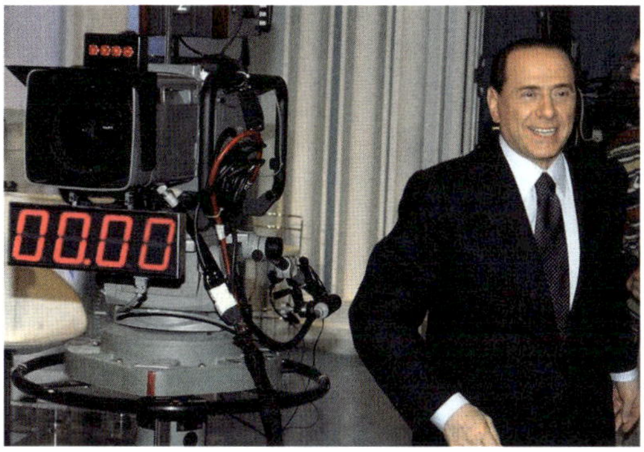

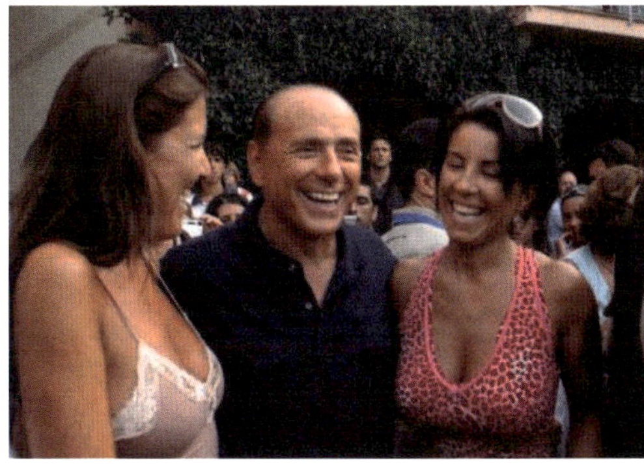

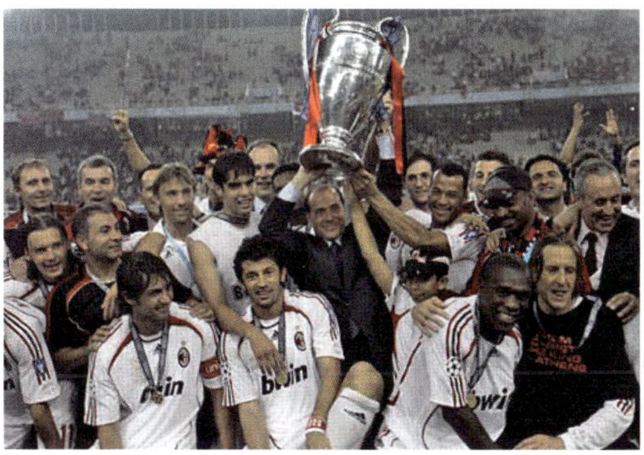

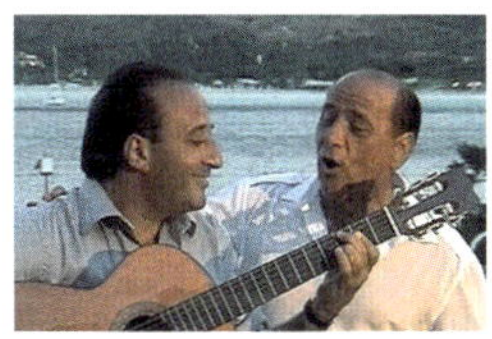

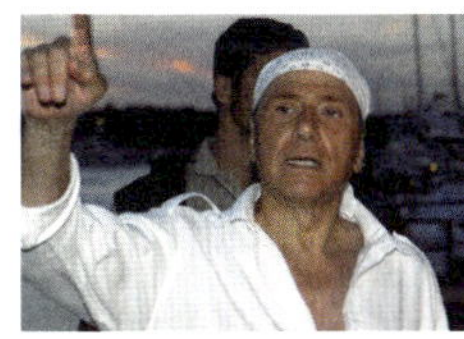

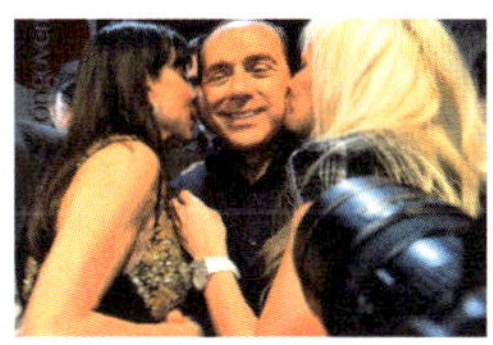

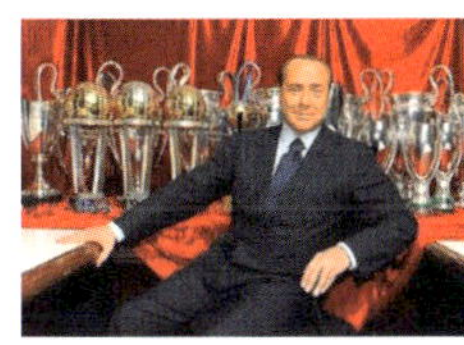

Character traits and gestures

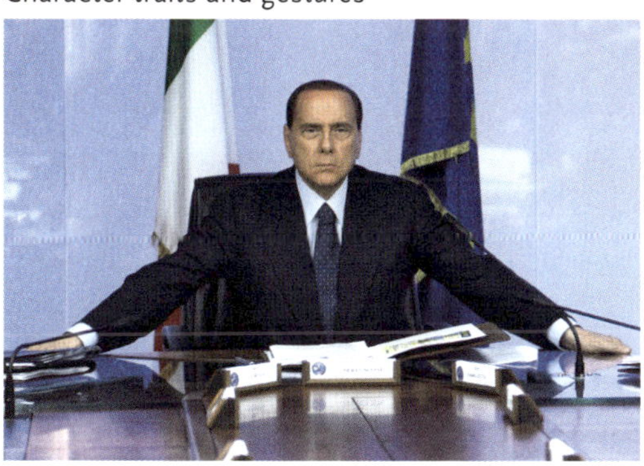

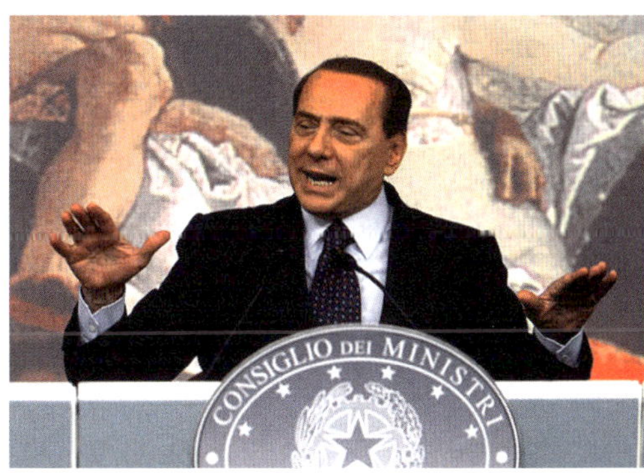

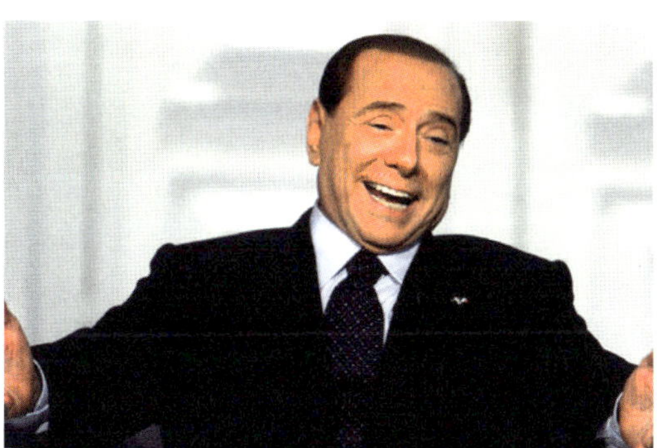

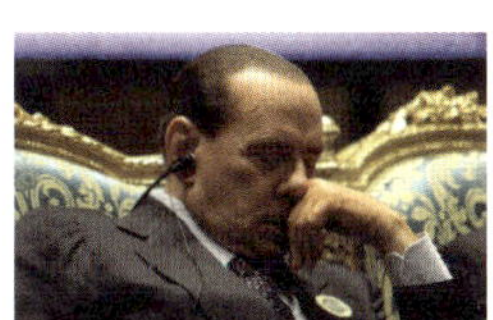

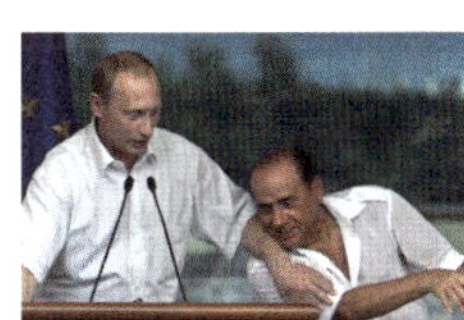

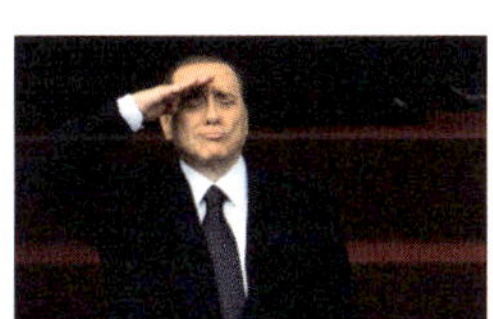

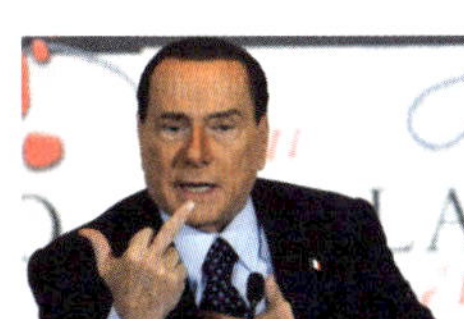

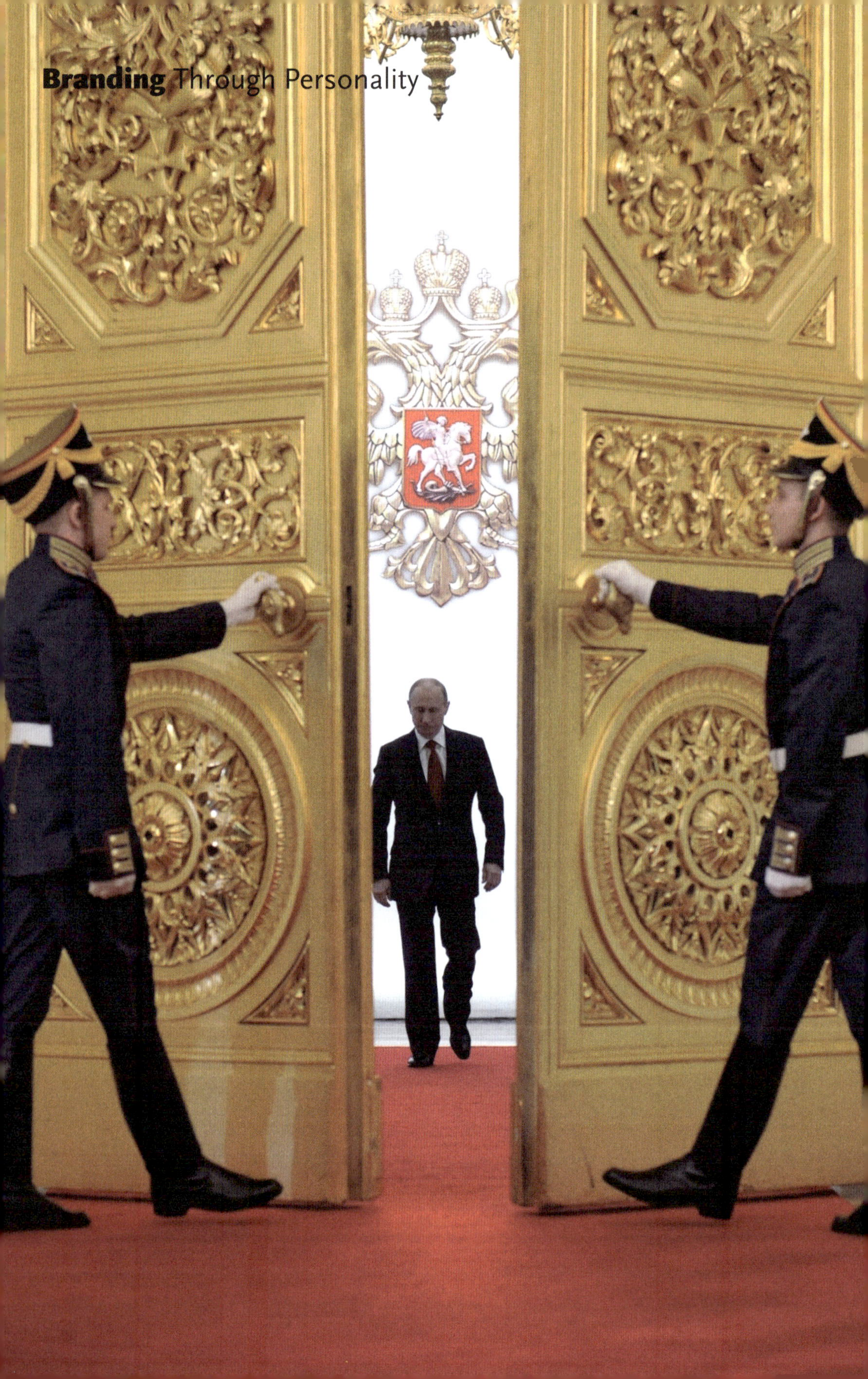

Family/partner

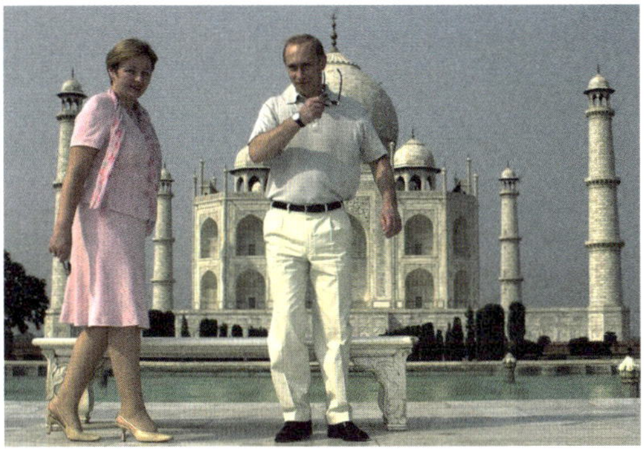

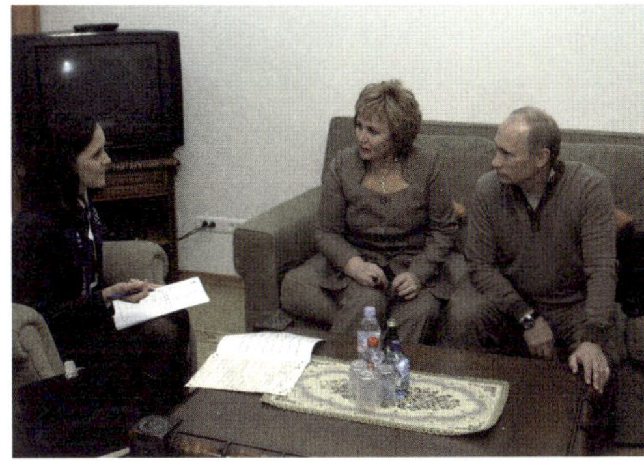

Children

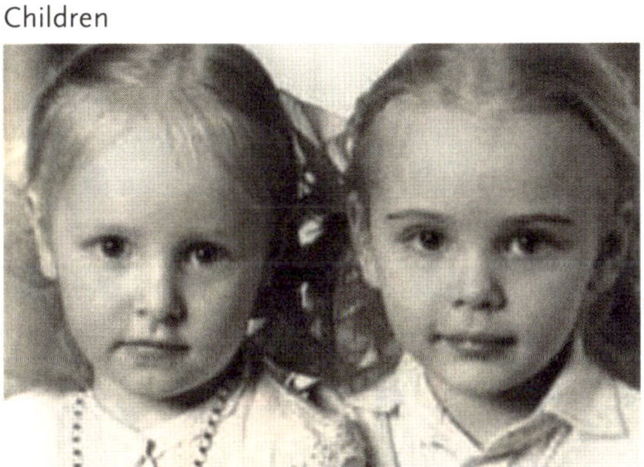

Branding Through Personality

Pets

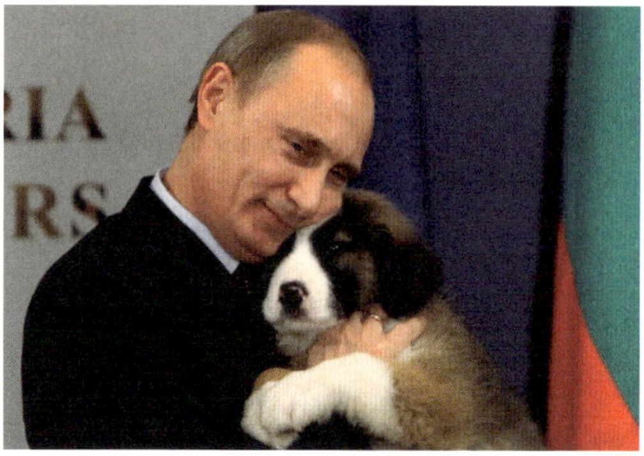

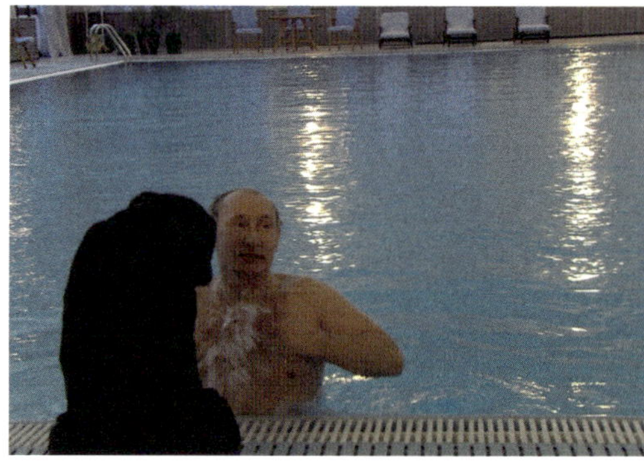

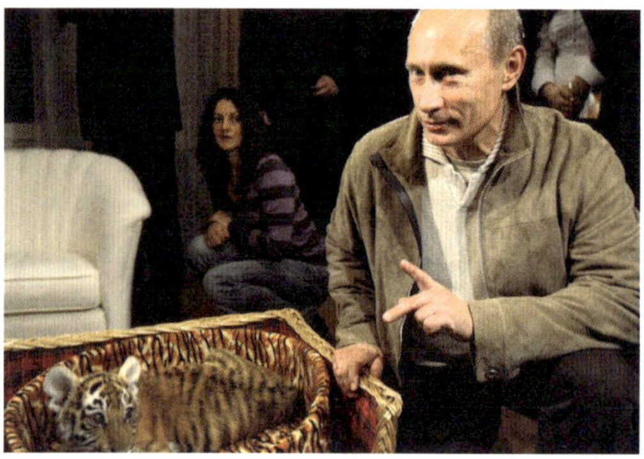

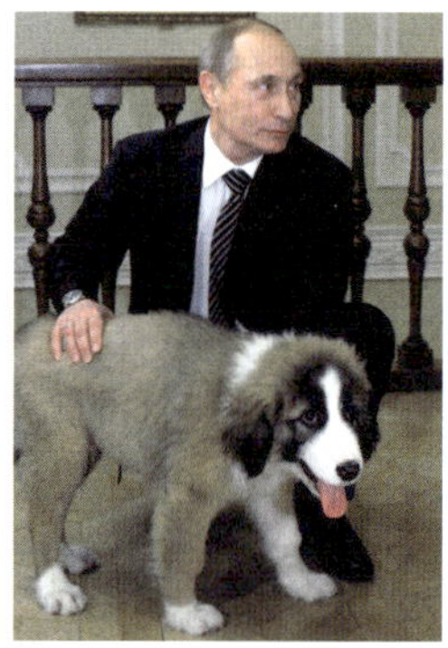

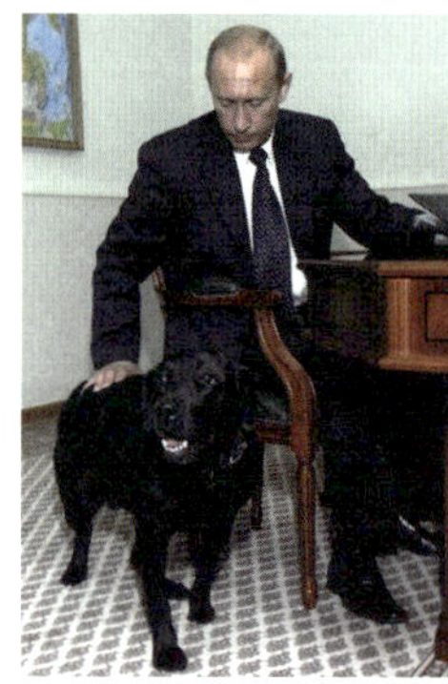

Friends

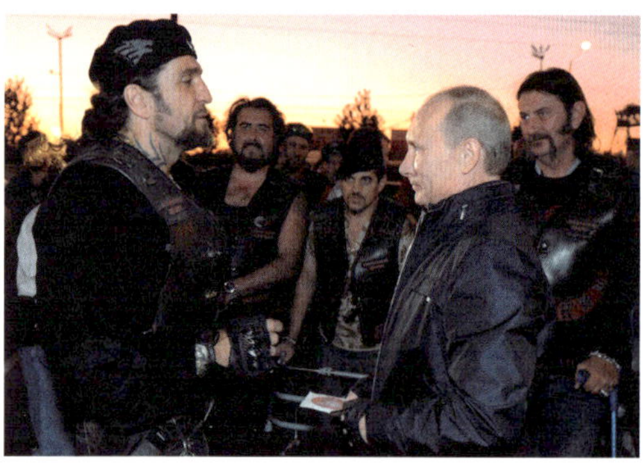

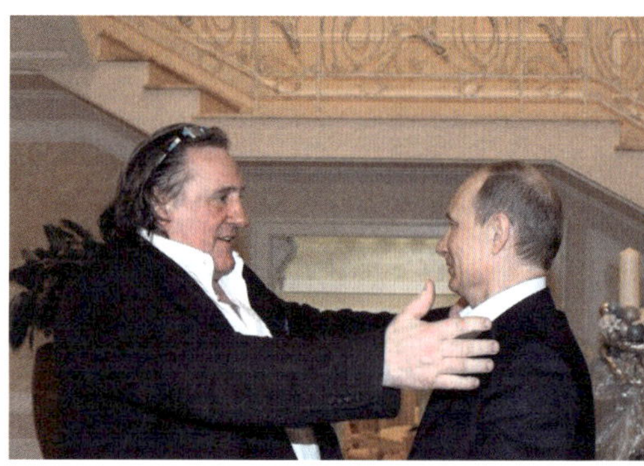

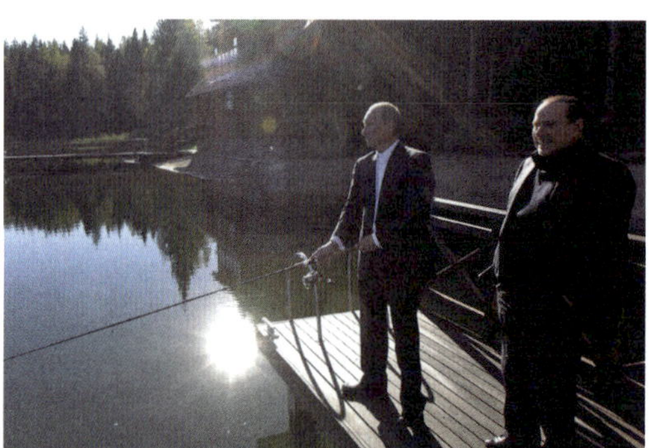

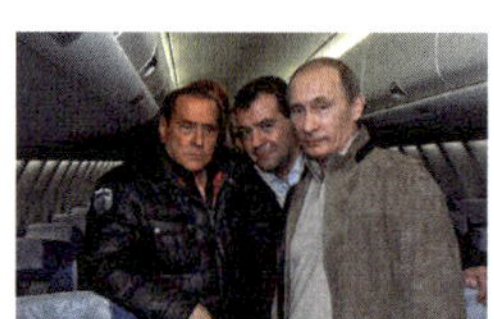

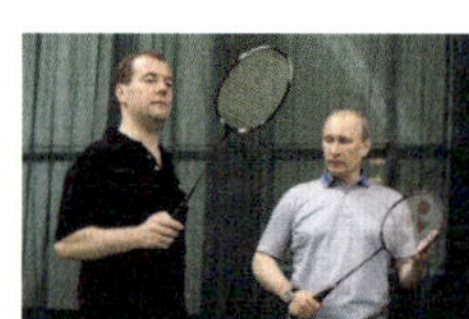

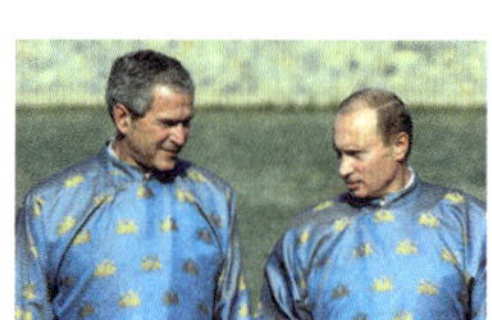

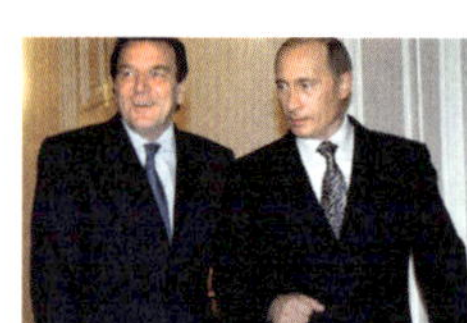

Hobbies

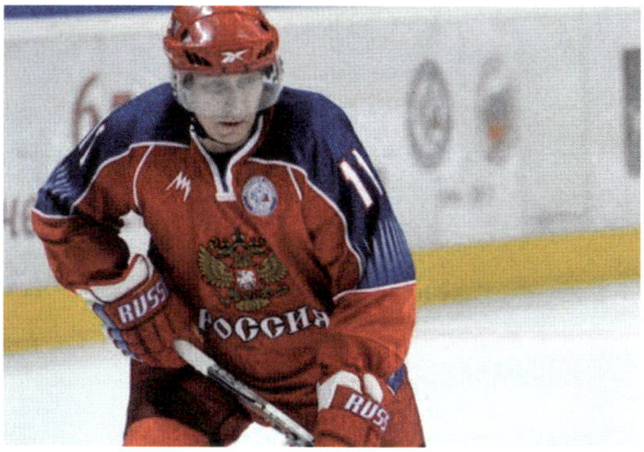

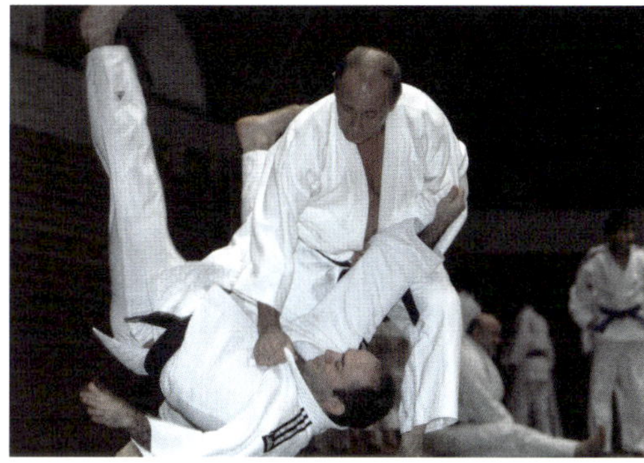

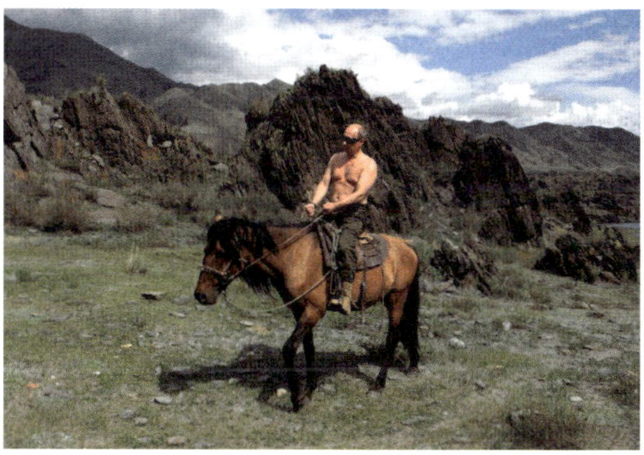

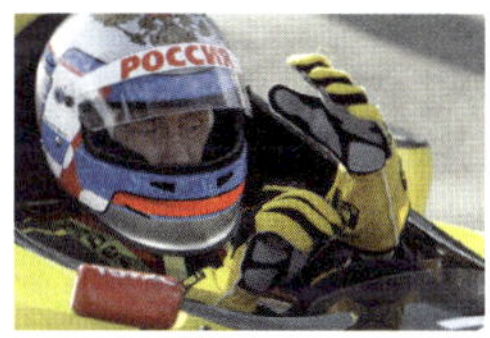

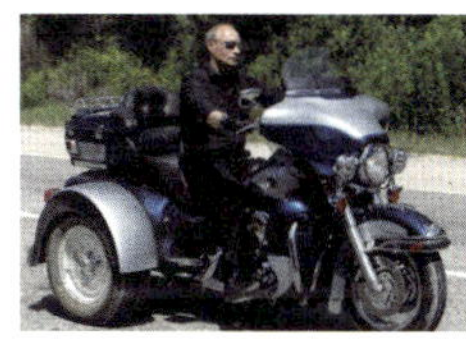

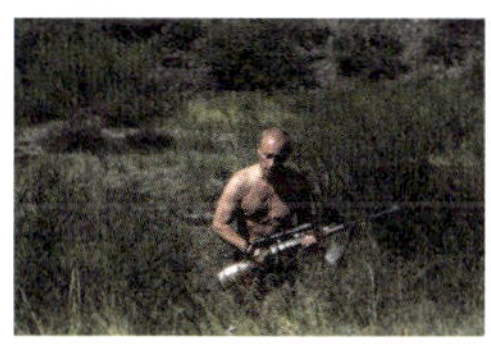

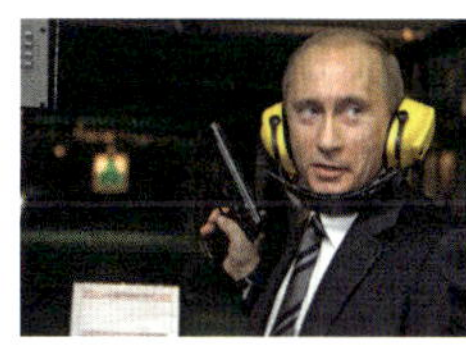

Character traits and gestures

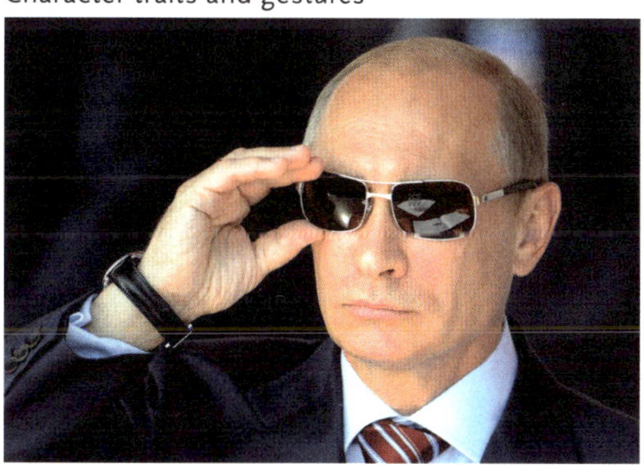

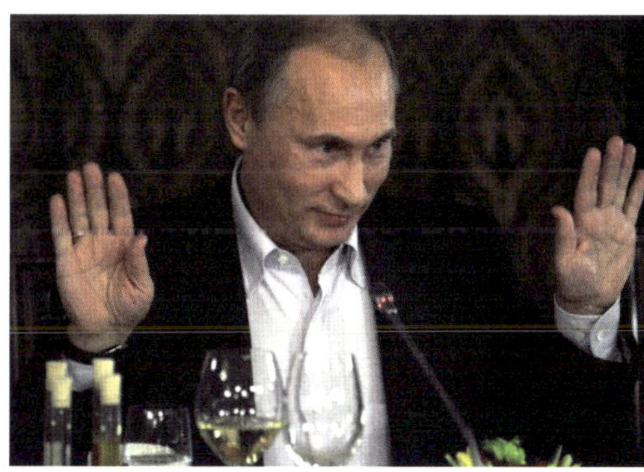

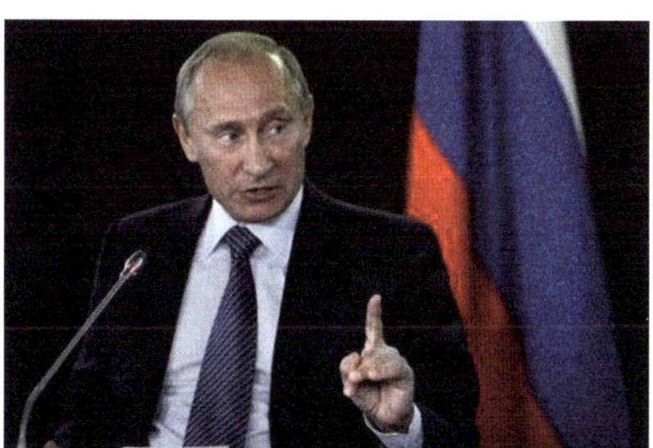

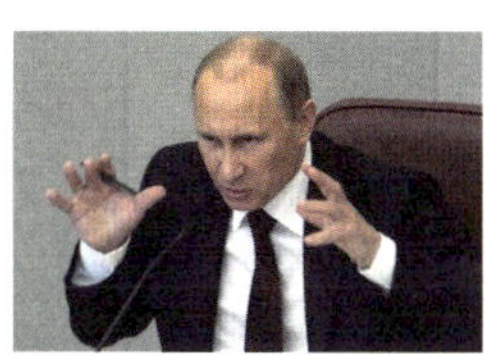

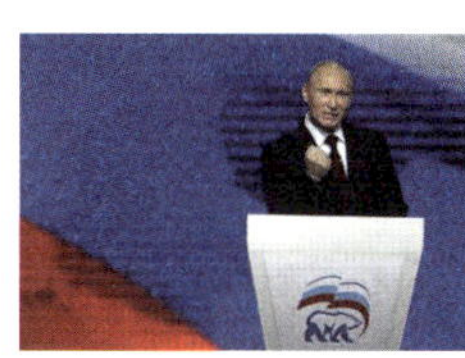

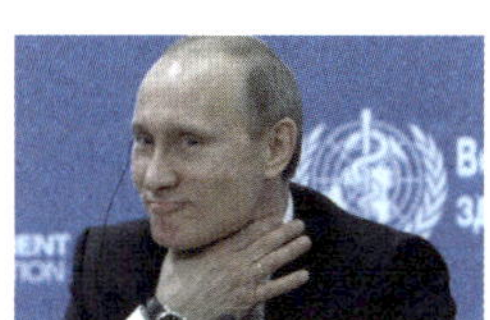

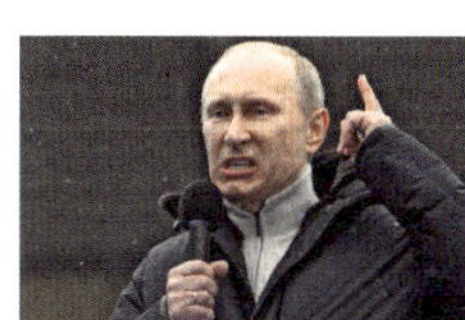

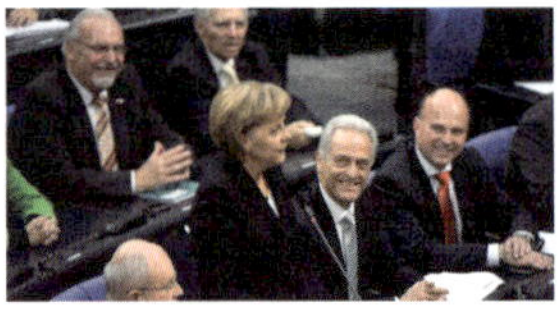

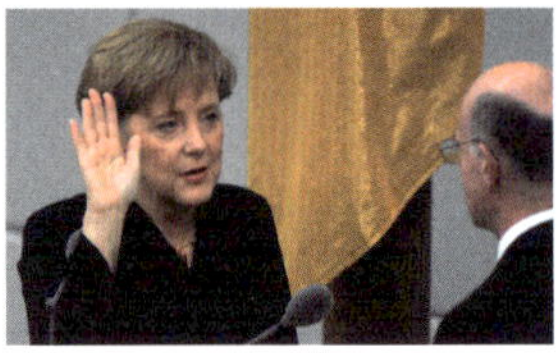

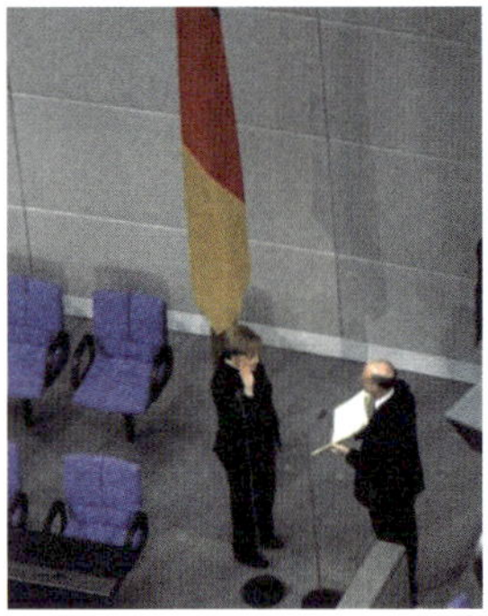

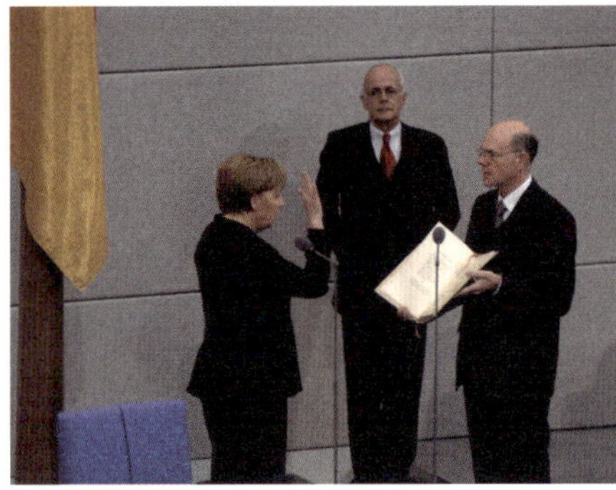

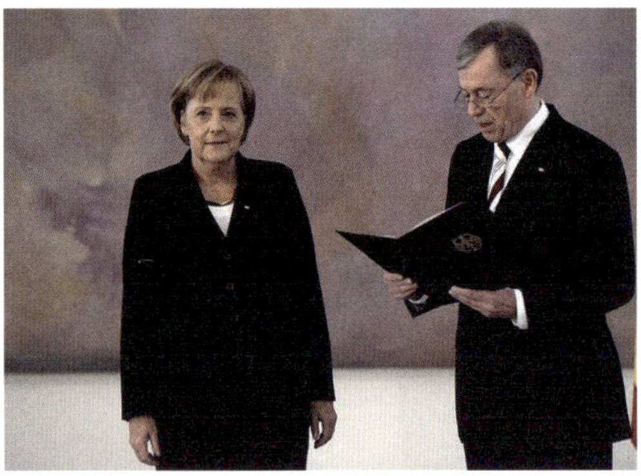

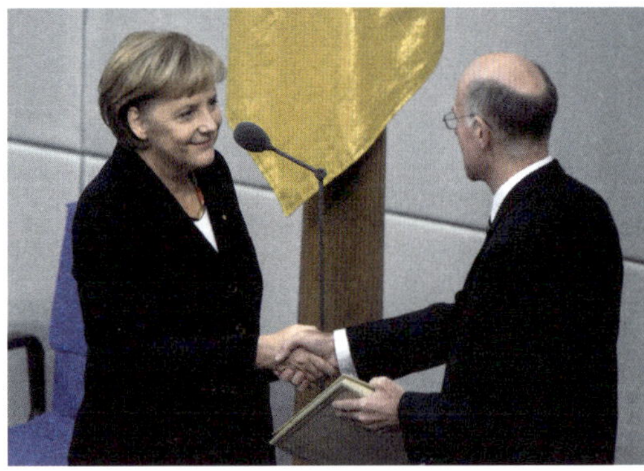

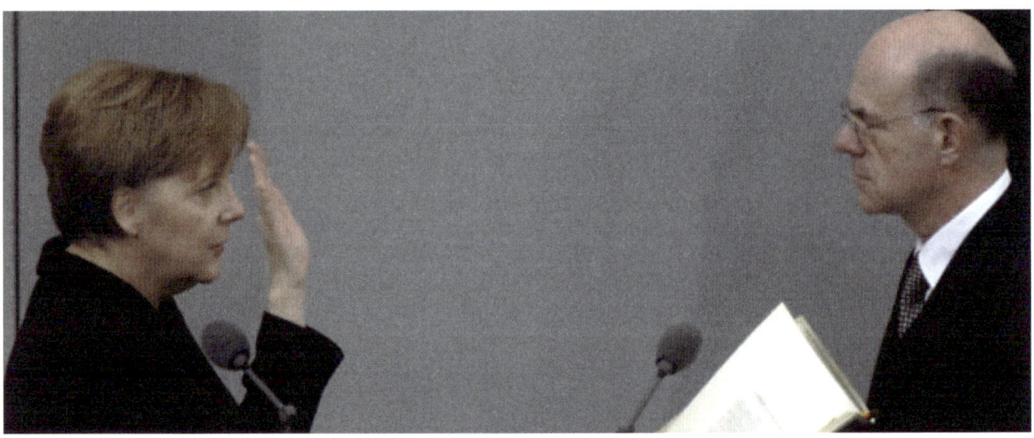

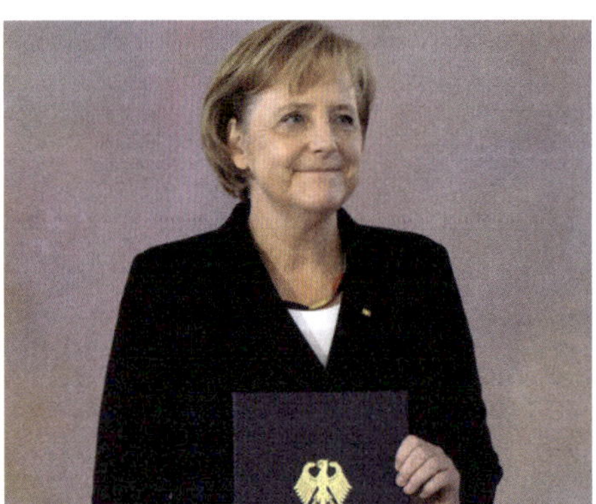

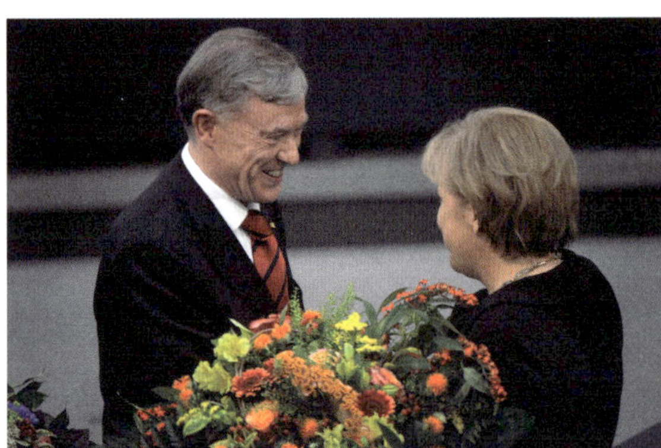

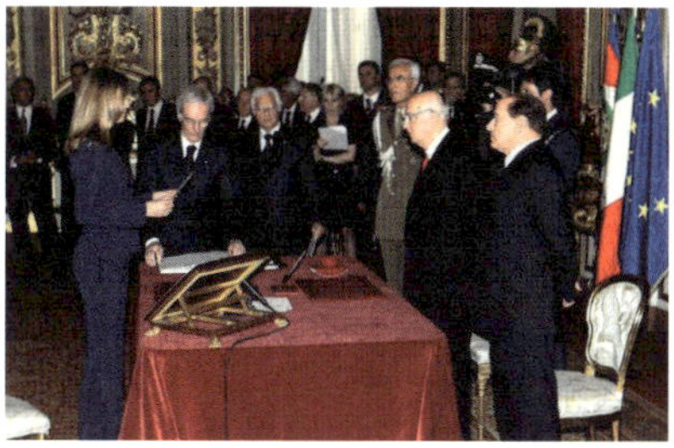

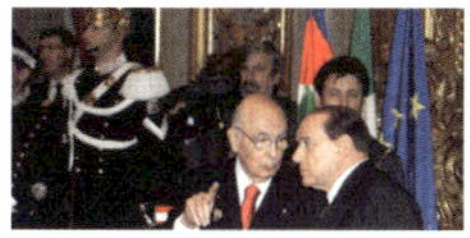

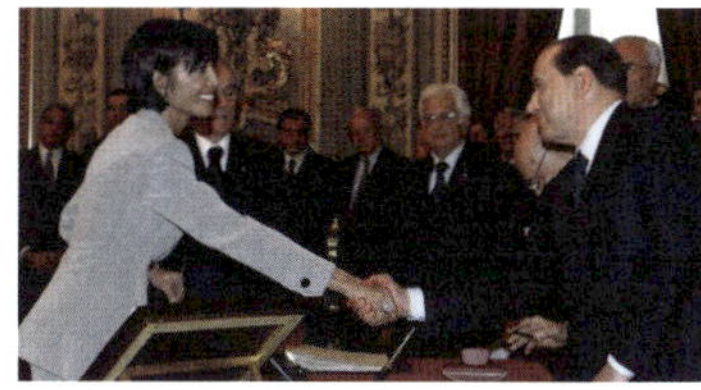

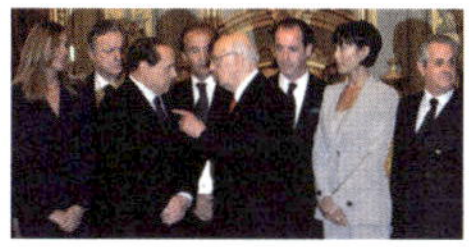

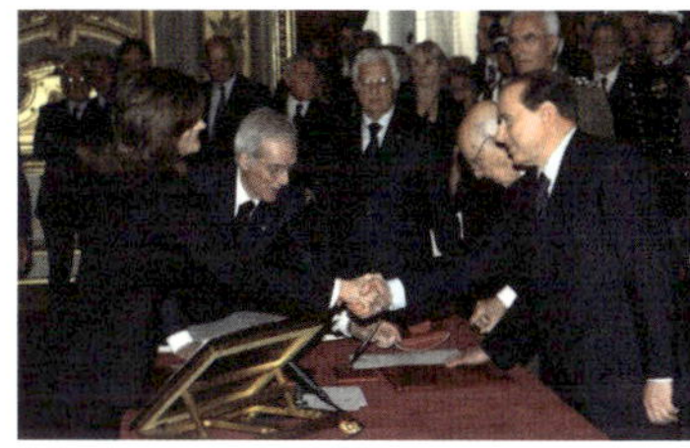

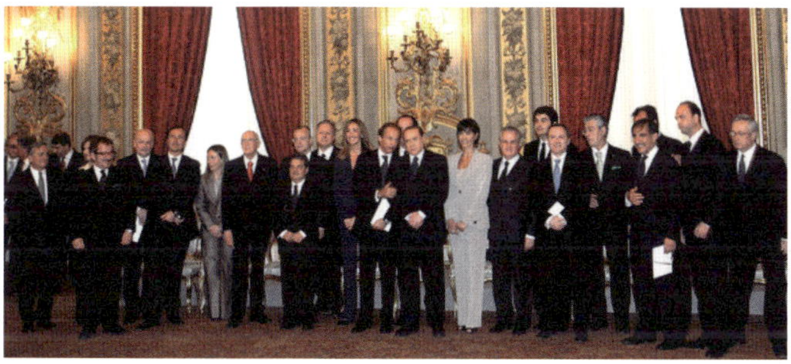

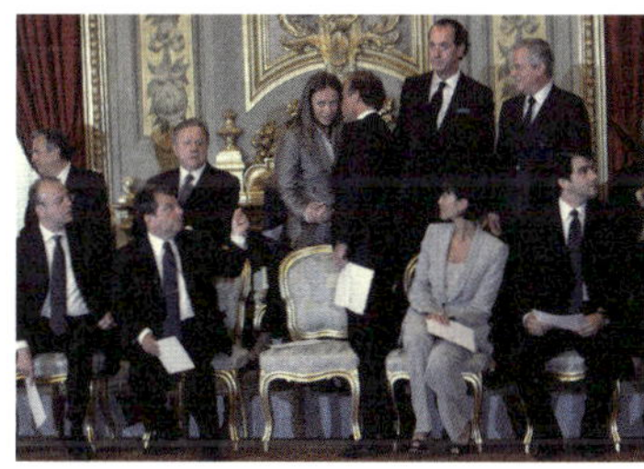

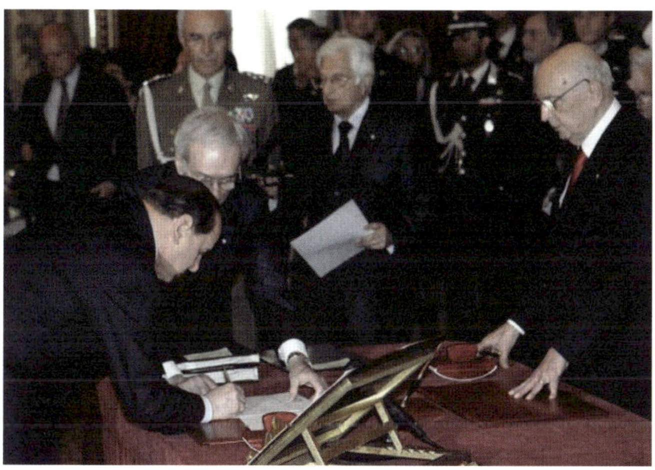

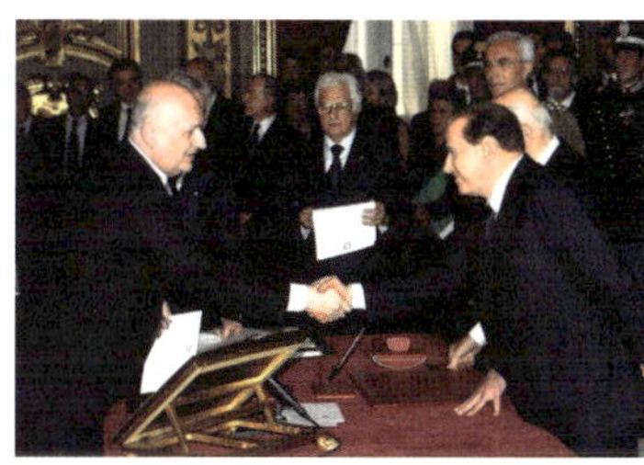

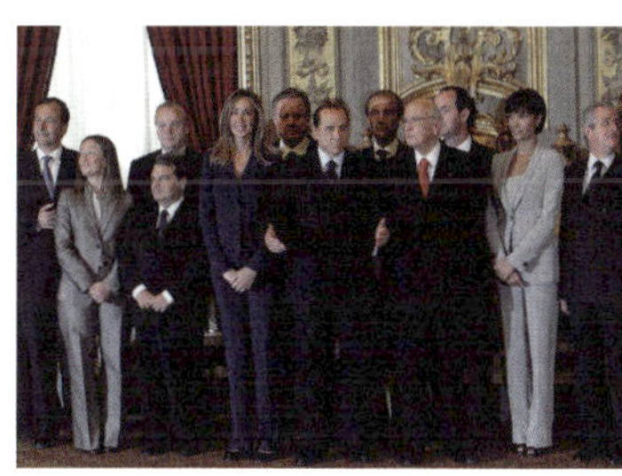

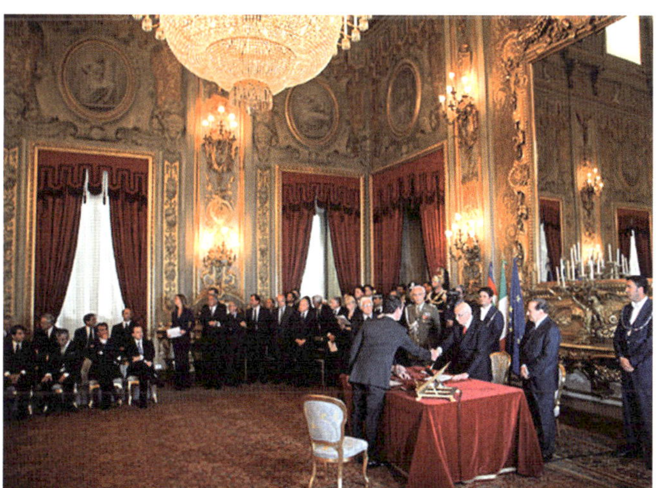

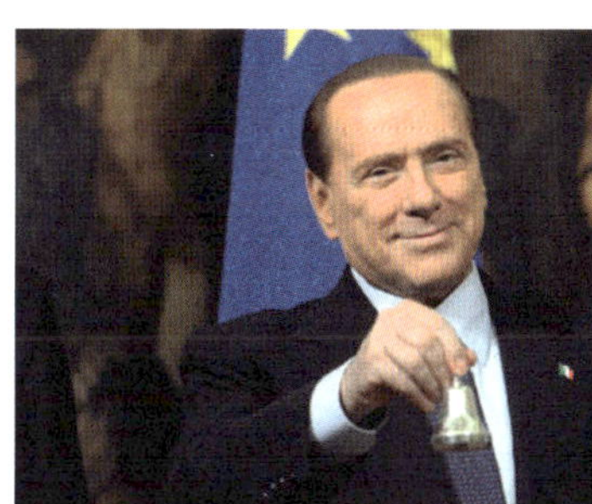

Branding Through Staging

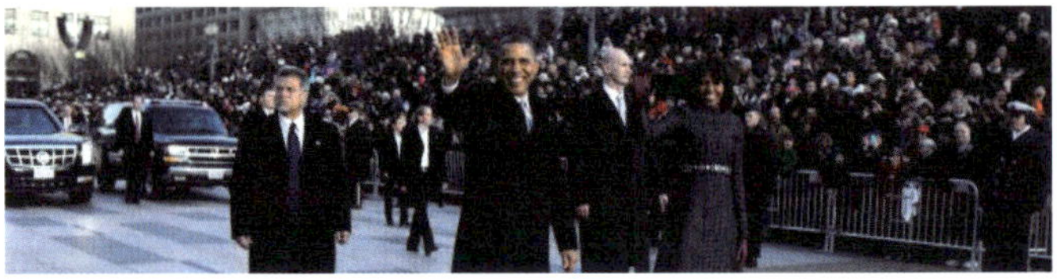

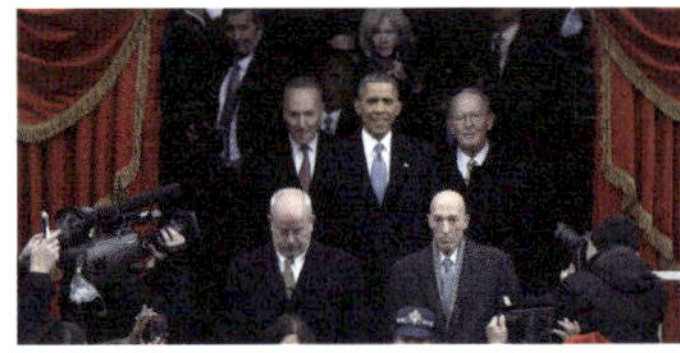

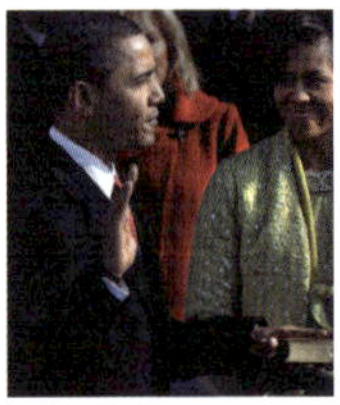

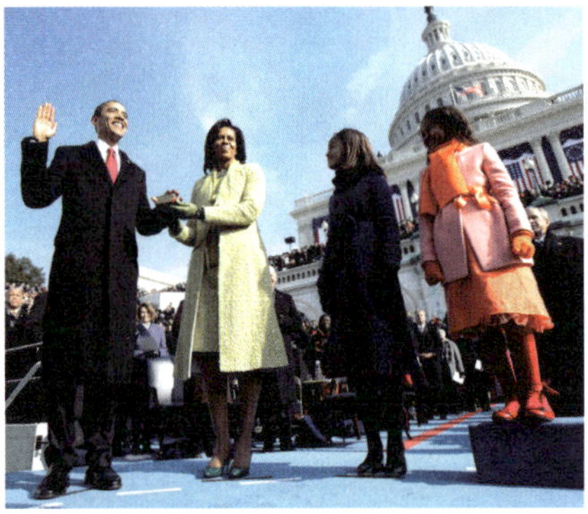

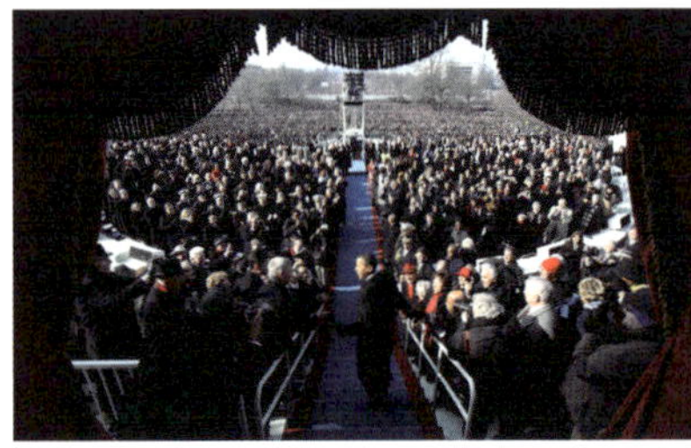

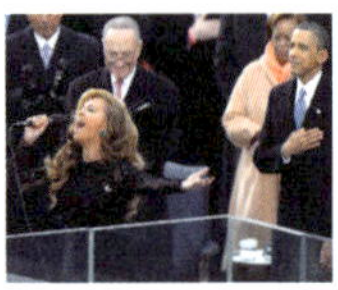

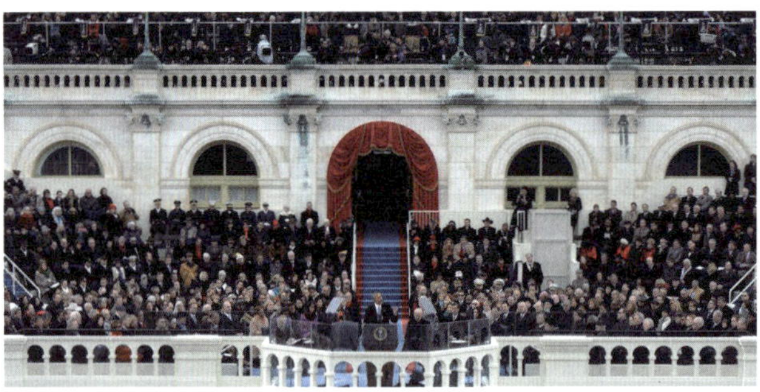

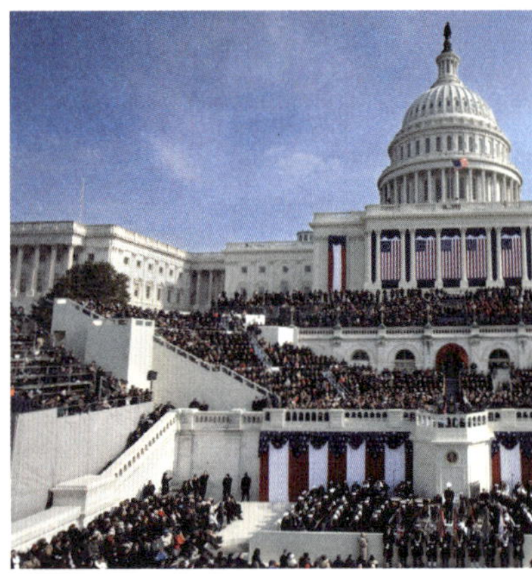

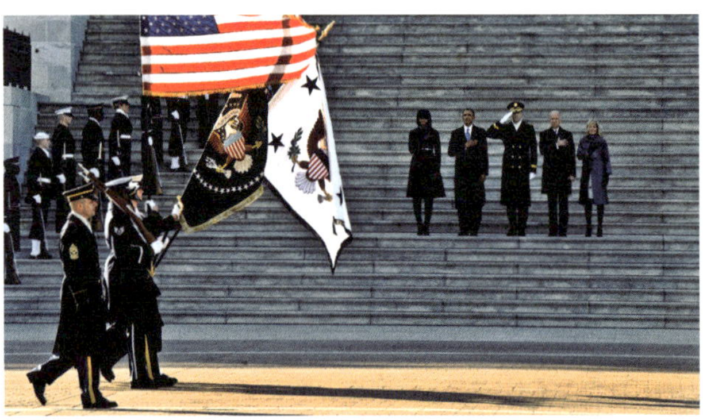

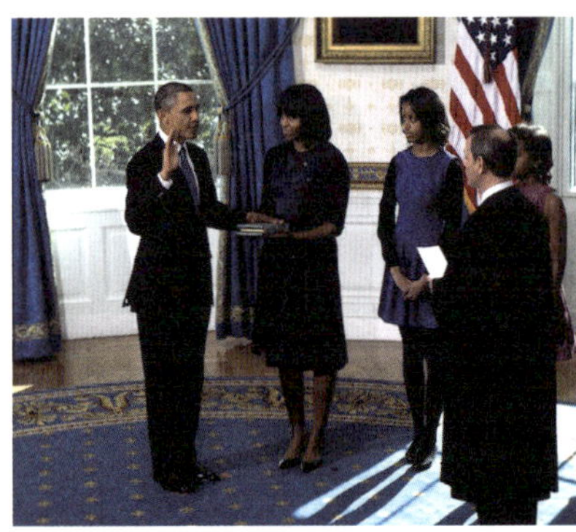

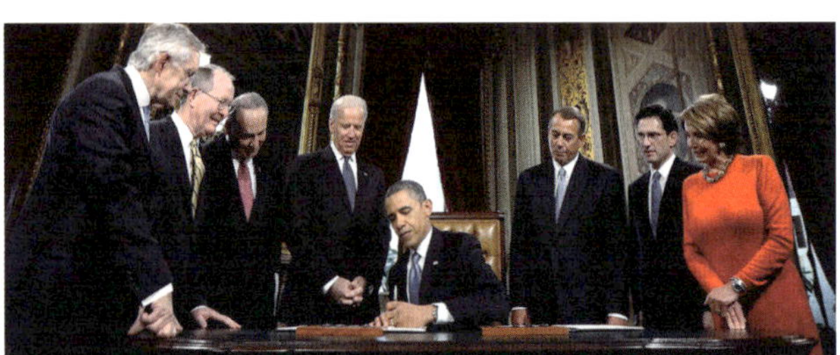

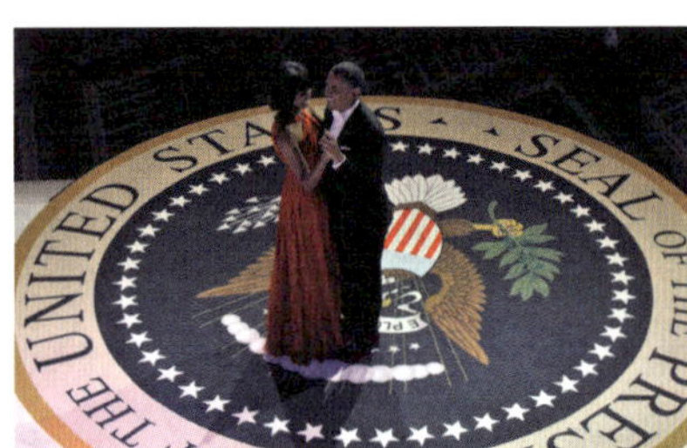

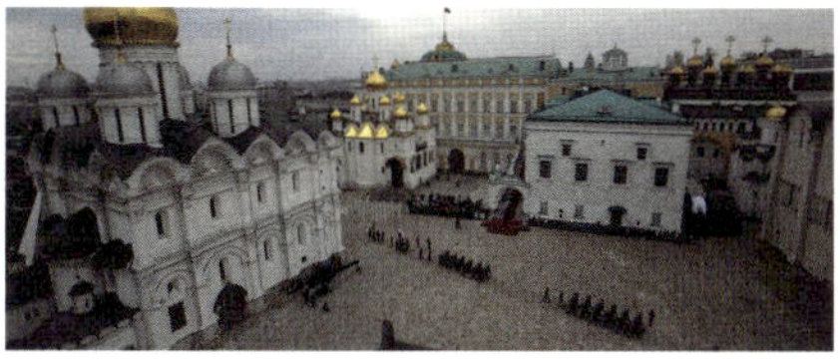
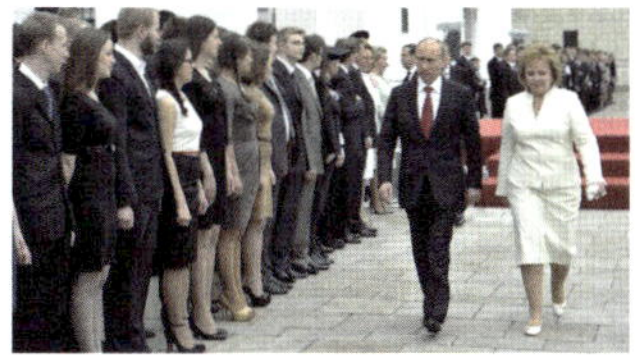
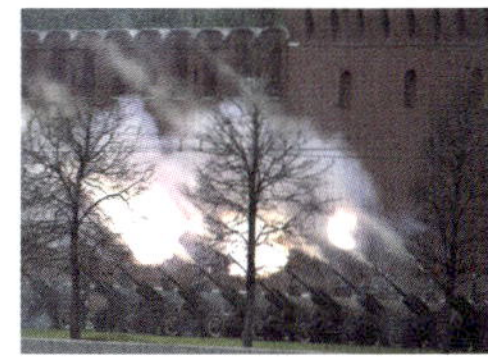
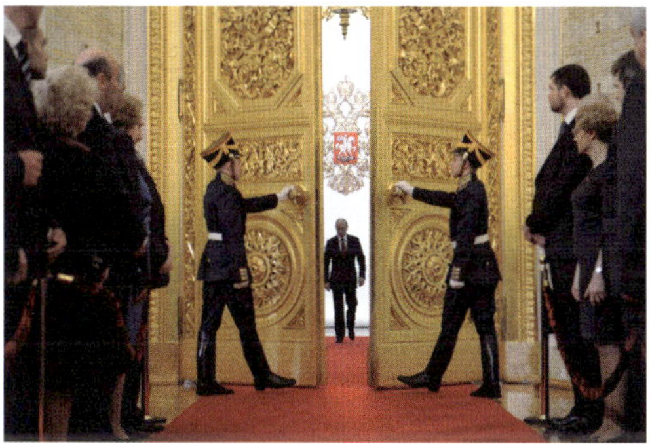
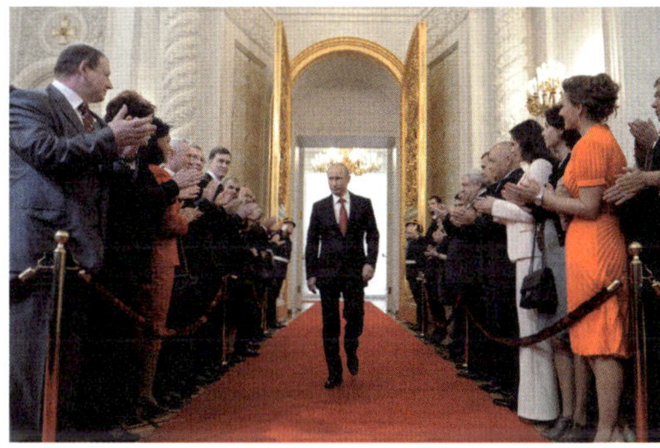
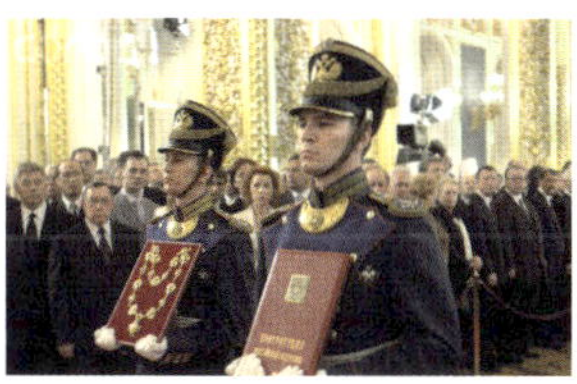
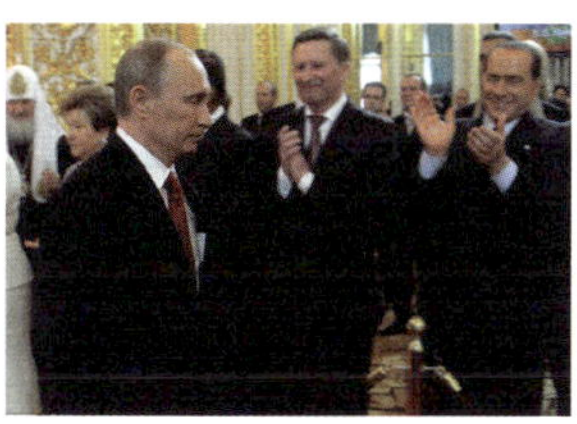
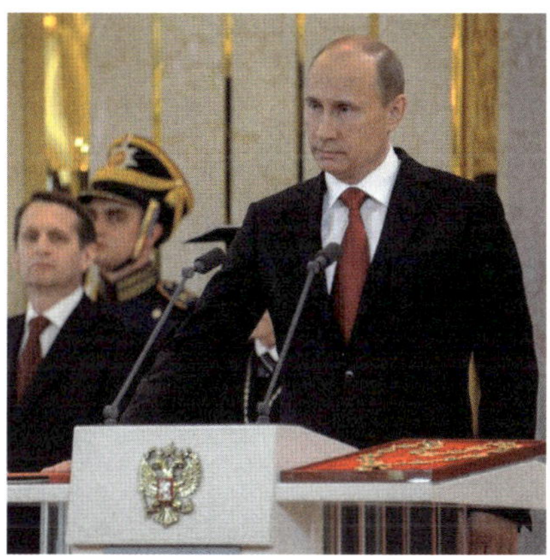
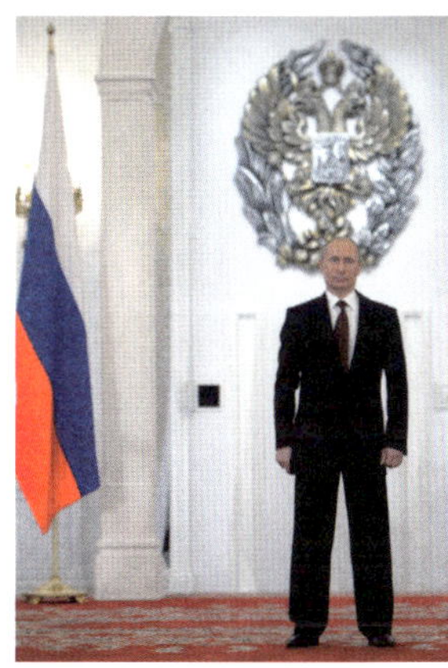
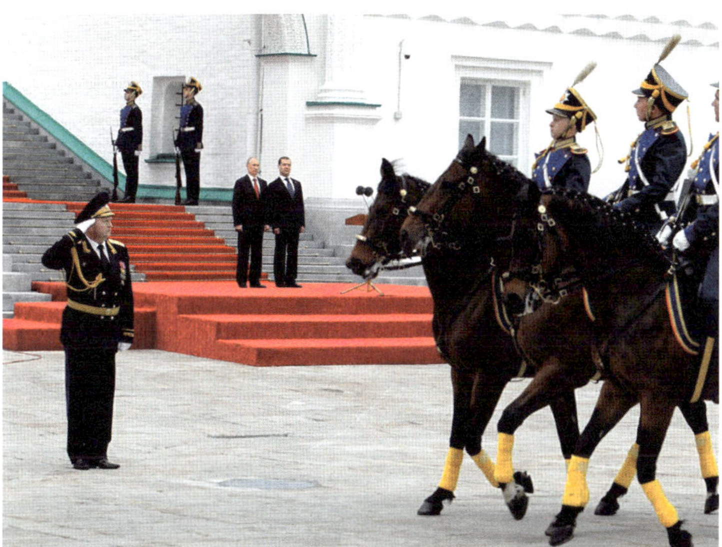
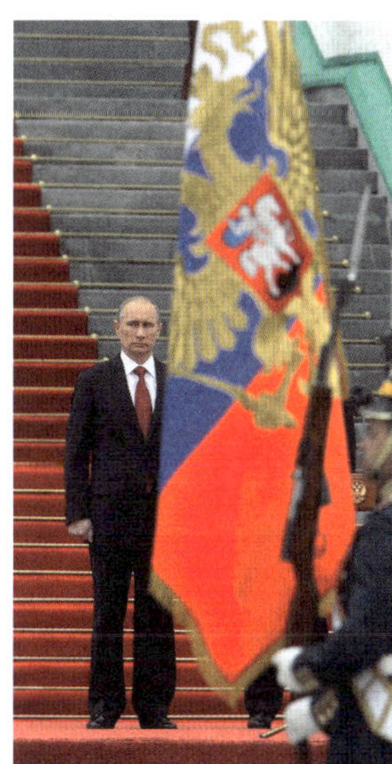

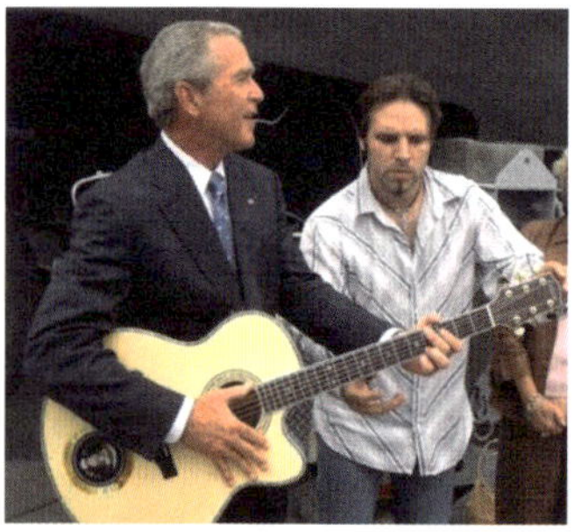
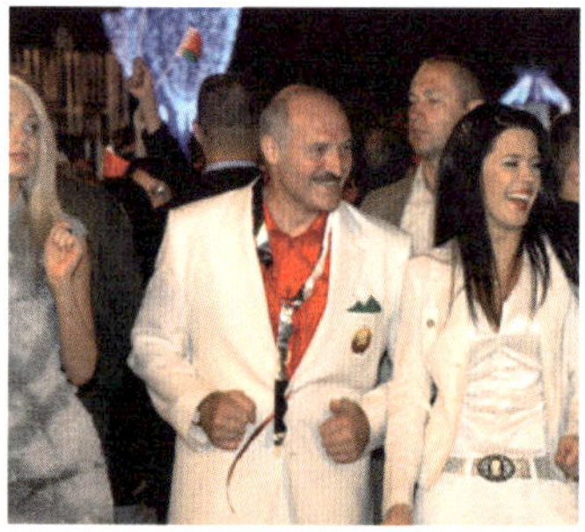
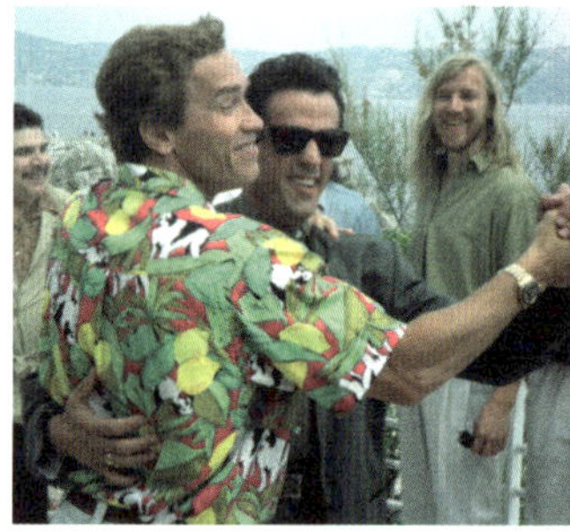
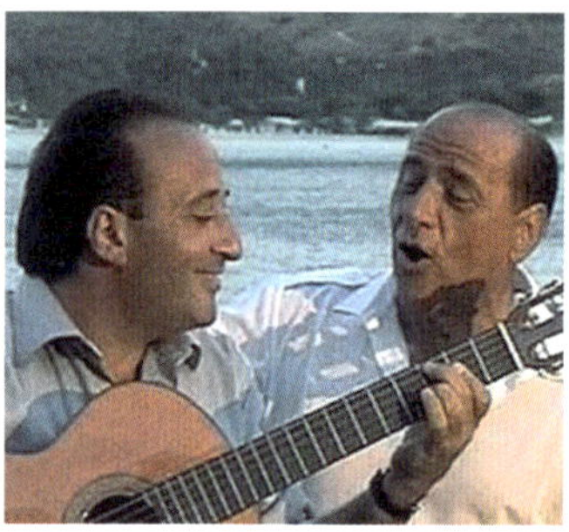
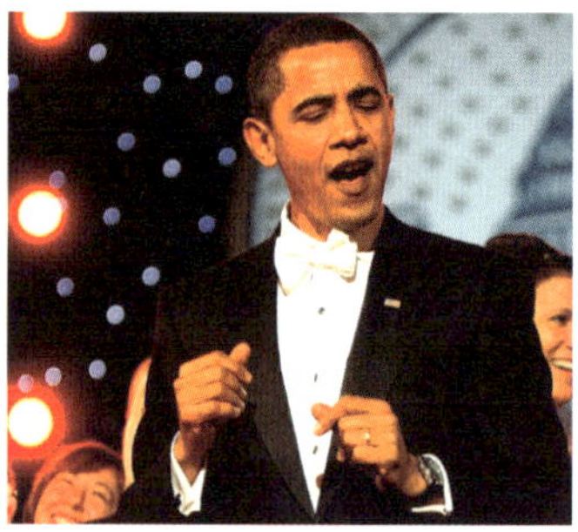
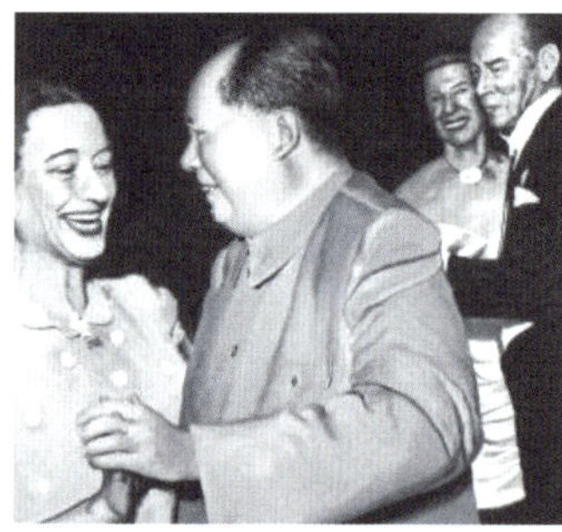
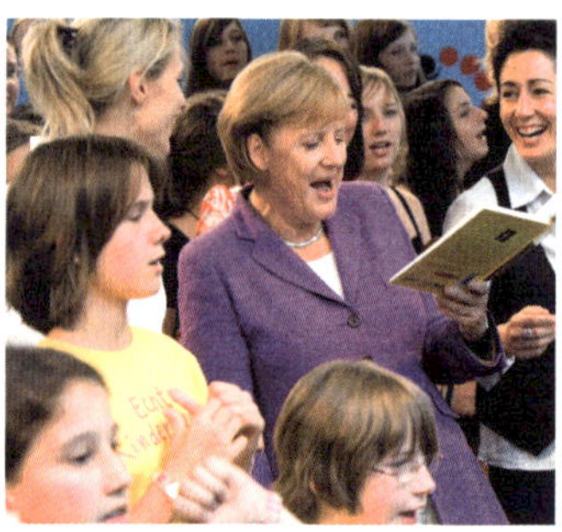
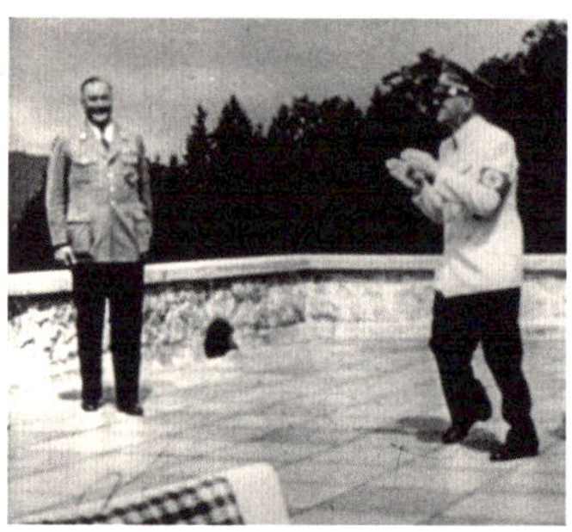
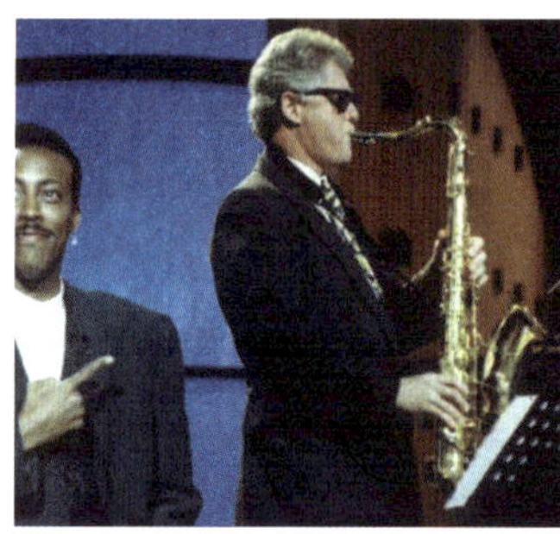
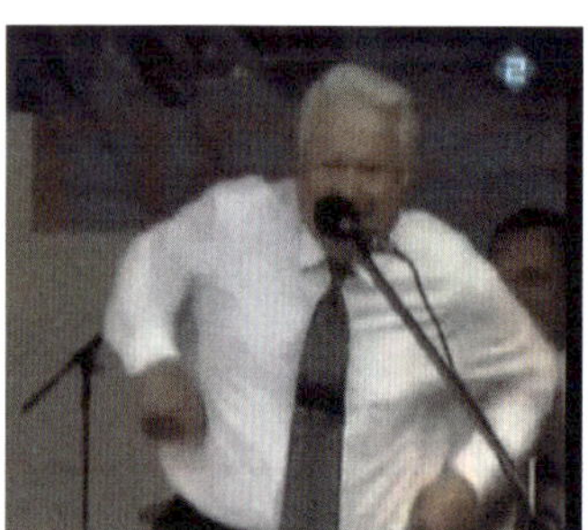
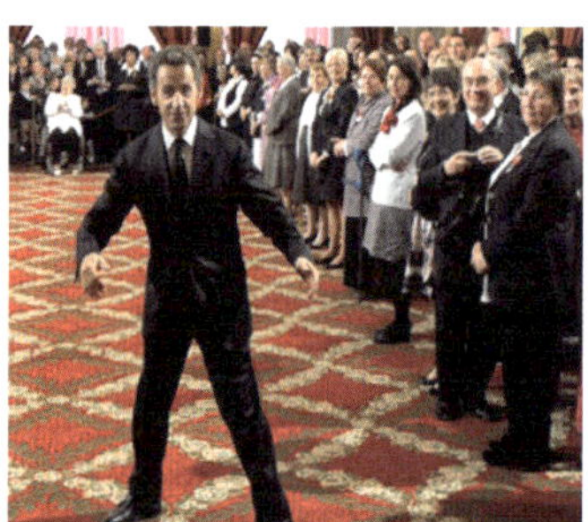
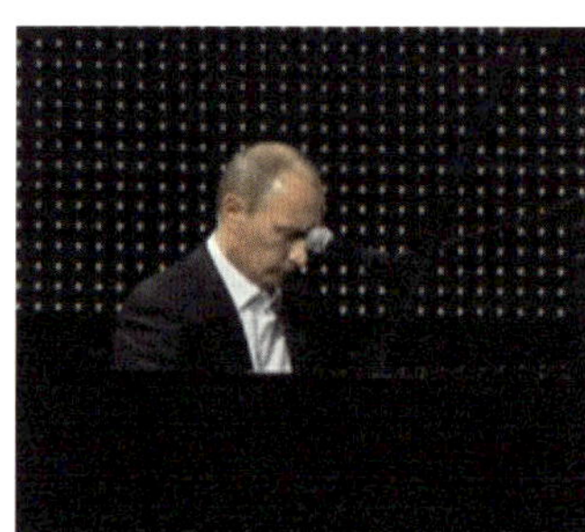

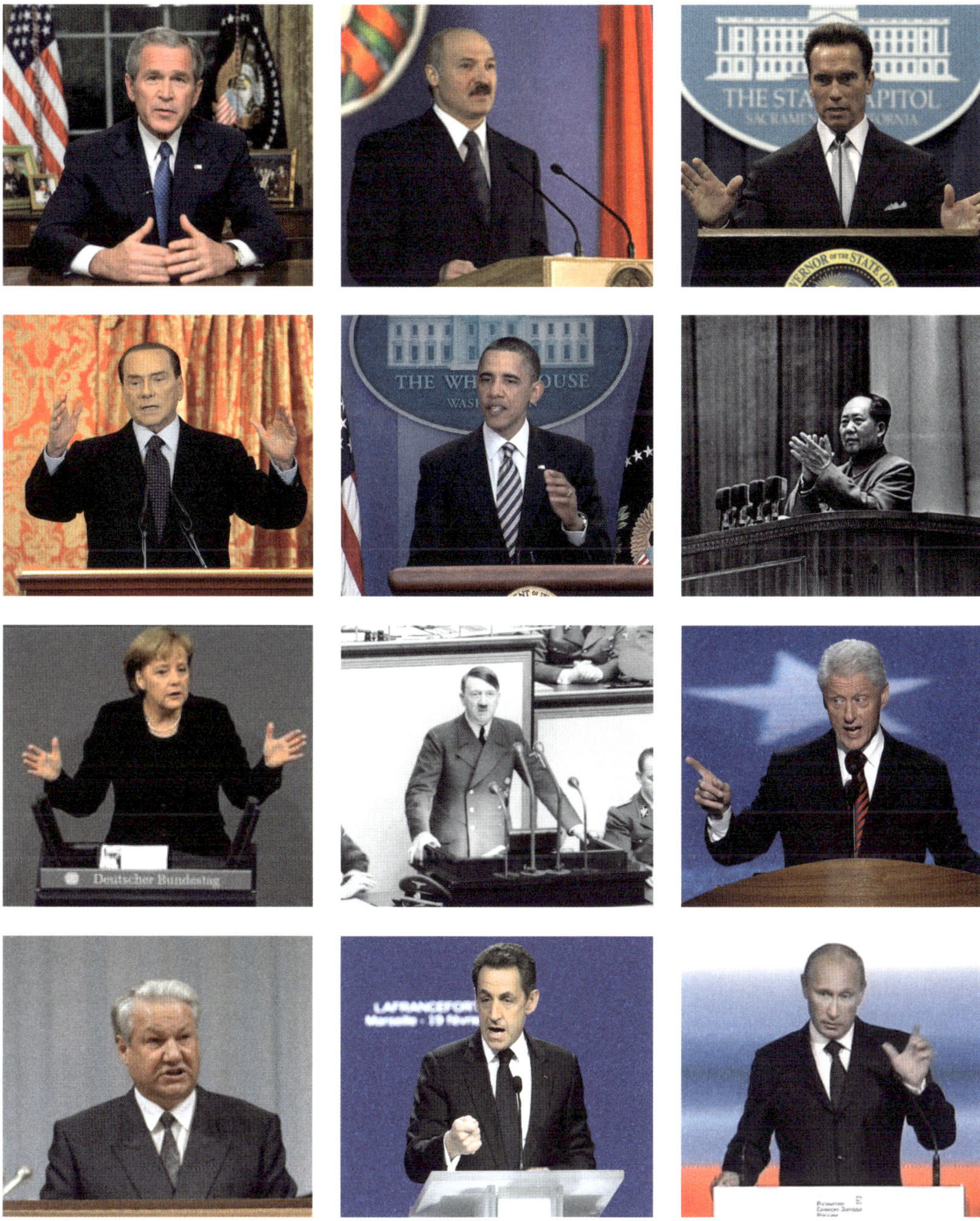
Deutscher Bundestag

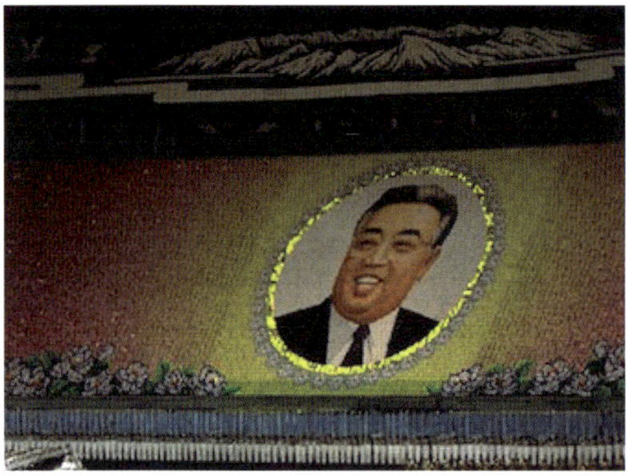

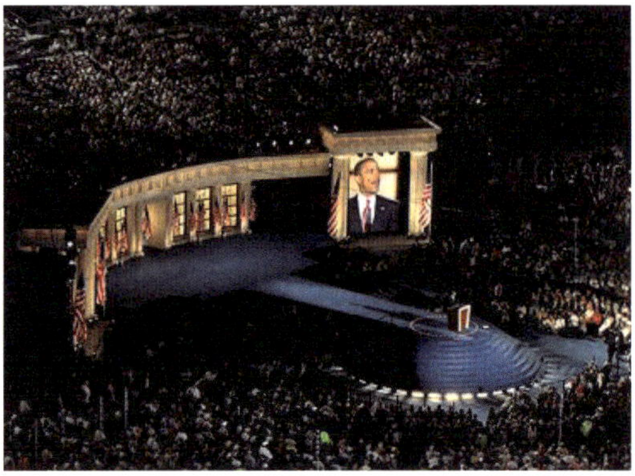

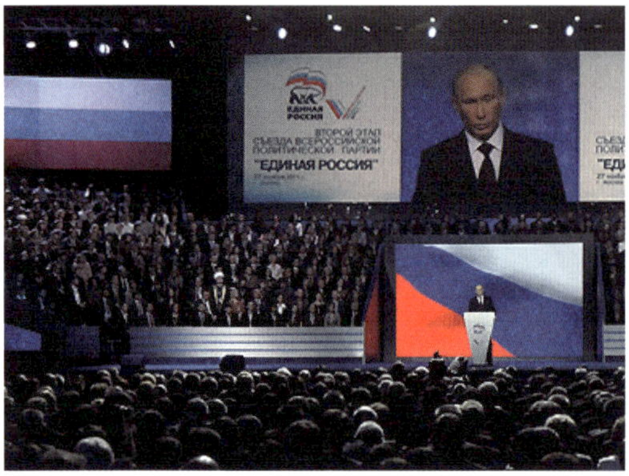
"ЕДИНАЯ РОССИЯ"

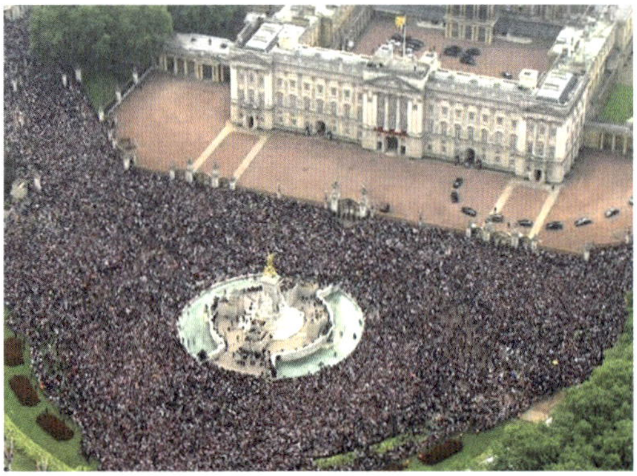

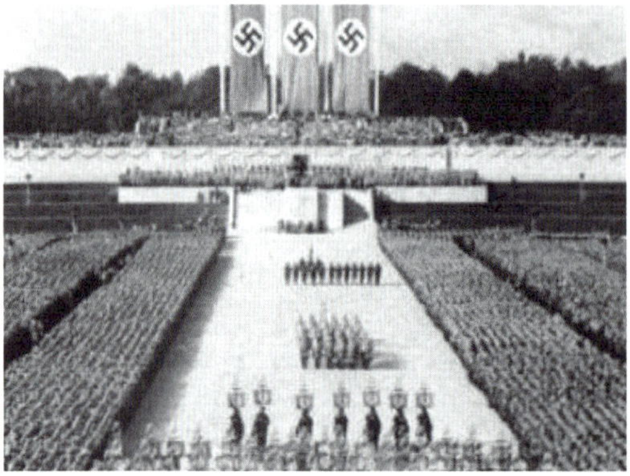

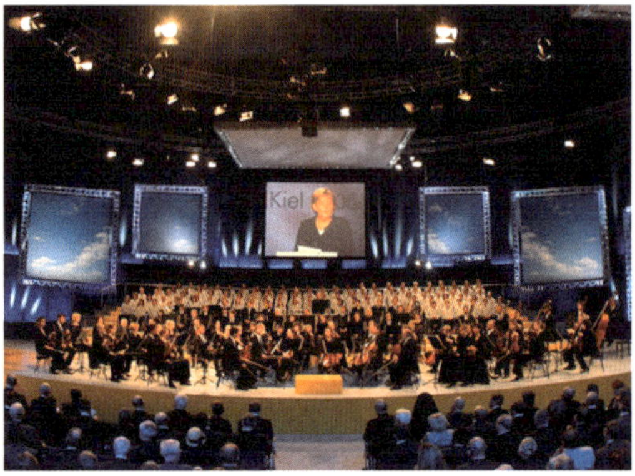
Kiel

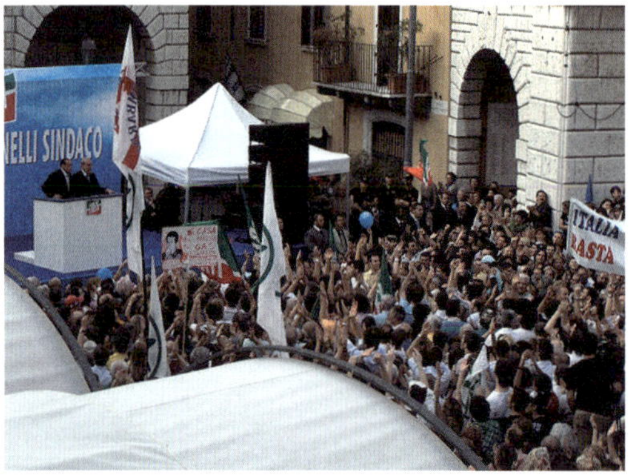

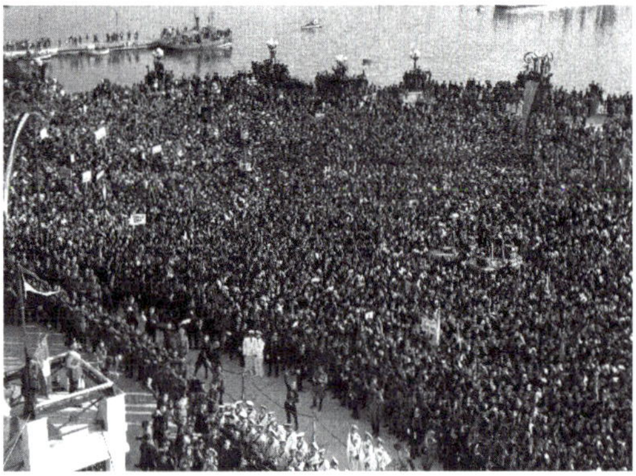

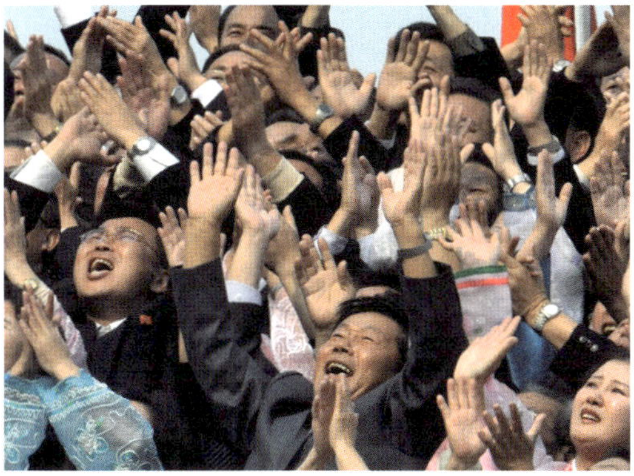

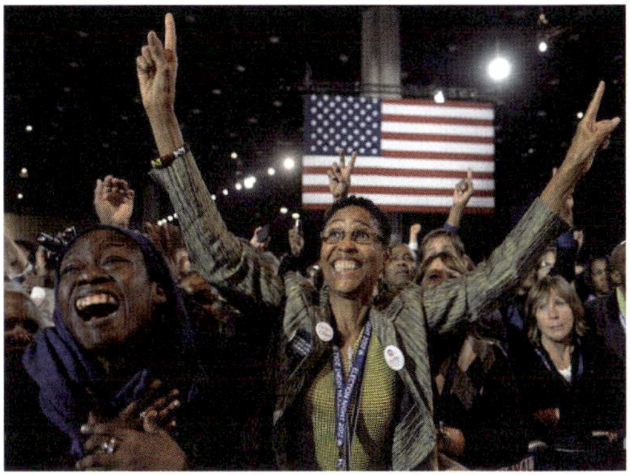

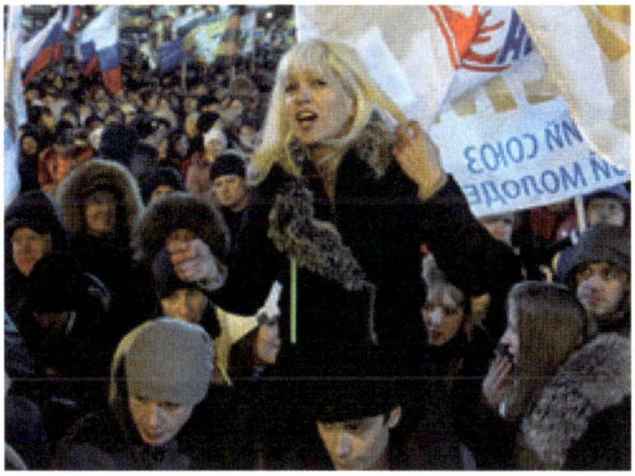

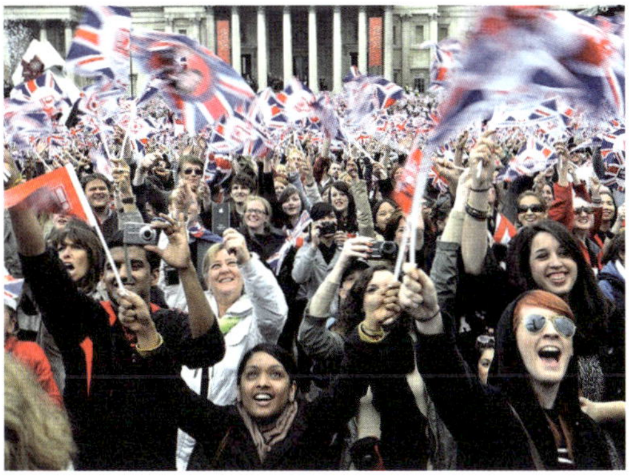

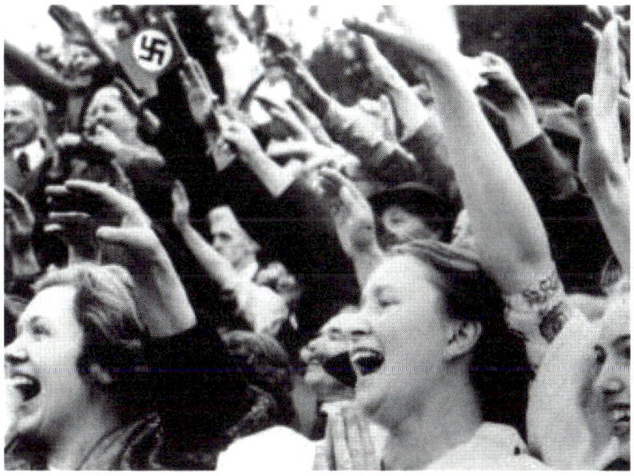

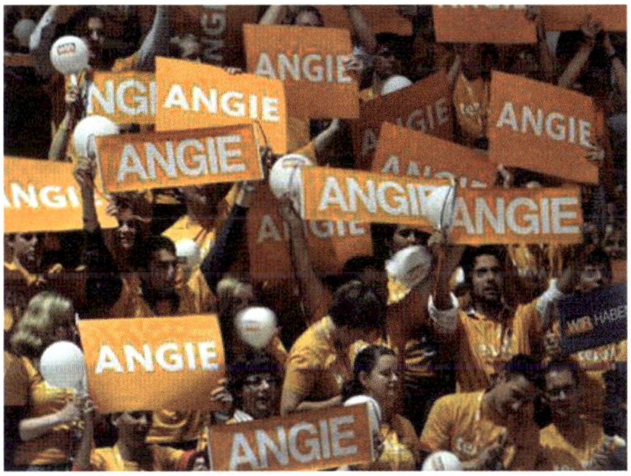
ANGIE
ANGIE
ANGIE
ANGIE
ANGIE
ANGIE

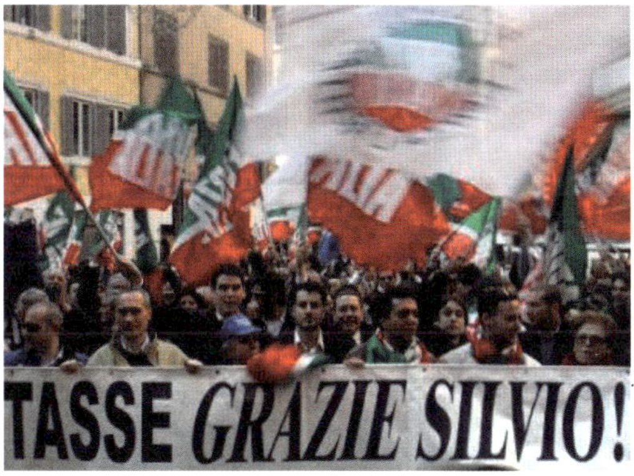
TASSE GRAZIE SILVIO!

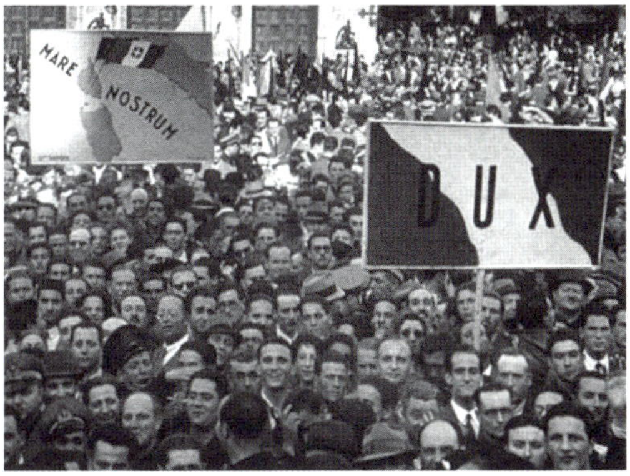
MARE NOSTRUM
DUX

Branding Through Emotion

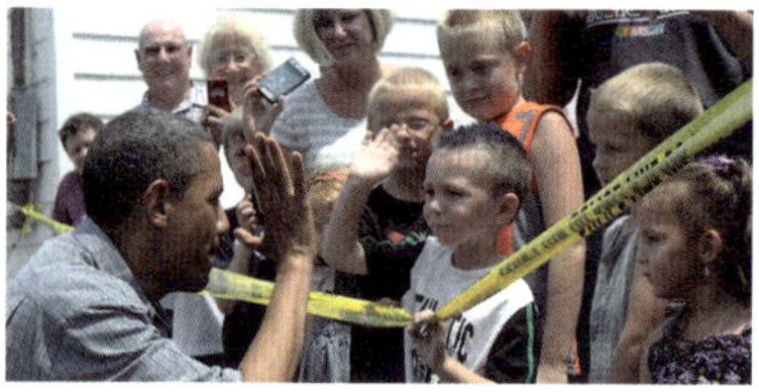

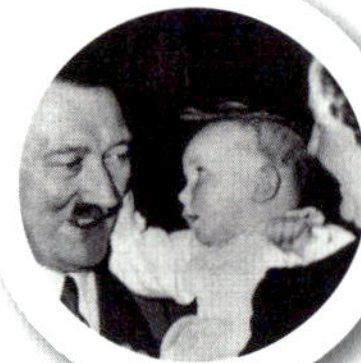

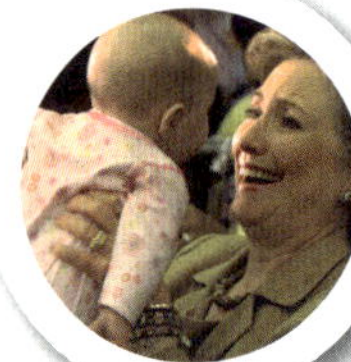

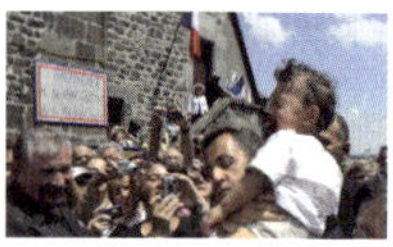

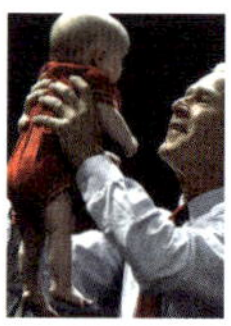

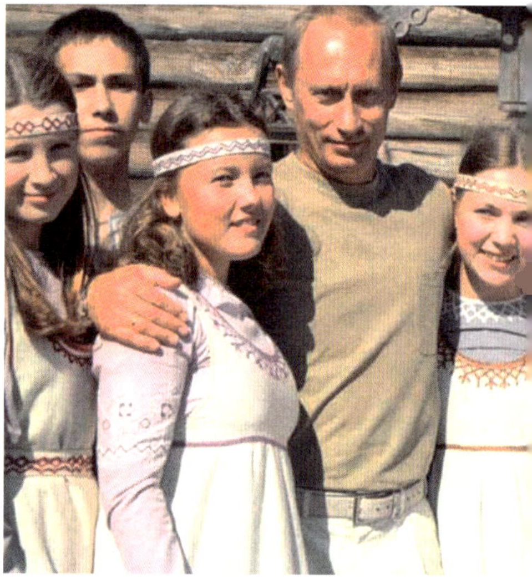

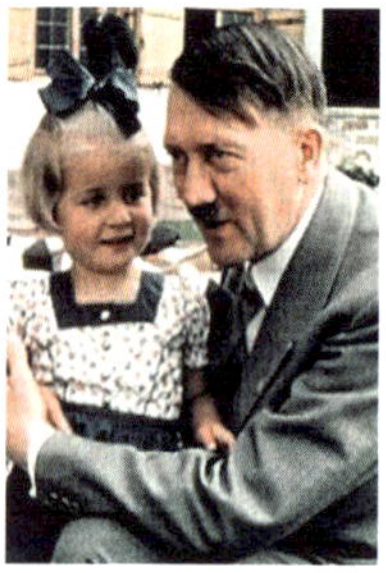

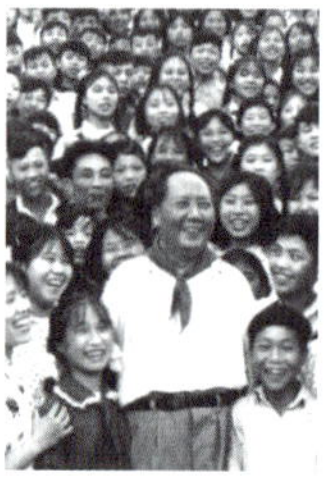

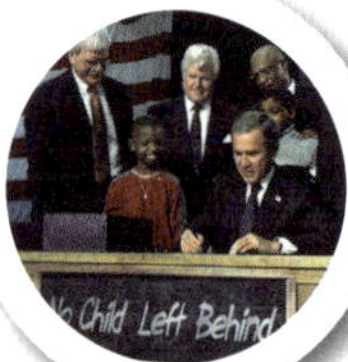

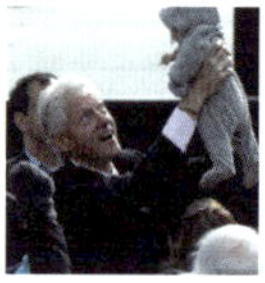

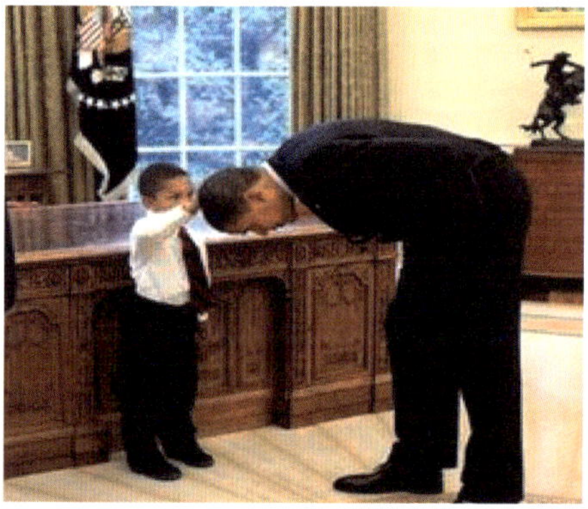

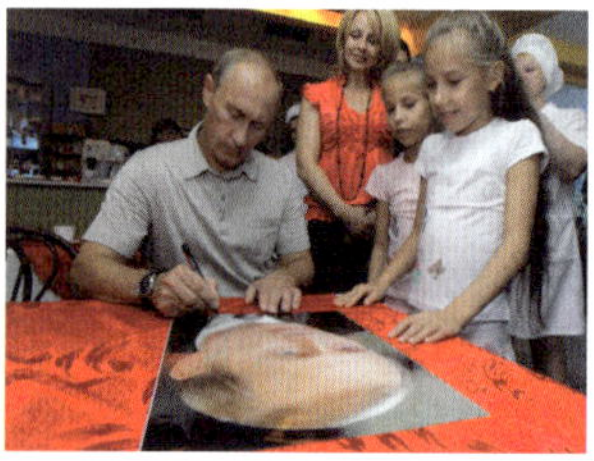

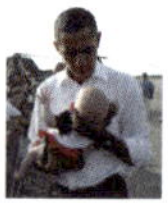

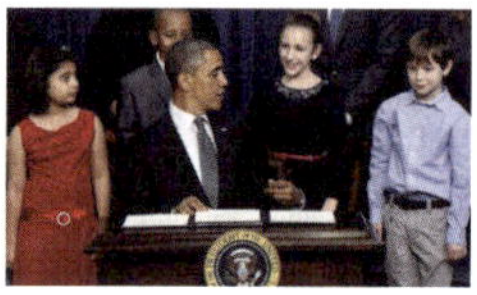

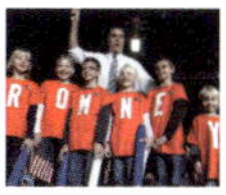
ROMNEY

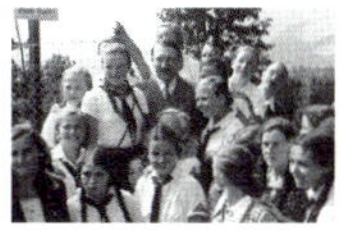

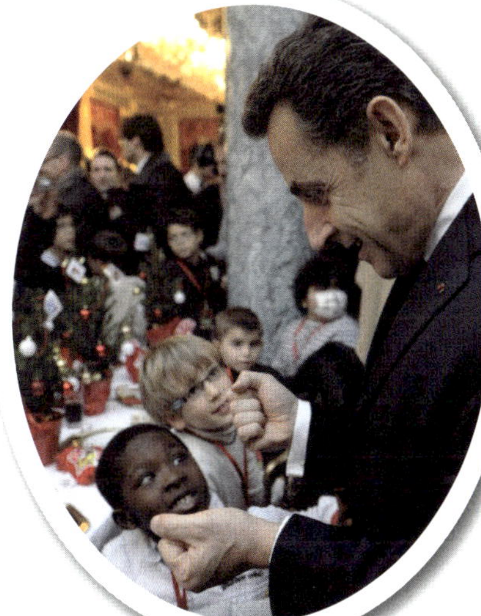

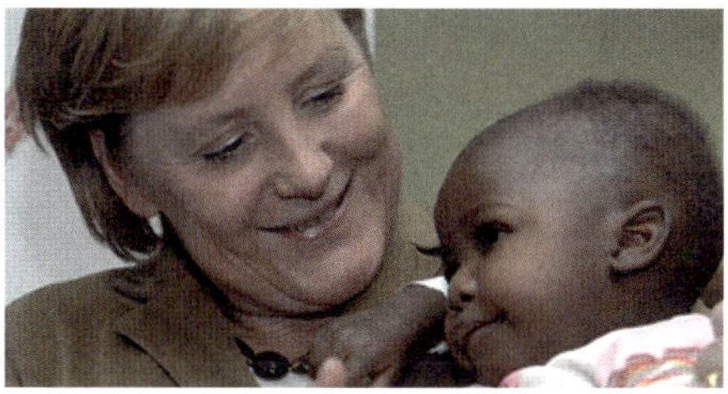

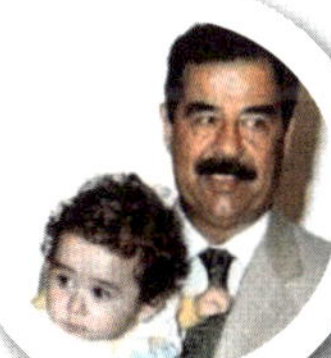

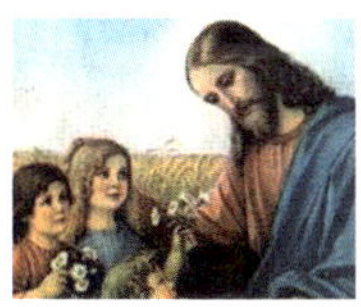

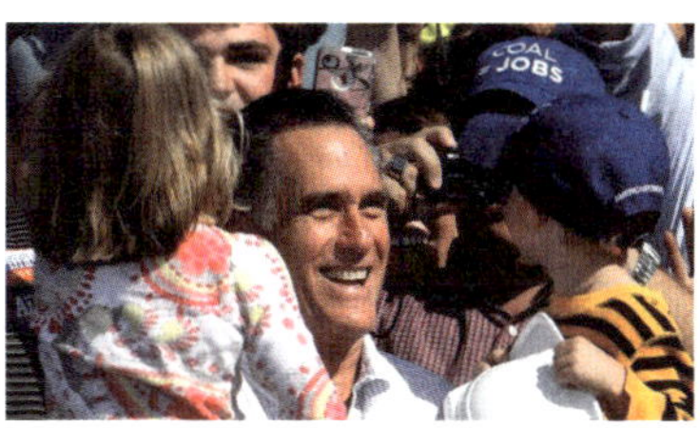
COAL
JOBS

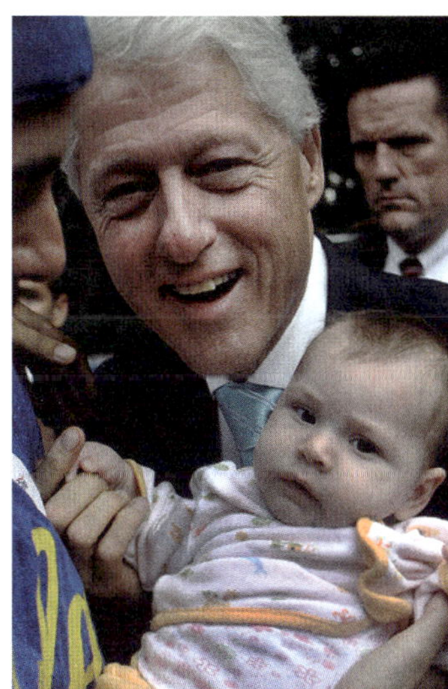

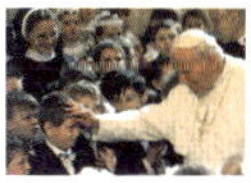

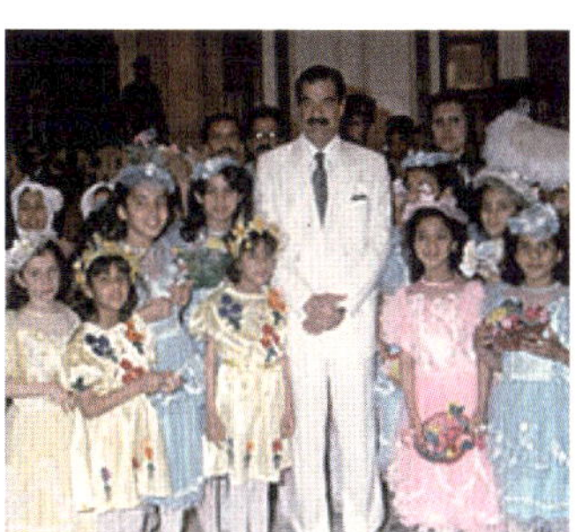

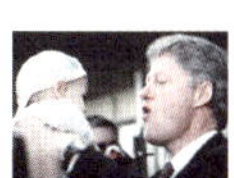

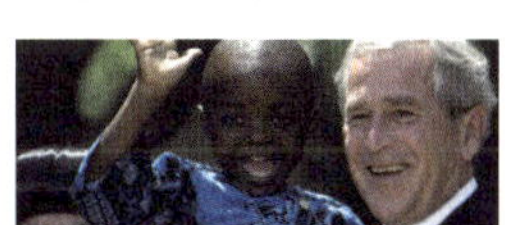

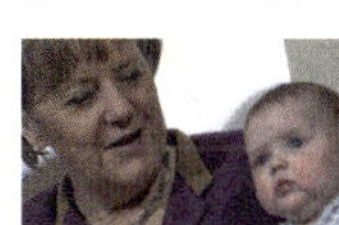

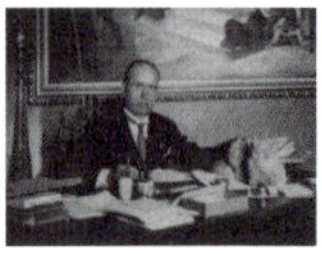
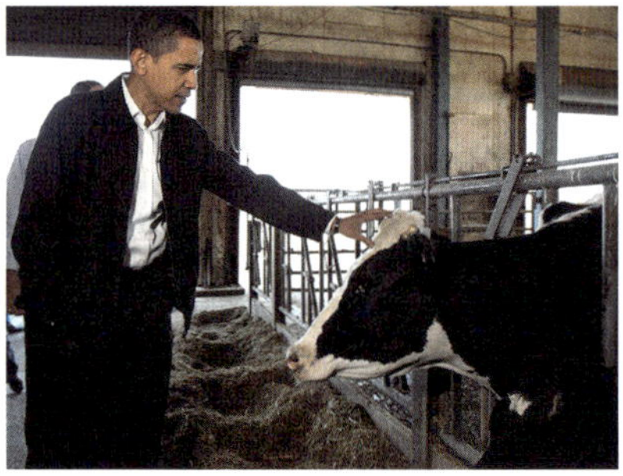
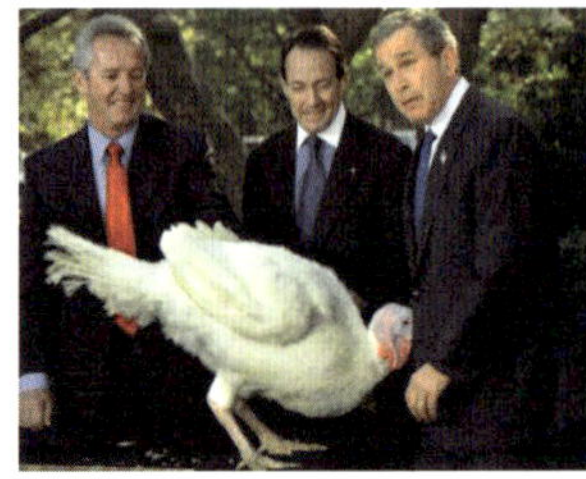
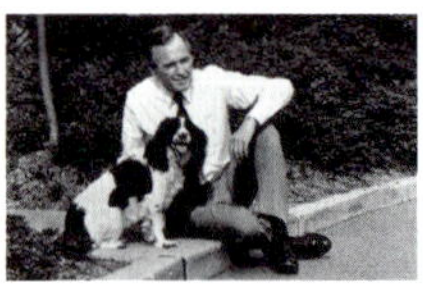
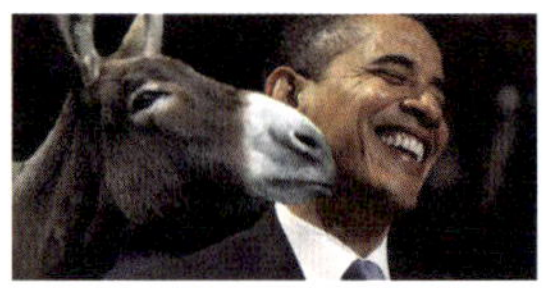
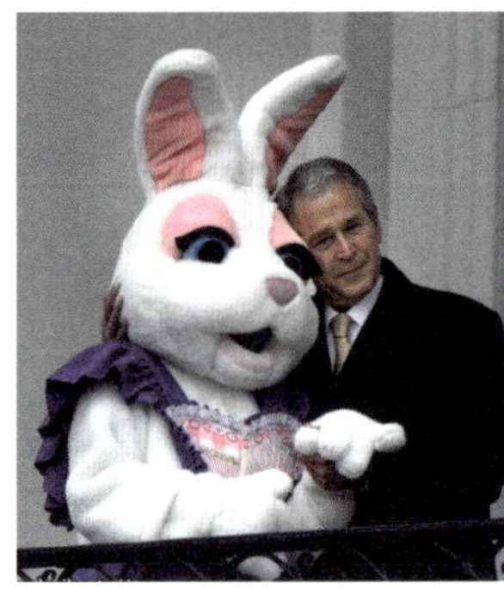
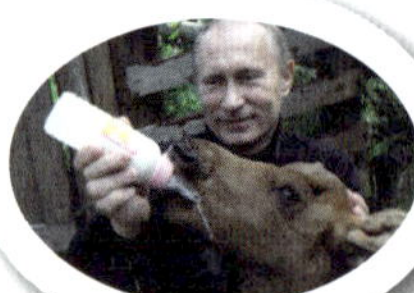
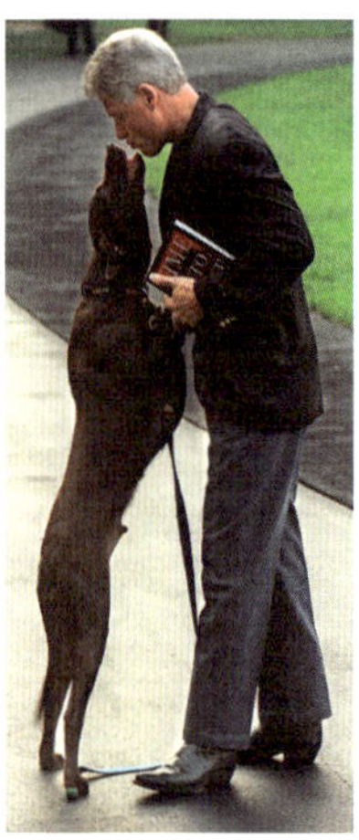
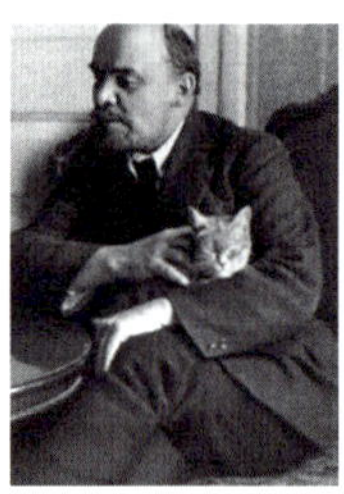
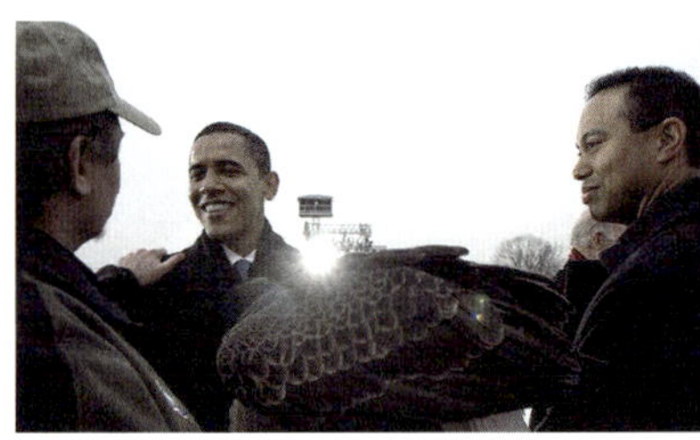
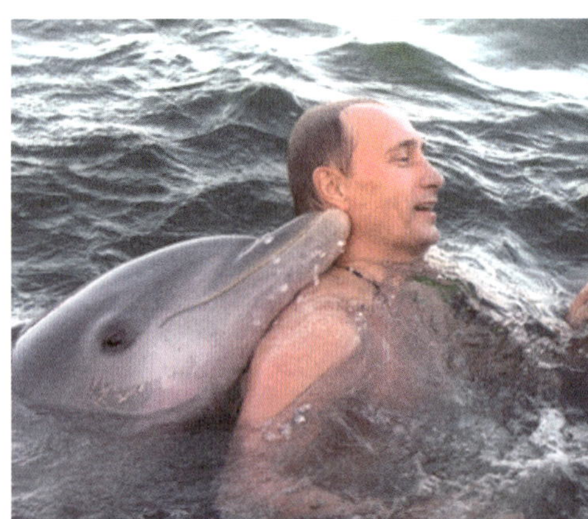
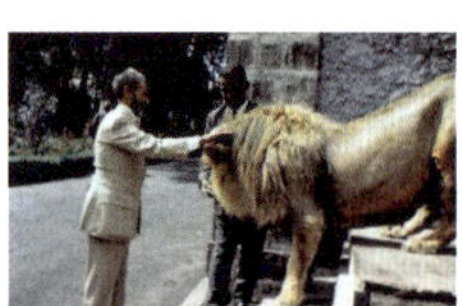
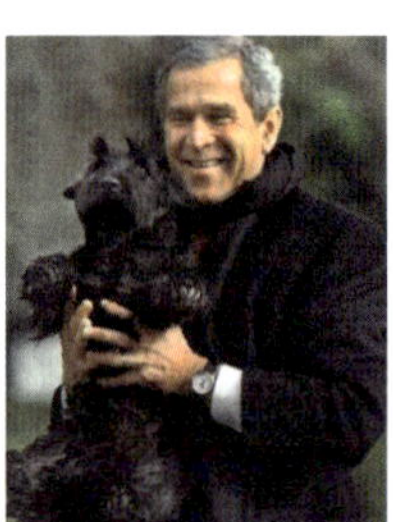
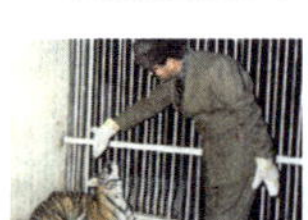

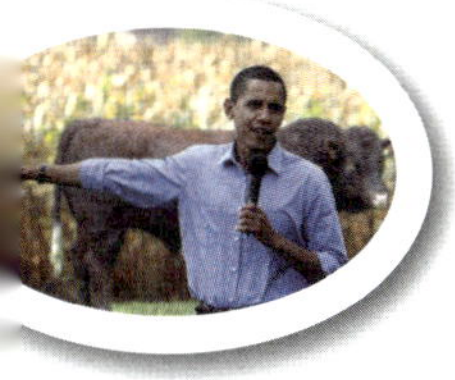
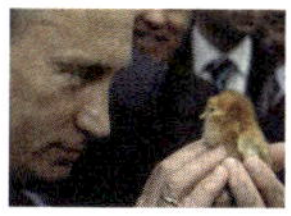
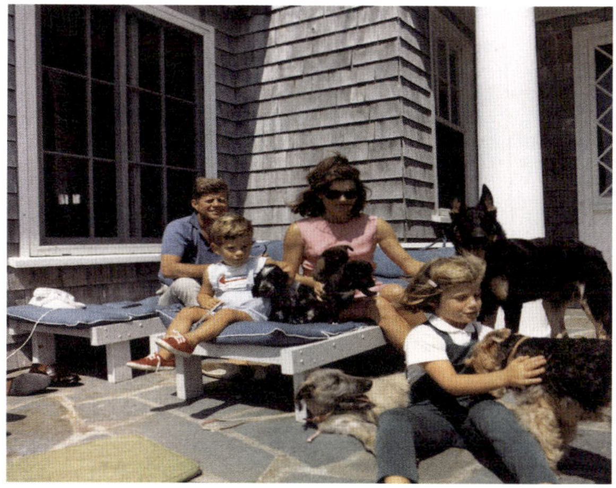
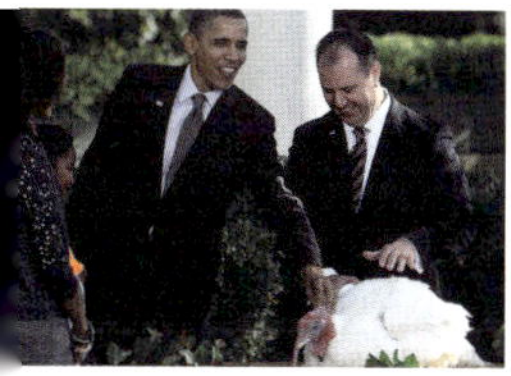
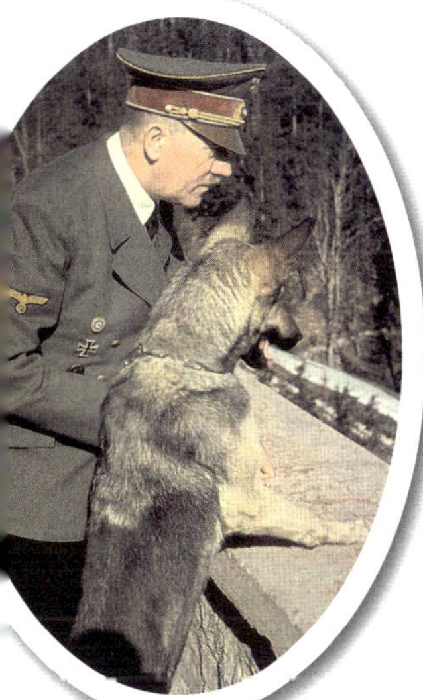
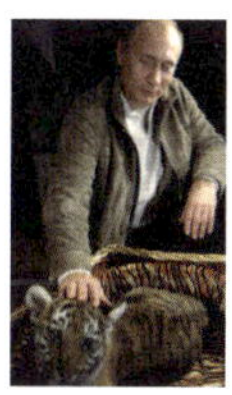
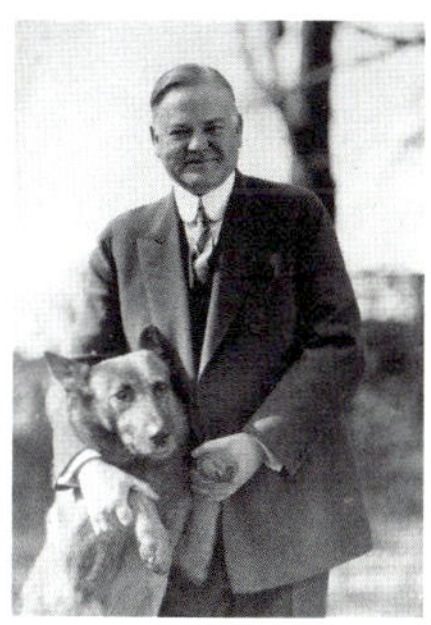
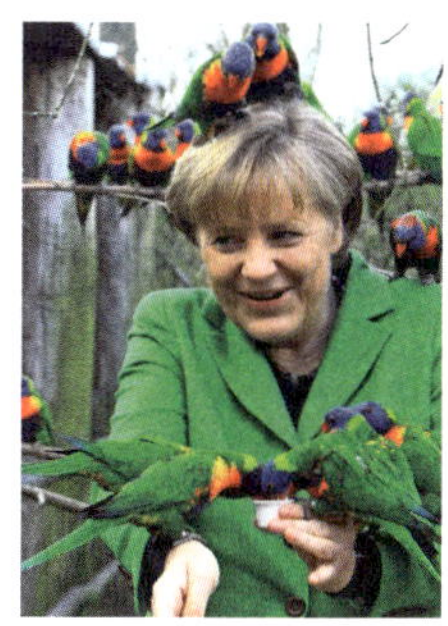
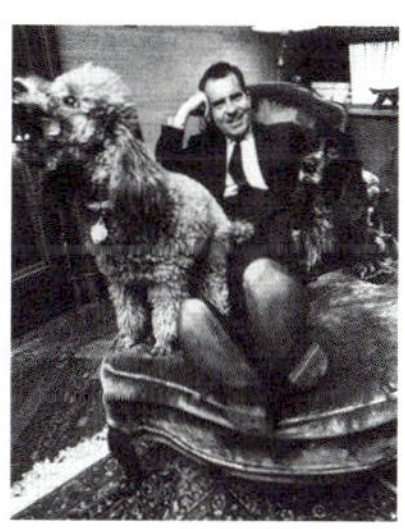
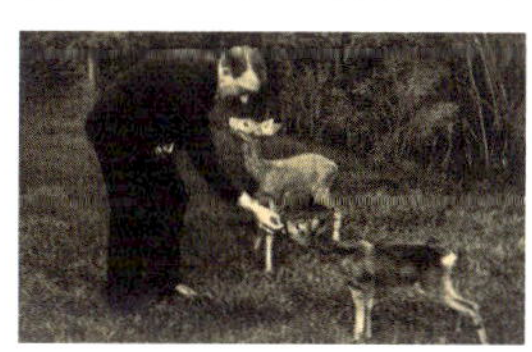
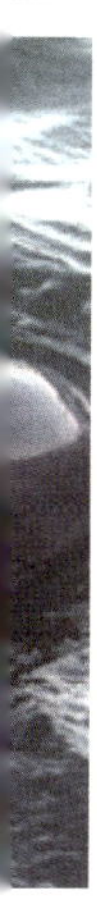
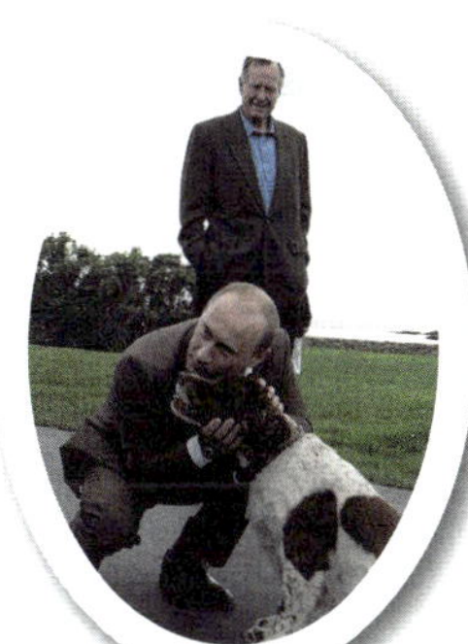
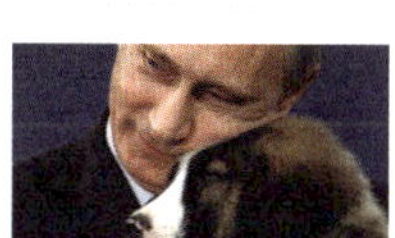
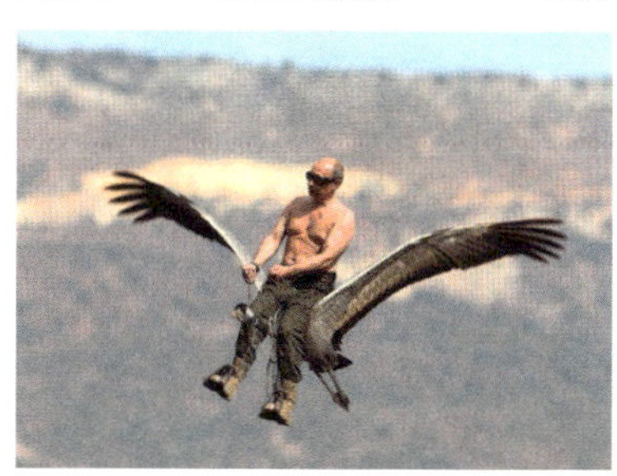

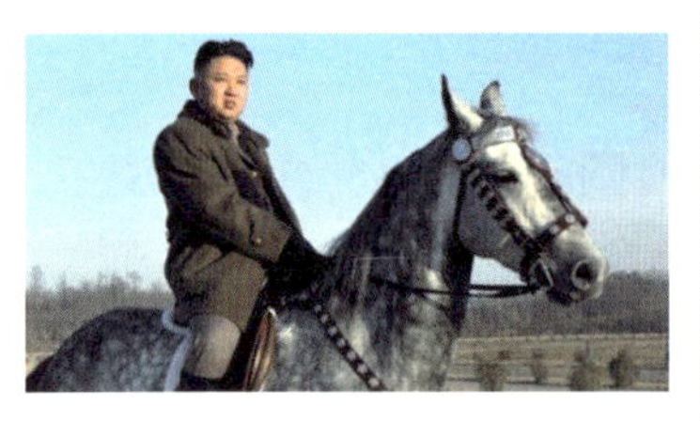

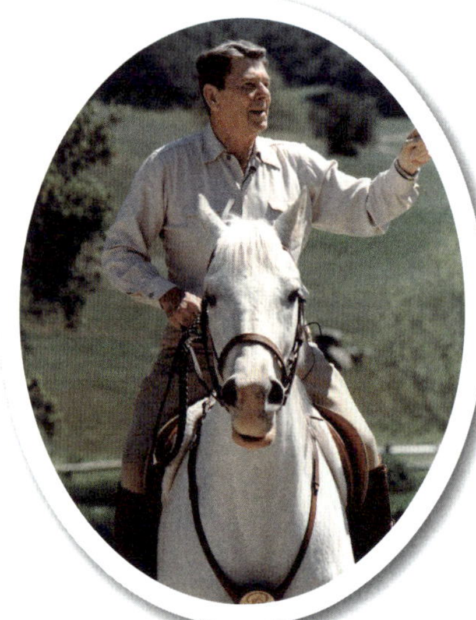

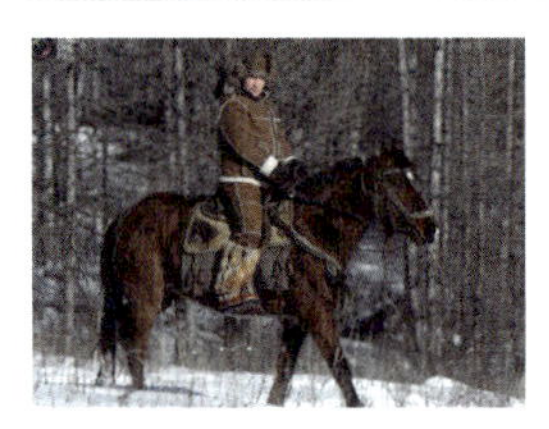

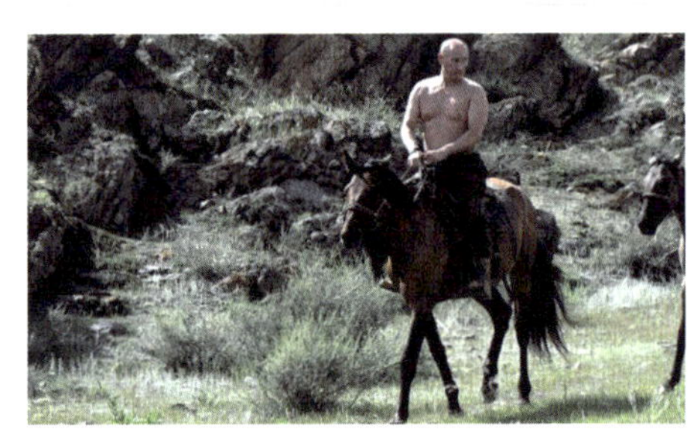

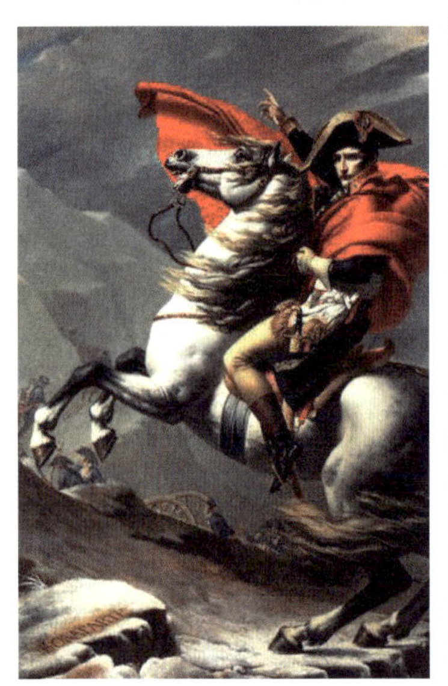

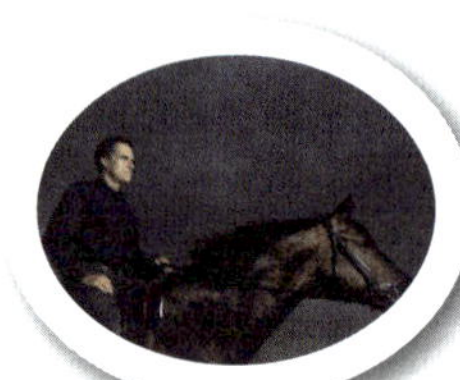

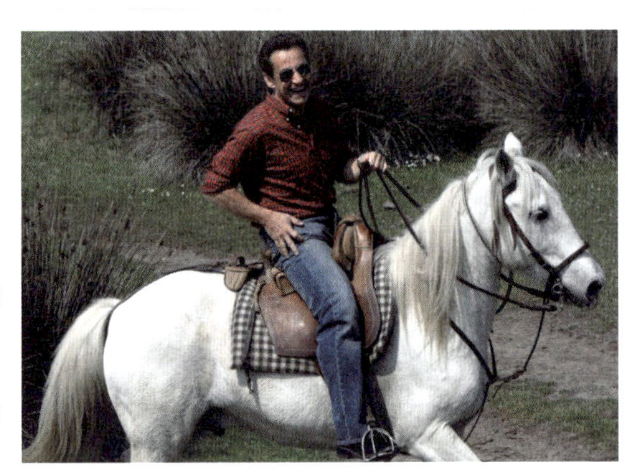

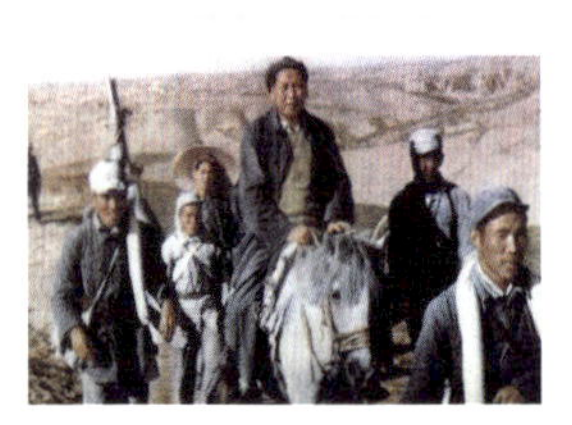

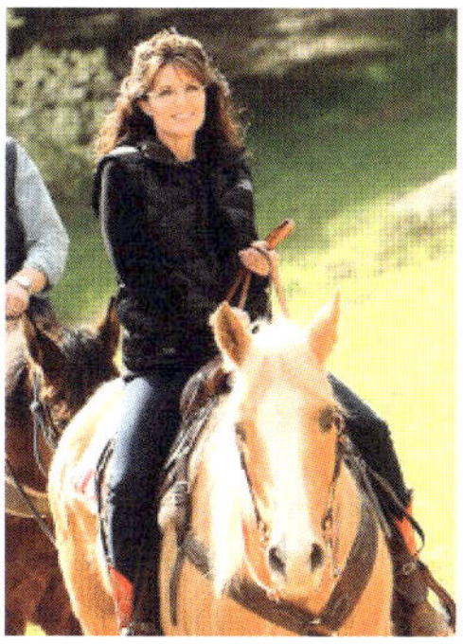

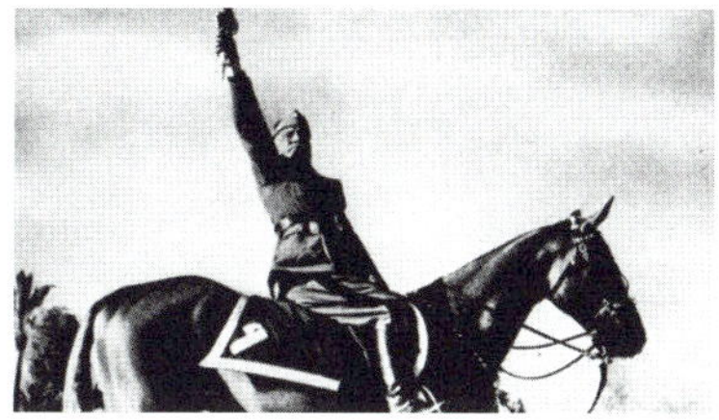

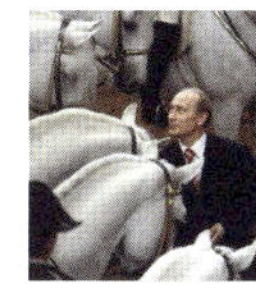

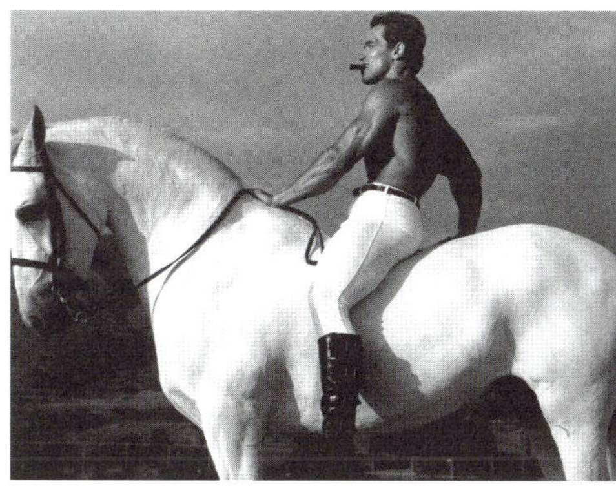

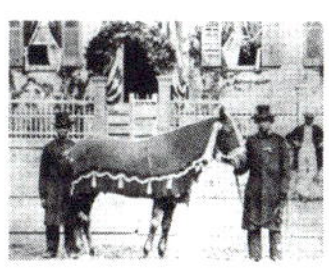

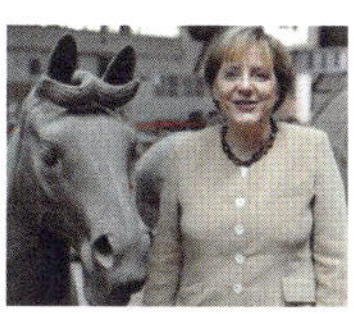

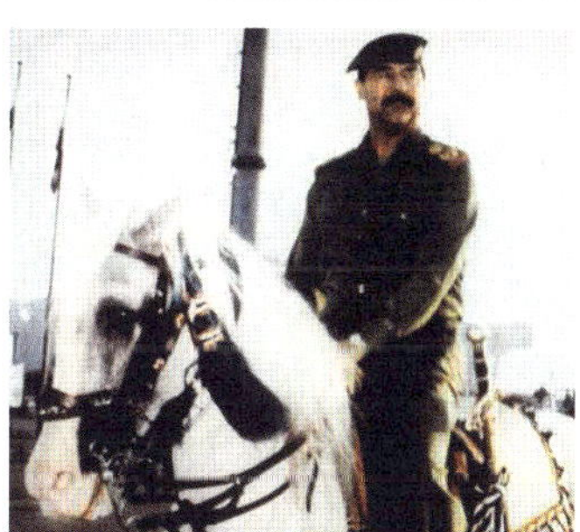

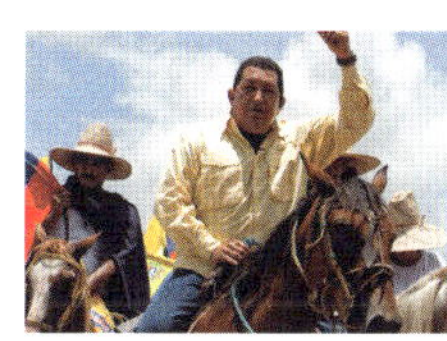

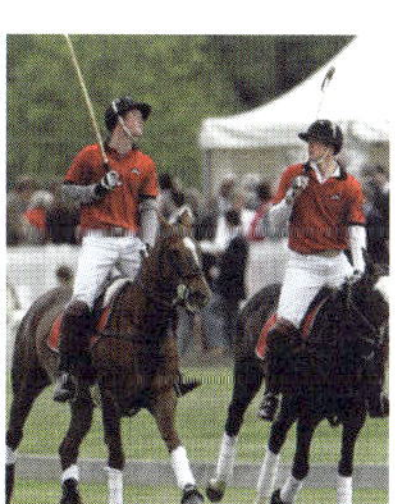

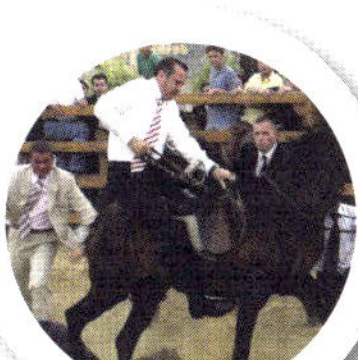

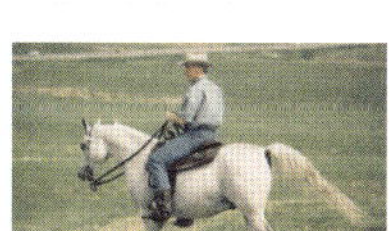

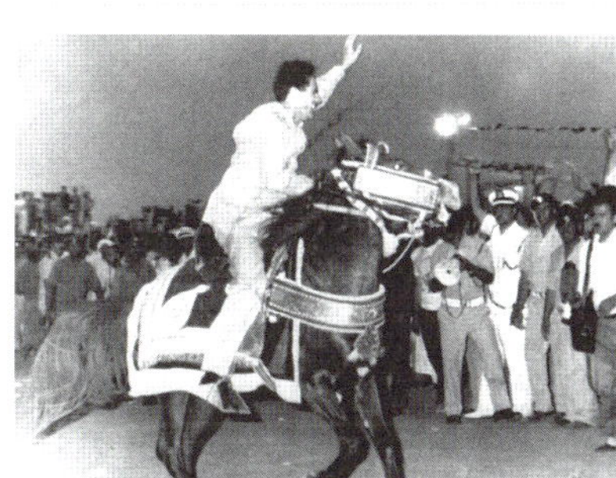

ST

Everything Must Go! An Approach to Contemporary Ceremonial Writings

Sébastien Thiéry

In the city, the subject is not particularly fashionable. It is anecdotal. As a matter of fact, it does not even arise. Issues related to the visual communication of local communities are allegedly nonexistent. Behind the images produced and peddled in the name of the city we inhabit there is supposed to be nothing but a simple mechanism, whose reasons have long been lost in administrative limbo. Individuals are all unconcerned as they pass by these barely noticed, hardly noticeable images, casting a glance at them that is of no importance. As a result, these signs, "logovilles" (or "city-logos," "branded cities") and municipal insignia arouse nothing more than a feeling of vast insignificance. Citizens quite naturally turn away from these objects that boast neither quality nor consequence, in order to aim higher and nurture their interest in politics by addressing more serious topics. In short, the visual communication of local communities is a trivial subject.

Inside the city, it is customary to address the subject while executing menial tasks, thereby conferring on logovilles a strictly instrumental value, a practical dimension. In offices, it is commonly believed that these visual elements provide at best a decorative dimension during the holidays. In their daily routine, municipal employees absentmindedly apply the same familiar sign at every turn, on envelopes and neatly prepared papers. Sometimes, however, an agent struck by some unspeakable thought manages to attribute to the object the power to attest. This revelation of a magical operation is undoubtedly ambiguous and testifies that, for the agent in question, something else is indeed taking place in the depth of the sign, beyond its banal usage. The municipal employee overcomes and fights such an impression; after all, these visual objects are no more than a simple administrative convenience, just a few details of color on a piece of paper whose importance lies elsewhere. Nothing decisive, as we know, could emanate from an object that is, all things considered, without mystery, and whose only requirement is to be efficient; in other words, distinct from the signs produced by neighboring organizations.

When it comes to the city, in the conferences of authorized professionals and in the graphic design studios where these objects are produced or "updated," people readily concede that the current standards tend to cause one to gag. In those contexts, it is in good taste to mention the poverty of these signs, which come from a long administrative—and hence reactionary—tradition. It is in good taste to mention the bland, plastic perfume of the contemporary logovilles invading our urban space, and to deplore, here an act of visual pollution, there a propaganda operation, but without availing oneself of the tools to measure the nature and extent of either problem. In any case, these signs are usually left alone and are rarely given full attention, maybe for fear of stirring their emanations and of encouraging their spread. People end up agreeing on the most unexciting features of the logoville: terribly institutional, sadly municipal, and definitely mundane.

In every corner of the city, everything leads us to dismiss logovilles and other public community communication campaigns. Everything discourages us from turning the problem into a major political issue. Move along, folks, there's nothing to see here! We invite ourselves not to face what is going on inside these signs, even though, far from disappearing, they remain or even proliferate, as testified—sometimes ad nauseam—by the documents gathered in the present book-document-manifesto. This is an opportunity then to reveal something that escapes our thoughts but takes hold of our eyes. In order to face up to it perhaps.

I. Staring at the Subject

We no longer make history. Therefore graphic designers think they are free in their art, that they, artists at work, are free to invent the very foundations of their own activity. As each generation re-elaborates its own mythology, they post on the door of their studios: "tradition, no admittance." Which kinds of knowledge can then be summoned to demonstrate that graphic designers are indeed playing with fire, as they grind up the signs that incarnate an institution? Nowadays, the eye keeps that obscure knowledge, that enigma (in the literal sense of the term) to itself, and we can no longer take it away from it. We can no longer believe our own eyes, and they know it. We are blind to what they see, and we boast such blindness as proof of our extreme modernity: we are free from any scabrous responsibilities, and all we perceive from our eyes' own testimony are indications of pleasure or displeasure.

In order to abandon blindness and grasp what is at stake, we must address the tradition that is our own, and admit that we are part of a heritage of craftsmen who, several centuries ago, used to produce *figuralia*—a scholastic term meaning "things that give shape, that mold." Since Roman antiquity, *figuralia* have taken the form of images and sculptures, engendered by institutions and addressed to everybody, with the aim of putting a face on references and identifying a common space. Placed under the eyes of all citizens, *figuralia* manifest "fathers and markers" (*pères* et *re-pères*), to paraphrase Lacan. Thus, the art of *figuralia* is based on a hidden know-how that makes graphic designers similar to lawyers, insofar as public images function as silent legislators. In our iconophile tradition, to work on the unique material of the images inspired by institutions through public procurement is indeed to touch the very heart and soul of the body politic.

Seals, those sovereign, masterfully engraved marks, are a recent reminiscence of these fantastic, seemingly otherworldly figures. Extraordinary and straightforward, the public image is literally sacred; that is, it remains an aloof presence and could never mingle with the world of individuals to which it is addressed. However, when "connected" to people by a form of rituality that is enacted, in particular, through seals and their social recognition, a public image literally pertains to religion, to *religere*. It is the locus of an emotional and political contract, the locus of the projection of the self as a participant in a historical community. Seals are evidence that a public power is at work, that the here and now is governed by a collective subject transcending the multiple interests of its constituting individuals. A loss is accrued at the exact point where we relate to these images: the loss of the fantasy of limitless power experienced by every individual. The seal is the face put on the boundary on which any collective adventure depends. To paraphrase Giorgio Agamben, the seal, hereby described as the imaginal component of the law, is at the heart of "the ceremonial and liturgical apparatus that has always accompanied" the Western political adventure (*The Kingdom and the Glory: Homo Sacer II*). It pertains to a theatrical know-how that, throughout this centuries-long political adventure, has produced the best and the worst.

The topic addressed here regards the problems faced by the designer of a public visual communication project, namely the problems pertaining to *figuralia* defined as fragments of the political arena. For the graphic designer, being on topic means addressing the question of how to give shape to a public space, a shape that should express the existence of a common good, since we find ourselves in a republic. It therefore means literally giving life to a subject that takes on a shape and a name in the form of a singular visual space that is at once common and exceptional—in other words, solemn. The confrontation with this subject leads to the formation of fellow citizens, contributors who share its name and face. Because the face of that public subject, by the magical operation of multiple rituals, obscurely resembles and therefore assembles them.

The accumulations of visual objects addressed in the present work translate our own detachment from the ritual requirements of *figuralia,* and our decline into a production of signs without mystery, as if they had been drained of what constituted their stature as otherworldly monuments—although they maintained that status, being elements of discourse that cannot be ascribed to a physical person. The conversion is perpetrated, the common face is disfigured: the city is a product like any other, its inhabitants are particles without a common address. Since the early 1980s, in France, the trend of logovilles has been steadily growing to such an extent that a considerable proportion of the 33,000 French communes have their own logo. The act of collecting and presenting in such a form these countless signs shows that the semantic poverty is equally radical in one and the other. Whether in small French communes or great European capitals, the strategies are marketing oriented and consider their public as "targets." Thus, depending on the audience to whom they are addressed, the images change in standing without changing their logic: contemporary programs of visual identity claim that there are no citizens, that is to say a group of subjects gathered within a common space of dissension, but rather only consumers conglomerated by the mechanical effect of a search for individual pleasure, comfort, material possessions, and leisure. The image is not addressed to a collectivity in what is properly "out of the ordinary" about it, but to each of us, in a would-be familiar and convivial proximity. Thus, the image invites us to form a society of "anybodies."

Through their programs of visual identity, cities battle one another on the field of competing signs, in the abstract universe of political marketing. In their striving to be "attractive," they explicitly confirm that what is at stake politically is precisely to attract, and that the logic of accounting lays down the law. Without any quality, singularity, or name, the city is, in the French term for a supermarket, a *grande surface* both literally ("a big surface") and figuratively (a *Wal*marts, as in the walled town of yore), designed to be as large as possible in order to attract masses—of workers, consumers, and investors. This dominant, unvarying logic produces identical images in that they express the same disastrous zeitgeist. In tune with the precepts of modern, upbeat marketing, images are presented in a palette of variations on the same theme of mass infantilization. The wholesale presentation of contemporary examples like Berlin, Bratislava, or even Madrid, testifies to the implacable nature of the project. In their capacity as "makers," graphic designers bear immense responsibility for this disaster, a responsibility that cannot be mitigated by the role of the commissioning agent: an art of resistance, inspired by the tradition of *figuralia,* should be constantly sprouting from graphic design studios, summoned to create what should not be created. Such an injunction, incidentally, presents the paradoxical characteristic of being cumbersome while remaining empty in terms of contents: the discourse of the commission has become largely insignificant and irrelevant, as if no one were actually voicing it. The subject has even vanished from the text of the commission specifications, which mechanically replays a marketing mindset applied to public affairs. Thus, the specs issued by a large French metropolis invite the graphic designer to produce a "logo that should give off enthusiasm and warmth, and take off from a quirky approach,... more marketing-like, in order to inspire warmth and loyalty."

Clearly then, local leaders consider their communities as products to be sold to individuals who, in turn, are regarded as user-consumers. From that point of view, the logo is one of the weapons put at the disposal of a political staff by a caste of professionals who, in the best schools of communication, learn the recipes for corralling human cattle through images. There is the ultimate refinement: programs of visual identity are easily implemented as "campaigns" and quite naturally are thought of in an event-related dimension as well. Thus, when the opportunity arises, major capitals conduct marketing operations that consist in re-inventing their brand as one would with an image produced during seasonal sales or for the launch of a new range of products. As a sign of the times then, the institutional image abandons the obsolete sheets of writing paper, to be thermal-glued on spin-off products and placed on aisle-end displays in supermarkets.

II. The Paradigm of Anonymity

The political arena is where the spin-offs of the sign-brand, conceptualized time and again by philosophers, is manifested: the aim of the sign, self-sufficient and entirely virtual, is no longer the consumption of the object it designates, but its very own consumption as a sign, thereby excluding from the symbolic exchange any manifestation of the reality it is supposed to designate. It is rather like wearing an "I Love NY" T-shirt without ever having been there: tourism becomes a simulacrum, and cities, like Hong Kong for instance, develop exactly like a brand and try to achieve substantial benefits through their image policy. This is what is at stake when branding is applied to cities, leading—as current events illustrate—to cities trademarking their own name as if they were brands. The shared awareness of the scattered consumers of the same brand becomes the ideal form of political sentiment.

When standing before the alluring sign that has been mass-produced by a dynamic institution, we face the desertion of the world, as underscored by Baudrillard and numerous other scholars. In such a game, which is no longer a secret, the communications manager plays the role of the ambitious product manager, but it is graphic designers who sell themselves as creators of a visual solution, depriving their profession a little more of the memory that once gave it its badge of honor. The sign is no longer mysterious: clear and uncomplicated, it is proclaimed like an acronym or a jingle, and signals the presence of something to be consumed with benefits, in pictures, something profitable. The nameless city offers distraction in exchange for a promising investment or, at least, for an expensive visit, and the graphic designer plays the role of the go-between.

The campaign developed by the city of Amsterdam definitely achieved a highpoint in terms of disasters. It combines the patterns of acronyms and jingles, the characteristics of a large brand operation, the so-called spin-off strategy, and the reference to a particular kind of modernity through its very obvious nod to the then unrivaled slogan "I Love NY." Maria Roszkowska's simple play on that iconographic universe makes us understand to what extent the image is marketing-inspired in its now classic version, that is to say in the version produced by major international brands; but it also shows how, at the end of the day, what might appear to be a radically Dutch campaign can be endlessly repeated and still function perfectly well.

However, by making the "I," that is, the "self" of the target-consumer, stick to the space of reference to the point of confusing them in the image that is placed there like a mirror, the campaign tells us something more: that the place left vacant after the explosion of the public subject is being filled by the multiple faces of the individuals who constitute the target-crowd and are placed in front of the silent image. On the one hand, what seems to be at play here is a height of indeterminacy, suggesting that the city is boundless, potentially extended over the entire world—in other words, constituted by the totality of individuals to whom it is addressed, just like any other multinational brand. On the other hand, the campaign demonstrates the narcissistic horizon of a company where everyone gazes at their own reflection in the space of reference and is connected to everyone else by the same condition of solitude, of being debased citizens invited to share the signs of power with the promise that they will also share its effectiveness. Potentially global, the community is constituted by an aggregation of solitudes. In these conditions, all that remains is the sad pleasure of consuming more and more, in an attempt to compensate for what is missing.

An anonymous entity, the city then develops according to a logic of a conglomeration of consumer-individuals deprived of any form of common space. But one need not go so far in one's search; the definitions have already found their way into the texts issued by the ministries, as in the case of the latest reference text issued by the French secretary of state in charge of city policy, a green paper that defines the city as "an urban unit comprising more than 2,000 conglomerated residents." Administrative language usually goes right to the point and, in this case, clearly expresses a logic of accounting applied to a cluster of bodies.

What in France we call a *métropole,* a metropolis, is probably the future form of that nameless city, in other words, a large-scale conglomeration without boundaries, whose extent depends on the development of urban consumerism: shopping zones surrounded by a proliferation of suburban houses. Then, whether in the sign that has become a brand or the territory that has become a zone, the political does not occur, and one can no longer speak of residents in terms of subjects constituting an urban community through their mutual confrontations within a common space; rather one speaks of "city users"—distinct individuals or groups using the city as a means of communication or as a commercial space.

The framework is no longer that of a city-producer (of languages, spaces, shapes, objects), with a face and a name in which we recognize ourselves, but that of a form of urban consumerism, in which citizens are invited to dissolve their identity to the point of reducing themselves to mere customers. In other words, the city is no longer written but develops, and graphic designers are summoned to contribute to increase the pace of such a development. Any other consideration will be perceived as a reactionary attitude.

Choosing to resist—this is what graphic designers might consider doing in the wake of such a document. To this aim, they should organize in the urban space an actual "vigil of memory," from which signs would have to be constantly reinvented or even reanimated. Such a vigil turns out to be the very basis of the political question facing graphic designers, whose mission should be to reactivate the enigmatic art of *figuralia,* those "things that give shape, that mold." In order to respond to the constant threat of the collapse of architectures of meaning.

9

Logotomized City (or Patrick Le Lay's Victory)[1]

Jean-Pierre Grunfeld

> If the signs vex thee,
> oh how the things signified shall vex thee more!
> RABELAIS, *The Third Book of the Heroic Deeds and Sayings of the Good Pantagruel*, 1546

> "On the day when I know all the emblems," he asked Marco, "shall I be able to possess my empire, at last?" And the Venetian answered: "Sire, do not believe it. On that day you will be an emblem among emblems."
> ITALO CALVINO, *Invisible Cities*, trans. William Weaver, 1972

Foreword: The Term "City"

Now that they are spread all over the world, a variety of radically different urban realities are called by the same name. Let us agree upon what we mean by "city."

During the Renaissance, a new way of accommodating groups of humans developed in the hills of Tuscany and the plains of Flanders. Citizens reinvented themselves as city dwellers. They created stone forms that were "masterful, correct, and magnificent,"[2] solid and void elements whose combination organized the choice between "public" and "private" spheres. They built upon the legacy of ancient Greek or Roman cities. They enriched such a legacy with new techniques and political visions. Everywhere in the well-off areas of the Northern Hemisphere these arrangements contributed to the advent of democracy and then to its consolidation. They did nothing to reduce political conflicts or social tensions. At certain points in history, they welcomed these conflicts in the form of barricades or the storming of the Bastille, celebrations of the people or triumphs of the aediles, the town officials. Monuments regularly accentuated these moments.[3] Kings lived in the city outskirts: Sans-Souci, Windsor, or Versailles.

The destiny of these cities is tied to a circumscribed geographical area and a short historical time span. Born in fifteenth-century Europe, confined until recently to the Northern Hemisphere, this urban form, the form of "our cities," is not reproduced on the entire planet.[4] Except for its colonial reproductions, that is. For centuries, this urban form has dominated and served as the model for human settlements all over the planet. It is now in a minority position.

The conurbations and metropolitan archipelagos taking shape in the poor areas of the Southern Hemisphere—whether "emerging" or not—are of a different nature. They are different in size, structure, and form. The same name cannot possibly apply to them. It is a misnomer to call "city" the juxtaposition occurring inside contiguous spaces in which tens of millions of destitute rural people find refuge.

As these people are chased from their arid countryside by even greater poverty, their countless forms of overcrowding sheltered by tents, planks, tires, or corrugated iron "do not a city make," far from it. Whether we are talking of vast slums or ever-expanding townships, the presence of a few rich neighborhoods, of a few air-conditioned, gleaming steel-and-glass towers at their center does not change the phenomenon. "Naming an object inaccurately means adding to the unhappiness of this world."[5] Despite piling up tens of millions of very poor people in the same space as a handful of extremely rich people, Lagos, Bombay, or Mexico City are not "cities." And it is uncertain whether they will indeed ever become such.[6]

As for the Western city, one cannot exclude that its peculiar urban form may be disappearing. Its virtues are much more vulnerable than what is suggested by the concrete, glass, and steel materials that have come to replace stone and brick. Its commodification is speeding up and increasing the risks of its own eclipse.

This is where the logo comes into the picture, contributing to the erosion of the sense of belonging. A city that has become a brand, reduced to the sole dimension of its own profitability, is a city in danger of perishing. At best (or worst), it can become a museum. Mass tourism, that "impossible voyage"[7] and great consumer of logos, has begun its work of undermining the city.

It is essential that we recall here the consubstantial links that connect, as they always have, the brands, their logos, and geopolitical and geostrategic violence, if we wish to describe their devastating effects on the city.[8]

To begin with, the transition from a humanity that was still predominantly rural less than fifty years ago to planetary urbanization has taken place suddenly, over a few decades.[9] In Europe, the young men fighting World War I were mostly farmers, just like the young Texans or Midwesterners who landed in Normandy thirty years later. In 2012, consigned to their neighborhoods by unemployment, drug dealers live, fight, and die in the planet's megacities.

Young executives, those fast-paced nomads of the world, live in their high-security villas, a stone's throw from the *favelas*, townships, and ghettos. In these common geographies, the signs of territorial ownership—logos—recount and emphasize class differences.[10] Slums, inner cities, or gated communities, ghettos for the poor or for the rich,[11] all of these—often adjoining—urban spaces constitute new theaters of operation. Technological revolutions, urban revolutions, and revolutions go hand in hand.[12] The city is the privileged venue for displaying the signs that accompany and celebrate these revolutions. Until recently, the city limited itself to accepting them under rather strict rules of occupation.

In France, everything changed in the 1980s. A paradigm shift or "upgrade," as they call it today. My generation called it an "epistemological break." [13] Elected local authorities, fascinated by money, subordinated policy considerations to economic ones. A meeting with a couple of shameless admen is all it took. Together, they came up with the following syllogism: the city (or an idea, a party...) is a product, it must sell itself; advertising helps to sell products: therefore, the city must resort to advertising. The ineffable, Rolex-sporting, ad executive Jacques Séguéla persuaded a histrionic politician that his city was "exceptionally gifted." [14] Twenty years later, after spending millions of euros on the creation and promotion of a city logo, the unemployment rate "remains higher than that of comparable conglomerations." [15]

Of course, commodification devotees can repeat the refrain that the other conglomerations had better logos. If only the phenomenon were happy to be inept and harmless, merely destined to feed a few uneducated graphic designers from local firms or international agencies, paid by gullible or lenient elected officials... Unfortunately, the help given to the process of commodification, that is, to the disappearance of a well-defined and fragile artifact (the city), produces deleterious, possibly irreversible effects.

As soon as cities or territories (districts, regions, countries) start claiming to be products to be sold on the market, they logically adopt the attributes of brands. What are the effects, the ravages of these impositions of symbolic violence on such vulnerable systems of human settlement?[16] Cities and capitalism have entered an era of virtual exchange. The struggles are changing their medium, and the fractures their nature. They are shifting to the rights and means of digital access.[17] It is less a matter of material ownership over these new technological objects than access to the "culture" that allows one to master them.

This points up the importance of the transition that is shifting the city from the role of a sparing receptacle for the signs of commodity to the commodity itself. The process of transmutation of the city into a brand makes use of a major weapon: the logo. The brand, the logo, and their later roles have their own genesis, their own history. What follows is a concise attempt to disassemble the weapon.

The Logo As a Weapon of War

Since its inception, the brand has been inextricably linked to war. And since its inception, the logo has been conceived and used in categories associated with conflict and belligerence. In this respect it is radically different from the symbol that unifies and connects.[18] The logo expressed, demonstrated, and ensured an affiliation—to a clan, a tribe, a belief, a territory. The uniform (livery) bore a logo (coat of arms) to show one's affiliation to a group or reveal one's exclusion from the community (the yellow badge of the *rouelle,* then the yellow star of David). When the individual moved to a different community through upward mobility (ennoblement) or betrayal (changing sides, turning one's coat), they took on a different sign, and became a different person. We are familiar with the terrible image of the degradation of Captain Dreyfus, his stripes and medals ripped from his jacket, his sword broken. Only then does his conviction become visible.

As a sign of distinction, the logo was initially incarnated in the literal sense of the term, worn on the naked body, i.e., scarifications, tattoos, or make-up. Adversaries or rivals faced each other in duels. There was no possible confusion when men squared off in "single" combat. All that was required were the signs of affiliation to the respective clan of each champion (herald or hero). Achilles' shield vs. Hector's armor.[19]

As combats increased in complexity, and as the planning of war operations started involving the strategic cooperation of large, organized collectives, the discipline of signs could no longer be avoided. For the sake of the survival of a Roman maniple or century, uniforms and emblems, brands and logos made their first appearance. It was necessary to recognize and be recognized by your own horde, gang, or troop. Identifying signs and passwords.

There was the superiority of the Roman legion's system of signals and its eagles over the Gallic tribes. The moustache, if it was ever sported by the Gauls at all (which is uncertain), was a collective feature that was too low in intensity. The Gauls lost for lack of a rallying sign.

The Logo As an Act of Faith

It wasn't long before acronyms and logos won their first battle. In 312 AD, the day before a battle, the pictograph of a hideous instrument of torture, the cross, appeared in the sky above Emperor Constantine. Add a slogan and you are all set: *In Hoc Signo Vinces. IHS:*[20] two thousand years later it still works. From these inaugural moments, the whole structure of the system of creation was there. A complex thought and word were reduced to their simplest possible expression. An elementary icon summed up the idea. A simplistic, effective image ended up replacing the concept. Too complicated. Summarize, summarize, there will always be something left. No more reason, no critical thought: Pavlovian reflexes and reptilian brains are sufficient.

That helps when one wants to divert or deny the message. A handful of centuries later, the dealers of the Christian brand and its Catholic subsidiary waved their logo of mercy in the face of the tortured and the maimed, at the foot of the stakes and gallows. Jews, witches, and relapsed saints who burn well and burn bright must be given one last chance to join the group (or Salvation, as it was called). Freethinkers moaned while they were being thrashed or broken on the wheel—the logo would take care of their souls. If anyone refused to swallow the idea and adore the object, the logo would be their last vision, with the horrific impossibility of changing channels.[21]

The Logo in the Fray

The long-term establishment of the necessity and role of the summarizing sign dates back to the first forms of conscription.

At the Battle of Bouvines, yokels on foot accompanied their lords, who rode on horseback protected by the anonymous steel of their armor. In order to avoid striking their own masters, serfs needed to recognize them quickly and clearly.[22] Immediately identifiable signs had to be worn on top of breastplates. This is when visual techniques of form reduction and color brilliance were developed; in other words, heraldry. Heraldry catalogues anticipated dictionaries of logos. The savagery, subservience, and stupidity required for the compression of forms and limitation of sense quickly found their department of research and development on the battlefields. From the oriflammes of Agincourt to the flags of Verdun, not a few have died under the logos of their motherlands.

Those times of chaotic brawls, when the sign unequivocally designated friend or foe, handed down to us the basics of the polemic vocabulary still used by advertisers nowadays: campaigns, targets, and strategies...

In the merciless wars waged by products and their lords, Citroën (André) vs. Peugeot (Jean-Pierre), Apple (Steve) vs. Microsoft (Bill), Coca-Cola vs. Pepsi, Adidas vs. Nike, logos are like projectiles, and their virtues are measured by their capacity to infiltrate our shattered consciences.

Later still, competing oil companies applied the same tricks to their first gas stations. Red circle or yellow shell, drivers must barrel toward the sign. No need to understand, all you needed to do was salivate. With its *armes parlantes,* or canting arms,[23] heraldry invented and perfected the play on words and images that admen took up in the 1920s. The shell designated the name of the fuel,[24] just as a grass snake (*coluber* in Latin) designated the acquired nobility of the French family Colbert.

The Logo and the Temperature of Wars

After the "heat" of the deadly world wars, the signs used in the "cold" rivalries of universal commodification were put in the service of fierce competition. Of course, one should be glad that economic wars do not systematically turn into armed conflicts. There is no doubt that the transition from physical to symbolic violence considerably reduced human losses and suffering. Such a relief is short-lived. The "peaceful" transition from hot reality to cold virtuality converts the modes of exercising brutality, delays or dilutes their consequences. Competition continues to kill, but at a distance, through images and shows. Coldly, slyly.

New missions are then given to the logo. With the cold, products are no longer the heroes. They give way to corporations. The idea is to create "brand worlds," more extended in space and time. To inspire trust and sympathy towards an institution cleared of its profit objectives, a "citizen enterprise."

The company transcends and incorporates any seasonal object—whose obsolescence is planned—in order to foster a kind of patriotic or religious fervor. The logo no longer suggests what you should have, but indicates who you should be. The consumer is Coke or Pepsi, Apple or Microsoft, Nike or Adidas, Mercedes or Honda... The logo is the mark of a style, a way of life, a culture.

These planetary strategies of war, in which brands replace nations (Apple the American against Samsung the Korean), are more insidious but no less intense. The invasion of brands and their logos precedes and consolidates political wins and losses. McDonald's, Coke, and Levi's certainly did more to bring down the Berlin Wall than diplomacy or ideological discourses. Desires of consumerism, kindled by logos, take over imaginations and territories, pioneers of dreams of freedom. Initially they are undoubtedly less deadly than tanks. Later on, they prove quite useful to focus desires and frustrations on products and objects and away, far away, from politics. This is called alienation.

The conquest of the eyes, hearts, and urges prepares territorial occupation and consolidates protectorates. There is no empire without a triumph of the logo.

The Diluted Logo

It is no small paradox that, in our new, increasingly global and imperialistic systems of identity, the logo plays a diminished role. In order to impose a brand world, more universal categories must be preempted. What is the logo of Coca-Cola today? The signature, the white-on-red ideogram which can be seen deep into the townships? The shapely bottle? Or, more generally, the color red? According to Frédéric Beigbeder, who knows all too well the hand he is biting, the rival company Pepsi went with the latter hypothesis and intends to trademark the color blue.[25]

More seriously, the maneuvers concealed behind the euphemizing tactics of the creation of new logos must be looked at carefully.

Gaz de France, formerly a public utility, was bought by the Suez group, then gradually replaced with the brand Dolce Vita. Under this new flag, the fight can be taken to any and every front: prices can be raised, the old core activity can be abandoned for more rapidly lucrative ones, and so on. The former water company Compagnie générale des eaux, now disguised as Vivendi or Veolia, can become a transport group or an audiovisual production society. The French public administration Postes télégraphes et téléphones—"PTT" when I was a child—has been privatized and dismembered to become La Poste, then Banque postale, France Telecom, then Orange. As the company shows increasing reticence in respecting its public service obligation of delivering mail, it can tackle banking activities. Under its unremarkable color and appellation, the "traditional" telephone operator can "diversify its activities" by creating pay-per-view television channels. All these manipulations are accomplished with the help of visual systems that tend to appropriate a few universal invariables. A constant in terms of identity must be as stable as the products are ephemeral. By becoming more abstract—more "conceptual"—brands and logos place themselves at the service of unmentionable realities. There are many suicides "at Orange."

Banque postale attempts to trademark the blue and yellow of its logo, in competition with LCL (the camouflage dissimulating the former Crédit lyonnais bank, plagued by worldwide insolvency). In these maneuvers, whether big or small, the logo is restricted to the accompanying role of a typographic auxiliary. Precious, but no longer vital.

In order to establish an unverifiable legitimacy, which sells better than any measurable performance, commercial companies disguise themselves as free institutions. Public interest becomes a mask for private interest. Acts of sponsorship are marked by logos. In turn, due to cost cutting, public institutions dream of becoming companies and brands. They resort to visual stratagems. Doctoring the books and codes are accomplished thanks to the disguises made possible by *costumes graphiques,* or "graphic outfits," like criminals dressing as policemen to commit a hold-up.

The Invading Logo

Which one is more worrisome: the profusion of mediocre signs invading the public space and penetrating the innermost intimacy of private spaces—a profusion vertiginously multiplied by the performance of "new" technologies—or their increasingly overbearing character in the service of global consumerism? How can one resist the invasion of commercial signs in every sphere of human thought and activity? How can one stop these signs from reducing humanity to its mere capacity for economic absorption?

For this is the major negative comment—yet by far not the only one—that can be addressed to this system of intrusion and interference: it dictates codes and imposes fashions. It includes or excludes according only to solvency criteria. Without financial and/or cultural capital, no salvation possible! Signs besiege, images assign. Of course, merchants, alongside their henchmen and lackeys, "symbol manipulators,"[26] do protest that this is not so.

Global affluence and rivalries, with their pervasive pictorial representations, ensure the freedom of consumers worldwide. The perspective of the "free fox in the free henhouse."[27] The dominant class can always find a few dominated to bribe in order to improve the aesthetics of their ascendancy and gild their opium pills. The logos are the excipients. When the product is God, the logo becomes its prophet.

Very early on, a communication expert admitted that "if you tell a lie big enough and keep repeating it, people will eventually come to believe it."[28] The advice is not lost on "wealth creators": the globalization of capital can happen only through the endless multiplication of the logo and its ever-multiplying iterations.

The Logo in the Net

With the emergence of ICT,[29] the swift improvement in the technical means for the spread of lies and stimulations allows a triumphant capitalism to strengthen a process of exponential growth.[30] One cannot overestimate the effects of these acts of "symbolic violence,"[31] committed for the sake of establishing a worldwide system. Local accents and vernacular cultures are not welcome in the midst of economic and ideological frays. Brands and their logos provide the semantic logistics of a vast enterprise[32] of euphemization and reification of human relationships.

The process is not new. From the day it was born, the gas of capitalism expanded to fill all the available economic space by any possible means. The caravels and carracks of Columbus, Vasco de Gama, or Magellan, marked by the logo of the cross, occupied the whole known world. Gold, spice, and silk trade, icon business. Murder of the Aztec eagle, destruction of the temples. On ruins and in the dread of silences that are still with us, in the heart of colonial cities, the winners established a network of churches and cathedrals, gas stations of the One True Faith. Before becoming the logo of a range of merchandise (mugs, ashtrays, T-shirts, scarves, caps...), the

Union Jack used to wave over a savagely exploited empire. All of this temporarily ends with the two worldwide butcheries of the twentieth century. The iron cross vs. the star-spangled banner and the red flag, the swastika vs. the hammer and sickle.

At the time, nations had not yet entrusted their power to global companies. After the fall of the Wall and the end of the Cold War, the brands took over. The global freeze of nuclear terror was followed by a multitude of local conflicts. Behind each and every one of them, we find competing economic interests. The method has not changed. Thousands of poor people (in the South) engage in mutual massacre without even knowing each another, for the profit of a few rich people (in the North) who know each other all too well.[33]

Benefits and dividends fight behind masks. It is the death of ideologies and great narratives. The storytelling of companies and their bosses serves as the specifications for logos.

Religions come back to life in their most intolerant forms. Extremisms need recognition. Here comes the revival of the three main logos of the monotheisms at war: crescent vs. cross, star of David vs. crescent. World traders are quite comfortable with these distant massacres, on the margin of ideas, confined to the outskirts of the world. *Business as usual* and *Coca-Cola über alles.*

"Puvate and Priblic"[34]

In the context of globalization and of the frenzy of exchanges that accompanies and nourishes them, the "public" and "private" spheres[35] have long stopped being airtight. In their transition from the "graphosphere" to the "videosphere,"[36] interpenetration and confusion undergo new developments. Identical spaces and architectural structures accommodate the same social classes as they roam the planet. In a world that is being covered by "non-places,"[37] where "class struggle is becoming place struggle,"[38] the signs of control, guidance, and affiliation proliferate.

In the suburbs of the world, I am never sure whether I can recognize my own house, pavilion, and shack. I need to improvise a few moderate signs, my own brand. I am never sure whether I can tell my supermarket from the others: the same logo over the same boxlike store. I can no longer tell whether I am in Paris, New York, Johannesburg, or Tokyo. I drive to the same Apple Store in the same rented car, before driving back to the same room in the same hotel chain, reached from the same airport to get on the same plane.

The same bar code, the same magnetic stripe, the same microchip grant access to the same privileges—or deny it: discrimination strategies of credit or subscription cards, Platinum, Gold, Silver...

If I fail to have the right signs, I face non-differentiation and indifference. Without a few discreet signs, I no longer know where I am: I am indeed *Lost in Translation.*[39] The logos come to my rescue and take me back to my familiar, recognizable spaces, as a willing prisoner of my own system of signs. Universal "logotomy": if I have the right image, I can keep deluding myself that I am the one watching Big Brother.

Branded Cities, Branded Bodies

Advertising cannot be exempted from the eroticization of bodies and the degrading representation of the female body. The logo cannot be acquitted of both carving deep into the flesh and intruding into the skin of cities. The same movement connects tats and tags, bodies covered with tattoos and the walls covered with graffiti. For fashion victims, sporting a logo on their clothes or accessories is not enough, not anymore. Too ephemeral, too distant from the skin, not intense enough. The act of possession must be made permanent, integration must be incarnated. Twenty years ago, ornamental pins were sufficient. Worn on jackets, caps, or lapels, they indicated the affiliation and conformity of taste of their owners. The logo of a French antiracist NGO, featuring a tiny yellow hand, was one of the stars of the those days. Anxiety has increased with the fear of losing one's job, home, life. We are no longer sure that our affiliation to a group is durable. So we embrace the logo, we eat it as if it were the communion bread of a new era.

Anxiety of territorial dispossession plagues the prisoners of our inner cities. Beyond the belt highways and bypasses live the tribes of insolvent consumers. Logos no longer bring enough notoriety and benefits to their brands. Excluded from luxury consumerism, banned from the places with a high concentration of logos—the Champs-Elysées, for instance—deprived of their territory, poor people in city outskirts create their own brands and logos. Those to whom nothing is given must conquer each sign, even if this means invading the centers where branded objects are plentiful.

The longing for spatial ownership is expressed by marking the spaces that one will never possess. This is the main reason for graffiti tags or drawings, the self-produced logos of the destitute.

The wretched inhabitants of the city, secluded in its marginal outskirts, fashion-deprived, with their truly tired bodies, search for the shapes of their dreams in order to gain an acceptable identity. The logos are inscribed on their walls and into their skins.

Institutions are unsure about the attitude to take when facing such a tide of signs of existence and territorial possession. I once attended a council meeting whose agenda included the purchase of a graffiti-cleaning machine and a grant for an exhibition of "street art"—a demagogical formula by which elected authorities and "community organizers" think they can buy civic peace. Eventually, both initiatives were approved.

After decorating costumes and designating cities, today logos are incorporated. Absorbed by the same process of reification, cities and individuals become logos. This happens at the price of forced banalization. An identical sign is endlessly repeated: the same body,[40] the same profile, the same skyline. Global anorexic thinness, the towers of every city center on earth, built by the same ten architects, all winners of the same Pritzker Prize, all dressed in the same black uniform. The planners of the planetary city travel in the same planes—in the same first-class cabins—with the top models of planetary fashion.

The Era of the "Brandosaurus"[41]

After the end of the Soviet Bloc and the emergence of BRICS countries, especially after China's transition to state capitalism, a special welcome was extended to ICTs. The city is the set of planetary television.

It becomes the privileged venue for the great maneuvers of the triumphant stage of capitalism. At regular intervals, and with increasing frequency, cities, traders, and logos intermingle in furious orgies.

The logo-city welcomes logo-people. For the length of a planetary show, the city prostitutes itself to the brands displayed on sculpted and doped bodies. A super-logo and a ghastly mascot are created for the occasion. In 2012, London's city planning advertised the long-term impact of its evolution due to its hosting the Olympics. And yet, by the IOC's own admission, a group of about ten brands—the main sponsors, whose investments must be ensured—dictate the organization of the spaces and the behaviors therein. One can imagine the joy and pride of the workers of the steel plants of

Gandrange and Florange as they contemplate their owner running in the streets of London, carrying the Olympic flame, wearing a white tracksuit with the logo of the Games. They must be even more proud to know that he is building a tower named after himself, almost after them.[42] The brands of investors are printed in the flesh of the new global gladiators: the chests of billionaire football players and buttocks of doped-up bicycle racers.[43] The televised close-ups on their sweat and blood enhance the color of their logos.

Sandwich-board athletes show off their muscles inside stadiums named after insurance or airline companies.[44] Admen and agents of "top-level athletes," the new *lanistae,* trainers and managers of contemporary gladiators, sell the television rights: pumped up biceps and pain under the magnifying glass of the camera. Then, for a moment of glory, an instant of victory, the best looking among the medal winners directly promote the brand. Sponsors analyze the media spin-offs and turn a profit on investment returns.

Only laws of exception can temporarily keep the brands at bay from the space of world television,[45] or banish them from the historic sites protected by "rankings." In order for the signs to subside, you had better be on UNESCO's World Heritage List. And even that may not be enough!

Logos for Life

As one can see, the transition from physical rivalry to brand competition brings along with it peaceful connections. The side effects of this pacification through aesthetics are worth considering. A reflection on how brands invade the city—understood as the space of both everyday life and politics—cannot be isolated from the analysis of how they impose their presence on our private lives.

Brands infiltrate our bodies and souls from our early childhood. Videos in maternity wards: milk producers and laboratories are on the lookout.[46] Back to school: all the children, in their early alienation, demand that their parents provide them with the appropriate signs of group affiliation. This injunction is renewed every year by the commandments of fashion and the diktats of marketing. The anorexic figure of teen models, the perfect, hairless skin of the heartthrobs of the moment... the parade of standardized happiness is repeated every season.

The dictatorship of style requires updating one's wardrobe at an increasing rate, reaching a peak during clearance sales. Household objects and their integrated obsolescence lose their function and establish themselves as status symbols. Cars are a "way of life." The price is of no importance, as long as you own the brand, the only one, the right one: the latest.

Such an endless flow of unnecessary injunctions addressed to the body is all the more irritating as it happens in parallel with a desertion of everyday life and its uses. One should analyze the list of the places and situations from which the signs of quality, useful signs, are absent. This is the most subtle and violent way of exercising power. In the name of a false virtuousness, dominant structures let the dominated struggle in a jungle of badly designed forms, obscure signage, incomprehensible acronyms, anonymous logos...
What an expression of seriousness and economy: the poverty of signs adds to the signs of poverty.

Our most valuable documents—those regarding our own identity—bear logos of low birth indeed. Passports, residence permits, driving licenses, and family record books are unlikely to present any sign of modernity. Oldness becomes a form of arrogance, ugliness is deliberate, neglect is premeditated: the only spaces where typographic excellence—including logos—would be dutiful, have been deserted by it. The problem reaches its most grotesque and dangerous form in workplace safety posters.

In a word, all that concerns lives, desire, Eros (the insolvable) is abandoned for the morbidity of accounting calculations and financial interests. Merchandise and its selfish glaciations are warmed up by the servility of signs.

The Distinctive Logo

The logo functions as a sign of exclusion as well as affiliation. It embodies Sartre's formula "Hell is other people." [47] Commoners, forbidden to bear a sword and go by horse, could not exhibit their coats of arms, were prohibited symbols, and excluded from the "house." Grade-schoolers stamp their feet in front of supermarket shelves. Their parents are summoned to buy the designer object of the moment, terrified by the risk of exclusion. In the playgrounds, only the signs of conformity ensure integration within the group, "the guys," and access to "compliant happiness." [48]

Logos allow you to join a restricted group, whose very existence implies the visible discrimination of another, differently branded—or, even worse, naked—clique. Thus, health ministers assume that banishing logos will lead to a refusal to buy cigarettes. End of the love saga between Raymond Loewy and Lucky Strike: in 1940, Georges Washington Hill, the "legendary King of Tobacco and one of the giants of corporate America," paid Raymond Loewy $50,000 to redesign the brand. By 1952, more than fifty billion of the newly designed packages had been sold.[49]

The same goes for the "fashion-within-fashion" mechanism of collectors. Planetary logos generate affiliations that are too vast, too indistinguishable. A few minimal shifts in color or shape, a spiced-up logo, and *voilà,* for a season, the brand, the trademark makes it into a more exclusive club. The club rules according to Groucho Marx: "I don't care to belong to any club that will have me as a member."[50]

We find the same double contradiction in the logo. Designed to rally, it serves to exclude; designed to set something off, it *indifferentiates.* The deliberate poverty of the plastic vocabulary reduces the number of possible combinations. Thus, overlaps become inevitable and analogies proliferate, thereby eliminating the differences. If we observe a plate showing, in alphabetical order and on the same scale, a series of a hundred or so logos created to identify sport shoes, sodas, political parties, cities, regions, what have you, it is impossible to tell what these logos represent without looking at the captions.[51] All of these "visual identities" launched only to achieve so much anonymity!

The Logo-City

For French territories, cities, and regions, heraldry's return to grace dates back to the "Révolution nationale" of Vichy. From 1941, mayors and prefects appointed by the Vichy regime assigned a blazon to their municipalities. The coats of arms of cities and provinces (the departments were overlooked, due to their disreputable revolutionary origins) preceded and prepared the arrival of logos in the 1970s. Most of these coats of arms had been ordered to "update" an approximate historical expression. The aim was to adapt it to contemporary times, which is to say to remove it from history (half-baked as it may be) and take it into the wonderful world of competition.

The 1970s saw the inception of a planetary process that transformed services, ideas, and cities into merchandise, ipso facto subjecting them to the same treatment tested on detergents and Coca-Cola.[52]

Forty years later, everything seems to indicate that the process was successful. Political parties, universities, hospitals, public transportation, museums—not one domain of the public sector, the ideas or the exercise of democracy, all formerly exempted from trivial commercial concerns, was left untouched. Generosity or calculation, profit or donation, writer or football player, university or grocery store, hospital or department store: every moral value has become a brand, every public service has been transformed into a slogan and logo.

This vast enterprise of introducing free products on the market and confusing values takes place in the shadow of logos. It is accompanied by a necessary mechanism of banalization and euphemization. A normality, a normalization of names: "The cathedral, the triptych, the opera aria, turned into 'resource deposits' for an improbable 'leisure industry,' would become the signs of that insidious technocratic barbarism, which comes directly from the practice of concentration camps."[53]

While enterprises try to achieve an increasingly controversial legitimacy by becoming "citizens," political authorities are frantically racing towards "corporate logic." Car manufacturers and their advertising agents are selling ways of life as well as historical and human depth, while territories are aping 1980s commercials by turning into brands. They lack both the economic and intellectual resources to do so. No matter, the fantasized models of "corporate management" implemented by politicians who, for the most part, have never set foot in a production structure, become the ultimate ratio for the promotion of cities.

The Disarmed Eye, Illiterates in Power

This raises the question of the competences and skills of elected authorities, local civil servants, high-level bureaucrats, tiny agents with the authority and power to command and decide.

In France, at no point in the curriculum are students taught the skill of reading signs. Just a little in primary school, nothing in secondary and high school, and even less in the institutes of higher education, where tomorrow's deciders are trained. On the one hand, an illiterate person cannot be blamed for being unable to decipher a text. On the other, one wouldn't dream of making him or her the editor of an official journal. However, this is precisely the case of public deciders, "visual imbeciles" armed with nothing but their own taste to impose signs on the public space. All the power and no knowledge.

It is worth noting that the teaching of signs still has an "artistic" status (graphic design, typography, photography, and so on) and is dispensed in the schools of fine arts. No postgraduate program, no pathway to universities, no equivalence, no research. French manipulators of symbols are relegated to "artistic" positions, unlike in Italy or the United States, where the training is clearly academic. This guarantees no ideological independence, only a minimum cultural standard. It also proves that it is possible to achieve an adult relationship between the public contracting parties and the designers of signs. The surreal dialogue between visually illiterate backers and ignorant professionals is not inevitable.

Pseudo-studies, as expensive as they are useless, serve as an alibi for judgments of taste. As for assessing the mechanisms and effects of images, words, signs, and their combinations, the task is assigned to polling institutes. Falsely scientific, truly scientistic, these institutes are as high-handed as they are incompetent.[54] Their role is to persuade advertisers—and sponsors—that their investment is worthwhile, and to consolidate the power of agencies.

Covered by state-of-the-art ideological umbrellas, brands and logos can thus "prove" their efficiency. Unsurprisingly, they have no difficulty in conquering territories that are suffering and going through an identity crisis.

The Imposed Logo

The last thing to be advertised for sale is public space itself, the territorial collectivity (country, region, department, and city). The French Republic is branded "France," the capital of Alsace becomes "Strasburg the Europtimist,"[55] its university "Unistra," and the rival university is called "UPEC" (Université Paris-Est Créteil). Designed by a territorial marketing agency, the brand "Bretagne" (Brittany) was launched the same year.[56]

"Territorial marketing" has become an academic branch, glorified by business schools and taught in poli-sci. An old swindler's trick: whitewashing through respectability.

This pseudoscience accompanies capitalism in its crazy phase. In that out-of-control spiral, visual stridence alone can stand out in the cacophony found at the hearts of cities. Times Square as the visual archetype of urbanism, the POS promotion of global finance: flicker of neon signs and stock market scrolls.

Brand owners and logo designers know it well: the urban space is the ideal venue for affixing signs from which no one can escape. They know that the "captive" consumers of their dreams (ah, the housewife under fifty!) have developed effective defense and avoidance strategies. The presence of brands and logos on the dominant media is endangered by the possibility of channel surfing. The show goes to a commercial break and off the victims rush to the bathroom! Worried, the TV host implores, "Do not leave! Stay tuned! We will return shortly!" The advertiser catches up on buyers thanks to the forced porosity between private and public spheres: what they have not seen while sitting on their couch, they will have to see in the streets.

The paradox is extremely violent: we are better armed against aggressions in our intimacy than in the public space. Impossible to escape or hit the remote. Stuck! And no way out! The inescapable out in the street vs. the choice of channel surfing.

The systematic occupation of the public space allows the merchants and their overzealous auxiliaries, "manipulators of symbols,"[57] to use and abuse their dominant position. The logos float all over the public space, like ice cubes in the increasingly chilly waters of "selfish calculation."[58]

In private law, confusing the interests of a company with those of its CEOs is a punishable crime known as misuse of public funds. Analogous charges should be applied to the misuse of public spaces.

A French Illusion

The petty bourgeoisie of France wants to believe in its capacity to keep brand wars at bay. Better informed, less gullible, helped by culture, protected by ad hoc associations and a stable economic standing, the best representatives of the middle class (the famous "privileged socio-professional categories" of marketing) can become better consumers and consider themselves free from any form of alienation. This Swiss-style neutrality, this combination of cultural capital and economic affluence, allows them to be "smart," even "organic" consumers. So much trendier.

Things and their standardized expression can be observed from a condescending, distant perspective. Alienation is other people. When Naomi Klein's book came out in France,[59] it was considered good taste to regard it as a charming, exotic exercise. The excesses described by the English-speaking Canadian author applied only to the Empire. French culture and public services—the best in the world, of course—would protect us. The widespread sponsorship of every possible cultural activity (exhibitions, museums, festivals, etc.), the invention of PPP (or public-private partnerships) to finance public infrastructures (stadiums, hospitals, theater venues, etc.), the "autonomy" of universities: all of these episodes are indicative of political disengagement.

In these deserted fields, brands and logos thrive. A city whose value is measured only by the standard of economic profitability dissolves into worldwide commodification. We used to talk about planetary cities, now what we see are flourishing, gigantic duty-free shops.

This is a game that small French cities are bound to lose (every year, it becomes increasingly difficult for Paris to remain in the rankings established by the economic journals).

Medication for "AllerLogogy"

This rather hopeless world that I describe with all the excesses of passion, all the outrageous and unfair stances of a pamphlet—I am guilty as charged—is not immutable. The increasingly exacerbated contradictions of today's winners are generating ever-wider cracks. There is a system of checks and balances, and it is growing. The present book is a proof of this.

Strong systems of domination tolerate a reasonable amount of protest and questioning on their margins, the very demonstration of their tolerance. The threshold is quite low. However, "a single spark can start a prairie fire."[60] The citizen/city dwellers who believe that the system is unfair face the same choices that the dominated face all over.

You can comfort yourself with the illusion that the geopolitics of logos is harmful only in its perverse effects in the margins; that, by changing a few parameters, these signs can serve the public interest. Agencies in the English-language sphere have taken this idea and the practices that derive from it quite far. In the morning, you work for the greater glory of a laundry detergent; in the afternoon, for a perfume. This leaves you some time in the evenings to place your experience and abilities at the service of humanitarian causes. The techniques, mediums, and codes remain the same: the confusion of genres can prove quite profitable indeed.

For the 2012 edition of the Fête de l'Humanité, an event organized by the French communist newspaper *Humanité,* Euro RSCG offered to create the poster "free of charge." What remains of the French Communist Party must have been very naïve or very shrewd to believe that a multinational, which announced for 2012 "a net income of 120 million euros (an increase of 9 percent compared to 2010)," [61] would be willing to do anything "free of charge."

Our symbol manipulators put as little effort as possible into these maneuvers to burnish its image. Changing the subject was enough. The height of hypocrisy is reached by Benetton and Toscani. The aesthetic treatment of social issues is directly used to sell sweaters. Analysis and (d)enunciation of such a combination of cynicism and cleverness would be no small challenge indeed. It is easier when one of the authors comes clean.[62]

Others, like me, believe that the causes of the "weight of the world" [63] are so deeply set that their effects can be eliminated only at the price of replacing them with others.

Which doesn't stop one from working with the enemy and polishing one's symbolic arms while waiting for the advent of truly democratic powers.

What is the hope? To see our cities newly liberated both from the obligation to please the consumers who are destroying them and from the market, returned to their role as catalysts of human relations, cleared of their brands and logos.

Notes

1 “There are many ways of talking about television. But from a ‘business’ perspective, let’s be realistic. Basically the job of [the French national television channel] TF1 is to help Coca-Cola, for example, sell its product.... For an advertising message to get through, however, the television viewer’s brain has to be receptive. Our shows’ mission is to make it receptive. That is, to entertain it and relax it in order to prepare it between two messages. What we sell to Coca-Cola is available human brain time.... Nothing is harder than obtaining that availability. That is where permanent change is found. You have to be constantly looking for programs that work, following the fashion, riding the trends, in a context where information is speeding up, multiplying, and becoming banal.” Patrick Le Lay, *Les dirigeants face au changement. Baromètre 2004*, Paris, 2004.

2 “Architecture is the masterful, correct, and magnificent play of volumes in light.” Le Corbusier, *Towards an Architecture*, trans. John Goodman, Los Angeles, 2007; originally published in French in 1923 as *Vers une architecture*.

3 “Contrary to what one might think, a city’s primary engine is not economic but rather political. The city is the base of public power, as well as its symbol and tangible demonstration. Through the organization of its structures, the city represents—in all its majesty—the powers of justice, regulation, and harmony to reign over the land below. To accomplish this, the city must be monumental.” Georges Duby, Introduction to *The History of Paris in Painting*, ed. Georges Duby and Guy Lobrichon, New York, 2009, p. 9; originally published in French in 1989 as *L’Histoire de Paris par la peinture*.

4 “The history of the city is the history of different forms of organizing space. The city does not exist, only cities exist. The *polis* of ancient Greece *is not* the Latin *urbs* and even less the *civitas;* the medieval Mediterranean city *is not* the baroque city; the modern city *is not* the contemporary metropolis, and the latter *is not* the city we live in today. The Mediterranean city is anticlassical ... it grows with use in the temporal determination of its functions. The modern city is the *violent* overrunning of that, in other words, it imposes on the space-time of the medieval city a theoretical Order, a theoretical Form, ever more clearly based on the synergy between industry and market, the space of production and that of exchange and consumption. The timeframe of the production/consumption relationship governs all the other timeframes. Its logic is applied everywhere, in the hospital as much as in the theater. It exercises a ‘hypnotic attraction’ over every other function and aspect of collective life.” Massimo Cacciari, “Nomades en prison, réflexions sur la post-métropole,” *Le choc des métropoles*, Paris, 2008, p. 244.

5 “‘The logic of the rebel is ... to insist on plain language so as not to increase the universal falsehood.’... Naming an object inaccurately means adding to the unhappiness of this world. And, in fact, the vast wretchedness of man ... is falsehood. Without knowing, or without yet saying, how it is possible, he knows that the great task of man is not to serve falsehood.” Albert Camus, “*On a Philosophy of Expression* by Brice Parain,” in *Lyrical and Critical Essays*, trans. Ellen Conroy Kennedy, New York, 1970, p. 238; originally published in French as “Sur une philosophie de l’expression,” *Poésie* 44 (1944).

6 Mike Davis, *Planet of Slums*, London and New York, 2006.

7 "Recently the architects of the 'Disney Corporation' won a competition for the redevelopment of the center of New York City (Times Square, Fifth Avenue, Central Park).... Perhaps such a movement, taken to its conclusion, runs the risk of killing imagination and drying up the imaginary, translating something of the new types of paralysis affecting life in society. In urban space, and generally in social space, the distinction between reality and fiction becomes blurred. Town planners, architects, artists, and poets ought to be aware of the fact that their fate is linked and their raw material is the same. That is, without the imaginary, there is no city, and inversely. From that point of view, society and utopia are intertwined. The imaginary gauges the intensity of social life." Marc Augé, *L'impossible voyage. Le tourisme et ses images,* Paris, 1997, pp. 168–70.

"Nowadays another invader is forcing himself on us and he is ambiguous, being both expected and feared: the tourist. All city dwellers are more or less business-minded, they look to attract the tourist, establish an exchange with him, a commercial exchange to say the least, yet for each of them, only a tiny fraction of tourists attain singularity. Indeed, in people's talk and actions, the tourist is a plural being who treads the earth, erodes lived space, lays siege, and comes to take the place of the aggressor simply because of his numbers. This is the new shapeless and proliferating occupier against whom one must constantly reconstruct an identity, basing oneself on a personal depiction of monuments." Daniel Fabre, "Gavroche et l'Éléphant ou Vivre avec le monument," in *L'abus monumental?,* Paris, 1999, p. 278.

8 "In Western Christian thought, our connection with the image and images is indisputably bound up with what is the basis of our freedom and concomitantly with anything that endangers that freedom to the point of annihilating it. It is easier to forbid people to see than to allow them to think. One decides to control the image to guarantee the silence of thought, and when thought has lost its rights, the image is accused of every ill under the pretext that it is out of control. The violence perpetrated against the image, that is the question. In the violence of this entire debate around the visible, we must understand that the violence of the visible is due to the war that is being waged against the image, the war being waged against thought.... To defend the image is to oppose everything that eliminates the otherness of the gazes constructing the invisibility of meaning. The power of the image is equal to the voices inhabiting it. It is no coincidence that images of war now inevitably mobilize the producers of images. People now commonly speak of image wars because the violence of situations involving aggression is immediately linked with the management of the visible and the transmission of discourse. The battles being fought on screen summon citizens to think of the visible and the invisible as decisive questions in political analysis. It is imperative then to take educating the gaze seriously, for any war today becomes a chance to wage war on thought itself. To conceive of the image is to answer for the future of violence. To accuse the image of violence at a time when the market of the visible is taking effect against freedom is to do violence against the invisible, that is to say, to abolish the place of the other in the construction of a seeing together." Marie-José Mondzain, *L'image peut-elle tuer?,* Paris, 2002, pp. 88–90.

9 "As of this year over half of humanity lives in cities. Nearly seven hundred new cities, accommodating over 250 million inhabitants, have been created since the 1990s. Megacities of over twenty million inhabitants are taking shape. Tokyo and Mexico will soon be followed by Mumbai, Dacca, São Paulo, Karachi.... For the UN, 'the twenty-first century will be the century of cities,' and this urbanization of the world is overturning the economic, social and ecological balance of the planet." Grégoire Allix, "Depuis 2008, la moitié de l'humanité vit en ville," *Le Monde,* October 24, 2008.

10 "Spatial identity can be viewed as the whole of the values attached to a space (be it a place, area, or network) that constitutes a reference employed by one or more of the actors who regularly use it to distinguish themselves from other actors. It expresses a logic of separation, classification, discrimination of signifying entities within the world of phenomena.... The identity of a space does not exist sui generis but is constructed, collectively invented by the actors of a given society who then may have the tendency to naturalize it in their use, make it an unchanging essence, at the risk of distorting, for example, what historical science has to say about the origins and development of a space. The identity of a place, area, or network... can thus be a matter of a mythical construction and constitutes one of those numerous mythologies peopling the acting imagination of human groups. In those cases, spatial identity is a powerful instrument at the heart of the rhetoric employed in the qualification and classification of objects of society by social actors, and in the justification of their actions. It notably allows one, in connection with the discourse on limits, to successfully carry out the work of dividing up a stretch of space and specifying singular spaces. This applies with particular intensity to the protagonists in the field of politics, but, beyond that, every actor is concerned by this work." Michel Lussault, *L'homme spatial. La construction sociale de l'être humain,* Paris, 2007, p. 93.

11 "If the poor have their 'ghettos'—also called 'shanty towns,' 'slums,' 'projects,' 'estates'—the non-poor enjoy the possibility of regrouping among themselves according to their income levels." Thierry Paquot, *Ghettos de riches. Tour du monde des enclaves résidentielles sécurisées,* Paris, 2009.

12 Henri Lefebvre, *Le droit à la ville,* Paris, 1968; idem, *La révolution urbaine,* Paris, 1971.

13 Louis Althusser, *For Marx,* trans. Ben Brewster, New York and London, 2005; originally published in French in 1965 as *Pour Marx.*

14 "Advertising is simple, sometimes simpleminded, but it has one real quality, it is a seller of happiness... Woe betide him who sparks the debate." Jacques Séguéla, quoted in Oliviero Toscani, *La publicité est une charogne qui sourit,* Paris, 1995, p. 64.

15 "The unemployment rate of the active population of Greater Montpellier remains higher than that of comparable conglomerations. Combined with jobs that are globally less qualified than elsewhere, it partly explains the fact that household incomes are relatively weak and marked by very broad disparity. In Greater Montpellier, the richest households enjoy incomes that are eight times greater than the poorest incomes.... In the conglomeration as a whole, a decrease of 16 percent in housing starts has been recorded between the 1990s and the recent intercensal period. City centers of comparable conglomerations have likewise recorded a decrease in the growth of their pool of main residences, but in less drastic terms." Bernard Tailhades and Olivier Tasqué, "Les chiffres clés de Montpellier Agglomération," INSEE, the National Institute of Statistics and Economic Studies (June 2010).

16 "There remain Western cities, London, Vienna, Rome ... Paris, but also Saintes, Dijon, Sarlat, Quimper, Colmar.... All of them, however, have been hit by the new agents of urbanization and offer resistance according to the solidity of their fabric, vocation, and the determination of those who are governing them and living in them. It is no coincidence if, since the 1960s (Malraux's law of 1962 on protected sectors), the concepts of historical urban groups and urban legacy have now joined that of the historical landmark. Forged in

England in the second half of the nineteenth century, these concepts only won recognition in France when the worst threatened. In a word, the city is becoming a historical landmark and [a] question arises that splits in two, i.e., how is one to both preserve this legacy and take on the future of the non-city that is coming after it?" Françoise Choay, *Pour une anthropologie de l'espace,* Paris, 2006, p. 42.

17 "The transition from industrial to cultural capitalism already is challenging many of our most basic assumptions about what constitutes human society. Old institutions grounded in property relations, market exchanges, and material accumulation are slowly being uprooted to make room for an era in which culture becomes the most important commercial resource." Jeremy Rifkin, *The Age of Access: The New Culture of Hypercapitalism Where All of Life Is a Paid-For Experience,* New York, 2000, p. 11.

18 "The *sumbolon,* from *sumballein,* to bring together, throw together, originally referred to a *tessera hospitalis,* a hospitality tessera, a fragment of a cup or bowl broken in two between host and guest, who would then transmit the pieces to their children so that they might one day recover the same relationship of trust by placing the two fragments side by side. It was a sign of recognition, meant to make up for a separation or span a distance. The symbol is a conventional object whose reason for being is to connect minds and bring subjects together. More than a thing, it is an operation and a ceremony, not of goodbyes but of reunions (between old friends who have lost touch with each other). Symbolic and fraternal are synonyms. That is, one does not fraternize without having something to share, and one does not symbolize without uniting what was foreign. The exact antonym of symbol in Greek is the devil, he who separates. Dia-bolic refers to everything that divides, and sym-bolic everything that brings together. The image is beneficial because it is symbolic. That is, remembering and reconstituting, to use equivalent terms here. But to re-embody, by virtue of the mechanism of incompleteness, it needs to include a hidden partner in the game. Make a connection, do good, but only the reference to an elsewhere, a distant place, a third symbolizing party allows an image to establish a link with its viewer, and, on the rebound, between viewers themselves." Régis Debray, *Vie et mort de l'image. Une histoire du regard en Occident,* Paris, 1992, p. 60.

19 Véronique Lostoriat Delabroise, "Le Langage du corps dans l'Iliade," *Kentron* 17 (2001).

20 Brendan Behan's pious grandmother thought that the initials stood for "I have suffered."

21 "A common world has been built that has defined its culture as a simultaneous articulated management of the invisible and the visible. People were passionate about the image. To call the life of the image of the Father, that of Christ, by the word Passion is perfectly in keeping with what is at stake in terms of the icon. The Passion of Christ, that is, the Passion of the image, played out in the image of the Passion. It is a crossing of the darkness to the final triumph. The history of the incarnation is the legend of the image itself. But nowadays an odd anxiety has been added. The power of the image would be that it impels us to imitate it, and the narrative content of the image might therefore directly do violence by making one act. It was once blamed for making one see, and from now on it is accused of making one do." Mondzain, *L'image peut-elle tuer?,* p. 16.

22 "Only the rich are well protected. The greater their power, the greater the worth of their fiefs, the heavier will be their armament, the less their ease of movement, and the less visible their faces. The skin of those princes who have gone so far as to armor their

horses cannot be seen, which for all intents and purposes renders them unrecognizable. Hence, the importance of rallying signs: the cries, the banners held up next to each captain, the heraldic symbols sewn on the 'coats of arms,' which are types of surplices of light material that flap over the armor but which tear quickly, soon turning into tatters, and whose ruin makes strangers out of those wearing them.... Every fray is a tornado of emblems, a din of calls and invectives, and, in the wheat's trampled dust, a whirlpool of tangled signs." Georges Duby, *The Legend of Bouvines: War, Religion, and Culture in the Middle Ages*, Berkeley and Los Angeles, 1990, pp. 18–19; originally published in French in 1973 as *Le Dimanche de Bouvines, 27 juillet 1214*.

23 "I would like to draw your attention to a particular category of coats of arms, which were very popular in the Middle Ages throughout Europe, i.e., *armes parlantes*, or canting arms. This embodies a true writing with images.... Roughly one could say that arms are 'canting' when the name of certain elements—usually that of the principal figure—form a pun or make a sound connection with the name of the owner of the coat of arms. The simplest case is that where the name of the principal figure and the surname of the owner have a direct link, for example as on three Norman shields from the thirteenth century: Jean de La Tour bears a *tour* [tower]; Baudouin de Corbeil, a *corbeau* [crow]; and Raoul Cuvier, a *cuvier* [tub]." Michel Pastoureau, "Une écriture en images. Les armoiries parlantes," *Extrême-Orient Extrême-Occident*, no. 30 (2008), p. 188. In English, the name Shelley might show several whelks or shells; Wellwood, a tree springing from a well; and Keyes, a brace or trio of keys.—Trans.

24 "'It's not with that that you're going to make people love your brand,' I said to president André Charon. The instant I spoke those words, it suddenly clicked in my mind. Not taking time to think, I cried, 'Hey, I've got a slogan for you: "It's Shell I like!"'
"André Charon and his colleagues looked at me as if I were a Martian.
"'You're joking!'
"'No, not at all. Nothing looks more like a gas pump than another gas pump. If you don't create an emotional bond between your brand and drivers, you are not going to get people to feel the difference.'
"It was no use. The thought that you could declare your love to their pipes left those gentlemen aghast.
"It took a year—and only when, by an extraordinary coincidence I was seated at an official dinner next to the international president of Royal Dutch—before I was finally able to 'sell' him on my slogan. André Charon accepted defeat, a good sport. And that is how we managed to launch a visual campaign on that theme, with all the opinion polls showing that it was a huge hit." Marcel Bleustein-Blanchet, *Mémoires d'un lion*, Paris, 1998, p. 210.

25 "'Octave, do you remember on the Zanussi account you suggested a baseline with the word "happiness" in it?'
"'Oh yes... The legal department said we couldn't use it or something, didn't they?'
"'Yes! Because the word "happiness" has been branded by Nestlé! *Happiness belongs to Nestlé.*'
"'Well, that doesn't surprise me at all. Did you know Pepsi want to register blue as a trademark?'
"'What?'
"'Yup, absolutely true, they want to buy the colour blue, to own it. And that's not all. They finance educational CD Roms which are distributed free in primary schools. So children are doing their lessons in school on Pepsi computers. They learn to read the word "thirsty" next to the "Pepsi" colour.'

"'And when they look up at the Pepsi sky, their Pepsi eyes light up, and if they fall off their bikes they get Pepsi-coloured bruises all over their knees.'
"'It's quite clear to me. So long as there's nothing else there, advertising will take up all the available space. It's become the only ideal. It's not nature that abhors a vacuum, it's hope.'" Frédéric Beigbeder, *Was £9.99 Now £6.99: A Novel*, trans. Adriana Hunter, London, 2003, pp. 121–22; originally published in French in 2000 as *99 francs*.

26 A category described by the American academic Robert Reich, the secretary of labor under President Clinton, and used by INSS since 1997. Robert Reich, *The Work of Nations: Preparing Ourselves for 21st-Century Capitalism*, New York, 1991.

27 The expression is attributed variously to Marx, Jaurès, and Lenin. It is developed in the excellent book by the Quebecer economist Pierre Lemieux, *Du libéralisme à l'anarcho-capitalisme*, Paris, 1983.

28 Joseph Goebbels, 1933, following the Reichstag fire.

29 The acronym stands for "information and computing technology," of course. That is, the application of computers and telecommunications equipment to store, retrieve, transmit, and manipulate data.

30 "What is there to say, too, about what the philistinism of our upper echelons calls management, for private enterprises, and administration, for public services, except that the dreadful onerousness of their organization aims to render all human activity standard and reproducible, and thus empower those who have no singular practice? And what is there to say about brands, which are being spread everywhere, whose origins we well know: traces of the footsteps that the whores of Alexandria left behind while walking, printed in the sand along the shore, thus revealing their name and the direction to their bed?

"Along their duplicated walk, do we not come back to desire? What president of a major brand, replicated everywhere nowadays, is aware that he is—and if he isn't, I am overjoyed to inform him—is aware that he is, I repeat, the son of those Alexandrian whores? We have created an environment where success itself, where art itself, now depend more on reproduction than the inimitable. The major risk our children run is this, those whoresons, whom I have just reminded of their worthy lineage, are plunging them in a world of replicated codes; we are crushing them under redundancy." Michel Serres, excerpt from his response to René Girard's speech at the French Academy, December 15, 2005.

31 "You cannot cheat with the 'law of the conservation of violence': all violence is paid for, and, for example, the structural violence exerted by the financial markets, in the form of layoffs, loss of security, etc., is matched sooner or later in the form of suicides, crime and delinquency, drug addiction, alcoholism, a whole host of minor and major everyday acts of violence." Pierre Bourdieu, *Against the Tyranny of the Market*, vol. 1: *Acts of Resistance*, trans. Richard Nice, London and New York, 1998, p. 40; originally published in French in 1998 as *Contre-feux. Propos pour servir à la résistance contre l'invasion néo-libérale.*

32 Éric Hazan, *LQR, la novlangue du néolibéralisme*, Paris, 2006.

33 "War: a massacre of people who don't know each other for the profit of people who know each other but don't massacre each other." Paul Valéry, *Cahiers*, vol. 1, Paris, 1973.

34 "What is private, what is public? A limp giddiness takes hold of anyone who raises the question." Serge Daney, "'Pruvé et priblic' sont dans un bateau," *Libération*, November 2, 1987.

35 Jürgen Habermas, *The Structural Transformation of the Public Sphere: An Inquiry into a Category of Bourgeois Society*, trans. Thomas Burger and Frederick Lawrence, Cambridge, Mass., 1991; originally published in German in 1962 as *Strukturwandel der Öffentlichkeit. Untersuchungen zu einer Kategorie der bürgerlichen Gesellschaft.*

36 Régis Debray, *Vie et mort de l'image.*

37 Marc Augé, *Non-Places: Introduction to an Anthropology of Supermodernity*, trans. John Howe, London and New York, 1995; originally published in French in 1992 as *Non-Lieux. Introduction à une anthropologie de la surmodernité.*

38 Michel Lussault, *De la lutte des classes à la lutte des places*, Paris, 2009.

39 *Lost in Translation*, American-Japanese film directed by Sofia Coppola, 2003.

40 The canonical episode is the candid shot of Simone de Beauvoir on the January 3, 2008, cover of *Le Nouvel Observateur* magazine. A glimpsed moment of flirty intimacy, the archetype of nineteenth-century bourgeois painting, i.e., a woman at her toilette. Minor scandal. That body, too real, not perfect enough, above all not orthodox enough, just had to have some posthumous work done. To sell copies, the official organ of the right-minded left definitely wanted to show the bottom of a philosopher, but they had to touch it up, so to speak. And so we got Photoshop liposuction!

41 "On the surface, the power plays between millionaire athletes and billion-dollar companies would seem to have little to do with the loss of marketed space that is the subject of this section. Jordan and Nike, however, are only the most broad strokes, manifestations of the way in which the branding imperative changes the way we imagine both sponsor and sponsored to the extent that the idea of unbranded space ... becomes almost unthinkable. Jordan and Nike are emblematic of a new paradigm that eliminates all barriers between branding and culture, leaving no room whatsoever for unmarketed space." Naomi Klein, *No Logo*, New York, 2000, p. 59.

42 "Only two years were needed to construct the observation deck and giant work of art, an exceptionally short timeframe in light of the recent history of London's urbanization... For the preparation of the Games (2005–2012), the process of awarding construction permits for the facilities was entrusted to the Olympic Delivery Authority (ODA), instead of the municipality of Newham, where the Olympic site is located. The examination process was simplified, the consultation period shortened, and public hearings rendered impossible...

"The mayor and minister hoped in this way to imbue the Olympic site with a new spirit by mobilizing private capital. In doing so, they sent a strong signal to private investors who underpinned the post-Olympic urban renewal phase. Indeed, while Stratford is the focal point of the summer event, all the sites will later be the theater of a vast urban transformation orchestrated by Greater London and financed by the developers, like the redevelopment of the Canary Wharf docks (Appert, 2012). Officially this is about keeping the promise of a post-Olympic renewal of the city, one of the reasons why London was awarded the Games.

"Rising to a height of 120 meters, the ArcelorMittal Orbit tower is an attraction that visitors have to pay to enter. They have access to two observation decks located at 76 meters and 80 meters above the ground.... The success of this new tourist attraction is uncertain. While the tower has inevitably drawn part of the 500,000 visitors who have been to the site daily, its viability, once the event is finished, is raising questions.... Why then construct a tower whose economic viability is uncertain? Behind the alibi of a tourist attraction and work of art, Orbit brings to light the modalities of the London municipality's conception of urban renewal. Like lots of other architectural projects that are dubbed iconic, the ArcelorMittal Orbit tower does not fit into any local tradition, no more than it echoes the territory on which it has been erected. Prominent and original thanks to its shape, this spectacular tower crowns the new Stratford and compensates an image deficit, what the building simplifications imposed by budgetary cuts could no longer supply. Commissioned by the new mayor of London and the British Minister of Sports, designed by Anish Kapoor, drawn up by the engineer Cecil Balmond (Arup), and financed predominantly by Lakshmi Mittal, the tower is simultaneously part of a 'starification' of the architects and artists, a political statement, and a branding of the site for life after the Games. It is at one and the same time government fiat, a completed project to be highlighted in an artist's or architect's portfolio, and an unmistakable landmark.... This is about deploying an entrepreneurial program that offers investors, developers, and future occupants a new territory that has been cleared of its negative image and wastelands, in order to minimize the financial risks borne by the private actors after the Olympic Games. In the absence of major public projects, Greater London is expecting the private sector to construct all of the 6,800 apartments and 130,000 m^2 of office space that are foreseen between 2013 and 2025. The commercialization of the Olympic site has already begun. The royal family of Qatar has acquired half of the apartments of the Olympic Village and will have them transformed into luxury housing." Manuel Appert, "La Tour Orbit à Londres, faire-valoir des Jeux?," *Métropolitiques,* September 12, 2012.

43 This nuance itself was abolished in the waning days of the summer 2012 season: "It is all over for the self-imposed constraints that pro football had respected for years in order to standardize practices and temper as much as possible the image of players done up as Christmas trees. From now on the clubs will be able to go beyond the former limit of six sponsors and take over locations that had been banned until now, for instance, the 'back of the shorts'—marketing euphemism for the buttocks.... Football invented nothing. From boxers to women volleyball players, it is ages since brands first came to life on the backsides of high-level athletes. According to Franck Massardier, the head of Madewis, one of the official logo printers of League 1 football, handball is one of the biggest consumers of fleshy ads. 'We tell the clubs to print the sponsor five centimeters below the drawstring and select plain lettering. The transfer also has to be very thin because of the central seam. And for that location, you're better off with a brand having a short name, between five and eight letters at most.'" J.L.B., "La L1 retourne son short," *L'Équipe,* August 10, 2012.

44 The reader should absolutely listen to François Morel's broadcast on France Inter, June 8, 2012.

45 In the name of public health, the tobacco brands that were chased out of Formula 1 racing were quickly replaced by energy drinks.

46 At the foot of the cradle, Dr. Carole Rougé—we see immediately that she is a physician, she is wearing a white smock and a stethoscope around her neck: a walking logo—financed by Gallia labs, tells you everything you need to do—and especially buy—for baby's health.

47 Jean-Paul Sartre, *No Exit*, New York, 1946; originally published in French in 1944 as *Huis clos*.

48 François Brune, *Le bonheur conforme*, Paris, 2001.

49 "In the original package, the famous red spot (called the target) appeared on one side of the package only. The other side was used for factory identification, federal regulations, inscriptions, etc.—items of no interest. All this text I transferred to the sides of the package, liberating the back area for a second red target. Thus, a package lying flat on a desk, a wrapper discarded, would inevitably display the brand name." Raymond Loewy, *Never Leave Well Enough Alone*, New York, 1951; repr. Baltimore, 2002, p. 148.

50 Groucho Marx, *The Groucho Letters*, New York, 1967.

51 In 1995, the association Ne pas plier (Do Not Fold) gave a series of lectures at the Centre Pompidou. For the series Isabel de Bary and I analyzed the logos and visual identity handbooks of four hundred French communes (districts or townships). We also came up with the word "logotomy."

52 "There are those who are in on the game and those who aren't. And I believe that's worth thinking about; so is the contempt implied by psychological techniques. Whether it's selling *soap* or winning votes, there's no psychological technique that doesn't start with contempt for the buyer or the voter; otherwise it would be useless. Here the whole man is at stake; the system is a totality.... There's no free play, no give-and-take, and that's why even a small disagreement with the system leads any artist to a *recantation*. So we come to the essential question: how can we keep psychological techniques from destroying the quality of human intelligence?" André Malraux, speech of March 5, 1948, published in *The Conquerors*, trans. Stephen Becker, Chicago, 1992, p. 194.

53 "In the vocabulary of the camps, a detainee was *ein Stück*, a piece. When one of them died, the SS would say, 'We're short a piece. There are only 213 *Stücke*, whereas there ought to be 214...' The individual entering the camp was not called *ein Zugänger*, a new arrival, but *ein Zugang*—a new delivery.

"This abstract vocabulary of technical efficiency has now invaded our daily existence.... Soon people will no longer shy from employing the term *gisements* ('deposits') to talk about the intellectual goods that are museums and monuments, elements that make up the nation's cultural legacy when these are viewed from the perspective of their market-oriented use.... It can be found still in the endless recourse to euphemism, which characterized the language of the Third Reich and today characterizes the vocabulary of naked economic rationality. People speak of *dégraissage*, 'cutting away the fat' and 'downsizing,' where not long ago it was a question of individuals being forced into unemployment. *Dégraissage*, 'degreasing,' the image is that of a machine being cleaned of its impurities. When related to the body, however, *dégraissage* regrettably conjures up the *Figuren* of concentration camp life, where the deficit in the daily intake of calories left the prisoner with a life expectancy of fifty to sixty days. The results of these 'cuts' in contemporary society are probably neither spectacular, nor rapid, nor probably as tragic as all that. People are not left to die of starvation. They are only left on the verge of. It is just as cruel, however. The homeless person and the welfare recipient, lost in the crowd and almost invisible, are the 'soft' version of the *Kretiner* of the affluent society." Jean Clair, *La barbarie ordinaire. Music à Dachau*, Paris, 2001, pp. 34–36.

54 Pierre Bourdieu, "Opinion Polls: A Science without a Scientist," in *In Other Words: Essays Toward a Reflexive Sociology,* trans. Matthew Adamson, Stanford, 1990, pp. 168–76; originally published in French in 1987 as "Les sondages, une science sans savant," in *Choses dites.*

55 "The brand 'Strasbourg the Europtimist' was created to rally the actors of the territory's economic development. It is now up to its partners to appropriate and use it!... Due to metropolization, competition is increasingly stiff between cities. Nationally as well as on the level of Europe or the world, cities are elaborating elements to distinguish and differentiate themselves. Their strong points must be highlighted, their markers pointed up.... The logo 'Strasbourg the Europtimist' embodies and sketches out the values and philosophy of a true signature of territorial attractiveness. Modernity, confidence, creativity, enterprising spirit, ambition, and partnerships are reflected in this logo." Cécile Marter, preamble to the *Charte graphique* (Visual guidelines), "Strasbourg the Europtimist," Direction du Développement économique et de l'attractivité, Strasbourg, 2011.

56 "Today, January 27, is a great day for Brittany. While this territory of over three million inhabitants will welcome more than 26,000 new residents each year between now and 2040, the Region has decided to give itself a brand to highlight its image and increase its power of attraction in Europe and around the world." Press release, Agence CoManaging, 2011.

57 See note 7.

58 "The bourgeoisie, wherever it has got the upper hand, has put an end to all feudal, patriarchal, idyllic relations. It has pitilessly torn asunder the motley feudal ties that bound man to his 'natural superiors,' and has left remaining no other nexus between man and man than naked self-interest, than callous 'cash payment.' It has drowned the most heavenly ecstasies of religious fervor, of chivalrous enthusiasm, of philistine sentimentalism, in the icy water of egotistical calculation. It has resolved personal worth into exchange value, and in place of the numberless indefeasible chartered freedoms, has set up that single, unconscionable freedom—Free Trade." Karl Marx and Friedrich Engels, *The Manifesto of the Communist Party* (1848), trans. Samuel Moore in cooperation with Friedrich Engels (1888), http://www.marxists.org/archive/marx/works/download/pdf/Manifesto.pdf.

59 Published in French in 2001 as *No Logo. La tyrannie des marques.*

60 An ancient Chinese proverb adopted by Mao Zedong.

61 Havas press release, Thursday, March 1, 2012.

62 "Dear Subcomandante Marcos, My name is Oliviero Toscani and for the last ten years I have designed the communications campaigns of the United Colors of Benetton.... For many years now Benetton has chosen to use a large part of its advertising budget to speak out about the most dramatic subjects of this century, AIDS, war, racism, intolerance. A way of demonstrating that a great industry is also a 'social actor,' and that it can foster an intelligent dialogue with 'consumers,' who, for all that, are human beings above all." Oliviero Toscani, *La publicité est une charogne,* p. 198.

63 Pierre Bourdieu, ed., *The Weight of the World: Social Suffering in Contemporary Society,* trans. Priscilla Parkhurst Ferguson et al., Stanford, 1999; the English edition is an abridged version of the original French published in 1993 as *La misère du monde.*

There Are Cracks in the Walls...

Annick Lantenois

Action worms its way into the cracks of reality in order to transform it.[1]

This text is based on three preparatory visual essays proposed by Irena Bockaj,[2] Maria Roszkowska, and Ruedi Baur as preliminary topics for reflection. Their adaptation to the format of the present work and the development of the ideas of their authors may skew one's reading of the following text without, however, changing its underlying concept in any way.

These essays are meant to take stock and record the "symbolic poverty of the identification systems of European territories." Their pages are terribly loud. And that noise is paradoxically a discourse. Or more exactly, two discourses, one superimposed on the other. There is the discourse that underlies the production of these signs, and a second one that is bound up with how that discourse is laid out on the page.

The former is constituted, not by each isolated sign, but by their daily interconnection—in which we are all evolving, whether consciously or unconsciously, with vigilance or indifference. This first discourse also tells us that, no matter their graphic "quality," signs are never mute.

The present essays constitute the second discourse. There are three critical essays on the identity of the state institutions designated by the term "territories," written by three authors—Irena Bockaj, Maria Roszkowska, and Ruedi Baur. The final result of their coming together is a discourse that seems to translate an observer's perspective, an objective perspective from above. And yet, these essays do more than merely observe. They suggest that, from the very beginning, there was the certainty of finding something that, all things considered, was not sought but rather experienced as a given.

1 Vladimir Jankélévitch and Béatrice Berlowitz, *Quelque part dans l'inachevé,* Paris, 1978, p. 143. My thanks to Marie Bruneau and Bertrand Genier for temporarily suspending their meditation before the ocean to carefully re-examine and discuss the present text.

2 Pages 240 to 241: excerpts from "Don't Insult My Neighborhood!," a comparative study of the signs of contemporary nationalism in ex-Yugoslavia, Switzerland, and Belgium by Irena Bockaj. This research was made known to the authors invited to contribute to the book.

"Don't Insult My Neighborhood!"
Irena Bockaj

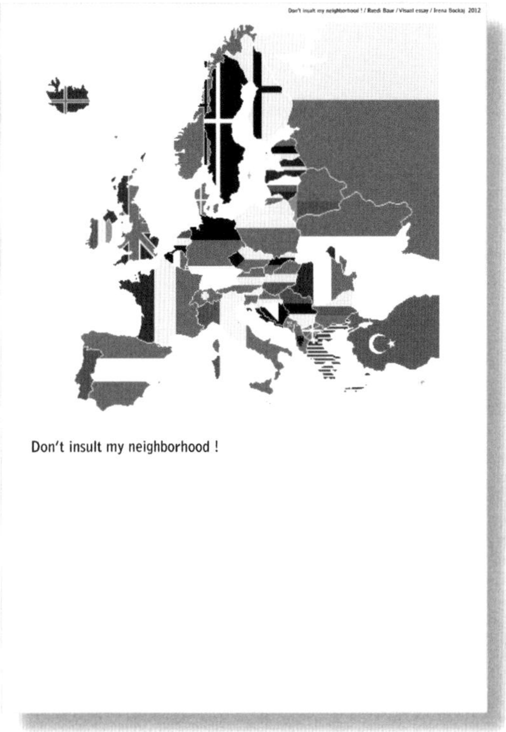

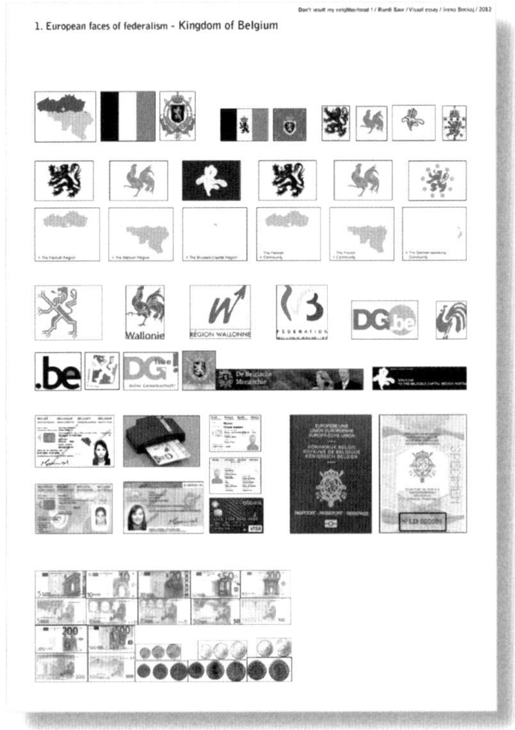

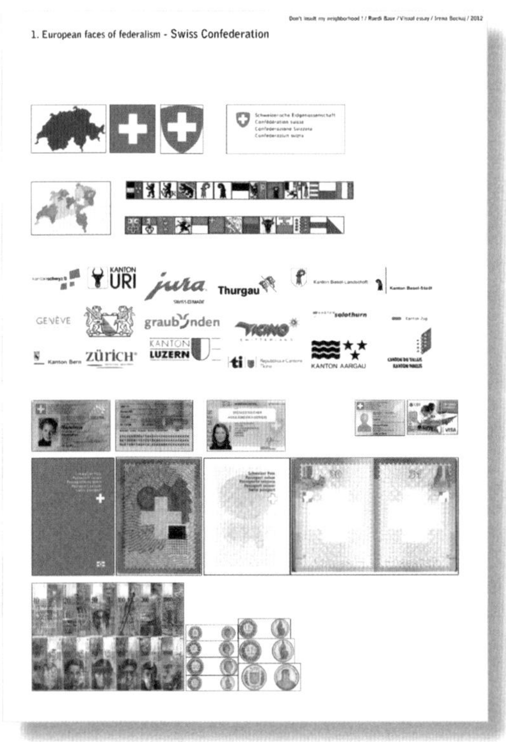

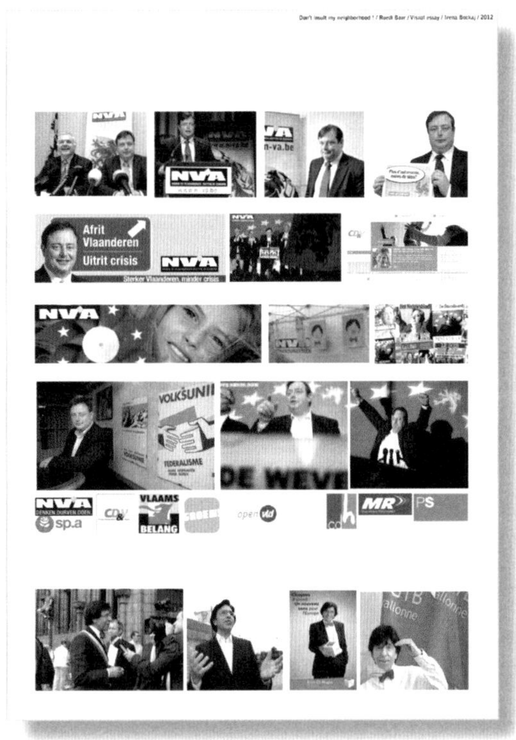

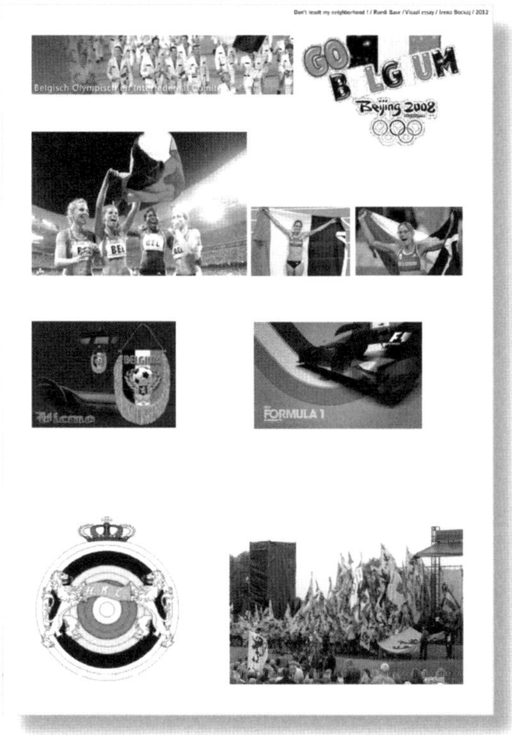
Don't insult my neighborhood ! / Ruedi Baur / Visual essay / Irena Bockaj / 2012
Beijing 2008
FORMULA 1

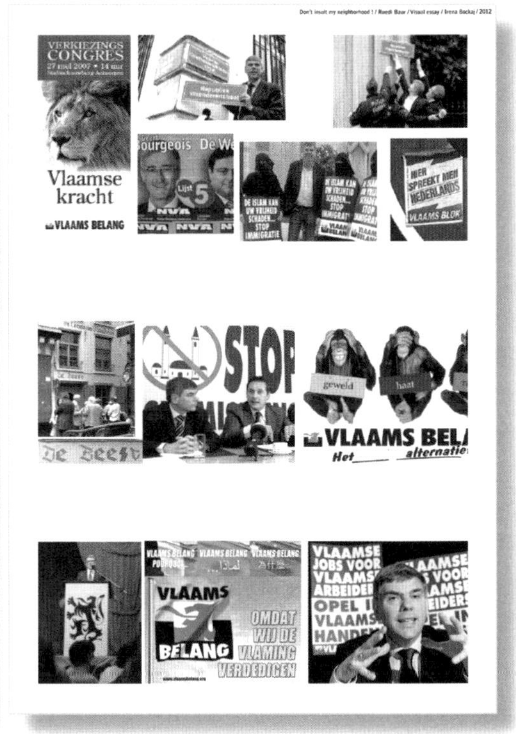
Don't insult my neighborhood ! / Ruedi Baur / Visual essay / Irena Bockaj / 2012
VERKIEZINGS CONGRES
Vlaamse kracht
VLAAMS BELANG
STOP
geweld
haat
VLAAMS
BELANG
OMDAT WIJ DE VLAMING VERDEDIGEN

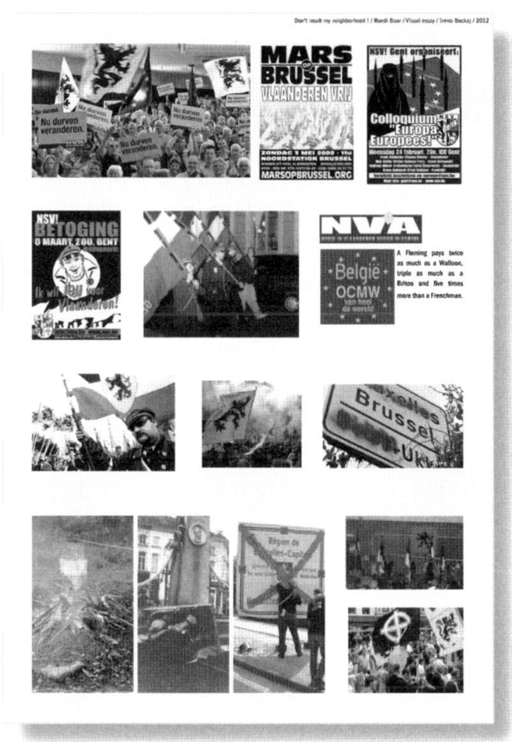
Don't insult my neighborhood ! / Ruedi Baur / Visual essay / Irena Bockaj / 2012
Nu durven veranderen.
MARS
BRUSSEL
NSV! Gent organiseert:
Colloquium "Europa Europees!"
MARSOPBRUSSEL.ORG
NSV!
BETOGING
NVA
België
OCMW
van heel de wereld
A Fleming pays twice as much as a Walloon, triple as much as a Briton and five times more than a Frenchman.
Brussel

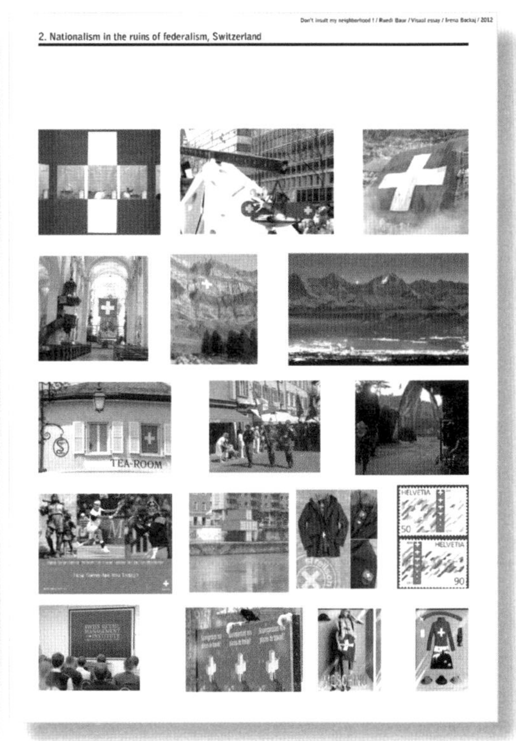
Don't insult my neighborhood ! / Ruedi Baur / Visual essay / Irena Bockaj / 2012
2. Nationalism in the ruins of federalism, Switzerland
TEA-ROOM
HELVETIA
50
HELVETIA
90

Rather than an assessment or a "perambulation,"[3] they constitute a demonstration. These essays are a construction whose aim is to demonstrate a given, a certainty.

The organization of signs, sometimes in a parodic mode, their juxtaposition, the succession of pages that allows one to compare them, the use of comparative tables, the insertion of maps, the authority of titles, the laconic nature of commentaries—all of these factors contribute to the scientific demonstration of institutional symbolic poverty.

This demonstration of the "symbolic poverty of the identification systems of European territories" has a point. Considering that they have been produced at ENSAD (École nationale supérieure des arts décoratifs)—a flagship school for design training with international visibility—and in the light of the studies on cultural, social, and symbolic poverty[4] that nourish the perspective of their authors, such a demonstration can only find a favorable echo, in that it makes such poverty visible. But is it accurate?

If this is the case, then these visual essays describe an appalling state of affairs, because they are presented as a self-evident, open claim. Everything is said in a double page. We knew it. I knew it. And I plunged into the interpretation of this discourse, equipped with my own references, oriented by the titles, commentaries, and layouts.

Three visual essays: a case-by-case review of the signs tasked with asserting the identity of "territories" (cities, regions, states) and to signify their legitimacy and authority. An aspect of the visual landscape of institutions.

What do we learn from this demonstration?

The rendering of this landscape tells us that there is a tension between two trends. The first trend is the erosion of the sovereignty of the State,[5] a deactivating of the legitimacy and authority of state institutions, in conjunction with the privatization of entire sectors of the public domain, and with the deregulation of social relations.

3 Ruedi Baur, introduction to his essay "L'absence remarquée du drapeau de la planète," study document provided by Ruedi Baur and Sébastien Thiéry, that is the origin of the present text.

4 The term "Misère symbolique" ("symbolic poverty") is drawn in particular from the following texts by Bernard Stiegler, "De la misère symbolique," *Le Monde*, October 11, 2003; idem., *De la misère symbolique*, vol. 1: *L'époque hyperindustrielle*, Paris, 2004, and vol. 2: *La catastrophe du sensible*, Paris, 2005.

5 See Zygmunt Bauman, *Identity: Conversations with Benedetto Vecchi*, Cambridge, UK, 2004.

This trend is inscribed in the larger process of globalization and commodification of all human activities, a process that now dictates its own rules. Among these rules, the mobility imperative (imposed on tangible and intangible goods as well as people) contributes to deactivating the paradigms that founded, during the Enlightenment, our Western conception of community life.

Deactivation of the role of the State, globalization, commodification, mobility: the situation causes and is caused by the way in which our experience of time is structured by the notion of speed, [6] whose alienating character becomes all the more efficient as it tends to cancel temporal and historical depth to the benefit of a self-devouring, "omnipresent present." Change, novelty, events, and competition: together, these norms constitute the framework and motor of the "contemporary experience of a perpetual present." [7]

The second trend revealed by these visual essays is the violent assertion of identity-related claims in nationalist and communitarian discourses. Such claims can be interpreted as a reaction to the Western desire to "own the world" [8] by turning it into a commodity, a desire that levels out the differences "to the point of leading to ... *a revolt of difference*." [9] These discourses are all the more dangerous as more and more people are excluded from the normative framework. Homelessness, poverty, unemployment, political, economic, and climatic migrations—the suffering of millions of destitute individuals are all a mirror held up to the citizens of the world, to millions of other people in near poverty who, for fear of exclusion, become a breeding ground for nationalist and communitarian discourses. Their power resides in their archetypal answers, engaged in an ideological rewriting of history that is all the more effective as it provides a stable, controllable, and simplified answer to the complex issues, dynamics, and uncertainty of our world.

Is it appropriate then, for the research launched in these visual essays, to apply the term "territory" —which implies the existence of boundaries—to state structures, or are we running the risk of involuntarily helping to fuel nationalist and communitarian discourses? Or should we abandon the term and run the risk of endorsing the economic logic of leveling out any difference, the logic that underlies the globalization process?

The obviousness of the demonstration provided by these visual essays is powerful. But beyond obviousness, the question of its accuracy remains a matter of discussion. It is all imposed in a disembodied

6 See Hartmut Rosa, *Alienation and Acceleration: Towards a Critical Theory of Late-Modern Temporality*, Malmö, 2010.

7 François Hartog, *Régimes d'historicité. Présentisme et expériences du temps*, Paris, 2003, pp. 18–28.

8 Georges Balandier, *Civilisations et puissance*, La Tour d'Aigues, 2004, p. 30.

9 Ibid., p. 24; emphasis in the original.

form: no names are provided with regard to the agencies, designers, structures, or anyone willingly involved in design, production, and distribution. This absence of names is also the absence of the economic network of communication agencies, the absence of its structure and mechanisms; a network which connects the different densities of power attributed to agencies—depending on whether they operate on an international, national, or local level—but also the network between agencies, studios, and workshops, between salespeople, "creative people," and designers. Moreover, does this absence run the risk of eluding the question of responsibilities? Of inviting us to accept the idea that, after all, the system alone—in other words, nobody—is to blame? And, consequently, are we running the risk of ratifying the dominant discourse about the fatal character of the violence of our present?

There is hardly any chronology.[10] Or, rather, there are only silent chronologies. One can observe a break in the evolution of signs (the passage from coats of arms to logos), but the absence of dates or chronological ranges tends to reduce the complexity of the process of identity transformation. Dates and ranges would help us integrate two additional levels of information. The first pertains to the relations between the production of signs and other systems (whether technological, scientific, linguistic, etc.). These relations crucially contribute to outlining the range of underlying reasons of a crisis that has affected not only our identities but also our paradigms as a whole. And such an absence of dates encourages a formal approach that runs the risk of reducing the analysis to the "quality" of the signs or systems of signs, and of overlooking the discourse that generates them. And attempting to qualify their quality would amount to overestimating their autonomy—on the one hand, from the discourse they are supposed to translate, and, on the other hand, from the larger network of visual productions that influences their reception.

The second level of information considers two stages in the evolution of identity signs: in the second half of the 1980s, the logos created by communication agencies were not yet inscribed in a global process of branding. They had yet to become systems of identification. As for the expectations of municipalities, with the

10 Except in the essay "Les capitales européennes en compétition. Évolution de l'identité de Peugeot," study document provided by Ruedi Baur and Sébastien Thiéry that is the origin of the present text.

exception of Montpellier, the logo alone was apparently supposed to crystallize the issues pertaining to the reorientation of identity narratives, under the pressure of industrial and economic mutations. The passage from coat of arms to logo concerned the majority of cities, regardless of their importance. Elected officials were the ones who commissioned the work, took part in the negotiations with the agency, and had the final word on the matter. On the other hand, the decision no longer to elaborate mere signs, but systems of identification that addressed the strategy of transforming cities into brands, was a phenomenon of the 2000s. A more detailed study would allow one to measure the extent of such an evolution, and to confirm or refute the process of constituting "centers of excellence" that reconfigure the geographic economy of France in particular.

ONLYLYON: a system of identification, a brand. In the everyday life of the city, this brand tends to take the place of Lyon—the lion—in the continuity of the coat of arms. Or, more precisely, the lion becomes a secondary sign of identity, subsumed into a network of visual actions and productions developed for establishing a brand. Originally, "ONLYLYON is the product of the territory's economic governance, organized into Grand Lyon L'Esprit d'Entreprise (GLEE)."[11] In 2007, the year when the campaign was launched, ONLYLYON was an autonomous structure, in which the city was merely one of the thirteen partners alongside the Lyon Area Economic Development Agency (ADERLY), Lyon Airports, Lyon's Chamber of Commerce and Industry (CCI), the General Employers Confederation for Small and Medium Enterprises (CGPME) for the Rhone region, The Rhone Chamber of Trade and Craft Industry, Lyon's Congress Center "La Cité," the Rhone County Council, Eurexpo, the Greater Lyon Council (Grand Lyon), Lyon Tourism and Conventions, the Lyon-Rhone Movement of the Enterprises of France (Medef Lyon-Rhône), and the University of Lyon.

The aim of the structure was "to address the state of affairs observed by the partners: despite its strengths and assets, Lyon still suffers from poor identifiability and from an image and recognition deficit. Consequently, the city does not enjoy the prestige and economic returns it deserves." The second stage, launched in 2012, should allow, according to the press release, "to consolidate the implication of some key partners in the projects of ONLYLYON: • The City of Lyon and Greater Lyon Council, for local anchorage and culture; • The Center of Research and Higher Education (Pôle de recherche et d'enseignement supérieur PRES), for training and research; • Lyon's Chamber of Commerce and

11 All the quotations about ONLYLYON are drawn from the press release "Promotion internationale de l'agglomération lyonnaise. Nouvelle image, nouvelle ambition," http://www.onlylyon.org/docs/2293-1-dp-onlylyon-bd-pdf.pdf.

Industry, as well as managerial organizations, for companies. The aim is to develop together new forms of action (about ten, starting from 2012) under the banner of ONLYLYON, in order to allow multiple actions and better synergies."

The conditions of design, structuring, and distribution of the ONLYLYON brand are based on an act of blurring, or even displacement. Such a confusion does not concern the role of elected officials in the everyday management of the city ("local anchorage"). It rather concerns the sphere of initiatives and decisions: Is that the economic sphere? The political sphere? Who is in charge and in control of orienting the future of Lyon within the Rhone County Council? The merging of the City of Lyon and PRES under the term "key partners" is also a merging between mostly immaterial activities (culture, training, research) that are liable to be capitalized upon in direct relation to the local economic fabric incarnated by the Chamber of Commerce and Industry. By an alphabetical coincidence, the Movement of the Enterprises precedes the University in the list of partners...

The instance of Montpellier is exemplary of this act of blurring. In the 1980s, "Montpellier la Surdouée" ("Montpellier, the exceptionally gifted one") became the city's trademark. This trademark was decided by one man, Mayor Georges Frêche—and not, as in the case of ONLYLYON, by an economic network (despite the politicians' agreement). In both cases, the tools were marketing-derived, but the displacement of the sphere of initiatives and decisions remained in the field of politics: "Montpellier is Frêche's city. Almost a year after the death of the Man (with a capital M) of the city, his impact remains very palpable.... He wanted Montpellier to be great, emancipated, and dynamic. He won his bet. The concept of 'Montpellier la surdouée' has lived up to its promises: today, it is the eighth city in France."[12] Notwithstanding the suspicions of megalomania attributed to the man, the choice of organizing and developing a city according to a marketing logic is rooted in the same logic that brought François Mitterand and his team to hire the advertising executive Jacques Séguéla to design his 1981 presidential campaign.

Here is another act of blurring. In January 2011, the "Bretagne" (Brittany) trademark was launched: "in a global context of competition between territories, the image of a region plays a crucial role, claims Jean-Yves Le Drian, the president of the regional council. Although Brittany enjoys clear notoriety and a friendly image, it must increase its appeal, especially among those promising economic sectors that do not necessarily associate Brittany with performance."[13] The trademark covers the regional council, Brittany's economic agency, and the regional tourism committee.

12 Clémentine Monperrus, "Montpellier. La 'surdouée' tient ses promesses," *L'Expansion*, October 22, 2011, http://lexpansion.lexpress.fr/economie/montpellier-la-surdouee-tient-ses-promesses_265584.html.

13 "Lancement de la marque Bretagne," press release, http://www.bretagne.fr/internet/upload/docs/application/pdf/2011-02/dp_marque_bretagne.pdf.

The discourse underlying these campaigns is rooted in a breeding ground of mutations that developed throughout the 1980s, at different rhythms and under different forms depending on the country. In the 2000s, pressured by the extension of the norms of rivalry, competition, and evaluation into every sphere of activity, such a discourse became radicalized. The projects of politicians were replaced with programs for the rationalization of (European) economic geography, and therefore of places of production, in particular immaterial production. This rationalization corresponds to a territorial organization extended to the whole planet by the economic logic of globalization, thereby becoming the territory of this logic.

What is the leeway of graphic design with respect to this economic-based will to control all the activities of a "territory"? Should we not then make the distinction between design and designer, the profession and its actors?

Is there a risk that these visual essays may transform such a demonstration into a wall? A smooth wall, without any bump or crack, compacted, opaque, a wall in which all the signs are the same: the representation of a bulldozer-like system. And such a wall is all the more opaque as the demonstration aims to be transparent. Any attempt to imagine something different would come up against such a wall. How can we not feel crushed?

In 2004, the Swiss National Bank launched a competition for the design of new banknotes. The theme was "Switzerland open to the world," with "Switzerland being presented as a whole, as a country open to the rest of the world and as an international meeting place."[14] An artistic commission was conveyed, headed by exhibition curator Jean-Christophe Ammann. In November 2005, the commission carried out the selection: the project by Manuel Krebs (Norm) won first place: "The chosen images are relevant and all address difficult issues (e.g. AIDS). In addition to being very clear, the proposed designs are universal and will remain topical in the future. The sense of cohesion in this homogenous series is very strong, with the themes moving from the microscopic to the astronomical (from red blood cells to the universe) and the relationship between the obverse and reverse of the banknotes proving very perceptive. This portfolio is the type that breaks with tradition, offering an element of surprise. The semantic value is very pronounced. The only point not in its favor is that certain images could lead to confusion."[15]

14 "Swiss National Bank presents banknote designs," press release, http://www.snb.ch/en/mmr/reference/pre_20051123/source.

15 Jean-Christophe Ammann, "Remarks on tasks of jury and on results," news conference, http://www.snb.ch/en/mmr/speeches/id/ref_20051123_ammann/source

Second place was a draw between the projects of Manuela Pfrunder, of which the jury wrote, "At a cursory glance, the designs may appear somewhat dull," and that of Martin Woodtli, "very original in terms of graphic design. The designer plays well with the messages he wishes to convey and masters the use of symbols. Despite this, however, the designs on the lower denominations lack originality and clarity."[16]

The Swiss National Bank published the evaluation of Ammann's commission,[17] and promised to come to a decision by spring 2006. However, it was not until February 27, 2007, that we learned that "the bank board of the Swiss National Bank has decided, on a proposal by the Extended Group Management Board, to proceed with the preparatory works ... with the graphic designer Manuela Pfrunder, joint runner-up of the idea competition."[18]

Between the selection made by Ammann's commission in 2005 and the 2007 decision of the board of the Swiss National Bank, tensions had risen around the iconography selected by Manuel Krebs. In an act of emancipation from traditional imagery (portraits of personalities, monuments, or lyrical landscapes), the graphic designer had favored analogies between the infinitely big and the infinitely small, the dialogue between scientific disciplines and the representation of life (fetuses, organs), and therefore, death (AIDS, a skull).[19] And the jury decided that Manuela Pfrunder's proposals, with their "references to nature, sports, and science, were better suited for manufacturing."[20]

The bank's management justified its rejection of the choice of Ammann's commission by pointing out various technical difficulties inherent to the manufacturing of a banknote—security constraints and manufacturing difficulties. The press, however, understood that the decision was a political one. A news anchor of the RTS channel commented: "The new banknotes were supposed to represent a fetus, a dead person's skull, or the AIDS virus. In the ensuing outcry, all of this is gone. The Swiss National Bank has abandoned the project of the controversial series." In the report that followed the news, Peter Rothenbühler, the editor-in-chief of the Swiss newspaper *Le Matin* and one of the most virulent opponents to Mr. Krebs' project, issued the following statement: "This is mostly a relief. I am very happy with the National Bank's decision to withdraw

16 Ibid. The reproductions of banknotes are available on the website of the Swiss National Bank, http://www.snb.ch/fr/iabout/cash/newcash/id/cash_new_result/.
17 Ammann, "Remarks on tasks."
18 "Avancees des travaux," Idées Suisses website, http://www.idees-suisses.ch/billets-banque-suisses/billets-banque-suisses.html.
19 See reproductions of the banknotes, http://www.snb.ch/fr/iabout/cash/newcash/id/cash_new_result/.
20 Bernard Wuthrich, "Des billets de banque tout neufs," *Le Temps*, January 3, 2012, http://www.letemps.ch/Page/Uuid/1a85e6b6-3569-11e1-8b16-9fdd903a14aa/Des_billets_de_banque_tout_neufs.

this banknote project. A banknote is like a country's calling card, in a way, and I could see no connection whatsoever to our country's identity and image in those banknotes. Death, destruction, and illness are no topics for a banknote, I think." The journalist concluded: "Instead of human organs, the National Bank's management has selected the creation by the runner-up Manuela Pfrunder. She addresses the theme of 'Switzerland open to the world' from the angle of tourism: the backs of her banknotes feature paragliding, skiers, and snow cannons."[21]

The year 2007 was also a federal election year in Switzerland, which saw the UDC—Christoph Blocher's xenophobic party—winning 30 percent of the vote.[22] Such a result was not a coincidence, that is, it was rooted in Europe's fertile ground of nationalist and identitarian far-right movements, which have continued their expansion up to the present day.

Although the banknotes were supposed to be printed in 2008 and issued in 2010, the operation was postponed to 2012.

The technical explanations put forward by the Swiss National Bank seem indeed unsatisfactory. It is quite likely that the bank has given in to the political pressure of the nationalist and identity movements incarnated, among others, by the newspaper *Le Matin*, which featured a long interview with Marine Le Pen in 2012.[23] However, what interests me most here is the crack introduced by Ammann's commission. Beside the bank's representative—Roland Tornare, the chief cashier and director of cash, as well as head of the project for the "development of a new banknote series"—the commission gathered several personalities from the world of Swiss art and culture, notably Jacqueline Burckhardt, the cofounder and editor of the art magazine *Parkett* (Zurich/New York) since 1983, president of the Swiss Federal Art Commission from 1998 to 2006, consultant for site-specific artworks on the Novartis Campus in Basel since 2006, and, since 2008, director of the Sommerakademie at the Zentrum Paul Klee in Bern; Chantal Prod'Hom, the director of Lausanne's Mudac since 2000; Jean-Frédéric Jauslin, the director of the Swiss Federal Office of Culture since 2005; and Bruno Monguzzi and Werner Jeker, both graphic designers.

21 "La BNS présente ses nouveaux billets de banque," *19:30 le journal*, February 26, 2007, http://www.rts.ch/video/info/journal-19h30/1591439-la-bns-presente-ses-nouveaux-billets-de-banque.html.

22 Psykotik, "Pourquoi c'est l'extrême droite qui a gagné en Suisse," *Agora Vox*, October 30, 2007, http://www.agoravox.fr/actualites/politique/article/pourquoi-c-est-l-extreme-droite-30846; Ian Hamel, "Suisse. La droite dure remporte les élections," *Le nouvel observateur, Rue 89*, October 21, 2007, http://www.rue89.com/2007/10/21/suisse-la-droite-dure-remporte-les-elections.

23 Marie Maurisse, interview with Marine Le Pen, "Freysinger trouve que je ne suis pas assez radicale contre l'islam," *Le Matin Dimanche*, February 12, 2012, http://www.lematin.ch/monde/Freysinger-trouve-que-je-ne-suis-pas-assez-radicale-contre-l-islam/story/24809796.

Such a crack in the selection process may seem insignificant and pointless at the end of the day. Nevertheless, gathering these people was like introducing a grain of sand into the wheels of a mechanism and making it malfunction, if only for a moment…

* * *

Great Britain: over four million surveillance cameras.

In 2008, in London, the band The Get Out Clause selected eighty of them (in the streets, in a bus) and organized a concert in front of each camera.

Under the Freedom of Information Act, the musicians claimed the footage from the agencies that managed the cameras. They then used the footage to produce a clip. The street took the place of the stage and the clip was distributed online via the website Dailymotion.[24] The clip made the most of the characteristics of surveillance footage: black-and-white images, low definition, the lead singer looking in a specific direction…

Michel de Certeau would no doubt have been interested in such a misappropriation of a tool of control, a tool all the more powerful as it was placed there with the consent of an important part of the population and in the name of security. "Everyday life," he tells us, "invents itself by poaching in countless ways on the property of others."[25]

Both examples—the misappropriation of a surveillance camera and the selection of the Ammann commission—are cracks in the wall of the dominant discourse about the fatality of our world, as well as in the wall of the discourse produced by these visual essays. These two instances are interesting in that their authors come from different environments. The members of the Ammann commission, whose authority is unimpeachable, were gathered in their capacity as professionals and experts in the field of art and design. I do not know whether they reacted to the Swiss National Bank's rejection. In the second example, the crack was the act of unknown kids without any means (to finance their recording), of amateurs. I don't know whether their clip, produced by misappropriating a surveillance camera and distributed online, had any favorable impact on their music career. Of course, this second example is not directly relevant

24 "The Get Out Clause—Extrait du journal de 13h de France 2 du 8 mai 2008," *Journal de 13h*, France 2, May 5, 2008, http://ma-tvideo.france2.fr/video/iLyROoafY2kG.html (accessed May 21, 2013).

25 Michel de Certeau, *The Practice of Everyday Life*, trans. Steven Rendall, Berkeley et al., 1984; repr. 2011, p. XII (italics in the original); originally published in French in 1980 as *L'invention du quotidien*, vol. 1: *Arts de faire*, Paris, 1990, p. 36.

to graphic design (or so it would seem…). However, the practice of misappropriating political or commercial posters, for instance, with the critical aim of turning their discourse against them, originates in a similar intent. The point is that these visual essays reveal only the tip of a complex situation—namely, the strategies of the institutions—while overlooking the poaching practices and other individual or micro-collective tactics aimed at the appropriation of the public space. Admittedly, this would be an extremely difficult task, requiring a considerable amount of resources and time. In other words, how do these signs and systems of visual identification affect the inhabitants of a city? How are they assimilated—or not? By presenting a construction articulated by signs derived from decision and negotiation processes, these essays deny themselves those grains of sand that are so many reasons for hope.

It would be a tall order to imagine that graphic design could change this state of affairs, and that a graphic designer could influence, in the course of negotiations, the bulldozer of "territorial marketing strategy" [26] endowed, as in the case of ONLYLYON, with an annual budget of 1.6 million euros.

What are our options then?

Part of the answer might depend on how graphic design is taught, especially in public art schools—those which I am most familiar with. To reconsider this educational aspect raises the following question: is graphic design a discipline?

"A discipline," according to Michel Foucault, "is defined by a domain of objects, a set of methods, a corpus of propositions considered to be true, a play of rules and definitions, of techniques and instruments." [27] If we answer in the affirmative, then are we not running the risk of defending a conception that is implicitly assumed to be ideal and, therefore, the only legitimate one? Would that amount to defending a certain idea of culture, sure of itself and of the productions it generates, whereas the very foundations of such a conception are deactivated by commodification? This pressure forces us to

26 Following the terminology used in the ONLYLYON press release, "Promotion internationale de l'agglomération lyonnaise."

27 Michel Foucault, "The Order of Discourse," trans. Ian McLeod, in *Untying the Text: A Post-Structuralist Reader,* ed. Robert Young, London, 1981, p. 59; originally published in French in 1970 as *L'ordre du discours.*

reconsider the foundations of our conception of culture. Moreover, the order of disciplines—their hierarchy, organization, structure, isolation, and, therefore, their identity—is no longer self-evident and is currently undergoing a critical process of redefinition and positioning.

The language of graphic design slides, slithers, and worms its way inside a diversity of human activities as soon as there is a need to convey information, knowledge, or content. The uncertainty inherent to the diversity of situations does not easily lend itself to being confined to a preexisting framework of "ready-made" solutions and answers prepared for the sponsors. Should graphic designers then be defended on the basis of their capacity as "experts," in the sense that their competence and practice thereof are tantamount to having authority and the right to judge? As we all know, defending the artist, designer, or intellectual based on the claim that they are pioneers, heralds, holders of truth and a trailblazing clarity is a tactic now consigned to history. Historically, graphic design has been a tool of regulation, rationalization, and circulation of people as well as material and immaterial goods acquired by industrial societies. This suggests a continuity between the historical foundations of graphic design and its contemporary concerns. However, the continuity is reduced to a mere utilitarian dimension as soon as the utopias endorsed by historical designers no longer serve as artistic, intellectual, and ethical frameworks. Training graphic design experts would therefore perpetuate and update the figure of the herald and pioneer, of the one who knows vis-à-vis the crowd of those who don't. It would mean training individuals whose sensitivity to grains of sand is undermined by their certainty of possessing the accuracy of expertise, the clarity of the answer. A graphic designer is neither a herald nor an expert. Should we speak of a loss of the power to act, to influence the visual landscape?

Of course some skills are specific to graphic design (typographical drawing, layout, interface design, etc.). It also goes without saying that the discipline has a history. But when this history is freed from formal approaches or a museum conception, it tells us that graphic design is inextricably linked to language and the media. This is precisely what we learn from a cross-examination of the visual essays and of ONLYLYON's press release: words and images are tools used to construct the narrative of a fictional world. The fiction, however, conceals the violence of rivalry, the exclusion generated by competition and ratified by politicians. Today, the power to act requires an understanding and control of what is at stake in language and the media.

If this is the case, is it not in our interest to redesign and adjust the orientation of our schools' pedagogy? Should we continue to approach graphic design through an overdetermination of practice, to the point that students, often with their "nose to the grindstone," end up reproducing existing models, whether historical ones or those currently in fashion? Should we not rethink the training through an association between the new material configurations of our present (economic networks, modes of production, etc.), the status of language and the media, and the new field of action imposed on graphic design by these new reconfigurations?

If we return to what is presented in these visual essays, what needs to be critically assessed is not the form so much as the foundations of a discourse that defines the choice of means and forms; we must assess a dominant discourse that tends to level differences, to produce a "ready-made," ideal universe, and that tries to impose on all of us, no matter our background, the truth about the fatality of the system. It is therefore no longer graphic design as such that must be questioned, but rather the attitude of designers/individuals faced with that kind of demand. The issue, then, would no longer be to welcome the students on the grounds of our own certainties, but to ask what motivates individual novice designers to become professionals.

In a 2008 article, André Gorz analyzed the current crisis of capitalism. He defined what he called "an annuity of novelty, rarity, exclusivity." This annuity results from the attribution of immaterial qualities to products, which thereby acquire a status similar to that of an artwork. Companies thus "compete for the launch of new products, models, or styles with the originality of their designs, the inventiveness of their marketing campaigns, and the personalization of their products." [28]

As early as 1947 László Moholy-Nagy described a similar process: "Thus, 'design' today is generally a bid for quick sale, usually nothing but an exterior cloak around a product. Its main characteristic is to be 'different' although the function remains the same. The industrial designer today is called in to 'style' or 'fashion' a product already engineered, and the more often he changes a 'design,' the more he is supposed to have contributed to the salesman's success." [29]

28 André Gorz, "Le travail dans la sortie du capitalisme," *EcoRev. Revue critique d'écologie politique,* no. 28, 2008, http://ecorev.org/spip.php?rubrique194

29 László Moholy-Nagy, "New Method of Approach—Design for Life," in *Vision in Motion,* Chicago, 1947, p. 34.

László Moholy-Nagy addressed this assessment by putting forward the need to define "a new method of approach," in which "The idea of design and the profession of the designer has to be transformed from the notion of a specialist function into a generally valid attitude of resourcefulness and inventiveness which allows projects to be seen not in isolation but in relationship with the need of the individual and the community."[30] In order to avoid instrumentalization, this spirit of resourcefulness and inventiveness needs to be rooted in a global reflection on the complexity of our world, a complexity doubly amplified by a constant process of transformation, by the movement of this process, and, with regard to graphic design, by the diversity of situations. Three elements must therefore by considered: the widening gap between our slow capacity to assimilate the far-reaching issues and consequences of these transformations, the dynamics adopted by this process of mutation, and, finally, our own experience of time, defined by norms of speed, and special, spectacular events. We must also believe in the actions of individuals operating in their own field, in their practice-based attempts to transform things, in their knowledge and experience of venues and situations. Although their attempts may be doomed to fail, they nevertheless correspond to memories that, once brought together, eventually constitute a common memory. Then, in order to recognize this action, we should accept being modest—without giving up on our ambitions—and stop postulating the ignorance of "people" (sponsors, readers, users, etc.).

The modesty required for the successful implementation of projects can be summed up in two different definitions, both of which could apply to graphic designers and become the foundation of their training. Norman Potter invites the designer to remain a student, "The serious student of scholarly bent who 'reads' the subject and may make a distinctive contribution to theory or criticism. By the word 'student,' therefore, I mean those who still question what they are doing, and ask why."[31]

The second definition, whose radicalness I would stress, is the one proposed by Jacques Rancière, based on a criticism of the traditional conception of knowledge and its transmission, "What the schoolmaster knows, what the protocol of knowledge transmission teaches the pupil in the first instance, is that ignorance is not a lesser

30 Ibid., p. 42.

31 Norman Potter, *What Is a Designer?*, 4th ed., London, 2002, p. 14.

form of knowledge, but the opposite of knowledge."[32] The ensuing distance is then "the metaphor of the radical gulf separating the schoolmaster's manner from the ignoramus's, because it separates two intelligences: one that knows what ignorance consists in and one that does not."[33] And in order to maintain a distance that is the guarantee of his or her status, the schoolmaster must "replace ignorance by knowledge, he must always be one step ahead, install a new form of ignorance between the pupil and himself."[34] This way of conceiving knowledge transmission is a form of "stupefaction" opposed to what we wish to grant our students: access to intellectual emancipation. In other words, we wish them to be aware of their connection to history, to a certain idea of design, but also to be free, in terms of resourcefulness and inventiveness, from the reproduction of models. The teaching ignoramus-designer should help novice designers shape their capacity to ignore anything that hinders their emancipation: the supposed "inequality of intelligence."[35]

Pedagogy would then train students, not for a profession as such, but for an attitude, the attitude of ignoramus-designers, unaware of the supposed intelligence inequality separating them from sponsors or readers. In other words, training should consider graphic design no longer as the profession of experts, but as the prerogative of emancipated individuals endowed with specific competences (mastery of visual syntaxes). Their critical approach to the word, marked by questioning and uncertainty, would orient designers' conduct and allow them to make their choice rather than passively enduring any kind of situation. Putting forward the figure of the ignoramus-designer may also break with that representation of life after school students call "real life." As if the "reality" of life found its true sense only in a kind of fatality; as if students had no other choice than to accept or refuse that fatality, positioning themselves outside or above it. As if, all things considered, there were no space for invention outside school or the system. Ignoramus-designers

32 Jacques Rancière, *The Emancipated Spectator,* trans. Gregory Elliott, London and New York, 2009, p. 9; originally published in French in 2008 as *Le spectateur émancipé.* See also *The Ignorant Schoolmaster: Five Lessons in Intellectual Emancipation,* Stanford, Calif., 1991; originally published in French in 1987 as *Le Maître ignorant. Cinq leçons sur l'émancipation intellectuelle.*

33 Ibid.

34 Ibid., p. 8.

35 Ibid., p. 11.

could pave the way for inventiveness and resourcefulness, because they would be free from a predefined conception of graphic design.

Today, one of the conditions of such an emancipation would consist in approaching graphic design through a movement of transformation, displacement, and reconfiguration, a movement that would force us to rethink the distribution of roles and the founding paradigms of graphic design, an open language, a "second text"[36] to be structured inside the negotiation. The critical approach of the ignoramus-designers would bring them to analyze a design of relations rather than one of "objects" as such, thereby reconsidering the nature of negotiations between being and things. They would find their place in the process of deactivation of the transmission model of communication, defined in 1949 by Claude Shannon (active transmitter/passive receiver), and to which one could also associate the dichotomy knowledgeable designer/ignorant sponsors and readers.

The conception of a design of shifting relations, a progressive conception supported by the appropriation of critical tools and, therefore, by the mastery of language and the awareness of the influence of the media upon our behaviors, would then constitute a possible answer to authoritarian discourses about truth. Such a conception would also allow us to rethink the complexity of the network in which specific, local situations are inscribed. It would allow us to accept this movement, no longer as a consequence, but as a decisive factor of constant reconfiguration of the roles and statuses; the movement would no longer be perceived as an effect, but as a state of affairs. Likewise, graphic design would no longer be conceived as a discipline with well-defined boundaries and creating its own experts, but as a language whose syntax is determined by the relation between the designer-individual and the world; an individual with specific competences, sensitive to the cracks produced by experience of the equality of intelligences.

36 Emmanuel Souchier, "L'image du texte. Pour une théorie de l'énonciation éditoriale," *Cahiers de médiologie,* no. 6 (1998), http://mediologie.org/cahiers-de-mediologie/06_mediologues/souchier.pdf.

"Branding," Faith, and Experience
Pierre-Damien Huyghe

Since the early 1990s the existence of *non-lieux,* non-places, more or less everywhere is readily admitted. The expression obviously owes a great deal to Marc Augé's book of the same name,[1] which was able to draw attention to a number of places that are poorly socialized, even non-socializable, or in any case unsuitable for developing the links of traditional sociability. Augé saw in the frequency of non-places the major element—the essential mode of appearance—of a new era, namely, "supermodernity." The negative character of the term he came up with remains a problem, however. What we must come to understand is that in fact—starting with its name—it is a matter of judgment that at heart rejects it.

I shall be arguing two points then in this regard. On the one hand, I would like to establish that this so-called supermodernity is bound up with a sudden, more global growth in terms of landscape. This sharp growth not only affects places that are devoid of humans and that we would like to pass through without having to pay any mind, but also, because the view is being peopled, as it were (an accumulation of more or less aggressive signs and logos, for example), this growth tends to determine the complete field of our relationship to objects. Is this entire trend inevitable? On the other hand, I want to offer a critique of the negative aspect of Augé's concept in order to raise that kind of question. Indeed, to know that the urban strata currently developing are doing so by implicating places and practices without any positive aspects hardly helps one to live in those strata. Rather it makes one want to take refuge in spaces protected from the incriminated movement, if any such spaces remain. This is precisely the problem, the whole problem of this search for a refuge: Is it still possible to really separate—I repeat, "really," not "imaginarily," not "nostalgically"—separate places and non-places? How did the latter, if they are radically negative, manage to come about? And how can one—not justify, that is not my intention—at least understand their growth?

1 See Marc Augé, *Non-Places: Introduction to an Anthropology of Supermodernity,* trans. John Howe, London and New York, 1995; originally published in French in 1992 as *Non-Lieux. Introduction à une anthropologie de la surmodernité.*

The term "supermodernity" does not only describe the qualities of a spatiality without place. What is at stake is also of a historical nature. It leads to involving the phenomena it studies in a period logic whose final phase would mean going far beyond an earlier phase that had been able to form places. As a result, these places, these true places, these places that are positively places, are conceptualized against the present in the register of a maintaining. It is this conceptual obligation that bothers me. That is, it tends to disarm those who would like to do something, who would like to change things. The possibility of having an intention *today,* even the slightest one, in terms of what is going on is permanently in doubt. Recalling a phrase that László Moholy-Nagy coined in his day—"designing is ... an attitude" [2]—I see as an issue the positions of principle vis-à-vis what is taking place. What is growing in the world can do so with a greater or lesser degree of desolation at first, "inorganically" as Moholy-Nagy would have put it, which doesn't mean there is nothing to do *with* it. Having read Augé's book, I indeed have a hard time seeing what might be done with the non-places he defines, except keeping them on the fringes of spaces that hypothetically enjoy a better reputation. But if the incriminated phenomena involve not only the hypothetically marginalizable areas of spatial growth, but also, as I have proposed just now, the displays of businesses and the commerce in objects, is that still possible? The most probable hypothesis is that they have wormed their way into all areas and that in the end nowhere are there places like before.

To get back to our analysis, let's take a look, or take a second look, at some characteristic element of this supposed supermodernity, for example the space of highways as it is embellished by those standardized signs that "tell" us that, thanks to a pitiful iconography which is itself standardized, a little further on no doubt, although not right there exactly, invisible in any case, *in passing,* is found this or that interesting monument, notable site, cultural space. These signs are *annonces,* [3] advertisements, something announced. They

2 See László Moholy-Nagy, *Vision in Motion,* Chicago, 1947.

3 The French term here comes from the verb *annoncer,* to announce, and indeed means "advertisements" (*petites annonces,* for example, are "personal ads"). But the term continues to have its sense of "something announced." The author exploits a number of these meanings throughout the rest of his article, but it is not possible to render them in English.—Trans.

are installed ahead of a possible experience, a visit that, if it does take place, would stop highway passengers on their way. But this experience does not happen most of the time. Highway passengers are essentially passersby; the highway is not made for them to go out of their way or stop, and only rarely do they indeed go out of their way or stop. Is this a bad thing in itself? The problem doesn't lie in the fact of passing by (a highway landscape can be beautiful even in crossing it, in the tracking shot created by the passerby); it lies rather in the dual constraint introduced by the composition formed by the sign and the highway, by the paradoxical association of the two. While the latter invites drivers to speed by, the former suggests that they take their time, linger, dawdle.

This experience does have its consequences. On the one hand, in its way it entertains passengers, separates the horizon of their thoughts from the horizon of their perception, forces them to turn their minds for a moment to an elsewhere that escapes their lived experience, and instructs them to enjoy a diversion that they have not consented to themselves. On the other hand, and this is what I shall especially stress for the whole of my analysis of branding below, it devalues the very space in which it is standing at the time. There is a repercussion with the signal: it shifts the place or thing where it is posed away from notability itself. That is why I strictly spoke of a phenomenon of "advertisements," of things being announced. The effective operation the sign carries out is not theological, strictly speaking (the place indicated is basically not religious, and when it is, it is presented rather as a part of our human heritage). It is metaphysical, however. Or rather evangelical. A piece of news is announced, hypothetically good news, that of a world that is not immediately present, an "other," substantial, notable world, substantial because it is noted, a world with which the addressee is initially connected in spirit, something that cannot occur unless the world here and now, the one not announced, not advertised, is more or less devalued. Here and passing through "here" plunge into a kind of prosaic indignity. They are destroyed by the advertisement. The sign as it is, removed from any function in and for the passage itself (it has no raison d'être as far as traffic safety goes, for example), implies at heart a hypothesis in terms of the site. Endowed with its icon, the sign along the highway is, in its intention, quite different from the more traditional signs located at the entrance to or exit from a village. Those transform the latter into a locality, a *lieu-dit,* with emphasis on the *dit*, the "said" part (a locality inscribed in a linguistic reference point). The sign along the highway does not attach the same importance to the place where it stands. Because it mentions an elsewhere that is by definition absent from current perception, it instantly tips the area into a kind of anonymity, and deprives it of the chance of being associated with a name; in a word, it despairs of the fact of being "there," for the moment the only fact to truly present itself to the eye.

A phenomenon of the same kind (paying no mind to reality in its present, sensuous aspect) occurs with the visual signals of the so-called brand companies. These signals are connected with products that are not necessarily separate from a material or functional point of view. Visual identity, the graphic shop window, aims less at perception than identification. It justifies the techniques involved in production and implementation, which go on to slip from genuine attention. If it were a question of creating that attention, the generics, as they say at the pharmacy, might be more frequent in contemporary commerce. In the world of brands, what counts is notability, *spirit*. This movement tolerates various instances of neglect as to the statutes and qualities of the objects themselves. It is often a certain carelessness in production—a relinquishing of one's concern to a certain degree—that makes it possible to inject value into description, the logo, and branding. Proof of this law, in France notably, lies in the number of shopping areas that have sprung up on the fringes of historical centers, on the way in and out of urban spaces. The proliferation of signs there is inversely proportional to the interest of the architecture, which is uniform and mediocre. Apparently, quite apparently, this architecture elicits the feeling that it is worth nothing by itself. It is not essential. What counts and must count much more is the advertisement it embodies, the sign surmounting it.

In the end, the world of brands in its way admits the dreary character of the mass produced. To borrow an expression with which Frank Lloyd Wright in his day thought he could justify both design and architecture, I would say that the branding of spaces as well as objects requires a certain absence of the "rhythm of Form." [4] Would productions that display formal differences that are notable in themselves need to be pointed up as these now are? It is *also* the

4 Frank Lloyd Wright, *An Autobiography*, New York, 1943; repr. Petaluma, Calif., 2005, p. 347.

uniformity of the highway—its formal constancy—that leads to the tourist sign. The question then is to know, if possible, what maintains such a sense of uniformity among us. Why, with all norms of security and all hypotheses of functionality being spelled out and respected, do highways, including at their rest stops, resemble one another so? Why are supermarkets nearly identical, save for their signs? Why do dairy products stand out more for their images and the graphics of their packaging than for their taste?

I have no doubt that these questions are the result of a certain economy. Only that economy is not as up-to-date as it appears. Old practices of religion and faith resurface there, albeit unrecognizable in their most obvious aspects. The word branding itself still recalls the brand and its fiery uses, including some religious ones. As for the word "economy," in the early centuries of Christianity it referred, in terms of circumscribing human behaviors, to the consequences that could be drawn from the administration of an assumed mystery, that of one sole divinity existing in three distinct registers. And in a way we have come back to a relationship to the economic realm that is suffused with mystery before we have anything to do with it. Even though we sense we no longer need to arrange our affairs in accordance with the divine, we are still capable of placing our trust in the signs of brands and believing in the virtue of the names, codes, or signals adorning the face of products. We even buy them solely for that reason at times. Occasionally we leave a shop equipped with a so-called loyalty card, one for the faithful, as it were. That such an expression doesn't seem odd to us suggests just where we are. Nietzsche's famous phrase declaring and recognizing at the same time that "God is dead" precedes by only a little the birth of such brands. The specific spirits of the latter, when brought together in shopping areas that make a cult of them, constitute a novel pantheon of multiple pagan divinities. Each of us, by a sign or logo, is called to sacrifice a portion of our time to the exercise of a belief that makes us admit that this or that product possesses a particular virtue, this or that brand-name computer, for example, is worth more than another, although its components are manufactured in the very same way, even in the same place. So we are still practitioners of one faith or another. Moreover, the Nietzschean observation proves strangely contemporary with the increase in importance of a kind of value that is able to go beyond the two-sided use value/exchange value of so-called classical economists, namely "fiduciary" value.

What is such a value? "So-called fiduciary money," Georges Blumberg writes in the *Encyclopedia Universalis,* "is a money whose nominal value is superior to its intrinsic value." In other words, it is a money without a realizable equivalent, a money that is mainly credible. "Commonly," Blumberg adds, "fictional values are called fiduciary, that is, values based solely on the trust granted to the person issuing them." [5] One should note the subjective character of the relationship defined here. It is the issuing party that determines the trustworthiness of what is issued. Initially then this trustworthiness must be established, produced in the mind. In the fiduciary register, the decisive thing in the end lies less in the content of what is issued than in the attachment to the principle that there is an author and that author is worthy of our faith. Hence the importance of defining an effective element (a name, outline, graphic image, color) that is likely to be supposed or imagined as guaranteeing a personal connection with value by way of a specific line, a signature. Basically this means nothing more than the following: "There is a signature and you can trust it (*you can, you may trust him*)," even though the intentions and interests of the signatory remain beyond our understanding.

Two truths come to light here. On the one hand, the fiduciary order with which branding is historically connected excludes from its essential center of interest an entire part of "realizing" (it is not about understanding, or making sense of); and on the other, there is no need for authentic forms to be organized on its behalf. That is, the register of the "figure," according to its old name in rhetoric, is enough. These two elements in fact go together. The formal completion in the order of things (the reality of the Latin *res*) is no more sought after than understanding, since it does not enter the principle of fiduciarization that those to whom it (fiduciarization) is addressed are aware in a way of what is playing out. Thus, the movement I am conjuring up here contributes for its part to the fall in the value of experience that Walter Benjamin echoed in a different context in the last century. [6]

5 Georges Blumberg, "Fiduciare," *Encyclopædia Universalis* (online), http://www.universalis.fr/encyclopedie/fiduciaire (accessed May 15, 2013).

6 "... experience has fallen in value." Walter Benjamin, "The Storyteller: Reflections on the Works of Nikolai Leskov," in *Illuminations,* trans. Harry Zohn, New York, 1988, pp. 83–84; originally published in German in 1936 as "Der Erzähler. Betrachtungen zum Werk Nikolai Lesskows," in *Orient und Occident.*

That such a movement dominates human commerce today does not make it however the inevitable future of the entire period. If in order to analyze it I insist on mentioning several concepts that are part of a long history (like that of "figure" just now, or of "economy" earlier), I do so to bring out the possible consistency of an attitude that is also historical, though divergent at heart and less devoted, dare I say, to "performing" this or that belief mechanism than perfecting this or that component of reality. The very notion of "supermodernity," a notion that suggests in its very name that the modern phase of our history is today a thing of the past, does not afford enough of a chance to this consistency. Indeed, nothing is certain in this regard. Of course, what dominates us currently might be thought of as the return of an obsessive fear—that is the hypothesis we ought to attach importance to, as I have just suggested. And of course what haunts us in this way doesn't appear to us bluntly. "It" comes back to us in a modernized and hence unrecognizable guise. But what we misjudge in this way is what one part of the modern period had managed to render passé. What part was that? Why, modernity itself, modernity strictly speaking, the modernity that strove not to throw itself on everything that could pass for recent, but rather to measure the distance from the present—"modern beauty," as Baudelaire called it—in things themselves, works of art and operations. That a highway all in all is not a road "like before" and that contemporary interchanges, to take one last time an example selected by Augé, don't allow for crossroads of days gone by is not enough by itself to justify rejecting them in the name of landscape culture. To manage to cultivate them with regard to their present functions is indeed one of the issues involved. Yet these functions are specific; in other words, it is no longer about bringing people together or presiding over localizations, but rather ensuring that people indeed pass and movement occurs. That such functions can be elaborated and shaped right up to the level of a possible beauty, and that, elaborated and shaped in this way, they are in a position to enter culture—any number of shots in photography or film has already taught us this. Nothing guarantees that this effort is enough, or that beyond turning something into images, there is no longer anything that is worthwhile doing. One thing is clear, however. Our world in large part today, though given over to the functional at times and to the fiduciarization of values at others, and in both cases abandoned by any concern for form, is a world of passages;

and by presupposing the desolation of that world, we help to render it desolate in fact, heighten the negligence it is liable to, and complete the process of leaving it to the forces that only prosper at the expense of reality.

In the seventeenth century, Spinoza had already posited faith as a kind of adhesion to the literal meaning of expressions that exceed our understanding.[7] He established that this kind of adherence possessed a practical aspect, i.e., it obtains through obedience what one could not obtain through intelligence. It is that sort of relationship that brand advertising can spark. The little we make of reality today does not exclude all practical sense. It is an action in itself. Generalized branding has an adversary that it is acting against, namely movement, both physical and spiritual. Substantially denying passages their share of freedom (a whole possible area where thought can wander), branding wants to win over the mobility that the contemporary world is capable of. Quasi signs, signals, and graphs affixed to objects, no less than tourist signs along the highway, readily grant passersby the leisure of their stroll. They mean to grab whatever part of idleness that may be lodged in them. Through sheer force, however (and I insist on the term "force"), their operation is neurotic. They tap into or tie up an energy that might otherwise invigorate, an energy that is flexible in theory. When all is said and done, the advertisements from the world of branding are a product of that kind of prevention that goes with fear and mistrust. A strange anxiety undermines and drives them at the same time, which prohibits experience or only admits it forewarned (advertised in this sense also), as if it always had to be explosive or in revolt itself. This is not the case. The world of experience is the world of receptiveness. It doesn't expect that nothing will be done that can surprise or awaken it. It expects respect.

7 See Spinoza's *Theological-Political Treatise,* 1670.

Against Disposable Territories: A Preliminary Critical Approach to Systems of Territorial Identification

Luc Gwiazdzinski

> The city must never be confused
> with the words that describe it.
> And yet between the one and
> the other there is a connection.
> ITALO CALVINO, *Invisible Cities*,
> trans. William Weaver, 1972

"Vertigo" is the word that immediately comes to mind when contemplating the hurly-burly of logos and territorial markers that now stretch out before our eyes. "Apprehension" is possibly the feeling experienced when facing the visual gimmicks and simplifications that are on display, and which are unable to express the complexity and depth of our territories and the plurality of our individual and collective identities. "Paradox" is the term—borrowed from Yves Barel[1]—inevitably associated with the observation of the dialectical dynamics at work through these representations between the I and we, here and there, opening and closing, real and virtual, local and global, reality and its representations. The cabinet of curiosities on offer these days is at once a kaleidoscope reflecting at will the spirit of the times, a disparate collection of the contemporary world, and one element from a karaoke culture[2] that partakes of the commodification and de-realization of the world, revealing a different geography of territorial representations that is added to the palimpsest and offers us the chance to delve into the complexity of living and building a common experience. We find ourselves in what Guy Debord has called the "spectacle,"[3] an inverted image of reality that implies that truth is a moment of falsehood. The separation between reality and representation no longer exists in

1 Yves Barel, *Le paradoxe et le système. Essai sur le fantastique social,* Grenoble, 1979.

2 Dubravka Ugrešić, "The suppression of knowledge, of the past, of continuity, of cultural memory and of the cultural hierarchy, and an inconceivable speed these are the key features of karaoke culture," in *Karaoke culture,* Paris, 2012.

3 Guy Debord, *The Society of the Spectacle,* trans. Donald Nicholson-Smith, New York, 1994; originally published in French in 1967 as *La société du spectacle.*

the continual commodification of our realities. Our world no longer exists in terms of the reality of this commodity, but conceals its own nature from itself. The world no longer exists as world, but as simulacrum. "[And] certainly ... the present age ... prefers the sign to the thing signified, the copy to the original, fancy to reality, the appearance to the essence."[4] How did we get to this point?

A Postmodern Context

Glocalization. We are facing a deep transformation in the way we relate to time and space.[5] The growth of the worldwide market and of direct international investments, the formation of major economic blocs on a continental scale, the generalization of economic interdependencies, the boom in new communication technologies, the increasing number of information networks in real time and on a planetary scale, the erasing of geographical distances, the contraction of time and space, the general increase in mobility, the weakening of the nation-state and the ascent of local powers: it is the dawning simultaneously of the "internationalization" analyzed by Michel Beaud,[6] the "globalization" described by Robert Reich,[7] the generalization of Fernand Braudel's "world-economy"[8] and Olivier Dollfus's "world system,"[9] the "global village" predicted by Marshall McLuhan, and the local and the "invention of territories," to borrow an expression coined by Paul Alliès.[10] In a word, we have entered the era of "glocalization."

Shattering. Territory as a topic has never been so widely discussed, yet our living space has never been so torn apart, even alienated.

4 Ludwig Feuerbach, preface to the second edition of *The Essence of Christianity*, trans. Marian Evans, London, 1854; originally published in German in 1841 as *Das Wesen des Christentums*.

5 Luc Gwiazdzinski, "Temps et territoires. Les pistes de l'hyperchronie," *Territoire 2040*, no. 6 (2012), pp. 75–95.

6 Michel Beaud, *Le system mondial hiérarchisé*, Paris, 1987.

7 Robert Reich, *The Work of Nations: Preparing Ourselves for 21st Century Capitalism*, New York, 1991.

8 Fernand Braudel, *Civilization and Capitalism, 15th–18th Century*, trans. Siân Reynolds, vol. 3: *The Perspective of the World*, New York, 1984; originally published in French in 1979 as *Le temps du monde. Civilisation matérielle, économie et capitalism XVe–XVIIIe siècles*.

9 Olivier Dollfus and Roger Brunet, "Mondes nouveaux," in *Géographie universelle*, vol. I, Paris, 1990.

10 Paul Alliès, *L'invention du territoire*, Grenoble, 1980.

Increased mobility has shattered the classical frameworks of everyday life and citizenship. The specialization of space into living, shopping, leisure, training, and work areas forces us to move further and further away. We must realize that most of our contemporaries now live in large cities, those *outre-villes,* "cities of the beyond," or cities beyond the city, in Paul Virilio's definition.[11] The way we use and experience space is becoming increasingly fragmented. We flit between the territories of this "city *à la carte*" through tunnels and transit areas, "non-places"[12] charged with little emotional investment. The cartography of our lived-in space is more akin to an archipelago, delimited by uncertain boundaries and connected by networks, than to an ideal living area or a city neighborhood. One of the consequences of this increased mobility and imposed nomadism is that a majority of people no longer vote where they live, but where they sleep. The famous "living zones" have often become no more than "sleeping zones." Our IDs are evolving. It seems difficult to find an anchoring, an affiliation, as today we often live multiple lives in multiple spaces. It has become difficult to say where we are from, to which territory we belong. Boundaries have become more uncertain. There is no longer a unique feeling of belonging. Between their neighborhoods, their towns, and the world, individuals now function on multiple levels of affiliation.

Disorientation and loss of meaning. We are simultaneously going through a genuine big bang of organizations and territories, and an acceleration of time. Our society suffers from "time illness,"[13] and its members are subjected to the dictatorship of emergency, the injunction of the duty of memories, and the absence of projects for what we wish to be a sustainable future. Today most of us live in the suburbs, those "specious spaces" that have uncertain urban qualities. The state has gradually withdrawn, along with the public services to which its citizens had grown attached. We are all aware that postwar gains are gradually being called into question. France has involuntarily become a "commentary power," torn between its

11 Raymond Depardon and Paul Virilio, *Native Land: Stop-Eject,* exh. cat. Fondation Cartier pour l'art contemporain, Paris, Arles, 2010.

12 Marc Augé, *Non-Places: Introduction to an Anthropology of Supermodernity,* trans. John Howe, London and New York, 1995; originally published in French in 1992 as *Non-Lieux. Introduction à une anthropologie de la surmodernité.*

13 Jean Chesnaux, *Habiter le temps,* Paris, 1996.

new role of "hotel"—the Michel Houellebecq outlook[14]—and that of an old Nation, comfortably established behind its own borders—following Régis Debray[15]— and it seems more affected than other nations, its citizens obsessed by their own decline and subject to what one might call "ante-pathy." Between an idealized past and an uncertain future, between their territorial roots and the call of wider horizons, our contemporaries seem ill at ease, disoriented, and in need of reassurance. The crisis they are experiencing is at once social (due to increasing disparities), spatial (due to urbanization and its ensuing tensions and unbalances), economic (exacerbated competition), and, finally, cultural (for the difficulty of integrating an ever-shifting identity in a country where the state has always played such a special role). The loss of meaning and the disorientation are affecting society as a whole, its institutions, observers, and citizens. These are the drifts and dreams of a society locked up in the immediate present—a form of eternity—in which emergency and proximity appear as the essential dimensions of time and space, and from which great narratives have disappeared. The world is plunged into doubt while denying its own disarray. It seems entirely mobilized in simulacrum, stupor, and attempts at reproduction as a defense against its own fears. Movement, noise, and speed make us intoxicated with the present moment, but do a poor job at concealing the hard time we have in visiting the different pasts, projecting ourselves into the future, and building long-term projects together. The repetition of sameness and nothingness makes us prisoners and highlights the void and nonsense around us. This is the particular context in which one must consider marketing strategies and the advent of "territorial brands" that, incidentally, do not necessarily correspond to existing communities or institutions.

Egotrip. As Andy Warhol prophesized, "In the future, everybody will be world famous for fifteen minutes."[16] In the early 2000s appeared Naomi Klein's renowned study of branding, whereby "The traditional spaces reserved for advertising have become too restrained for logos

14 "For me, France is just a hotel, nothing more," Michel Houellebecq, November 5, 2012.

15 "The border as a vaccine against the epidemic of walls, a remedy to indifference and a safeguard for the living," Régis Debray, *Éloge des frontières,* Paris, 2010.

16 Andy Warhol, catalogue of his retrospective exhibition at Stockholm's Moderna Museet, 1968.

influenced by a galloping expansionism."[17] It was already too late. The territory was already going through "a turbulence," to quote the title of an essay by geographer Roger Brunet.[18] In a few years, the ego-machine spiraled out of control, leading anyone to believe that they could gain the kind of phony renown that temporarily singles you out and elevates you above the common mass. Marketing and its professionals jumped on the bandwagon. Suddenly, individuals, organizations, and territories wanted to wink at the maps of standardization. Marketing turned its attention to territories, starting from the international megacities, the end-aisle displays of this new vanity fair. They died not all, but all were sick.[19] The "brand bullies" have struck our communities, from the megacity to our regions and down to the smallest of our villages. There was no choice but to exist. "To exist ... is to differ, to be different,"[20] if we are to apply Pierre Bourdieu's analysis of the notion of distinction to organizations and territories. Just like our contemporaries, territories and their officials dream of their fifteen minutes of fame. Spin doctors and other communication and marketing consultants looked into our slumbering local communities and told them to enter the lists. They provided the pictures and linguistic elements to try to turn these communities into winners. The contest is about who is the greatest and most beautiful. "Euro-the-best" and "Eurocities" come out all puffed up from their facelift. At the great globalization ball, the toad quickly ends up taking itself for Prince Charming. Magazines have become the display cases for the rankings of combatant territories, unequally armed on the battlefield of international competition. They help us identify "winning" territories[21] from the "losers." Everywhere, territorial competitiveness has replaced territorial planning and development—even in the terminology wielded by DATAR (Interdepartmental delegation for territorial planning and regional attractiveness), which had briefly

17 Publisher's blurb for the French edition of Naomi Klein's 2000 book *No Logo,* Arles, 2001.

18 Roget Brunet, *Le territoire dans les turbulences,* Montpellier, 1990.

19 Jean de La Fontaine, "The Animals Sick of the Plague," 1678.

20 Pierre Bourdieu, *Practical Reason: On the Theory of Action,* Stanford, 1998, p. 9; originally published in French in 1994 as *Raisons pratiques. Sur la théorie de l'action.* See Pierre Bourdieu, *Distinction: A Social Critique of the Judgment of Taste,* trans. Richard Nice, London and New York, 1984; originally published in French in 1979 as *La distinction. Critique sociale du jugement.*

21 Georges Benko and Alain Lipietz, *Les régions qui gagnent. Districts et réseaux. Les nouveaux paradigms de la géographie économique,* Paris, 1992.

turned into DIACT (Interdepartmental delegation for territorial planning and regional competitiveness). "Mirror mirror on the wall, who's the fairest of them all?" Like Snow White's looking-glass, the world is summoned to decide between the parties involved. The first inventory of the visual identities of territorial communities is an opportunity to question this territorial competition, the symbolic poverty emanating from it, and the risks it poses for life in a collectivity and the production of territories.

A Discourse for the City and the World

Urbi et orbi. The global economy and the redefinition of the role of the state have led to a dual movement: a decompartmentalization of actors and functions locally, and an opening up of territories to what is international.[22] The question of territories and their representation is inscribed in a binomial play between here and there, international and local, "I" and "non-I," "me" and "us." Territories are called to adapt to the demands of the local population and actors in search of reassurance, as well as the demands of companies, tourists, researchers, executives, students, and global creative classes[23] in search of new destinations. Global economy and territorial development are not opposed but participate in the same dialectic movement in which representations, emblems, images, and brands are involved. *Urbi et orbi,* to the city and to the world, the old papal tag applies.[24] We must produce a discourse directed inward and one directed outward, one for the city and one for the world. Thus, beginning in the mid-1980s territorial communities have launched an increasing number of initiatives in the field of local economic development, while simultaneously attempting to deploy international strategies.

Marketing and branding strategies. Thus, under the joint effect of globalization, European integration, and decentralization, territories are now competing against one another. They must become attractive,

22 Luc Gwiazdzinski and René Kahn, "Mondialisation de l'économie et développement des territoires. Relecture d'un paradoxe apparent," *Inter-régions,* no. 179 (1994), pp. 14–20.

23 Richard Florida, *The Rise of the Creative Class: And How It's Transforming Work, Leisure, Community and Everyday Life,* New York, 2002.

24 Luc Gwiazdzinski and Gilles Rabin, *Urbi et orbi. Paris appartient à la ville et au monde,* La Tour d'Aigues, 2010.

i.e., attract and retain human, economic, and financial resources. As a consequence, collectivities devote themselves to “territorial marketing,” defined as “the effort to increase the value of territories confronted with competitive markets, in order to favorably influence their targets’ behavior with an offer whose perceived value is durably superior to that of their competitors.” [25] In other words, territorial offer is adapted to demand. The notion is often associated with other corporate terms such as “lobbying”—which characterizes, for instance, the work of collectivities that established representative offices at the European Commission in Brussels—but also “project approach,” “territorial intelligence,” “territorial watch,” or “forecasting.” Territorial marketing does not sell a service or an administrative partition, but rather a destination to targeted clients: investors, managers, executives, and families. Territories are put on the market with a strategy, an operative plan, tools for steering and facilitating decision-making, as if they were a brand of laundry detergent or the launch of a new smartphone. Local communities and their secular arms (tourist and development agencies) have become full-fledged economic and tourism operators. This gradual transition to branding strategies involves both public and private actors. In a society affected by a competition-and-uncertainty complex, the brand is there to reassure, prompt a feeling of identification, and express ideas. After Lyon in 2005 with ONLYLYON, for the first time in France a French region, Brittany, created its own brand in 2011, thereby turning its territory into a product. They are now promising us that Alsace will soon have its own brand. Hopefully it will manage to escape the “five-*C* syndrome”—*colombage* (half-timbering), *coiffe* (headdress), *cigogne* (stork), *choucroute* (sauerkraut), and *cathédrale* (cathedral)— humorously skewered as the constituent elements of Alsatian identity by the historian Georges Bischoff. [26]

Urban planning for purposes of communication and event planning. Branding is not merely a question of images, symbols, and representations. A branding strategy whose aim is to transform a conglomeration into a major European metropolis has a feedback effect on the urban fabric and on the organization of social collectives. The

25 François Gollain, director of Agence régionale de développement d’Île-de-France.
26 See Renaud Dorandeu and Luc Gwiazdzinski, “Cartes postales,” *Saisons d’Alsace,* no. 132 (Summer 1996).

ensuing competition, playing out on an international scale, has an impact on the territory and its inhabitants. You must work hard to earn a reputation of being exceptionally gifted (*surdoué*) and gain admission into the inner circle of the territories that count. Once again, symbols replace reality, and clichés conceal complexity. A form of communication-oriented urban planning develops and spreads in the magazines. In every capital, iconic architecture is placing beautiful, lone objects signed by the planetary stars of the discipline. From London to Berlin to Montpellier, rows of steel-and-concrete monoliths have invaded the cities and the pages of periodicals. Tramways are spreading, serving both the people who ride them and the revived image of the cities they crisscross. Bike-sharing systems soon follow. Franchise signs are transforming the city center into a reassuring, open-air shopping center, while the shopping center is transformed into a city center by borrowing the latter's codes for its setting—fake sidewalks, benches, fountains, fake smells, fake bird songs, and plastic palm trees. The "faux war" predicted by Umberto Eco[27] is in full swing. The will to exist is also expressed through the advent of the city as an event venue.[28] Each major city needs to bring its people together, become a community and a territory, and signal its own presence to the world by organizing a cultural and attractive event on an international scale. These major events, like the Olympics or the World Cup, doubtless partake in the process of "aestheticization of the world" that Walter Benjamin had sensed coming[29]—the process of turning into an aesthetic object something that had no vocation whatsoever to be one. The dominant aesthetic modes imposed by globalization, theatricalization, the spectacular, and the kitsch are now applied to territories.

Geographic mutations. Even geography is transformed by such a generalized competition. According to promotional brochures and thanks to high-speed trains, you are just a few hours from anywhere. Better still: thanks to tricks of perspective, astounding processes of anamorphosis, each territory finds itself at the heart of Europe, the center of gravity of the continent, or rather the market.

27 Umberto Eco, *La guerre du faux*, Paris, 1985.
28 Luc Gwiazdzinski, "Chronotopies. L'événementiel et l'éphémère dans la ville des 24 heures," *BAGF*, no. 3 (2009).
29 Jean-Michel Palmier, *Walter Benjamin. Le chiffonnier, l'ange et le petit bossu*, Paris, 2007.

We are not far from the omphalomania that Roger Brunet decries—the capacity of any godforsaken hole in the wall to take itself for the center of the world. Cities everywhere want to be in their best light, in a nocturnal cosmetic competition that bathes the world ad nauseam in a yellow glow, as deplored by the lighting artist Yann Kersalé: "I am critical of the notion of an urban lighting plan that emphasizes too much, with too much effect, yet with too little sensitivity and hardly any possibilities for rediscovery." [30]

The city seems to shame the deciders, who remain hidden behind their own idea of modernity and the verdict coming from outside their walls. Even topography, which seemed eternal, is evolving under the repeated blows of marketing campaigns. Thus, the village of Chalons becomes Chalons-en-Champagne, Saint-Dié is transformed into Saint-Dié-des-Vosges with its International Festival of Geography, the department of Basses-Alpes becomes Alpes-Haute-Provence, Côtes-du-Nord turns into Côtes-d'Armor, and Bas-Rhin regularly reflects upon its own name faced with the emergence of Haute-Alsace. Newspeak translators continue their work, exercising their talent on individuals, groups, times, and spaces. Inhabitants have become actors, yesterday's big shots have become members of the "civil society," local companies set themselves up as "stakeholders," the market is a "convivial place," the multipurpose hall has metamorphosed into an "Espace André Malraux," the former industrial area dreams of becoming a "Technopolis," the music festival is a "Territory of Music," the senior-year party in high school becomes a "Nuit du bac," in an escalation that cries out for deeper analysis. In an air-conditioned world, marketing experts have turned their attention to the seasons, which, as we all know, no longer exist. No single summer in the city goes by without sand beaches, big beach umbrellas, games of pétanque, and beach volleyball tournaments. No urban winter without an ice-skating rink and a Christmas market in front of the train station or the town hall. From Paris to Longwy, between touristification and local mobilization, everyone is adapting to these new standards. After Roland Barthes elevated the Tour de France to the rank of saga and mythology, [31] even May 1 with its International Workers' Day seems affected by folklorization,

30 Jean-Louis Pradel, *Yann Kersalé*, Paris, 2008.

31 Roland Barthes, *Mythologies*, trans. Annette Lavers, New York, 1972; originally published in French in 1957 as *Mythologies*.

patrimonialization, and aestheticization. Everywhere, the one-off holidays are aestheticized, the exceptional rendered sacred, overshadowing ordinary, everyday life. The celebration becomes a possibility of meeting others in the postmodern city, a moment of exchange, an experience and an occasion lived in common against the fragmenting of times, spaces, organizations, and forms of mobility, a break from the pressure of time and the dictatorship of emergency, a pivotal temporality to counter the gradual erasure of great collective rhythms.[32]

Limits

Brands, logos, emblems, symbols, landmarks, and other totems are indicative of the zeitgeist, materials to be analyzed, mirrors that magnify and distort the habits and customs of our contemporary societies. They force us to consider potential risks and limits.

Dangerous simplification. The first fault we can deplore in these attempts to induce visual identification is that they naturally lead to a simplification of the world. We must first acknowledge that we are akin in a way to the characters in Borges's "The Aleph,"[33] who are struggling to understand the universe. Confronted with complexity, a term that Edgar Morin describes as "a problem word and not a solution word," we cannot make do with simplified world maps. We cannot accept not being able to grasp the totality of time and space around them. We must also realize that we ourselves take part in the spectacle through which "the ruling order discourses endlessly upon itself in an uninterrupted monologue of self-praise."[34] Finally, we must not forget that we are the ones directing our outlook on the world. "That is entirely up to you, she will be what you want her to be, if you think she is beautiful she will be beautiful, If there is evil in your heart you will only see demons."[35]

32 Luc Gwiazdzinski, "La ville par intermittence. Des temps de la fête à un urbanisme des temps," *Cidades* 8, no. 13 (2011), pp. 317–35.

33 Jorge Luis Borges, "The Aleph" (1949), *The Aleph and Other Stories*, trans. Andrew Hurley, New York, 2000; originally published in Spanish in 1945 as "El Aleph."

34 Debord, *Spectacle*, p. 19.

35 Gao Xingjian, *Soul Mountain*, trans. Mabel Lee, New York, 1995, p. 93; first published in Chinese in 1990 as *Lingshan*.

Caricature. A territory is not a yogurt. It cannot be reduced to an image and a slogan. A territory is not the isotropic, homogenous, smooth space that some would have us consume. It is a rocky space that takes time to cross, tame, and appropriate. It is a multilayered pastry that cannot be reduced to a slogan and an image. It is a complex human and social reality, a "layout of material and symbolic resources, capable of structuring the practical condition of existence of an individual or a social collective, and, in turn, of informing that individual or collective about their own identity." [36] Territorial identity cannot be reduced to a few clichés.

Credibility of the image. The second fault we can deplore is doubtless the power of the image produced and the way in which it replaces a text. "To visualize is to explain.... We can no longer legitimately oppose a speech to an image. Visibility cannot be refuted by arguments. It gets replaced with a different visibility." [37]

The masking effect. A metamap of logos and brands is overlaid until it is masked and removed from the physical geography of the lands, plains, mountains, and rivers, as well as from human geography.

Rotation. In this system of fast rotation, visual identities follow one another according to a logic of accelerated obsolescence. The naming of a new general manager of services, of a new president, often corresponds to the deployment of a new logo, a new identity for the administered community and territory—city, intermunicipality, or department.

Copy-paste and trivialization. From one medium to the other, communicators appear to be presenting endless variations on the same message. In this media circus, images of shampoos mix and merge with those of cities. Same smiles, same hairstyles, same female models who flatter us because "we're worth it."

Mise en abîme, fetishism, and gadgetry. Is there any meaning left in the flag or logo, endlessly repeated on hundreds of objects as if

36 Bernard Debarbieux, in *Dictionnaire de la géographie et de l'espace des sociétés*, ed. Jacques Lévy and Michel Lussault, Paris, 2003, p. 910.

37 Régis Debray, *Vie et mort de l'image. Une histoire du regard en Occident*, Paris, 1992.

part of a fractal visual identity, a mise en abîme of the city and its representations in an industrial copy-paste? When we look at the European flags adorning the trinkets labeled "Made in China" in the window displays of souvenir shops in Strasbourg, Luxembourg, or Brussels, we cannot help but imagine the garage sales that are the inevitable destination of all these mugs, caps, candles, spoons, watches, and bottle openers. From a larger perspective, we may consider how territories become reduced to gadgets, to frivolous and disposable objects, thereby increasing their own commodification.

Symbolic poverty. We have reason to worry about symbolic poverty,[38] i.e., the loss of individuation resulting from the loss of participation in the production of symbols, the fruits of the life of our intellect and senses. These distorted symbols and images do not replace politics. The progress of extremism is not merely based on exacerbating unhappiness, but also benefits from the huge void in the political debate. It is just as dangerous to fail to give a meaning to the Europe currently under construction.[39]

Risks

The missing piece. "The citizen was recognized by the fact that he had a part in the religion of the city, and it was from this participation that he derived all his civil and political rights."[40] Residents are rarely invited inside picture or brand factories. Participation, co-construction, and collective intelligence remain empty concepts waiting to be filled with meaning.

New boundaries. The mechanisms at work for the mobilization of local actors can contribute to the emergence of new boundaries between the inside and the outside, others and us. As reiterated by one rebellious territory in eastern France, "Upper Saugeais has no boundaries; it's everybody else that's limited." The umpteenth

38 Bernard Stiegler, "De la misère symbolique," *Le Monde*, October 10, 2003.

39 Luc Gwiazdzinski, "La manipulation symbolique," in *L'appel de Strasbourg. Les régions en prise avec l'extrême droite*, ed. Bernard Reumaux and Philippe Breton, Strasbourg, 1997.

40 Numa Denis Fustel de Coulanges, *The Ancient City: A Study of the Religion, Laws, and Institutions of Greece and Rome*, trans. Willard Small, Boston, 1874, p. 258; originally published in French in 1864 as *La cité antique*.

paradox is that graphic representations appear to be rediscovering the notion of boundaries. Like a child outlining with a color pencil the limits of a country, a region, or a city, representations insist on borders. It is a strange paradox that our contemporary world, dominated by an ideology of generalized decompartmentalization and free circulation, is also a world in which walls and barriers are erected, "as if borders were Hydras." [41]

A possible island. Better still, territories often seem to be aboveground, free-floating entities with no visible connection to the rest of the world and their neighbors. They are similar to islands, protected from the rest of the world by a strange emptiness.

Symbolic abduction and withdrawal. We have reason to worry about the symbolic abduction of some banners and symbols by extremist movements, [42] as in the case of the French flag appropriated by the National Front party. There is as much reason to worry about the parallel developments of marketing-oriented territorial representations and politically oriented ones, both preaching an inward exclusionary focus, even the hatred of others. A "symbol" designates anything that connects and brings together, as opposed to the divisive nature of an "evil spirit." In that sense, the maneuvers of extremist parties are diabolical, in that they manipulate national or regional symbols in order to divide, identify, designate, and erect walls between individuals and groups. As they navigate between memory and history, nation and nationalism, these parties are increasing their symbolic raids on the abandoned resources of traditional parties.

Looting. There is also reason to worry about the way in which multinational communication companies extract images, like multinational mining companies overexploiting a local deposit, subsequently leaving behind a depleted subsoil without measuring their impact on territorial ecosystems.

Boomerang effects. There is reason to worry about the discrepancy between the idealized image of a city conveyed by marketing and a reality which can blow up in its face. Such is the case of Strasbourg,

41 "Murs et frontiers," ed. Thierry Paquot and Michel Lussault, *Hermès,* no. 63 (2012).
42 Gwiazdzinski, "Manipulation symbolique."

between the Christmas lighting of a superstore attracting visitors from the world over to the city center and cars being set on fire on New Year's Eve.[43] By definition, "reality is what we were not expecting."[44] Since then, Grenoble, a center for innovation, has taken up the torch, with a news agenda constantly focused on crime and Sarkozy's famous "Grenoble speech."

Balkanization. In a context of exacerbated territorial competition and local actors endowed with increased democratic legitimacy and competences, there is a serious risk of territorial "Balkanization." We need to prevent branding from contributing to a situation in which each territory sets itself up as a "new duchy" and, in doing so, sketches the outlines of a new feudalism and a "new Dark Age," in the words of Roberto Vacca.[45] Similarly, the emergence of "city-states," forgetful of their own surroundings under the pretext of implementing an international strategy, must be held in check. Positioning themselves in international networks does not exclude a local and regional anchorage.

Increasing inequalities. Even though they resort to methods, concepts, and a vocabulary borrowed from the world of economics (prospective, strategies, project, competition, territorial marketing, branding, etc.), territories are not companies. Accepting such a competition without proposing any regulating mechanisms means accepting an increase in inequalities, the existence of "winning territories" and "bankrupt territories," just like in the private sector. Such disparities are increasing between regions that are unequally armed in the competition between urban and rural areas, or between the neighborhoods of a single city. This model of unregulated development produces divisions that are already deeply affecting our territories.

Challenges

How can we escape from the space imposed by brands that are confining us in a caricature? How can we go beyond these world

43 Fabrice Dhume and Luc Gwiazdzinski, "Violences urbaines et representations," *Hommes et migrations*, no. 1209 (1997), pp. 101–7.

44 Henri Maldiney, *Regard, parole, espace*, Lausanne, 1994.

45 Roberto Vacca, *The Coming Dark Age*, trans. T. S. Whale, New York, 1974; originally published in Italian in 1971 as *Il Medioevo prossimo venturo. La degradazione dei grandi sistemi.*

maps, these new geographies that condition our localizations and movements? We must praise complexity when facing the "dislocation of shaping," in the words of Georges Balandier.[46] The transformations at work require that we change our outlook on three major challenges in terms of representation and reading of fluid territories and organizations.

The challenge of the topological space and enlarged citizenship. Already we no longer inhabit the same spaces. The "metric space" of the distances we were once used to, the space where we had an address and could get our bearings, the space we could walk over and measure off, that space has been doubled by a different, "topological space," introduced by the use of information and communication technologies, and in which contemporaries all live together like new neighbors. That addition forces us to rethink everything: politics, institutions, our laws, and ways of living together.

The challenge of hypermodernity.[47] We must learn how to think about things in terms of their complementary rather than opposing nature, in terms of their complexity rather than in a binary, sector-specific manner. It is possible to develop together technologies and the sense of the human, the ethical, and the ecological, to imagine globalization and local development, to reconcile the social, the economic, the environment, and culture in dialectical approaches. One does not exclude the others, on the contrary.

The challenge of hybridization. Times, spaces, and organizations have shattered. The postmodern images of fragmentation and an archipelago have taken hold, even as old certainties and stable figures are being erased. We are past the time of organizations, professional trades, of one workplace and one home, of "monochromatic" activities. The borders between work and leisure have become permeable. Venues and spaces can no longer be intended for a single activity. We must learn how to address the versatility and hybridization of venues, times, and organizations. We need and should forge alliances and set up collaborative projects, to elaborate, share, and build together at all levels.

46 Georges Balandier, *Le dépaysement contemporain*, Paris, 2009.
47 Gilles Lipovetsky, *Hypermodern Times*, Cambridge, UK, 2005.

This will certainly require the creation of new unifying narratives on the scale of our old countries, territories, cities, and neighborhoods, the elaboration of open and innovative platforms and of smart territorial factories, in order to work on new imageries and on the emergence of a new kind of citizenship. In a fluid and mobile society, it would be illusory to try to create a match between *urbs* and *civitas,* in an umpteenth attempt to outline a "relevant territory" and its institutional machinery. We must consider the instability of our environments, create the conditions for the occupation of spaces and times, imagine a public space on multiple levels—from the individual neighborhood to Europe—and change our outlook in order to invent the new figures of an "augmented, mobile, and ephemeral citizenship" on the life scale of the temporary users and inhabitants of our territories. [48]

New Directions for Tomorrow

Assessments and challenges aside, the time has probably come to remind our "marketers," who talk about us and our territories in terms of targets and products, of a number of convictions formed in the past few years:

· A territory is not a disposable product, nor is it soluble in the massive enterprise of world commodification. Territorial identity is inscribed in a long temporality, in the spirit of Fernand Braudel. [49] This is not a time of emergency, immediacy, commodities, the disposable. We must fight against the obsolescence of humanity. [50]
· A territory is not only a destination. It is an inhabited territory.
· A territory is a complex system. Its multifaceted and heterogeneous nature cannot be conclusively reduced to a single image, monument, or landscape.
· A territory has a depth, a dimension, and a weight that prevent it from becoming a disposable product in a rapidly rotating system in which the sole horizon is that of obsolescence.
· A territory is primarily composed of men and women, temporary

48 Luc Gwiazdzinski and Gilles Rabin, "Les défis de la citoyenneté augmentée," *Libération,* February 23, 2011.
49 Fernand Braudel, *Identity of France,* trans. Siân Reynolds, London, 1988; originally published in French in 1986 as *Identité de la France. Les hommes et les choses.*
50 Günther Anders, *Die Antiquiertheit des Menschen,* 2 vols., Munich, 1985–86.

inhabitants and users with different life histories and trajectories, as well as conflicting needs and interests that must be reconciled.
· A territory is a living system that cannot be frozen, once and for all, in an ideal and eternal representation.
· A territory is an open system with hazy boundaries, interacting on different scales with a larger environment—not a closed system folded upon itself.
· A territory is a reassuring image, an actual or symbolic anchorage point in an uncertain world in which we all question our own identities.
· Reality is also "that something we bang into." Even as we try to conceal problems and smooth the rough edges, cultural, economic, or social reality is quick to tug on our sleeve, knock on our door.
· Elected officials and their communication strategists come and go, territories remain. They change and evolve with extraordinary adaptability and resilience, a quality in which researchers have only recently started taking an interest.

Let us remind the top officials and other makers of territories that ideal cities do not exist, that the best is indeed the enemy of the good, that things were not better before. Setting aside the needs of the economic stakeholders and the injunction to adapt conveyed by discourses and images, let us not forget that those who inhabit these territories also have rights. Essential indeed is the "right to the city" in this regard, defined by Henry Lefebvre as "as the highest form of rights: liberty, individualization in socialization, environs (*habitat*), and way of living (*habiter*) and to live there.... The right to the *œuvre* (participation) and appropriation (not to be confused with property but use value) was implied in the right to the city." [51] So is the inscription of this right in the urban chart of the Council of Europe.

Let us remind everyone that, wherever they live, their everyday behavior has an impact on the making of territories and cities, intended as venues for the "maximization of interactions." [52] To both fight stereotypical representations that weigh down, mask, and manipulate, and escape the geographies that marketing, the

51 Henri Lefebvre, *Rights to the City, in Writings on Cities*, trans. Eleonore Kofman and Elizabeth Lebas, Oxford and Cambridge, Mass., 1996, pp. 19–20; originally published in French in 1968 as *Le droit à la ville*.

52 Paul Claval, *La géographie culturelle*, Paris, 1995.

economy, and tourism impose, we must start upon a journey to discover the wealth and plurality of our cities and territories, crisscross our great metropolises to meet their inhabitants, rediscovering otherness. Experience teaches us that a developing, attractive, and pleasant territory is first and foremost a territory in which people can meet. A city is sized up through the senses more than through any census.[53] This is a new way of adopting a Neo-Situationist position in the wake of Guy Debord: "We did not seek the formula for changing the world in books, but by wandering."

More than images, slogans, and brands, we need a dialogical democracy, new imageries and common narratives, and a new contract of trust at every level of our lives and cities. Miguel Torga's *the universal is the local without walls*[54] sums up what our territories could become, offering a clear new direction for tomorrow.

53 Luc Gwiazdzinski and Gilles Rabin, *Si la ville m'était contée,* Paris, 2005.
54 Miguel Torga, *L'universel, c'est le local moins les murs,* Bordeaux, 1986.

Don't Brand My Public Space!
On the Symbolic Poverty
of the Representational Systems
of Territorial Collectivities

Edited by Ruedi Baur and Sébastien Thiéry
Civic City, Head Genève, EnsadLab
A project of the research series by Design2context

Design: Maria Roszkowska
Editorial office: Maria Roszkowska
Translations: Daniela Almansi, John O'Toole
Copyediting: Jonathan Fox
Lithography: Civic City
Paper: Munken Lynx, 130 g/m²
Printing and binding: Kösel, Altusried-Krugzell, Germany

Lars Müller Publishers
Zürich, Switzerland
www.lars-mueller-publishers.com

ISBN 978-3-03778-348-1

French edition also available:
Face au Brand Territorial
Sur la misère symbolique
des systèmes de représentation
des collectivités territoriales
ISBN 978-3-03778-354-2

Printed in Germany